AWAKENING TO THE LIGHT

By the same author

The Fire and the Stones
A Mystic Way
Selected Poems
The Universe and the Light
A White Radiance

Awakening to the Light

Diaries – Volume 1
1958 – 1967

NICHOLAS HAGGER

ELEMENT

Shaftesbury, Dorset • Rockport, Massachusetts
Brisbane, Queensland

© Nicholas Hagger 1994

Published in Great Britain in 1994 by
Element Books Ltd
Longmead, Shaftesbury, Dorset

Published in the USA in 1994 by
Element, Inc.
42 Broadway, Rockport, MA 01966

Published in Australia in 1994 by
Element Books Ltd
for Jacaranda Wiley Ltd
33 Park Road, Milton, Brisbane, 4064

Cover design by Max Fairbrother
Design by Alison Goldsmith
Typeset by Pat Laker
Printed and bound in Great Britain by
Biddles Ltd, Guildford & King's Lynn

British Library Cataloguing in Publication
data available

Library of Congress Cataloging in Publication
data available

ISBN 1-85230-505-3

CONTENTS

"The struggle of the self to disentangle itself from illusion and attain the Absolute is a life-struggle....What is the nature of this mysterious mystic illumination?...The illuminatives seem to assure us that its apparently symbolic name is really descriptive; that they do experience a kind of radiance, a flooding of the personality with new light....Over and over again they return to light-imagery in this connection....The metaphysical mystic, for whom the Absolute is impersonal and transcendent, describes his final attainment of that Absolute as *deification*, or the utter transmutation of the self into God....He emerges from that long and wondrous journey to find himself, in rest and in work, a little child upon the bosom of the Father....Here all the teasing complications of our separated selfhood are transcended....In that mysterious death of selfhood on the summits of which is the medium of Eternal Life, heights meet the deeps: supreme achievement and complete humility are one."

Underhill, *Mysticism* (1911), Methuen,
pp229, 249, 415, 443

In order to discover some of the major categories under which we can classify the infinitely various components of experience, we must appeal to evidence relating to every variety of occasion. Nothing can be omitted, experience drunk and experience sober, experience sleeping and experience waking, experience drowsy and experience wide-awake, experience self-conscious and experience self-forgetful, experience intellectual and experience physical, experience religious and experience sceptical, experience anxious and experience care-free, experience anticipatory and experience retrospective, experience happy and experience grieving, experience dominated by emotion and experience under self-restraint, experience in the light and experience in the dark, experience normal and experience abnormal."

Whitehead, *Adventures of Ideas* (1933),
ed Northrop and Gross, CUP, p845

"Mysticism is direct insight into depths as yet unspoken. But the purpose of philosophy is to rationalize mysticism: not by explaining it away, but by the introduction of novel verbal characterizations, rationally co-ordinated. Philosophy is akin to poetry, and both of them seek to express that ultimate good sense which we term civilization."

Whitehead, *Modes of Thought* (1938),
ed Northrop and Gross, p924

"We shall not cease from exploration
And the end of all our exploring
Will be to arrive where we started
And know the place for the first time."

T. S. Eliot, *Little Gidding*

INTRODUCTION TO VOLUME I

These *Diaries* were not written for publication. They fulfil the same function for my poetry as Coleridge's *Biographia Literaria*, Yeats's *Autobiographies*, Kafka's *Diaries*, and Gascoyne's *Journal* did in relation to their work. They help the reader to understand the poems. In Volume 1 the reader can see a poet's discipline taking shape as I learn to take charge of my experiences and motivate myself, as I find myself as a poet. The reader will observe a poet behind the scenes, groping through false starts towards the work he should be doing, producing *The Silence*, *Archangel* and *Old Man in a Circle*, transforming himself spiritually and in the process throwing up the concepts of the chapter headings.

These *Diaries* also state a Mystic Way: my own journey from mechanism to metaphysics. They follow the events I have narrated in *A Mystic Way*, but contain the different perspective and detail of entries written on a specific day. The daily entries show a young man on the Mystic Way in many different situations and kinds of experience, in many postures and poses, and contain snapshots of a mind taken over the years from every conceivable angle. These *Diaries* are distinguished from all other works by their daily search and their successful journey from unhappiness and craving for purpose to a mystical position. They show a journey from confusion to certainty, from despair to hope, from darkness to Light, from Hell to Paradise. While Volume 1 ends before the Paradise is attained, the movement is clearly present.

These *Diaries* attempt a philosophical self-definition. They amount to a work of process philosophy. The philosopher is in process, in a flux of Becoming from day to day, and is groping towards Being, which in several entries he glimpses, although his full apprehension of Being will fall within Volume 2. As he proceeds through time his ideas and perceptions change. Each observation and reflection must therefore be related to his present position and stance within a changing process, and many of the more sceptical observations in Volume 1 will be contradicted by the more metaphysical observations of Volume 3.

Rereading these early *Diaries* now, I am struck by how from the very beginning I seemed to have an inner knowledge of what I had to do and of where I would go, and some of the earliest entries anticipate developments that took place years later both in myself and in the current affairs of the Age. For example, I see that I predicted the post-Modernist movement on 20th January 1965 before I started *The Silence*, which is arguably the first post-Modernist poem as well as the first Neo-Baroque poem; and there are several predictions of a coming European Union (such as the entry for 19th January 1967), which anticipate the European Union we are now citizens of. It can now be seen that in the 1960s I was at least 25 years ahead of my time, and my gropings towards a new Baroque Age (a mixture of Classicism and Romanticism), a new post-Existentialist philosophy of Universalism and a post-Communist world order must be seen in that perspective. Here can be found the germs of the work that became *The Fire and the Stones*, and the concern for my fellow human beings throughout Asia which resulted in my support for a benevolent world government that puts an end to famines and wars.

The entries are selections from writings that have survived. Certain key points in my life, which I have described in *A Mystic Way*, passed without any reference or comment in my *Diaries*. Confronted with this almost arbitrary body of work, I have adhered to strict principles. I have put in anything that aids an understanding of my literary, philosophical or historical work. I have included anything which shows my development from a sceptical Oxford position to the metaphysical outlook of my Metaphysical Revolution and Universalism. I have omitted anything of a personal family nature, and anything which can hurt any living person.

These *Diaries* record an inner development against a background of events. At first they show a young man who is disenchanted with his life and who is seeking something beyond him which he associates with eternity. At Oxford in 1958 and in the holidays I had already awakened to this "something beyond" and was at odds with society and changed from Law to English in 1959. In 1961 I married and began my search among other cultures, religions and civilisations, beginning in Iraq. No Diaries for this period have survived. In 1962, back in England, I attempted writing, living with my in-laws in Dulwich. I spent all our money and we elected to go to Japan; I took short-term jobs, as a gardener in Dulwich Park and a library assistant, while I waited. My father died and everything seemed to have gone wrong. I had only £5 in the world, but found I was a Professor in Tokyo at three universities: Tokyo University of Education, Keio and Tokyo University. My boss, the Representative of the British Council, was the philosopher E. W. F. Tomlin. I taught the Vice-Governor of the Bank of Japan one day a week and was eventually made tutor to the younger brother of the present Emperor. I was exploring the theme of eternity in a novel, which was not going well.

In late 1964 and in 1965 I underwent a development, purging myself and turning to poetry, writing *The Silence* and remaking myself as a writer. I had my first glimmer of illumination. This development coincided with the arrival of the novelist and writer of short stories, Frank Tuohy, in Japan, but otherwise I was on my own, and without any objective yardstick by which to measure or interpret what was happening to me. My research among different civilisations and cultures took me to China and Russia in 1966, and I deepened my vision and produced poems such as *Archangel*, which predicted the collapse of Communism, and *Old Man in a Circle*, which anticipated the European Union. I did not know that when I returned to Essex at the end of 1967 I would lose my way and that there would be a swing back into inner darkness. It would be several years before the development begun in Japan could be seen to be the beginning of an illuminative way and a lifetime of inner growth.

Nicholas Hagger
14th April 1994

OXFORD: CHOICE AND WHOLENESS
October 1958 – December 1962

1958

13th October. A dismal day at Oxford surely rivals a dismal day in London in its effect upon the will to energy and life. On such a day the depressing drabness penetrates to the very core of being and fills the interior with its external atmosphere. The mind wears boots and the disposition is heavy and listless. Such a day was today. Even the lecturer caught the infection by not arriving at his lecture. The Union introduction was prolonged and sweaty.

I came away feeling at odds with myself and the world and hastened to seek the solitude of Smiths' bookshop, where I found an opportunity to recover myself in the quiet anonymity of a bemackingtoshed browser. There I was seized by the longing to give vent to the tremendous store of vitality which was pent in the pit of my stomach, the desire to *do* something, to shake off the sluggardly reception of my surroundings and feel the satisfaction of an achievement….I left Smiths, turned left at the doorway and entered Marks and Spencer. I stood and observed the assistant…in the shelter of an angular arch. I resolved to approach her and staking all on one throw, like Caesar's adviser, sink or swim. But I knew, deep down inside me I knew, that I would never do it. Not never do it, just not for the present. Which amounts to the same. It was as if some irrevocable force had pitted its supernatural resistance in my path, and drained the power of action from my limbs. I was powerless, totally incapable of satisfying an intellectual behest….I was shattered and constitutionally broken. Without so much as an effort I turned and made straight for home, my mind a blank. I dived into my room in the depths of my nature. Something had drained the glass of my confidence. I felt alone. I felt myself.

Perhaps the cumulative effect of this morning's episode was partially responsible. I was reading in my room when the awful starkness of my situation suddenly confronted me. I picked up the book. It was on Roman Law. I turned it over and reopened it. Could I have been reading this? I put it down, and unsuccessfully visited David (Pitman) with a view to learning the name of his English tutor. And all the time things seemed to encroach upon me, to efface me. They annoyed me by insisting upon imposing themselves.

I took my gown and walked to college. I was conscious of a burden hanging upon me. With bowed head I paused before knocking on the Law tutor's door. The awful predicament in which I stood made itself known to me. I had reached the stage in my life when the road divides. The next 60 years was contained in my crooked finger. This realisation overwhelmed me and anguish flooded my being. Arts or the office. My hand fell. Myself or people. I knocked again. Myself and people. Impossible. I listened. There was no answer. I felt weak. I turned and returned. My mind was made up. I walked the turning of my choice, but not that of my will. The hour of my destiny had passed, leaving me considerably stronger than before. I revived and entered lunch in better spirits. But all the way through I wished the tutor had called in response to invite me in.

15th October. I have just returned from taking Susan, the girl I met on Monday evening (13th), to see a mediocre production of *Waiting for Godot*. I livened myself with a couple of beers before meeting her, but as soon as the curtain rose on the two God-neglected tramps my spirits began to sink and my face became longer and longer. It seems that Beckett infects me with his attitude of resignation, his struggle in spite of.

By the interval I could stand it no longer. I thought I should go mad. It seemed as though a nauseatingly familiar theme had returned to plague me with its past associations. I turned to the young lady, and with a few hasty words of apology hurried her outside into the chilly but comforting night. I believe she wanted to stay, but it was quite out of the question. I was on edge and very agitated. As we searched for a coffee bar, I gave vent to my feelings by discussing the play.

I was thunderstruck at what had happened to me. Why could I not return and hear the second half of the play of the man who, a few months earlier, was my favourite playwright and to hear whom I would have travelled half Europe? It seemed so frightfully trivial, horrifyingly unreal, to see these characters, reputed to be suffering the lot of mankind whose representatives they were at this particular time and place, moving around like pawns, like puppets. For as long as ten minutes I was gripped by the "total world-view" (for want of a better name) in which I was situated outside time and space and received a tremendous insight into the condition of both actors and audience. I kept muttering to myself "Why, Why, Why?" For those ten minutes, which took ten hours to pass, I utterly failed to see the point of anyone wishing to write a play on the subject of universal misfortune. For ten minutes I saw things as they are.

We did return to see the last half hour, but I was resigned to my advantage and looked on at the stage with merely an objective interest. When the awful lines "astride a grave and a difficult birth" came up I even failed to gasp.

It is impossible to diagnose the mental tone of the experience, as to whether I loved or abhorred life for those ten minutes. Time stood still. I knew it was ten minutes because I looked at my watch at the end of them. I felt one with myself, and a tremendous peace and desire to cease striving entered upon me. How could the poor girl realise this? She is more acute and intelligent than some, but why should she above all others be able to come within nine hundred thousand miles of understanding me?

17th October. How these little men enrage me. They are insignificant and boorish, and yet they behave as though they comprised a very reservoir of experience. What especially arouses me is the dual interpretation of the essay's function. The man who is content to copy passages from a book (or maybe two books even) differs from the man who actively wills to impose his personality upon a viewpoint, as much as the learned counsel with his notes of wisdom and original thought differs from the clerk of the court, whose function it is to copy, second-hand, in an experience once removed, the words which fall from the counsel's mouth. The practical man will protest that he *has* a mental level of his own. I disagree, he has the mental level of a worm, of a camera, of a stoppered sieve. The contrast between these mental planes is as violent as Moussorgsky's brilliant portrait of the two Polish Jews...."Unto him that hath shall be given: from him that hath not shall be taken away."...Why cannot the small men, *how* cannot the small men realise that they are among the "hath-nots".

23rd October. I went to the Union Society debate this evening a wavering Tory. I left it a confirmed Socialist. Conscious of my responsibility I listened to a poorly reasoned argument on whether the Trades Unions are used to the detriment of the national interest. Last week my vote decided the debate. I came to a decision and voted against unilateral nuclear disarmament: the motion against which I voted was defeated by 291 votes to 290. This week's debate convinced me of the evils of capitalism and the rights of the worker "by brain or hand", and the conception of the national interest as the happiness of the individuals of the country, not maximum production at minimum costs.

24th October. I am one who went a different way. My only hope is that I shall live long enough, as did Keats and (James) Dean, to achieve the fulfilment of my mind's desire.

28th October. As I sat reading, I suddenly realised why James Dean was the rebel without a cause in *East of Eden*. Before, I had thought that the rebel without love was intended as the answer to the rebel without a cause, that all his problems are objective. Now I know that he stood outside the stream of life and asked why. Love is the answer only in so far as it is one way of getting to grips with existence. The striving for purpose can be partially satisfied by God, or by any other creed: but these remedies are objective.

I now know that it is possible to get to grips with existence through subjectivity. To think existence is fatal. The man who asks why is sunk. Living is loving. The lover completes my existence. I can hardly bear to wait until I see Di at 2.30 this afternoon. At long last I have solved the mystery of existence. A year's bitter experience has been rewarded by a glimpse of the way back. My struggle has not been in vain. Loving is living. Dean wanted and lacked the love a father withheld and consequently felt discontented: his women proved no alleviation to the general dissatisfaction that he felt with the world. He felt that what is offered is inadequate and fails to serve as an insufficient incentive to live. All this is fatal. To think is to annihilate. The enormity of this truth, discovered solely by my own experience, has strengthened me. All notions of freedom are sacrificed to living. Living to the full leaves no time for questioning. When we question we are not living to the full. To analyse is to destroy. The tunnel is subjectivity, not objectivity, and loving is one of the many media to the world-harmony. My whole life must be devoted to securing the maximum harmony. Loving is living, as Dean discovered.

5 p.m. I caught a leaf, yellow and turned up at the edges, and wished. The setting was ideally Arcadian, the river quiet and still. She knew what I wished. I was astounded at the purity of it. Had it been any other woman my wish would have been base. But it was D. Lord, take not this cup of happiness from my lips.

5th November. Guy Fawkes Day. What D means to me was brought home by a review of the French film *Les Tricheurs* depicting the escapist youth of Paris, shirking life and responsibility in the endless rotation of an amoral, nihilistic, self-deceiving society. Their values are jazz, cars, whisky and women. They are aimless and purposeless, but theirs is the supreme renunciation of bourgeois life. For the last two years I have played at bohemianism. Yet am I any better than the true bohemians? Have I any purpose? Uptil now, no. But for some mysterious reason I have now grasped life in both hands....Marriage is no longer a reprehensible bourgeois institution. I have found something more permanent, more stable. D is unlike the last 25 women. I love her as a person, not as a body. No longer do I share the bohemian way of life. But o Lord, keep me not from bohemianism.

30th December. I sat in a reverie for 45 minutes after lunch in the depths of despair. My enthusiasm for my work has gone. A pallid listlessness has immersed me in its irresistible cloak. I do not think I am well. After last night, there is nothing in this world which I have not experienced. My heart was set upon reading English, but I feel so tired, so enervated by events and life, that my poor bones are not capable of the effort involved in catching up on two terms' work. My study is becoming automatic, I have lost faith in my abilities, confidence in my results. The only reason that I go on living is because I can't see sufficient reason for dying. I have forgotten how to smile, alone. I can smile in public. I can get drunk with others, and I can talk when I want to. But my energy will only permit me to sit and rest in a long caverned warehouse rigged with tables and artists, or a Soho coffee bar such

4

as the Partisan with its chessboards. I am weary. I am forgetting how to love. Everything is gripped in the folds of a seasonal frost.

1959

4th January. (Ainger) the (Methodist) Minister cited a passage in *Daniel* where Shadrach, Meshach and Abednego reaffirmed their faith when threatened with the furnace of Nebuchadnezzar: "Our God, whom we serve, is able to deliver us and will deliver us from thee, O King, but if not, we will not bow down and worship the idol you have set up." He applied this in its modern context to the literature of despair by citing the *1st Epistle of John* on love. God is love and is a moral conception, not an intellectual one.

One could see his conception of God as the unifying force of society where love of neighbour satisfies the platonic idea of love and vice versa. He evoked great pathos from the idea that nuclear weapons could prevent us from seeing 1960, and there was a notable absence of reverence as if we were doing God a favour.

Criterion of poem. Taste (sensitivity), discrimination, judgement – the poet's personality, imagery, insight, compressed meaning and logic.

1st February. (Norwegian) Anne came round this afternoon quite unexpectedly and played at seducing me. She has a marvellous technique, no doubt the end-product of a vast pool of experience. The type of woman I should want to marry would have to match a keen, critical intellect with sexual awakening. These two requirements are imperative to any intelligent person but are not easily found (and charm and understanding of me).

Once again I find myself forced to choose between a total commitment to life as I find it, including the rigours of a course of study which has not my full interest, and the theoretically more attractive posit of a spiritual purgation in the form of temporary retirement and thorough self-examination. In the absence of God these are the only forms of motivity. The endless drift is by its very nature an escape; it is a preference to avoid a definition of the issue.

The issue is, what must one do to make life attractive and worthwhile? What touchstone or objective point of reference has one to prevent one from ending one's life this very minute? Is Existentialism the solution or merely a form of escape? Then I am living ethically as will, but unethically as a moral Christian being and even more unethically as a man striving to eliminate the self which panders to the world. Surely the question is which is the better and more satisfying way of life. Both involve an exaggeration on (sic) experience. But whereas the one is humanistic, the other is stripping to the essentials.

Living is laying bare the flesh through the surfeit of unnecessary garments which clog the issue. Surely the question depends on a consideration of the necessity of human relationships; can one live in complete solitude? I wish I could have more time to myself.

Undated (before April 25th). The alternatives open to me are (a) to leave Law *now* but I should have to take English Mods in the Summer term i.e. in two terms instead of three which will mean extensive reading throughout Easter (Paris) and summer vac, and my work so far would be wasted academically; (b) to leave Law after Mods which would exonerate me from English Mods and leave me to work for English finals; (c) to leave Law after finals which means I would earn straightaway and enter the admin. side of (say) BP at a lower rate than if I qualified as a solicitor; (d) not to leave Law at all which means the intolerable degradation of running errands, no pay for 5 years, the subordination of my irrepressible artistic impulses, the possibility of doing something I shall regret all my life, the possibility of industry (definitely *not* private practice) and abroad, the likelihood of too much filing and bourgeois life at home in the industrial midlands.

Questions: (1) If I read English *now*, with a view to writing or going into industry, what will be my job? Probably as inartistic as Law, less well paid – advertising or examining underground water patches in Northern Ireland. (2) If I were not at Oxford now, what should I do? Either keep on with my Articles and pray for finals after a four and a half year sentence, or give up and go away for good to make my living ultimately by writing. Life at the office would be directed towards the evening's reading, and the chance of my mental development would be lost among managing clerks of 60 who have never heard of English Literature and think it's a synonym for the ledger.

In short, why don't I like the Law? Academically (1) because it leaves too little room for originality – you can't disagree with the book and there are not enough points of view; (2) because I don't like interfering with past (dead) people's private lives in learning up (and revelling in) their misdeeds (case law); and (3) it is a cramming course based on an object (facts in book) instead of the subject, my mind. Practically (private practice) because (1) there is too much running around, making arrangements, etc. and not enough steady work; (2) every letter must be inserted with the right file and be sent to the right department; (3) there are too many errands to counsel and courts; (4) we talk of clients' affairs in hushed whispers as if they comprise one's whole horizon; (5) practical law deals with dead people and not life. On the other hand it is occasionally interesting (but so are a lot of other things) and provides opportunities for meeting people (though many will be octogenarian grannies); life at the office is petty with its departmental rivalries (but you'll get that in any office which is all the more reason for not working in one).

A final question. Would I rather give up money at 25 and a qualification in a subject which does not really interest me (but can do occasionally) to live a precarious life? Yes, if it's my own life.

25th April. Now that I have broken completely and finally with my past, perhaps it is beneficial to consider the impact of life on the Oxford student who will not take himself under control. Woman was created for man to fertilise, and no certificate, witnessed by a marriage registrar and his decaying clerk, will convince me to the contrary. Only by sleeping with women, drinking heavily, and indeed doing our damnedest to secure our early death through excess vices will it be possible to look back from our deathbed and proclaim (through much effort and coughing): "It was not in vain. I have enjoyed myself. I have lived."

3rd May. Last night I visited the Union cellars and lost all sense of the time-scale as I propelled Wendy in what seemed a preparation for the Bacchic ceremony. The evening passed as swiftly as the day.

Suddenly it hit me, overwhelmed me. Resistance was utterly useless. I was in the relentless grip of an all-sorrowing world-sickness, melancholia. My body turned into a contaminated instrument before my very eyes. I felt – quite bluntly – dirty. I realised in a flash of sickness that my capacity for appreciating beauty and value, and for achieving the deeper human emotions known as love (when two human beings go into and outside of the world of time to commune in a world of absolutes and ecstatic pleasure), was clogged and bemired by sordidly superficial substratas of ultra-human contact. There is a difference between contact and communication. Perhaps (contact) is a preparation for communication. Last night, it became an indiscriminate "feel-apparatus" which debased me.

And yet, ironically, embedded in the mire was a jewel of priceless worth to extract which I would have moved mountains for all my lack of faith. I felt I could marry W, and so transform the surface of the stream (reflecting the faces of the gazer) into the bed visible beneath the surface. The responsibility for a perception of surface instead of bottom lies, not with the watcher's eyes, but with the light – an objective influence. Could it be that this jewel, a timeless reality, could prove an objective value? Would it enhance life, my life, from its present external superficial debasement to something rich and strange? Would I find value anew?

Then depression centred over me, so heavy that I collapsed beneath it. I tottered into Kingsley's room after 11 p.m. having walked the streets for some time. He tried to dissuade me from suicide, but it was no use. This was a compulsion not choice. Lack of value was lack of life. I ran back to my room, formed a noose of W's belt and tied it to the clothes' hook at the back of my door. I put a very unsteady chair underneath, drew the curtains, wrote a note, and climbed onto the chair. It was one o'clock. I wondered what clock had just struck it. Then, my foot on the end of the chair, my eyes fastened upon Hamlet's soliloquy which lay open upon the table, I leaned forward until I choked. I felt faint. Just as in the doctor's everything fades away and begins to whirl round and round in concentric circles, and one feels hot in the head and weak in the knees, so I began to sink, I wanted to belch – or was it to breathe? I had resolved not to live. As my head grew hotter I thought of Stavrogin – he was hanging behind the door; was it from

7

the door? Still, it was too late to find out now. By now I was leaning with my feet against the door (on the chair) and my neck about two feet from the top of the door. All that remained was to kick the chair and hope that the peg held (and that no one would wake and cut me down). The strap was holding superbly.

So this was it? Kafka's words "like a dog" invaded me. I thought with no little annoyance that I would be one of the ingredients of the suicide rate for 1959/1969, a printed figure on a piece of paper. I thought of breakfast in hall that morning, when I would be in possession of all the world's knowledge. It made me sardonically indifferent. Then I thought of my family, for the first time, for an hour. Of my mother struggling along. Would this cause her death? Would it disrupt the family. I didn't know. I couldn't tell. Did they love me? I knew they were fond of me. I burst into tears, went to bed and wept for half an hour.

19th May. I affirm my love for Rosemary. Something black and dark inhabits my room. I think of the best line of poetry I have written "An eye-sorrowing fixation is not enough to save a world".

27th May. In *La Belle et le Bête* Cocteau takes the myth of the handsome prince entombed in a beast's body as a punishment for his lack of faith. The archetypal younger sister relegated to the position of Cinderella emulates Christ and in redeeming her father's life (for an act committed on her behalf, in this case stealing a rose) establishes a personal relationship with the Beast founded upon sympathetic understanding. She perceives that the Beast is half governed by all his magical attributes. Her integrity is put to the test, and her loyalty redeems the prince, who discards the Beast's visage (his penance satisfied by an act of faith which is very nearly love) and assumes the mask of her former lover.

The myth is therefore essentially Christian and finds its basis in the heroic-romantic ideals of purity and chastity; the monster is the Nietzschean animal inside us all which tends to lust, yet in this instance conquered by, or rather succumbing to, the initial love of the helpless maid. To be effective love has to be active and efficient. The myth marks a spiritual progression which finds its own rewards and judges the sister by the shining light of her example.

24th June. Midsummer Day but my infection is the natural prolongation of my natural state. Only 24 hours after I first met Margot....The transfer of our attentions from the Randolph to my room followed logically. She needed no prompting....I was surprised at the apparent absence of the nausea which chooses to beset me in such a predicament. Far from crying "Sordid" I was nearly crying "Yea".

11th September. My relationship with Polly, as short as five days but intense, has left me in a state of nervous excitement. The tragedy is that I should have to make a choice between her and Sonia…, and that I should choose Sonia though I appreciate Polly's point of view. She has strong Catholic tendencies. She is the prettiest girl in Loughton, this stagnant pool. I cared when I saw her in the pub the day after I chose. It hurt, and I ran away into the night.

But having chosen I can feel nothing for S—, nothing. P has elevated love to the sacred, and elevated me with her infection. "It's only natural," she said "but all you men complicate things, you fuss and worry." I feel unclean but she said that I was one of the cleanest people she had ever met. I have renounced an idol for a toy, and the toy fills me with nausea. Disgust. That's the tragedy. The irony is this, that as soon as I find someone with whom I can establish a real communication I must needs turn tail and run.

23rd October. And what is Subud? A resignation of self to God, a loss of identity, an arbitrary though tenable division of the soul into material, vegetable, animal, human and after, a dying away from violence.

25th October. Either-Or. What is it? What is the cause of my present condition? Last year I came up, ruined by my fanatical interest in the inner problems of life. I could never gain a foothold in the landed aristocracy. I isolated myself from the outset by a refusal to compromise. My change from Law was historically an error. It has moulded me into a different pattern. It has increased my diffidence; I feel uncomfortable with people. And yet I feel superior. It has cut me off from conventional conversation. It has made me more unhappy.

And yet the change was only a logical stage from a pre-existent step. My personality will not stand up to the steamrolling force of outwardly turned College men. Introspection has heightened. I feel unhappy, but know not where to seek happiness. I am more alone. If only I could feel the security of a Law degree. And yet I should feel disgusted with myself for failing to realise my potential power to think. Intensified thought turns against itself and annihilates hope. It is the uncertainty of the future that is partly to blame.

A writer's life is hard. It is a lack of direction. Recently I have felt a sense of destiny at hand, driving me forward, but I know that in less then two years my course will have ended and I shall have to make a decision, doubly obstructed by my decision to reject a training offered to very few people in the modern world, entailing a great sacrifice on the part of my father. Life is too transient. I have nothing to define it by. If I had a wife to work for I could deceive myself into hope, but I haven't; and I wouldn't. Unless P. "There can be no disparity of marriage like unequality of mind and purpose", haunting words which fill the soul with terror.

Two years, and then, the gap. What am I to do? I am limited by what I am. I select acquaintances, and cannot bring myself to make my entry into the Public School set. I have been to a public school. But I feel outside of their temperament. My values are different. They will receive top jobs in the Establishment. It is far more preferable than living the disorganised life of a B or a G, or of a poor writer. O God, the time for decision is now, now that Tchaikovsky has made my soul weep with self-reproach. What am I to do? Forget the acquaintances I seem attached to. Devote more time to balanced people. I am surrounded by neurotics. K—, R—, H—... all people who will never make anything of life, who will suffer life as it comes, unless luck is with them.

I am wasting time. I read but feel restless, whereas only a year ago I devoured what I could lay hands on. The novel is a discipline to which I voluntarily submit, not a motivating power any longer. Why am I like this, I who was the symbol of hope? Why do I refuse the loud conversation and future acquaintance of the Public School set? Why do I dress in black shirts? Why do I see so much of a group from which I am divorced in interests? Why do I not play games as I used to? How important is "The Search" to me? Have I renounced all hope of love...?

The answer is to be sought in my past. Not the influence of the solicitor's firm, though this may have accentuated my futile inferiority. I read avidly and enjoyed life to a certain extent. But I was surly then. I was miserable and depressing, unappreciative and inconsiderate. I was also objectionable because the set of ideas I found were an objective truth which coincided with my own experience. I was lonely then, and am lonely now. But I can tolerate my own aloneness better now. I can learn to forget. And I will forget more if I see less of the bad influences on me. Nor was it D—'s influence: I wanted to have women and he merely pointed the way. Nor Sartre's: I sympathised with him before I read him. I cannot point to a definite point of time when I became unhappy, where I saw through life. At school I chose Law because the day was distant and I could think of nothing better.

I blush on occasions if unprepared. I have been told I am beautiful by three women since the beginning of this month. This reflects an assumed self-confidence, but it is precariously balanced, not on inferiority because intellectually I am not inferior: socially I am the equal of those with whom I must mix and accept. I am solid middle middle class. So I have a barrier, but my mind is inadequate to the demands made by physical reactions. I am shy in a crowded room, unless I can avoid hearing my own voice. And yet I can dominate and devastate any given one or two people, or a small group at a crowded party. Basically I am diffident in my opinions.

Was it a mistake to change subjects? The change came at a crucial point in my life when I needed a mental stimulant, a subject-in-itself. But the mental life is not a purpose: it has the reverse effect of intensifying the search for a purpose and therefore heightening the effect. Aimlessness is too sordid. It is the unrelatedness of events which makes me a slave to time. I must learn to love life. But I need sorting out. I will not feel hope until I know either hope or despair.

26th October. I am so very near a solution. A positive Existentialism requires a purpose to relate its otherwise meaningless acts. The individual's immediate goal is to transcend his immediate state as man and become God. But the effort, the struggle, is rendered meaningless unless it is founded on the realisation of something which will give meaning to his life. Each choice must be part of a plan, directed towards an end: otherwise it is an insignificantly ineffectual protest. The freedom of choice and action must cease to be an end in itself.

We have however reached the age of the bourgeois Superman. A man can only become a Superman by doing something. He must have some psychological love to impel the effort. The question is what must he do, and what will he become. The answer is different for everybody. It must be founded on experience, not an arbitrary idea. It is my preoccupation to solve this problem. The days of the social Superman are over, for Lampton (in *Room at the Top*) is not a Superman. The question is, can a man become a Superman without being great? And how? And how will his responsibility, formed into a workable social ethic, be affected?

Is God an end in itself? Does God want to be God, in fact? What do we mean by God? Supreme will, in a limited sense. Perfection. The Absolute. And hence, technically unrealisable, the founder of the divine plan – or rather the being (immaterial) unfairly, some may think, held responsible for this world.

27th October. Did life just happen? Does it just happen that we're going to die? Is there no purpose? To think this would be the most terrible of all solutions to me. I have just been talking to a literary friend who denied a God. I am a fanatic. I have a fixation. But the roots go deeper than this. At least I have one redeeming feature: I could have been a hypochondriac. But am I?

I remember Polly's words, "I have never met anyone who spoke more about death than you." O God (if you exist) what a curse to set upon me. Immediate alienation. P.W. would not ask "why". I am different from him. I am different from J.H. who would ask why. I want to know. No one will tell me, but that will not stop me asking.

I agree that unless one believes in God there is no purpose for Man as a race: but I disagree that there is no purpose for me. We must all "work out our own salvation with diligence". What is mine? Humour, the ability to see life as ridiculous. And I believe it is. So I need no humour. Then why not commit suicide, why indeed?

I have forgotten how to enjoy life. I must learn anew.

5th November. Today I mistreated Margot abominably. I mistreated Mina abominably too. Yet both seem to like it. Why should I do it? The cause, I think, is to be sought in my fundamental awkwardness. I am frustrated because I cannot make polite conversation as I should like to. So

I have to express myself in terms of aggression and moroseness. I am not basically morose. In the last week the role of the sexes has been reversed. I want to be alone. But whenever I get to my room Margot is there. I resent her intrusion on my right to do as I please.

I don't think I am surly if a girl fails to show interest. Then I am charming and out to win. But if the whole relationship is settled at the beginning, then I put up barriers. I push her aside. The morose man is not liked.

7th November. This evening I thought I should meet Margot at 7.45. 8.30 came and she still had not appeared. I went to a party in Magdalen after being turned away from another. I could have had G. I left her, sitting alone in an almost empty room while (Michael) Horovitz danced with another woman. I called on M but she had not returned since leaving early this morning. I found a jazz session with the others, but J.B. wasn't there.

Last night I wanted to weep when M began to read *Snowflake*. Then I was moved by the horror, almost terror, that she has the mind of a child, and can articulate no better than a child of 12; also by pity for her background, her unhappy life, her need to be cared for. With these conflicting emotions I took the initiative and consequently proved successful, despite the distraction of a gurgling water-pipe. Our whole relationship was placed on a different footing. I only met her last Saturday.

16th November. M did not arrive tonight. Fate guided me to the Randolph. I felt "all in". M called me back as I left with Ricky, and waited while I had a drink. She was very drunk. Against my will I bought her a vodka and orange. As I took her away she met a girl going back to Cambridge, and left with her. Before she left me, she said "Kiss me" and repeated her request several times when I refused. I complied. In the bar she talked of suicide. "You have a great responsibility, Nick, me. I'm your purpose."

18th November. "How can anyone so logical have emotions?" I will contest this. I will have emotions – even if it means getting up early and looking at Nature. Yet my moroseness is not just an act. And that is the alarming thing about it. Perhaps my surliness is also defiance. In M I defy womankind as Raskolnikov knelt to Sonia as womankind. I have been thrown out of gear, temporarily. I am not a balanced person.

Once I can re-establish a regular sequence I shall be happier. Not happier though, because happiness is not then in question. By forgetting that I am unhappy I may find a negative, but nevertheless valid form of happiness. I must feel fresher. Intensity of passion purifies, cold pleasure (my sort) corrupts. Tonight when Mina comes, I will be passionate. I have made the mistake of being myself. I must act. To succeed involves hypocrisy. I must be jovial. I must feel. Life is feeling, and I must feel.

OXFORD: CHOICE AND WHOLENESS (1958 – 1963)

19th November. M is in Holloway. She will come up for trial on Thursday, a week today.

20th November. M will stand trial for theft. She is not a member of the University, but she believes she is. Theft.... She has been wanted by the police for some time. And I knew....

(Lord) H, the man I met in Spain, had a bad crash last night and could not lecture on Bullfighting this evening.

1960

28th January. There may be a possibility that I love Kate. I first saw her a week and a half ago. She has a Greek face, a dark skin with black eyes and black hair. She has a very becoming smile. She has a way of showing her teeth slightly when she speaks, and gives the impression that tears come into her eyes. She is attached, I believe, but not very strongly. Having seen her I made endeavours to speak to her, and was finally introduced in a coffee bar. As usual I had nothing to say, and ignored her. She seems quiet, though she associates with rowdy people. This afternoon I entered somebody's room for tea and there she was. At first I ignored her, to conceal my embarrassment. Then I ventured to speak to her....

Undated (between 28th January and 6th February). P's auburn hair is unusual for me to like. I seem to prefer dark women, though I am unable to confess a Dark Lady. She has an attractive pout. She is too conscious to the extent of pettiness. She will want to know what I am thinking of. She doesn't like being ignored; and yet she says that a man who pays too much attention to her is probably insincere. She has too much of the superficial. Her actions belie this, but not her thought. She is too tenuous, too shadowy.

K is harder – in my imagination she carries off whatever part she plays. She is more attractive perhaps, certainly more intelligent, though P has a native intelligence almost unequalled. There is less of the mysterious about P, so paradoxically she is more solid. Perhaps she put me on a pedestal. I always seem to come down to her. I have a year and a half in which to make up my mind. But the very thought of marriage makes me shudder. Children, responsibilities.

6th February. The future awaits. Life is part of a pattern or flow towards a goal, for me. My immediate tasks are to diagnose what I have to say to other people, and become associated (without contributing) with a group of writers.

Undated. It makes me weep that people have to deceive themselves into thinking that their lives are profitable and enjoyable when they are near enough to me, and loved enough by me, for me to weep for them. If I had the money I would drink myself into a stupor tonight. As it is I have to

13

remain horribly sober in the knowledge that life will not change, while I torment myself and prevent my pen from stopping and changing to poetry (for me an artificial solution, for the emotions I want to write down are too strong to be controlled with words or to control words or to be refined into form) by piling up instance after instance of terrible suffering and inane hopes. I want to write about people; I can't see it happening and that's why I should be drunk. I must forget P in the summer. I don't need anyone. No one is important. But I'm just empty and afraid and sick. I'm not a misfit. I'm a good mixer when I don't pay too much attention.

I have no hopes, and my one ambition (to write well full time, with a beautiful woman to help and understand and love me, and to live in comfort without compromise but not dangerously) seems out of joint. But I will not die. Because in setting down a hope, something I value slightly now (though it's only living a futile and tedious and anguished life in comfort) I have given myself a standard by which to measure my future failure and disillusion, if and when I discover that I have no talent for serious writing at all. I will write about people and ideas only in so far as they bring those people alive.

17th April. A minor attack of glandular fever has ebbed my responsive powers to a placid surface of suppressed horrors and emotional tensions. I am ill, I know. This afternoon I felt like an old man buried in leaves brown and faded, though they only reached my ankles. The forest failed to move me despite the buds of spring and the new sun. I need a rebirth. I don't write enough. If I could write during the emptiness that comes each day, in sickness or in health, perhaps I would approach myself more closely. But I don't. Instead I sit and stare at the ceiling. Or I walk alone among people I do not know. I try to escape. But just now I watched Margot Fonteyn, and the grace brought tears to my eyes. I am tired but I can still respond. I have lost values. Will I ever write? Do I want to?

The struggle for something to hang on to less ephemeral than a woman's embrace or a few ideas is never ending. Life will be intolerable if I do not change. Turning from external diversions I have no inner faith to turn to, I cannot believe, with Coleridge and Kierkegaard, that the leap of faith can become an act of will because truth is subjectivity. The need is there, but I won't satisfy it. Intensity of life, the ability to be involved, is perpetual suffering in the present. The man in prison longs for his release, and then for his return. Only present suffering or hardship makes the future worthwhile.

It is Easter Sunday. The cross for me has always symbolised not the resurrection, but a renewal of life based on a voluntary submission to suffering; and the equality of soldiers, harlots, privileged and unprivileged people beneath it; also an exemplary humiliation for an idea; also a submission to worldly government on the confident assurance that the spirit will triumph. Not salvation for all, or the justification of God's ways to man. I would like to write further on this and the possibility of self-respect in modern man (Dostoevsky's *Underground Man*) and the falsity of worshipping a God in whose existence it is impossible to believe without compromising one's own honesty, and also on the way existential freedom can become a system, but I am too tired at present. Let me cry. Emptiness must be faced above. Are people slugs?

25th April. Sibelius after six weeks' absence.

26th April. I have just seen *Ashes and Diamonds*, and before that Mary came. A strange unrest is striving for an outlet. A world that I thought had died has been turned over in me, and its recalling to birth is painful. I thought that the longing for a world of action based on an ideal had embodied itself in the past that is buried. I want self-contained independence, free from a need to define myself in terms of other people – but love. Above all I want to climb out of the wheelmarks of comfort, expectancy and assurance and wade through the slough in search of a destiny more vital, more precipitous and therefore more dynamic and responsive than my present fate.

This film of heroic action and martyrdom makes poetry and art seem insignificant, and it hurts. It makes all seem transient and threatened, and it hurts though the labour pains are the necessary precondition to this new state. It accentuates my emotional deadness and dissatisfaction for I am in a better material, financial and privileged position (with a family too) than the Polish patriot or Party idealist. The hero died running away from his past, in the person of his friend and superior officer. He too felt the need for permanence. Is it necessary to accentuate the transience by reliving his circumstances first. He shows up Keats' artistic solution and my futility. I want to weep, but there is an emptiness, a sense of something missing in me. Was it the film producer's design to provoke this response?

9th May. Two sparrows making love in the gutter, the male hopping on the female's back and fluttering briefly before climbing off and watching. Process repeated. The female darts away to a tree in mock escape and the male follows, stopping his journey once on a roof ridge.

29th May. No creation has been possible today. I have not felt in the mood. I had the first glimmerings of insanity. I fainted over my desk after a particularly tense and alone afternoon: as I sat in my chair everything began to flutter and my body escaped from the control of my brain. I seem to have less control over my thoughts each day now. I dread the prospect of insanity, not for the stigma attached to it but from the way it will affect my work. I visited E on Friday, a conversation with some of the patients in his mental home confirm that my weakness for inventive fantasy (not fancy, "inventive" denoting a use of the creative imagination) aligns me with many of the inmates.

Nonetheless, there are times, more and more frequent recently, when I

15

genuinely believe that I have something to say on man's attempt to approach the divine in him. Art should do more than record the sufferings of the artist's fellow beings. It should however avoid too ready solutions. I am so tired nowadays. A routine would be advisable.

I have fixed on the final form of *The Serpent-Hunter*: precision of words, symbol and image, and a welding of subjective thoughts, action and conversation and the Serpent-Hunter's wife's viewpoint can be the only medium. The ingredients I have tried singly without satisfaction.

30th May. Words received gratefully as completing my self-containment: in reply to my "Parties are unimportant" – "what is then?" and "isn't the Jazz Club?" "Get the naive idea out of your mind that you can plan your life" (meant seriously and said contemptuously). Very well. You are not part of my world.

7th September. First a note on what I aim to achieve by keeping this "diary". Most significantly, I suppose, to watch my impressions and to see whether, over a long period of time, my grasp over my responsive apparatus becomes any surer. In fact, to assist in the search for a pattern. Also, to preserve a desire to write about episodes, something I have seen, that I could not incorporate immediately into a story. The desire comes and goes ephemerally, and the creative enthusiasm is probably no more enduring than half the time it takes to find pencil and paper. I want to watch myself trying to live, and to find out more about the ways I set about it.

I realise how fragmentary a solution this attempt will be, and how necessary and difficult it is to avoid the pitfalls of narcissism or self-dramatisation. I will endeavour to be faithful to the event or the impression, and to write as unself-consciously as in me lies. This is my record. When I come to read it through, bearing in mind its piecemeal composition, perhaps I shall have the satisfaction of noting how much more mature, how much more integrated (in one piece) I am than when I began. That would be ample reward.

5th October. I have just arrived in Oxford, to camp for a few days before finding a room for the year. The strain that has built up over the last few days has unleashed itself. I have been unable to stave off tears the whole afternoon. I cannot think of any rational explanation for this. I think I have been living at too high a pitch, too often alone, with nothing to enjoy.

I suppose I have had what amounts to, in psychological terms, a breakdown. The main symptom was a feeling of impotence: it took me 20 minutes to turn the switch of the electric toaster, tea took one and a half hours to prepare, and consisted of two slices of bread, a slice of cake and a cup of milkless tea. The image was of a net of steel closing in upon a figure rooted to a rock.

A feeling that it is impossible to compete for anything. Sordid, squalid

Oxford: nobody caring whether you live or die, with the the only relief in fusty academic conversation which means so little or its counterpart and opposite, superfical badinage. At such times I think I will never be a writer: the energy is undermined; one's actions drag weights of quartz.

Alone. I was alone yesterday in the Forest, watching the leaves fall one by one from impersonal trees. It struck me that the whole universe was organised along super-fine lines, that as the leaves dropped off each year so we die and the whole principle, man, lives on through our children. It is the survival of the kind that matters. But somehow mind was thrown up, a great consciousness of inquiring, seeing beyond the rhythm and therefore past its obvious nature. Mind, the source of suffering and death.

One can imagine how society was created. Groups of mindless, instinctive beings, rising and falling, corrupted by the need for protection and organisation, defending themselves against nightraiders when they should be sleeping at ease. Becoming self-conscious of their rights, having to worship, seeking to know their status in the world – and so mankind is turned from survival as part of Nature to a pretentious house-and-gable dwelling, post-human, above but in Nature. We are of the universe and not *in* it. But today this is never felt.

I am tired. I must escape into the woods from this room. Perhaps I shall work. Suffering requires the mind's distraction through complete absorption. Perhaps I am ill.

10th October. A reading of Jung has shown me how much I have in common with him, despite his insistence on the death of individualism. He recommends the individuation process (mandala dreams) for the middle-aged, but I think I am nearer to middle-age than to the youthful preoccupations of idealistic love. Let me very tentatively attempt my own diagnosis – paying special attention to the danger of accepting the "shadow", the precondition of the personality's development. To achieve this I shall have to accept Jung's terminology and archetypes, and rest content with a conscious level only, for the whole of his analysis is directed at eliciting from the collective or personal unconscious information which influences the conscious. This is only a starting-point.

17th October. Needless to say the examination was never written down. What matters is wholeness. It is mine to plumb the extent of what I am given, to know not only my range but also how best I can express myself with what I am given. (D.H.) Lawrence was right, but his range was so narrow. He knew it though. He described Dostoevsky as a stinking rat. Both are equally right. Lawrence described the moral code in literature as old hat. He is wrong. What matters is not the programme of a theory of art, but the actual creation in a style which is adaptable enough to include everything that takes me nearer truth: the unconscious imagery, the social world, all the ordeals we poor suffering mortals have to undergo.

This style must be capable of including realism, rational revolt, and the most beautiful experiences we are capable of having. The question is "how to accept". Every experience is important, on every level of the personality which takes me nearer that end. Hitherto, like Larry in O'Neill's *Iceman Cometh*, "I was born condemned to be one of those people who has to see all sides of the question. When you're damned like that, there comes a time when the questions multiply for you, so that in the end it's all question and no answer."

I have to make up my mind whether or not to commit myself. Detachment....I stand for too little. I stand for too many generalities. I should have some belief that is important to me. As yet I cannot commit myself, because to do so would be to avoid many major issues. Commitment involves exclusion, whether it be in the sphere of politics, art, religion, or way of living. I cannot say as yet, "This is the right (and therefore only) course." My criteria are too general. Commitment leads to Puritanism. It needn't, but in my case it would.

I suppose it is my task to give hope (irrational hope) to an age of rational revolt and doubt without the aids of religion (in the established sense). An unenviable task.

Back to Existentialism, though not in the false ego-advancement of the will-straightjacket.

18th October. Once again I feel depressed and lonely: empty, despairing of any worthwhile feminine friendship, and convinced that the rest of my life will be passed in trying to spend time with no creative urge to thrust me onward. Purely material considerations have never ceased to worry me. I have no money.

1961

Early 1961, undated. After seeing the stars in the mystical moment of naked "motion and spirit", hearing the fish jumping for spangles in the blackgreen canal, the dog baying, the reveller's distant melodic monologue, the swan sinking to rest; how is it possible to fit man into the universe and make his life significant? Mysticism depends on insignificance. That's why the Easterns have no tragedy.

What threw up mind and brain? What holds the stars to a fixed course? What makes the fish jump? Is the will to live mechanical and atomic? What principle of life enabled creatures to adapt themselves to sea, air, earth, trees?

How did the life-principle become conscious and therefore mind? The physiological side of brains, in animals and humans and reptiles. Gilbert Ryle's contribution? Has science the answer? (1) Stars, (2) energy (cf Freud and mind). Go to physics.

Undated. The personality brings with it the illusion of oneness through the body and the mind in reflection. Its disintegration escapes the conscious mind because its many-sidedness often reveals itself (to others) when the mind is not self-conscious.

Ayer and Ryle refuse to recognise the mind-body problem – Koestler is right.

Undated. The spiritual side of marriage.

Does greatness in literature depend on inflation, of passions? Can the sordid be great and have an overpowering emotional effect? Can greatness come through contempt, or must it come through sympathy, admiration, reverence?

Undated. The slag-slope past the railway bridge (to Port Meadow) curved away to the stile at the bottom. Suddenly I became aware of the hedgerow to my right. I stopped and leant on the faded white railings, looking into the sea of green. Yellow banded fly-bees, nimble and nearly hatched, were crawling among the white nettle-bells and the parsley. One was squatting on the spikes of a maroon-pink thistle. To my amazement the whole row was alive, crawling with something – alive, no matter how unindustrious; something with a mind, intuitive or instinctive, but still a mind.

30th May. Conversation with Ricky in Randolph. Ideal "not-desire" existence, performing acts which are not acts because no significance can be attached to them, e.g. massacring 500 (Arjuna). Raskolnikov, Stavrogin, Kirilov are all invalid because their motive was to act without a motive. Self-discipline leads to "not-desire" selfless irrational existence. The phenomenal world is all illusion, so there can be no moral condemnation of massacre. Humanitarian values are illusory, wrong.

The Yogi performs acts which are not acts because they are completely unmotivated by desire or freedom.

Ricky believes he has no position. Sooner or later he'll have to exclude certain desires as he begins the journey through discipline to his ideal state (that he hankers for).

The whole question is, what value can we place on the reason? With Ricky I agree over rational/emotional judgements and commitment to a radical line and no one truth (Kafka), but I'm not sure on the extent to which we can live our lives outside a rational pattern. (Was Eichmann a Yogi?) Practical memory and the creative mind work rationally.

If we try to live consistently, anti-Rationalism is harder. If we live in hope and court the Great Unknown, yet emphasise mystical intuition (which may be high blood-pressure) while preserving a veneer of rationality in our behaviour, consistency is easier. The reason demands consistency yet we know a very great part of experience is irrational.

30th May still. The old question – the extent of detachment and commitment depends on how illusory the personality is. Huxley embodies this dichotomy in world thought, conveniently summarised into the pagan and Christian West on the one hand and the East on the other hand.

Ricky is the reverse of the Humanist, though to pin him down would be to insist on consistency. He is inclined to believe with the Christian that this life is not all that important – not wholly fair because a good karma depends on actions in this world – but in the stages near enlightenment, evaluations of actions cease to have importance.

Should action be evaluated in terms of some moral scheme, and if so, to what extent? Certainly a "whole personality" depends on the reduction of greed and craving (Aldous Huxley's later hates). Only by detaching oneself from cause/effect, external stimuli, desires, wants, needs can one see what one is.

How far should one's observation of people, and its portrayal in novels and plays, judge behaviour in terms of an anti-greed/craving standard? Or should it explain (analyse) behaviour?

Freedom and bondage. Huxley: "As soon as you think you're a Yogi, it's a sure sign that you're not a Yogi."

I am a "Jungian".

How to reconcile science and imagination, reason and irrationalism. They can't be reconciled? No systems – just an individual certainty for me.

The trouble about marrying into money or society is that the man with values automatically betrays his values, having to put up with sophisticated idling about people and things.

Undated. The night where no men work – St. John of the Cross on death. Philosophy = Rationalism/Empiricism, Idealism/Realism, Intuition/Logical Analysis.

Ricky creating a brand image of himself as obtuse, then destroying it by what he says.

The buried life exists at intense and trivial levels depending on the degree of self-consciousness; yet self-awareness can promote intensity. I am intense because I am aware. Or am I aware because I think awareness comes first in the child? So I am aware/I think/I am. Otherwise thought is a conditioned abstraction. At its worst level it is detached from awareness. Aware thought is the summit of mental achievement.

Chaos is negative energy. Can a man love his neighbour as himself, yet not tolerate human stupidity?

The Outsider can't be a saint because he can't love – but the validity of mysticism?

The Outsider as a figure is to be condemned. Yet how attractive he is in his detachment.

Detachment/involvement.

Jimmy Porter – we must choose between this world and the next.

Perhaps there comes a time when we can think no further: then we search for images to express our thoughts in a new way, to give it a new dress, a new change of clothes. Then the thought is buried in its suit. But do we deceive ourselves in the process?

"Was I really wrong to believe that there's a kind of burning virility of mind and spirit that looks for something as powerful as itself. The heaviest, strongest creatures in this world seem to be the loneliest....That voice that cries out in pain doesn't have to be a weakling's does it?" John Osborne, *Look Back in Anger*.

"Michael Robartes holds in his arms the loveliness that has long faded from the world....I desire to press in my arms a loveliness that has not yet come into the world." W. B. Yeats.

"And the end of all our exploring/Will be to arrive where we started/And know the place for the first time." T. S. Eliot.

In all our dealings with people, we either love them or we understand them or we judge them or we help them. So it is with the novelist.

Types of mysticism.

1. Outer. the heightened flower. Cf awareness (mescalin). Lawrence and Hopkins.
2. Inward. Subjugation of self by discipline for attainment of a reality beyond "reality". Subud, Huxley.
3. The experience by the Worcester College lake, unsummoned and unexpected: timelessness and permanence.
4. Apprehension of qualities of love and hope and faith through passion. Dostoevsky's Alyosha.

But, how much is weak frontal lobes?

Reason and Intuition. Division and Unity. Time unreal, Evil unreal (Arjuna). Cf Humanism.

Love can so often be paraphrased. It is used of the whore, of a one-night free woman, of an infatuated adolescent, of a passionate young woman, of a frustrated middle-aged man, of sister-brother and mother-son, of God.

Soul as a value word of the highest man is capable of.

3rd September. Yesterday I asked for excommunication; the priest was reflective, though it was morning, and the atmosphere was sombre. He told me it was impossible. "I admire your integrity, your perception," he said quietly. "I have a great respect for them. I'd feel betrayed if you accepted God's word before you were sure." There was a silence, and we both made a pretence of thinking.

7th September. After my letter to Tom D. Yes, I'm a bit of a fascist in my outlook on the spiritual working classes. Why do these things matter so much? Why can't I stop caring? Sometimes I want to weep when I see an "unsaved" soul walking in the twilight of redemption, in the groves of this earth.

Clarity and superficiality, confusion and communicating the heart. No, I will not surrender to academic clarity. I will not divest the idea of its flesh, present merely the skeleton. I want the whole Body of the Idea, a snarl to Heaven caught in its echo and made eternal in art.

Now the vastation is about me, the restlessness, the heaviness in my heart, the tiredness in my brain. I'm grieving for something, what it is I don't know and cannot think. It's as though the earth were about to heave a sigh for man. Yet I know no man, not in my present mood. I know only a feeling. The heart-scalding tears that want to come divest me of thought – and already I exist, in my felt agony – yet words, words, totally meaningless and gladly so.

One hour later. Two weeks unfecund, lying fallow, waiting impregnation. I await the flicker at first, then the fire. The emptiness and nothing throw up the buzzing creativity, which is born of the void, like the earth from God's void, a dark stretch of starless womb, and a puncture of hope.

My life is the most valuable thing I have. I only realise this when I am nothing, annihilated. It is a gift, an imperfect gift, a gift in need of repair, in need of the care of deft fingers, the fashioning potter, of love. But let us not make the mistake of attributing the gift to a donor.

12th September. Conversation over the telephone for one and a quarter hours with Jill from 10.00 to 11.15.

She told me that Michael was dead. He died three weeks ago, she hadn't been told until after the burial. First she said that he was thought to have committed suicide. Then she said it was a heart-attack, on a rubbish dump. He was found dead. She hadn't been told.

If only she could realise why they hadn't seen each other for 18 months (she hadn't visited him after Greece). The guilt. "No one under 35 or 40 will do for me, and he knew me, has known me since I was five. It was so real. He was a real person. He took me for what I was, he wasn't concerned with problems. It would never have happened, I'm convinced of it, if he'd seen me. If he'd seen me once, he'd have come back to me. He was part of me, and now that he's gone, I've gone to the grave with him, my mind, my writing. I can't read books any more. He's gone, and now that I've known beauty and reality once, everything else will seem superficial, contemptible. And now that I've created my Hell there's no escape. I've missed my opportunity. Only once was I happy. I had a chance, and now I'm living a posthumous existence, life is meaningless, and I'd sooner be dead than decay."

The thought of Michael in a horrible waste-land grave was terrifying to her, she wanted to dig him up. "Will you help? You're as a man should be, you're the only real man besides Michael I've ever met, and I must confess I was a little in love with you, a lot then, but now I can see it's only Michael who was my love. Will you help to dig him up and bring him back home? I'll bury him in Yorkshire."

I said it might be a bad thing. Apart from desecration, and possible (judicial) sentences "to see Michael again, let's not flinch, decaying and rotten might have a terrible effect on you, might damage you for the rest of your life". "Yes I had thought of that, slightly. I blame myself, despise myself. If I were to respect myself, I'd have to kill myself, shoot myself."

"Jill," I said, "if you decided that anything after Michael was second best, a falsity, and you went out and did it, I would feel sorry, I would shed a tear, but I would respect you, and I would admire you. If you decided to live on, I would also admire you. But my advice is superfluous. It tells you more about me that about your situation. In two years it will have receded."

"I can't envisage living the second-rate," she said, "repeating Michael with others and getting nothing from them, despising them because they're not Michael. Nicky," she said "I'm going to ask you something that will make you furious, that will set you against me for good. Can I come with you, to Baghdad? I know you're to be married (I kept Ricky up all night, and my phone bill came to £14). Just to live near you, to begin again, to talk to you, I wouldn't interfere."

"No," I said. "It's impossible. It didn't work in Greece, and it won't work there. You must accept yourself, Jill, and stop building cosmic tragedies out of the regrettable....You're one of the sufferers, you wanted the ideal happiness, yet wittingly or unwittingly you were an agent in its destruction. You rang me up for help, help in carting a dead body from one dung-heap to another. Now you're wanting another kind of help: you want me to do your living for you. Well I can't, and I'm not going to. You must do that for yourself, alone, having accepted that you're Jill, and not Cathy in *Wuthering Heights*, or Heathcliff. I'm sorry for you Jill, and I give you my genuine, though useless, sympathy. It's you that has to do the getting better, you that has to recover."

13th September. Mrs. Swann came in with her wedding present. She held it apologetically. "If you don't like it, you can always change it." She sat and talked to father "I'm delighted you can go to the wedding, really de-light-ed." Her quick-slow nervousness suddenly exploded as she hunched in a panic, "I must go now," and she was up and retreating to the door.

In the kitchen, as I made coffee, I heard the story. Perhaps she still hasn't overcome her husband's death; she's certainly lonely. She is Dr. Mautner's secretary. She occupies the room that John Mautner died in: the old kitchen now converted into a bed-sitter 12 x 8, with a kitchen 4 x 5, her whole furnished flat. Mrs. Sh— has the upstairs flat. When the Canadian couple were there, there was gaiety and laughter, and she could go up for a bath and have some human contact between the end of surgery (7 p.m.) and the beginning next morning (8.30 a.m.). Then they went . Mrs. Sh— came in, a separated woman with a daughter Jill (a nurse at the London) of 21. She herself is a matron at the Forest Hospital, and soon after arriving she went into Hospital for an operation – cancer. Nine months elapsed, then another, breast cancer this time. She came into lunch with us before leaving for Hospital. "I must go quickly," she said, "I have to pack." She went, but the whole afternoon you could see her at the bottom of our garden, planting sweet peas along our fence. She was in Hospital for eight weeks, and the sweet peas grew.

Mrs. S, huddled in her room, waiting for my mother to go and visit her, any time after her solitary meal. She asked my mother if she could give me a pepper-mill for my wedding present. I don't take pepper, so I suggested a butterdish. My mother told her "Nicholas will pay you a visit to tell you what he wants." She opened the door and warmly pressed her face into Caroline's, extending a hand and shaking Caroline's, for thirty seconds. Tonight she said "Caroline is really beautiful – really beautiful, charming. I'm so pleased." And she genuinely is.

I had a touching letter from solitary, partially blind Miss R—, my old schoolteacher at Oaklands. "I am sure that your life will be a very full one and a very varied one and I am so delighted to know that you have found someone with whom you can share it and so enrich it. I shall always be interested in your doings."

Life for B.D. Rhodes is reading a *Gazette* for cricket. He has a spiritualist wife who attends séances.

Miss Attwood. A library assistant, first at Loughton, now at Buckhurst Hill. What makes her tick?

Mrs. Holden (cf Miss Harris) and Mrs. Gower?

The Youth Employment Bureau, the flat at the back.

Mrs. P—'s warehouse for candelabra, lampstands. The wasps' nest smoked out by the Public Health Inspector.

A change in attitude. At school it was the heights ("per ardua ad astra") implying mediocre lowness. Now it is the depths ("de profundis") implying mediocre superficiality. Yes, the criterion has shifted too. It is reality now, not loftiness.

The idea splintered into fragments.

The novelist must help his readers. He is driving the car, because he knows the way, and he must show them the landmarks, the interesting buildings, the scenery and make clear what each is. To fail to do so is an impoliteness.

There's a pattern there; I can see it, dimly, on the bottom; but there's a wind, and the surface of the water is ruffled. I must wait for the calm; the hardest thing to do. It's a miracle, that any man can write of the tempest from the quiet night of his room. Perhaps it's imagination which separates us from the beast – not awareness. I can be another; the beast is just itself, with all its petty food-grabbing instincts.

"Recognise you're a consumer not a producer of culture, Nick, and you'll be much happier," said Kingsley; said the doorkeeper.

If only the Beast were capitalism as Alun Owen would have us believe, how simple everything would be. My advice to Owen – go and ask any psychiatrist where the Beast lies.

The classics – the criterion must be, in the final analysis (which is daily, yearly) how much do they tell us today, i.e. for all time: for the gap between one age and another is irreparable, the cycle does not return. But, is it possible that history repeats itself, under the guise of changing fashions, manners, environmental progress. I sometimes think that the struggle of human nature is eternal. We see it differently in different ages because our knowledge and conditions differ on the stained glass. Yet the spirit that moves the medieval passion scene is the spirit that moves the dreamer in his South Ken bed-sitter.

14th September. I was walking from Charing Cross to the tube station on the embankment. On my right, a high building. On my left, trees with twittering birds fleeing from autumn. I looked up at the ravine of blue sky, suddenly there was a cawing, and the sky was covered with moving objects, moving to the right, shrilly shrieking.

I walked on. Outside the station entrance a man in a battered hat and spectacles was preaching from a stand marked "Catholic Guidance Guild". No one was listening. A drunk, or a tramp, slept against the wall twenty yards from him.

When I arrived at Leslie's for supper, I saw a photo of Leslie's father. The same face as the speaker.

7th December. My strength is in the observed incident with psychological undercurrents. Agreed, 14th March 1965.

Undated 1961-2. Children playing with a lame bird throwing it into the air.

Organic form (Coleridge); a form within life (Gide). Another writing problem: entering within the hero's consciousness, and having to explain things not within his consciousness at the moment.

The vision stands out against one mood; so does prayer, meditation, a purpose.

On Jewad Selim (an Iraqi artist): "He was a master." "You knew him?" "Ye-ees." A long drawn out breath. "Showing the moon was his trademark. His diamond necks. A vision. But he trusted abstract art to get life out of it."

Sartre v Camus. Sartre: political engagement. A man's freedom is nothing if he's not engaged because he must make a meaning. He is the sum of his actions and hasn't a good or bad nature. Camus: quietism.

"If God does not exist, everything is permitted" (Dostoevsky). Moral awareness throws up God, is not dependent on theology: or is moral awareness thrown up by God? (Cf Leibniz, Hume.)

2.

LONDON: DEATH AND PURPOSE
July 1962 – November 1963

1962

4th July. All my life I've spent struggling against mother. Mother's social "charm": at the age of 8 I saw through that humbug, and didn't want my schoolfriends to see because I feared they'd find me ridiculous.

All my family have substituted kindness and duty for affection, because of their Puritanism. I wanted affection and closeness, but had substitutes: security (financial and emotional) and "treats" instead....Arrangements, what will you do next? I have successfuly thrown down the father-figure and am now autonomous. Has the damage gone too far, has the Puritan lack of affection ruined me for life? My standard is "What has a meaning?"

My *Long Day's Journey* will be written in blood, about a mother who lost six children, dominating but unaffectionate, coming to realise this; a father whose whole life has been affected by his leg – his inhibitions, his defiance, his retarded education, his "normality"; a diabetic son who will never escape, who is discriminating; and the rebellious artist refusing to surrender what he is for what they think he'd like to be.

How much of the consequent suffering can be dispensed with? The heavy, wordless numb feeling.

One can't wash one's hands of one's parents, because of duty. Yet one ought to, because I've outgrown them as a bird does a nest. If only they weren't so kind (money, encouragement, etc).

C: "Sleeping with you is loving you so much that I want to give you everything I have yet at the same time take in everything that you have to give me, just wanting to accept everything."

"It's not what you do, it's what you are" (anguished cry to parents).

5th July. John. The motive in talking, not what's said, interests him. He draws nourishment from psychological problems, not philosophical ideas. Whether the universe is irrelevant or not has nothing to do with him. If he met Barnard there would be embarrassment and small talk: an unwillingness to share in the sufferings of others (inadequacy), parasitic observation without internal dynamo. Tristy digs out the suffering in others, but is sufficiently insensitive not to share in it. John can share in it, but he doesn't get at it.

The introvert/the extrovert.

"God, Christ, the cross, the universe, reality is nothing compared with human relationships."

6th July. Two disturbing dreams.

(1) I am walking up a fort, with medieval soldiers, and Kaseem (or Qassim) is brought bound and noosed, in tears and full of Christ-like innocence, to execution, at the orders of Macmillan and Sir Anthony Eden, who are there. The mob hate him. I think he is to be jailed, and although I hate him, I go up to him and speak Arabic to him to comfort him and tell him that I'll make his prison life easier.

Between the fort and cliffs is a valley. The next thing is Kaseem hanging from the cliffs, still struggling because the noose isn't tight. All mock him. I go down into caves beneath the fort and look up. His feet are above me. He looks as though he'll fall. I return to the fort, take a rifle, and, in defiance of the military, shoot accurately, so the rope breaks above his head.

Then I'm wanted. I'm hiding in the caves two feet high, one leading to the next through small openings, descending like a tunnel. A huge loaf of bread, still warm, lies between each cave. I wish I weren't hunted.

My crime is that I've sympathised.

(2) I'm driving students back somewhere. I park the car at the top of the cliff, and the car shrinks so that I can hold it. I have to descend by climbing down a corkscrew spiral with little to hold on to. I know those in the toy car can see destruction 2,000 feet beneath. At one point I have to cling on to a pole with my legs and I'm too terrified to continue; but feel my responsibility for those in the toy car. Someone is asking me about something from the sky, and I call out "Hawkyn the Active Man", and then discover I'm reading *Piers Plowman*. I put it down, it drops below to the rocks. I have to proceed on the dangerous descent.

A plot certifies experience. My aim in *Tristy* is to throw up a man to show the significance of experiences, to relate them without a plot. *Tristy* could be subtitled "Moments", perhaps "Unmagic moments".

17th July. Another dream about Kaseem. An older man showed me an escape from my room in Baghdad. It led to a fête. Kaseem the opener. Army and guns. Three men hanging, one died on the rope saluting, all Army men like Corin Redgrave in Wesker's play (which I saw yesterday). Then mud, rain and I boated through jungle with C while others got wet and muddy. Elephants and grotesques. The traffic. I was afraid of shooting.

20th July. I have just made a decision which may alter my life. I've turned down the (British Council) job in Hué (North Vietnam). Far from feeling the calm elation of freedom and exhilaration, I feel a quiet despondent fatalism, from which the only escape is work, work which no one, in their right mind, will want to see, hear or read.

The Far East hangs before me like a forbidden peach with a jewel inside it. When you see that life is subjectively meaningless, it's objectively meaningless, and vice versa.

The thunderstorm in literature from *King Lear* to *A Burnt-out Case*.

C dreamt a coffin was being made for me, of pure white. It was shiny, streamlined, beautiful.

"Il y a toujours l'un qui baisse et l'un qui tourne le joue." ("There is always one who kisses and one who turns the cheek.")

John: "We only like people because they don't impinge on our weaknesses." "Whether people realise it or not, their courses always have to pay dividends of happiness." Drink is poison to him. A stranger, changed personality.

18th August. Dream. I was at school with Caroline and her mother. Senton and Will were in an illegal section of the police called "the Whippies" (a throwback from Jordan's *Spearhead*) – they were unhappy and had been abused. S— referred in a conversation with someone else to a text in T.E. Hulme's *Speculations* (a throwback from my conversation last night in the pub). On the school wall in BSI (Big School room 1), beneath Archbishop Harsnett's bust, I saw the text in Roman letters, "DEBEO VOBISCUM DEO" ("I owe, or have a debt, to you and to God"). The "Debeo" faded as I strained to look. It took on the significance of a divine revelation. I explained the words to Caroline and her mother, but couldn't understand why S— had quoted a Greek reference, in Hulme. I wanted to point out that it was in Latin, and that I owed nothing to "you" or "God". Then I realised the truth of the text. I owed everything to (Chigwell) School for having made me a rebel and everything to God by his non-existence, thereby giving me my platform for my writing, everything I've written. But even so, this neat interpretation left me with a feeling of acute discomfort. My attention had been attracted to something I had neglected.

The strange accuracy of the subconscious really makes me despair and want to believe in determinism and total scepticism.

31st August. Walk to the (Strawberry Hill) pond. A green grasshopper: four legs, four "teeth", two pushers, brown and white eyes, two antennae; orange, blue, green dragonflies; silver birch, beech, oak; toadstools, mottled green; lilac, heather. Autumn is beginning.

The Church of the Holy Innocents (High Beach) is surrounded by bracken and silver birch. Two inscriptions: (1) "Pause ere thou enter, Traveller, and bethink thee/How holy, yet how homelike, is this place./ Time that thou spendest humbly here shall link thee/With man unknown, who once were of thy race." (Cf *Little Gidding*, for content.) (2) "Whosoever thou art that enterest this church, leave it not without kneeling down and saying a prayer to God for thyself, for those who minister, and those who worship here."

28th September. A spider eating above a fly it has rolled up and spun round with its back legs. Eight legs altogether, and two minute crab-like pincers in front, which it holds to eat. Body like a prepuce, brown and pink (death's head marks). It ran on the cobweb. Cf a lizard in the East.

10th October. The disgust I felt at killing a rat. The cat had it, it wriggled, and I hit it with a mallet, feeling the horrible human-like squelching, shutting off feeling, going through mechanical action.

5th November. After the outing to lunch at Gorringes – the selling of my old corduroy suit for a paltry ten shillings because it had the moth in it – my mother sat down on a Victoria Station bench with J and F, ever considerate for C's pregnancy. Of course I sullenly made C buy a magazine to establish independence. A prostitute passed us; an Italian sharper, out of a job, sat on the seat in front of us. And beneath the safe conversation – of arrangements, refusing sixteen shillings and only taking four (fares) – I thought with grief of the world mother excludes, which threatens her, the world of street-soliciting, men whistling at C from house-scaffolding, a world where jobless lay-abouts sit on seats outside public lavatories. This world bears no relation to Buckingham Palace, the gilded paint on Buckingham Palace gates, the gloss of the fireworks.

27th November. Reuby. "Fatherhood is a more worrying business to the father than to the mother!"
Mother: "I said, 'I don't mind if I have a bunch of carrots so long as I have something pretty soon'."
"Argie", I gave her that name when, in trying to say "Margaret", I erred. Also my attempt at Grannie: "Gaga". I always associate gaga with Dada.
Grannie's house called St. Anton after her one trip to Austria. The provincial isolationism which finds its way onto the gate of successive houses: so we preserve our memories. But what happened in St. Anton?
"Gurgle gurgle goo-ga, that means you are very nice." An old letter from my father.
Frost crunch in the forest.
C's dreams: recurring pattern of the laughing dark-haired woman in red who seems good but turns out (to everyone else) to be evil.

2nd December. Old Waalf S— is in a Mental Hospital. The boys called "Wart" (= What?) after him, and drove him in.

4th December. I am a puritan: too much potential, and refusing to accept my mediocrity, arrogant to assert my assumed superiority.
The egotist who marries the silent woman.

11th December. I want to become a scientist and work on chemical biology – the atoms within the cell of body and brain: "What is life?" "What is your greatest regret?" "Not having been a chemical biologist or a brain physiologist. I want to be everything, everyone."

AWAKENING TO THE LIGHT

Father had a stroke last night.

13th December. Not allowed to watch the birth at home at the last minute
– C's panic under gas. Began 7.15. Second stage approaching already at
9.45. Labour pains should be one every seven minutes. With her, one in two
minutes. The 35 second pain. Sterilising water, linen, an old blanket. The
nurse, sister, doctor, "Push down." "One long push." "That's it, and again.
Quickly, well done." Old newspaper and brown paper. Sterilised disposable
surgical needles. White transparent plastic gloves. "It's warm in here."
10.45. "Oh it does hurt." 10.50. the cry. As slippery as a floppy fish after
shoulders. A daughter. Then the burning of the after-birth, like a sheep's
heart elongated. C not seeing anyone – just wanting to take orders.

The steel coat hanger clanging on the door.

Father: a lumbar puncture. Spinal fluid. Doped with phenobarbitone:
fear of blindness.

Dirty nappy: cry of discomfort. Not feeding: cry of anticipation.

The Life-Intelligence at work: (1) Breast milk after 48 hours – baby has
enough inside it to last 48 hours; (2) juices from placenta (after-birth) into
baby's stomach through umbilical cord; (3) no teeth so as not to harm
breasts.

Father: "I keep on thinking of your words, 'It won't be long now'." He
nearly died. My father: 30 years ago (before he met mother) after terrible
pain he went blind in his right eye.

"It takes a man to make a girl" (popular saying).

Metaphysical problem: futility, religion, purpose.

A poem: "Will the ice-cold Rationalist in the dusk/Of the world pray to
the sun that is spinning away?"

Flower bulbs used as ashtray. False teeth. Aunt N—, a marmalade out
of grapefruit peel and oranges.

Father: A man dying, calling. A screen, a tent. The char: "I knew it – 'e
'ad too much fruit."

The screen opposite. "He's on the bed pan." The priest went in. "Is he
helping?" (Holy Communion for death).

All the while I was watching the tramp opposite. He died because he
wasn't in a private ward.

U.S.E.	(i.e. United States of Europe):
1946	Zurich, Churchill
1947	Marshall Plan
1948	Benelux
1948	E.E.C.
1949	Council of Europe
1950	European Coal and Steel
1950	French Government European Army
Dec 1955	Messina Conference
1957	Rome Treaty

LONDON: DEATH AND PURPOSE (1962 – 1963)

1958	F.T.A.
May 1958	De Gaulle to power
August 1961	U.K. wants to join.

1963

31st January. When I make my name, then my problems will begin and I'll look back at the freedom and peace of now with a sad yearning.

Grotesque images: carnival head, masked face, band, laughing women looking for pleasure. Prostitutes luring sailors like sea-nymphs.

3rd April. "In the desert you can see clearly, but there's nothing, nothing save sand and dust and heat and discomfort and pain."

"At 2000 feet the sea is veined like wallpaper or the sand at low tide: the white glare is excruciatingly other."

The September crocuses on Mont Orgeuil – Biblical lilies in the field: there lizards are protected.

A flash light and whirling disc (stroposcope) 2 cycles a second faster than your own alpha rhythms (i.e. just off frequency) can drive you mad (raises alpha + 2). Brainwashing.

Harold Nicolson: "Poetry deepens my feeling, novels broaden my experience."

13th April. Knobbed lavatory glass like limpets.

14th April. "The bars clicked and twanged and the red began to glow." Electric fire.

My parents' visit by car. They brought: 8oz jar of coffee, 8d, Easter egg for C, canopy, *Gazette*. Father: "I'm swaying like a drunk man." Dr. Walker: "It's cheap at two shillings isn't it?" Father feels pills have set him back.

17th April. Socrates executed for saying there's no God, Christ executed for saying there is.

19th April. My father has had a brain haemorrhage and is on the (B6) danger list in Whipps Cross Hospital: a struggle for life. His speech.

Father: calling the nurses darling. "Opportunity H" (= Heathfield, the specialist he has faith in who was on holiday). Red card for danger list. Weeping. Too ill to talk.

20th April. Title of novel: "Between Ormuzd and Ahriman". Two parts of man waiting to jump out like two hungry tigers.

Dad: talking but confused. "Comfortable night" i.e. no doctor (but he says it was a rough night). No vomiting. The paterfamilias: "Get off my back will you? Get off my back."

21st April. All mankind is my brother. Each man wins for himself the moral awareness to take upon himself the suffering of his brother and alleviate it. When Grimau was executed, my brother was executed. Even though Grimau was a Communist.

The Hospital. I went to the Sister and she told me to wait until 3.30, so I waited. The others seemed to be waiting for a train: they had the same blank expressions on their faces as you see on stations, and occasionally one looked at a card.

Outside daffodils swayed and tossed their heads in the wind. My father was absent, barely with it. He greeted me as though he had met me in a dream, without emotion or surprise, and his handshake was limp. In the cot he looked like a child whose defences had gone and he didn't understand me when I said: "Isn't it a rotten business."

22nd April. Summer image: a tractor threshing grass, throwing it dancing in a green surf-wake.

Fourth fit: convulsions. Father is now senile in a fantasy world: milk spilt, spoon, can't light pipe, no matches, no tobacco in hand. Trying to go home so looking for shoes. Going to films at end of ward. Introducing Robert to strangers: "Can't remember your name." In a hotel. Tragic. An intrusive vein has split in his skull. Tests at Barts. Barium meal (follow solids in blood-stream on X-ray). Operation next week.

"They're all coming to see me." How much is it ethical to lie to a dying man?

23rd April. Mother explained: father thinks he's at a banquet, and the old Barnet treasurer is supposed to be there. His treatment: angiogram – dye to affected blood vessel in brain which will be cut out; lumbar puncture: to show bleeding in brain.

24th April. To the Dulwich Group of Poets last Wednesday. Outside; a walker "nursing a baby", and a smell of mown-grass. Downstairs halves of bitter only. Upstairs: chairs in an arc on the creosoted floor. An old woman, blonde, with a saucer leather hat. An old man carried in and placed on a chair. Every time he coughed his useless leg swung and his heel caught the floor. He smoked a pipe and couldn't reach the ash-tray.

"The East rose from his subconscious like a dripping god from the sea." In my writing I cut the jigsaw pieces to shape if they didn't fit.

29th April. It rained: the cherry-blossom had strewn damp pink petals on the ground, and the lush-green horse chestnuts held up their phallic candles and each leaf-clump drooped like a seven-fingered hand clutching downwards, and high up they resembled the stars on tomatoes or strawberries.

On the line steamed a pair of khaki drill trousers, and the association was of a man hanging. (Dolls hanging on door handles.)

LONDON: DEATH AND PURPOSE (1962 – 1963)

1st May. It rained all day and then the clouds went and in the window across the road there was a blinding evening sun that dazzled all watchers' vision.

5th May. Angiograph. Father: two heart attacks. Pain: injections, tablets. Cardiograph. General weakening. Head, heart, legs all affected by blood stream.

A man with broken shoelaces.

A little boy sat in the gutter and pulled the heads off dandelions. By his feet was a rusty iron horseshoe.

7th May. "In the old language T contracted cancer of the soul."

Dream: "He had been what used to be regarded as a disembodied 'soul' in heaven, and that disembodied 'soul' had cancer."

Read Huxley's *Doors of Perception*. The perception is sharpened under mescalin – but this must not be taken to adduce proof for the Brahman.

11th May. Mrs. King stayed three and a half hours and finished Part 5 of *Mandalas*. After I glued with Grip and Fix: in its green carton it looks like white ice-cream, and I applied it with a spatula.

Cynic: "What a good man." Social and ethical plea for "goodness".

Juben: epigraph in the passage in St. Augustine about burning for hell.

Tristy: "Every man is my brother." Suffering for others in Hospital but can't suffer himself.

Yesterday my father had a heart attack, his third. Injections, tablets, cardiograph. General weakening: legs, heart, brain.

12th May. Visit to my father: I had a quarter of an hour before Mother and Argie and Frances came after Jonny's confirmation, looking churchy. He said he was round the bend for 4-5 days. Another heart attack; he looked well in spite of it. The clot moved from his leg to his heart, and he felt a crippling pain and struggled for breath. Reading the paper. Behind the screen lay a corpse, and from the far end of the ward a dying man's groans drowned much of what I said. He's still on the danger list.

The Forest was dark and dank and murky: hornbeam, hazel, pussy willow, elm catkins, tender beech.

Clot on lungs now. He saw writing on the wall in English and French. No crispness, no hope, no colour in the Hospital.

25th May. Ezard at the Long Bar 7 p.m. He was an hour late because he forgot the situation of the bar. He bought me one last pint I didn't want and was promptly sick and left his book behind. His "bourgeois pleasures": sex, drink, cigarettes, TV.

26th May. Went to Loughton. My father had moved: more suspicious.

He talked to Robert about Warrington Gardens, then the new car's insurance policy, then about the WG Association of Tenants. I contributed a few mundane remarks at the end.

27th May. Began at (Dulwich) Park. Last night, a dream of success, or escape? I was running and jumping down a long hill in Jersey with Ezard, pursued by horses with knife-riders, passing horrible incidents, e.g. executions. Then I was jumping and leaping and I was higher than the telegraph poles and pushing down other people floating high and proving that they were standing shoulder to shoulder. I wasn't giddy and I dazzled all the others, and a Sophie-like woman who met me off the plane came up when I got down. (Out of body experience in sleep?)

Park: I was given the task of clearing the sorrel and ground elder that grew in last year's peat (which came from Somerset); they sprout in the many heathers before the rhododendrons (with pimples of glorious smudges on their lips) and the azaleas. John the park-labourer: "Ready ter do a bit er hard grăft (or crăft) are yer?"

28th May. All day it rained, and I sat alone in the shelter and watched the bubbles float down the lawn-gutter and explode against the obstacle of a piece of paper, and it was no compensation that I was being paid 5 shillings an hour. I felt cold, wet, depressed. There was a temptation to despair: I have £8 in my P.O. account and two bank accounts; I shall not be paid until Thursday week. Now there is a temptation to despair: 8 months' work has left a crust on my brain, like the peat on the beds; I've tried to begin *Juden* (my next work) in desperation but was too physically tired.

30th May. A cold morning developed into a sunny day and a hot afternoon. "Dodge ve guvnor and go 'an 'ave a drink – gow awn!" C came. Marshall fell off his bicycle after "'aving 'ad ve rats". "Wiv ve LCC it's not what yer know but who yer know." Overheard: "I fancy a li'le bit er ve uvver." "I fink I will." Incessant patter about theatre stars and film stars. "At Christmas, I 'ave a little kiss an' a cuddle, but vat's all." "I've never met anyone what reads poetry." The Foreman: "What I want when I retire is a cruise, a whisky and ginger ale within reach, and I shan't trouble anybody." Materialism. The tree-pruner won £7,000 on the pools and didn't hold a party.

31st May. A hot day. I worked in my vest beneath the mauve and white lilacs and dug the earth. You make a trench first, and put the earth in a wheelbarrow; then you turn the earth over in front and thrash with the side of the fork. When you've finished you fill the trench (which has moved with you) with the earth from the barrow. Bellis daisies and polyanthus. Red spider's eggs on a green maple leaf.

C. last night: "You've become remote. You've withdrawn from the world. You only answer out of politeness."

1st June. A wasp woke us up at 6 a.m. I hunted it and killed it.
Walley suffers from gout.
"Distance lends perspective to art."
Preaching one thing, practising another.
Ricky rang. Graham Wallis is dead, a week last Thursday. Liver complaint, which drinking didn't help. He had a pain and went to a chemist for a drug and bought a barbiturate which is fatal for people with bad livers. In the country. His parents attended the funeral, no one else.
Ricky: Gita arrangement revised, now she can have boy-friends, his piqued pride: "Illiterati non minus nervi rigent" (Montaigne on Ovid).
Kingsley: Laing of the *Divided Mind* recommended a psychiatrist in New York who has debunked his theories, e.g. his own image of himself as the lean ascetic scorning worldly pleasures. Now taking Claire (daughter of art dealer) to Russian Embassy, fighting for the daughter of Sir Hugh Cassons ("making the scene with her"). Has given up Subud ("sitting in draughty drill halls waiting for a message from the Absolute") for the flesh.

2nd June. Charles Nunn's fellow schoolmaster trying to get through to boys on ancient Egypt: "And just remember that if you had been alive then, your whole life would have been spent in dragging a huge block of stone from lower Egypt to the royal pyramid, and after you'd been pulling it for forty years when you got there, you'd find it was too small and you'd be sent back for another one."

3rd June. A slip from the Oxford Radcliffe Camera: "Man's Unconquerable Mind."
Poem: "I dreamt I saw the altars
            Burning in the night.
            And in the Christian rafters
            Shone education's light.

            "I dreamt I saw the people
            Groping in the dark.
            And on each blazing steeple
            Sang a dawning lark.

            "I dreamt I saw the sunrise
            Burst upon the land..."
(Incomplete as the inspired fragment ended there, awaiting the development to a metaphysical vision which solves the last two lines.)
Suggested end:
            "And with a haloed choir's eyes
            Sang an angelic band."

From a *Hymn to God*:
    "We praise Thee for the chromosomes,
    Which weave the threads of life...."
The Group-Captain told to shut up for being noisy and provoking the dogs.

7th June. Jill has rung three times, like the Erinyes.

8th June. I wrote *The Great Pyramid* first version quickly because a lodger was coming to take over my room at 6. I wrote it between 4.30 and 6. Then the lodger decided not to come. Now for the second version at 7.30.
    "Our ropes are ropes of brotherhood."
    V. Woolf: the novel deals with the particular, the drama with the general.
    Ezard on a Cabinet Minister: "A man of his importance doesn't worry about his purpose in life – he's much too stupid."

9th June. I've never got on with the rationalists – Henry James and Jane Austen – because experience is never shown, it's always off stage and narrated by the rationaliser.

12th June. The hottest day of the year. Seed-grass. Three seasons: spring planting, summer planting, leaf-sweeping. Indian bean. Bay-tree (cf laurel), yew, plane, two holm oaks, two wych elms, maple, forsythia.
    For a Conservative Public Opinion Poll I stated that I'd like to see a Labour government now.

13th June. This morning: "How are you?" "Broke – just a dollar!" And he got his dollar.
    The initials on the seats in the shelter. One said, J.E. The men in Virgil's *Eclogues* carved their loves on trees. Yew-eyes.
    Another book by Colin Wilson. Reviews: "Colinwobbles", "Another dose of the Wilsons."

16th June. The church battle between C of E and Methodist youth clubs. P's car smashed outside his home, £40 damage. In the coffee bar opposite St. Mary's, policemen in threes.
    Father: "I'm a slug". Grannie reading the *Methodist Recorder*. Notice (put up by Frances): "Goodo, Daddy's home". "The Hagger flag", touchingly spontaneous.

20th June. Bowls: all the regulars in the rain. The season for grass games is the last day of April to the last day of September after which grass can be renovated or returfed because it's stopped growing.
    Story: A man sells his Tut-ankh-Amun figurine to pay for his writing, later tries to steal it back and kills in the course of it. (An auction at

Sothebys.) *The Missing Tut-ankh-Amun.*

Fine weather: a pigeon soars up, flaps wings, glides down.

Bad weather: rooks circle up and up.

Overheard: "The rain's eased off a lot to what it was." "This tea ain't worth two pennyworth of cold piss." "Gor bless me, I could ride bare-arsed to Streatham on this saw and I wouldn't feel a scratch." Two squirrels at a litter bin. Otto the Boxer, male, treated like a baby.

25th June. A drawing of a face. Fields overgrown with weeds beneath the trees. Tree branches in the brain, with personalised birds pecking and warring in shadowy leaf-calls.

Wednesday. Is there anything self-revealing in this drawing I wonder? Was it an accident that I put the birds in the unconscious areas of the brain? And gave them sour faces? And why the mournful lips, the enigmatic eye? Beauty and asceticism and doubtful melancholia?

26th June. At Rosedale school, grass-cutting.

7.35. I am utterly exhausted and depressed, and all my endeavour seems either doomed to failure or pretty valueless anyway. I just can't seem to affirm. Now, it's the little things: BBC TV2 seems full of organisation-centred men I don't want to meet, judging from the *Sunday Times* supplement; I've written to the British Council to ask for Libya and I don't want to go.

All week so far I've been too tired and depressed to think properly and now my eyes are closing.

27th June. Gordon – looking over shoulder for fear of war-planes.

On spastics: "It makes one wonder, oh yes. You wouldn't think it was humanly possible to live under them conditions, but they do you know, they do. I couldn't, it makes you think."

On mowers: "As I said before I mean we're all learning aren't we, I mean we might learn something, I don't know what. I mean it's all technical isn't it? We live and learn don't we, ay, ha ha, I mean all you got to have is patience."

On a dreamer: "Hey, they tell me it's telstar, ha ha!"

30th June. Wrote *The Missing Tut-ankh-Amun.*

2nd July. The Philby scandal breaks – cf Blake in Beirut.

"Every act of freedom leads to a new enslavement."

The LCC worker at school "can't touch the earth or weeds, only the grass".

Grass smounders inside as it turns to manure. Hence African fertility?

The safe world of a child: it calls and its father appears, like a genie responding to the lamp. Nadi: "da-da" for a game, "mu-mum" for a want or need (hungry, bath, grizzling).

4th July. I took some books off my shelf and browsed: *Brothers Karamazov, Under Western Eyes, Reprieve*. Read the Penguin *Dictionary of Quotations*.

A Marxist, a Catholic, a sceptic, an angry, an inspired debate on love by a mystic – it's a wonder I manage to take up any position.

Depressed: abandoned *Mad Dictator*.

6th July. Socialism v Christianity. Man has evolved higher than he deserves. I've flirted with the Scientific Revolution; now I must take the side of the mystery and concentrate on the respect for the person, in spite of what underlies it. Socialism drags man down by asserting that all men are equal irrespective of what they do. Negationism, anarchism, disorder, atheism, socialism – all are pro the devil's advice, the coercion of human conscience.

"Socialism is first of all concerned about bread. It appeals to science and maintains that the cause of all human misfortune is poverty, the struggle for existence in the wrong kind of environment" (Dostoevsky).

"Disorder now reigns everywhere in society, in its affairs, in its leading ideas (which for that reason do not exist), in its convictions (which do not exist either), in the disintegration of family life. If passionate convictions do exist, they are only destructive ones (socialism). There are no moral ideas left, not a single one remains" (Dostoevsky).

Cf (1) "Every man is my brother." (2) Create your own values. The basic disorder which socialism can't remedy.

Boys learn from experience, girls have instinctive powers of perception and wisdom.

11th July. Carter a former Superintendent of the Park, is now the *Observer* critic on flowers, and he lives in Peckham.

If God exists, how on earth could he have created the wood-louse? This morning I spent half an hour on hands and knees, observing the futile backwards and forwards motion to no end. Can there be any other creature in all existence which is so apparently unpurposive and stupid?

12th July. Mrs. Coates on Kaseem's execution. Kaseem came out at the salute and just said to Arif: "I saved your life, you save mine." No pictures of Arif now; so that he can't be recognised? Yusef Abood (Dean of the University of Baghdad) is in prison.

14th July. The smell of wet sweaters, evoking the cricket match at school that was interrupted by rain.

I have too many ideas. They rape me every day. Last winter I tried to become more physical by training myself to think in images, but this was a compromise, for the image is a physical equivalent for the idea. Now my need is for purely physical description. Perhaps it would be a good "idea" if I took to writing purely physical poetry with the occasional concession to ideas in an image.

Style, for me, is limpid simplicity, but I always seem to overburden my sentences. I wouldn't call any sentence I've written this year simple. I must be precise, economical, lucid and simple.

15th July. There are times when I think I am very near to religious faith. I see the necessity to believe so much: the concepts of sin and redemption raise man up, they give a significance and meaning to his life, they make every choice a choice between good and evil, and above all they condemn the vulgarity and superficiality of our civilisation, with its anti-spiritual values. Yet I can never swallow "Christianity". Often I go to the opposite extreme and berate it with unwarranted violence. I can't swallow a salvation or a damnation in an after-life, I can't swallow a personal God or a divine Christ. And so sin and redemption I have to feel ethically; and their value, and man's value with it, is just not so high. I have long formulated this position. It's only in the last year that I've *felt* it; or, more pretentiously, *suffered* it.

The trouble is scepticism and discipline to no end don't lead one to control one's life in the moment, as faith does.

Buy Oxford book of Rhyme; book on Poetic Accentuation and Syllabism. (It took me another 10 years to get round to buying this, 16th August 1975.)

17th July. Japan. Interview 11.30. Board 4.00. C— is an overgrown baby, author of a novel and non-fiction work on Malta. His story of the lecturer in Japan who was told he was to lecture to the beginners. For an hour, he said slowly and simply, "This is a pencil" and so on. At the end he asked if there were any questions and to his horror a boy stood up and asked him in fluent English what his attitude to Joyce was. He'd been teaching the postgraduates.

A real roasting at 4.00 – on my methods. For future interviews: they like you to mention the British Council library and to say you'd consult your predecessor for the syllabus.

My Tutankhamun can't be proved. He's real and definitely 18/19th dynasty. Mr. Shore said "That's right", or "They're all right", or "It's not wrong."

18th July. "Socialism" from "socius" (Latin), "companion, ally". State provision and subordination of the individual freedom to the interests of the community. (1) Treat every man as your brother. (2) Equality of opportunity. "Progressive" in what direction?

22nd July. C's dream: Our house on fire. Signifying the bursting out of love? But at 11.30 a.m. this morning railwaymen set the railway bank on fire and a woman ran into the front garden to ask if C (who was on her own) needed help. Precognition?

Tristy: disillusionment of optimism, caution and pessimism as he develops. His wife looks at security and bourgeois possessions. "It's what we are, not what we've got." He has too good an imagination.

28th July. Home. Mother has a nip of Benedictine before meeting people. She has much to endure, e.g.: Dad's illness and retirement.

The letter from (Sir John) Biggs-Davison (M.P.) in a polythene bag, and the reverent order of 6 *Gazettes* for the retirement announcement and the secret pleasure at the tributes.

Grannie wanted Argie to discuss her will at 6 a.m. this morning, lying in bed. Nadi has a sixth sense of the proximity of death and nearly cried (cf Nadi's attitude to father). Argie asked pointedly to Nadi: "Will you prop up your old mother?" and Grannie replied quickly from her sick bed, "Yes she will, I'm sure she will."

Visited school (Chigwell). I drove the car to the New Gym and got out and came face to face with the Head. He was tolerant and patronising and asked formal politenesses like "Did you like the Middle East" gazing far out over the playing fields. The casual disinterest did not suggest six and a half years' passage of time.

30th July. 10 a.m. Shumoto, a funny little man with no sense of punctuality or interviewing, e.g. he didn't know what the post was, he thought it was for the end of October instead of the middle of September and he thought I was the only candidate and said "See you in Tokyo" – much to C—'s discomfort.

1st August. E. M. Forster's themes: "How can men and women remain loyal to their generous and best impulses in a world which inevitably imposes mere conformity with its coldness, its cowardice and its polite deceit? How can men achieve a good relationship with nature and with other men, and avoid the self-sufficiency which is based on various forms of pride, or hubris or hardness of will?"

4th August. Ricky at 5.50 brought Gita, a mellow laughing girl. Patrick married Bridget Bardot's sister and travels to and from New York fixing up films. Gita: "Ricky feels uplifted after he has seen Nick" – told to C in the Ladies.

5th August. A novel based on Corvo: *The Lost Englishman*. This idea came to me as I read between jumps at the LCC horse show. It left me in a state of subdued excitement for the rest of the day as I planned, censured and speculated.

6th August. An aristocracy of the spirit (sensitivity and awareness) but not an aristocracy of the body, of the material, the inherited privilege. Avoid being a member of the spiritual working-classes.

Brecht: "No, unhappy is the land which needs a hero." (The hero as a rebel against his government.)

Corvo: "I had done so much; and I wanted so little."

7th August. The generosity of a school cleaner: she gave me nine shillings worth of sherry. That is pure socialism of the heart: the kindness and instinctive generosity that lies outside party systems and organised politics.

10th August. Father. 10 p.m. Robert telephoned. Another stroke. Father is in Whipps Cross. He has been unconscious for five hours, and may not survive the night.

It may be as well if he dies. Retired prematurely, a burden on mother, loathing his "sluggish" existence, he is tired of life.

What will happen to mother? What will her emotional reaction be? Will she become more religious and sociable, or will she withdraw and drink? Will she turn to her sons rather than to her sisters?

Will J run riot? Will the experience of seeing my father scream in the front garden affect Frances?

Com-passion is deeper than sym-pathy; it's strange that passion should have connotations of both love and suffering; it suggests that to love is to suffer.

I wait, but can do nothing. May it be painless, and for the best.

11th August. Saw father at 2 p.m. He was dazed, did not know where he was, but slowly pieced it together. "I don't want to die – there's so much I want to do for Frances."

12th August. Mother knows Dora Bella, to whom Elgar dedicated one of his *Variations*. If she is still alive she will be in her late 80s. Mother will arrange a meeting for me.

14th August. There was an air of silence in Dr H—'s surgery; it accorded with the folded hands medallion and the framed prayer on the wall. H— was an inquisitive little man with glasses, a middle parting, and a brown moustache, and there was an air of incompetence in everything he did.

After taking a few minutes in testing and retesting my blood pressure he stood up and with a look of pity said, "You ought to have a life insurance, you know."

Dad's paranoia again: in tears, feeling the whole world is against him. The responsibility of furred-up arteries.

In the last week there has been a reconciliation with mother, after 3-4 years of resistance.

15th August. X-ray, Waterloo approach. The drunk in the train who mentioned the mail robbery (Great Train Robbery).

I find it incredible that no self-portrait appears so far in these pages. I don't think I would like what I saw: pretentiousness, priggishness, culture-mongering, intellectual shallowness, lack of depth, rudeness, bad manners, gracelessness, coarseness, neglect of personal relations – I am free from none of these. I need more tolerance, more genuine kindness, more humility, more modesty. I need to respond to persons rather than their ideas; I need to be more morally strong in regarding actions and behaviour. I need to throw overboard the existentialist Sartrean cant of the moral-free act devoid of character.

18th August. Whipps Cross, Charity ward, 2-3. Father: BBC TV cameras and post office and radio have been broadcasting news of what he believes he's got, calling him "scum". The terrible thing is the suffering is real to him, so real that he has been screaming abuse at the ward. Only our visit could keep "them" away.

Last Saturday week: "I don't deserve this." Mother: "We never get what we deserve in life." O God, the disillusionment, the pain. And I, who have suffered least, am powerless to help. I am ashamed to record that the Forest, summer-fertile, was so peaceful near High Beach at 6.30 that I wanted to weep. I had no right to be so happy when my family was suffering.

25th August. Dad better.
"Yes, of course we wore black ties for when the King died." Jonny: "What happens if God dies?" (Smiling.)

28th August. Theme: man of thought becoming a man of action great in endurance; a hero.

30th August. "Grannie's not well, she's counting her money again." Mother: "I sold some music and got ten shillings for it."

5th September. Gordon informed on me in respect of last Friday, and said that it wasn't the first time. He's too stupid or cowardly or mad to understand what he's doing; ingratiation is his prime value. At all events I handed in my resignation and gave the Super a day's hard labour which proved to be my last: for I have a day due to me.

What have I learnt in the last three months? Primarily, I think, that I can endure the most arduous physical discomforts. Perhaps it requires a vein of coarseness to accept bodily discomfort among men who don't think. Anyway I now know that I am not as soft as I thought I was.

6th September. Secured a job at Kingswood library at £13 per week as opposed to the Park's £10.14s.

7th September. Loughton 3 p.m. Nursed Dad – pill (blue) at 9, pill (striped) at 10. M and J to prom, R to Majorca.

Poem. Society and the human condition: Rilke, *Waste Land*. 6 parts. Pagan/neutral/Christianity. Attitudes and prejudices of pop culture and lament for absence of classical values. Spiritual lethargy. Enlightenment. Energy standing for a basis to judge the dead and the stupid; aristocracy of intelligence and humanitarian egalitarianism.

(This was written in the room where my father died, written hastily while I was nursing him, he being left alone downstairs for the time of writing it.)

26th December 1965. Prelude to Freeman? i.e. *The Silence*.

8th September. To Maldon, where my ancestors triumphed in 991, 29 generations ago. Argie: "The sermon this morning: the man said, 'They say education can solve social evils, but Stephen Ward was an educated man,'" i.e. education can't reckon with human nature.

9th September. Started at the library: 9-1, 3-7.

Going to Tokyo. Unenthusiastic. The cable was tolerant: "Hagger acceptable. Accommodation adequate."

10th September. 9-1, 2-7. Processing books. JFR (Joint Fiction Reserve), MSC. NCL here (National Central Library). Distinction between "casing" and "binding".

12th September. Library, 9-12. I must prove my strength of will by refusing to have another cigarette. The next cigarette I have will confirm my weakness.

Succumbed 4.15 p.m.

Jill: at Ludham Hall with Michael. She had everything yet was too bored to want anything; she frightened men off with her nimble brain. My portrait of a lady.

After 2 years Jill seems to have mellowed. She is neater. She has eliminated her self-neglect. She offered me two shillings for her gin: I refused to accept it of course, for fear of appearing mean. Nonetheless she still cannot look at people, and for all her "friends" on the Continent and in the West Indies she is lonely enough to persevere with me and invite her mother too.

13th September. Library, 9-1, 2-7. 8.30 p.m. Dad had another stroke at 8 a.m. this morning and was unconscious until 4 p.m. Now he can move his lips, but barely knows what has happened. Will-power brings him back, but what suffering. The doctor would not allow him to be moved to hospital.

15th September. Father: "This is a parlous state. I really must apologise for letting you down. I am ashamed of myself." "You've not let anyone down."

The pond was a glory. Against the backdrop of suffering it endures.

Father: "This is the end." "No it isn't". "Yes, this is the end." A baffled hurt anger in his eyes. Trembling; another stroke imminent.

On Tokyo: "That's first class. Really first class. First class is best."

"I'm off now." "Oh, are you going to the office?" "No, to the station." "Oh yes, the station."

Four visits of one minute each were enough.

I have reached the stage of *Confessions of a Rationalist* where I want to rewrite 50 pages in Pt. 2. They don't make clear the point, which is the conflict between morality and existence, rationalism and being and feeling.

16th September. 9-1, 2-7. A letter from Ricky. I feel personally with him now.

17th September. 9-1. I have just fallen in mounting my bicycle: two cut knees, one grazed elbow and a painful left ankle, all of which I shall ignore on principle to prove to myself that I can master pain.

25th September. Went to the Dulwich group of poets: Howard (Sergeant), the only man to edit a poetry review (Outposts) which has not folded since the war; knows all the authors. Brian Johnson, the man who believes in narrative progression as opposed to story or plot, who is all technique and nothing to say – no theme, author of *Travelling People*. Zulfiqar Ghose, Indian poet who had two acceptances this last week; Edwin Brock, who has "reduced poetry to a stale marriage", full of bitter comments on his wife's profligacy, "piercing the eyes of my child's teddy bear" and so on. I heard from Jean that he was always being emotional in the street with his wife and trying to show how much they were in love as though to prove it to himself; a relationship founded on sand. He directed his poems to his mistress. George MacBeth: themes: the Bomb, fascism, his father who was killed in the war. He looked like an Edwardian with a moustache, a thin stooping body yet aesthetic carriage, steel-rimmed glasses. Palmer: the founder and hanger-on; a schoolmaster, review editor but no writer.

28th September. Mr and Mrs. Dawson. Mrs. D's paintings – a shell becomes a skull, an ear of corn is phallic, a detailed twig resembles a knobbly human bone. She makes her point about the community between the human and the natural with striking immediacy; whether I'd like to live with them, as I'd like to live with van Gogh's works, is another question.

7th October. Rang mother: father has been very ill, and is now better. His condition was very grave on Saturday 9.30 p.m., but he woke up at midnight better.

LONDON: DEATH AND PURPOSE (1962 – 1963)

8th October. Father given two days. Beer-drinking turned to convulsion and tears; defiance and courage while I watched hauntedly from the door. The goodbyes in darkness; he nearly died while I held his hand. Downstairs a TV tube went, and the picture shrank to a "postage stamp". Keeping up Jonny's and Frances's spirits with false banter. The total impression was of a pathetic loss of dignity before death.

9th October. To Oxford: Ricks told me he is awaiting literary murder from the Leavisites.
Port Meadow. I felt old; separated from my youth. Then I had joy and humour.
Ricks: "Are you using your novel as a quarry?"

12th October. John 7 p.m. Evil is imperfection – the absence of compassion and mercy.

13th October. Father has been in a deep coma for three days. Before he entered it he was very distressed: mother broke down in describing his mental pain. His breathing is laboured, every fifth breath is difficult. Frances is terrified of the closed door and nothing can induce her to go in. Feeding and the giving of pills are virtually impossible; phlegm has to be swabbed out of his mouth. The conversation tactfully omits the deed box, but stoically prepares for the funeral and cremation.
When will all this suffering reach an end and serenity follow? Why has all this suffering come upon one family?
Suffering has left us not happy but with an iron-hard constitution for gritty endurance, patience, resignation, and a determination not to be beaten.
A man in a deep coma can record voices and remember them later.

15th October. Father died at 7 o'clock. Leaving now. What resistance.
The family were drinking port when I arrived. There was an air of thankfulness in the regret, a thankfulness that was as much Christian as merciful. After the nurse went with an exchange of normal conversation I went up into the room. Mother said, "There's nothing terrible in death" and took back the sheet. The face was grey and peaceful, full of absence of expression. I felt a slight repugnance I wanted to control, so after she had replaced the sheet I asked if I could look at him again. She said "Yes" and went out. I took back the sheet and looked in the stillness, but the repugnance was still with me. I felt I had no right to see him at a disadvantage, I felt a Peeping Tom. So I replaced the sheet, turned off the light, stood for a few moments in the dark to overcome my fear (the muscles on his face had twitched slightly), then went out.
Downstairs no reference was made to salvation. We discussed the form of the funeral and distinguished a cross for a wreath. Robert dominated and

mother asked if I minded his taking over the arrangements. I said I didn't. Soon we had risked a joke or two, but the situation upstairs was not far away.

On the train going home I was only aware of the futility of his life. Born of an upper working class family (like Christ, his father was a carpenter) he was stricken by polio at 14 and never completed his education; his struggle to get on terms made him sing and develop his will and finally marry. Mocked and feeling more useless than most, he slaved in local government while six of his children died. Then when his dreams of holidays abroad were in his grasp he had four strokes and four heart attacks, endured acute mental agony and died without understanding what he had done to deserve it all. The futility of it all left me determined to justify his existence by making my name.

16th October. Father has been moved to a Chapel of Rest following a second doctor's signature on the certificate which is required in cases of cremation to prevent collusion. The papers have been notified: *Telegraph* and *Times* and *Gazette*.

The problem now is how to tell Frances. Robert dominated by assuming the responsibility. I resisted and said that in the interests of F's future security mother should tell her, stressing that Father is happy, that he went to sleep and did not wake up, and that nothing will change, except that he will "no longer be there".

The ashes are not to be returned for keeping in the house or scattering in the forest for reasons of sentimentality.

Frances cried for three quarters of an hour: "I don't think I'll ever be happy again." But she's got it out of her system.

Cause of death: subarachnoid haemorrhage.

17th October. Everything is a disorderly mess. I cannot leave for Tokyo before the third week in November at the earliest. My job ends, and the (Dulwich) house is due to come down on November 1st. I have no money, and must find a job for those three weeks to support my family. There's no job in Dulwich, and the house the Nixons are moving into will have only one room for us, so that I can't write. I must move to Loughton. I can't live in Loughton jobless now that father is dead – mother is too short of money. I must find a job in Loughton tomorrow. Then there is the packing which I haven't begun, the clothes to buy.

18th October. The funeral. Floral arrangements, the search for vases took up the morning. Three Austin Princesses comprised the cortège, and flushed with drink we followed the undertakers into the church; they carried the coffin on their shoulders, with their hands by their sides, one at either end and one in the middle, on either side. The coffin was placed on a raised trestle at the front. Afterwards we drove past men who crossed themselves or took off their hats to the Forest, and through the Forest to the crematorium.

Curtains hid the final surrender. The funeral party was sombre but polite.

Later, saw a maisonette and decided to buy it because it is within easy reach of Epping Forest.

19th October. "Bought" the maisonette. £3,150, of which I have at present £6 + some National Savings Certificates I had not thought redeemable. Hope to move in on November 2nd.

Mother: "It seems a week since yesterday. My sense of time has gone."

I have let mother into my life; I have willingly allowed her to strengthen my roots in Loughton, my nearness to her.

21st October. Atmosphere: "that baking hot summer."

My nervousness: my whole life, from my friends to my job and to my wife, has been governed by my nervousness in the company of people I do not know very well. Rooms make a tremendous difference. I am never nervous in a pub or any functional place; yet in a sitting-room, where the demands are for spontaneous small-talk, I become tongue-tied and mix my metaphors and stammer and relapse into long silences and pray for the impersonality of ideas to enter the conversation. Never once have I managed a long, successful, smooth-talk conversation without retreating to my room.

I am never nervous out of doors. Yet put me in a car or a house and I am immediately constricted.

Every person I meet has a time on his/her head. If I exceed this time (30 seconds with some, 30 minutes with others) then I get awkward and fidgety and want to be alone.

22nd October. A motto from an old book: ἀνδρίζεσθε ("andrizesthe", "be a man"). In the Buddhist, not the samurai sense – in the tradition of Yeats, not Montgomery.

23rd October. My father's death has strengthened my conviction that the condition of life is futile suffering and illusory hope. Yet in spite of my pessimism – my belief in the ultimate worthlessness of effort – I am genuinely glad to be alive and, as I said to Ricky, "would hate to lose the Forest in autumn". This attitude underlies *The Great Pyramid*.

Telephone call from E. Why does he irritate me? His attempt at superiority? His weakness? His coldness in always speaking his opinion even though it is not tactful?

His trouble: not psychotic (congenital) but neurotic (emotional patterns imprisoning), concerned with his excessive dependence on his mother, and also concerned with his pursuit of ideas at the age of 14 (because ideas were impartial and did not hurt).

He irritates me with the stupid people he sees, and the high-sounding

47

words he uses to describe them and penetrate them. E: "When I go into a pub, it's the background music I notice rather than the people."

26th October. Begin a novel: "X added the final touches to his bibliographical collage. On the board were 2 Vs in sleeves, pointing down to the record cover of *Sleeping Beauty*, which had a picture of a Romantic society. Beneath were *This Island Now* and *Plays for England*, between them *Disturbers of the Peace*. To the right the back tier pointed through *Anglicanism* (upside down), *Mental Hospitals* and *The Fraternal Society* to *Nudes*, the front tier from *The Church on the Corner* to *Jazz on the Record*. To the left the back tier pointed through *Living Faiths, Our Daily Bread* and *Social Aims and the Community* to the rather pessimistic *6001 Nights*. The front tier contained on the left a book of Christian essays on Christian understanding, and beside it *A Cure of Delinquency*. It gave X great anarchistic satisfaction that the word was 'of' and not 'for.'" My display for the Community Centre. In the centre, a photo of Lord Home.

The Group-Captain as a Neo-Darwinist. How can evolution throw up you?

Story *Clarence*, the queer bus conductor whose life's meaning is to touch passenger's hands when he gives them their tickets.

50 mins on Beeching's station.

27th October. Society is composed of men who are outside society.

Yesterday, the Forest: crinkling leaves, trees which lost their colour at dusk, the damp clammy mist which left my hands sticky. I was so happy that I wanted to cry.

The Romantic outsider-concept depends on a fixed, immutable society.

28th October. Fowler (the librarian), "You're a thinker *and* a man of action." As a result of our conversation I was able to form a law (which has its exceptions like all laws): a thinker is interested in action in so far as he lacks the capacity for action, and is disinterested in action in so far as he possesses the capacity for action.

In four hours I have found a shipping agent, agreed the ship, packed and sent off a triplicate inventory.

29th October. "Miss F has teeth like tombstones." They're huge.

30th October. 8.30. Now I know, life is one long disappointment and cheat and the old saying is true, "When you're on top of the world look out." Some petty little rule-man in the UDC (Chigwell Urban District Council) has found a slight crack in the wall of 9 Crescent View, and he's called it a settlement, as a result of which my mortgage has been turned down. God rot them. Oh the plans, the time, the effort – all collapsed. Will nothing go right? I've long since resigned myself to the calamities which befall the

Haggers but sometimes I like to think, just once in a while, that something's going to go right. Is that really such a luxury?

Could the settlement be a blessing in disguise? Could it bring the price down?

Let me return to ideas: they don't hurt you, unless they relate to the wounding human conditon.

31st October. Saw (Tim) Norris at auction. Bought furniture. Applied to Abbey National for mortgage, covering letter from Grannie. Wrote to prospective tenant to defer.

Mrs. Ezard: "All the strands in your life have come together at the same time." Yes, my father's death; job; demolition of the (Dulwich) house; purchase of my maisonette; Tokyo – shipping and preparation. Argie: "I hope you'll have time to do your writing in Tokyo."

2nd November. My theme – I have only one theme. Men with a lust for life whose existential faith requires them to praise and affirm as often as possible in spite of their trials and tribulations, and the futility of it all. The question that matters to them is "How am I to affirm?"

3rd November. Crébillon fils, *Preface*: "You will see in these memoirs a man such as nearly all men are in extreme youth, simple at first and without art, and knowing nothing of the world in which he is obliged to live. The first and second parts deal with this ignorance and his first experiences of love. In sections that follow, he is a man of false ideas and riddled with follies, who is still governed less by himself than by the persons whose interest it is to corrupt his heart and mind. You will see him finally, in the last part, restored to himself, owing all his virtues to a good woman. There you have the subject of *The Wayward Head and Heart.*" (1736/8.)

4th November. Crébillon: a pleasing comedy of manners, made possible by the fact that the hero is identified with traditional moral and social norms: love and learning the vices. Because the values are fixed and constant, as is all classical literature, an immense strength comes through. His characters develop and are in the round, for the most part, being neither good nor bad.

5th November. It's all off on the flat. I discovered today that no one will advance a mortgage on a freehold maisonette because of the covenants. I have been tricked by the vendor and misinformed by the estate agent, and as a result I am faced with a heavy legal bill for costs. Oh what a waste of precious time! So much effort – admittedly only for a possibility – and so much futility. Mother: "I don't think there's any bad news left to give you." I: "Don't be so sure."

Ben (a cousin) died.

Yesterday, such exhilaration; today a deep depression.

6th November. The flat is on: private mortgage and £400 reduction by Mrs. Baker.

7th November. Moved to Loughton.

8th November. Last day at library. Went into a squalid pub in Camberwell and saw the races.

11th November. Shyness leads to egotism.
John read an account of a Buddhist fire-martyr and related the Eastern scorn of the body and devotion of the mind to me and Ricky and Kingsley – and associated himself with the Western indulgence of the body and lack of discipline.
Shock-uprooting tactics. John: "I have been influenced by you, but soon we won't be in shouting distance."

13th November. Arrangements and John – historical pattern.
What is the point of "why"? "Both you and Ricky are religious, whereas I, because of something physiological perhaps, some gland which doesn't secrete as it should, am not. It just doesn't worry me. I'm indifferent to it."
"You give my attitude a philosophical label. It doesn't mean anything very much to me."
Ricky's letter: "I have an ineradicable conviction that there is some point to it all." I was meditating on this when I walked in the Forest and remembered the Life-Intelligence, and Mrs. Dawson's remark, "If God exists, he doesn't have to be good – like Hardy's God it can be neutral or even evil." Suddenly I lit up and became terribly aware of the trees, the mallards, the water-boatmen – life. What is the point of life? I asked. If there is no point but just a blind law that life reproduces, all is futile, what is the point of living? Evolution to higher consciousness. And what is the point of that? What is the point of the Life-Intelligence? Does there have to be a point? Yes, I decided. It was inconceivable that so tremendous a scheme should be to no end. Then I realised that if there was to be a point to the Life-Intelligence, and if I was acting on the assumption that there was, then I had faith. Faith in what? I did not know, I do not know. Faith in some higher consciousness? Could there not be some principle in the universe which cannot be reduced to science and which had some end we will never know? Then I realised the immense significance of my discovery. Throughout I have acted on the assumption that there is a point to the Life-Intelligence which lies behind its forms, of which we are one, and that the point can be deduced from this plan. But the point will never never let us know its end.
26th December 1964. This experience, coming just after the despair and nihilism caused by my father's death was the beginning of my shift towards metaphysics, which continued in January 1964 with Tomlin and gathered force in November and December 1964 and was denied 30th April 1965.

2nd June 1965. False: the Life-Intelligence is a metaphor, my body is not literally a form. Or so my rational intellect tells my intuition.

4th February 1975. Nearly a decade later. False again. Intuition right, reason wrong.

14th November. The British Council clothing allowance of £100 got me off, but apart from that the total finances I possessed when leaving England amounted to £5.

3.

JAPAN: SCEPTICISM AND ETERNITY
November 1963 – November 1964

15th November. Airport arrival (in Tokyo): the ceremonious delegation
that went wrong because my air freight luggage was late and Nadia cried.
I shook hands with a scraping Professor Kuriyagawa holding a blue blanket
and a yellow teddy bear. "Your appearance will, I am sure, be most
acceptable to the students, Professor Hagger."

16th November. Tony Rainer as a man who left Nuffield after one year
of a 3 year contract, he should be interesting. He combines clarity of thought
with a confident but rather drab personality. "I discovered the dead-end of
economic rationalism." "Anyone who says he is a rationalist just hasn't
tried being a rationalist, he'd know how impossible it was." Aspiring poet
with all the critical jargon, but will his training hamper him too much?
    The bowing at the University. (Tony R shook hands with a menial by
mistake). When I came out the mother of a boy who had thrown himself to
death off the University roof encountered the Dean. She was distraught but
she bowed for 30 seconds.
    The visit to the house, a little ceremony with various officials. Irie, "You
do not teach until next week, the week after next. You have plenty of time,
there is no hurry."

18th November. Spending spree at department store. Moved house.

19th November. Tomlin, disconcertingly like Profumo. The ill-assorted
luncheon – the dogmatic self-important linguistics Professor with an earthy
front and his bitchy wife, monopolising the conversation about mutual
friends and then turning to me and saying "And what are you doing here in
Tokyo?" My revenge in the end when I talked metabiology with Tomlin and
excluded him into silence for half an hour until leaving was an embarrassment.

20th November. Irie called to give me my times. "Oh I have not taken
off my shoes. Does it matter?" "Our University begins at 8 o'clock but we
thought Mr Hagger would not want to get up that early so we have arranged
for him to begin at 10.20." Nameplate.

22nd November. Found my way to the British Council by subway, took
12 books from the library and arrived home airless and exhausted to sleep

and then to discover that I shall not be expected to lecture on Monday. "Mr Hagger to speak frankly, please wait a little." It seems the main reason they want me is to turn up for lunch twice a week so that the staff can ask me questions.

23rd November. The artist makes us feel what he wants us to feel but does not insist that we ought to feel it (in which case we lose touch with the imagination and come down to ideas and opinions); he makes us see the complexity of many of the concrete human situations to which moral judgements are undoubtably relevant but which do not lend themselves to description and analysis in straightforward moral terms – makes us see situations in depth as we cannot often, i.e. shows us how it happened.

"You want to be an artist? You want to disturb men's peace of mind? Why?"

"As soon as a man's back is turned the Japanese pass a compliment: "He is a very kind man"; "He is a very interesting man."

A Japanese lecturer will keep a class waiting for half an hour rather than leave the room without being first dismissed by the guest of honour.

24th November. Shopped and wrote *Criticism and Values* which may not be necessary but is as well to have up my sleeve should I suddenly be thrust upon a large audience.

Two misunderstandings: (1) On TV, an Englishwoman says "My husband likes the girls." Anxious consultation by the Japanese, then after 10 seconds, "We hope that Mrs. — is not angry with Japan?" (2) Kuriyagawa shows me his old MSS with immense tenderness and because the subjects (Runic Inscriptions, medieval Latin grammar) convey little to me I say, "I must be careful that my fingers don't make the pages dirty." He rushes to the tap which gulps four times and then gushes, spraying water over his trouser turn-ups, and waves his hand and beckons me. He thought I meant, "I must be careful that the pages don't make my fingers dirty."

Ginko trees (which produce gin).

25th November. Began at Tokyo University of Education. The rain turned the paths to brown mud and brought out black umbrellas: my blue umbrella was inappropriate. Met various members of the Department. Narita and Sakuraba and Saito. Learnt of Kennedy's death from Kuahara with immense shock. No lecture.

"Enjoy." Kiyooka, "You will find my wife very interesting, I hope you will enjoy my wife."

"Take." "I am afraid that not many students can take your lectures."

Kiyooka: "Oh yes, I stayed in Oxford and visited St. Nicholas's College." "St. Nicholas's?" "Yes St. Nicholas's." Ando: "No doubt there will be a St. Nicholas's College in a hundred years' time, in honour of Mr Hagger here, but at present I am afraid there is no St. Nicholas's College."

26th November. Ishi do-ro = stone torch-basket.

At Keio. Kuriyagawa a very kind old woman. Ando attentive and hospitable (though he landed me with a lunch that was not of my choice and which was totally uneatable – chicken noodles very long in soup). The lowness of the standard is reassuring. Not much preparation required. I must expect 70-80 a class however, as my periods are "compulsory". Presents from Kiyooka.

The haunting sculpture "Nothing" (= Eternity) which Spender liked when he was here. The sacrosanct speech-hall near which one must not smoke, built for accoustical effect by Fukuzawa. Meeting with the President (a famous economist) and Director of Finance (an eminent Christologist).

When are the Japanese being polite and when are they being sincere?

27th November. At Tokyo University of Education. Later, to department store with Kuahara. Established the circumstances governing my appointment. Five lecturers were interested and Kirkup (who had left Kuala Lumpur) formally accepted, requiring the University to reject four; no one would take responsibility, so it was considered best to write to the British Council asking them to recommend Kirkup. The British Council and Kirkup had quarrelled, so the British Council said they would rather recommend Mr Hagger. The Japanese reaction, "He is better than Kirkup." Then I arrived and spoilt their party. Now they are accepting the situation.

Narita is all powerful, and no lecturer will speak against his opinion. He admires vigour. ("Mr Hagger is the most vigorous, the friendliest and the most accomplished lecturer in the Department.") So he may be on my side.

Kuahara wants to go to England, and I can recommend him to the British Council, so he is on my side out of self-interest, although he is my Assistant and is older than I am, and only earns £23.10s a month.

28th November. Irie called and discussed the students' ignorance. Like Mr Porson (who disturbed Coleridge's *Kubla Khan*) he interrupted me on *The Expatriate*.

29th November. Officialdom and the telephone: although a telephone can be removed from a house to an institution quickly, it takes months for the reverse to be effected. Toyama guarded with regard to the syllabus, which is much simpler than I feared.

30th November. Finished *The Expatriate*. I am far from satisfied with it – it challenges the modern ear too definitely, and I've used syllabic form rather than stress, which I now think is a pity. Somehow it is not liquid enough, not that such a subject can be really liquid, a felt disintegration before the lack of a spiritual truth and death, and the shifting basis of the hero's rationalisations which therefore have no firm foundation. I also feel

I have not succeeded in portraying the hero as I set out to portray him. I've been too sympathetic towards him, he's not self-important enough. As I was aiming for a tension between sympathy and judgement, that may not be a bad thing.

My problem in poetry now is: how to relate life to poetry – how to get rid of the formal barriers yet preserve the form? To be colloquial and stick to monologues? Could I not extend the range, preserving these conditions, in *Life Cycle*?

1st December. Wish to write a complementary poem, *The Expatriate's Enlightenment*.

The religious idea: detachment and subjugation over the lusts, etc. Self-perfection the only way.

Yeats's father to Yeats: "You would be a philosopher and you are a poet."

2nd December. Broke the ice with two lectures, one on Eliot and one which ended up as a discussion after a ceremonious walk brought us to an empty room. In between I ate tempora-subba with chopsticks and outlined the Leavis-Snow dispute for the benefit of the staff.

3rd December. Two lectures at Keio University. Tried to break down the barriers of formality with a familiar attitude. Kuriyagawa: "You have boiled up the students." Had saké and tempura with Ando and Kuriyagawa afterwards.

4th December. Met Fitzsimmons, an American poet at the TUE (Tokyo University of Education). Grey hair that stands up, a Rilke-esque moustache and brooding eyes make him look much older than 38. "I've gotten rather tired of it all."

(1) A man is overwhelmed by a particular aspect of the whole, a personal or historical or social need, but he shouldn't put it in an art-form if he's going to propagandise some spurious solution.

(2) Complexity: "it's not as simple as that"; "you've given two of many ultimatums." Danger, private language.

(3) The old notion of "character" is outdated, there is no continuity. Keep name of a character and sequence of events (what people do reveals character) but make interpretations subjective and weave them together and have monologues.

"You don't increase in maturity as you grow older, so forget that misapprehension."

5th December. Rewrote *The Expatriate* and wrote the *Pilgrim*.

Kuahara brought my contract to be signed. How nice to have things done in this way!

6th December. Three lectures at Tokyo University of Education.
Yeats: "There are only two themes worth writing about: love and death."

7th December. Marked papers in composition for British Council Scholarship. In the evening Buchanan called and we drank a quart of saké and and got ourselves thoroughly tight. His confession that his maid has been his mistress for years.

8th December. Interviewed professional men for British Council Scholarship. Lunched with Eland and Tomlin: very embarrassing as no one would talk. No good stories.

9th December. Two lectures at TUE and received some salary. Then the party. The Japanese loosen up after a drink or two. No formalities thank God, though I had to make a short speech of thanks at the end. The Assistant Professor who disgraced everybody by toasting me although he wasn't the right person.
Later Buchanan insisted that I am like Shelley and I showed him some poems to show that I am not. The Japanese think I'm a budding, rather eccentric, English poet, apparently.

10th December. Two lectures at Keio: 50 and 70 attended. Afterwards was waylaid for a metaphysical discussion by students, then taken to a bar by Ando where I ate warmed pike (delicious), then a dish called "tsukimi" (= appreciating the moon) of seaweed and ground plant-roots, and finally the most revolting jellied oysters which slid in a sickly fashion down my throat whole. The flattery and compliment game, and the effect upon one's own vanity.

11th December. Conference, 3 o'clock, TUE (Tokyo University of Education). Made my speech to the Faculty. Narita: "The Dean is a scholar in Freud. Does he know Freud? I mean, do you know Freud?" "Please come to my home. And are you...?" There is another Hagger – a Japanese Hagger at the TUE, a specialist in Zen Buddhism.
Went to Sanseido book shop in Jimbocho and bought two books.
Later Buchanan and Keikosan brought Emiko our new maid. She will begin on Friday.
Note from Fitzsimmons: "Please call me Friday evening or Sun – Fri before 8 if possible – like to see you Sat and give you some information."

12th December. Went to Isetan (department store) and bought several things: an electric toaster, an umbrella, a dictionary and so on. Gas cooker installed.

13th December. Three lectures at TUE and an address to the English-

Speaking Society at lunch-time. Afterwards was taken back to a student's*
"attic" and made to read a thesis on "What sustained Keats's existence."
Full of quotations and irrelevant detail that was quite laughable and made
me seriously wonder whether I couldn't fake a bogus study on Wordsworth
or "T. S. Eliot and the search for religion" or something to obtain the £20
a month extra for a Doctor's degree. Could this be combined with a series
of critical essays on various men of literature, called "Critical approaches"?
    * 3rd December 1964: Munekata, who is very loyal to me.
    Ate "gomoku dsuski" for lunch: cold rice, assorted vegetables and
seaweed.

14th December. Met Fitzsimmons at 6 at Myogadani.
    1. Form. Significance = meaning and points to form; but significance is
two-way (from you to object and back) whereas meaning is three-way
(from you to object to third unknown). Cf response and criticism.
    2. The Novel. Fitzsimmons is interested in different explanations of a
man, I am interested in *the* man though I may be interested in an illusion.
Lack of continuity, suggested by (1) knowledge or ignorance of events and
the impact of awareness of those events, (2) age, e.g. contrast the day before
he went into prison with the day after he came out. Different people know
fragments e.g. sailor clinging to wreckage claiming responsibility for
motivation, though he may be shock-crazed and fulfilling a dream; a
woman wanting a baby by a handsome strong man – can she use him?
Extreme situations because normality contains violence and horror which
is only averted by conventions which sometimes break down. No good/bad,
responsibility; no one to blame, things happen. No esoteric or intellectual
elements which can be got at source. Suggest thoughts by describing
objects outside in the way a thoughtful man thinks of them. Create patterns
for the reader to create details.

16th December. Met Fitzsimmons at 5.30 at Tokyo Central, outside
subway. Fitzsimmons: "Watch out you don't get ill – all artists believe
they're indestructible." Wisdom beneath a deerstalker hat and a beat-up
donkey-jacket. Process/plan. Reconcile purposelessness/development and
cultural/physical/metaphysical (= "why we are"). "Humans are the only
creatures who are disappointed." The breakdown of Christianity won't
leave a ripple because of behaviour patterns, e.g. Japan has no religion but
social norms and Zen and practices which mock abuse of strength. "Feeling
your being flow." The Japanese admire mechanisation and don't care about
metaphysics. They worship Noh and Kabuki because it is Japanese, i.e the
West is metaphysical, the East is materialistic.

19th December. C: "Never mind if she cries." Never mind about my
concentration.
    Shinto. Yoyo-gi Hachiman (war-god) shrine, Shibuya-ku. A hill, pines.

57

Stone shrine, to-ri ("bird-home"), kagara dance, dogs ("komaine = imaginary dog). Shrine: latticed wood ("ichimazu goshi"), curved roofs ("shinden zukui" = structure in shrine style), streamers (5: red, yellow, blue, mauve, white) to ring closed bell over donation box. You clap twice, pray, clap twice again after summoning the God, then the crows call "Ah ah ah". Before, wash hands in a trough near a neolithic hut of straw and wooden gate; small shrine at back for "inari" (fox). China foxes, red aprons on stone foxes, fried bean-curds ("aburaage", fried oil) placed for God to eat.

Orange trees. Protection from evil spirits. Shinto has lost its meaning, is now a wedding ceremony, not a doctrine. And so the Shinto-grove is a place of (1) desperate search for reviving meaning, (2) ritualistic exhaustion.

20th December. Buchanan came in the evening and talked generally. His record: army, embassy, 17 years' teaching. He is going to Hong Kong to stay with the Consul-General, husband of an ex-pupil of his. The wife turned up in the rain in October 1966. "I give my money to my maid/mistress."

The Celestial Dragon (symbol of Heaven). Ryo-an-ji ("dragon peace-temple"); cf kiomizu dara ("sweet/holy water temple").

21st December. Visit to Nishiwaki, rather a vain, conceited man; awkward and solitary at first, while Ando delivered his rebukes: "But Professor Nishiwaki is an authority on Joyce", etc. When Nishiwaki said that reputations were imposed I took him up on it and made out that his was not deserved. Ando: "But Professor Nishiwaki's reputation is earned, he is a technical innovator." Nishiwaki: "I write for my reputation!"

Then Nishiwaki began to get drunk on whisky. He presented me with his poems and read aloud *January in Kyoto* (cf T. S. Eliot reading *The Waste Land* with commentary!) and said bitterly that only second rate poets got the Nobel Prize (sour grapes) and that he would nonetheless accept it if he were given it "for Japan's sake". Ando: "As Professor Nishiwaki is unpredictably drunk..." Nishiwaki: "I want to kiss hands with Mr Hagger and toast his figure, his face, his hair, his knowledge and his mind. He is the greatest Englishman, a real scholar. I am seldom wrong in my intuition, but one day you will be the greatest man in England – and not only England, all of Europe. One day you will get the Nobel Prize." This theme was repeated throughout the evening. Ando: "Professor Nishiwaki is not a sychophant." Nishiwaki: "Never forget, make the public come to you on your terms. Impose your will on the public. As Wordsworth said, teach the public the taste by which you are relished."

Readings from Joyce and (Dylan) Thomas and Nishiwaki of course and then to first a low-class then a high-class bar for saké and brandy. I arrived home rather unsteadily: the stars were fascinating, very bright.

Five senses writing, tactile prose.

JAPAN: SCEPTICISM AND ETERNITY (1963 – 1964)

23rd December. These hard clear sunsets with indeterminate colours.

24th December. A day of interruptions: I took ¥955,000 to the bank in horror of being robbed, and as soon as I got back Buchanan took us out, after giving us a blanket and Nadi a teddy-bear. We ate raw fish at Hill-Top Hotel. We got back at 3 and then Narita called at 5, bringing whisky and grapefruit.

An unexpected change in the temperature made me sweat: apparently it will be cold and wet tomorrow.

Narita: "*Saturday Afternoon and Monday Evening*. I mean *Saturday Night and Sunday Morning*."

9.54 an earthquake. Where the epicentre was I don't know, probably in the Pacific. It sounded as though a tube was going underneath the house. For ten seconds the floor shook, then the walls creaked, the windows rattled and the glass in the bookcase rang out. Then it got worse and I thought the ceiling was coming down. I stood up. C was frightened. She stood up. I should have gone to the door but instead I went into Nadi, who was still asleep. It was like walking on a motor-boat that has no list. Then it stopped.

25th December. Tomlin's party. Tomlin got slewed: paper hats, the fortune-telling fish (Tomlin was cold and dead), mottoes. The kitchen staff went wrong: brandy not lit, no brandy-butter. Whisky, champagne, wine, cognac. Tomlin has been to Ghadames and is a Christian.

Buchanan waiting when we got back.

Lunch: The Christmas pudding mishap, rehearsal went wrong. Tomlin is a shy man who has to go out, open and close the lavatory door, then return – all to indicate that he's busy.

26th December. Buchanan came to dinner. He was a Lt. Colonel in the Signals Section.

27th December. 12.40 Two loud bangs – a vertical earthquake. The windows shook for a few moments and then all was over. Emiko (my maid) pointed to next door and said "Mistake". It's loss of face to admit that Japan has these phenomena.

30th December. At Nobe with Buchanan. Kwenon (Kannon) goddess of mercy. 17th century, newly cleaned. The sea booming. The hut, the thatched roof near it; saké on the tatami. Photos. Binoculars and naval movements. "Your sense of direction is good."

Buchanan's trouble with the geisha, left Keikosan, blackmailed by geisha's father. Keikosan's policeman brother pulling him out of it, so now Buchanan looks after two of Keikosan's brother's three children.

Boyce (my predecessor in this bungalow) the corruptor and pervert, three women a day and a fetish for two sisters at once. Blackmailed, but

Narita's response. Buchanan's book on Japan would be titled "Yes and No." Are they honest, are they moral? Yes and no.

1964

1st January. Was violently sick after bloated over-eating at Narita's: octopus, mokshi with seaweed. Went to bed at 9 p.m.

4th January. Tomlin to dinner: talked from the point of view of the history of science – necessary because concepts change meaning, e.g. 17th century matter in science, 18th century philosophy. Pre-Socratic (no division between supernatural and natural) and pre-Cartesian (no division between mind and body) views of Nature, which is One World in which we are monisms that can be seen in three ways, organic, psychical and spiritual (all other concepts to be swept aside). So we are a part of Nature; there is no hostile Existential universe. Oneness with Nature eliminates the whole epistemological debate since Descartes (e.g. Berkeley).

Justifications. (1) The greatest argument for freewill and value is that I can say "I value freewill" – these cannot be relative and man-made because no machine could rebel, it conks out and a mechanic tightens a bolt. So they're part of the Absolute. (2) Beware of a confusion of categories, e.g. what I am thinking about *Ode to a Nightingale* bears no relation to the permutations of lights in a mansion; it hasn't been proved that information is stored in the brain-cells. Information can't be passed on by genes or nitrogen in DNA, Crick has faked it and seen it in the wrong terms. Intensity of thought bears relation to electricity, but not its quality, e.g. there is as much electricity in a bad pop singer as in Mozart. If I'm just conditioning, I'm my environment, not me. So who (not what) is doing the thinking? We are a manifestation of the Absolute as we live in One World; i.e. argue from the intellect, not emotion or experience.

To what extent does knowing the Absolute help us to live our lives, assuming that death does not affect the spiritual part of ourselves? We're here for a reason, there's a plan, the reason is not revealed, so we must seek.

Tomlin debunked Humanism ("a swindle"), Existentialism ("naive, contortionist" and "We could have told Sartre that Existentialism was a Humanism without having to read his book"), (Kingsley) Amis ("a good mimic, I will say that for him"), Jung ("The archetypes should be in the conscious like Plato's forms, why did he have to stick them back there?") and Carstairs. False gods include natural selection.

Why does one rebel? Why did the first cell undergo mitosis? These are the two fundamental questions of philosophy: value and science. "No, if God does exist everything is permitted, because we can sin a good deal and be forgiven." Would Tomlin be so rationally metaphysical if he'd suffered so much as Dostoevsky? Yes (19th June 1975).

5th January. I'm undergoing an upheaval. My temperament cries out for the metaphysical – the dignity of mind, freedom, rebellion, value, all force me temperamentally into a metaphysical position. But I can't take a life after death, no matter how you dress it up; I can't take the Absolute value of effort, the concern of an infinite Absolute. My intellect, my feeling, my instinct – all rebel against that. Yet why do I rebel? Why have I the awareness to rebel? Because I've a metaphysical being in me? Turmoil, turmoil, turmoil.

The point, to Tomlin, is to attain the Absolute.

Tomlin: "Not having a metaphysic is committing mental suicide."

Sartre: his denial of God requires a mechanistic position which he denies by asserting the primacy of freedom which he can't hold because he denies God.

Why not raw freedom? Why a rational system? (Which is what Tomlin's is.)

6th January. Introvert the pagan ideal: nobility and heroism in terms of self-perfection, not action.

Tomlin: if we are all One and part of a One and value is spiritual, then God has value.

Is linguistic analysis of value?

If I am organic and psychical and spiritual then Reality is organic and psychical and spiritual.

The key is the genetic code.

9th January. To Yokohama for my trunk.

10th January. V. H. Mottram. Personality depends on thalamus-cortex dominance; sense/mind and the "spiritual". Pragmatism: "what difference will it make to you?"

Alfred North Whitehead: "Scientists who spend their life with the purpose of proving that it is purposeless constitute an interesting subject of study."

Neo-Darwinism: proteins as link between dead matter, viruses and living protoplasm. Biogenesis: life cannot be spontaneously generated from dead matter.

Mystic experience of Unity: everyday "I" and real "I".

I have thought all day about the great divide between Science and Religion – between cold, arid Mechanism and the vitalism of the One I so want to believe in, and I have come to one conclusion: science can never explain why.

Yet we are for the most part machines: how much are we machines, where is the raw One-force of the Life-Intelligence, and how does it come to be in the brain?

11th January. My trunk arrived and with it this diary.

16th January. Universe. To Newton and Leibniz the universe was a harmonious machine, everything orderly, predictably necessary, purposive. But existence is gratuitous, contingent, i.e. there is no planned evolution to some purpose, except what individuals make of it.

All novels record experience in terms of "consciousness". All traditional novels make traditional assumptions about "consciousness". The overthrow of these traditional assumptions calls for a revaluation of traditional experiences.

Journalism and sociology are the two enemies of the novel.

The Absurd: what cannot be reduced to reason or logic. We greet it with laughter, the French with tears.

What threw up rebellious value?

17th January. On a life-centre. To live positively and avoid drifting one must have a centre. Without this concrete dream, will-power gets you nowhere. Most people are content with the rhythm of work, entertainment and domestic ambition. If this is not satisfying, there is a need for a life-centre. The more you feel the need, the more its salvation is suggested, for you see things through the form of your salvation: a painter wants to paint the truth about the faces he meets. In searching for the need's solution, it is necessary to abandon one's notion of one's own past: a being with limited talents, a third secretary. The dilemma of pride. If one succeeds one is a genius of vision and originality, if one fails one should have kept to one's station and is one of history's fools, a man of hubris. The vision is normally associated with originality: Einstein, Gaugin, Joyce. It is this which links situations and history, and prevents one from ossifying morally.

On Eternity. Belief in an eternity is the highest thing that man is capable of, and also the most primitive. All the profoundest books of our time are approaches to eternity.

There are two approaches to eternity, the objective (relativity, biology and Whitehead, physics) and the subjective (the mystics, Eliot's *Four Quartets* and significance, Kirilov's "I know eternity"). No scientific discovery is going to abolish subjective experiences, only objective concepts, i.e. an eternity in which a subject can share is still possible, but an eternity in a subject that survives a subject's death is not possible.

Power over self is still possible, but if human beings come to an end in death then life and the universe are meaningless and purposeless, and all civilisations have no goal. Therefore Materialism rules, and there will be no "spiritual" power (cf the finite) – putting it very simply.

The denial of eternity is not a terrible new weapon, and would only be a "moral problem" (U.S.) to a genuinely religious man.

Man's thirst for spiritual power and religion.

Quotations on Eternity.

Blake: "Eternity is in love with the productions of time."
           "He who kisses a joy as is it flies

JAPAN: SCEPTICISM AND ETERNITY (1963 – 1964)

	Lives in Eternity's sun-rise."
Shelley:	"White Radiance."
Dostoevsky:	"Immortality."
Eliot:	(1) "To be conscious is not to be in time....
	Only through time time is conquered."
	(2) "We cannot think of a time that is oceanless
	Or of an ocean not littered with wastage....
	We have to think of them as forever bailing...,
	Not as making a trip that will be unpayable."
T. E. Hulme:	"Mechanism is the obstacle a saint must surmount."
c.f. Eliot:	"But to apprehend
	The point of intersection of the timeless
	With time is an occupation for the saint...
	For most of us, there is only the unattended
	Moment, the moment in and out of time."
	Eternity in literature: compare significance.
Spinoza:	"We feel and know that we are eternal."
Shelley:	"But the pure spirit shall flow
	Back to the burning fountain whence it came,
	A portion of the Eternal."
cf Marvell:	"And yonder all before us lie
	Desarts of vast Eternity."
Blake:	"To see a World in a grain of sand
	And a Heaven in a wild flower.
	Hold Infinity in the palm of your hand
	And Eternity in an hour."
Vaughan:	"I saw Eternity the other night
	Like a great ring of pure and endless Light."
Keats:	"Dost tease us out of thought
	As doth Eternity...."
Coriolanus:	"He wants nothing of a god but eternity" (V iv 25).
Hamlet:	"All that live must die
	Passing through nature to eternity" (I ii 72).
Eliot:	"The sea is the land's edge also, the granite
	Into which it reaches, the beaches where it tosses
	Its hints of earlier and other creation....
	...The salt is on the briar rose,
	The fog is in the fir trees."
cf Spinoza:	"I understand Eternity to be existence itself."
Wittgenstein:	"If by Eternity is understood not endless temporal
	duration but timelessness, then he lives eternally who
	lives in the present."
	"Is a riddle solved by the fact that I survive for ever? Is
	this eternal life not as enigmatic as our present one? The
	solution of the riddle of life in space and time lies

outside space and time. Not how the world is, is the
mystical, but that it is."

Tithonus:	anti-eternity.
Huxley:	pro-eternity.

18th January. Wrote an essay: "What is the theme of the *Waste Land* and
how does Eliot handle it?"

19th January. What really appeals to children's sense of humour is the
adult world breaking down, e.g. the car wouldn't go, Smee in *Peter Pan*
(tearing the sewing).

A wearying weekend.

20th January. Ekkehard spends all morning sitting and reading and
thinking: Frisch, Kafka, Dostoevsky. He only looks about 28 but he must
be nearly 40: his memories extend long before the war. "My life is too dull
to record."

The profundity of living through a new dimension. Today I reread *The
Grand Inquisitor* and my intellectual resistance was weaker than ever. I
want to value love and forgiveness as the highest expressions of existence
– I already acknowledge that they are – but I can't do it through the Christian
framework. But how I'd like to.

My life-centre is shifting, I'm living through a new part of myself: a new
awareness. It's not dry and arid and rational, it's warm and there's a deep
wonder and love at the heart of it that makes me involved in things and not
consider my petty pride. Who am I? Who?

21st January. Sometimes death terrifies me; when my circulation stops
in a finger, as it does three or four times a day, I cannot help seeing that
finger as part of my lifeless corpse. Any day I may die – never has this truth
been so real to me, never has it been less of a rational attitude.

22nd January. Tomlin and Colin Wilson make a corner, cf Shaw and
Yeats – the metaphysical, opposing scientific materialism with religion.

Clearing away the ground for a philosophy which is Vitalism rather than
Mechanism.

Develop towards a metaphysical position: "You can't explain man."

Self-change and Mechanism are incompatible. But.... (Any ism or
scientific theory must acknowledge that fact.)

23rd January. Going abroad is an effortless accumulation of experience.
You freshen your senses on even the most mundane walk, and the slightest
triviality is a manifestation of a strange culture.

The quality of an author's mind: certain minds are indispensable to me,
I feel unhappy if I don't have those minds on my bookshelf, and even if I

don't share them for a week there's comfort in the knowledge that they're there.

Read Whitehead.

25th January. Speight's lecture on T.S. Eliot's *Murder in the Cathedral*. I feel a disquiet from being with the wrong people.

26th January. To Nobe. Read *Heart of Darkness* in the Yokosuka train. It made a tremendous impression on me. I quite understand how Eliot must have felt in his deck-chair on Margate Sands.

Buchanan's godmother was Mrs. Patrick Campbell, and when he was a boy he knew Maud Gonne and met Synge and Shaw in Dublin, and also the Irish revolutionaries, e.g. James Connolly.

The two Wastelanders of the 20th century – Eliot and Greene – both draw the expression of their tradition from the *Heart of Darkness*. (Cf Greene's *Heart of the Matter* and *A Burnt-out Case*.)

27th January. Evil is excessive egoism, for egoism is at the root of all harm. Evil, then, is a lack of value; and the greater the lack, the greater the evil seems less of a lack and more of an independent force, as at Auschwitz.

Attack on Scientific Materialism, which contains the causes of all evil by denying value. No matter how far away the metaphysical alternatives seem, I must attack it at all costs; I must work towards the Absolute at all costs.

Whitehead: the contradiction between Mechanism and self-determining organisms.

28th January. The Doomed and the Dying, i.e. doomed Scientific Rationalism and dying Metaphysics.

The Mechanist and the Metaphysician.

So Adrian Hohler (from Oxford) is living two roads away from me, and I thought I'd escaped Oxford once and for all in coming out here. Vae victis!

31st January. Adrian: "Tomlin's theories are more preposterous than Mechanism."

3rd February. Talked with the notorious Mr Togo who proved to be unexpectedly shy, charming and intelligent. He has the reputation for being the Communist leader of Kyoikudai (Tokyo University of Education). "Until the war we pitied the Chinese. They were inferior to us and we felt sorry for them. Now we acknowledge their plight."

5th February. I'm at war with society. I want to master it and force myself from its stupidity. I shall do it by making a million out of its stupidity, its vanity.

Met Fitzsimmons, who is suffering from pemphigus (an internal allergy) and is kept alive by cortisone, which means insanity, ulcers or total remission. His New England background, his Michigan security of tenure. He has been betrayed by his body, his boils and burns. The artist can't run a family and earn money.

In philosophy he was anti-Tomlin because he affirms a physical basis of everything and no Absolutes, because all is dependent on the environment; "Plato, Aristotle, Aquinas and Descartes are the villains of history, chopping everything up and falsely labelling." Organism is not "what has an organ" but "what energy can form a compound and react" (as matter is energy) so he is anti-Mechanism and anti-Vitalism which divide into life and matter.

The environment; we can never never never never escape it.

6th February. Whitehead's definition of "organism"?

Earthquake 8.20 last night: 3 on a scale of 7. Very short, but a little rattling at the end that was quite frightening.

13th February. "The Silver Age". "Decaydence", a student's misspelling.

15th February. Corrected Keio papers.

18th February. Fitzsimmons: "Art is something that involves the whole being, not just the intellect" (i.e. reason). We drank saké, not beer, and went on to Manos in Akasaka. Russian kitchen, Embassy men. Ako: "When I feel like it; yes, I feel contempt." "I like it and charge money."

22nd February. Have been reading Bacharach's history of composers in four volumes. How many men have created out of loneliness, horror and starvation, and for how many the reward has been madness and early death. There's a warning in it. It's the Artistic Wager, this sacrifice. What leads men to do it? Not the gratitude of future generations, I'm sure of that; just one blind upward-driving need-thrust, just one obsession. It's as though the body has to get even with the spirit for ridiculing its limitations.

The subconscious has its own language and characters, like Chinese, and to interpret it one has to learn the language and characters.

29th February. Accepted Todai (Tokyo University) on Wednesdays. (Professor) Hijikata, flattering and obsequious. Tomlin gives a free hour a week. Rainer: "Often I'd like to become a part of a mountain, a snowflake or a drop of rain, just to be permanent."

Nadi's fall. Segawa's visit, then a drunk Buchanan, full of repetitions – trying to impress with stories of what he was supposed to have told his hates.

Adrian's stammer and nervousness; his manner and front. He would be lost in situations which aren't dignified.

JAPAN: SCEPTICISM AND ETERNITY (1963 – 1964)

1st March. Read Powell's A *Question of Upbringing*. Polished style but very external-social view of character, no extremes, no interiorisation, no treatment of aloneness. An immense distance. As much relation to the possibilities of reality as a dancefloor has. But nonetheless interesting, although characters are so ordinary, although theme and title are so self-evident.

20th March. I have been reading the lives of the Great Murderers (Kürten) and trace many sex-crimes to a physiological glandular disorder whereby sexual satisfaction is dependent on the sight of blood. No "moral" law can judge such a man "guilty".

22nd March. Comic possibilities: a shower of a fire station ("where's my helmet"); the indisciplined which should be disciplined. Also a businessman killed by a fire caused when his match broke in the course of an attempt to light his cigar; the monstrous out of the ordinary, with a certain amount of bizarre social justice.
Beethoven's violin concerto: the peace, the ineffable moment, quite incommunicable. As earlier this evening I walked beneath a violet dusk and was touched by the carnal nakedness of the moon, an immediacy I could not communicate.

23rd March. I have not a great mind, but I have a greater vision than anyone else I know. I have never doubted that I shall be great: I always think of myself in terms of great men and feel disgruntled unless, after reading something that impressed me, I have not done something equally good within half an hour. I work too hard, much too hard. There's a singing in my ears now from the strain of doing everything, yet I won't slacken. I shall die from overwork: perhaps because I know this my greatest enemy is impatience. Yet relaxation is my greatest fear; it's too like sloth.

25th March. Self-creation by one's actions. A man begins as nothing and ends as a powerful spiritual giant – through his own freedom – conquering all his faults. He creates himself as a human being out of an intellectual despairer, creates himself a man out of a nihilistic experimenter.
A dying man reviews his life, the self-creation that has gone into it. In his deepening contact with death he realises that it was not in vain and comes to understand the meaning of suffering: "To exist at any price."

31st March. Visit to Ochanomizu dental hospital. Poor C; rows of chairs and lights and drills, and tiled walls. C fainted but drilling continued.
Bought Toynbee. Am very preoccupied in the rise and fall of civilisations at present. Poised as we are on the collapse of the 21st perfected civilisation, I can only hope that the barbaric tongues of the decadent Silver Age will throw up one golden writer in me.

67

3rd April. A party. Mrs. Witt-Diamant, founder of the San Francisco U.S. poetry movement, had a love affair with Dylan Thomas. Tomlin, complaining he has no time to write but upset when not invited: lonely since he agreed to a divorce. His wife has custody of their child and has remarried an Italian.

4th April. I always feel lonely the night after a cocktail party: a socially-centred person must feel lonely when alone all the time, an itch in his heart for contact with people, no matter how superficial a contact.

The cherry-blossom fertility-vegetation ceremony; radio bulletin on the progress until the sakura (cherry blossom)-party in Ueno Park outside the many-layered temple.

Love is like civilisation: the initial energy, then the decay, the preservation of the status quo.

5th April. 10.45 a.m. An earthquake just as I was filling my pen. My chair was pushed up a little and there was a swaying sensation as on a ship: it lasted three seconds at most.

Classical style: not a word that is not necessary.

Buchanan's dress-maker.

Adrian has received a black mark from Cortazzi, Chief of Chancery Guard, for driving too fast in the (British) Embassy Compound. Apparently this can affect his chances of promotion.

9th April. I'm learning Japanese from my daughter: "Kochi-koi", "come here".

Rickyisms:

W. E. Henley: "I am the master of my fate,/ I am the captain of my soul."

Clough: "Say not the struggle naught availeth."

Clare: "My friends forsake me like a memory lost."

Livy: "Vae victis!"

Donne: "I am mine own Executioner."

11th April. Lunch at Kiyooka's; saw Fukuzawa's treasures: wall-hanging, boxes, gold soup bowls, special plates.

Poem written two hours before his death: "Yuki sugi te/Mata furikaeru/ Aki no kaze." = The Autumn wind, having gone too far, turning back and looking behind. (Fukuzawa Yasokichi.)

12th April. Last night, in bed, my wife asleep, I felt the old terror of dying. I can't get it out of my mind now. Whenever I relax to sleep after a hard day's writing I lie on my back and place my hands across my breast in a dead man's position, close my eyes, and imagine remaining like that for eternity, not existing. I must stop doing it.

JAPAN: SCEPTICISM AND ETERNITY (1963 – 1964)

Neo-Classicism + Neo-Romanticism – is that the new movement? Both the fixed and the unlimited.

15th April. Diagnosed acute inflammation of middle ear by a German-speaking ear-nose-throat specialist: oil and water syringe caused it, he said. New novel by Golding: *The Spire*.

Buchanan has just brought me his English version of the specialist's report: I shall go deaf very soon unless I have an operation soon; 5 days treatment to be tried first. This is the fulfilment of Keogh's prophecy, made when I was 8: that nothing will prevent me from going deaf at 30. Ear-treatment has progressed since then.

And so the one surviving-healthy member of the Haggers is threatened. Effects of cathocycline: a rise in temperature, lethargy.

17th April. To the Japan-British Society in evening. Anthony Powell, all bum and Oxford accent, talking too much. "I still don't know how it's done." "You have to bum around and live first." "I've got enough material for another 30 years, it's organising it that's hard." "Novelists fall into two types: those who produce and reduce, and those who produce and add. I'm the second. An idea is excruciating for me. I write it in 30 words, then 90, then 300, and that's my day's work. I can't churn it out." "My great theory is that experience is all the same for everybody." (Cf Joyce to Djuna Barnes: "A writer must never write about the extraordinary. That is for the journalist.")

The speech of Nakajima: "Mr Powell is very popular, if not as popular as Mr Somerset Maugham." E. W. F. Tomlin introduced to an admirer who did not say a word.

18th April. Tomlin: "Talk about *Four Quartets*, he hadn't four words to his name."

To Sanseido to look for books.

Earlier Emi (our maid) asked to leave. Long talk on the veranda, explaining it would be mutually beneficial in view of my financial position. "Smiling parting." Emi doesn't like a maid's job, feels she doesn't understand enough. Very good trier really.

Emiko went: feel strangely depressed. Somehow she provided security, though she evidently saw me as security-provider for this house. The house feels emptier, more lonely.

21st April. The situation. We never fear the concrete, only the unknown.

Large boil in my ear has left me doubled up with pain. Can't eat, can't talk, feel like Job. When I cancelled Keio Iwasaki, who didn't understand, asked whether it was due to alcohol. Earlier ear specialist: "Did you have any alcohol last night?"

22nd April. Second day of boil – complete apathy, energylessness, boredom, pain.

Tailless cats. (Manx cats). First mosquito.

25th April. Aching left ear now. Toothache, jaw ache, glands, neck ache. God.

26th April. Lunch with Edmund Blunden who proved to be an aged, shock-haired hook-nosed man with beady eyes; suffering from chronic asthma with a perpetual shaking hand that made beer-pouring very difficult. He was strangely timid, not just gentle. Often he would begin to speak then stop, if he had to compete against another voice. He spoke in a quiet undertone, little above a whisper. With opinions, he is the least self-opinionated man I have met, and will listen contentedly to a heated argument on Lear without feeling any need to intrude.

He was slightly paranoiac (e.g. "People are saying I was pro-Nazi and pro-Communist") and has an old man's fear of functions ("I don't know anyone at this cocktail party tonight"). Likes his beer and everything comes back to cricket. ("The Greenes have made some fifties between them.") Often pathetically helpless: "I'll be cut off back in England, it's a long way to the station and I don't know anyone who has a car. Perhaps Auden will help." His agent is Peters ("another cricketer").

Of Greene: "He directs his own life and can smoke opium without getting addicted; he is in touch with fighting." "He is quiet. He has a passion for Literature without considering his own contribution." Of Clare, poems about Epping Forest. Talk of the Owl (public house, Lippitt's Hill). Of Owen: "He never told anyone he was a poet when in the front line."

I kept on imagining that he was going to die on the tatami matting, that the three of us would have to lay him out.

(He spoke at some length about Shakespeare's retirement in Stratford, and said that Shakespeare must have continued writing during his retirement, and that somewhere in Stratford, in some attic, there is a trunk of his last writings in manuscript, waiting to be discovered.)

27th April. Irie asking about Coney Hatch, mentioned in Galsworthy's address: "If the advance of science continues, the whole nation will be queueing up outside Coney Hatch."

Dr. Ozenberger, timid, small Jew with bald head and spectacles and incongruously white coat. No word when I went in and told him. "Show me". "Lie down" "Shall I take my shoes off?" "Why should you? We're not in a mosque are we? It's not tatami in here is it?" Later: "It's nothing. Been worried? Is this important to you?" (Suggesting that nothing worries him any more.)

28th April. Ears got worse as I had to shout to a second class of 89.

The dinner party in the former Bolivian Embassy. ("If I dig in the garden I'll find packets of heroin.")

29th April. Infection of middle ear again. The wheel has turned full circle. The Rechabite (total abstainer).

4th May. Everything is suddenly green: ivy and willow and cherry-leaf green.

Flower arrangements, ikebana. Existing 1,200 years ago, an art by Ashikaga Era, most flourishing in Tokugawa Era. Originated in Tokonoma.

Main theme ten-chi-jin = heaven-earth-man, all in a unity for Zen meditation. Flowers to symbolize "Heaven", "Man" and "Earth": stem = Heaven, twig on right bent sideways = Man, lowest twig or branch on left with end slightly bent so that it points upward = Earth. Stalks and branches in odd numbers because even numbers considered unlucky.

The modern school Sōgetsu specialises in abstract arrangements not only with flowers but also with rocks, wires, paints, buttons, etc. "Surrealistic ikebana." "Hana" includes blossoms and flowerless trees and shrubs.

7th May. 11 a.m. to Tomlin. Irie had to be taken, though he's met Tomlin twice already: no introduction was necessary, and I was just rather redundant and went off to the library.

Later, an evangelising Irie talked Quakerism. He is an Emersonian and Monist as opposed to a Dualist and visited Dr. Suzuki to check disparities on Tuesday.

An earthquake – I thought – in the middle of my seated British Council debate with long-winded Mr M talking through it and everyone smirking and casting furtive glances of alarm at the swaying floor. No earthquake felt in Bunkyo-ku or reported, however, so I record the situation.

16th May. Wrote "essay" all day.

At Todai: "What is the universe? We cannot answer this question, because we are part of the universe" (Zen). Schiller: "Uber sentimentalische und naive Dichtung." "The sentimental man imposes feelings on flowers, the naive man sees a flower as it is."

17th May. Old Japanese Folk Songs. (1) Aizu-bandai-san. "Hā/-Aizu-bandai-san wa/takara no yama yo/ Sasani kogane no é /mata narisagaru / Ohara Shosuke-san/nande shinsho tsubushita/ Asané, Asazake, Asaya (Asa-bobo varita) ga/ daisuki de/ Sorede shinsho tsubushita /a multo-moa motto muda." "Oh, Mount Bandai in Aizu is the treasure mountain. Even the leaf of bamboo grows gold. Mr Shosuke Ohara, he lost his fortune. Why? Because he was greatly fond of morning sleep, morning drink and morning bath (or sex). And so he lost his fortune. Chorus: Oh it's

71

quite natural, quite natural." (2) Kusatsu-bushi. "Oisha-sama demo,/Kusatsu no yu demo/ dokkoisho/ Koi no yamai mo/ Korya naoryasenu yo,/ choina, choina." "Even by the specialist or even by the hot spring at Kusatsu, love-sickness (the disease of love) cannot be cured." Also another version: "Kusatsu yoi toko ichi do wa oide/ dokkoisho/ O-yu no naka ni mo korya /hana ga saku yo choina choina." "As Kusatsu is a nice place, you should visit it at least once; even flowers will come into bloom in its hot water." (3) Soran-bushi. "Yaren soran, soran soran, soran, soran/ hai hai/ Okino kamome ni shiodoki kikeba/ Watasha tatsutori é/ nami ni kike, choi,/ yasa, en-en-ya-sa-no,/ dokkoisho,/ A dokkoisho." "When one asks the seagull how the tide is (= the time of the tide), then the seagull answers 'I am the bird going away so ask the tide itself.'" Sung by fishermen – soran = "heave-ho". (4) Kurodabushi. Saké song = soldier song. "Sake wa nome, nome, nomunaraba,/Hinomoto-ichi no kono yari o,/Nomitoru hodo nomunaraba, /Korezo makotono kurodabushi."

18th May. Typed all day, outside lectures.

Geisha: "mizuagé", "breaking virginity", when a geisha is taken on by a danna (-san), = wealthy millionaire client, who buys her out and puts her in a house to become his second wife. Not to be confused with "fude-oroshi", = using the calligrapher's brush/penis for the first time. Compare "karyu-kai" (= "the flowery-willowy world") and "akasen(-kiuku)" (=red line, the prostitutes' quarter formerly permitted by law). The caste-system is still in operation: "mizushobai", "the water business", which includes bar-hostesses and restaurant proprietors. Flirting: the word used is charm – "iroke" (literally colour-hue).

19th May. Philosophy of "micromany" = attention to small objects. Claimed to have been invented by a Keio postgraduate.

Japanese dancing to the sami-sen.

The Japanese doctrine of aesthetics in relation to nature: mono-no-aware. Much scholastic speculation about this, but it contains the idea of world-sadness, the Weltschmerz, and therefore the Japanese sentimentality. It is supposed to be a requirement in classical Japanese writing. An expression of it is in the festival at the full moon of autumn, "skimi" or "tsugimi", looking at the moon. So a group of Japanese can break off from jazz and look at the moon for ten minutes, then return to their jazz.

20th May. Met Fitzsimmons in Shibuya. Discussed a film we'd make. The fantasies, memories and illusions of a dying man: his roles and masks as philosopher, artist, statesman; his struggle for power and renunciation. His self-creation, his self-unification, overcoming the conflict between his sensuality and asceticism, which he relives, against a background that is a region of his mind, e.g. a waste of snow, an intimate pub. His final recollection of all the opposites in himself until all becomes a blur and he dies on this note of illusion/reality. Techniques: into an eye, through to a room's keyhole, through to another scene. The maze, labyrinthine form with an apparently incoherent connection between rooms. House/head (*Gerontion*).

Fitzsimmons's poems. "A trivial subject soon ceases to be trivial – like the crack of a door widening when you push it open." "Sand trickling/down:/Through fingers/grudging every grain./Mounded miniature of suns/Mound of tiny/deaths:/The moon dips low/To beckon in the sea."

(Shoeseller) Freddy Durrant died. Memories from the 1940s: X-rays green (an X-ray machine for seeing if shoes were too tight, you could see the bones of your toes), the red face, the smell of new leather, the pipe and bushy eyebrows, "the currant" (we used to chant "Freddy Durrant ate a currant").

22nd May. Met Ando at Shimbashi. The sumo wrestlers in their wide-sleeved robes, their top-knots. Sagasan and Norikosan. The geisha's cart or rickshaw (jin riki shi = man-power cart) which looks like a London gasman's canvas tent on wheels – the broken cellophane and the split, flapping canvas yet the impossibility of seeing inside. The old iron carriage in the foyer of the Viscount near Dentsu Building, and the girls looking for men to take them home as taxis are difficult to come by. The saké-pourer's stock-saying: "We're single (dokushin = bachelor = alone body) for tonight." The sensual indulgence and frankness that could never take place in Puritanical England; the rooms in the Japanese restaurant and the earthen wall which takes a year to make and has been a traditional part of Japanese architecture for 500 years.

24th May. Kamakura. The Dai-butsu (Big Buddha), serene and and aloof in a grove turned into a bourgeois horror: picnics, group snapshots, parades of high school students beneath banners. The rings for hair, vaguely green; the pimple on the forehead, the pierced ears with their exaggerated lobes, the curled lips with their sneer of indifference, beneath whose expression the hands seem redundant.The lotus in modern art in front on either side. The large straw-thonged sandals hanging hopefully and jarringly to the left.

Later the lobster restaurant: the tanks of fresh lobsters where you take your pick. The black volcanic sand-ash, each one a moon, the salt smell and the dry bladderwrack and a brooding sun-numbed sadness I could not associate with anything in particular.

Okayama sorted out: Baker going in my place as the British Council cannot pay expenses.

Climbing in to Adrian's window: a box, rope, and the wooden strut outside the upstairs window were the main factors.

25th May. "A man with a blink and an accent."

27th May. Wrote *The Oceanographer at Night*.

28th May. Tsuchigane: "We Japanese smile at foreigners, and sometimes we respect them, but often we despise them, secretly."

31st May. Conversation on civilisation with Tony. The decline of Western civilisation is reflected in the progression of all arts and philosophy and science to an abstraction that can go no further. The West has developed scientifically but not spiritually and all the forms are dead: the new science is a symptom of decline, not the emergence of a new civilisation, though scientific discovery is part of emerging civilisations. Prophets arise to arrest the decline of civilisations and are hailed for their direction by the next civilisation as being before their time whereas in fact they are very much a part of their age. They do not suffer from pride if society believes them right (the disparity principle). The old analysis of civilisations, e.g. by Toynbee, doesn't work today: communications have improved. The next stage is the spreading of Western civilisation throughout the world while Western civilisation becomes more decadent, a process that can continue for 100 years at most. Then the bomb, an interregnum of anarchy and chaos, and the new civilisation begins with the energy of the survivors.

1st June. Japanese superstitions: thumbs under at funeral because thumbs symbolise parents; don't cut finger-nails at night or you won't see your parents' funeral; don't lie down after meal on tatami or you'll be reborn as a cow (which is not sacred as in India); don't go to sleep with your head to the north (dead men do); shi, 4 = "death": even numbers unlucky; salt purifies Devil (as in sumo), so it is used after marriage or in new house.

4th June. The fans like table-tennis bats in the Bank of Japan. Ekke liked my poem and urged me to have it published: *The Oceanographer At Night*.

The Japanese opening: "Thank you for your kind instructions, and will you be able to...?" Always, the dutiful thanks, eyes brimming with gratitude, for the precious time which sensei has generously set aside for deigning to trouble with his poor students. One day I'll tell them "I'm only doing this because I need money." The effect would be one of shock – shock that I had broken their social norm.

5th June. Night in Nobe: the jungle sounds: frogs croaking, birds whooping, owls hooting, cicadas. The Japanese house. Decorations: jars, shells, red nude on the wall head down, lanterns. Fans. Red pine wood and yellow wood. White papered doors.

Hishinouma the patriarch and the fishermen. Yukata – man's kimono: blue the predominating colour. The yellow-straw "igloos" on boats, the well outside the house.

JAPAN: SCEPTICISM AND ETERNITY (1963 – 1964)

6th June. Nobe. The rain, drumming on the roof. The Shinto temple with pictures of the Russian war showing the Japanese winning: the 15 dead commemorated on the boat of Eternity and the fish of life. Wild strawberries, Chinese dragons. The huge hill behind it. The cemetery with its coloured bell on a "ladder", the emptiness beneath the topmost stone to symbolise Japanese Nirvana.

The fantastic Milky Way and the darkness of the ravine, the invisible sea and the distant red light.

7th June. Nobe. The sea-shore littered with squids, sea-slugs, starfish and jellies. The threshers separating the chaff and the pile of grain, their cooly hats and the useless electric fan as a winnower (no battery). The frogs in the paddy fields and the women wading, scattering salt (?) and fertiliser (?), and weeding.

The climb up to the pylon. Large coloured spiders. The brilliant butterflies. The snake "yamamori" (= mountain adder) in red and black and yellow, after I said, "This is snake territory." Our tentative lobs with pieces of wood.

The hornet that intruded and the terror Adrian revealed: Adrian's moodiness, his refusal to answer often and his desire to be alone. The frivolty I associate with Oxford. Adrian: "I'm interested in facts, not patterns."

10th June. British Council party. Mrs. Ishibashi poetess, specialist in Yeats. Hijikata talking about Eliot and dropping his cigarette. Tomlin complaining that he's no time to write and arousing my curiosity as regards an "interesting" job. Rose Falkenstein, whose "palace" has a structural defect.

13th June. A farewell party for Fitzsimmons at the Mikasa Kaikhan, Ginza, at 6.30 p.m. Excruciating: half an hour at the table before any beer arrived: 14 either side. The blunders. Irie's speech: "And we hope that the time will come when you know what we really think about you." Silence. Fitzsimmons. "That's what we call an ambiguous statement." Irie. "Oh." Fukuda, "I've nothing to say." Narita, refusing to talk all evening. Mrs. Witt-Diamant, trying to reform the system for Enozawa: "Can't you let him have three hours for study?" Deathly silence. Mrs. Witt-Diamant: "You're not a Quaker are you?" (to Irie, who is). Fitzsimmons talking about Ginza bars before the Japanese, especially about the women. Worst of all, perhaps, the Fitzsimmons and Mrs. Witt-Diamant talking about Japanese stupidity: you say in good Japanese what you want and the Japanese reply is, "I am sorry I do not speak English." Mrs. Witt-Diamant, to assistant: "Does he speak Japanese?" "Yes." "Glad to hear it."

Jean Fitzsimmons: detachment beneficial to her, has been alone. Re Barbara, "She's a prude, she won't let any man plunge deep into her, figuratively speaking of course. She wants to be a Great Mind and has not the softness to attract men. She's not a woman. She has a neurotic fear of sex." Barbara wants to go to the U.K. to study Blake.

The incident: Fitzsimmons's luggage piled solemnly and ceremoniously by the Japanese between a chair and a steel cupboard: all dropped, knocked over by Fitzsimmons. "Get a fishing line." Fitzsimmons as 2nd class archer, with his Zen bow. Miyajima or Hiroshima for fire-walking: tread hard on cinders.

16th June. The earthquake 160 miles north of Tokyo, 5 on a scale of 7, at 1.01 p.m. In Keio, the 2nd floor windows began rattling, then distinct waves passed across the staff room floor, each of which I rode: the tables and chairs all shook as though a poltergeist, or dozens of them, were at work. It left me feeling slightly seasick, and I was giddy for about five minutes after. It lasted 1-2 minutes. Immense damage in Niigata Prefecture. My reaction: not to get up, it would have been cowardly. The reassuring sheepish grin of the woman by the door.

Narita's immediate reaction when I met him in the subway: "Thank you, thank you for...." Then he remembered he had nothing to thank me for and was trapped into an embarrassing dithering silence by his Japanese thank-complex. On parting there was a mix-up: I bowed and he extended his hand, I extended my hand and he bowed – until we finally made it shaking hands. His list mentality. "And what about Kermode?"

18th June. Ekke (my German colleague): "I make the stones speak."

20th June. A title: *Children at the Gate*. Will the veiled sister pray.

Eliot's distinction between prose and ordinary speech. I must evolve a dramatic prose that purifies and heightens ordinary everyday speech.

Technique of selection by omission rather than by inclusion: omitting what is irrelevant and showing only what is relevant to the theme, thereby liberating the drama from time and place, cf TV and films.

21st June. His mouse of a wife in his palace of a house: to Akiko, "what thoughts do you want to hear from sensei?"

22nd June. I have become more formal, less friendly. In class I am at my happiest when the atmosphere is remote, when there is no personal chit-chat. I am retreating, protectively, I am taking advantage of the barriers afforded by my position.

Shy with two people at a cocktail party, but not shy before 90 people at Keio.

The earthquake at Kyoikudai: the tilting and rattling.

23rd June. Pitakabesa and the Botah religion: presumably he failed

Responsions, moved from Worcester (College) to Hertford after passing there the term after I took over his room; presumably the legend of two Pitakabesas was apocryphal, and originated as the result of an unfortunate misunderstanding to which his shyness contributed. Miss Morita of Keio met Pitakabesa when Ando was at Oxford.

24th June. Epigraph: "To the head expert with sail and oar/The sea was calm" (Eliot).

Zen life:
- 4.30-5, 5.30-6 sitting
- 6 or 7 breakfast, rest
- 8.30-9.30 labour
- 10-11.30 sitting; rest
- 12 lunch; nap
- 2 labour
- 4-5 sitting
- 5.30 or 6.30 supper
- 7-8.30 lecture
- 8.30-9.30 sitting
- 10 bed.

25th June. Every day recently I have been aware of my vow: to become England's greatest writer or shoot myself. This wager lies behind everything I do, everything I think. I prepare myself for it. I say to myself "I must do such and such a thing because in ten years' time it will be invaluable to me." It's an absurd dream, but I know that it will come true, because I believe in it; and if I go bust, I have the reassuring thought that I'll go bust in a big way, once and for all: I fear death, but if I break my vow I will die, I will die.

26th June. Haga (i.e. Hagger), the Japanese Zen scholar, introduced by Irie. The Zen techniques: the search for unity, the unity between subject and object, beyond the comparative world.

Counting to 100, then let stray thoughts pass through: "live through your soul."

29th June. Met Waterstone at the Tokyo Medical and Surgical Clinic and got a lift back in his Embassy car. He was having three injections and his ears blown out, having swum and got sand in them. "I went to see Father Milward yesterday." Milward suffering from TB, is not allowed to read: he lies in bed composing sonnets which he writes himself.

2nd July. The Governor's woolly speech for the National Bankers' Convention – 10 pages of long ungrammatical sentences that read like the vomit from a book on banking and which was justified as being "in technical language".

3rd July. Foreign Office party at the Han-Nya-En, the former house of a Foreign Minister now run as a restaurant by the F.M.'s wife: springy green grass and about four wings, brown polished floors and tatami, Chinese roofs, lights. Koto played like a harpsichord or spinnet. Dancing. Waterstone, "I approved of the left-hand samurai"; her nobility and dignity and bearing. Mask-dance, then the baseball-dance. Later Adrian came with a camellia from Waterstone's garden. It smelt like a peach. Adrian's stories, he backed from an advancing woman into a pond, emerging with duckweed up to his knees and, moving on, he fell through a Japanese paper wall into a staid party next door full of speeches, left hissing through his hole. Waterstone: art seems an imaginary world, most people don't recognise that it's the real world, the artist's view is so true.

5th July. My dream: in China and execution inevitable in a number of various forms, e.g. hanging. The Chinese buildings I saw and would like to see again.

6th July. Barbara insists she doesn't attach too much importance to the mind, yet admits to being Puritanical. A disparity between her image of herself and what she really is. The choice between womanhood and academic career.

About Tom. Soft Puritanism beneath the tough Rabelaisian exterior. Scoptophilia stamped down by Puritanic disgust, hence Rabelaisian remarks to try to get rid of Puritanism, e.g. "she'll get screwed with her clothes on" (after B refused an egg).

What J put up with: time short and J doesn't like his poems.

9th July. Ekke: "You talk like a materialist (about the brain) but you're interested as I am in the psychology of saints."

Party for my British Council class. Miss Harada's dream in which she heard everyone say in English "Heaven is ours": "What does it mean?"

Adrian here when I returned. Debate on my poem *Twilight*. "What concretely goes on in meditation? Isn't self-perfection a pleasure like eating or Olympic running? Isn't thinking about the purpose of life a pastime no different from thinking about history?" If you haven't felt the need you don't know.

10th July. A stream of morning callers: Munekata, Enozawa, and Kurieda of Chiba.

Abroad one's sensitivity decreases and observation increases, the decrease in sensitivity being due to the fact that one is constantly being looked at as a foreigner and therefore has to put up barriers and exclude. A foreigner therefore gets a false impression of Zen atmosphere?

To the Dojo, or meditation centre. Garden overgrown, towels and washing on the line outside the main room downstairs with polished boards.

Haga smoked a cigarette and fanned himself by the combed ash-pile. The lecture heard cross-legged in 2-3 rows. My stiffness: I could hardly get up at the end and was in agony, which I managed to control. The koan. A man hanging onto the top of a tree with his teeth is asked by his Master "What is the truth of the teachings of Zen?" and he must reply. My answer, "I've gone beyond cause and effect and can deny gravity: the truth is to hang onto this tree with my teeth without falling," i.e. faith. "If you haven't found the answer by the time you go to bed sit up or die in bed if necessary." Christianity's division of body and soul is wrong; they're one in Zen. Beatings for spilling a grain of rice which is Buddha-nature. It must be given to the birds after being spilt. The hypnotic song on satori that demanded a response: four truths – pursue satori for others, be anti-lust, be pro-wisdom, be pro-self-perfection for self so that self-love leads to the love of others. Teaching downstairs while my legs eased, then the sitting: relaxation, the sadistic beatings accompanied by shouts of "Kura" (= "hey"), the bells to distract and to waken and to summon to Master to answer "koan"; bad answers are rung out.

Munekata's depression: "I know myself better. I'm a coward and don't like discipline, don't like constraint: Zen is inhuman."

My reaction: effort worth reward in terms of relaxation but not necessarily satori.

The materialistic self-service restaurant: the flying bug and the huge moth and the beater's twitching fingers.

11th July. Parable. Zen koans, but even the Master does not know the answer. "We have mastered the koan after years of struggle" – the official explanation, i.e. we know enough to tell a wrong answer.

"He should answer and risk his life for Zen."

"If I can hang onto this tree with my teeth, I can get my teeth into Zen, for Zen is the tree" (said while holding the tree). He doesn't need to speak, he knows. Ask Master whether either of these would do. "The Master speaks through his body."

14th July. Buchanan's visit: Maud Gonne was his godmother. He finds it difficult to remember recent events.

Reading Adler: the test situations and the life-style which dominate our idea of ourselves and explain our neuroses, paranoias, grandiose images.

20th July. To Kogenji temple. The tombs: many-sided prismatic statues to the Buddha, the Master, bald, bespectacled, yukataded – with a sharp, cunning Donald Pleasance look. "No service necessary." The caretaker, a scrawny old man, a carpenter, with arm-veins so varicosed that you could get a coin beneath them. "Every bone of my ancestors is here, since 250 years." "Ko-on."

Kogenji, = high place struggle temple. Also Gokujuji, = country protection temple: 1,000 years old, and the lead was nicked from the roof when the war was lost and the temple had failed in its function. The Daibutsu (Big Buddha) is in a Zen position.

Worn out by cathocyclene, an antibiotic proscribed by *Lancet* as too toxic: feverish and overstrained and depressed.

21st July. "Tropical ear": humidity produces wetness which attracts bacteria and leads to boils; cures are antibiotics, drops developed by a research doctor in Hong Kong, Enavid.

Bergman's violence in *Through a Glass Darkly*: a new element in him – the death of Esther, the madness of Coline. The writer, whom Ricky saw as myself: detached, confessing in his diary that he would like to observe the effects of his daughter's illness dispassionately.

C: "Your diary is written for publication." I: "No – I write too elliptically (and illegibly) for that: I use a shorthand." Besides, who would be interested?

23rd July. For 20 years' time. Either a Proustian novel or a Proustian autobiography. "The Loom" (patterning threads). From now I must reflect meetings with the characters of *The Loom* in this journal.

24th July. Buchanan's first appearance on the beach at Nobe in a "jinbe", a yellowy hat with a twisted brim, and binoculars round his neck. An eyepatch and he would have looked like a pirate. Later, at the Drive-in, he echoed Hemingway's confrontation with violence: man is bored and needs excitement to keep him alive. He is anti-idealism (and very anti-"morals and religion"): would fight in South Vietnam because he liked fighting, not for the ideal. Thought of becoming a professional soldier.

The bath 110°F: you burn when you move.

On the way to the shrine at night, Buchanan: "If I were writing a novel about Japan, I'd concentrate on the conflict between East and West, and show how the Japanese have discarded the useless parts of their code since the war and retained the useful parts."

25th July. Read Koestler and got sunburnt on the beach, so much that in Tokyo at 8 p.m. my legs went completely stiff. Buchanan's friend, Billy Hill, nearly 80 but in a swimming costume with his dog, a millionaire in soap; Buchanan hadn't seen him for 10 years. "How are you Billy?" "Ah, Buchanan...." "You don't look a day older." "You do."

26th July. The meeting (to discuss "The hero: some problems in British fiction"), to which I limped, suffering from acute leg-burns and swollen ankles: I sat and read at the conference table to about 30. Questions revolved to a great extent round the problem of "detachment". The Japanese seemed unaware of it. I insisted that it was a part of criticism, and not an extra-literary value. Toyama's question, "Is it possible to establish any definite rules of criticism?"

Later, sitting on the sofa with two ice-poultices around my ankles, trouserless.

27th July. The meeting: main point, religion is of two kinds and Existentialism is not equivalent to religion because it focuses on different areas of experience, e.g. choice, existence, responsibility.

1st August. Travelled to Nobe: queues on Tokyo station, waiting half an hour because train full: another wait at Yokosuka. The Chinese brocaded doll Nan was given temporarily at the Drive-in, Kurihama.

2nd August. Restful day. Read *The Bell* and *The Europeans*.

C on me as a "serious young man"; which is how others see me. I don't need friends and seem mature to them. I would like to explore this further here, but am writing under her nose.

3rd August. A walk into the jungle: incredibly brilliant butterflies, blue and black dragonflies, hawks and an occasional peasant bent solitary in a valley, tending to his paddy. The black snake that trailed away.

7th August. A novel: *Felix and Edward*. About a frivolous artist and a serious visionary of ambition.

Tsuchigane, after I'd given him his instant coffee: "We only have instant coffee in Japan. This is good." The preoccupation about gaijin (foreigners).

8th August. My dream. Colin Wilson comes specially up to London to meet me but wouldn't let me tell him about my novel; he doesn't seem interested. He wants to take me to a night-club. Then I am with him in a seminar of "friends" I have not seen before. I tell them about Japan: they are unimpressed and bored, and I have to persist. Then, in the course of conversation, Wilson says: "I think you're on the brink of insanity." His statement is approving – the implication being that I have genius – but I am deeply shocked. Is this a warning? Is my subconscious warning me that I am already showing the signs of insanity?

9th August. Another day trying to write in an immensely humid heat: rain later in the evening.

10th August. Left 7.30 and took the night train at Shinjuku. It divided unbeknown to me and I went on to Fujisawa, where I waited half an hour before making the one hour journey to Odawara, thence one hour to Gora by mountain train. Arrived three quarters of an hour late, barged into my lecture for the last quarter of an hour.

Afternoon, toured Hakone in their car. Evening a hot bath in their hot sulphur spring talking with a TUE (Tokyo University of Education) linguistic Professor and Miles; meal; then home by express.

John Miles, a sad man, divorced from his wife: "she analysed herself out of his marriage" having got under the influence of a therapist, a woman. He has a column in a paper with 100,000 circulation in California and writes for his children. During the war he got to primitive Bali. "One day you'll be world-famous. You've had an interesting life." His dread of mosquitoes and encephalitis.

11th August. Had a wisdom tooth pulled: the cocaine injections into the tooth; tooth feels like a stone, quick heartbeat. The rapidity of the drillings, giving you no time to be alarmed. Hypnotism: "You will feel no pain."

12th August. Gum trouble revived: pyorrhoea. It affects lower jaw causing all the teeth to become loose; the only remedy, to massage teeth with a toothpick every day for life. I returned home armed with 1,000 toothpicks.

My bodily ailments: ears (drops), gums (toothpicks), teeth (pills), sunburn, corns.

Hakone. Arrived 8.30, was introduced to the 100 teachers and made a short speech, bathed in sulphur, ate with Muto sycophanting solemnly beside me, yukata-ed, drank beer, slept on the floor next to Miles. Miles' gems: "Anyway, I've had a stomach upset since I came here" (to the staff room). "A wisdom tooth and seven fillings, you must have a strong constitution" (in the middle of the night). His lapsing from obscure meditative silences.

15th August. It took me three and a quarter years to understand Zabov (my brain physiologist) from June 1961 when I first dreamt him up to the beginning of August 1964 when I finally understood him in Nobe: during the course of these three years he has appeared in *The Peace*, another novel whose title I temporarily forget (the Baghdad novel), and *Mandalas*. I've written thousands of words in his mouth. The present novel *Soul-Destroyer* must be the most reduced novel ever written, in terms of what has been left out. To me he has become so central a symbol that I often think of him when reading the paper, etc., as though he were a friend, like Ricky.

16th August. A walk in Chinzanso (= Mansion on the camellia mountain).

I must not get impatient; fame is there, down the road, and with it, more important, financial success that will liberate me from extra-literary work – at least, that will offer me the option of a liberation. Self-belief and patience.

This world of fallen vision.

JAPAN: SCEPTICISM AND ETERNITY (1963 – 1964)

18th August. To Nikko with C and Nadia. Did a great deal: saw the Toshogu Shrine, with its fantastic detail; the Kegon Fall and Lake Chizuka. Also went up the ropeway to a beautiful pine forest. Met Mrs. Witt-Diamant coming down: she was just off to Yumoto for a hot-spring bath, with her housekeeper.

Read Iris Murdoch's *Flight from the Enchanter*: good analysis but very trivial happenings. Her approach to the novel is similar to Huxley's in *Point Counter Point*.

21st August. Wrote all day but not very profitably, it seemed: mainly emendations.

I sometimes wonder how successfully *The Soul-Destroyer* recreates my inner life, that is, how satisfactorily to myself I have objectivised the priest and the mature scientist in myself and the tensions they cause me. As both are so evidently symbols (for all Zabov's reality to me, his reality is the reality of a flesh and blood symbol) I am not sure that the book succeeds by the standards of the novel: for all that it has power, I believe, a quality by no means common today.

The butcher delivers meat wrapped in a bamboo leaf.

23rd August. To Chiba: the inevitable error after the immense calculations: I waited on the platform while Kurieda waited by the barrier. There's no doubt, I'm learning more from these seminars than do my students. Yesterday afternoon I knew nothing about sentence stress or strong and weak forms or rhythm, whereas the students evidently had a good grounding already. Amano's careful diagram, combating the ferroconcrete buildings on either side of me with hideous aerials on the ivy wall.

Alienation from self: a novel about a man alienated from himself, not understanding his dreams and his actions and not having the capacity to understand them; one of the unself-developing hollow men, a Teddy Boy perhaps, a symbol of the vulgarisation of which alienation is so essentially a part.

24th August. The bookshops – how I love them: the excitement at finding 12 volume Proust for only ¥4,500 and Bretall's edition of Kierkegaard (an anthology) for ¥1,020. The bookshops give me a peace: just to be in contact with books is sufficient, there is no acquisitive mania.

Why do I feel an exile? What is the need in myself that I am fulfilling by choosing the life of a voluntary exile? Undoubtedly, a large part of it is my inadequacy. I feel confident in the presence of those who cannot speak English, the language barrier makes me confident: yet the presence of one, just one, Englishman or an American contorts me inside so that I feel like a figure from Rodin. So I have exiled myself from the familiar to banish this contortion, my nervousness. The triumph over my nervousness depends on a life of exile. Nonetheless, I still feel an exile: the peace I feel among dumb ciphers of human beings is also, somewhere, an obscure pain of separation. I have not rejected England as completely as I like to believe.

A theme for my autobiography: why was I so nervous of the world at 18?

25th August. I have been reading through my *Diaries* and am impressed by how little of the truth I reveal. I do not lie, but I conceal. I am too aware of causing pain if this is read by the wrong people. Perhaps I should keep this *Diary* under lock and key in the interests of the whole truth about myself. The sacrifices of liberty imposed by marriage.

Read Kazantzakis's *Christ Recrucified*.

26th August. A memory: Travelling back from a boring day in the solicitors' office, feeling hot and sweaty and depressed, filled with a sense of the unattainability of women and my dreams, I met a notorious boy who had sat next to me in the Latin class at school. He smoked, drank and never worked, translated from a crib on his knees. He had "changed" and was anxious to impress me, showed me Sartre's *Existentialism is a Humanism*. Immediately I saw my salvation in the free choice and act. Being too poor to buy the book, I borrowed it from a library the next day, and set about forcing myself into situations I feared: talking to women for example. Each day I had to make a choice that would overcome my nervousness. A week later I returned to the library and saw shelves covered with books I had not read. I made a vow, that I would read them all.

Two months later I heard Colin Wilson speak in the Fleet Street coffee bar, and I vowed that I would know so much about metaphysics that he would want to invite me to his home. That week was perhaps the most crucial in my life: without it, I would not be here (i.e. in Japan), and I would not be what I am.

Note. It was in the autumn of 1957. I think the two outstanding periods of my life have been October-December 1957 and October-December 1964.

My dream. Adrian's brilliant monologue, which I reluctantly conceded; Waterstone piercing the moon with a pin to give relief to his eye; and was operated on by the Worcester football captain, Fred, who later went berserk, killed three people and shot himself; the Embassy not wanting me in their building.

27th August. Adrian's first visit for a month. His account of singing hymns to the sun at 5 a.m. on top of a mountain in Kanazawa, from a Shinto shrine.

Later, hypnotism. Without doubt I have hypnotic power I never suspected. Even the first time, when he sat in the chair, I had him snoring within 10 minutes. The second time, when he lay on my couch, I got him to obey simple things after half an hour. He felt pinned like a mummy in a coffin, enfolded by layers of soft cloud-like cotton-wool. His attempt on me was not so successful. The art is largely word-timing, making the suggestion before the subject takes a breath: also no lights, no third person in the room, no counting (which is a challenge to stay awake). He was aware of me only as a voice, a voice he trusted.

28th August. Black Magic shop in London for the Tarot.

1st September. Karuizawa. The station and the town's main street lie low, but further back the hill climbs among trees to Sunset Point in Gunma Prefecture. From here there is a magnificent view over four rows of jagged peaks below your feet: misty and black like an ink-drawing. Ando's hut was behind a small café whose owner is about to become a Shinto priest to preserve a family tradition 400 years old. The Shinto shrine next door is half in Nagano Prefecture, half in Gunma. We walked down to the town through the forest and got soaked, sheltered in a hut above a rugged mountain stream. The mist that rolled down. In the Chinese café the waitress was surly and the proprietor, who emigrated from Shanghai and had grey-white hair, had to be woken up when we wanted to pay the bill.

Shinto: essentially a fertility-religion incorporating the land (gods and pantheism), sex (the phallus on the do-ro) and religion, which has grown out of the land. The to-ri as gate to the god of the mountain originally, so climbing is an act of worship. "Rokkon shojo" = 6 roots purification, said when climbing. The 6 roots are the 5 senses and talking, each has 6 subdivisions = 36, x 3 for the past, present and future (adoption of children, etc) = 108, which is the number of times the Shinto bell rings on New Year's Eve. The Indian influence of the bell and the elephant, Shinto being all inclusive.

2nd September. Located the "thank"-complex: Narita's "thank you, thank you" on greeting is a mistranslation of the Japanese "dormor, dormor", which really means "I'm very pleased to see you."

Since reading *The Four Quartets* again on Monday I've been pondering on the problem of time and timelessness. Timelessness, how much I would like to acknowledge it: the apprehension of eternity and time would be a sufficient justification for struggling with the meaning of life for a thousand years. But alas, I still feel that Eliot's suffering from an illusion when "eternity" is perceived in time. What is perceived is not eternity but significance, or history.

My reading and my philosophy are very contradictory: my philosophy denies eternity (though I'd give anything to be able, one late afternoon, sitting quietly, to say "Yes, I acknowledge you", and mean it) whereas my reading is all intimations of eternity. A writer is at his intensest when writing of eternity: I must somehow achieve a similar intensity without the fact of eternity but with the sense of significance.

The mythological element behind *Mandalas*: the resolution of opposites in the centre, the myth of the descent, the shadow and the anima and the abstraction. It's not perfectly present, at present. "The still point of the turning world."

4th September. In accordance with Kierkegaard's "Rotation Method" I have put *The Soul-Destroyer* away and am returning to number 2 of the trilogy, *Juben*. *The Soul-Destroyer* is far from complete, but judging by the fertility of my subconscious during its year's fallowness on *Juben*, I am confident that December will bring the necessary corrections, gradually. I am amazed at the extent to which *The Soul-Destroyer* has changed this vacation. One cannot force writing, it comes of its own accord, if one waits. And the Rotation Method is more crucial for small novels than for a large one, as there are few characters and staleness comes after eight weeks or less.

Trilogy themes: certainty, evil and renunciation. Minor themes in common: puritanism, body-mind, values, the descent, the lower part of oneself, the double-being, parental estrangement, exile.

5th September. How a foreigner would see Japan: bowing, shoes off, geisha, hospitality and presents, too Westernised. (But, Kyoto.)

Tony. Worried about his mother, was dragged off to church twice while in England, and prayed for the congregation to reach God. ("If you believe and it does you good, why worry about honesty?" The pragmatic argument.) Tony's joy at being back in Japan. "I don't deny the existence of God."

What is my conception of God? At the most, as an impersonal force whose only evidence is in my own existence and all existence. I still maintain, reluctantly, that prayer is a self-deception, that God is not an automatic telephone-exchange in command of every language in the world, though most fluent in Latin. The efficiency of prayer is in the prayer's resolution, which may certainly be increased (for many people) through objectivisation and projection outwards. In this respect, for a man of thought and vision, prayer is a dishonest substitute for meditation, and the commands of God a dishonest substitute for personal ideals.

6th September. Paul Tillich distinguishes belief and faith. Belief is accepting something on skimpy evidence. Faith is an affirmation of something more important than oneself, something one is prepared to die for: it may be a god, e.g. money, or it may be God. God, then, is Faith, this sense of conviction, this feeling of service of something higher than oneself. What is the object of God, if God is faith?

In my case this something more important, this something higher, is my writing. I am convinced that I obey a voice from deep within me, which does all the creating while I merely record. It is my god, but I do not see that it serves any useful purpose to call it God or to bring in Christianity and such dubiously historical events as the Resurrection.

I have however a nagging doubt that I, who have been a flagellator of logic, am living too entirely through logic in my insistence on science and the physiological basis of thinking. If I develop it will surely be a development away from honesty in the name of the defeat of logic. For the tragedy of the twentieth century is that logic and honesty cannot be separated, and one cannot live through logic.

No earthquake since June 22nd.

Worn out and full of negative emotion.

7th September. A memory. Father's logic on the engagement ring: "Get a good one, because I want your marriage to last."

9.30 p.m. Worn out, tired, depressed. Without a doubt I've written myself to a standstill; my fields are exhausted and need to lie fallow. Perhaps it is a good thing that term is beginning, bringing the winter and clear-headedness.

"Learn something of everything before studying everything of something" (Prof. Maeda).

"The deeper the soil is cultivated, the more fruitful the seed will be."

"Mono-no-aware" = some feeling of pity or sadness: it grew out of pre-Buddhist, manly "masurao-buri", in the Heian era.

8th September. Bukou yosai = Japanese (eastern) spirit, western civilisation.

"The goldfish peddlar calling 'Goldfish' always reminds me of Miss Fusa, one of my relatives, sitting beside the brazier with the goldfish at her head." The kitten which disappeared and the Japanese who tied a piece of paper to the door-handle with a poem: "I will keep waiting forever like this on this snowy day. Now this paper has become somewhat dirty and yellow.... I imagine it is still on the door and moves in the early autumn wind."

Reason for Japanese dislike of Western metaphysics: coming from farmers, they like natural phenomena to correspond to their feelings and feel more intimate with Nature than with humans, and have never sought to recreate Nature artificially into a metaphysical system, so their real religion is not Buddhism but Naturalism or Pantheism.

"We can make progress only so long as we are not satisfied with ourselves."

10th September. My "back to the womb" tendencies are unmistakable. I have no copy of Freud to hand and can't analyse myself on this count. But it's clear that unconsciously I must be more timid than I think, and must feel the need for a Pinteresque retreat to safety in darkness that is warm. Woman the earth-mother and mother-substitute. What effect has this upon my metaphysical cravings in spite of my anti-metaphysical ideas?

Birth trauma. Freud enthused over Rank's book at first, then had second thoughts. To what extent did he adopt it* finally? I must remember to get particulars of my birth from mother: how long it took, whether there were any abnormalities or complications.

*He didn't. They quarrelled and separated.

11th September. To Seibus: the Hell of the 3rd floor with its waxwork dummies crowding into the consciousness.

T. E. Hulme. The Renaissance placed Perfection in man, yes, but what evidence is there for believing that values are absolute and "outside man"? How can there be absolute values? Treat Perfection as your God, yes, and acknowledge that it is absolute and quite unattainable by man, but how do you explain that man can partially perfect himself through "discipline and tradition", as we see from the saints? Only through the Pascalian belief in the misery of man without God and in the total helplessness of man (the "prolegomena to Pascal").

Hulme attacks the humanist age from the point of categories, not through notions of a goal, and in this he is with Tomlin. But although I sympathise with his aim there is something in his argument I can't swallow, and I think it is this: he does not deny that man can perfect himself partially, yet he suggests that this perfection can only come through subordination to an Absolute, through the religious attitude, and he does not say whether this needs God's help. His argument is incomplete.

Nonetheless in extremes he is a good influence: the identification of perfection with progress is an awful fallacy. Again I am confronted with my schizophrenia: wanting to believe Hulme right, but being unable to accept him totally.

12th September. *Juben*, the first of the trilogy, is about the failure of humanism, and the "religious" temperament. *The Soul-Destroyer*, the second is about the failure of individualism. *The Lost Englishman*, the third, shows a possible solution in the "negative" way of renunciation.

I am utterly divided, yet the division stimulates me rather than enervates me. Compare Yeats's remark about poetry being written out of the argument with ourselves.

Hulme. The issue: is there a perfection down the human road, or is perfect goodness a kind of Platonic ideal that is divine and apart from the human world, an Absolute?

Cannot man approach perfection, even though he never attains it?

All I did in the first version of *Mandalas* was to restate the history of thought since the Renaissance: it was as though I was writing at the beginning of the Renaissance. My ignorance, which seems unlimitable. I sometimes wonder whether any discovery is new: every thought has been thought before, and more profoundly. Cf Rilke, "Is it conceivable that every thought that has been thought is wrong?" "Evil is an imperfection of good":

the standard here is human, human goodness, not the unattainable divine perfection and goodness. Compare Tomlin's value. "God is an ideal that is perfect."

13th September. Perfection cannot be found in the world: only in men's minds. Return to Plato.

Colin Wilson's weakness. He is against humanism, but his solution, Existentialism, is a humanism. The conflict is not between materialism and religion, but between humanism and religion. To subordinate man to an absolute or not?

If two days' thinking about a problem gets one no further, it is fair to say that the problem is insoluble by thought. The problem can only be solved by experience. What in my experience is anti-humanistic? What in my experience could be anti-humanistic?

14th September. Russell: "The man who overvalues himself is surprised by failure, the man who undervalues himself is surprised by success."

15th September. The quarrel at Keio. A ferrety little man with shifty eyes inveigled his way into the staff room and tried to flog me two prints of Hiroshige for ¥700, claiming they were originals. I told him that the originals would cost at least ¥20,000, and that his were reproductions. Whereupon an elderly sensei, who had been reading, stood up and told the sharper to clear off. The sharper answered back, claiming that he was a representative of the publisher Kenkyushas. Whereupon both began to strike kabuki attitudes (hand across heart, hand into pocket), take deep breaths and speak with immense volume without raising their tone. In the end, sensei banged his straw hat (possibly panama) and walked away and out of the room. The reactions of all present: pacifying the sharper and getting him out, then standing round in an embarrassed silence, feeling humiliated before me, the gaijin (foreigner).

Later, I attended a rehearsal of the *The Merchant of Venice* in a Buddhist temple. Students lay around on the tatami listening to the Old Vic recording and brewing tea that tasted of teak-wood and smoking, and the prompter squatted on the altar. The gold Buddha on high viewed proceedings with the detached indifference that was being accorded him.

16th September. Adrian feels annoyed that whenever he lets his dog out, it finds its way to us. He keeps the dog in the wood-shed, lets it roam the streets and won't show sympathy to it because of its ear, and still expects it to be affectionate. A guard-dog and a pet have very different psychologies. "If he calls again, don't let him in."

Adrian wanted to invite a newcomer, Pertwee, to dinner, and rang up the Embassy and was put through to Popplewell: invited Popplewell to dinner before he realised the mistake and recognised Popplewell's voice.

Popplewell: "No, I simply can't come after that." (This after a hesitation, "I'll be a little late", etc.)

On Hulme: perfection is a direction, not an Absolute. Other words for "perfection", e.g. achieving a goal. To be based on experience.

17th September. A memory: my homily to the Holly Bush (Loughton) one Christmas Eve; dared by John Ezard, and suitably inebriated, I asked the pub men to reconsider their motives for celebrating the birth of Christ and suggested that Christ was glad to die. All listened for five minutes before there were dissenting cries and I was escorted to the door. All this was within 150 yards of my home. There is a link between that Christmas Eve and my presence here (i.e. in Japan) as a lecturer.

18th September. Restarted at Kyoikudai (Tokyo University of Education). Buchanan as nervous as ever. "Ye-es, I spent most of the vacation outside Tokyo." Uchiyama as usual doing nothing behind his desk. Fubara. Kuroda, whom I inadvertently addressed as "Mr" instead of "Professor". Later got fitted for a suit.

Taxed regarding the "life-force": real issues out of words that can be explained away.

Talk with Narita. Bitterly as regards himself, and enviously, "How lucky you are to have something you like doing. I'm sure you'll make your name." His consolations: the American Professors he meets, the first editions he buys. On depression: "Both Fraser and Quennell got depressed during the rainy season and went home, breaking their contracts."

Fubara's question to me for NHK "Why do writers like Japan?" The answer I can't give: because the pay's so good and there are so many vacations. Writers: Blunden, Empson, Quennell, Fraser, King, Kirkup, Thwaite. What have they in common?

19th September. Borrowed A. R. Jones on Hulme from the British Council and bought *Further Speculations*. I'll get to the bottom of this man in another week.

While walking to Jimbocho from Ochanomizu I was perturbed by my age. It seems I'm growing older and nothing is being achieved: Wilson and Brooke had both made their names by the time they were my age. C: "But Wilson and Brooke weren't doing what you are. If you were doing what they did you'd have got something published by now."

20th September. Received news of Uncle George's death on September 9th. I did not know him well, and quarrelled with him or resented him the few times I saw him – resented his bourgeois complacency – but for all that since his first heart attack old scores have been forgotten and I have thought of him as a person in pain, and I now feel depressed. The futility of existence, vanity of vanities. A death always induces in me a feeling of the transience and powerlessness of human life, a profound sadness that is probably pagan in its origin. Somewhere in my heart I weep not so much for the man as for the predicament.

21st September. Am writing this in retrospect and remember nothing – no action, no feeling, no thought: this is because I'm worn out. Got especially interested though in phenomenology and existential psychology.

"There is no town like London to make one feel the vanity of all art except the highest" (E. Pound, *Letters*, ed Paige, London 1951, p41).

"Every creative writer worth our consideration... is a victim: a man given over to an obsession" (Greene, *Lost Childhood*, p79).

23rd September. A slave's day correcting 97 Keio (exam) papers.

T. E. Hulme's two periods: Bergsonian and evolutionist, then the static period of original sin when perfection was outside the plan. Which period do I select?

No tribute from me to Sean O'Casey in these pages. *Autobiographies* remains, alas, unread on my shelves, and I know too little about him to mourn him.

25th September. The typhoon: great gusts blew off corrugated iron, then developed into battering eddies that made you reel: my lecture 10.30-12 while wooden sheds disintegrated and the windows rattled.

26th September. Irie's visit, full of eulogies on the nobility and happiness of my family, saying how great he's sure I'll be. His insistence on "light" which is impressively revealed in his face and his being. His related insistence on Zen: the Master does not know the answers to the koan (cf my parable!) and is not interested in words: that's the point, any answer will do if the state of the heart is right, e.g. "Oh let me drop" said in the right tone.

27th September. Worked on *Juben*, redefining Lasco. There is still something about this trilogy that I have not grasped, though the idea is good.

Tristy – life of action and contemption. But be contemporary, about 1960 England.

Ibsen's *Ghosts* on NHK: the faking over Oswald, whose inherited syphilis takes effect in an attack so sudden and melodramatic and dramatically convenient that I wonder whether my whole attitude to Ibsen must be overhauled.

I seem to grow deader and deader each day.

28th September. A struggle with the opening passage of *Burnt Norton*. "What does Eliot mean?" I was surprised at the intuitive understanding C had of it, e.g. what might have been, Libya (which we could have gone to).

The issue: Eliot does not make clear his attitude to the opening. Does he approve of what might have been being an abstraction? Later he says, "Concentrate on the present and forget the past and the future if you want your significant moment." Yet the rose-garden is connected with what might have been and what has been and is presented as something positive, not as an example of wasting time. Perhaps Eliot is stating a paradox: consciousness is living in the present, but significance is awareness of the past and what might have been, the awareness being in the present. Stated too vaguely, but something of the sort.

19th November. I have since understood this passage, which treats time as a process, and therefore represents the anti-eternity view.

30th September. Mrs. Witt-Diamant to dinner, enhanced by Tony who did not think her very bright but who agreed with her misinterpretation of Camus out of politeness. ("Don't ask why, just be" – there's no need for an external purpose behind the universe.)

Why have I become so "anti-American"? Prejudice aside, I think it's partly due to the constant misunderstandings that make the Americans as different from the British as the Japanese. For example, I think they're vague and generalise too much possibly because I'm not used to equating "moral" with "religious". Consequently I ask "In what way" or "What do you mean?" and am told I'm being pedantic. So semantic differences and differences in standards which they accept as part of the American dream and which I question, and their aggressiveness – they alienate me from them. I've also noticed that they tend to listen to facile ideas with interest and dismiss (by my standards) far more original ideas without understanding them.

1st October. Torn this way and that – now Hulme, now Eliot, now Kazantzakis, whose Zorba has left me flushed with life and filled with a determination to go all out for healthy vision and to hell with the "Buddha" in me. But when, oh when, will I cease to be seized, fired and ravished by such different visions – when will I be immune to influences and have my own vision, nothing more. Will it be then, when I'm dead in all save my body, when words have become mechanical toys and I have no vision to express?

I have succeeded in discarding the Greene influence, another of those useless ghosts that hindered me. The exorcism has been *The Quiet American*.

Roghudi, the Calabrian mountain village 6 miles from Riggio, where classical Greek is still spoken, having survived Roman and Italian influences (according to Professor Gerhard Rohlfs of Munich University). Others think the dialect springs from the Byzantine reconquest 6th-8th century AD.

3rd October. I am retreating from the world: walls are being built up. I want to feel for the whole world.

92

JAPAN: SCEPTICISM AND ETERNITY (1963 – 1964)

4th October. Book title: *The White Radiance*. (Shelley's "Life like a dome of many-coloured glass/Stains the white radiance of Eternity.")

Decided to write a book in the future on Self-Development in Literature, applying it to living. Active and contemplative lives.

26th December. A book on the literary representation of self-realisation?

A remark of (the librarian) Fowler's in the library: "Poets write about eternity. If you're not writing about eternity what are you going to say?" My retort: "The 20th century has destroyed eternity." Was I right?

5th October. "We think to live; we do not live to think."

Kuahara's boy seems to have TB. Much coughing in the morning: his wife is in hospital with the strain. All the same he wanted to know if she is a "nominalist" as opposed to a realist. (Nominalism: doctrine that universals or abstract concepts are mere names. Realism: universals or general ideas have objective existence.)

The Counter-Renaissance by H. Haydn. Thesis, that the Renaissance developed out of the scholastic Middle Ages, which were interested in classics, so that there was Christian humanism and humanism. Nature-Reason. Against this state of affairs the irrationalists – Montaigne, Shakespeare, etc. – rebelled, and it was only after their rebellion that the Scientific Reformation took over. T. E. Hulme?

Toff, confiding manner and no greeting: "Got an awful bollocking the other night because I wasn't home until 1.45." Personal titbits whispered in your ear in lieu of greetings. Working class, slightly surprised and open-mouthed. A comic character. Vices: women and borrowing money, he owes £300 to people in Tokyo. "Didn't expect to pay tax on my car." Irresponsibility.

6th October. Torn hither and thither again: Life-Force or mechanism? Metaphysical system or no? Tony's meeting with Tomlin at which Tomlin said "Without organism there can be no universe" i.e. no watcher? "Life must have been created." Tony wants to debunk the concept "spiritual".

T. E. Hulme: "Belief in mechanism constitutes the obstacle which the saint must surmount." "This struggle with fundamental unbelief." The 19th century "nightmare of determinism" (*Speculations* p173).

7th October. All day, struggling with Hulme, Gurdjieff, Eliot, Nietzsche, Shaw, Whitehead, trying to get something straight.

8th October. All morning, working on Hulme, Shaw, Whitehead and Bergson, assessing biological truth and incompatabilities and seeking a system. The result: a definite commitment to an anti-mechanist position, which I shall defend from now on at all costs, because I must: a saint's surmounting. I shall deny myself mechanistic reading for a month to get criteria that can argue against mechanism. In the paper there was mention of a monkey that has been taught to drive a tractor. I did not permit even this to shake my commitment, and said "This is no proof of mechanism in humans."

Furthermore, I have committed myself anew to a position I held before I went to Baghdad, and somehow lost: never to seek a system, but to work from my experience, rejecting speculations I cannot prove as a waste of time and not allowing science to interfere except in the physiology of the brain, when I shall concentrate on the oxymorons.

The Vice-Governor (of the Bank of Japan) is very penitent because he told me that haiku and tanka were the same, whereas the tanka has 31 syllables: he realised his error in the North when looking at a monument of Basho's with a tanka on it.

Toff's duplicity: deliberately seeking out the traffic when with his wife to strengthen numerous alibis and combat her intuition.

2nd June 1965. Rejection of systems is necessary to writing development (28th October) but somehow ignored in November and December.

9th October. Narita's visit. His gossip (Empson sacked for making advances and attacking a chauffeur), his invitation to me to stay in Japan indefinitely.

The snake-fascination: it mesmerises a frog, which cannot move; then, while the frog is screaming in terror, it eats the frog alive.

11th October. Truitt's party. Sam Francis and Paul Jenkins, with a grey-white Dostoevskian beard and an ascetic face. Matsumi Kanemitsu claimed to have met me in New York. A gallery of Huxleyan caricatures: the old parading as young and the young trying to look mature; pseudo-cosmopolitan Japanese, totally unrooted, and U.S. servicemen, trying to conceal their ignorance of art. The stripe-picture which looked like a woman's dress design. The pub-seats round the hearth in the strangely English room. Mrs. Witt-Diamant.

The distance between U.S. and English cultures, the English being far more complex.

How many people waste their lives, living out of habit or duty.

13th October. 10.30-7.30 no cigarette: this because of (Dr) Morton's report: internal wheezes, etc. I feel very remote and can hardly focus, but I'm determined to sweat it out and finish smoking: a disgusting, expensive habit which has become a drug, keeps me underweight and is ruining my chest (as though Tokyo soot isn't enough without making it worse). But I can't relax.

14th October. 9.15 p.m. The crisis: nearly 36 hours without a cigarette and my body is struggling, crying out for nicotine, bargaining degrees: but I clench my fists and grit my teeth and sweat it out, although my vision and my balance have been affected. This is the test of my will. At all costs I will not be as weak as other men: I will give up smoking and thereby symbolically renew the discipline over my life I had before Oxford.

9th December. Gave up but am not sure about renewing my pre-Oxfordian discipline.

15th October. 9 a.m.-11 a.m. wasted, lying on my bed refusing to give in: I will not give in, on no account will I give in. This is a test of my will-power. I shall be my body's master, not its slave. Now I must concentrate. Gather your energies and concentrate, as you did when you meditated last night. Dependent on a plant-leaf like tobacco? Come on, grow up.

16th October. After a day fighting nicotine went and bought myself some snow-darks and left for Fuji with Adrian and Tony.

17th October. Up (Mount) Fuji from the lakeside ryokkan (inn), Adrian's car having failed to climb successfully. Took the 9.30 bus and reached the 5th stage at 10.30. Had until 3.15 to reach the top and return to catch the last bus back. Climbed to within 1,000 feet of the top then turned back.

The clinker and ash and rock; the snow, the blue sky, the cloud beneath, the sun. The conquest of the mountain, going higher and higher, a symbol for spiritual ascent through effort, will and determination. Adrian's feminine emotions: affection, brutality, conquest; the crater-vagina imagery, the permanence. A mountain symbolises something to each climber: each climb is a private conquest.

The rarefied air at 9,000 feet and the shadow when the sun set behind the crater: the sudden chill and the meeting with the bald Mexican who had a sow's bladder full of saké.

The bar we visited and everyone disappeared because "the gaijin (foreigners) have spoilt the atmosphere".

18th October. 120 hours without.

"Hot rain", radioactive-silver, fell hard and cold on my damp sweater as I gathered the milk.

Poets who visited Japan: Blunden, Empson, Quennell, Kirkup, Thwaite, Bottrall, G. S. Fraser, William Plomer, R. Hodgson, George Barker, D. J. Enright, Francis King.

19th October. In the staff room my account of Fuji was received with incredulity. "Oh, he has climbed our mountain: was it not too cold for you? You did not find our mountain not to your taste?"

21st October. Todai deserted so went to Jena's and bought Colin Wilson's *Sex Diaries*, which I read in the evening in between going into Pound's *Hugh Selwyn Mauberley*, especially *E. P. Ode*.

22nd October. Promoted as the Governor's sole speech-writer.

Toff insisted that my train was his, in spite of half a minute's argument to the contrary, and pronounced himself "a nut" just short of Iidabashi station. He really is idiotic.

A general feeling that I should be writing and making my name but a nasty feeling of powerlessness and hopelessness: too much work, just too much, for me to write a word before next week.

23rd October. It is feared that (R.H.) Blyth (the Zen authority) is critically ill, too ill to sign his contract in hospital. The incongruous tone in the staff room: the solemnity and the indifference that was almost farcical, e.g. Kuahara poignantly, "I have heard that he was educated perhaps at London University" (i.e. not Oxford), and Narita: "He must be about 70." Kuahara: "No, 65.", Narita: "No, 70. He retired from Todai perhaps five years ago." Kuahara: "There is an official document in the Administration giving his age as 65." The man's dying, and everyone's quibbling without any real feeling.

Irie on my visit to Okayama: "Why not take a holiday? You work too hard with your beautiful standards you set yourself as regards the students. Why not take that Monday off."

24th October. One often dreams of the devoted teacher, expiring after 40 years' service in Japan with crowds of students round his death bed and more still to mourn him when his coffin is carried on high through the streets. The business of Blyth shows that the reality is quite different.

Seven and three quarter hours writing speeches for the Governor's tour of the Far East.

25th October. Connections, e.g. the wartime Japanese bank note (which I was given in a Morrison shelter in the garden of the old Oaklands at Trap's Hill, Loughton) and Japan. And "He's as safe as the Bank of England" (of Bill Robertson, the Chelsea goalkeeper, in a Chelsea crowd when I was 10), my image then of a Bank being realised in Tokyo 15 years later. The two points or moments, one pointing forward and the other back, which I constantly seem to find: they are the pattern, or rather the outline of the pattern, that runs thread-like through our lives. Moments and bridges between moments.

26th October. Memories: Julian Road (Folkestone). Miss Whitworth, "Mr B" chasing us, old Caroline across the road with Miss Mapleton, always ill. The next door garden, the significance of the owner's names, and the stone against which (my cousin) Richard and (my brother) Rob and I played cricket. When? In 1947? 1948? 1949? I know Richard was at his prep school, and talked of Ricky Metcalfe; that would be some clue. And Mr Baker (the preacher) "sliding down a mountain", the telescope and the peculiar smell in the South Downs buses with their strange tickets. And Kingsnorth Gardens, our run, and the ball among the flowers.

It was then that I met the potash man, Rex, who cycled blindfold through Folkestone and found a watch: he dominated my childhood, squatting among his charcoal on the promenade and telling the future by sortilege with his great wise beard. He was wisdom incarnate. Was he behind the vision I had in Tw*ilight*, I wonder.

27th October. Saw a letter from a sensei to his pupil: "Dear Mr Sekinaga, I think you should realise that there are many problems still unsolved by scholarship.... Yours, T. Fujita." Two sheets typed in English. The same pupil had actually taken the bother to copy out and learn my poem T*wilight*; it evidently struck chords in him somewhere, which was gratifying to me. I still find it ludicrous that I should be taken so seriously, as when Muto asked me to lecture on my poem at Fujisawa.

Later read Wilson's *Sex Diaries*: atrocious as novel-writing, but interesting as another "critical" book.

My dream on radioactivity. It was over 500 and when I went out everyone was disintegrating, the flesh being eaten away. I know the same was happening to me but I had to continue walking and looking, for this was all plague and pestilence collapsed into one visibly symbolic affliction: moral ugliness and physical deformity.

28th October. Writing theme: the sickness of our contemporary culture, and suggestions as to its health (the theme that preoccupied Eliot and Pound); the levelling down in England at present, commercial and industrial society, its rootlessness, modern superficiality. Contrast with modern attitude, dissatisfaction, the divided mind, loss of religious purpose.

Language. The gulf today between literary and spoken language has been bridged by making language too colloquial (Amis and Co). A return to literary language is required while preserving its roots in colloquial language: how can this be done? Not by writing as the Movement writes, but rather by "imagism" renewed.

Explore both these problems of theme and language, especially language.

2nd June 1965. A new phase begins. This is the beginning of the development in my writing which, aided by Tuohy, has become more realistic and everyday. In 1964 (October)-early 1965 a development took place in my writing. It wasn't just that I turned to poetry; I was turned to poetry by facing problems I had not really faced before, and by an increase in maturity. On 1st November I accepted the squalor of contemporary civilisation.

Grannie's reference to "the man in charge of Labour."

29th October. A dream after reading Priestley's extract on post-Serialism: I was walking up a sand and gravel drive to a vast house with a conservatory and back door, without Nadi but with C; father was waiting to greet me but I was returning from Tokyo and had not seen him for two and a half years; as we shook hands I said "You're looking well" and he said with sad cheerfulness, "No, I'm dying."

Letters to Japanese. News about the weather, e.g. "It's very cold but fortunately the chrysanthemums are out." "I'm very sorry I have not written for a long time." Message: "Please take good care of your body." Begin: "Greetings."

30th October. Blyth's death reported, with a shock-haired photograph. Narita's absurd comments: "I hear it was a nervous breakdown, since April. I have not seen him for some months." "Now there are only two foreign teachers at Kyoikudai (Tokyo University of Education)."

I must think again about the social history of England. What is the particularly significant feature since the War? The "emergence" of the working classes (as mirrored in the 50s drama) and political disillusionment: the Angry Young Man on the left (cf ND) who is the descendant of Bakunin, perhaps, or, on the anarchistic side, of the nihilists? In England there is no older order to overthrow now, as there was for the Russian nihilists like Nechayev and Chernyshevsky, but the descent is still there.

Today we protest against triviality, standardisation and socialisation and stress the individual. It is the levelling – the dream of the more idealistic nihilists – that is our energy today.

An essay on modern England: the Russian Nihilists and the decay in standards.

31st October. The contemporary ideas that have been concerning me recently: the sickness of our culture and contemporary social history. Have come out Tory from a cultural point of view. Spiritual laziness is caused by industrial and commercial society, pop-culture and mass communications.

Read Golding's *Spire* in Nobe. His techniques of concentrating on the outside (a vague state of mind) and of making the familiar strange by refusing the cliché, e.g. six lines of imagery to convey "He woke up". Golding the paraphraseable.

The walk with Tony, the climb, the coloured spiders. Later Tony's insistence that he was indifferent to existence, which was neither unbearable nor good: he did not mind whether he was alive or dead next week.

1st November. The village shattered by the motorbike, roaring its power in echoes down the well. The curious peasants.

Reflections on city/country. Deep, emotional and responsive country versus superficial, rootless city. Is all civilisation a destructive process, corrupting the intimacy between man and nature and substituting alienation in the name of education, rootlessness in the name of sophistication? Can I come out on the peasants' side, like D. H. Lawrence, in spite of the fact that my living depends on cities?* Can I confess that I am continuing the corruption by superficializing the students' emotional responses, not deepening them? Is the City problem a 20th century problem in so far as cities retained an intimacy during the 19th century that it's only possible to find in slums today? Has the impersonality of the city caused the death of Christianity? For any hard-hearted man could pity the starving and the frozen in Dickens's London or Dostoevsky's Russia, but it takes a saint to love a family in a block of flats with no education and £3 a week.

* No. City-life is irreversible.

My achievement the last two days. Reorientation to accept what I have hitherto shirked and sought to escape in my writing: the squalor of contemporary civilisation.

2nd November. Two ways of looking at the universe: seeing it as an example of the insignificance of man, which is usual, and seeing it as an example of the significance of man, for man has "existence" (= consciousness) and the universe has not.

A memory: the Boys' Brigade.

3rd November. I seem to have lost the power to work. I am completely exhausted, both mentally and physically: almost too tired to write this at 4 p.m. and I've already slept or dozed an hour this afternoon. I have no energy or vitality, yet I am tense. Perhaps it's connected with giving up smoking. At all events my stamina is quite pathetically low and I have no staying power. And I feel thoroughly depressed.

The problem of anti-rationalism. The universe cannot be expected to make sense rationally, in which case the world ceases to be familiar and man feels a stranger. This is the effect, as Camus saw it, of broken-down belief.

I despair, I despair, I despair. If ever I make my name, I must never allow myself to forget today, the nihilism, the indecision, the despair.

2nd June 1965. Dying away?

4.

SPIRITUAL DEPTH AND CREATIVITY
November 1964 – June 1965

5th November. From now, a desire to Saxonise my language and cast out those stilted Latinised abstractions. Like Hopkins, always prefer a word that has an Old English root unless I am using the abstraction for a particular effect. Above all, be concrete and particular in communicating my experience. All our intellectual and spiritual and psychological terms meant physical things in Old English and Latin: recover the physical sense whenever possible, and perhaps renew my study of Old English. If only I had appreciated the full significance of Old English at Oxford: I feel as though I am just ready now to go up to Oxford, having completed my preliminary studies. Trofimov, Trofimov.

A thought: the ubiquity of the lower middle class, with its material prosperity and spiritual emptiness: their take-over of Great Britain, their suspicion of education.

6th November. Thursday 5th p.m. The reception for the London Symphony Orchestra in the Tokyo Bunka Kaikhan (Festival Hall). Sir Arthur Bliss, with blue eyes, shaking me by the hand unintroduced: white hair and moustache, cf Elgar and Sibelius.

I am leaving for Okayama. Speaking before 500 people on a platform I have always dreaded. It is my Room 101. I have nightmares about being on the platform and having nothing to say. I must go and conquer this, my greatest fear; I must master this situation which six years ago would have been the most terrifying experience of the year. Amen.

7th November. A wretched train journey. I was given a sleeper but the train had no seats and I had to write notes for my lecture. Therefore I had no option but to haul myself up the steel ladder and lie on the top bunk, variously on my front and supine, where, contorted, I wrote until I was defeated by cramp. Then I lay precariously, as though on the top of a cliff, while the train jogged, jolted and lurched, shielded my eyes from the powerful centre-light and tried to relax. In vain: I arrived without sleep or breakfast, my attention scattered, and too nervous and tired to talk in anything but the thinnest voice.

Sister Ellen Mary was very doubtful, but revalued me when, after Zen concentration, I united my attention and gave a decent lecture to 300 girls (only 300 because there are no classes on a Saturday and each would have to travel specially, one third as much as four hours). Sister Frances, the submissive nun who struggled, was gently humiliated by Sister Ellen Mary. What tragedy lay behind her eight years? The stamp of spiritual beauty upon a physically beautiful face and my feeling of uncleanliness in the silence.

Hiroshima, cradled in mountains, and starkly flat. The waterways, the ryokkan (inn) near the Kinza: my two baths in my luxury suite which I bargained for ¥2,000.

2nd June 1965. How much of the metaphysical movement to December 27th began here rather than after I gave up smoking?

"The nun's eyes": this has become a stable point in my thinking, that "spiritual" depth is possible, no matter what science says.

8th November. Up at 6.35 a.m. My early morning visit to Miyajima ruined by crowds of schoolchildren and the fact that the "famed torii" was faded and much less impressive than its photographs. Hiroshima Park, which I approached from Aioibashi: the Peace Museum, with its simplicity. The picture gallery of atomic scientists (looking like criminals), models of the explosion in a matter of fact tone. The epicentre 600 metres up. The hypocentre a hospital yard. The ball of fire, the burns, the keloids. The infernal nuisance of being unable to book at short notice in Japan: hence I had to travel 1st class all the way back, including the Tokaido line from Osaka at 125 mph.

Dream (not mine): a paradise and a stream that is pellucid, with shiny pebbles on the bottom. Wish for a simple mind, for everything to be uncomplex.

9th November. At Kyoikudai (Tokyo University of Education) polite "sensei" (professor) questions: "And was it fine at Hiroshima?" said in a respectful tone that is disproportionate in its seriousness to the triviality of the subject. This is the strangeness of Japan: the incongruity between tone and subject.

The strange letter from Munekata, pouring out his feelings about Dr. Blyth. At the end on page 6, just before the abrupt transition to me, the truth leaked out: "I was the only student to attend his last lecture."

C and I harmonious and attuned, sharing jokes, especially sensei-jokes. e.g. "Dear Mr —, The most important thing in life is to study hard." I record this stupidity because I ignore the happiness I have with C, which is frequent, if often negative, and concentrate on the misery.

11th November. The blue sky. One day I shall not see the blue sky, though it will exist. Therefore, though it changes, it is permanent and I am ephemeral. The relationship between man and the blue sky has nothing to do with the reason. Yet the sky has no meaning without man.

The evening at Hijikata's. Hijikata met us (Tony and me) at the station in yukata and scrapers and a blue beret; shuffled home like an onion-seller. The embarrassing dinner with his wife, two sons (our age) sitting in silence while Hijikata talked about his acceptance of death and Eastern philosophy ("consciousness is a bad thing, unconsciousness is what matters"). Tony's two faux-pas: "Sixty-five's very old" and "No whisky now that I've started a beer – you should really have wine after sherry" (Hijikata having no wine in the house). Also, Tony's tightness with money.

The Hijikata swords, which should have been turned in to the U.S. authorities: the ceremonial sword and the killer, made of layers of steel. The rapier for hari-kiri: the painful insertion into left side, slit across, then up, which was generally anticipated by a stooge's striking off the head when the sword had been accepted, i.e. when the honour of the recipient had been saved.

12th November. Rather fed up because the Bank of Japan driver quite needlessly got me into a massive traffic jam and lost me half an hour, after which I got soaked in a downpour, not having an umbrella. The last straw was when I reached my room and found that a 50-man orchestra was playing full-blast in the next room, so that everything I said was drowned. This sequence might be a good comic scene.

A memory: being on holiday in Bognor in August 1945, going out to buy a newspaper for my father; the sunny day, the headlines "H-bomb". The *Telegraph* of course.

13th November. Does one inevitably run into people of the same temperament as oneself in unlikely places? After meeting Fubara in Nobe, he turned up in a squalid café near Hitotsubashi theatre, before I went to the Keio *Merchant of Venice*.

You had the truth in 1957, seven years ago (reading the best of European civilisation) and your higher education has been a slow process of losing it, of being distracted from it. Regard it as confirmed, and for God's sake, write from the inside: write what you would have written in 1957, taking advantage of your developed mind.

27th November. Compare *Mimesis*.

14th November. 2.55 p.m. a violent, vertical earthquake. The ground heaved up: it took me two seconds to realise what was happening; then I threw down my spectacles, jumped up, flung open the door and rushed into the sitting-room where C was sitting, dazed and motionless. Nadia's face was one of profound astonishment and alarm. By that time all was over. Another ten seconds would have brought everything down.

The humanistic ideals lead to spiritual pride and to the isolation of the individual in the prison of self: you acknowledge the need for a religious attitude, so present it. There is no necessity at this stage to go further.

When I'm finally disillusioned with people I will achieve God.

SPIRITUAL DEPTH AND CREATIVITY (1964 – 1965)

15th November. The five university drama contest. The melodrama, the St. *Joan*, the popular *Christmas Carol* (appealing to the audience), the unrealistic *Medea* and the draggingly slow Wilder play. At the end there were ugly scenes. We left the hall quickly to avoid the losers. Bernie Trink, the bum in a corduroy jacket who scandalized the Japanese: film-critic, chess-player, "poet" and lover of a Thai girl. His suggestion for the closing address: "I think we can all agree that everyone's had a completely futile day." Smith's counter-suggestion: "Speaking as the captain of nuclear-submarine Sea-Dragon...." There was great merriment among the judges who were called upon to decide the result of months and months of effort, and before whom the actors cringed with fear.

The earthquake was like a twitch; it tore down one's foot and released it, having twitched it in the earth.

16th November. Gordonisms: "Anyway, what's it got to do with you?" "What?" "Whatever it is." And: "So what do you know about that?" A Toffism: of tea. "Oh, have you made it then?" Both of these came to me quite naturally as I adopted their personae: that is to say, I've come out with both today, to C.

Toff's loneliness and desire to impress: his quarrels with his staff. ("And I told them, I let them have it, I blew my top.") Also: "I like a night like this."

Earlier, his frankness about his marriage, "I love my wife, but I'm not in love with her. She's hurt because I got involved. She said 'I wouldn't have minded if you'd gone and screwed a whore and had a good washdown afterwards, you wouldn't have got involved.'"

17th November. I seem to get more and more tired, more and more bloated with stupidity, more and more indolent. I really do despair. Yet I still know* that I am undergoing some spiritual preparation for the magnum opus I shall write: quite seriously, I know it, in spite of all these superficial distractions. Become more alive: you should have no time to sleep. Alertness, alertness. I saw you relax today. You shouldn't have time to relax, except when you teach. Your working day should be exploding with vitality.

* 2nd June 1965. Amazing premonition.

Earlier, strangely ran into Munekata at Tokyo Station: he was strangely embarrassed, presumably on account of his letter.

18th November. "A New Britain", the cry of the mid-1960s: the theme of art will be the preservation of individuality.

Dostoevsky understood that the Church has adopted the position of the temptations, which Christ refused.

I could so easily have become dead in Japan. I'm already an insider.

Imperceptibly, I've allowed that to happen. I must detach myself, in the interests of life, and write about what is relevant: spiritual power, the advances of science and the need to combat them, the need for purpose, modern society and the purpose of the individual. And stop being so sleepy-headed, so well-fed, so other-directed.

If necessary give up your Professorship and take up a gardening job in the University front quadrangle. Wittgenstein did it in a monastery. Live in chaos.

19th November. Live in chaos, then you will create your order. This worked in Baghdad, and the reverse is working here: you live in bourgeois order and your life, which is crucial, is in chaos. Stay here until February 1966 to avoid English fuel bills, yes, but do not stay longer, or you will be so stuffed with intellectual (i.e. rational) facts that you will have no spiritual life. Remember, you are not an intellectual but an Existentialist.

Modern life: the barrenness, the tedium. A theme as old as the hills, but I can't help wondering whether modern suburban life isn't worse than any other day, even the tedium of Chekhov's provinces. Worse by what standards? The beginning for a book.

Write out of ordinary everyday experience, at all costs.

20th November. Bought Toynbee (volumes) 1-10 at Kinokuniyas, much to the amazement of Mr T, my graduate student, who was kind enough to come with me.

Earlier, handed back the proofs of the new report on TUE (Tokyo University of Education) to Irie. My comments included a reference to an ambiguity: "established"/"founded". "Oh, but this is ambiguous in the original writings, so we can only hope to translate it ambiguously." What could be nearer to the spirit of *The Fallen City* than that? Also Irie's hushed compliment: "You have examined these writings more closely than anyone else, and the University must be grateful to you."

Buchanan's little party down at Nobe, "I'm having Penson of the Embassy down – will you be coming down? Will you come in for a drink?"

Letter from Grannie. On the Labour Government: "There is nothing we can do about it and we must make the best of it."

Awakened 2 a.m. Saturday morning to an earthquake, a very long, rumbling shake; lay and listened, sleepy and insecure. The fourth in one week.

21st November. From my letter to Rob: "Although I'm in principle on the side of social justice I view the increase in egalitarianism that a Labour Government means with doubtful feelings. Having detached myself from England I can see there's a take-over going on, a take-over by the lower middle classes, and traditional cultural standards are dropping. We're now in the Silver Age and (as in egalitarian Rome*) inevitably in decline. And all (Harold) Wilson's talk about a New Britain is just another way of saying that the decline is going to proceed more rapidly. I loathe financial Toryism and complacent self-interest but I think now that the Tory party (regenerated) may be the only party that can delay the decline."

*3rd December. No, as in Greece in 30BC the Golden Age of Rome/ America is yet to come and may be approaching now.

As a result, wrote *And Scholars will Ask* (cf yesterday's purchase of Toynbee and last night's reading about Silver Rome). A poem that would be very unpopular with Leftists as it attributes the breakdown of Western civilisation to increasing egalitarianism and spiritual emptiness.

Before that spent all day working on the historical groupings of 20th century poets, from the 1890s to the 1960s, and felt on the verge of breaking through into a new poetic technique: this is an exciting time for me, poetically.

22nd November. To Nobe. The train which closed and went as I was passing from 2nd class to 1st class via the platform, with C. Stove-cleaning when we arrived until I went to see Buchanan and Penson, whose first conversation was about Chinese restaurants in England and most of the proprietors beings spies. After drinking whisky returned and read Toynbee volume 9.

Poems. *The Night*: effort and the final ice-cap's dark. Original Sin: Auschwitz, refuting the innate goodness of many. How can a generation that has survived Auschwitz still believe in human goodness and perfection?

The idea of Nemesis.

23rd November. To the jungle with Buchanan and Penson, both of whom had to think of their hearts. The bamboo was a glory beneath a brilliant sky, and there were gentians and corn violets in the horseshoe valleys, and the familiar shrikes. Penson and Buchanan sat in a cabbage field and Buchanan photographed me climbing a pylon to see the sweep of the misty bay, a photograph that will probably dog me. An illuminating character-touch. Penson in opening a Kirin beer-can, sprayed foam over the ceiling, the Japanese paper-doors and me while Buchanan said in a ruffled voice "What *are* you doing?" The accidental and unexpected is a good measure of character. Good for a satire on the British: the crazy walk with each separating and photographing cabbage patches, and the inefficient attempts to be inconspicuous at the beer-party afterwards.

Later, my exhilaration: the wind beating down the beach, sweeping the sand with the foam, flapping my trousers like sails and parting my hair like grass, while the waves pounded and thudded the beach. I felt at one with everything and ran and danced on the wind (for I was alone) and laughed and chased my shadow for joy at being alive.

24th November. Style. Aim, to be vital and energetic. My paradox.

Classicism is social-centredness and my individualism belongs to the Renaissance, though I believe in Original Sin.

Romanticism is to be equated with Individualism: ignore this term, attack it, and substitute "Modernism"?

My fear of being deemed Romantic, yet my inability to escape Individualism. What else can I do if all the traditional certainties have decayed, leaving the individual no acceptable link with the whole? Should he subordinate himself to a lower middle class society, or should he carry on his own private rebellion?

"Vulgarization" or brotherhood and humanity? I have felt the Congo massacre very deeply.

Is not the U.S.A. the Universal State that is absorbing our culture as the Roman Empire absorbed Greece? Hence anti-Americanism? Pro-tradition?

25th November. First day of Fujisawa seminar. Met at the station by Muto, a teacher aged 45 who asked my age. "I think you must be older than me, you are a Professor," he said. When I disabused him he looked startled and said mechanically: "Oh that is a surprise. You are a Professor and you are younger than me." I agreed. Later I lectured on critical appreciation of prose and verse and encountered a hostile, stony silence. Muto had completely misled me (as I later heard he had misled Miles who lectured in the same atmosphere on the difference between Japanese and American humour), for his praise of the teachers proved to be bragging about his dream-world and he really wanted something very simple. He was hoist with his own petard and serve him right. But there was more to the teachers' reaction than incomprehension. They resented my youth, for the youngest of them was a dim-witted 40. It gave me a strange feeling of power to talk on, with apparent insensitivity to the atmosphere, forcing them to listen, in complete control of their physical presence, and to assail them with remarks like *"Ozymandias* was written when Shelley was 25" and "Eliot revolutionized the whole tradition of poetry when, in 1910, at the age of 23, he wrote *Prufrock".*

Later, after Todai, met Irie, had a very polite coffee ("No, let me pour") and examined, once again, his inscrutable "writings" with their teasing ambiguities. The question after my lecture: "How did you become interested in poetry?"

26th November. Second day of Fujisawa seminar, and for the second day running, up at 6. A more friendly atmosphere, but still a degree of hostility in the first lecture. The composition I saw, in the manner of a parable by Kafka, written by "Mr No Name": "A student came to his teacher and said, 'I am the son of a peasant and when I return home each evening I do a peasant's work and will become a peasant when I finish my studies. Why should I learn English?' The teacher answered from the course of study as prescribed by the Ministry of Education and sank into the depths of emptiness."

Got going on *Mimesis*, which is considerably more portable than Toynbee. Had only one hour at the Bank of Japan, in which time I wrote to Bertrand Russell on behalf of the Governor, so stopped at Kitazawa on the way back and bought (Jung's) *Modern Man in Search of a Soul*.

A memory from 1957-8: (the solicitor) Brickdale's letter written in modern Greek and on pederasty. "Can you translate – I don't know what it means." I read it, gave it back saying it was too difficult, got up and left. Later I discovered that Brickdale reads modern Greek.

27th November. Lay in until 7.20. At Kyoikudai (Tokyo University of Education), was amazed by the students' progress in criticism: very unJapanese aggressive criticism of poems from the point of view of rhythm and rhyme. Buchanan's love of Joyce and his determination to read *Finnegan's Wake* before he dies: his delight at discovering that *Finnegan's Wake* is based on Celtic poetry and can therefore be regarded as being (printing aside) in Homer's genre.

28th November. Wrote a poem to go with *And Scholars will Ask: Odi et Amo*. Not quite satisfied with the ending yet.

A great change is taking place in me. I can't pin it down but I know it's a change for the better, a kind of maturity: I am, day by day, becoming more aware of my task and of what I inherit, I am founding my writing more on society and placing myself more within a tradition.

29th November. Have spent the last two days solidly reading Toynbee, raising questions, answering them and moving on. So much seems to have come clear: the significance of a Pax Americana; our similiarity with Greece in 30BC; our role as spiritual power between the material "Romans" and "Parthians", the pattern whereby a new religion is thrown up by unfavourable material conditions and by disintegration, the possible aim of civilisation being to create higher religions (I am not sure about this); and the falseness of seeing barbarian ages as heroic ages. "Spiritual" nationalism. Civilisations: spiritual aim or futile? I am eager to read the "Darwinian" Spengler to see the pessimistic theory work itself out, and notice my ten for a desert island would be: Toynbee, Whitehead, Nietzsche, Kierkegaard, Dostoevsky, Eliot, T. E. Hulme, Camus, Kafka, Shakespeare*: all being pro-religion and anti-materialism, for the most part.

Vast changes are taking place in my outlook as a writer, and my vision of the world is being deepened immeasurably so that I have that dimension of our society I lacked: the historical dimension of man's historical relationship with the universe in relation to his individual ephemeral existence. I see man in his civilisation, not just man in a particularly squalid and vulgar society that has gone rotten.

*Afterthought. Also Yeats and Rilke, making twelve.

30th November. At Kyoikudai (Tokyo University of Education) a discussion on the wisdom (so called) of age in Japan and on the need to reject the whole idea. In the afternoon worked on Spender, Edith Sitwell and Dylan Thomas's A *Grief Ago* which is really incomprehensible, at least impossible to paraphrase: written when he was 21, four years younger than I am now; when I think of the earnestness of my outlook at 21, and the romanticism in it, I wonder.

Although I find cocktail parties irksome (especially small ones) because my opinions are generally dismissed or patronised, I'm not over-anxious for the fame which would sanctify them: I want historical fame, I'll admit it, but not particularly fame in my own life-time, though it would be nice to know of the historical before I die.

1st December. At Keio. Later rather depressed by Adrian who asserted that our culture is not disintegrating, asking where, when, how, why, saying that the lower middle classes do not dominate our consumption, that on the contrary we have advanced in so far as the proles can now read whereas in the 18th century they were illiterate.

To what extent is my attitude towards the Debdenites (on the working class fringe of Loughton, Essex) purely emotional and without intellectual backing? I think in images and have visions. Do these disappear when subjected to precise questioning, or is the subject so nebulous that it can only be considered concretely (as I've considered it) and not rationally? Why and how does a Labour government make a difference practically?

Romanticising the working classes and seeing only their virtues; they are there and that's that: but our culture exists independently of them?

"Socialism doesn't approve of the vacant face."

2nd December. A turbulent day, full of self-questioning about *The Soul-Destroyer*, irritatingly interrupted by Todai which drove it underground but did not eliminate it. Which side is J. S. Lawrence on? On the side of eternity or on the side of anti-metaphysics? He ought to be the new science, and the priest ought to symbolise "the Spirit", particularised in Christianity. But it's not as simple as that: he is a mass of contradictions, as I am. This may be a strength, if I am to follow *Mimesis* (by Auerbach), but I must get a clearer idea of what he is after. E.g. has he a sneaking longing for eternity (as I have) though he knows it to be hopeless? Is he a reluctant discoverer? Does he long for an age of certainty, in which eternity is eliminated, but, after he has achieved it, find it totally unacceptable, because civilisation and the universe cannot be so purposeless? On August 15th I wrote "It took me three and a quarter years to understand Zabov." Now, three and a half years later than my invention of him, I still have not understood him in his new garb as J. S. Lawrence.

3rd December. Another turbulent day of reappraisals, likewise interrupted by classes. My trouble is I'm torn between two parts of myself, the objective scientific and the anti-rationalist (which is often pretty primitive as well as seeking the Higher Religions), and I cannot resolve these two sides, no matter how much I censure my reading. (I am still reading anti-rationalist books only.) I can achieve a compromise in art – perhaps that is the "neat" solution I long for and always reject; perhaps the artist is a man torn by two incompatible forces with no hope of a resolution, and perhaps he creates out of his despair at achieving certainty.

If J. S. Lawrence reflects this part of me, there is little hope for him, for having achieved "certainty" his anti-rationalist side would continue to pull: he cannot eliminate one side of himself. And yet he doesn't believe in eternity as a survival – only as something that he can experience. So why is he so reluctant to deny eternity?

My view of man is man in relation to his civilisation and to the history of the universe, not merely man in relation to contemporary society or to "other people". This is the distancing I need to avoid the Romanticism that goes with individualism, man as the centre of the universe. This is a very important discovery.

5th December. From Thursday, Classicism is man subordinated to something higher than himself, society or God. My form of Classicism is man subordinated to the historical processes of civilisation – growth, breakdown, disintegration – and to the history of the universe from nothing to nothing, or at least to the history of this earth.

"J. S. Lawrence is the victim of Modernism which is a way of regarding self-division today." To what extent is this statement rubbish? Why should self-division not find its way into art in the 19th century? What form of vanity is it that permits us to believe how peculiarly different the 20th century is?

Cricket memories: linseed oil, vellum bats, and the smell of rain on your white sweater.

6th December. British Council scholarship interviews with the Healeys, Tomlin, Baker, Collcutt and Tuohy. Found Tuohy a very prosaic man*, thinking in facts with nothing to say and a very abrupt introverted manner that disregarded everyone else. Of course he's very shy underneath, and his aggression is a kind of defence-mechanism. His corpulence and cheek-jowledness do not flatter him. It is conceivable that I might come to like him and know him more intimately in the future, but I record my first impression: of a man who lacks passion and truly creative imagination and who is too severe in his front to have true warmth.

6th April 1965. Retracted but interesting.

Mother's letter: "The winter jasmine is out in the garden, and I have hyacinths in flower indoors." (Written 29th November.)

7th December. A comic episode at Kyoikudai (Tokyo University of Education). I went to have a pee, and because one of my postgraduate students came in, had to wash my hands for fear of giving the impression that Englishmen are unhygienic. There was no towel, so I went out of the door shaking the drops from my right hand. At that moment the Dean passed. We meet very seldom and we always shake hands. I shot my right hand behind my back but he had already extended his hand and I had to shake it. The Dean went on, his right hand wringing wet, feeling as though he'd shaken an old dishrag.

Compare two days ago. On Saturday I was walking and thinking when a girl said "Good afternoon". I responded mechanically, and taking her for a student asked "Do you live round here?" and this I repeated. It was only 30 seconds later that I realised she was our new next door neighbour with her hair done differently: I had not realised, on the one occasion I had seen her, how like one of my students she looks.

8th December. After a wearying day at Keio, talking about Surrealism, the New Apocalypse, and Sprung Rhythm, I spent the evening arranging a year's cuttings. A ritual preparation for a vacation's writing.

There is a swamp at the bottom of all our minds – a fetid swamp of evil that is responsible for the Congo, for Auschwitz, for Japanese atrocities. We are responsible for this. Compare Conrad's Kurtz looking at Europe and crying out "The horror, the horror". The Kurtzes are responsible for the Congo.

9th December. The radio broadcast for NHK, on English Literature: a free talk for 20 minutes. My damned nervousness at the beginning, the predictably thumping heart during the count-down and the paralysing shortage of breath. When I began talking, it was as though I was in a nightmare, my voice coming from far away, with myself detached and observing what I was saying. After about 20 seconds I realised I was talking rubbish – apart from the fact that my voice was quavering and faint and I felt rather sick. Of course I had to stop it all and begin again. Thank heaven it was a recording. It was all right the second time: it's as though I need two minutes to get warmed up. How can I eliminate this infernal paralytic nervousness? By practice? How would I react on TV?

On my way back from the studio bought Berdyayev's *Dostoevsky* and revived in myself the wound, my cleavage between spirit and matter, fidelity to science and fidelity to my vision. This reflected itself at Todai (Tokyo University), when I spoke of the 20th century cleavage in Western civilisation between analysis and intuition.

10th December. A day of great mental conflict, or, as I would prefer to call it (now that I've resolved it) "spiritual conflict". Without doubt this is a momentous time for me. This last six weeks (since I stopped thinking about cigarettes?) I have been undergoing some development that is obscure, even to myself in its extent. Sometimes I fear I'm giving too much ground.

I think it's some sort of a centre-shift, at least a shift from my old way of looking at things. Now for example, I acknowledge: (1) the spirit, the life-force and original sin as metaphors ("live by metaphor") and, taking Sister Frances the nun as my text, believe that belief in a fake produces "spiritual" or "self-realisational" depth although the spirit as an immortal part of ourselves does not exist, and believe that this depth is good and necessary, no matter how undivine Christ is (Christ the symbol); (2) that Eliot & Co have all sided with the spirit in principle to declare their antagonism towards materialism and humanism, i.e. have lent their names to the official "spiritual" organ, the Church (metaphysical belief) and have achieved depth (cf Eliot's verse "Will the veiled sister pray") but no static states; and (3) that spiritual depth need have nothing to do with eternity because it is man's self-realisation, which is man's aim in life, and in comparison with which most men haven't been born yet.

2nd June 1965. Did I exaggerate the importance of these months? This trend ended on 27th December 1964. Looking back I can't help seeing all this as (1) depending on a false notion of what I termed "the spirit" and (2) coming from a certain inner desperation that could have been satisfied artistically, but wasn't. Between October and December I advanced to God's frontier, then turned round and walked away, preferring to live in futility by art.

13th August 1965. No, another alternative: see July and August 1965 and the entries about Rank.

11th December. On Thursday, I said I had "resolved" my conflict by acknowledging the spirit as a metaphor and by declaring myself in principle on the side of the spirit. In fact, of course, very little is resolved. There is still the inevitable tension to and from, with me torn between. Nonetheless, my development is of crucial importance to me as a writer for it gives me a point, a purpose: to bring a new spiritual depth to man in spite of his inability to participate in eternity. Words fail. I want to say what I mean by self-realisation, but words fail. Yet I do know that the way up the ladder of perfection does not begin at Tomlin's cocktail party, to which I must now go.

Later, after Tomlin's, expounded my new creed of "live by Metaphor" to Tony, stressing the need to take sides in principle either for or against the spirit. Tony's objection: if the spiritual is self-realisational, then a scientist can take part in it. To which I would reply, Of course he can, that's not what matters. What matters is that one should have the attitude that self-realisation is more important than scientific truth; and that any means of realising oneself is good, so long as one realises oneself.

12th December. At Tomlin's yesterday, the mandala which belonged to

Mrs. Hollie. Tuohy failed to meet his welcome party-cum-delegation and spent the next party picking up objects that other people dropped. Father Milward's alert eyes behind his spectacles, and the way they contradict his self-deprecating manner: which reminds me of somebody I once knew and can't remember, the rather formal, bogusly polite manner of who? The high-pitched voice? The rather ferrety appearance? Who does Father Milward remind me of?

The lights went out for 30 seconds: the hush, the glow of a cigarette, the restrained panic, the sudden terror of being alone in the middle of 200 people you couldn't see.

My refutation of all academics who belittle Toynbee: "I don't apply academic standards. I'm interested in thinkers who suggest patterns, as Toynbee does, because they generally have a bearing on my living. Offer me an academically brilliant thinker with no relevance to my living, and an unacademic thinker who is far too general, and I would choose the latter if his thought has a relevance to my living."

13th December. To Nobe where we encountered Tony. My walk with Tony in paradisal valleys with sweeping views of the sea. Talked about Higher Religions and was astounded to hear him maintain, quite seriously, that he had come to Japan to found a new religion with Hayasaka, of all people. I said that a new religion was possible but would not begin to work for 600 years as it was harder to deify the secular beginner, the Buddha, Christ ("I am the Son of Man"), Mohammed (his gullible soldiers), and that the likeliest candidate apart from Soka Gakkai were Gurdjieffism and Subud. In the course of all this he told me that he had to decide whether to go into economics permanently, i.e. whether he should turn his back on irrationality. I told him a story about the Day of Judgement. "And when God answered 'Truth is irrational' there was a cheer from the Absurdists, the artists and the saints and a howl of protest from the mathematicians and the economists, whose spokesman began 'Objection your honour, on the data presented to us'."

In conclusion I said of Gurdjieff, "It doesn't matter whether his theory of higher centres is right or wrong objectively, it doesn't matter how academically ludicrous it is. The only judgement can be made after trying it for 20 years. Ridicule it (or yourself) if it hasn't worked then."

14th December. Returned properly to *The Soul-Destroyer* which I see I put aside on 4th September. Since then I have experienced much, the struggles concerning Hulme and Perfection (September-October) and my commitment to a religious position, the first entry being on 8th October and culminating with this last week via the disintegration of Western civilisation. This is I feel, a good time to return to *The Soul-Destroyer* as I had not consciously admitted at the end of August the position that Zabov takes up. I am changing the form a good deal. Part One will be "The Spiritual

Autobiography of J. S. Lawrence" and will end just before the priest discovers about Te Deum. Part Two, the Priest's MS, will begin before the experiment and will conclude at the end, being divided into "The Lamb" and "The Sacrifice". Perhaps the most powerful point I am trying to make now is that the religious attitude does not depend on eternity, or rather, that the whole question of eternity is irrelevant as being objective. Self-realisation is what matters. I only hope that the last three months have brought me added depth and insight.

26th December 1964. This is a startling discovery, if it is true. For in that case there is no reason why "religion" should depend on Absolutes. In fact the theme of religion should not be worship but self-realisation. A man who has realised himself will not worship false gods. So the purpose of the universe may have nothing to do with the purpose of humans. The "purpose" of humans (not according to any God) is self-realisation.

Is it possible to teach Dostoevsky and Rilke at any university here?

15th December. An evening with Keio students, interesting as my conception of Romanticism and Classicism emerged in a bar: it is of two kinds, first T. E. Hulme's, second Amis's individualism = romanticism, so that the two clash. Original sin and society or original sin and the individual. I am still slightly drunk as I express this, and admit that my expression is not clear, so let me repeat that there are two standards, one in terms of original sin and the other in terms of society, and that both have to be taken into account; and that in the case of the individualist striving for a perfection he will never attain they clash.

16th December. On my way back from Komaba met Martin Collick, whom I last recall seeing in Holdsworth's room, November 1958, at a tea-party for 9. (When Ando gave me his card yesterday, I could not place him.) Could I have foreseen six years ago that I would spend one and a half hours talking with him in Tokyo? He is at the University of Sheffield, Centre of Japanese Studies (and as he has no students he is engaged in research and will visit Japan every five years for nine months). He is married to a Japanese who lives in England. We talked about the Japanese and finally about Zen, which he said he could not understand. Like Adrian he asked "So what?": in other words, what, literally, is enlightenment like? When we left I took away with me the impression of a prosaic, factual man, very nice and very sound, but not very stimulating. Compare Tuohy: the link between prosaic and shyness.

17th December. Three stages of consciousness in the *Four* Quartets: indifference, heightened moments, e.g. the rose-garden, winter lightning (hints and guesses) and finally the saint's consciousness: our glimpses are what a saint sees all the time.

Only half an hour at the Bank of Japan, during which time I received three large books on Japan from the Vice-Governor, who is on-discharging, and then went to Sanseido and bought Eliot's *Notes towards the Definition of Culture*, which is very relevant to Toynbee.

18th December. Gave a lecture, then went to the Bank and spent an hour sitting in a coffee-shop reading Eliot on culture, instead of giving my second lecture which I had cancelled last week. Eliot's thesis reflects something I have been groping towards: individual/class-group/society. Europe's civilisation and the way a culture disintegrates according to Eliot are similar to Toynbee's principle for civilisations: a widening of the classes and a splitting of class cultures so that there is no one culture all classes share in. This is evidently so today and our cultural disintegration is evidently connected with Christianity; cf Leavis who sees English Literature as replacing it.

Eliot's difficult distinction between culture and religion: they are not related or identified; rather culture is the incarnation of religion, i.e. the tangible expression of the religious spirit? What of Humanist "culture"?

Don't forget the mission of Europe, which is to produce spiritual power when the material power has gone into other hands.

19th December. With Tuohy to Nobe. A packed train, but a walk as the sun set into the horseshoe valleys and after splitting a large bottle of whisky a walk to the sea. On writing: timing is necessary for light novels. Thinking through perception, because a work of art is a proposition in feelings and perceptions to which you can say "Yes", which he got from Wittgenstein. (Wittgenstein: "At the end of *King Lear* you say 'Yes'.") Dostoevsky gets people who have ideas, and the people are strongest. How? How does he make it organic? A work of art cannot be paraphrased: all paraphrases are inadequate (also Wittgenstein). No novel can be set in Japan because "no communication between two people has taken place". "English fiction presupposes sincerity and you can't write about a liar." Of dialogue, "English people don't talk in paragraphs or even sentences."

20th December. With Tuohy to the shrine with the Russio-Japanese etchings, and then up and along the ridge through thick bamboo, finally plunging down with high earthen walls on either side. On writing: a novel is quite different from a moral fable, a novelist shouldn't have a programme, i.e. any Gurdjieffian ideal. There should be a bedrock of realism, i.e. observation (cf Kingsley Amis's "I am a *Roman* Catholic", an impossible thing for a Catholic character to say) and realistic detail and atmosphere. Readers make assumptions so experimentalism such as Robbe-Grilletism, which questions the assumptions, is unnecessary; what is needed is imagination. The 19th century is preferable to the 20th century because the 19th century writer can understand an experience, as the 20th century cannot.

On life: I said, either the first cell came out of nitrogen and carbon, or it didn't. If it did, there's pattern but no purpose; if it didn't, there's the idea of higher organisation. Anyway some notion of acquired characteristics is necessary to explain the development from ape to man, acquired over generations but still measurable. "It is not a novelist's business." "Avoid, at all costs avoid being conventional." "People are neither good nor bad, that's the point to remember." "Read back once a week, not more often than that."

On December 14th, a year ago, my notions of what a novel should be were challenged by Fitzsimmons. Tuohy is not so expansive but I feel he might have an important bearing on what I write. I have penetrated his facade but slightly.

21st December. The trouble with England is that you don't know how anyone will behave: your next-door neighbour may give riotous parties and your daughter may be seduced anywhere. All social norms have broken down. (The 19th century has these?)

The Hagger theme: the descent into oneself, which is necessary for maturity and which unites one with one's subconscious enemies.

22nd December. A good morning's writing stressing "what I have always known", in the course of which my idea of "phases" emerged. This is something I've believed in for some time without articulating: the evidence being in this journal. Briefly, the idea is that there should be no spiritual developments to static states, only spiritual phases, each contradicting the other. I should like to believe that these phases can find a root in a static state not strictly imposed and allowing the phases to continue; that would be my argument against materialists who ask "Why embark on the spiritual if it's just a set of phases without a direction?" Anyhow it's quite clear to me that I have in many ways a very full "spiritual" or self-realisational life in terms of these phases, though no spiritual life in terms of a static state.

The prime question is not "How true is it?" but "To what extent does it bring significance into my life?" Though for an honest man an untruthful thing is often not significant.

23rd December. Adrian's experience when being asked insistently to sing although being tone-deaf: he stood up and shouted out the only words he could remember, those of the Albanian national anthem, and said at the end that it was an old Gaelic folk-song. ("X referred them to Joyce's *Finnegan's Wake* and gave an additional discourse on the origin of Sprung Rhythm and early Welsh poetry."…)

I have also decided to change the title (of Th*e Soul-Destroyer*) to*The Eternicide*, to avoid obvious ambiguities, and to make J. S. Lawrence as sympathetic as possible, this being a departure from the old alienation idea.

Don't make it too symbolic. The composite personality or cultural forces idea is good but can deny reality or humanity to it. Think very carefully before having Te Deum in the basement and J. S. Lawrence upstairs under the priest's hole.

24th December. New light on the "culture" problem. If specialisation and lack of communication and cleavage is a symptom of an unhealthy culture, is not the so-called "two culture" dispute between Leavis and Snow just another manifestation of Eliot's thesis? If they argue against Eliot they surely mean different things by "culture".

6.40. A rumbling earthquake that made me feel quite sick. I predicted this as it got warmer, and notice that there was an earthquake on Christmas Eve last year.

The New Year decorations: straw, pine, fern, an orange or lobster, a red and white fan. Also the tall bamboo canes with branches on either side of a building.

25th December. The theme of *The Eternicide*, which cannot be paraphrased, very falsely is: "that self-divided scepticism, having killed eternity and worship, leads to materialism unless it commits itself to the religious side, there is no middle way." Hold onto it like fury, and don't for God's sake lose your humanity.

A sudden unity of vision: make Mrs. B a mad visionary who reflects the sickness of the whole (*Blighty*, 3rd October 1966), and write it in the third person, which is quite possible as J. S. Lawrence believes he has made his discovery. If J. S. Lawrence is divided scepticism he can't in any sense be the modern Christ, the lamb who is sacrificed, not even in the most brutally ironic sense. Eliminate the Christ theme? If religion does not depend on eternity (but needs Christianity as an ally) there is no need for J. S. Lawrence to hang himself or to be depressed or to be destroyed. The whole must triumph over the parts.

Tomlin's party, for 15 connected with the British Council. Very Christmassy with candles, turkey, crackers, carols, and a jumping monkey, but a miscalculation on Tomlin's part compelled us to spend a long time in silence listening to some indifferent folk-music: everyone was clearly very embarrassed. I sat with Tuohy who was rather subversive, and said, when I stressed on the way home how kind it was of Tomlin, "But when an evening's a success one doesn't say that." Tuohy is brutally honest.

26th December. Felt rather lethargic after the drink at Tomlin's and speculated about the universe: is there an alternative to the "chance or purpose" issue? Can one believe that an accident has pattern and yet that it has no purpose? Can one believe in a very complicated accident, in which man with his complicated brain is fed and warmed from his environment, and yet assert that it has no purpose, that it was not designed? I refuse to believe that the plan is without purpose, but (and here I believe I repeat my entry to 13th November 1963, my last day in England, a very important discovery for me) deny that it is a purpose that can affect my life or that I can share in, because it is not a purpose that takes account of human beings. Is that really so illogical, is it a fuzzy compromise that is untenable? After all, a purpose suggests someone to purpose it.

I have just reached the origin of Existentialism: existence is, there is no one to purpose it.

27th December. Compare 13th November 1963, the notion of God as "some higher consciousness."

27th December. All this wrestling with purpose and I wonder, am I in fact struggling with God? Is God the idea that defeats one's intellect, the notion of the plan? (Not the creator of the plan, for God is the plan, without the plan of the universe there is no God, and so we, as members of the universe, are now in God?) This is surprising, that I should put it this way, for the concept of "God" carries ridiculous notions, and after all the ridiculous things said about it, is so completely obvious: the point of the plan, that cannot be experienced without the plan – in short, life and the universe. In which case, the philosopher would retort, the concept of God is redundant.

I see now however that this unknowable has been symbolised in the *Old Testament*, and that the Higher Religions and their prophets are merely directing attention to the plan (with symbolic solutions perhaps) and are ways of feeling the religious awe which is expressed symbolically in worship. Jettison therefore the notion of a God outside creation: vaguely out in the universe. God is creation, the plan, and the point of it is symbolised in the notion of God. This is so difficult a notion of God that (to parody Eliot) I am not sure that I understand it myself: I certainly do not think I am struggling with God, for God is not concerned in whether I struggle, God merely is, the purpose that cannot affect my life, the purpose in which I do not share. Am I slowly becoming Christian? I don't think so. Is this merely a restatement of the God=Nature mechanism? Have I stumbled on something that I have not understood? Compare Kafka's *Castle*.

De-symbolize the Higher Religions and make a study: the impossibility of expressing awe of the point of the plan and purpose without symbols.

28th December. Yesterday's entry conceded a day of despair that was solved in the evening just before Adrian came by a flash of inspiration and again my vision united.

This has given me an insight into my own methods of creation: I have an image, or a set of images, which I then try to understand and sometimes the images clash with the logic and historical symbolism. Image and logical modification, in that order: that is how I create. And creative failures are due to the failure of my logical modification.

29th December. I have so rich an inner life these days that I have no space for what has happened to me. This must be one of my most creative periods so far. I am teeming with images, and new graspings. Such a state can't last, and I am dreading the inevitable crash and hope that it won't come before January 11th.

30th December 1964. A day of distractions: the tape to be sent off, the attempt to get in touch with Nan'undo, then (the) Osborne (book) coming, then booking tickets for Kyoto. (The official forms for the New Tokaido line, the people sitting in the station as though it was war-time except that they had boredom on their faces.)

I now have the unpleasant task of taking stock of the year. I left England in despondency (in spite of my experience on the last day), my father dead and only £5 in the bank. Since then I have become progressively more pro-religious and anti-scientific. My grasp is firmer, my control surer, I have become more mature as a writer in so far as my "individualism" now has a firm social basis and is not least related to contemporary society and culture. So there has been a two-way movement, an increase in spiritual penetration and a heightened awareness of social trends. I have a long way to go, but at least I have improved. Which is to say that the dream is slowly becoming a reality. If nothing else, this *Diary* is a testament to the possibilities of Self-Development.

31st December. Oo-misoka = great pay day, and for me the Day of Self-Reckoning. At 11.30 p.m. it looks as though the year is going to end in artistic deadlock. Anyhow the themes that find a place in the past year are artistic doubt and planning, metaphysics versus materialism, dreams, observations of Japan and parties and probably others. I am struck by the fluctuations of my mind: everything proceeds in phases. Therefore I am not convinced that one can believe in Self-Development beyond an intensification of mind within one's phases.

2nd June 1965. This disbelief in Self-Development I have disproved in my poems. There are phases within a development, runs on a particular subject, or theme, the conflict depending on one's self-division. I am hopelessly self-divided, but can resolve my self-division in art: consequently have not had too much conflict in 1965.

Wrong in 1964 over Self-Development. Wrong in 1965 over other things?

1965

1st January. Year of the Snake. Theme for a short story, *The New Man*, about a man injured in a car accident who loses his memory and looks on the world with divine vision and can't understand why man's consciousness is so blind. In the end he's locked up in a mental hospital. Before the knock on the head he was as mundane as the others, an office worker. He has to

118

be re-educated into Western civilisation (having lost his conditionings) and in the end refuses, declaring all society is mad, that everyone must be blind not see that the purpose of life is to contemplate the wonder of existence. ("How can they not understand it?")

Toyama's visit. His rebellion against Fukuhara will be to write a manifesto arguing for analogy against example or illustration (which kill a thesis and make it ephemeral): my suggestion that he should include Eliot and T. E. Hulme, and my point that there are two traditions in essay-writing, the pattern-tradition and the factual tradition, both of which have different aims and must not therefore be judged in terms of each other. My attack on the "factual" school, which is strong in Japan as it is a Japanese characteristic to be factual: also my attack on rationalism and linguistic analysis, insisting that they must yield to experience. (Don't trust categories.) Toyama's description of a Japanese relationship after our walk: "moments of intense happiness, just flashes, which make us value our distance: we can tell by the blink of an eyelid." Cf Tuohy, "Nothing has happened between two people, therefore no story."

I have felt these flashes with Toyama: certainly something has happened between us. The intensity and sincerity of our relationship is something I find quickening.

2nd January. An image for a writer on his life: "hauling myself up a cliff, and the higher I got the more people came to watch underneath." ("And the more remote I was from them.")

I am reliving the process of belief. For example, today I arrived independently at two thoughts that have been held for 2,000 years by Christians – that all men can only be equal as members of a *Civitas Dei*, the great idea, and that a thought is quite different from the electricity it is contained in (but cf radio thoughts in a radio wave, although without the thinker the radio wave would contain no thought). I also speculated again about the Whole Man, the artist-philosopher-scientist-saint, my ideal, though it is impossible today. The final statement of the poems.

On my walk I considered the New Year rituals: a man with a snake's (dragon's?) head and dark red mane did a Bottom-like dance to a drum and a quick flute outside each house; after the man with a large bag collected money. Perhaps the snake-man represented the Devil who was kept away by the white pieces of paper and the protective straw.

3rd January. A day of distractions, the distractions being Adrian who came first at 10 a.m., then at 2.30 to take me to *For Whom the Bell Tolls* and then stayed until 9. Objected to Roberto Jordan in the film because his motivation wasn't dealt with thoroughly enough. It wasn't made clear whether he was in Spain for the idealism or for kicks (to combat futility) and so the last night (love and death after the sunrise) lost a lot of poignancy: it could have been a statement of the human condition as well as being a realistic portrayal of a last night. Adrian: "There's a situation and one can go back behind it indefinitely – one has to stop some time."

Got Part 1 of the novel straightened out and wrote a great deal between 10 p.m. and 12.30 a.m.

4th January. A day of revaluation, the archetypal "Faustian" story reinstated. I have faced the weakness in my commitment to a religious position: if the "spiritual" is only to be followed metaphorically, like "life-force" and "Christ", and if it is equivalent to self-realisation, why follow it at all, since nothing survives death? What incentive is there? Last week (25th December 1964) I wrote "Religion does not depend on eternity." But it must, that is what I've discovered today. Otherwise it is open to the objection: why bother? Only because it is a pleasure, like eating? Self-realisation and self-development and contemplation and the "seventh degree of concentration" must depend on the notion of immortality or eternity, otherwise all life is futile. Eternity is crucial to purpose. Religion does depend on eternity.

And so I reluctantly concede another point to the metaphysical and still, cowardly as I am, refuse even to think of taking the leap. How I manage to write anything with such tides of self-questioning in me is incredible. But, if man evolved from the ape, and if apes do not share in eternity, eternity must have evolved. Perhaps it did. Perhaps eternity is only bestowed upon those who are sufficiently conscious to deserve it.

But, can it be experienced?

5th January. Tuohy last night: the distinction between presentation and explanation (cf Tom Fitzsimmons); Dostoevsky presents people who explain. Cf Tolstoy's *Kreutzer Sonata* which is full of explanation, like Sartre. Tuohy on "I" and 3rd person narration: "the Japanese are still at the stage of finding things in drawers." The rule, how much you know: the confidence. Christian names. "Ancient Mariner's eye" which you never know you've got. Aesthetics and beauty being a "socially taught thing", with reference to the Heian period and mono-no-aware.

To Kyoto by train. Flying low over a sleeping city at dawn; the sun rising in the misty mountains, the curly-tiled roofs slumbering on; the vision that a Second Coming might have. The station food, city-specialities. The various shrines and gardens on the sides of the hills: Ryoanji, golden and silver pavilions, the shogun's castle (Nijo). Kiyamachi and the swindling ryokkan – pay ¥1500 down and a tip for the tea, "¥100 please": I walked out and found another ryokkan for ¥700, tea and bath all in. (Taxis and entry fees had taken a lot of money.) Over dinner, the rugger player: 1936 All-Japan captain, fearfully drunk and boastful. Nogame Ichiro was his name: it means "Number one on the field".

6th January. To Nara. The park or forest, with Tempyo shrines scattered beneath a blue sky. Horiyuji and the Japanese party, throwing coins, clapping, praying, and watching to see if I was looking (as I was, staring quite shamelessly). The peasant bus back to Nara, no one sitting next to the gaijin (foreigner, me); the bumpy road like the road to Pylos. The deer. My poem on the shrines after seeing the death-stones lining the steps and all culture as dominated by death – man in the forest erecting trophies to conquer death. I wrote it in an open-air restaurant, my fingers freezing, sitting beside an ineffectual charcoal brazier, with white glowless-charcoal buried in sand.

An accident-prone day. The streetcar in Kyoto went into a car, causing me to take a taxi to catch my train: and the 5.22 train back was delayed until 6.50 by switchboard and wire-failures, so that I had to stamp around Kyoto station in the freezing cold, cursing the designers for not building a waiting-room and trying to read (with numb fingers) Iris Murdoch's *An Unofficial Rose*. The queue for refunds in Tokyo. De-cobwebbed by the fresh air, but eye-achy. *The Death of Ivan Ilyich* which I read yesterday (Tuohy's copy).

7th January. Buchanan's party in the Japanese restaurant. Buchanan was pretty slewed at the beginning and went round pouring saké for everyone and hugging the various women and lamenting that Barbara hadn't come. Emery, the *Times* correspondent who was at Bancroft's until 1951 and who obviously is luminously bright, with a very powerful memory and a very aggressive mind: his Swedish wife. His story on datelines: UPI breaking etiquette by writing the earthquake report under a Niigata dateline, although the correspondent was in Tokyo.

After, my dream. A voice, my own, saying "My novel objectifies internal conflicts and symbolizes inner self-division." I must choose whether *The Eternicide* is to incorporate the priest's doubts.

8th January. Toynbee's *Schism in the Soul* with its alternatives: abandon/ self-control, truancy/martyrdom, drift/sin, promiscuity/unity, archaism and futurism/detachment and transfiguration. "The spiritual experience of schism in the soul is a dynamic movement, not a static situation" – compare my entry on phases (see 22nd December 1964). Undoubtedly a divided society produces a divided mind/soul, as our society has produced in me, and I find it rather thrilling to justify converting the macrocosm into the microcosm on the grounds that I am reflecting the historical "truth" of our time.

Tuohy. "Explaining suggests I know something that you don't"; limiting to a week-end in a novel – where do you stop?; don't lie; characters never represent historical forces; Uriah the Hittite; "D. H. Lawrence's Christ gets there too easily, Dostoevsky would have made him argue back."

Statement and showing.

9th January. Visited the British Council to collect files, saw Tomlin, talked and returned in depression, filled with the futility of Tokyo life (Tomlin, "the years pass so quickly and things don't get done") and the hollowness of my job, my life. Felt terribly vulnerable, and could hardly put up the necessary defence when a student greeted me in the bookshop after. Since then I have felt a quiet despair. Did I catch it all from Tomlin? Is it possible to catch depressions, and was Tomlin disguising a depression beneath his "warm" external?

A rather depressed day, writing to conceal my depression.

10th January. A day's writing on progress to conscious states of mind, which I compared later with Eliot's "hints and guesses" when preparing Eliot. There is no doubt about it, Eliot has faked no evidence. On the evidence he provides he affirms eternity and I don't, that's all. Yet I feel myself weakening and weakening. The unity of the world, the inexplicable "energy" or life in every sense-form – these are things I've experienced and rejected on speculation. This evening I took up Whitehead's *Science and the Modern World*, intending to read some of it with my postgraduates, and discovered: "Religion is the reaction of human nature to its search for God." Call it what I like, I am "seeking God" and am experiencing spiritual life.

Today threw up the concept, which I may abandon, of philosophy X, a ladder to a more conscious state of mind.

11th January. A day torn and racked, interfered with by classes. It began when I read in the paper of the discovery of a "brain depth probe" in a hypodermic, something I predicted word for word at least three years ago. It continued when I picked up Grey Walter's *The Living Brain* again and discovered the extent of his impartiality, which I had not realised. Mind or matter – is mind dependent on matter? They are clearly both similar as they interact, so is it mind and organism?

Sometimes I feel that all this meditating can only have the effect of self-brainwashing. The thing is, I will never know, but I shall always want to know and worry at it.

12th January. Another day of suppressed despair. All the time I know that I've lost my faith in J. S. Lawrence's machine; and faith on my part was the motive behind the writing I did last summer. I now think the whole thing a foolish fancy. I should be writing about the modern city and about the relationship between a spiritual man and an intellectual, not about sensational things which are too fantastic to happen. This, and the fact that I know so little about brain physiology and higher mathematics, are what restrain me. Write about experience, not philosophy and beliefs. Write about the scientific, yes, but don't make it so horribly self-dividedly complicated. Yes, a day of despair. At this rate I'd never finish anything.

14th January. Krishna's words in (Eliot's) *Dry Salvages*: the object of contemplation determines our state of mind, i.e. the highest object of contemplation produces the highest state of mind, spiritual being.

15th January. A holiday for Adult's Day. Wrote on Lawrence's self-creation. This mirrors my own self-creation, which is by no means at present complete but which has begun since I came to Tokyo. I was thinking of this parallel last night, and got the idea for a novel in which the author interweaves autobiography with the copy of the autobiography; I believe B. S. Johnson and Gide have thought of or experimented with this idea. As a result I had a wretched night last night, dozing and dreaming that Eliot was my next door neighbour, that he was dying and didn't like Tuohy, etc. – a great deal of rubbish which irritated me and has left me with an insomniac's head today.

Eliot's objection that he is not a static stater: "we must be still and still moving."

16th January. A very disturbed day: first Toyama, then letters which had to be written, then my resignation to Todai (Tokyo University) and the Keio exam questions which had to be typed out. As a result I did very little writing, but was able to formulate my aim, which is to write about states of mind experiencing. Seek a form not in mythology but in experience, for the poem on Western civilisation.

To what extent can you give an experience and an interpretation (part myth/belief), and yet make the interpretation entirely different from the experience, separate from it? Eliot did it in "hints followed by guesses". To what extent also can you give complexity to the whole by working something at two levels e.g. modern Tokyo in states of mind; contrasts with ancient glory and rustic values in states of mind; symbolism of the closing of civilisation and spiritual power in states of mind.

Mythology is frozen experience.

17th January. C went to Nobe to pay the rent, I went for a walk with Tuohy up to the Catholic cathedral and to Chinzanso, and then he came back home with me to collect the *Telegraph* obituary of Eliot. We discussed various things: Eliot ("he's doing the same thing as Graves, he believes that poetic experience is the same as incipient religious experience" – I disagreed); Tolstoy (on stating as opposed to showing – "the Russians state with such power and conviction"); Hardy: "Hardy had the power to generalise his private experience." (See 31st January for the full significance of this remark, i.e. you don't ask "so what?" Why not?) He distinguished the vacuum-cleaner from the cultural mind, which led to a discussion as to whether $E=mc^2$ is the subject for a novel and necessary to culture, his answer being no, although our knowledge of culture is arbitrary and there are no defined limits as to what English culture is (classical and European but what after that?). "Snow is talking about one culture and scientific

123

knowledge which can't be used in poetry", e.g. Prufrock and the patient. Compare: "Eliot lacks cadence, e.g. the generic 'the'." John Hayward, a cripple, who replied when Tuohy said he'd visit him, "Yes, but you know you can't meet Mr Eliot." Tuohy's frequent objection: "He hasn't felt it, he's got it from books."

18th January. Artistic techniques: the extent to which personality matters in literature and the extent to which the communication of an emotion depends on the reader's having had it. I developed an idea I had at Kyoikudai from Eliot: that we have no continuous identity beyond a superficial connection, that otherwise we are states of mind whose quality of existence depends on the object of contemplation, and whose duration does too.

Cf *Prufrock*. Eliot presents state of mind and reactions; we have to guess the rest. Cf Fitzsimmons: "When I want to describe a character's thoughts, I describe what he is looking at."

19th January. Taught Owen's *Strange Meeting* and then *Prufrock* to the 3rd year at Keio, the theme being the composite personality (cf Kafka, Pinter, Beckett) and the divided self in 20th century Literature; taught the Movement to the 4th year.

An autobiographical novel, taking certain moments and relating them to the past. The poet deepens experience, the novelist broadens it, so the poet needs fewer experiences for an autobiographical poem.

20th January. On the way to Todai bought Pound's *Cantos* and Snow's Rede lecture, which I read on my return in the evening together with *A Second Look*. It's all in Eliot and as Tuohy said on Sunday, Snow's talking about one culture and scientific knowledge, and $E=mc^2$ is quite useless knowledge to a writer, it's not experience. Nonetheless I was very interested in his distinction between the industrial and scientific revolutions, and in his "attack" on Modernism on the grounds that it's interested more in the individual than in society. I can see that my Modernism (the composite personality and states of mind) is going to be challenged by myself in the next few days, so I record the characteristics of Modernism as pointed out by Lukács – rejection of narrative objectivity, dissolution of the personality, ahistoricity, static view of the "social" condition – and Snow's distinction between the tragic individual condition and the meaningful social condition. I think I agree with Snow up to a point (the point being that "social" life is a pretence against death, a magic notion of collective humanity, though material standards have to be raised for the poor) but my leftism is blighted by my feelings about what levelling off will do for us. As regards Lukács' four points, I don't practise the first three and wonder whether there is to be a post-modern (i.e. Modernist) Movement that will not practise the first three.

SPIRITUAL DEPTH AND CREATIVITY (1964 – 1965)

21st January. A day of hard work and much talking, most interestingly at the Bank of Japan with Oshima about the present cultural divide between scientists and the arts and the attempt of the (British) Labour Government to solve this by creating more places for scientists at universities.

Reflections on form: a broken form for a fragmentary view of the world, which Modernism implies. So how do I see the world, as a whole or in fragments, with all the traditional certainties broken, and experience remaining? How much confidence have I as a thinker, and to what extent does Modernism depend on a broken society, which I am not reacting to? I read Toynbee in connection with a review of (Colin) Wilson's latest book, in which (as I have long suspected he would) he (Colin Wilson) comes out for Evolutionary Humanism, for all his praise of T. E. Hulme and the religious attitude, and was called a futurist: the progress from archaism (in my case archaeology) to futurism, on to transfiguration, which is a really positive force, and which is confident, certain, and perceives as a whole.

22nd January. A crowded day. Met Adrian at 8.25 in a steaming bath, was given a present by Sakuraba, a book by Irie, advised Moritani, my religious maniac, and heard Buchanan provide me with the framework for the Lost Englishman. (He is going to buy land and build in Nobe and slowly retire, living with Keikosan and renting his property in Tokyo, so my "history" takes place after he has withdrawn from Tokyo and is something of a legend – a meeting between "I" and the Lost Englishman together with interior monologues.) How to make interiorised writing readable?

Then introduced Toyama to Emery and talked on Nationalism and the possible rise of militarism. Also thoughts on symbolism in an age without any widely shared symbols: symbols cannot be ready-made, their interpretation should be made clear by the context in which they grow.

My themes: the victory of the spirit and the meaning of suffering: dignity.

23rd January. Read some of Pound's *Cantos* and decided that I shall make a study of Modernism, its causes and the attitude to living it expresses. To what extent does it reflect chaos outside in society, like Existentialism? I.e. to what extent is its condition a breaking society? For today the problem is not the break-up of traditional society but the break-up of the traditional "spiritual" view of man, which has survived the break-up of traditional society. That means the break-up of the certainties that evaluate man's experience.

24th January. To Nobe. The sea dominated by light, diamond-explosions, pure white, and the smaller sparkle and glitter of billions of crystals in the sand, and the fire in my head as I walked and the lights jumped like neon, describing patterns. The receding moisture after the ebb of each wave, like an ebbing cloud, and the splutter of bubbles. The pummice-stone you can break in your hand, and the shell-kernels, preserved from millions of years back. The Lost Englishman's house on the hill, derelict among the firs, the bamboo, a rusty lantern and a view since partially blocked by a white house, the rattle of the sea-wind on the broken pane. The sea seen from the top of a horseshoe (valley) towards dusk, pure white save for the rock, between the V of the hills, so that the strip of land above it floated on mist.

25th January. In a society whose symbols are stereotypes, the need is for fresh, precise, particular, individual experience, questioning the values of the mass which the mass would not allow, raising the quality of life, restoring the psychic or spiritual which is in danger of being lost from our mechanistic society. So the priest is a reactionary, traditional archaist who doesn't like the present and who misjudges J. S. Lawrence as the new type of machine-dominated man (spiritual barbarian) who is our future (electronics, atomic energy, automation) and who is for these "psychic forces", (and who) has in fact kept himself free from machine-consciousness and is rather revolutionary, a futurist who unlike the priest (who dreams of Georgian England) embraces the modern city as a Modernist. So the priest dreams of Epping Forest, and knows that J. S. Lawrence will replace him; sees himself as preserving values that the machine will destroy. Hence J. S. Lawrence's ideal is wholeness. Neither understands the other; both have preconceived ideas. (Cf *The Owl and the Nightingale*.)

T— took me home, lonely and trying to understand why, in spite of all his trying, he can never persuade a girl to allow him to be unfaithful to his wife. "I don't have something and I'm trying to find out what it is. She suspects, but she doesn't know, but it's all right."

26th January. Plans for the future. I want to return to England in February 1966 to get the atmosphere of Labour England: I am determined not to lose contact. Would TUE (Tokyo University of Education) agree to have me back? They would have to pay the money for someone else; why not me if they are sincere in inviting me to stay "as long as you like"? The British Council has agreed to renew my contract, so I would get the subsidy and tax exemption; apart from the house, the main benefit of TUE is the power I have over the syllabus: at no other foreign university anywhere in the world could I teach T. E. Hulme and T. E. Lawrence and Pound.

A letter from Ricky made me think of the requisites for the new Existentialism: a belief that civilisation is declining, an interest in the human condition, and individualism (with a social basis), a determination to reflect the conflicts of the 20th century but to do it through states of mind and experiences. Later got the idea for *Experiences or Experios*: a group of autobiographical poems relating experiences that are apparently arbitrary by association and creating a pattern out of my life so that when seen in terms of each other the experiences assume depth. The conception is to be cyclic and is to contemplate and interpret experience, the occupation of the saint. This is quite revolutionary.

SPIRITUAL DEPTH AND CREATIVITY (1964 – 1965)

27th January. Since last night I have written three experiences and feel that this search for a pattern to my own life is quite original in conception: Pound, Betjeman, Wordsworth, Tennyson – none of them built a jigsaw puzzle out of experiences: and Eliot's *Four Quartets* is very different. Now that I have discovered that the best material for poetry is from my own past experience I must take myself seriously as a poet, not regard myself as an occasional poet. Experiences 1-100 should be possible by the end of the year. The trouble is, can I publish if I tell the truth? And if I don't tell the truth there's no point in writing. Ideally I should feel free to tell exactly what happened in the Oaklands garden at night in 1959 or 1960.

Bear in mind for the novel that the U.K. is supposed to have an affluent society that is not fully modernised, that "Modernisation" is the slogan of the Labour Party.

28th January. Wrote and am pleased with the physical words. This is a great improvement in my style, one I can only attribute to my increasing stylistic consciousness during this last year. Some of the words now ring out like a blacksmith battering an anvil, so my style is muscular and energetic and has the authentic ring of a genuine half-crown. But remember the awful turgid, jargoned, mannered, abstract style you're trying to leave behind and don't get complacent. And sharpen your observation. Every day, remember, at least two precise, detailed descriptions to yourself of a scene or an object or a person. I discovered that my Experiences or Experiments are in fact *Life Cycle*, a Meditation or Introspection. So physical is the present scheme that I could not recognise the original *Life Cycle* with its abstract Rilke-esque conception in ten elegies.

29th January. The essence of *Meditation* is that it is cyclic and another day it might all be different, for one might start at a different beginning, yet would the pattern be different? Probably. Yet not basically. Bear in mind, "Like all meditations, I got off the subject." And the possibility of meditating on one subject, so Meditation 1 is on freedom. Meditation 2 on spiritual life, etc. Each to have 100 poems. The bridge idea.

Buchanan sees me as a Shelley looking for Mary Godwin.

30th January. Catch the waves of the meditating mind, reflect the delta rhythms and K-complexes as the meditation gets deeper. Interpret experience in terms of other experience. Give it depth not in terms of mythology (like Eliot's Fisher King and Joyce's *Ulysses*) but in terms of itself. The detachment of meditation enables me to fulfil my ideal of "spiritual unravelling treated anti-romantically". Also it is an investigation of post-war society.

You have avoided a choice between poet and novelist, but it may come to a choice, and be prepared to choose the poet. One's own experience is always superior to other people's or fantasies. The 20th century has

127

undermined the whole conception of action in the novel. Any extraordinary action is laughably ridiculous.

31st January. Tea with Tuohy, who, as usual, had nothing good to say of anybody and was interesting. The main points: Resonance: what makes a poetic line poetic? "So what": what is the relation between the particular and the general, the familiar and the strange, that makes the reader interested? Tuohy is pro-general, I rather pro-particular. Of my Meditation he admitted it was original but countered (rather obliquely) the possible objections: it's difficult to write out of ordinary experience – Eliot moved away from it; free verse only works if it comes from a strong personality like Lawrence's; it might mean nothing to anyone else, because what of the diagram; narrative is a bore in Wordsworth; inflation; you can't put "Sartre" in a poem without destroying the resonance and making it funny – the difficulty of being serious. I countered all these objections and maintained that the subject of poetry must be one's own experience, deepened by itself not mythology, and made unromantic by irony, detachment, deflating, juxtaposition. Consider other means of distancing. Tuohy's criterion for any work of art: does it work, e.g. "It works in...." His criterion for writing a story: "I'm going to see how real it is to the people round about." Of a scapegoat festival near Nara, the scapegoat receiving "ons", then being purified in a shrine (cf Camus).

Also: "Leavis wrong about machines (it's better to work in a factory than peel potatoes)." Eliot's distinction between the man who suffers and the artist who creates is because of his first wife.

1st February. "Why should anyone want to read your Meditation?" "Because I give particular experiences of freedom which have a general appeal, a universal appeal: other people should be able to say 'Yes, I too' and respond to the poetry." ("My words echo thus in your mind.") So it is anti-impersonality.

The device of masks or roles to achieve the effect of a multiple personality and thereby generalise my experience. I have realised the power of mythology to generalise private experience.

2nd February. A crowded day. Wrote, then went to Keio to set the students a report for their examination, as they are going to boycott the university to protest against the £230 entrance increase.

What will come out of my poems will be this point, that in ceasing to rebel I have created myself, and that rebellion is only possible if your life is macrocosmically or God-centred, not if it's microcosmically-centred. For the genuine microcosmic is indifferent to the outside world of action: he does not rebel against it. (Compare my secret disgust at Trink, who was a yardstick by which to measure my own conformity.) On the other hand, paradoxically, one cannot create oneself unless one rebels, for otherwise one is not an independent being but merely the extension of someone else's will.

3rd February. A very busy day. Wrote, then went off to the Jimbocho bookshop and bought Rilke's *Malte* and Hesse's *Steppenwolf*; arrived late at Todai (Tokyo University), told the students this would be my last day as I wasn't paid for after 10th February and wouldn't do their exams for nothing, rushed through *Little Gidding* and *Look Back in Anger*, went to the Finance Department to settle payment and discovered that Todai are paying me to the end of March "as a present". Went home feeling guilty, read the *Observer*, prepared for Friday's three lectures and tomorrow's British Council class.

Let the reader do the creating: all I should do should be to give the reader the patterns. A novel is written in the mind of the reader.

4th February. Wrote. At the Bank Fukuchi told me that he was in Nagasaki when the A-bomb dropped. He was sitting away from the window with his back to it and saw an orange flash like lightning, felt the earthquake. "It was all over in a second." After, he went out and walked the twisted streets among the dead and the suffering. "It was hell, all groaning." One man was digging in the rubble. He stopped and told Fukuchi that he had been on a trip in Kyushu and had returned home. "That's my wife", said with control, but shocked. Fukuchi 's friend went in search of his daughter who worked in a factory beneath the hypocentre. He knew nothing of radiation and died a week later. "The worst thing of all was waiting for the next one. For four days we waited as there were no communications." As he talked I wanted to weep but not with shame. It is no doubt very naive of me, but I feel suffering strongly, especially archetypal suffering: someone like Tuohy is pretty detached, but runs the risk of being blasé.

5th February. Behind the scene politics at Kyoikudai (Tokyo University of Education). The first idea I had was when Irie said "Congratulations". I said "What for?" "For being appointed to royalty or isn't it decided yet?" It later appeared that TUE had a meeting and recommended me as candidate, and the Imperial Household was most interested: this for the position of official Tutor to the Crown Prince, to succeed Blyth. Later Kuroda asked me various questions: the TUE is of course pushing me for prestige. I shall now think no more about it: it is an interesting situation, but as I am only a candidate it does not really concern me.

The novel treats Part 1 from the religious mind, Part 2 from the scientific mind.

6th February. Wrote on Isaiah in the modern pub. Then read Eliot's *Family Reunion* for Monday's class, collated it with *Burnt Norton*; then wrote up something on "Is Jimmy (Porter) a hero or a neurotic?" This while flurries of snow swept past the window, then stopped. Very tired. Have slept little the past three or four nights, and have kept going with coffee.

My writing career will be the poems, which will show the retreat from the world of action, to the *Eternicide*, which is set "in a green shade" (Marvell) and on to *Mandalas*, which also takes place behind the world of action. Remember my ideas about phases. (I completely forget my own inspirations within two or three months. Hence the careful documentation here in these *Diaries*.)

7th February. Having found my poetic form and released all my poetic energies on January 26th, I think I may at long last have found my novel form. I have been trying for a long while with states of mind, experiencing, but have so far conceived of them as being linked by a narrative, in the case of *The Eternicide* contributing to two parts which balance each other. Now I wonder, could I not replace narrative* by contrast and juxtaposition, changing the person "I" to "he" for example, in order to achieve a Picassoesque effect of approaching the hero from every side at the same time? If I retain the "composite personality" idea, macrocosm giving way to microcosm, and write solely through states of mind experiencing, will I not gain? Is this not the only way of expressing what I want to say, to concentrate attention from the outside world to the inner world, yet not to be lost in the inner world, and to telescope time and place? Note: the significance of the concept "the inner novel". Check this with Tuohy even if he pinches the idea: find out about Faulkner, Joyce, Beckett.

The important thing about my Picassoesque idea is that the time-differences are determined by me and not by the character. I am therefore pasting emotions and times together.

Layers. A "Scrapbook technique". Cf a collage.

The object of experiment is not novelty but to release creative energy, to split the atom.

*Narrative jettisoned: states of mind relevant to the theme?

8th February. This official Tutorship to the Crown Prince (like my appointment to the TUE) reminds me of Kafka. Everyone is congratulating me on "being asked" and no one has asked me. Was it not like the man who waited years, daily in expectation of being summoned to the Imperial Household, and all on the strength of one rumour? Or is that not in Kafka at all, but an echo from some remote dream I once had on some afternoon walk? Anyhow, the authorities in the Imperial Household have, like the authorities in the Castle and the authorities connected with the Great Pyramid, taken an interest in me, unworthy as I am. In Meditation 1 use this parallel to write the only Kafkaesque poem.

Rang Tuohy. Going to see him tomorrow to have my new inspiration debunked.

9th February. For my "Scrapbook" technique or "collage", preserve narrative (even if I am meditating in narrative), just narrate by juxtaposition, the object of each section being to reveal the state of mind experiencing of the character. So no analysis, no objectivity. Disjointed, fragmentary blocks rather than a continuous flow, transitions being as sharp as required.*

Later: rather undecided about this technique, and also the balancing idea – every sentence of Parts 1 and 2 will have to be in different styles, which is a tremendous technical strain on me, and after all I am doing the writing. Tuohy: "Get the damn thing finished."

Tuohy was rather depressed, talked of his "neurotic sloth" and was self-effacing in the same way as Ricky often is: told how at 18 he had visited a schoolmaster and was left alone with his mistress, and could think of nothing to say so she lit a cigarette and burnt away the hairs on her legs. About writing a novel in contemporary Britain, "I just can't see it, I'd have to go round with a notebook." His insistence that he is a minor writer. His insistence that Eliot, Pound, Joyce, Woolf were more dedicated than anyone writing today. On Eliot: Eliot reacting against Pound, the importance of undischarged sexuality.

*3rd November 1965: this idea I have applied to the poems (i.e. *The Silence*).

11th February. At the Bank wrote to the Governor of the Bank of Korea apologising for the murder by a Japanese of a Korean trainee. Then in extreme weariness from a late night performed a free act. Ann our baby-sitter last night complained she couldn't go to Oxford because she had no A levels; I said Tomlin would give her a reference, saw Tomlin who said he would, and changed the meaning of Ann's life within one day. After that, rushed to Sophia, entered the Piro Shoten at 6.25 to have a quick coffee, and at 6.28 had three vases full of earth knocked over me and the whole bar silently awaiting my reaction. I went on reading, but had to leave. They would not believe it was because I had to teach. My punch-line on entering Tuohy's dinner party for Stover, "Have I got vine-leaves in my hair?" (An echo of *Hedda Gabler*.) Tuohy on parodies of novels, but nothing really interesting emerged because Stover is a cultural anthropologist and an SF anthologist and dominated the conversation.

Last night at (Fred) Emery's.

13th February. Wrote poem on Gawain. At 7 p.m., Mrs. Patterson rang on the door to tell me that my car light was winking – and the battery would be wasted. The conversation that formed itself round this while we traced the owner of the car, in the meantime Dr Hatamura (neighbour) was hiked out of his bath.

Without doubt, the key to my life is my nervousness. And the most influential events in my life are those which increased or reduced my nervousness, my diffidence. My marriage, my rebellion and search for freedom, all were motivated by nervousness, but I can't really motivate the nervousness.

14th February. Wrote, combining the Scholar Gipsy with the Lotos-Eaters and Bridges. I am very tired as a throw-back from last week's chaotic disruption of my sleep, and I am not satisfied that I have written it well.

15th February. A day spent recasting the novel. At present in despair. I'm on the side of the older generation and point out the dangers of the new generation. In a complete mess and now I've got to go and teach my dumb British Council classes.

Later: I wonder whether I'm doing the right thing in trying to make it real. What would Kafka's *Castle* have seemed like if he'd tried to make it completely real?

Taken by surprise when told that my nail-spot would bring me a present: blushed abominably – when will this come to an end?

17th February. From Rilke: "You will understand that it was only by jumping the rails in the most rebellious and aggressive way that I could take possession of my own temperament and blood....What I write as an artist will probably to the last somewhere show traces of the rebellion by means of which I entered into my own" (13th March 1922, letter to Bodländer, Br Bv p129).

Later Adrian's party. The essentials of a good party: good organisation, good people, good surroundings. The neurotic drawing attention to himself to dominate by asking "Is it really my entry that's caused the silence?" and so on. The daughter of the Persian Ambassador who paints at the TUE and the room full of nudes below me. John W who left Shell to become a Jesuit novice for two years (not three as he read Greats at Oxford). Why did I get so stupidly drunk? I really must give up cocktail parties. They are quite useless and drinking is an awful waste of time.

18th February. Hangover but wrote one of my best poems so far. Everything happened, including the "postage stamp". All day, tired and depressed as a result of my hangover. I must stop drinking too much. Weeks go by without my having more than a beer or two, but at a cocktail party I drink whisky after whisky. It's childish. This is a pausing time for me. I progress through leaps and bounds: great strides forward (as October, November and December) and then rests to consolidate, to put into practice what I have discovered in my straining (e.g. the 100 poems). The resting brings a complete change in my attitude to living, so that I seem to become infertile generally, apart from my writing. No great ideas seize me, but my writing is sound.

19th February. Invigilated. Taking stock of myself. My self-creation will not be completed until I die but a fundamental change of attitude is my relative loss of interest in the macrocosm, which I can now do without. The delicate balance of marriage: independence, not causing suffering, satisfying needs.

20th February. Wrote. Then went to coffee with Tuohy, who lent me *The Ice Saints*. Nothing much emerged from conversation, save that Eliot's *Waste Land* was referred to as "The Ravings of a Drunken Helot" by the T.L.S.

Tuohy's negative vision. He always picks on the worst as being the most truthful. So, his account of the Festival near Nara: "There were a quarter of a million people, you had to pay to see the scapegoat, and there was nowhere to pee." Also Poland: the people are ordinary, everything's boring and tired. It seems to me that Tuohy is making a writing-career out of going to places he doesn't like and then saying in effect what a waste of time it's all been. Tuohy's vision is not completely truthful as it denies energy and vision.

Corrected 60 exam-reports from Keio.

21st February. Wrote: by the seaside in the vestibule by the Acheron. Then took Nadi for a walk in the park. The scum-smell of the grey-green sewer, the frothy bubbles and drifting débris. The stones at low tide, which depends on the flowing from benjos. Parody this through (Eliot's) "the salt is on the briar-rose,/The fog is in the fir-trees" (eternity and time). Compare the Thames-smell. Make the poems more surrealistic. That is, be wholly whole, let yourself go more.

22nd February. A busy day. Finished my exam gradings and took them into Tokyo University of Education: posted Keio papers. Saw Toyama. Then went to the Bank. Saw Popplewell. Then went to Jimbocho. Bought a number of books e.g. 3 Waugh, 3 Woolf, Beats. Then returned to Tokyo University of Education. Saw Enozawa, rang someone and took taperecorder back home. Then went off to teach. A day gone, a whole day, and nothing to show for it except exam gradings, arrangements and business chores.

23rd February. Spent all day writing on a church jumble sale. The poem took me longer than most. For some reason the sounds wouldn't go together at first, and I had a number of words left over at the end – "organ", "flowers", "painting" – which wouldn't blend in.

One of my strengths is, perhaps, an ability to suggest that latent, disintegrating tension beneath a normal, conventional situation. I think this can best be expressed surrealistically.

You only write poetry by releasing enough poetic energy to be able to write regularly. Regular poems are essential for a good poet, yet most of the poets in the 20th century have been occasional poets.

Later, tried to write a hack article on the Angries for *Study of English* but found it impossible. After genuine creation, intellectual (i.e. rational) crap stinks.

24th February. After 19 days of waiting I was informed by Kuroda that the Crown Prince has changed his mind and appointed an American to teach by a new method once a day: all boxes and squares and arrows. Harada said I was next in line and was sorry it had got out, I have lost nothing and have assured myself of five mornings a week until July 8th when my poems will be finished. The only prospect I have lost is of a holiday in the U.K. next month, which is a pity as I'd have liked to research for my poems. All else is prestige, and if I care about that I should despise myself as a snob. (Didn't I give up Todai to write?)

Nonetheless my conviction that nothing is certain until it happens has been reaffirmed. I cannot ignore disappointments (and the reactions to sudden despair by doing mechanical things like drying-up or playing with a carpet-beater) in my poems.

25th February. Yesterday I wrote my ideal reaction, not my true one. The truth was, I felt depressed all day, even when (Professor) Hijikata was talking about Eliot and Chinese philosophy (yesterday) evening. I tried to suppress this and rationalise it, but there was still a heavy disappointment. I did raise my hopes slightly: I hoped that the University would be round my little finger so that I could return to England. "Let us sleep now" (Owen).

All reopened after the Eliot Memorial Meeting, to which I took my class. Met Tuohy and went with "the gang" to the International House for a drink with Narita. Narita told Tomlin who hadn't heard a word about the post. As a result he's "gone into action" to block the American's appointment becoming official. Tuohy came back and drank. Judgement on Southworth who I was to meet the next day. His "disguised hand."

26th February. The conference. Terribly dull and some 20 nervous men from all over Japan whose faces twitched and blushed when they had to speak. Agenda: welcome, staying on, books on English, teaching large classes, crazy films, general discussion, etc. Lunch with Tuohy and Rainer. Later went back with Tuohy. Talked about Kafka. (I read a quotation from *The Dyer's Hand.*) His confession that his superego/parental conscience had driven him to descend, not ascend; i.e. to sin and the warm Mediterranean and Japan. Do saints come from families where mother is a whore and father a drunk? On to Baker's party after drinking with C. Drank a lot and talked about cadence with Tuohy (= "carrying on" – amateurs end-stop), also consonants and punctuation in Eliot (glib lack of tipping over, the "family solicitor").

Tuohy: "A summer school would be the ideal place for a murder."

27th February. Second day of conference. Even more boring. Agenda:

summer school, classes in Spoken English and English Literature. Little reaction. Painful flogging of trite ideas, capably MCed by Baker in Tomlin's absence, whose performance made me realise I should never be able to enter the Council. I felt like a Kafka character, literally crouching under my chair in embarrassment and twisting and writhing in the presence of the others. Admittedly I was very tired, not having slept until 2 for the last four nights but everything outside seemed to be a calmly rational nightmare. Now I prepare for two parties, feeling I've wasted two days and compromised, or rather been compromised.

Got drunk. What a senseless waste. Was belaboured by Corbett at Taylor's.

Tuohy drank too much at Tomlin's and went home without waiting for me, very slewed.

28th February. Ill after vomiting saliva all night. Food poisoning? A chill? Lay in bed and read all the papers and *Encounter* and thought about the article which is supposed to be written by March 3rd. But did nothing.

Then Toyama came about 4.30. I corrected a letter of recommendation, heard him about the Eliot article, and the Crown Prince. Briefly, public opinion wants an Englishman because the British have a royal family. Also Koizumi is pro-British. The announcement will be made in mid-March and he first knew in mid-January.

Adrian's farewell, given by Ransome-Williams. Killing time until the Chinese dinner. The spinning centre to the table, sitting next to millionairess Miss Azo. The silence. "Instead of saying 'There's an angel passing' the Poles say 'A policeman has been born.'" The break-up at 10.45 and Adrian's suppressed emotion. Home with John Walker, the Jesuit priest to be, in 10 years from now. (It would be 13 years if he didn't know the Greats syllabus.) Patrick: "John's voice is like Nick's."

2nd March. An embarrassing situation: Kirkup has been awarded the PEN Club prize for a poem about "rejuvenated Japan", and Tomlin, the man who turned him down for my job, had to go and receive his $1,000 cheque for him and was photographed.

My article on the Angries has made me believe I am living in the equivalent of the 1780s: awaiting a new Romanticism following a new French Revolution and a new rebirth in 1798 – back to the common people. All nonsense because our civilisation has become more uniform? And more decayed?

The S—s. Quick, alert, full of mimicry and associations and remembered jokes, while I sat confirming my own stupidity, tired and dull. Compare Ricky "Why am I so thick?" The consolation after their show of self-confidence was the self-doubt of Graves:

> "He is quick, thinking in clear images;
> I am slow, thinking in broken images."

But is it true that he becomes dull and I become sharp? At all events we are two different types: the contemporary and the Modernist perhaps.

3rd March. Be contemporary: give the feeling of contemporary living even while you are interested in the self and thinking in your – mistrusting your – broken images.

Theme for a novel. A man with an allergy against himself, not recognised by his children, or by himself, without identity, seeking (Fitzsimmons). S—'s account of G. On arriving in Kyushu he held an exam and failed 80% of the students: refused to retract and stopped going to classes; then fell in love with and raped a student, came to Tokyo to force the banns through and met A. Very unbalanced.

Think out something on the novels. You are twisted up inside: the energy is not flowing because although you have the subject matter you have not found your form.

A day of great tiredness and scrappy progress, posting article, handing in grades, writing letter, making a list of short stories, writing notes for *Two Classes of Man* and not getting down to the poems.

4th March. Wrote on the office and Cynara (who is still in South Africa?). To the Bank of Japan, then taught. All a waste of time and nothing emerged.

The novel is going badly because I want to be contemporary yet can't be, want to be realistic yet can't be. Something is very wrong. What?

5th March. Wrote on Cy Laurie's. Not as satisfactory a poem as I would have liked at this point – the theme requires a link between rebellion and breaking out of isolation, whereas mine isn't really about rebellion, rather existential choice.

Later recorded three or four of my poems. They took two minutes each and didn't sound too bad, though my reading will have to improve.

6th March. Wrote the vastation and affirmation at Nobe.

An article for me. A study of poets who have written before their 30s, showing how bad poets become after.

In the 20th century Owen died at 25, Brooke died at 28, Eliot wrote *Prufrock* aged 21-3. In the 19th century Keats died at 25, Shelley died at 30. Byron died at 36, but wrote little after 30 save *Don Juan*. Coleridge was 26 and Wordsworth 28 in 1798 when the *Lyrical Ballads* were published. (Wordsworth was no good after 1807, when he was 35). Browning was no good after 30 (1842). Arnold was no good after 31 (1853) save for Dover Beach. Earlier Shakespeare's sonnets were written before 30 (1593), Sidney died at 32. Donne was good 1592-8 (he was 26 in 1598). Marvell wrote *The Garden* aged 30+ (1651-3). Exceptions: the 18th century poets, Yeats and Hardy.

7th March. To Nobe. Walked into the horseshoes: the badger-holes or are they human? Then the walk by the sea.

Tony rather subdued, but mentioned his feeling of strangeness which is not so evident in Japan. I said it was like feeling one was a beetle and having to pretend one was a human being, and coming to Japan meant one could live life like a beetle. T's "motive" for marrying a Japanese would be that it would symbolise his strangeness. I am not affected by Japan; is the language barrier a way of keeping out the world?

Felt ill in the afternoon and huddled in my raincoat over a stove that threw out virtually no heat. Was it eating oysters or the fresh air or some sign that Fitzsimmons saw and which, I sometimes fear, Barr and Tony see when they say I'm not looking well, that I'm pale and drawn? Remember that evening, after Trattner (President of the Oxford Union) went when I imagined myself trading my health over in return for creativity.

Tony: "What is the energy you have, and what caused it?" I: "It's creative energy. It can be channelled into various things, religion, physics, literature, but it's creative energy that does not depend on energyless society."

(Cf Tuohy's disillusioned vision, and his failure with energetic people.)

8th March. A letter saying that Grannie died a week ago on Monday 1st at 11.10 a.m. I have of course been prepared for this, but feel a sadness, even though she was 90. So many of my memories are related to her: scooting in East Grinstead, the coloured matches and toy soldiers on the tiled window-sill, the knife-grinder at the bottom of her garden. The family, which always seemed so strong, feels weaker: only Argie and my mother are left, apart from Aunt Flo: the three sisters awaiting their own turn. Mother's rather pathetic attempt at boldness. Argie is free at last.

"As Grannie apparently died from a fall, there may have to be an inquest. If the post mortem shows that she died from her chest condition then one will not be necessary." (She had just recovered from pleurisy). "The funeral will be at East Grinstead on Friday at 12 noon, followed by a family lunch at the Felbridge Hotel."

Poor Frances. She was with my father pruning roses when he screamed and fell back; and had tea with Grannie the day before her fall – she fell on Wednesday February 24th. Most children are shielded from the horror of sudden death or illness until they are old enough to understand.

C: "The family are like an old clock that never gets started. Occasionally something jolts them, and the hands are moved, but it doesn't go."

10th March. All day rewriting, finishing and typing the article on Eliot. In the course of doing this I discovered how historical Eliot is. Notably, his heroes tend to be Europe, e.g. Gerontion, the Fisher King – both symbolise Europe, and the Multiple Personality device is a means of achieving this. Hence his obscurity: his readers are thinking individually and not historically.

Have I not a poem on Britannia's exhaustion? I am doing it in the novels; why should I not apply the historical vision to poetry, using English geography?

Last night C said again how much I'd changed and attributed it to Japan. "You always wear a suit, you're always prepared for visitors, you're correct in your dress."

11th March. Barbara: "My body is me – you can't separate mind and body. Why should I let anyone into *me*?"

12th March. I've tightened up in this last year, I've got more nervous. I'm tense all the while and more creative than I have ever been. That nervous outburst on Monday is a warning: if I get too tight I shall be flirting with some form of hysterical madness.

Tom (Fitzsimmons)'s distinction between meaning (a 3 part relationship between self, object and meaning) and significance (a 2 part relationship between self and object). My loss of meaning was not a return to myself.

Each man's talent is like a wave flung up on a shore by creative energy, then advancing until the force is spent: all that remains is what was flung with it, the forms. One day in about 5 years' time I shall wake up to discover that I can no longer write poetry, that this tremendous energy in me has gone.

The dog howling at the police-car sirens.

13th March. Novels are about relationships and present people in contemporary society through realism and psychology. At present I practise a view of the novel as being about a theme, presenting arguments through symbolism and analysis, which is quite wrong. Think again but the subject matter of a novel, e.g. the theme of self-descent and self-creation by ascesis – how does it work out in practice and how does the theme of the monster work out? Remember my resolve to treat interiors by relating macrocosm and microcosm through symbolism and states of mind. To found a novel on experience uninterpreted and unromanticised.

14th March. As to the novel, can I not make J. S. Lawrence a realistic person who is going to hail in the future, but who can still die? Does this jar with (1) composite personality, (2) historical interpretation? I know the general conflict, but why the particular conflict? For great art grows out of the particular, which is plausible and convincing.

After a dreadful day – uncompleted poem and fiddling around on the novel – decided to write the novel in the 1st person, through J. S. Lawrence's eyes, as he describes his experience in terms of his ideal "Whole Man" and also his relationship with the dying priest. Theme: his self-creation after discovering his self-destructiveness and obsession with Beatrice.

SPIRITUAL DEPTH AND CREATIVITY (1964 – 1965)

The maximum energy in writing comes from the concrete and the physical, i.e. states of mind experiencing, so write *The Eternicide* as entirely in this way as possible. (Remember: philosophy X gave birth to the experiences in poetry).

15th March. Worked on the novel (still undecided between 1st and 3rd) and then went to the TUE graduation party at (predictably) a Chinese restaurant (Chinese being better than Japanese and less expensive than gaijin food). The sitting, the toast to begin beer, then standing and talking to various Professors and lecturers about the C.P. and the Mombusho's refusal of my application to succeed myself. When it came to the singing and neared my turn I nipped out with non-singer Fukuda and went to the Tokyo Prince Hotel near Tokyo Tower to see the first night of a crappy mystery play *Bonaventure*. As Pattersons' guests.

The overall impression from row E: everyone was there to be seen, their interest in the play was fake and judging by overheard comments ("What was in the box?" "No, she wanted the paper") they would have been out of their depth with anything else. Tokyo middle class society, no one having done anything and all nothing in England. Introductions: "He's of Shell", "attached to — Co." After, the dinner party upstairs above the Magnolia Room. The awful Scotts, snooty, snobbish, coarse, he from Liverpool, she from South Wales. Patterson to blame for mixing businessmen and academics. I was left wondering whether I should write about such drones and bores and follow Tuohy. But decided against it: the bourgeois are not worth the time.

16th March. My superego: rather on my mother's side than father's, stemming from mother's high standards, e.g. church, judgements, class.

17th March. Wrote amid interruptions, including Buchanan and a three hour trek round Tokyo to Tokyo University of Education, Todai (Tokyo University), British Embassy, Bank, Post Office. Aim for the complex layers that lie behind my personality and experience.

18th March. Considered poems. Lunched at the Bank of Japan in one of the inner precincts. Embarrassing silences, I commenting on the wine and the soup (which was filled with clams and shrimps), the steak and the Mt. Fuji ice-cream. I was sat in front of the picture so they could see me in all my beauty. Fukano saying very clearly what it was all for at the outset: "Under your supervision and guidance, Mr T and Mr O are speaking very good English and I am very grateful to you. Also everyone appreciates your letter-corrections – we discuss them and we always agree with you." (Cf Mrs. Hatamura, handing Nadia a present and saying, "We are sorry the building of our house made so much noise.")

19th March. Wrote in a rather slangy colloquial tone. The ideal parents. Society trying to conceal death and the tragic human condition.

20th March. Considered the novel and got in a mess. Visited Tuohy, who had flu, and had a long talk. On Gothic versus realistic: Gothic has a dream-like quality (cf Dostoevsky, *Radcliffe*). A novel should be all of one piece, everything to be built in. "A novelist is like a boa constrictor, he has to cover everything with his own slime." On symbolism: "The characters shouldn't know anything about it." On relevance: "If it's no different without it, leave it out." On 1st and 3rd persons: "Don't take a point of view and don't confine yourself by saying 'it seemed'." Form is something one grasps with one's own being. "There are no good novelists before 30."

On poetry. Free verse works best when it comes from strong personalities. Objections put by Bridges: carrying on, stress and accent difficult, structure of line. On pseudonyms: don't take one unless you intend to stick with it (because of publicity); and risk alienating family. Tuohy is "the one who writes dirty stories". One cousin took his first book back to the library in tongs.

Tuohy's parents: Irish Catholic and Scottish Presbyterian.

21st March. A dreadful night last night, tossing and turning, equating Gothic with new Romantic, distorting the World-Lord into writing too valuable to forget but ruthlessly determining to cut it out, excise it as a cancer which is arresting my growth. The end of it all, a faint-hearted determination to be as realistic in fiction as I am in poetry, a determination I must enforce by telling myself repeatedly not to write fantasy or flat characters or to depart from daily life, even though I've written whole passages I feel affection for. Find Your Voice.

Wrote.

The Keio graduation ceremony at the Chinese restaurant Kokusai-Hanton in Hotel Kokusai-Kankoh. Colourful kimonos. After a drinkless sit in the lounge, and a wordless introduction to Professor Ishii (Kuriyagawa's predecessor) we sat at one of six tables, four of which had sensei, until Ohashi arrived. The sensei had to speak first. I disagreed with Professor Ishii that I had lost the way because of Kaneko's directions (causing Kaneko to take the blame), thanked our hosts for the party, was sorry we would not meet again collectively but hoped we would individually. Then everyone had to make a speech: name, thanks to sensei and memories of lectures, future job and chatty remarks. Finally the Keio song. One of the students "I hear you are very young: I was very surprised."

22nd March 1965. Wrote. Then thought hard about the structure of "Meditation One". It began as an accident – accepting arbitrary meditation, but my infernal thirst for the greatest possible order and arrangement is trying to persuade me to rearrange the experiences and group them under themes in, say, ten blocks of about ten poems in each block. This will spoil the effect of the whole process of meditation, will it not? And will it not destroy the unity of the 100 poems? And the sense of discovery?

On Gothic versus realistic: how internal or how external do I want to be? Compare my attitude to Bellow, who writes as I would expect Ricky to write....Ricky's problems are purely internal whereas mine are/were problems of adjustment with the outside world. Do I want to stress loneliness through monologue, or show external events through dialogue? At all costs, however, my subject must be experience. States of mind experiencing. Another approach to the same problem: to what extent am I interested in the individual, and to what extent the (historical or social) type? (Cf General/particular.)

23rd March. Last night at Kurdi's, involved in argument with Husseyni, the son of the claimant to Palestine now living in Lebanon (where he has lived since the abortive revolution of 1936). The hostility to Churchill, the incredible battery of historical facts which I had not heard of: my colonial ignorance.

This morning, repaired my historical ignorance by turning to Fisher, and a flash of inspiration: Why not write a series of History plays showing the decay today? So (1) on religion, from the Inquisition, Luther and Anglicanism to today – a petering out; (2) Cromwell and the Restoration; (3) Italian and German Renaissance and Humanism (versus Medievalism); (4) British Empire and Commonwealth and loss; (5) 20th century World Wars; (6) social reforms and present socialism. Themes to show the loss in purpose of Western civilisation, and the way individualism has petered out leaving our institutions as forms, our democracy as a collective mess. Historical forces. Incorporate the decay of private institutions like the family. Or, more ambitiously, a complete history of all Christianity? 2000 years ago to the present? Showing Christ as a madman and Paul's accretions and later wars? Distinguishing doctrine and religious spirit? A vast epic?

In the afternoon spent £21 on books including Sartre's *Being and Nothingness*, Toynbee XII and *A Historian on Religion*, and ordered Gurdjieff. In the evening read *A History of Christianity* for my play. Wrote.

24th March. Had an inspiration as regards the novel. Keep the priest certainly, but do not have him conflict with J. S. Lawrence – leave that to the man of vision and uninstitutionalised purpose, who is the black sheep of the family and who asks what difference J. S. Lawrence's discovery will make. As an Outsider, he sees the aimlessness of the old man's house and Western civilisation and can point to the purpose.

Spent the rest of the day reading about the *Old Testament* prophets, dating them and seeing them in their historical context. Haggai and Zephaniah not referring to an unearthly Messiah.

Physical impressions: the old egg-shells round the stem of potted plants, why? The greeny brown muddy-white curve of the Edogawa sewer and the lasher beneath. (What is the smell? Every afternoon I ask. Is it a smell of canals or of the sea? Or of an exploding bubble?)

25th March. Wrote on the Queen's birthday in Baghdad and my obsession with priests.

In the evening to Noh. A Shinto roof, the stage. Much whooping and beating from knock-kneed and bandy-legged musicians. A flautist. Kantan's bed. The dress-attendant. The numbers flicked over. The bored expressions on the gaijin's (foreigners') faces: "Life is a dream" and enlightenment meaning nothing. The cameras and the whispers.

No Tuohy as he "had a relapse".

Go into church architecture: nave, transverse (transept), chancel, apse. Clerestory, sacristy; pilster, rerodos, piscina.

26th March. Wrote on Rex the prophet. Then went off into Tokyo. Post Office, Bank, British Council to see Corbett about the class next April, library about COI reference pamphlets. Met Tuohy and discussed arrangements for this evening. Then to Kitazawa to collect Gurdjieff. Met Alan Barr. An accident-prone day full of unplanned meetings, e.g. Toff.

With Tuohy and C to *Sunna No Onna*. A drink before and dinner afterwards at the New Hibuya. Tuohy: on the history of ideas, ideas depend on their age and circumstances in philosophy (we have the answers to questions) but this is not so in Christianity whose ideas are for all time. In the Middle Ages God was needed to make the seasons come in and the planets remain, and to rectify social inequality. On lack of education, uneducated people are touchy and resentful, e.g. Yeats. On making a film, it would be technically impossible in England because everyone is so uneducated, but it is the concreteness of the images that matters, e.g. renunciation by the Avon, commercialisation. Tuohy's style has a dying fall, which makes his vision seem more pessimistic than it is. "Sadness is not a permanent emotion, so a book infused with sadness is a neurotic book." Tuohy's obsession with death. "A young man doesn't think he'll die." My reply: "I do." The creepy *Sun* reporter who extracted the name of Tuohy's prize by asking "What was it again?"

On Fukuda: "He's articulate but not very intelligent."

27th March. Wrote on (Holy) Grey, then became dissatisfied with the order of the poems. Yesterday's poem belongs later; will correct the mistake tomorrow.

Existential thinking is thinking which shakes one because one is on trial and not safely protected by one's detachment. On religion. We have to redefine it today to mean spiritual power, but what concretely is this spiritual power in the moment? That was my test. Spiritual power is something one applies to experience, to control experience. Religion is the

142

regeneration of a number of metaphorical concepts without the dogma.

Tuohy's excellent point that the English separate metaphysics and ethics. Compare Ivan Karamazov's "If God does not exist, everything is possible," which is nonsense for an Englishman.

Poetry is at present more real than fiction because it comes from my own experience.

28th March. Wrote on the Philosophy Course and ascent. Something I must think about is, how did the priest come to symbolise higher consciousness, if he did? Through *The Outsider* and my reading? As an ally? Because there is no one else in society and the community who can be identified as a "higher consciousness man"?

An afterthought on priests. Have I, for the last 7 or 8 years, failed to separate religion and consciousness?

Later still: Do I see Bickford or Ainger in each priest, i.e. a friendly father-advisor? Am I repeating one relationship with F— and L— and M— and W— (cf older men). Or am I explaining why I can't be a priest? I don't know.

29th March. Wrote on (Colin) Wilson; inspiration dried up at the end, which will have to be rewritten. I feel very tired and sleepy. Is it the weather or the strain of the last few weeks?

On the novel. I am still dithering over Gothic/Neo-Romantic v realistic, except that the whole pattern has changed. Can I not do a Dostoevsky, choose a fantastic plot and work out the inner life of J. S. L, which was my original aim?

I have two approaches: (1) concentrate on inner consciousness and psychology and have fantastic externals if need be (spiritual or visionary realism); (2) concentrate on external plausibility after Turgenev, Tuohy, etc. and show the powerlessness of the inner consciousness and its position in a decaying society and age. In my bones I feel I should do (2): ours is not as violent an age as was the age of the Russian nihilists, nor is it an age in which the traditional or the Christian has so strong a defence, and one's consciousness is necessarily moulded by one's age. I may loathe our age and wish I were in Dostoevsky's, but I can't escape our age by writing as though I lived in Dostoevsky's: accept the age and contemporary life.

30th March. Wrote and hope I've got priests out of my system. They must be exorcised, cast out like devils. They offer me nothing with their fixed doctrinal attitudes which are substitutes for experience. Note. The theme of recommendations – everyone recommending something to me and advising me and I having to decide whether to accept or reject – comes from my essay on Langland.

At 1 o'clock held an exam at Keio. Sitting on high in judgement over 90 students, underneath a microphone without a switch.

Physical impressions. A cracked window-pane like a spider's web (cf the wire-crossings at Iidabashi).

31st March. Instead of curtains I hung three suits on coathangers from the curtain-rod. I took a long time to sleep. Silhouetted against the street-lamp they resembled three men hanging, and their shadows fell across my bed to the wall above me.

Wrote very scrappily, though got two good lines: one about a violin and the other about weeping arpeggios. Afterwards argued with C over land. I was very indignant to discover that 50 million acres (in Britain) are in private ownership and feel a social revolution is necessary, an ordinary land reform program such as every other country has had. C was pro-upper class, to my horror, though she surprised me by arguing well. Later corrected Keio papers.

Social revolutionaries in London, cf *The Possessed*? No, it wouldn't work today, there would be too many committees. (Compare Fourierism and Dostoevsky.)

1st April. Wrote on the prophet. (Most of it was written already.) Then wrote to Ricky.

2nd April. Wrote on Tower Hill and in the library. I have been reading through the poems and have discovered cross-references I barely noticed when I wrote: this would be quite impossible if I were writing of someone else's experience – this intuitive layering is something that one can only get from one's own experience. Although the poems need a lot of polishing they don't read too badly so stop despairing.

In the evening the British Council party. The central table, the students all standing round. Because I am leaving the Advanced Course they all supposed I was returning to the U.K. Tomlin's presence: his phoney farewells.

3rd April. Wrote on Dulwich Park. One good line about Belsen. Later thought up the idea for Meditation Two (later *Old Man in a Circle*), which will be a series of portraits of life in Modern Britain showing the decay of Western civilisation, the pettiness of suburban life (Toc H, etc.) and the meaninglessness of people's lives. In the suburbs, but bringing in the new towns, the doctor's surgery and so on.

Earlier a dream. I was on some kind of British Council course and had to give a vote of thanks. A single word or two would have been adequate, but I needlessly began to make a point which I had to abandon as it reflected I had not understood what Tomlin had said. My embarrassment, feeling judged by Tomlin. I walked back with Tuohy and came to a vast mansion, a kind of labyrinth-hospital. I went through hundreds of rooms (during which I met Argie) and emerged in a courtyard involved in a cross-country race, the (Chigwell School) Bean (Cup). This is imperfectly remembered, but I think the point is the immense complexity of the artistic career I am trying to embark on, which E. W. F. Tomlin and Tuohy represent.

4th April. What course for a poet who has graduated in English? 20th century Literature, criticism, discussion of foreign literature and the structure of British society and institutions – the social background of modern Britain – and a knowledge of English suburban society, and Toynbee.

My dream last night. The Vice-Governor (of the Bank of Japan) died and in spite of being anti-religious gave strict instructions about his funeral so that he would be received by God. After a service in St. Mary's, Loughton he had to be cremated at 5.05, 5.15, and 5.55, (in three parts); his ashes either put down the benjo (à la *Murphy*) or scattered by Ida of Todai on a dirt-track. Later I talked to Usami (Governor of the Bank of Japan) about death. When I returned home Auden was in my room, but I couldn't offer him whisky as Tony's friend "Hobdy" had drunk it, replacing orange juice. I was a poet, I gave Auden the (West Essex) *Gazette*, suggesting he might find subjects from the headlines.

The old geiser lying in the box in the front garden, like a corpse in a coffin.

5th April. Yesterday read Tuohy's *Ice Saints*. It's about Insiders and man in a group, whereas I must write about Outsiders and man alone. I must not let Tuohy influence me.

After: there was a program on TV about the mentally handicapped and I wept at the injustice of the fates of the idiots, and my mood took me onto injustice and suffering everywhere, and the pointlessness of it all if God does not exist and there is no after-life. I cannot understand it.

Later. Feel morosely anti-pettiness. I came to Japan to escape pettiness. That dog for the thousandth time barking at the cats. It's freedom I want, freedom from the hollow and the habitual.

Wrote. In the evening went to the cinema to see the Resnais double bill, Hiroshima and Marienbad. The ornate parts at the beginning symbolise brain cells, dendrons and axons.

6th April. Wrote on junkies. Of my poems: I have knocked up some 45-50 pegs, the robes will hang on them when I've got up the 100. Spent all day thinking about the structure of the poems, especially action and contemplation in my life, and read two and a half years' diaries, but to no avail. I want an experience to start me off on the theme of changing from the active life to the contemplative: changes aren't made like that, and I must communicate this.

Two images. Kantan hats, like hats from a cracker. The temple near Edogawa bashi (bridge), like an Indian army helmet with a spike (or a Roman gladiator's helmet?).

7th April. Wrote. I chop and change about theories for a novel, but why have I been so studiously against the confessional novel? Is not the *The Eternicide* a confessional novel, or is it a 3rd person account of a conflict? I think the latter, but at least the confessional novel overcomes particularities and plot and enables the writer to focus on experience and on truths to be drawn from experience. Revive the confessional novel.

In the afternoon read Wesker, and sorted out literary history and style syllabuses, apportioning texts. Went through catalogues looking for a paperback on Modern Britain, without success. In the evening drew up on a master chart the outstanding poems, bringing the total to 115, 15 to be rejected perhaps. A day of organisation, getting the impression of mastery.

An implicit device of mine: the shifting relationship between poems.

9th April. Tried to write but couldn't: tried to write on Trink but couldn't get into it. Perhaps it's the weather, which is very warm; perhaps it's my late night on Wednesday. Then considered the structure of the poems. At present they're all out of order.

Buchanan came at 5.15, and talked about tax and staying on. We then pushed him out and met Tuohy and saw *Red Beard* by Kurosawa. Tuohy came back for a meal and stayed until 1 o'clock dragging out skeletons from writers' cupboards, e.g. Greene, who is living in sin with Lady Walston (Lord W is coming here next month); Edith Sitwell, whose mother got two years for defrauding the poor in Edwardian times. I got the impression that most established writers are indifferent to writing (e.g. Spender, "I was never very good") and hope I won't get like that; hope my energies never dissipate.

10th April. Tuohy (cont.). Golding spoke on him on April 2nd and a tape is coming which I shall play as he hasn't a taperecorder. I correctly located the source of *The Ice Saints: Where Angels Fear to Tread*, with Tadeusz substituted for the baby and Rose/Strether for the two Ambassadors. On *Heart of Darkness*: the distinction between a quest and an obstacle race, the quest stressing the end. On death, people feel awe, not sympathy. My point that creative energy can throw up different forms, a church or a work of art or a university or Parliament. My vision of the world could almost be summarised as "the relationship between energy and forms". Cf Life, taking the form of the body? "Priests, doctors and writers never talk about their work at a cocktail party." (Tuohy governed by social rules.) Real time implies determinism – nothing has happened, e.g. Joyce; i.e. an event implies unreal time? and change? On the confessional novel: "generalised writing is not possible today." Tuohy's generalisations, e.g. "You can always tell a schoolmaster" to which I replied, "I've known schoolmasters who have been shy and haven't organised." "A character is like a child, he asks why he can't do something and you can't say 'Because God says so'." ("There is always a rival ethic to any established ethic.") "Methodism is what distinguished England from the Continent; England in the 18th century was very Continental."

As I was tired, went to see *Goldfinger*.

11th April. Taking up the point about life and its forms. If I see all creative energy as throwing up forms, which go dead, it would be quite logical to see life as a creative energy that has thrown up different forms, limited by their environment just as a work of art, a temple, or an institution is limited by its environment. Life throwing up propagating forms – which go dead – is it a possibility? An abstraction without any scientific foundation whatsoever – a metaphor, a symbol? The form housing the energy. Find an image for this, a better one than the sea flinging up on the land, each man being merely a wave following previous waves and to be succeeded by future waves, and many waves existing at the same time. This image catches the idea of energy, but no form is left at the end of it: a wave is futile, leaving only a receding wetness on the sand, nothing permanent – perhaps there are no images to express the permanent, only metaphors, because nothing in the world is permanent – unless it flings up some débris. Is man's individual energy linked to a vast sea of creative energy? On second thoughts this image is a good one. Wrote.

Also the image of the energy driving up weeds. Creative energy, bringing into being out of nothing through contemplation, is the highest form of energy there is. And all life is energy. Negative energy, positive energy, creative energy. The triad. And sexual energy? Libido? Cf December 27th. Cf Jung's *Modern Man in Search of a Soul*, p250: "It is from the depths of our own psychic life that new spiritual forms will arise."

12th April. Wrote on turbulence. Was dragged off with my co-operation to see the Olympic Film (an observation of emotions and reactions). On the way got two images: "neon-lighted bows in pale pink and red" and "noteless bars of telegraph wires." I really must try and find two images a day: I do this only very spasmodically. Later (at 12.50 a.m. to be precise) there was a strong earthquake. I lurched out of bed and stood near Nan in case the ceiling should begin to fall in: a great deal of noise.

To edit my poems properly when they are completed, I really should have some experience in film-cutting.

A letter in the paper: "Why do you wear your hair long? Is it to draw attention to yourself, or to advertise the fact that you are a non-conformist?" My answer? Number 2: to let everyone know that I am a beetle and not an ordinary human being, to get a distance between me and the world, and also because my long face needs long hair. So, for reasons of detachment and physiognomy. (To alienate to preserve my outsider-status?)

13th April. Wrote. Then prepared for lectures – need Wesker's *Roots* and *I'm Talking about Jerusalem*, parts of Fraser and H. Read.

147

The main feeling of the day was that I am a bourgeois writer, that my introspection is a privileged luxury and that I wouldn't stand a chance in a Communist country. A symptom of capitalism is decay – that's all I am, as a poet. I don't like it, but all I can do is write about it.

14th April. *Narziss und Goldmund*. The emotional conflict between spiritual and sensual men, though neither discover their true identities until the end.

Nietzsche was a Professor at 24. Will I ever be able to admit to being the same by mistake?

15th April. Wrote a poem. Then went to the Bank. Fukuchi agreed that spring is a disturbing time: the interior rhythms of winter are broken up from the exterior rhythms of summer. I feel mentally in between, neither intense nor objective. Some trouble about how to address the Ambassador. Answer: "Dear Ambassador" or, formally, "Your Excellency". Later read through my corrections of kyogen.

One thought, on anti-Americanism. U.S. and British policies are closer than they have ever been, now the the U.S. is colonial and Britain has given away much of the Empire. Anti-Americanism is therefore due largely to economic resentment and reduced status (3rd power). Europe and South Vietnam want the U.S. to get out of Vietnam. Only a policy with an end can keep them in; this policy to have some connection with natural resources and an anti-Communist defence-plan. Can such a policy be formed, and will it create the American Empire?

16th April. Writing a novel is like visiting a new town – you don't know your way around until the second time: reading a novel is like being driven through a new town, and the polite novelist will point out the landmarks because he's been there before.

Went into Tokyo University of Education. Corrected Harashima's Noh plays with him – how like Narita he was – and saw Irie who, after much politeness, said the Ministry of Education would not pay travelling expenses to U.K. Returned, discussed the future with C, and decided that unless someone offered to pay £750 for our return fare to England on leave, we should return for good in 10 months time, next February. I should move on. I've become an insider here, and have almost yielded to the temptations of comfort. I must not repeat experiences: I must seek what is new and go perhaps to Malaysia, or India; China being presumably out of the question. Or, the clearing in the jungle.

17th April. My dream last night. I was in a vast mansion of fame: C and I slept in the same bed as Toynbee, and in other rooms in this "hotel" were various writers. In a room off this bedroom there was a trapdoor under the carpet and a cellar in which I had seen (with Brooke) four ghosts. These ghosts resembled children and were "unreal". Later one came up into the room. I called Toynbee and we found it: a crippled child. Earlier, in the cellar, thinking it a ghost (did I ever cease to think of it so?) I had hit it around; was I responsible for the fact that it was crippled?

Interpretation. The cellar is my unconscious, the room my subconscious, the bedroom my conscious? The "ghost-child" symbolised some repression on my part that I have and should let up? Is this dream telling me that this repression is defenceless now, that it can be let up without any risk?

18th April. What I am witnessing in the course of these poems is the death of the man of ideas in myself and the emergence of the psychologist, interested primarily in understanding my experience, not in imposing a philosophy. Why people say what they do, rather than what they say: this approach is long overdue. An Easter-theme of death and rebirth. What has also emerged is the resemblance of much of what I have discovered about myself to a Jungian analysis. It is interesting that Jung is exceptionally interested in symbols and images, which I must study without being taken into mythology. Draw no conclusions, merely present experience.

Wrote a poem on the Bank of Japan and the Palace.

Later, prepared lectures. Reread parts of *La Nausée*, and thought about the various views of history put forward by G. S. Fraser. I must think out my view of history. The trouble is, I sympathise with so many conflicting views. Starting with the individual, like Existentialism, I feel for cyclicism, for immanentism in Shaw, even for historicism. I have the feeling that no one view is right. Later: all I know is that I am *in* history: history and experience are inextricable.

19th April. Went to the Tokyo University of Education and organised classes in *The Outsider* and 20th century poetry. Dr. Saito asked me to pun on tumbler/prostitute for one of the kyogen (farces). *Eigo Seinin* appeared with my article next to Tuohy's: also an incredible article by Kirkup, attacking Eliot's politics, his anti-semiticism, his upper-class Christianity, his policy in Fabers, etc. Also, a nasty reference to the "orthodox and unimaginative teachers" of the British Council, presumably to me, as I have the job he wanted. The man is quite evidently deeply resentful and completely at the mercy of his emotions.

20th April. Looking at my picture of my mandala I realised why I have always been excited by Eliot's death-rebirth imagery: I interpret it not in terms of the world/God alone, but in terms of the ego/the self – or two similar concepts, at any rate, cf April 18th – and I thought this thought today was new, whereas it had just been shunting round its circuit until the points changed and it could come out onto the main track.

Depth is connected with the unconscious. The more consciously social or rational an author is, the more unprofound he is.

Considered the end of the poems, then read Toynbee XII and reclassified civilisations. One thought in particular impressed me: not the Superman with his mutations, but the higher man. The earthquake this morning: "a strong disturbance in the earth" (radio). It didn't seem strong to me, though as usual I jumped out of bed to protect Nan. One killed.

7 p.m. Today has been a massive reconsideration of all the themes that preoccupied me last November/December: Toynbee, Spengler, Gurdjieff, Jung, Nietzsche, Whitehead – I have been reading them all, and would redefine the spiritual as "the inner workings of man's mind". Is there going to be a new spiritual revolution soon? Jung, echoing my idea of 11th April that spiritual forms are created by (psychic) energy. What share could I, as a poet, have in rediscovering our inner symbols (cf Toynbee IX)?

21st April. My poems will appeal because of the blend of inner and outer, or, as Jung calls it, progression and regression, the energy flowing as it should, quite uninhibited. For the depth-psychology, my justification is D. H. Lawrence's "new places of consciousness". My lack of a persona, my over-active and disruptive shadow. My anima, who I saw yesterday in the person of Marsha P—, an actress who has been in Tokyo 20 years and who was dressed like a prostitute in red silk trousers: her maternal black hair and dream-like response to me, taking me aside at the end of the party and talking to me.

22nd April. Last night, the party at John Walker's, for 10. Jim R— said, "I saw Marsha take you away yesterday, what did she say?" He then called her a bitch and said how she "gushed", referred to childbirth as a spiritual act and so on. "She was a second row chorus-girl in New York." He sided with her husband.

Later I dreamt I asked Tuohy (while a recording of him talking on the radio was going on the gramophone), "Isn't Ida Arnold Graham Greene's anima?" and tears came into his eyes as he said "Yes". (This is a throwback from Tuohy's article in *The Rising Generation*.)

Thursday. After the Bank of Japan, bought V. Woolf's *A Writer's Diary*, and (Colin) Wilson's *Rasputin*; then (after keeping the Bank of Japan driver waiting some 40 minutes) returned and recorrected Noh and kyogen until midnight.

23rd April 1965. A day of work for other people: 8.30-2.30 teaching and selling books (Wesker, Fraser, Scott), then accounting to Sanseido for £53, then correcting two Noh and kyogen until 6.15. After that wrote up the names for classes and read the *Observers*, at home.

Toyama: has disillusionment come to an end, because there is no reason to express disillusion if everyone is disillusioned? Will there be a new period of optimistic confidence in England, "the New Britain"? What are people in England thinking, and how real is the mood: how permanent will it be? Is it not an illusion: a rally before the Pax Americana perhaps? Will it not deceive people into blinding themselves to our general decay?

Kirkup has written another hysterical article in a magazine, all about himself and his "daring" non-conformism. Why can't he turn his invention into poetry or drama?

The tumblers' chant: "Guatten-ka?" (All right?) "Guatten-ja." (All right.)

24th April. Tired all day. I have been doing too much and apparently look ill: my eyes are yellow, not white, and are bloodshot; is that a symptom of anything especial? And I am coughing a lot. After I wrote a poem on Etna (the sexual symbolism that has fascinated me) I spent the rest of the day reading: Rasputin and thaumaturgy and pre-vision, then *La Nausée* and other books by Sartre I could find on my shelves. (Not *L'Être et Le Néant*, which I must go into some time.)

25th April. Began to write my poem, got the name "Freeman", but as it was such a fine day went to Nobe. The frogs, the B—s had taken the deck-chairs. Buchanan's arrival, our walk by the sea: the world behind green darks. Then the horseshoes: vetch, violets and that prehistoric plant in segments of 8 fingers. Buchanan, tired, went to sleep on the way back. Present-bound, having to bring one back for the neighbours.

Read *La Nausée* and, sitting in my first class compartment, feeling vaguely ill at ease with all this comfort, pondered subjectivity and objectivity.

Physical impressions: iron girders with nuts like limpets.

26th April. At Tokyo University of Education considered *La Nausée*, and distinguished two distinct experiences: (1) existence before essence, seeing the table/tree as an existent rather than as functional; cf Eliot's "timelessness": no nausea; and (2) contingency: if existence precedes essence there is no plan and no God and no reason why accidental things should exist and all existence is free: nausea. But clearly my tongue will not turn into a centipede and my hand will not turn into a crab (in Sartre, as a result of mescalin), so to what extent is my intuition objectively true? Is there a plan, the essence in terms of evolution, and to what extent does it violate my experience to affirm this? (Test by experience, not the reason.)

Later went to Morton and had diagnosed from X-ray the cause of my sickly childhood: T.B. and pleurisy, which has left my left lung twisted up with my diaphragm. (The calcium deposit for T.B.) The heartburns I have felt have been the tuggings on my lung. Nothing can be done, but it doesn't seem too fatal. This, though, is the true nausea: the feeling that all that I hold noble is dependent on a bloody mess of intestines and a squelching heart.

27th April. Wrote a poem on seeking snakes. This afternoon went to the bookshops and bought, inter alia, Spender's *Struggle of the Modern* and a brilliantly written book on *Vagrancy* in the Penguin Special series. Full of intensity, it challenged many of my assumptions and I am now full of self-doubt: is no one responsible, has anyone chosen, is the cult of unique personality (in whose tradition I am a poet) really a delusion to conceal the fact that I am not different from my neighbour, and is society responsible for alienating individual from individual? Thinking back over the wanderers I have met and romanticised, I think I would deny these conclusions, from what I know of them. On the other hand, one must be compassionate, which is putting it differently. Rasputin and the modern tramps – I think the solitude would do me good, I think ideally I should do it for a month or so (and making out in England would be very different from making out on the Continent). But remember the "diffusion of the ego", as the author of *Vagrancy* put it, which I felt in Dulwich Park.

28th April. *Vagrancy.* (Cf Dostoevsky's *House of the Dead.*) Wrote on working-class Jeanie. Went to the Bank of Japan as tomorrow is a holiday, then went to Ann Gegg's in spite of the rail strike. Tomlin's sister and son, clearly aware that Tony and I were Tomlin's employees. Tuohy's abruptness, almost ignoring at first, then, when I invited him back, saying "No" and going off in a taxi on his own, drunk. He's getting more money for an article on Hiroshima than he got for his first novel. Our future: Tony told me that Professor Hirai of Todai (Tokyo University) wondered if I would succeed him after spending six months in England.

30th April. A day of rushing around. 8.30-2.45 teaching, then correcting Harashima's two Noh plays yet again and paying off Sanseido, then to Dr. Morton and finally the (British) Council at 6 where I had 25 for my class on the social background and had to select 10: gave interviews until 7.45 then returned to a bath, too tired for any great thoughts. This weather, in between winter and summer.

After the abstract Bank of Japan speech: what am I trying to do with language – make it as concrete as possible, root it in experience, strip aside all the old, tired, abstract clichés and start again? Every word must count.

1st May. Prevented from going to Nobe with C by Bank of Japan. While I waited, having corrected the speech, an enormous raven swooped down onto the veranda, strutted and flapped idly away as I approached the French windows: in another age it would be a symbol of death.

The luxurious box of grapefruit to apologise, the insistence with which Tsuchigane bought my ticket at Tokyo station. The intense journey, revaluing my poems, reordering. The frogs at Nobe: the various frog noises – fluting (female?) like castanets or a roulette ball or a stone being shaken in a milk bottle, a jam jar: very resonant; and then the sawing. (The puffed-out throat-bag of a green tree-frog, sitting in a clump of paddy amid a waste of water – seen on Sunday.) The walk on the beach: the sapphire egg/cell. It glowed. I scooped it on to a ¥10 coin: under the streetlamp on the promenade it swelled and moved like a nucleus in a cell. When we put it on a saucer in the house, with some water, it drowned and I felt sad. The theme of futility. (Tony saying that intellectual excitement and having a bath were equal pleasures; that there is no scheme of values not based on enjoyment. My disagreement: self-realisation the value.)

2nd May. A glorious day. All morning I poked among the rock-pools at low tide, examining the way a starfish turned right side up, curling one tentacle over, two back and two up, the suckers groping for seaweed (a slight variation each time); and then observing a sea slug (squid?) in the process of spinning out a yellow thread of eggs from its back, and the way the male slug avoided it when its antennae had recognised it. Later in the horseshoe valleys I found various phallic flowers, one bulbous orchid in an off-pink and white colour, and one with an erect centre: red azaleas, red camellias. The newts in the paddies were black with scarlet bellies.

Organisation and futility; life is, there is no why; there are laws, there is no why. This is the nearest I can come to stating my present attitude towards existence: a creative urge, for no revealed reason; an urge that can create a luminous cell according to a law, but for no ulterior purpose, for life is for no ulterior purpose. Everything just is, there is no why. Hence man's absurdity, asking "why" when there cannot be an answer.

This is a denial of 13th November 1963 and of the metaphysical echoes last October/November. I am now in an anti-metaphysical "phase". No. There must be a why!

3rd May. A very wet day: tried to write in the Nobe bedroom, came home about lunch-time. My self-assertion with the taxi-driver, mainly because I knew it was a test-case to measure my weakness by, though I didn't like doing it: he drove all round Tokyo station, so that when we came back to the point where we'd started, the ¥100 for 2 kms basic was used up; when paying him I paid him ¥100 less than the total amount, and told him why. He was going to contest it at first, but he caved in. After – only 5 minutes after – I could not tell Aikosan (our maid) off for failing to post two letters and for failing to unbar the gates: two examples of shoddy maiding. Why am I so weak with people I know yet "strong" and "pseudo-strong" with strangers? And yet two hours before I told Tony he couldn't have his bridge party in Nobe on Sunday May 30th as Monday 31st was a holiday and I would be going down. Oh, what a contradictory person I am!

4th May. My dream. After thinking about my rootlessness all yesterday evening I dreamt I had returned to England for a short visit, and was confronted with a succession of people from my life as passers-by. I tried to stop some of them to tell them that I was a poet but they looked at me as though I was different from them, a different species altogether, and went their ways. Some laughed. I did not belong: all my past was before me, and I did not belong. I turned away.

At Keio, two short lectures and sales of books, then a long conversation with Kuriyagawa and Ando about my "unworthy successor", assuming I will have to leave Keio. The business-like manner with which Kuriyagawa got down to it all: names on pieces of paper while muttering his sorrow. Later I travelled to Tokyo station with him on the train. He confided, "I have very bad asthma fits in the night. It is every night now." His skin looked white and stretched, and as he gasped over his oxygen in the train I saw him as a dead man, as I'd seen Tony dead on Sunday.

Wrote a poem about rootlessness in England.

5th May. Wrote a poem about rootlessness in Tokyo, then worked for lectures. Did not go out at all.

I think I shall have a permanent stoop to the left side. Is it my imagination, or has my left lung/diaphragm hurt more in the last two weeks?

Will I write in the same way after I've finished the poems? I set myself to record my own experience without distorting a thing: will I find other people's experience – and imagined experience at that – cheap and unconvincing? Have I committed myself to real experience? One thing I do know, in the last few weeks I have moved right away from allegory, with its preconceived meanings and patterns and schemes: now, everything is in question.

6th May. Wrote part of poem on creativity/party. In the course of reflection, realised that my dreams of suffocation/strangling/hanging are connected with my difficulty with breathing when I was a child.

Read up on pleurisy and TB and discovered, to my indignation, that Morton has not told me the truth. So the bacilli in calcium can reactivate, and post-primary TB can lie ahead; and heightened resistance is offset by the allergy. It is strange, but I have always known that this lay ahead, I've always been prepared for it; and I now see why Morton recommended me to have a "general check-up every 6 months". Somewhere in the future I can see it, a large sanatorium: where is it, where?

7th May. Taught 8.30-2.45, arranged for Narita to visit Tomlin who had just had "a biff in the eye" (how the with-it words jarred with his formal tone), did a recording, went to the Embassy and collected some more COI reference pamphlets and the 1964 Handbook. Returned home, sorted. Time 6.30. What a creative waste.

Nan's secure world: "Dadda, Mamma, Nan-nan", all in a fixed hierarchy from top to bottom, all indivisible, permanently united.

Ideas are of no value before death.

C of boiling water. "I don't like it bubbling over but steaming in the spout." The sexual language.

8th May. All morning and half the afternoon spent on redrafting the poems in more or less chronological order. The total with omissions is 91, so I have to select 9 from the optionals: I also have to take account of the meditating mind – I must proceed by theme and groupings. A chronological grouping is better than a grouping by association in answer to questions of mine because a pattern can only emerge that way: otherwise I shall be in danger of imposing the pattern first. I must not start off with any preconceived ideas about myself; merely observe myself in situations, trying to recapture as exactly as possible what I felt at the time. Some faking is inevitable: it must not be deliberate.

A terrific heat is getting up as I write now at 4.25. There will surely be an earthquake. Will it be a great one?

To Nobe. On the train read Pound's *Mauberley* which gave me a bang. Over dinner talked with Tony about the psychological foundations of all World-Views, e.g. is *The Waste Land* merely sexual horror? Eliot as a fake, capitalising on his impotence and becoming a Christian. Why are people seekers rather than fatalists to whom events happen accidentally? What psychological thing prompts them? Are they still seeking for some meaning? My answer: in my case, my statement about the world is only an hypothesis; I must read everything (an impossibility) in case something throws some light and enables me to "know". Futility and intensity. Tony: "You're an Existentialist seeking experience: why don't you meditate on Nothing?" My answer: "Because I can't write about nothing."

On friends. I claimed each of us has heads, represented by ciphers, and we scan the world until we find actors for the robes and the roles; then follows an impromptu play, which is merely an inner drama projected out, though one can be affected if the actors rebel, as Ezard did. The role Tony has in my dream, successor to Ezard, the good mind and judgement lacking experience and living in a willless, fatalistic chaos.

9th May. Read Camus (is Meursault's revolt against the sun?) and Hemingway's stories. Also noted the common theme in the 1920s: spiritual emptiness and futility and impotence or sexual wounding. Eliot the Fisher King, Jake, Chatterley. "The Castration Complex in the 1920s" – discuss.

No sleep. Up at 7, returned by 5 and bathed.

10th May. A class on Camus's *L'Etranger* in which I found the four shots after the fatal shot puzzling. If the first shot is indeed a reflex "crime" against the sun, committed solely to get into the shade, isn't it far-fetched to introduce a notion of "accepting personal responsibility" with the next four shots? Would an instinctive rebel, aware only instinctually of the hostility of the universe, perform such an action? If this is not his motive it is not otherwise explained and is there only for the plot. To conclude, the four shots are either unmotivated or unconvincing. As to Meursault's freedom, he feels ready to begin life over again and is free from his previous feelings of unreality and now that his dislocated feelings have been healed he is no longer separated from the universe.

Later a deputation of new assistants called to introduce themselves and to get me to sign and write my date of birth: this last item was announced with some glee and I gritted my teeth, for there was no evading it, and wrote 39.5.22, almost hoping they might believe in a May 39th and that I am 42. Outside the door they all talked at the same time: the other side I instinctively searched my face in the mirror.

11th May. Did an hour's recording (unpaid), then gave two lectures to classes of 90. In the evening felt too tired to do anything save lie in a weary stupor.

The label I would give my poems: realism, "truth to observed facts and feelings." I am not sure that my methods of presentation are realistic but in every other respect I am a realist.

After lecturing on history at Keio, and posing Tolstoy's problem of Napoleon and the common soldier, the old old question, "Does history create men or do men create history?" I would like to think the latter.

12th May. Wrote. Remember a remark in this month's *Encounter*. "In his early poems Eliot created a world, in his later poems he kept a journal." What is my world? One of provincial, suburban life with vulgar and futile but nonetheless sympathetic people: a great pettiness which is a background to great strivings.

Once again, so tired.

The subject matter of my poems is not essentially very different from Joyce's *Portrait*: rebellion against family, self-creation and exile.

The American problem. If I am so fed up with England I should take the side of history, follow Auden and become an American citizen. The trouble is, I don't really like Americans, just as, perhaps the late Greeks didn't like the Romans: no displaced number one does really like its successor.

What am I fed up about? Objectively, difficult to say: the class-system, the injustice perhaps. In which case I should not back out, I should stay and fight them.

My "futile people". Not many of them know they're futile, they just live from day to day. Ezard has no ambition to better himself, and is content to live from day to day in Loughton, though he does know he's futile. They are futile in terms of my vision: which might be too severe?

13th May. Another idea as regards the poems. Shall I abandon the idea of calling them experiences and divide them into groupings by subject matter, connecting each experience?

The Fukihara Sangyo scandal and its effect on Usami, the Governor, who was president of the Mitsubishi bank when it was swindled out of £3 million, and who has acknowledged culpability by apologising to the Diet. The chaos in the Bank of Japan: Usami going to Osaka (and Tsuchigane had to go to the airport); Sasaki's beaming face, as though he were waiting for Usami to resign.

The British Council course of "Education". The rapid and intelligent questions, whose answers I had to find. The pain behind my ribs, like a long drawn-out stitch. Buchanan on the Japanese. The going through the motions, e.g. his two hour sit in the Hiyoshi staff room at full lecture rate looks good on paper. Sensitivity to self first. The contradiction of scrupulous honesty in personal dealings and a £3m swindle of the impersonal institution. The detail, not seeing the wood for the trees: long-winded grammar at the expense of meaning. The timidity, the refusal to take responsibility if something has not been done before. The need for 3rd person introductions in business.

14th May. At Kyoikudai (Tokyo University of Education). Narita's gossiping about the lovers of the former tea-girl, now working upstairs, and the number of abortions she has had: "the doctor is a brother-in-law of mine, so I know." At the British Council Tomlin's mistake over the telephone: "I thought I was talking to Sargent but it was Gauntlett – I thought it was strange: Sargent was supposed to be going tomorrow, not going into hospital; and I thanked him for helping me with the ball." To Gauntlett, with a dream-like lack of any attempt to impress, "Er, I thought you were someone you weren't when I was speaking to you just now."

The book on Eliot, which he wants me to contribute to.

Earlier his automatic sympathising and rejoicing on the phone, his set patter; Buchanan's proletarian conversation about the Grants and the difficulty of parking and "whippersnapper Thwaite"; Tuohy's moodiness in the library, almost a pointed sulk, really childish; grumpily condemning all films. What is wrong with him; and is he becoming a commercial writer, and does he know it?

15th May. On Joyce's *Portrait*, Stephen's exile. Escape means getting away, having the freedom to create, enlarging. Eventually there is a final coming to terms with one's country at a distance.

Changes in the poems: to be chronological, in 5 parts without each "experience" documented or numbered, no mythology, the device of Freeman. The idea of the poet as film director: a narrative of "moments" montaged and collaged together, the abrupt transitions showing the different moods and perspectives without a trace of any formal break's being indicated. Find out what objections Tuohy can raise to this. One difficulty: can I begin with Freeman's departure from school, glancing back at causes for his shyness and rebelliousness?

With Tuohy to the bookshops. "The novel, is never a mirror, true realism is impossible." No objections to my new idea. Of my name, "Isn't it the Anglo-Saxon messenger?" (Later Haigha and Hatta, which he confused as Hagger.) The students we met, and my immediate adoption of a sensei

157

(Professor) role that was rather mocking, to accommodate both Tuohy and the students.

16th May. I too was aesthetic in a rather ugly way, writing for artistic or psychological effects, quite indifferent to the modern world. And now, like Pound, I have said Good-bye to that old attitude.

Spent the day reading, especially Hemingway's *The Sun also Rises*. Compare Tuohy's remark, is Jake's wounding symbolic or is it technically convenient?

17th May. Rang Tuohy, gave two lectures at the Tokyo University of Education, then went to Maruzen to buy the COI paperback 1965. Returned home worn out, drank wine and went to sleep. A day existing like a vegetable and getting into cold sweats about leaving and not getting any work done. How nice it would be to stay on with a social role: I have noticed that one is enhanced by a role – one can grow into it, as one can grow into a suit that is too large. Or does one take the shape of one's role? Anyhow, I am certain that much of my contentment comes through having a role (as I have not in England) and much of my hatred in England is connected with the fact that I am not recognised as having a social role; like Jimmy Porter I am futile because there is no place for me. I must, however, leave: having a role does not prevent me from stagnating; I am an intellectual nomad, in the interests of keeping alive I must tear up my roots as soon as they begin to hold firm in the soil.

18th May. Finished rearranging poems, then went to Keio. Lectured on *The Waste Land* and realism in the novel, this second lecture being through a microphone.

19th May. After writing the K man and pumping Illingworth of the Information Service with obscure questions about the monarchy and the composition of the Cabinet and the figures of the Labour-majority, I corrected the NHK T.V. English scripts for September to December: a shockingly creative task.

The earthquake in *Akihibe*, connected with guilt and punishment. Compare *The Bridge of San Luis Rey*. Today, utter nonsense: but Ricky might say "How can you be sure?", for he acknowledges some notion of karma.

Tuohy's meanness with books – always borrowing rather than buying – yet his Lucullan dinner-bills: such a sense of values is based on arrogance, surely? The assumption being that he knows it all, that the books are less important?

20th May. Tuohy saying "The important facts are those you feel." My love-hate relation with Tuohy takes another turn. I am alternately irritated by his moodiness and secretiveness, his meanness in refusing to give from himself, and touched by his generosity in letting me share his impersonal literary knowledge, which is considerable.

21st May. Kept awake all night by a storm, which was 120 times as radioactive as usual owing to the Chinese fall-out. Fortunately my 3rd lecture was cancelled, but I was still awfully tired when we arrived at Tuohy's. His reason for celebrating: he is going into Penguin in his entirety. An argument developed in the Ueno tofu restaurant and finished later, concerning the organisation of life. I was trying to attack anthropologist Stover's smugness by demonstrating how little he knew about the practical things behind the life force metaphor – negative entropy as he preferred to call it; then by saying that it might be possible for man to advance himself by will. Acquired characteristics are passed on socially, not in the genes, but man's destiny could still be affected. Thence we got on to culture and civilisation and Toynbee, and tried to salvage what was valuable.

Did the hypothetical first cell contain the seeds of us or not? On evolutionary humanism, what about death, what about the fact that acquired characteristics can't be passed on in the genes?

Tuohy's remark to Tomlin about Porterish I—. Tomlin: "A most unfortunate business."

22nd May. Very sleepy. Considered the mood of the poems, then wrote a speech for the Governor (of the Bank of Japan) and went down to Nobe. The misty sea, the squids like cucumbers on the beach. The irrigated paddies. Conversations on freedom with Tony. He stressed pressures and motives and all that makes a situation complex. I stressed the experiental action, saying that one is free when one chooses one way or the other, irrespective of the pressures. In the poems I ask "How free am I?" and conclude that each free choice creates a new slavery, that one is the prisoner of one's past choices until the next free act and so one can never say "I am free": it is always a question of the next free act, of bringing new possibilities into being. My purpose in life: to master my experience by understanding it and living it as fully as possible.

The sudden moment of full knowledge about myself as I was about to cross the bridge: I stopped, looked at the bamboo and said "I must leave her" and felt a tremendous sadness. The idea of the pain I would cause made me feel sick.

23rd May. Last night. The stupid beetle, which returned three times to the trap from which I released it. This morning, the walk into the muddy paddies, hunting snakes with forked sticks. Saw five, caught two, one of which puffed itself up so that the red pattern became brilliant. A yamamori, I think it was: quite harmless in spite of its flickering tongue. Too drunk with humidity and fresh air to observe anything remarkable. Otherwise sat in my bamboo chair, hating myself for what I was thinking, and read and reread the last chapter of *A Moveable Feast*, dreaming over and over again what I should do to recover my freedom and wondering why I wouldn't do it.

24th May. At lunch, conversed about my poems in the role of sensei (Professor), something I have not really done before. Illuminating points, e.g. I changed to a historical view of experience on account of mood/moulding forces/London/complexity; and that a poem about society purely and simply is impossible – it must also be about oneself, saved from autobiography/diary by making the particular as general as possible, i.e. making it refer to a general situation or state of mind. Earlier, me saying that Kafka's God demands man to seek but refuses to reveal himself. Test this against the books in two weeks time. Also finding Hemingway's intentions about Jake – "I plunged into the fiesta concept of life" (*A Moveable Feast*) – thereby clinching what I said last week, that Hemingway does not condemn Jake's life in Paris, just as Jake is not meant to be a symbol for spiritual impotence: like Henry, he is the most religious of the characters in the book.

Toyama. On the movement in appreciating a poem: the poet translates the particular into the general, the reader the general back into his own particular, which might be very different from the poet's intention. Realism, as a photograph, does not last. One must treat the eternal problems, using symbolism and dreams (in which the general is dressed as the particular).

26th May. Like any artist (no matter how good, and for this there is no guarantee) I live in two worlds, one of vision, one of the everyday, and I should forget the vision when I leave this room, but somehow cannot: and so I show little interest in the everyday, especially when there are unreal states of mind inimical to my vision, e.g. the bourgeois unrealities of dogs, photos, indiscriminate T.V. and pop, being fooled by the commercial culture, all of which make my blood boil. (How they fill silences that would be unreal.)

27th May. Recast pt 5 of the poems. Went to the Bank of Japan, then to teach politics, the press, radio and T.V. at the British Council. When I got home I dipped into as many modern poets as I could find, trying to see how much they thought, how much they communicated experience; came out anti-Auden and anti-1950s, much of whose poems is thinking aloud: no communication of states of mind experiencing and oh, so much about the Greeks and in such mannered rhyme, and so lifelessly.

28th May. A day off work. Wrote. In the evening went to see *This Sporting Life*: Storey's love for the ape-gentle relationship, and the demanding wife to complete the triangle. (Cf *Radcliffe*). His use of feeling and strong situation, so that words are unnecessary.

160

29th May. A morning's seminar. After to the bookshops. Returned and rewrote the beginning and end of the poems.

30th May. Wrote while it rained and read a book on T. E. Lawrence.

31st May. On my self-discovery. The crucial event in my life was the loss of Paradise. I was alone, an outcast. Sport, archaeology, writing were compensations.

To what extent did I later will to be different, an outcast? (Cf my rebellion later.) I rejected this image swiftly and violently and adopted the opposite attitude, later growing my hair long. In Japan I feel at ease because all gaijin (foreigners) are ugly.

Can I do any more choosing of my self now, or are things going satisfactorily? On my will-philosophy at Oxford: basically I was right, as Ricky now realises, I think, judging from his last letter; I smashed because I had not interiorised it to art, and no doubt Ricky played a part in this process of interiorisation, though he also made me doubt an attitude that was basically right and certainly preferable to his of the "loaded dice".

My Paradise: the East Grinstead wood, the toy soldiers and coloured matches and the grindstone at my grandmother's; the scooter, the pond with swans; the large fir tree at *Beechholme*.

2nd June. A day of tremendous struggle, revaluation and progress. First read my *Diaries* from October 1963, and contrasted two positions in relation to metaphysics: "there must be a point" and "there is no point". Then, having written a poem on this contrast, I got onto the priest-obsession and found, to my horror, that I have been repeating myself as a writer since 1961.

C's painting: two heads from one body with both hands modestly covering the sexual regions, a man. This archetypal pattern for her changed recently, the two heads emerging from one, the front one being red and bloody and living, the back being black and dead. What does it mean? Are the two heads me and lover? Also the modesty: before one hand covered, the other was behind the back. What? And the white bird? She herself is puzzled and obsessed by this symbol.

The milk boy collected ¥200,000 a week early and absconded. The only house he couldn't bleed was mine: I told him twice to come at the end of the month at the proper time.

3rd June. Progress continued. Combined fragments into the end. C's change of heart about Japan. She would like to return for another two years somewhere else in Tokyo, in view of the conditions. I am at a loss. "Do what is real" is my criterion. But which would be more real: to go elsewhere and not be able to teach 20th century Literature or buy books or follow up contacts and perhaps have to teach in the mornings; or to stay here and write, assured of five months' holiday a year?

4th June. At Kyoikudai heard of Tomlin's anger about Kirkup, summoning Kuroda, ordering a public disclaimer or else he would sue for libel, getting Kirkup declared "persona non grata" by the Embassy. What an idiot Kirkup must be to carry his war on particulars into a foreign press which does not even know the whole. Buchanan had Miss Arai in Nobe last weekend. Toyama is starting a new magazine this autumn. One of my 3rd year students, Mr Kaneko killed himself a week and a half ago: a student came up to me, poker-faced, and said, "Please do not call the name of my friend Mr Kaneko in future, as he has died." The tone was matter of fact. Did a recording for the Language Laboratory. My contract reaffirmed that my status is that of "Foreign Professor".

In the evening to Godard's *Une Femme Mariée*. Techniques for poems: (1) making the reader see what I want him to see and nothing else; (2) "negatives", so that the body is black with a white light shining through eyes and hair. Technique from Beethoven's late quartets which I played afterwards: speed and slowness in passages, and transitions – short/long words. Godard is the detached spectator, the ironic observer. He increases consciousness and awareness but there is no feeling in his gaze. He says "Look", not "Suffer with".

5th June. More work on the priest-complex: my recreating failed priests to prove I was right. On change, energy remains constant, e.g. Donne, (St.) Paul and Augustine: the energy is adapted to another use; compare Yeats's choice between "Perfection of the life or of the work". As to my poems, beware of seeming complacent at the end or too involved in myself, leave everything unsolved, as of course it is.

My mind is not really Modernist: I feel too little despair, too little drift, I am too aware for that. I am an existential post-Modernist.

6th June. Began to write the fortune-teller. Had an inspiration about the search for self. In the afternoon lazed in a heat and read *The Trial*; seeing it like the *Castle* as a statement of absurdity: the world is, there must be a point – the very existence of the world suggests a point just as the very existence of a castle suggests an authority, as a law suggests a High Court. Applied the search internally.

Cf. Tony: "Why are you a seeker?" and "What do you hope to find?" Answer: I am baffled by the world, as to how it can exist without a point, but I do not think there is a point I can share in or discover. I hope to confirm this hypothesis, assemble all the evidence, and contribute something through absurd creation.

Write an essay: a meditation on the Meaning of Life in relation to 20th century literature and Modernism. "The longing for eternity". The rejection of it, the absence of a point.

7th June. On Kafka. His works are symbols (Heller) not allegories (Muir), and to translate the untranslatable (as a symbol is what it represents) the "meaning" is "The Absurdity of the World". How relevant the symbol is to my life is another question. K's attitude to the Absurdity is one of horror. "No point, but there must be a point." My reaction is the priest's: K is deluding himself by expecting to have real contact with the "Truth"; and I am not convinced that the "Truth" makes such demands on one, and K could reject his case and the two assistants and no unreality would have been accepted. In short, if one denies the existence of the Law/Castle, the search loses much of its delusion. If I say "There is no point to the universe and I do not expect there to be" then Kafka loses much of his hold over me. This is Camus's position, although Camus interprets Kafka at the allegorical level, in terms of God.

Yet can I really say that Kafka is not so relevant to me? I seek, not only my interior self but also somewhere a point and I don't like to admit what I have admitted, that the universe is pointless. My self-deception, perhaps? But, for me, to think otherwise would be a delusion, I can only believe that my purpose is within myself, and is finite and absurd. (Cf 24th May: wrong.)

8th August 1965. This reason, this irrational.

8th June. Concentrated on a poem, then went to Keio. Very tired, nearly lost consciousness at one point in the last lecture: very giddy. In the train stretched my lung in the course of holding on to a strap amid the rush-hour crowd. Was in pain for the rest of the evening, reading up on land, agriculture, housing, town and country planning and new towns.

Art: the search for perfection and "stillness amid motion."

9th June. Heard in the morning that today is the Queen's birthday, that there is an Embassy party 5.30-7.30. It was set deep within the Embassy, I believe in the Ambassador's own residence. On the lawn the other side of the red-carpeted hall there were some thousand people. Few strutted around, many were in formal dress. I was taken to meet Mrs. Kitchingham. The Council interview, I saying all the wrong things, e.g. that I am teaching a lot of Literature and so on. Tomlin: "A great pity about Tuohy's refusal: he could write 5,000 words."

10th June. A morning reading through my father's suffering and reliving it, being too involved to write.

11th June. To a film on Vietnam with Tuohy. The futility and pointlessness of the suffering, the torture. After ate and drank with Tuohy. On maturity: one's disillusion deepens (the process of disillusionment is connected with youth); maturity is detachment but "being able to go on loving", and recognising that there is a time-limit on all emotions; one has less energy

163

and one "wakes up with a hangover to remember 'God, I didn't get drunk last night'" when one realises one is middle-aged; also less "coming"; a novelist should live long enough to see things develop.

On suffering: one must accept pain, doctors do; he always feels inadequate in the face of great suffering, not having suffered in the same way; "I can't be nihilistic, I must believe in goodness, e.g. some man took my friend's name off the execution list." His final admission: "I am living a life of 'quiet desperation'."

On to Nobe, rather drunk.

5.

THE IRRATIONAL, THE STONE GARDEN AND WHITE LIGHT
June – December 1965

12th June. Nobe. No rain until later afternoon, but all was cloudy. Read Camus's *Myth of Sisyphus* and thought out my objections and my own position. I know that I am and that the world is, but I do not know why. All deductions will be hypotheses, therefore reject rationalism and systems and categories, and stick to experience: the narrow line between practical philosophy and psychology, proceeding from observations. The result is not irrationalism: there is no meaning of life that is outside life.

So like Camus I reject the notion of a point I can share in; unlike Camus and like Kafka, I still seek within myself. My objections to Camus are: (1) his scorning is unrealistic and romanticised and (2) his concept of the absurd depends upon his rational revolt in the interests of clarity ("Why?") – it is this that bifurcates Nature for Camus – whereas I am inclined to feel that Camus overemphasises man's desires. I agree that Camus correctly describes an "absurd" sensitivity that exists in Literature but I feel that he has failed to take account of another possibility, that it is man's questioning "Why" that is gratuitous and senseless, rather than that it is the world that is disappointing. Also, the world is disappointing in its lack of clarity, but one must be careful not to talk about the absence of God, for although God could be the clarity He is not necessarily so and I find the notion misleading.

13th June. Nobe. The centipede with legs like red rose-thorns, five inches long. The mess on the stone floor, the thorns in the stick. The three snakes, the cleft stick. The cow's skull on the beach, disturbing my subconscious which immediately thought it significant.

When I got home Tuohy came to return a book. His friendliness until he went out of the gate, then like Buchanan and Adrian he withdrew. Conversation over a drink mainly to do with not joining the (British) Council permanently. I had always suspected the Council would demand all the employee's time, even for University posts, and now I know. I shall never enter a system. Freelance and contracts or starve. That is one of the prices I must pay. This confusing lack of security, exhilarating and depressing in turns. But better than a secure death.

14th June. Articulated my quarrel with Camus. He stresses the rational too much, probably because of his feeling of being a stranger in an unfamiliar universe. So he asks why, receives no answer and complains of the "unreasonable silence of the world". But the approach from experience, as opposed to reason, is different: "I am, the world is, it is impossible to know why; reason will therefore take us no further so complain of the unreasonable questioning of man and don't pursue the reason any more; certainly don't found a philosophy on it." Man's rational desire for clarity is therefore a fruitless desire one must learn to live with, like death. But although I disagree with his methods (and his "compensation" of scorning); how much I agree with his conclusions. The bifurcation between man and the universe, the absence of eternity, the conception of hope as an escape – how right Camus is, judging from my experience. There is nothing to be sought in the outside world, the quest is within oneself: and here I get into territory that Camus would despair of. So what does it all come down to? Despair, senseless self-seeking and discovery, statement of my true situation in art and intense experiences as my particular brand of self-created values. Then return to the nothing from which I came. I emerged, I wrote my protest, then I returned. I also developed myself in order to write my protest. Pessimism. But if death is final, what else?

15th June. For my essay. "There is no search or quest. And those who think there are are deluding themselves. There are only distractions, escapes. I am recording this in spite of my own temperament which (perhaps because some gland secretes too much, or because of my struggle with my parents) is a seeker's. I am a seeker and I am writing that there is nothing to seek. And the materialists are right. They who were too lazy to seek have lost nothing by their laziness, while I have expended my energy in a futile cause." On the metaphysical temperament: is it because I failed to make the transition from adolescence, this wanting a metaphysical solution, or is it purely wanting to overcome ultimate futility?

On pessimism and "if death is final what else?": "Life is all, if death is final then life is all." Reading over the last few weeks I feel the gates are closing on all my escapes, or rather, all those gates I imagined ajar are firmly barred and locked and I am confirming my prison, I, the imprisoned seeker for an escape, am confirming that escape is impossible. There is no way out, none; I must accept the unpleasant truth of my situation, accept it completely, and say "life is all", "existence is all".

16th June. The tape. Mother in the background, supervising and guiding, adding pieces of information and correcting items of news with a demand for accuracy that is not merited by the triviality of the subjects. Behind them all, a silence, which emphasises the exhausting intensity with which they live the trivial. Ah, my intensity I owe to you; I should not disparage yours: but my intensity has found an object.

17th June. Wrote on the scream among the summer roses, then went to the Bank of Japan where, because of the financial crisis, everyone was very busy. Talked at length with Oshima about symbolism in Iris Murdoch, read and reread Felicity's magic rite in *The Sandcastle* while he scurried about his master's business, then went off to the gloom of the Cocteau café and watched the patronne from the corner. Went home to hear how Chinese MIGs were shot out of the sky. Is there going to be a war? Has Wilson traded Britain's voice for support for sterling?

What a fragmented day. Reading over what I have written I wonder that the mind can achieve any depth so widely is it stretched, from subject to subject. And moving from one subject to the next can never have been so swift as in the 20th century, or so total.

18th June. After the Tokyo University of Education and the Bank of Japan, an evening with Tuohy. The dispute over the bill at the Rosier: I asked for large beer, they brought small and charged the price of large, ¥200; the menu further said ¥200 a pint, which is approximately three small bottles. The "release of adrenalin", haranguing passers-by until the police-car arrived. Then to Manos. Then back home; Tuohy staying until after 2 a.m.

On writing. Journalists see one side, a novelist sees both because of his superior observation and perception. A writer is not with it, so why shouldn't Eliot have followed Gautier in 1918? (But did he discover it in 1922 or was it all due to Pound? Investigate the date of Amygism.) On the small audience of poetry. Existentialists have no sense-perceptions, they cannot embody their ideas. Gossip on writers.

19th June. Worn out after the late night and an early morning. Drafted out notes for my meditative essay on the meaning of life. This would be unashamedly as unartistic as *Notes from Underground, part 1*: should I do it? I can, now that I have exorcised the priest in my poems.

In the afternoon went to the bookshops and got everything except the one book I went to get, *Honest to God* for Thursday's class.

20th June. Wrote on being an unwilling exile, then went for a walk to Chinzanso. The ducks, the birds, the rabbits outside the new cathedral. In the gardens the priapic spire with bells behind the soft wall of running water.

In the evening read up on Romanticism; in particular it is "the mind that desires and the world that disappoints" as Camus, the rational romantic put it. The environment not satisfying desires in portraits of the artist, e.g. *Tonio Krüger* and Joyce. What else could make the artist feel so separate? *Tonio Krüger* between the bourgeois and the bohemian world. Cf Ricky's world-rejection and (Colin) Wilson saying "He sounds the archetypal Romantic" although Ricky would deny it. Cf T. E. Hulme.

21st June. While I was talking about the Romantic hero at the Tokyo University of Education C was accosted by a man who exposed himself.

Stephen D: "The contemplation of an inner world of individual emotions mirrored perfectly in a lucid supple periodic prose."

On friends. One has no friends, only acquaintances. I set too high standards for my friends, demanding an absolute commitment to my best interests and possibly giving too little of myself in return, so that when someone shows himself indifferent to my best interests I feel betrayed. Then I feel angry with myself for having trusted, for I should know better. The truth is, I have a need for a friend but have none, and Tuohy is in the same position. Essentially I am alone and must admit no one to the inner sanctum.

22nd June. Last night; the recital of Dickens by Emlyn Williams. His sound knowledge of what a foreign community will respond to, getting echoes from their memories; his digs about the cruelty of high society, the pettiness of dinner behaviour. After, Tomlin took me round the back with the Ambassador. The two man team I met...: the hulking manager, the little actor. On my way out I saw a familiar face smiling at me, beckoning, and asking "How's your play?" and I found myself talking to my anima (Marsha); her children, her stunning hair.

23rd June. A heat got up. By 10 I felt drained and couldn't do much writing; fiddled around on choice of exile. The changing social background, the petty provincial life in England, the futility of their existence, the up and coming anti-puritanical generation liberated by people like me who remain enslaved, mentally. The vulgar materialism of a declining power.

Later, read Robinson's *Honest to God*. So God is the ground of our being and Christ is the revealer of just that and prayer is keeping a diary in depth and the function of the Church is to make us aware of the eternal in our midst and there was no Creator and Jesus's prescriptions were only hints. Deny the Absolute or eternal, see depth and being in terms of existence, and nothing remains.

The emptiness of the post-Christian West. Man, the only thing that can fill it. Man, a being who will become nothing, seeking things that will compensate the loss of his being: intensification of his love of life, thorough self-knowledge, and the pagan values of heroism, honour, sadness.

24th June. Wrote on Freeman, private eye, and the vivacious woman and ate a late lunch while the Bank of Japan car waited. As I was about to change the doorbuzzer went and Kuroda stood outside in his suit: I in sand longs and a white shirt that showed the vest. His mission: Prince Hitachi wants two lessons a week. My reaction, one of mild irritation, and plotting to save my mornings for my work. So the Imperial Household, after teasing me with their rumours about the Crown Prince, is fobbing me off with (his younger brother) Hitachi; if I were a Beckett character or K I would feel insulted. Still, the teasing attraction of the Palace might at last be penetrable.

THE IRRATIONAL, THE STONE GARDEN AND WHITE LIGHT (1965)

At my class on Christianity. Robinson's courage yet his immense naivety, asking questions at 57 (?) which most ask at 17. No sympathy for the agonies of the Church from those atheists who, from the age of 17, went through the same agonies, and survived, without any sympathy from the smug and complacent Church. Also the influence of Puritanism. In my bath I asked, what values do I admire against the backdrop of nothingness, and my answer: independence, sensitivity and courage, and truth (cf. the Anglo-Saxon Wanderer's self-sufficiency).

25th June. At Kyoikudai (Tokyo University of Education). Tuohy's moodiness over the telephone, his attempts to be apologetic for it. Narita's politeness: "Come and sit under the window, it's cooler." A penetrating remark by Fukuchi: "We have no word for perfectionism in Japan because it is the norm, not the exception." To Dr. Morton for a routine ear-cleaning, the wax having been cleared with cerumol; but was discovered to have the "white fungus" I had last year – caused by the humidity; flocculosis, it is, in fact, reflected in dandruff and spots and connected in some way with my flocculondular lobes. My general low resistance. Bombed up with ilotycin (erythromycin), feverish, temperaturish, alive.

On rhythm. Connected with emotion: mechanical rhythm, mechanical feeling. An effect of any thought but can be used consciously; art; punctuation. Mood being reflected by the rhythms: the short, terse staccato; the languid leisurely gaze. On seeking: I seek the way to myself, I seek an answer to the question "Who am I?"

26th June. A discovery: My rejection of a social role in my third year at Oxford, and my independence, was linked with my anti-intellectualism, prowling round the intimate and squalid streets of Jericho with Trattner or alone, and being calmed by the workers' singsong on a Saturday night. I was anti-intellectual in my 2nd year, but rather fashionably so, e.g. my cry was "Sciolism", but I lived it in my 3rd year. This anti-intellectualism is also linked with C. How much so? E.g. the squalid digs I found first of all. Perhaps C gave me the strength to be anti-intellectual.

To Nobe. Read Hesse's *Steppenwolf* and *Demian* in between walks. The frightening kite as I approached its nest. My strictness with myself – sitting on the edge of the chair, refusing comforts: it derives from my puritanism, which is the factor that determined my spirituality; also my sensuality is a reaction. Japan helps you to shut people out of the inner temenos of your being. The doll's head on the beach. An image: a giant in the night, like the Kamakura Dai-butsu (Big Buddha).

27th June. The tropical storm all night, then the steaming night. After running away from the Fs on the beach, a long appraisal of my unsociability, my retreat from society because most contacts involve waste of energy, pretence and lies. Basically it is my nervousness, poet's shyness perhaps.

28th June. At Kyoikudai (Tokyo University of Education). On Hesse, the writer of the search within who never really defined what he was seeking; perhaps that was his theme.

29th June. I was able to tell Colin Wilson in January 1961 "I shall become a Wanderer and an Exile", and sure enough that is exactly what has happened. My father's reaction to the old house in Southmoor Road (Oxford): "It's a condemned house, this is shocking." Compare my nocturnal wanderings in Jericho, feeling comfort from the working class terraced houses and talking to a gelly-boy or an old lag in a pub. (The rhyming cockney slang on cards.) How clearly we understand the lives of others – the T. E. Lawrences and so on – yet how obscure are our own lives! I, groping for understanding, am probably already completely transparent to another.

30th June. My poetry is a poetry of self-discovery, a poetry of drabness for a drab society governed by science and technology, a deeply psychological poetry in an anti-metaphysical psychological age: a poetry of decline and debasement for a declining and debased society. (25th May 1992. Later my poetry became a spiritual tonic for a declining age.)

1st July. First meeting with Prince Hitachi. The obsequious men who appeared out of doorways in the Palace "hall"; the absurdly cringing Private Secretary. The bungling Prince, very uncertain of himself, holding out his hand at the wrong time, mechanical in speech; his indirect conversation with anxious glances at his Japanese teacher. The ridiculous departure, the Prince hanging around behind me while I made arrangements with a servant.

Asian smile, beware. "The Japanese smile to avoid offending others' feelings, it means nothing." The basis of Japanese politeness is not consideration for others but not offending others, i.e. keeping out of others' way.

2nd July. Tokyo University of Education, then to Dr. Morton's, travelling with Fubara who talked about the 19th century Japanese "Renaissance humanist" attitude of absorbing everything. Later Tsuchigane came with 24 scentless red roses and stayed till 11 o'clock straightening out points in connection with (the Governor) Usami's speeches at the honorary degree ceremony at Keio and luncheon afterwards. It is impolite in Japanese to be exact about numbers (because of the old samurai code).

Discussion with C about staying on for an extra year; this time being crucial to me, needing money, and Irie having left the door open for this.

(Earlier. Buchanan's haikus, e.g. "The sunray/On the broken glass/The hard glitter" and the more revealing "Her fig/My limp lily/What frustration" and "Her fingers/In my rough hairs/What ecstasy".)

3rd July. Revoked my decision to leave, the British Council approving. Essentially, I suppose, this is a decision for security against existential change. The situation is very complex and changes with what is focused on; it is too large to see as a whole.

Since the beginning of 1965 I have changed as a writer and the extra year would give me time to finish poems.

This depends on Tomlin's recommendation being approved by London. Irie's cry of joy; the Head of Department's relief at not having to assume the burden of finding a successor.

4th July. A walk to Chinzanso, picked a green fan-like ginko leaf. The nightmare strollers, intruders from a Bergman film. Their make-up, the drum and cymbals, the red and white barred banner, the exaggerated walk and fuss of Nan. The quiet shrines, a howling dog; the silent Cathedral in between the organ playings, the sloping grey stone walls suggesting tent sides, imitation catacomb. The towering uplifting tentpole of yellow and white glass and the spindly 'metal' cross. The geometric starkness, the abstract grandeur and human insignificance, and I was moved. Later worked on T. E. Lawrence for my class. Was the son of the claimant to Palestine (see March 23rd) the son of Emir Ali, the one who did not get a kingdom in 1928?

Tired, drained, yet emotionally very brittle.

5th July. On T. E. Lawrence. So tense that I was nearly moved to tears when reading aloud the scene in the hospital and the Dostoevskian murmur "Aman, aman": pity, pity. The 20th century has had agony and torture enough, but now in the 1960s the spiritual reality that agony breeds is impossible: hell has been sterilized and the great vision replaced by the unreal rubbishy pachinko parlour consciousness. There is no doubt about it, one can only write of what one knows, and what I know has a debilitating effect on me: a decadent culture and civilisation, a decadent writer – Pound's Hugh Selwyn Mauberley.

And is there any escape, the withdrawal into the desert? There must be to some extent, but there is always the return, and in the course of handing out what has been discovered in the self, one is living in a decadent culture, one cannot escape what one knows. One knows the outer decadence, and the within that might or might not be affected by it, so the message learnt in the desert goes "Know the within as much as the without." A stale old message, issued in different terms by the *Old Testament* prophets during the 8th century BC decadence. The themes of the 20th century: the divided self, the fragmented vision, the impotent hero.

Tomlin's polite clichés. He will ask the British Council to pay my tax and continue my subsidy.

6th July. A long meeting of two and a half hours with the Prince. He is very willing and co-operative and obedient, but I got into my usual tangles:

walking into the wrong room after my arrival and then having to go upstairs; saying to the Prince on the way down "Don't bother to come down" and when he didn't correcting him, saying, "That's English politeness and it means you do." His diffidence and nervousness. ("Shall I call the Duke of Edinburgh Your Grace? How should I address your Queen?") I, who two months ago could not distinguish a Baronet from a Knight, am now making minute distinctions in the order of precedence; I, who have always been paralysed on being introduced and mumble all the wrong words, am now teaching the Prince to be relaxed and confident; I, the striker of knock-kneed attitudes, have become the striker of confident attitudes in a psychological warfare the Prince understands.

7th July. To the Tokyo Club with Buchanan. In the bar he sat near the door, said the majority of members were Japanese diplomats and brought up the elections with I— so obviously.

In the car on the way home he told me that R (to whom, he admitted, he is going to send a report on the elections) was condemned to death in 1941 for espionage; when I asked him if there was any justification in the charge his reply was "Undoubtedly he did a lot of espionage both in the 1930s and after." Another curious connection, R was saved by K, Buchanan's present pupil. Met Bush, a bombastic bore, seeking to impress with swaggering swear words, until he talked about his years in the Japanese concentration camp, his torture, "I can see their faces in the subway today." His sad admission that after 32 years in Japan, because of the "on" system and defensive relationships of Japanese, he had only three friends. His naval background. Buchanan: "He's a Conrad character." He holds his knife like a pencil when dining. Buchanan: "I'm the most bogus teacher there ever was. My motto is, 'If you don't know invent'." "A little of him goes a long way."

8th July. Worn out after a morning with the Prince, afternoon with the Bank of Japan and evening at the British Council. Tangles again: telling the Prince to say to a vicar "I am a Buddhist" until he said "I am not a Buddhist"; and later, chatting in the hall to a chamberlain, I became aware of a girl bowing very low nearby. I gave a cheery nod and continued chatting until I noticed the horrified expression in the chamberlain's eyes and realised that the girl was the Princess. Got back to find an attractive card from Tuohy: mountain and lake and his telephone number. After the Bank of Japan, read *Great Britain or Little England* (a Penguin Special), especially the last chapter on the lazy, feckless, pleasure-loving, unambitious English: the conflict between the arrogant intellectual and the conventional English who will not tolerate him.

N's dolly twisted up in her wicker-pushcart, like a condemned woman waiting for the tumbril to start off for the guillotine.

THE IRRATIONAL, THE STONE GARDEN AND WHITE LIGHT (1965)

9th July. Exhausted. Sat wearily at my desk typing to keep myself awake after the strain and stresses of the last two weeks directly, and the last ten weeks indirectly. Wrote about the giant Buddha. What I am trying to do is to reflect the consciousness of our time of transition between the old and the new, between Great Britain and Little England. Contrast is important in a time of transition. The old glory which has decayed, and the new debased, vulgar slang which is, for all its impoverishment, perhaps more vital. So in language there must be a mixture of noble language and slang; and old and new attitudes must find a place, especially the change to technology and the conquest of space and their impact.

To Nobe, meeting Munekata on the way.

10th July. At Nobe. After a night of little sleep, a drizzle and white-crested waves. Resolved to cut out those books which have fastened to me and died and have impeded my growth – ruthlessly to cut them out with a knife of clear thought. Surgery is required to leave behind my arrested adolescence. My TB bacilli which have no active influence, my thin arms. Read Wilson's *Beyond the Outsider*, sadly noting his contradictions, his changed opinions.

11th July. Nobe. Overcast and a black sea. A battering wind, flapping my black shirt, my sand trousers. It swept up the horseshoes, swirling waves of rice with it. All Nature was adance – even the grass up the hills swept up like a succession of tidal waves – and standing amid it all, giddy with movement, I felt it was hard not to be a part of Nature, it was hard to feel an opposition between me and the world. Involvement to the hair, and then the spectator took over and observed the rice fields were patched light and dark green like velvet. The boat on the beach with the straw cover that resembled a Mexican hat; the buildings of Tokyo before Shimbashi, as though a child had been messing around with a box of bricks in some half dozen shapes: rectangles with squares poised on them, rectangles on their sides for blocks of flats.

Reflected on my poems. How unEnglish I am, both in my life and in my models. Freedom is a French preoccupation, choosing situations is certainly not English, and my rejection of England for a life-pattern abroad. Ah, but none of this could kill the basic reserve and modesty.

12th July. Wrote on Freeman's despair in Oxford and got caught up in a rhyme scheme I couldn't extricate myself from, although I tried to make it looser towards the end. A very difficult poem as it is not a complete experience I am writing about, but rather a bridge with loose ends that tie up later. I think I should change it, but into what I don't know.

13th July. After the Prince, and my not knowing the Duke of Edinburgh had written a book on birds and his personal complaint about his lack of privacy and my tangle when leaving to cap his ignorance of my arrival, wrote a poem, or rather, part of a poem.

I have abandoned philosophy for psychology, the universe for human relationships; to some extent at any rate. If not completely, Oxford is to blame: Ricky and Kingsley had a religious sense of God's absence, while Ezard and now Tuohy are definitely Cambridge in their disinterest in the universe.

15th July. From yesterday. The Prince's invitation to dinner, my successful ploy to keep off royal Dukes – when the younger sons of kings cease to be princes and become royal Dukes – and also why the son of the Duke of Kent is an Earl and not a Marquess (or does it go down every generation?).

In the evening, Tokyo University of Education farewell dinner for Fujii. Crippling – after an hour of sitting at the table without beer or air-conditioning, only 9 or so had turned up, excluding Fujii. Later, Kuroda's deliberate attempt to annoy Irie by asking the waiter to offer Irie beer, Irie being a teetotaller-Quaker. Irie may have arrived one and a half hours late as an insult to the Kuroda faction of Fujii. "This very important matter about the moving of Kyoikudai."

Irie's essay on Empson. "Oh," said I, "on Empson as poet or critic?" "Neither. To be exact, it is called 'Empson as Grandfather'." It sounded an invaluable contribution to scholarship to me. This item of news came after his saying how flattered he was to be referred to in my class: "Empson was Professor Irie's teacher". So he has spies in my class, eh? My speech about the tax situation and my dream which followed, reading a book "by Conrad" called *The Returning Ship* with my graduates, I saying "The ship symbolizes the soul." The story was original and I wanted to remember it to write it, but can't.

16th July. Tuohy. Most of the evening's conversation was about the difference between art and journalism. All art is artificial (not a pejorative word) and its relationship to life is parallel, cf imagery and algebra's relationship to arithmetic; anything really with it is journalism (Tuohy). I said there should be a balance between the eternal/general and the contemporary, and that a work of art was related to the laws of human behaviour, which should not be fantastic. After disagreeing, Tuohy agreed. Various fallacies on aesthetics, alternatives to Wittgenstein's proposition: "I agree with this, this relates to my situation" being the main one. The difficulty of writing drama because of the middle class lack of violence and because nothing happens and life is plotless. (But "art is independent of life." This is where I disagree.)

On poetry being a situation (me) rather than linguistically haunting (Tuohy). The big question, does the individual create society or vice versa (me)? Tuohy: "The artist catches the disease." I said one's view of art depends on whether one is a historicist or an Existentialist, and that five years ago I was the latter but am now not so sure; tend to be both. Tuohy attacked my term "poetry of self-discovery" on the grounds that there was no self to discover and one did not discover but presented; I countered, "But one discovers how one repeats oneself."

Also, the disappearance of Orwell's "knobbly" English, and Tuohy's feelings that the Japanese hate him some days, his admission of shyness and that writing is probably a compensation (cf Freud). Tuohy: Shakespeare felt a common soldier more deeply than Osborne and our disbelief in the divine right of Kings does not matter. So he disagreed when I said that Ibsen's determinism and Chekhov's decline bore no relation to today and could not be followed by middle class dramatists. "It's a question of cogs." Shaw writing and timing well.

17th July. To Nobe. Wet. The marmoushi (brown poisonous snake). Drank with Buchanan and Hardy in the café. Later with Buchanan, on Mrs. Empson's trip to live with P. D. S. in Hong Kong. Hardy's loose gestures, almost a sign that he has given up and is adrift.

18th July. At Nobe and returning home, reading Freud and thinking about myself after leaving the beach to write. I am pretty stabilised (i.e. adult, pattern already predictable) but my equilibrium (between cathexes and anti-cathexes) is based on defence mechanisms which are infantile: on repressions (failures), projections (blaming others and making excuses), identifications (modelling myself on writers), habitual displacements (e.g. C for mother) and sublimations (e.g. writing for energies without other escape) and compromises (writing?), reaction formation (oral dependence becoming independence), regressions (retreating) and probably fixations (standing still/adolescent as regards meeting people).

In short, I am a hotbed of anxiety, primarily I think, reality anxiety; connected with the external world. I do not feel Ricky's neurotic and moral anxiety so much, I can locate my anxieties and do not feel the need for self-punishment. Or do I? Anyhow, I am maladjusted in relation to the world and have retreated into a dream world of "myself as artist". I don't want to disturb this, but I cannot regard myself as mature, healthy, well-adjusted, and the very persistence of defence-mechanisms is a sign that the ego's development is inadequate and needs protection; compare my tendency to be uncompetitive. I don't want to disturb the status quo because my energy is flowing in the direction I want it to flow in, and a disturbance of energy in one part of my personality might change all that: the creative cathexes of the "id" might be blocked by anti-cathexes from elsewhere as they are id/ego, ego/superego.

In short, I would rather be a sick artist than a healthy, average citizen. (Kingsley: "Average guy.")

19th July. And this is the crux and is related to my ego-retarding. In Freud's terms I have failed to relate the image of myself with the real object in the external world: my id has distorted the realism of the ego's "reality principle", the "secondary process" and the reality testing and the process which distinguishes fantasy from reality and does not confuse the two. My "id" rules my ego, which explains why I have no mask, why I am uncompetitive, why I would rather write than assert myself, would rather be alone than have relations with the environment. My superego – the priest, my jailer – has also annihilated my ego and left it energyless, which explains my disinclination to stick up for myself in society.

Hence my reality anxiety and maladjustment, my shyness; hence all the defence mechanisms: not being able to face reality's failures, repressing them to protect myself from anxiety and frustration and thereby replacing realistic thinking; hence my liking for Japan, which helps to disguise the truth for me by making me a Professor, advisor to the Bank of Japan, tutor to a Prince, and also my vow to kill myself when I'm 40 if I am not successful: the superego's vengeance. So there was nothing courageous in Freeman's refusal to despair; it was compulsive. Anyhow, no matter what the cause of my dream is – self-importance and adolescent desire to be different or whatever – I shall not renounce it, although my writing becomes more realistic.

20th July. Freud, still. A deterministic view of my awakening in 1957: an outpouring of (repressed) energy, the dam having broken.

The more anti-cathexes, the higher tension level of personality, preventing psychic energy from being dissipated: I transform/sublimate this into writing. Writing as a reduction in tension, an ego-ideal cathexis retained from growing-up years because it was satisfying. An outlet for my social tension, now compulsive and drug-like.

23rd July. The rainy season continues. In spite of the cool weather I feel emotionally exhausted after a long searching week and today's attempt to write the centre of the mosaic and the contradictions it reconciles: roles as son, husband, teacher, "socialite" and poet; also as exile and failed saint; and father and friend.

In all my writing there is an insistence on the loss of the mother; in this case, connect the mystical experience of a presence in the night (pre-natal memories). My so-called metaphysical temperament is, perhaps, a disguise for my pre-natal memories of my mother's presence, so what could be more natural than to connect the loss of that presence (the trauma of my birth) with my anti-metaphysical ideas? Hence, perhaps, my feeling of strangerhood.

24th July. Wrote on the deterministic picture of Freeman, then went to Nobe, which was smoky and airless and overcast. Read *From Ritual to*

176

Romance and wondered what I could say about Eliot: attack his mythological vision and the view it expresses of sex, and defend free verse. Read Ira Progoff, especially on Rank, and found a confirmation for something I was trying to express all afternoon: that man is more than his Freudian instincts – he is both instinct and will and his relationship to "culture" too, i.e. he can create society and society can create him.

This fusion of the historicist-Existentialist opposites is very satisfying. Rank on the will to immortality, which is certainly true in my case, though I do feel that my aggressive will in 1959 has become sublimated into art. Rank's view of art, not as a neurosis but as an articulation of experience that everyone has felt vaguely.

On Monday, his lumbago permitting, I shall confront Tuohy with the Rankean "report on experience" and argue against the Wittgensteinian "proposition". Consider also the aim of will according to Rank, higher and higher consciousness, and the concept of the chosen self-image which Rank has salvaged from Freud, e.g: Perhaps I chose (and can therefore unchoose) the mother-image, and perhaps my repetitions are habits which I must unchoose. The relation between will and instinct. The historical nature of all psychology, which is negative. Back to existential psychology.

25th July. A fine afternoon. Met the Gs and the Bs from behind the reassurance of darks and agreed with C that I am too accessible to people like Tony and Adrian and so get used. This led me to wonder, am I imitating my father's unsociability, and is Nan imitating mine – e.g. her flight from the aggressive B—lings. Mrs. B looked like an Earth Mother with some three children or more clinging to various parts of her anatomy as she walked: a mobile family. Reflection: why do not strangers try to get to know me and would they try if they knew I was a poet? Or am I ridiculous and uninteresting to them?

On art. When one has read the report on experience one says "It has expressed what I have felt deeper and better than I could have done it." So with Fitzsimmons (1) what is it? (i.e. the experience); (2) how was it made? (3) So what?

26th-27th July. Zen with Tuohy. In the taxi, on the train, talked about Zen, as a retreat from an on-society (cf the egotistic West); or as an aid to martial skills; as higher hedonism; and as an objectively valuable aid to reflection and problem-solving. Tuohy: "It must be seen historically and socially." (Cf Rank.)

At Kitakamakura, the long wait for Miss Kobayashi, the walk in Tokeiji temple to see the tombs of (my ex-colleague) Blyth and Daisetsu Suzuki. To Engakuji temple, over the railway, much-bitten; no Master Asahina – one of many misunderstandings. A shaven Zen priest, completely genuine, with visions of old Masters sitting under banana-trees amid the mosquitoes achieving satori in two days: he therefore forbad us to wear socks. As a result, a prolonged self-torture in true Tuohyan conditions: sitting outside the meditation-hall, ignoring mosquitoes, beetles, a centipede, then being unable to sleep, and after all this being marched round the temple at dawn and being made to sweep the path near the benjo (the latrines). At times the self-torture became masochistic, with (suppressed) desires to ask for a beating; Tuohy thought it ritualistic rather than a punishment though.

A redeeming feature: the silence at dusk and dawn, the sounds unreal, intruding; the breathing of our lungs and the scraping of cicadas, and all a unity as the shadows moved.

Tuohy's clumsiness: falling in a heap on the floor when the Zen priest prodded his back with the stick, breathing stertorously during meditation, and when everyone had carefully placed their breakfast bowls on the tray, dropping his with a clatter. At night, the sweaty futons (floor-beds) and the light, and Tuohy's groan: "Three hours and then labouring? Oh God." Tuohy and Munekata (my graduate student): the one aggressive and the other watchful. Munekata clearly thought Tuohy spoilt it all by dashing back, as perhaps he had, and Tuohy's aggression was evident on the way down.

Tuohy: "A person is neither good nor bad, so don't judge in fiction."

28th July. This last week or so I have, without really realising it, overcome a crisis. I can see now that the Freudian view of the artist as a neurotic is the idea I should fear most: for acceptance means finishing. And what pressures there are to accept, especially as the old spiritual reality has smashed, leaving me with nothing by which to measure my traditionally heroic task save the community.

Rank is so right about this process of self-doubt through lack of spiritual conviction, and in seeing psychological self-analysis as a narcissistic dead-end of art if it is not related to the heroic and enduring. I have not accepted just because the heroic is denied (e.g. "I cannot live by Freud/There in his mirror/I cannot create/A towering image of man against a void") and I can see now that when I wrote these lines my whole "career" as an artist was at stake. Reading Rank has confirmed that.

Where I am still in danger is in regard to the enduring, the immortal. I am not so sure about this, but I think Rank is right in insisting that something must replace the old spiritual reality for the artist. I have always thought of the replacement as "mandalas", the inner power which exists in all men and which is beyond rational, psychological, personal, subjective concerns. I think Rank means something similar by his "new soul", the irrational dark psychic source, between which and the old spiritual beliefs man stands in transition. My task now is clear, to seek the enduring beyond psychology, to relive the old hero's life. I knew this before my poems (i.e. *The Silence*) began, and my poems are either a regression from or a preparation for this task.

THE IRRATIONAL, THE STONE GARDEN AND WHITE LIGHT (1965)

29th July. An insight into history, through Rank. What I have failed to appreciate is that we are now standing between two eras, between the death of the old animism and rational psychology (you cannot be rational about the irrational) and the birth of a new irrational of some kind, a new Existentialism. The Failed Saint, then, was connected with the old era of the soul; my fascination with writers on the side of the spirit (see October-December 1964) is connected with the new anti-metaphysical, existential "Spiritual" era (i.e. an era that bypasses abstract, rational, speculative metaphysics). The spiritual reactionaries who chose Christianity, e.g. Eliot, who cannot be followed, and the spiritual progressives who will rebuild more according to the idea our age needs most of all, the creative will and development beyond the reason.

So, to simplify somewhat it seems as though art and spirit will not be utterly separated for me, and my poems record a shedding of rational psychology, which is now part, not all, of them both. There will be no new religion, rather a new conception of man and a new attitude to life which concern the spirit.

30th July. Cicadas at Nobe. Like a dentist's drill; like a filling lavatory cistern; like pinball; like clockwork toys.

Poet v bourgeois and what is real.

2nd August. Existentialism is the New Romanticism. It will be based on (1) Individualism and (2) the limitations of Reason, to offset the smugness of science (reaching Mars but not knowing about existence) and because reason is founded on the irrational, e.g. contemplation, emptying self and existing and not knowing why. Two attitudes. Tuohy: "A question which cannot be reduced to reason is not worth thinking about." I: A question which cannot be reduced to rational understanding remains a question, and can be experienced irrationally, and can be important: reason can understand nothing that is important as regards existence.

Hence play down the reason. The reason does not have to ask questions about the meaning of life. The world was content until man came along, and Camus is wrong to expect a rational answer; the existence of his reason is unnecessary. Futility (rational), mystery (irrational). "It exists, there is no why", i.e. one should not look for a meaning the reason can understand.

Accept death and value life and everything which gives it value, as a pleasure. No rational complaint about death (and therefore life). Not darkness-self-darkness, but "I am one of many generations and am unimportant". An experience is real if...?

Psychology is very helpful in social relationships but the analytical conception of man is wrong, it is too static. Our generation can change its image unlike our father's generation because we have destroyed Freud. Our hope in this life.

What I know: death is final, reason can tell me nothing important; I live irrationally. Reason v living.

179

2nd-4th August. Monday-Wednesday. To Gora. The inevitable mess-up over the afternoon lecture: I was told to expect a practical seminar and found a hall full of people and had to give an impromptu lecture for three hours.

The ropeway and the sulphur-springs. The inevitable mess-up when I came to leave; everything prepared save checking the clock; as a result I had to chase the mountain train down to the next station. On the train healed a stammer: a simple technique of three deep breaths and some kind of faith or transference.

5th August. Last night dinner at the Palace after the two hour class, just (Prince) Hitachi, (Princess) Haneko and myself. The Princess came in without my being given any warning and after a few words we swept out into the garden through billowing lace-curtains. I kept ducking under pine boughs and making inappropriate remarks, e.g. "Are those nesting boxes for birds?" "No, they are my ancestors"; and of the golf-net, "Ah, an aviary – what birds are they?" "Tree-sparrows."

After admiring a blue-tailed magpie and having peered in vain for some water plant beneath the lotus I went in to begin a formal five-course Western dinner in a small room along one wall of which stood four ladies-in-waiting; the eldest looking like the Duchess in *Alice in Wonderland*. The Princess's vitality, constantly forgetting her position and remembering it, and the Prince, rather left out of things, trying to assert himself with an "I see". After taking a fish too many and nearly upsetting the pudding-salver I got away to brandy, and left at 9, after five hours of simplified English. On the way out Haneko gave me a pineapple (which, wrapped up, looked like a plant); and apologised for not inviting C. Higashizono (the chief Chamberlain) ended the evening by saying as I walked out of the door "How thoughtless of Their Highnesses not to have invited Mrs. Hagger."

And this morning the Prince was complaining that he wants his State visit to Britain to be informal but that it seems as though it will have to be fairly formal, for it is the Chamberlains' decision.

6th August. Miles said "Have you ever tried putting prose into poetry, breaking it up into stanzas?" and my reply surprised me as it was a sharp rebuke: a poem is more than stanzas, I said, and if it can be written as prose there is no need to write it as a poem; and what distinguishes poetry from prose is the intensity of the poet's vision, which is an entirely alien way of feeling from the prose-writer's, a concentration that could never be written in prose. To achieve this intensity and concentration in the way I want to, it is necessary to *live* the problems of the 20th century: only by *living* these problems will I be able to see them in relation to history and find out who I am, what my relation to society is, and what the meaning or purpose of my existence is.

To Nobe. Saw Tony, then went to drink with Buchanan and Penson.

Penson's Japanese daughter Doris and his "maid" keeping apart from each other. Penson's embarrassment. He therefore got slightly too drunk and talked too much. "Before the war, we had our spies..." and so on. Then he showed me the most important book in his life, a book his father always kept by him and which he found in a Kookaburra Club jumble sale in the 1930s. Ralph Waldo Trine, *In Tune with the Infinite*.* Buchanan. "You've never shown it to me." Penson: "I thought you'd mock me." Buchanan and Penson then speaking strongly about their opposite opinions on religion.
　*May 1973, which is now by my bedside.

7th August. Got windburnt on an empty beach and read on Jung. The theoretical proto-image, which cannot be verified by experience, but which is tremendously attractive as an idea: the acorn's dream of the oak, the Self having an image of a completed, individuated self, and the DNA of Crick. The question is, how much is given at birth and how much can be chosen? Compare Rank's life-will.
　One thing is very true, that man transcends himself by projecting into the future an image of himself and by being drawn towards this image; this is his sense of purpose, this movement towards the image. I would say that the image is chosen: I have chosen to be a writer, and my "shadow" will therefore differ from another's. Jung does not seem to be specific about this, judging from what I have read; he seems to suggest that it is not chosen, that it is biologically inherited like DNA, and is fulfilled when the potential is realised (cf Hesse's self-realisation, i.e. image-realisation), though he does not seem to say exactly what is realised. Hence he talks of "possession by the archetypes", which are independent of thought.
　Whether the proto-image exists and is fulfilled or not, I do not and cannot know; I do know that I am living as though it did, and although I think I have chosen my image and purpose, I cannot be utterly empirical and reject the possibility of their (i.e. image and purpose) being such a proto-image. Rethink your concept of freedom and creative will and see how much is conscious, how much unconscious.

8th August. Recently I have changed my attitude about what I have achieved since I came to Japan. Two months ago I thought I had rejected metaphysics once and for all and had moved closer to John (Ezard), who was wrong to say on my last evening in England "When you come back we'll be out of shouting distance"; 1964 was largely a false year. Now I think I have rejected Christianity and the soul and priests once and for all, but equally as much I have moved away from John's rational psychology, and this was what I was groping for in 1964 from October-December. My insistence that my problems were spiritual then heralds in my present anti-rationalism; and yet I have always been anti-rationalist, e.g. before my marriage, in *Tristy*; and so was expressing my temperament, perhaps.
　Anyhow now the point is that in 1964 I failed to make a distinction that

I have now made and now see the nun's eyes within the context of the post-Freudian conception of man. So that the theme of the poem (i.e. *The Silence*) must be my progressive anti-rationalism, by which I mean stressing that however useful the reason is in social problems or in solving problems, it is basically very limited and its place in the universe is not so very important, especially as it is an intruder.

On reflection, my "misunderstanding" on 2nd June 1965 was based on the question of whether or not there is a point in the universe, not how important a place reason has in the universe. I am anti any superficial rationally understandable purpose, but affirm that there are sub-rational/irrational experiences which seem to contain truth. My schismed soul: rational protest and irrational affirmation. (Cf 2ndAugust 1965.)

9th August. Let me try to place my view of reason in its context. I conceive of the brain as being a finite organ in which, at different layers, thoughts circulate. At the front and the top is reason. At the back and at the bottom, possibly, putting it very crudely, are thoughts that the "I" of the front-top is not aware of. The thing can function as a whole or in parts, in thoughts or in images or in both. Now the reason is inclined to think itself superior to all the parts of the brain. Out of pride it dismisses questions it cannot understand.

In contemplation, when the "I" has emptied itself of reason, one can understand that reason is founded on a silence and that the silence beneath is fertile, and that the questions the reason so glibly dismisses assume feelings of awe. Who is this I, floating on the silence? Who am I, who cannot explain or even understand why I am? Such are the rational equivalents of the question. When one confronts one's existence, one's reason is speechless with incomprehension. When one confronts the silent ground of the reason, the depths beneath the reason, in objective scientific terms the bottom-back, one's reason is speechless with incomprehension. One realises the blindness of the reason: how proudly it believes itself supreme, yet how it deceives itself.

The point is not that the silent depths can take one to the meaning of one's life, though I am not saying they cannot; nor that they can answer problems the reason cannot answer, though I am not saying they cannot; but rather that they are fertile, they can nourish, and one's conception of man must take account of their healing, life-giving properties. (Cf Adrian: "You mean it's a higher pleasure.") Reason and science and meaning – rethink.

10th August. A hard morning's writing: rewrote two poems, neither of which I had finished, one on the temptation and the other on the prophecy. When I finished I was pouring with sweat. Changed and took a taxi, with C and Nan, to Tokyo station. New Tokaido train to Kyoto. Met 5.30 p.m. by Mr Ukeda, Bank of Japan rep, and an air-conditioned car; were taken to the Yoshikawa Inn, where we dined in our air-conditioned room, Nan in her yukata.

THE IRRATIONAL, THE STONE GARDEN AND WHITE LIGHT (1965)

Every morning Nan gets up and sits by my side until I wake. She cannot sleep unless she has her ritual ribbon. She likes to sit in my swivel chair, put my glasses on, read the paper; she prefers trains to dolls. Her conception of "yoi yoi" (work) must be affected by what she knows, i.e. she can have no idea that I teach and must think that when I go out in a car it is to the sea.

11th August. Kyoto and Nara. A pampered day when I lived at a low level of intensity, a horribly complacent day of living through a Governor's mind. Left the air-conditioned hotel for the air-conditioned car at 8.30.

Drove to Nara. Got out to see the Todaiji Big Buddha and the Kasuga deer. Classic misunderstandings: "Can we go round here?" Ukeda: "In spring and autumn." Again, "Is this slat-style peculiar to Kyoto?" "A saké district." Drove back. Thoughts on images: the antlers in the Essex stream, suggesting the effigy of Adonis; the ishidori ("stone torch-basket" or lantern found in Japanese gardens) with candles, like human beings; the old crumbling wall, my excitement at the burnt gates. I, the poet of the self, working through opposites and intensity. Lunch at the Kyoto Hotel.

In the afternoon, to the 1,000 statues (Sanjusangendo Temple): they stood, with spoked suns behind their heads, in 5 or 6 tiers, silent, like a football crowd in a grandstand of the subconscious, and I felt the discomfort I felt among the silent dummies in Seibus (department store). After visited three gardens (Kyomizu, Katsura Imperial Villa and Heian shrine). The turtles. The Japanese lack of spontaneity: "In spring we gather together to admire the cherry blossoms and in the autumn the maples here." From the air-conditioned car to the air-conditioned hotel-room through manifestations of respect that were unreal.

12th August. Kyoto. Mr Ukeda was replaced by Mr Fukuzawa, a homberg-wearing, greying middle-aged man with a lot of hair and a loose mournful skin that creased easily into a smile; unlike fat, willing but slow Ukeda. Saw three gardens (Nijo, Kinkakuji, Ryoanji) and Arashiyama.

Was most impressed by my second visit to Ryoanji. I thought I saw what Soami was after: he was trying to express satori as a symbol, the point being that whether the stones are sea, clouds or earth, everything is one, and is of the same nature as the mountains or rocks, or whatever appears to be different; and that the borders around existence, the frame round the symbol, are quite arbitrary – the unity could equally as well continue indefinitely. Of course one's reaction is entirely subjective, but I felt my reaction was more than subjective.

Left for home at 2.22, arrived 6.00.

Later my dream. I entered a cross-country race without any training, just to prove that the will could do anything, and the record showed I came first by the fantastic margin of 15 minutes. I had no recollection of this, but knew only by the record.

C on my piercing eyes. A tall, gaunt, stooping hollow-cheeked man with piercing eyes – is that how others see me and how I cannot see myself?

13th August. Tried to write the nun's eyes passage, but couldn't. Felt drained by laziness, too slack.

As regards Freud, I must acknowledge that much of his work on the nature of the imagination and of symbolism is valid; what I object to is his static view of man, his rationalism, and his view of art, which can be overcome by grading levels of fantasy: the artist leaves one reality for a qualitatively more rewarding reality. Eliot: The great poet "out of intense and personal experience is able to express a general truth: retaining all the particularity of his experience to make it a general symbol."

The German Erlebneisdichtung and D. H. Lawrence. The inner war between the irrational and the analytical, with the analytical destroying itself in its quest to be certain.

The violent storm with two hours of blue lightning, now forked, now like lights being turned on and off by an impish and malevolent Being. My primitive fear.

14th August. To Nobe. Began reading for my 5,000 word article on Eliot. Hough's thesis that the Modernist movement lacked a central purpose, not being a spiritual movement like the Romantic movement: hence the confusions of Hulme, the stress on technique and sensibility (Pound and Woolf). It was "symbolism without the magic" and should be regarded as a diversion leading back to the main road. Compare Kermode's thesis, that the Modernist movement was a continuation and completion (?) of the Romantic movement via the French symbolists and the 1890s. Compare Spender, that it was a reaction against the Romantics but paradoxically acquired the subjective view of the imagination of the Romantics. Compare Conquest: an Anglo-American invasion and we should go back to the 18th century. Eliot: "When (a poet) theorizes about poetic creation, he is likely to be generalizing one type of experience." Is there a great incompatability between experience and the image, between the Romantics and the Moderns? If there is, Hough defeats Kermode. M. H. Abrams in his review of Kermode: "The central tradition of poetics... looked upon poetry not as verbal structure nor... as an image composed of images, but as a verbal representation... of thinking, feeling and acting human beings." Images to have their place in this. So I have generalised my kind of experience.

15th August. I have been undergoing some kind of a centre-shift. This has been taking place on and off for the last eight years, so there is nothing on the face of it to be surprised about: I am always discovering the irrational and losing it again. (One of the reasons why a fixed symbol like Christ is so useful: it is there as a constant reminder.)

Yet this time things seem different. I can feel the irrational all round my reason; it is a fact, something I can be aware of half a dozen times a day.

THE IRRATIONAL, THE STONE GARDEN AND WHITE LIGHT (1965)

Never before have I *felt* the reason to be so limited, so small, so unreal. Never before have rational abstractions seemed more pointless and artificial. When I think I catch myself feeling after a time, "all this stuff I am spinning means nothing really, it's irrelevant." So I have a horror (as I always have) of writing articles. They are impure in comparison with what I really want to write, which is like gleaming diamonds in a dark mine.

So too I feel that Freud's view of things is not quite true. What is below reason is not full of horrors necessarily; and although normality may be a medical ideal for a sick person, it is no ideal for a healthy person who can develop his whole being, both irrational and analytical.

16th August. Three hours with the Prince, then corrected a MS, then received Sakuraba for tea, then made a list of wines for the Prince, then fiddled at my Eliot article, wishing that I could write what I really want to write and not what decorum requires me to write, until I felt too sleepy to do any more. In short a day of inessentials away from my poems, away from my self. Two reflections: I rebelled against the outer form and sought the inner reality; and a good, but probably stale, image for the poet is that of a tree shedding leaves (cf an orange tree).

17th August. All day another poem grew in me, about the enfolding of the irrational in which the reason is a bulb. The stone lanterns. Reinterpreted the past. I rebelled against the outer form and sought the inner real.

I need images, desperately. They come to me, I drag them up like old car-bumpers, rusty and dripping, and all disconnected: incoherent images which I must cohere: roots and branches of a jagged forest, like the inside of a brain; a skull growing out of the Sciathos tomb; a buoy on the sea; a lotus on the pond; the four-sided clock of Lopping Hall (Loughton); the mesh of the streetcar wires and I, with clawed fingers, shaking my cage to get out. They come to me, but they are all the wrong images; they cannot catch what I want caught – want caught badly because I cannot catch it with my intellect (i.e. reason).

(Stuart) Holroyd's centre: resting in God.

18th August. At the Bank of Japan after a long talk with Fukuchi about Toynbee's "spiritual power", and connecting the new view of man hinted at in modern biology and psychology, talked with Tsuchigane about the Stone Garden.

It is a symbol, a kind of koan. It is also a kind of mirror: you see in it what you want to see – what you see tells you about yourself; the garden of subjectivity. Yet there is an objective message for the profound. The rocks seem permanent amid the flux of pebbles, yet pebble and rock are of the same material and are essentially no different; no matter what the pebbles symbolise – clouds, sea, earth – it is the indivisible unit of everything that they are: rock today, pebble tomorrow – everything is changeable, yet

185

everything is the same, and all Nature is one. To feel this with one's body-centre as opposed to one's reason, to abandon oneself to Nature and the atmosphere amid unreal forms which are a part of One with oneself, so that one might be living or dead equally as well, that is satori. The unity of all objects and life, the illusory nature of diversity and permanence in the outer world – those are the truths of the Stone Garden.

Combine with Toynbee: the illusory nature of all progress, disintegration awaiting the society for which the compassionate Leftists are fighting and should fight for. The centre of the mosaic is Unity.

19th August. Wrote on the nun in the morning and then went to Nobe.

Derivative images concerned me. I wanted an image to express the idea of two opposites, eternally at war, being kept apart yet held together by a centre, but what I found was inappropriate, e.g. the wheel; an axle and two wheels; a sector in a circle, orbiting moons; a man and his shadow; two mountaineers roped together; the well and wheel and two buckets; in balance, a see-saw; the winch on the beach with its turning shaft, and the bent backs on the winch-pole as they toiled in a circle, round and round, three of them. Also a Janus. The opposites of blind rational Professor and visionary Saint, and of C and myself (cf nothing v affirmation, male v female), for knowing the value of the irrational to my art, I projected my irrational out onto C, who is a constant reminder, like my cross; this interpretation I prefer to the mother-one, and is the answer to my "anti-intellectuality" (i.e. anti-rationality).

The centre of my marriage is perhaps the image I am seeking, i.e. the child, Nan, who holds together and keeps apart. Relate child and wheel, for I suspect it will have to be a geometric ideograph in the end. Three images of the Self: the four-sided clock-face of Lopping Hall (Loughton), fixed and continuous; the white orb of the sun in the station puddle; and the central Kannon (or Kwannon) among her 1,000 selves, each with sun-rays/spoked wheel behind their heads. Cf grass on head, instead of hair.

20th August. Last night got drunk at Buchanan's on two-thirds of a bottle of Scotch; slept only five hours in consequence and did not take a midnight swim.

Returned home in the afternoon because a typhoon is approaching; in the hot time of waiting for rain under a sultry sky, sounds travel, jets echo.

21st August. The subjective vision – that everything is evocative to the Self, that natural and artificial surroundings symbolise the deep patterns of the spirit. Of course, it is egotism. And I am egotistic in two ways: in feeling that what I have found in myself is valuable to others, valuable enough to communicate, and in my tendency to value my spiritual autobiography higher than, e.g. C's wishes. This is doubtless a fault, this egotism, but at present it is the only possible condition for me, for I believe that only by knowing myself can I know others and respond to others in the deepest possible way. Altruism begins the other side of self-knowledge, if it is the saint's altruism rather than the ordinary good-hearted kindness of the simple mind. The complete loving the incomplete – that is how I envisage the modern saint's love; and the incomplete will always say that such love is "pleased" or "complacent".

As to what I feel for others, sometimes I am overwhelmed by rushes of feeling with individuals – generally when I am ultra-aware and intense or when I know I am being kind or cruel – and I am sometimes overwhelmed by feeling for groups, e.g. beggars, bus-queues on a hot, oppressive evening and so on, but generally my feelings are controlled. This does not mean that I am cold, rather that I have the condition of all quality of feeling: a mature hierarchy that scorns the cheaper feelings.

22nd August. Worked on my Eliot article, as yesterday, while the typhoon approached, and saw myself in the context of Romantic and rational traditions.

The Romantic tradition à la Kermode stresses the image and revelation and organic form; the rational tradition à la (Yvor) Winters stresses statement and moral discourse and mechanistic architecture. And I am half-way between the two. Naturally a Romantic, I was pushed through a rational education, and the influence of (Christopher) Ricks, for example, stuck to a certain extent. I told him I was interested in "mystical" poetry at our first meeting, and his reply was "I must get you interested in social satire." I think I incline more to the Romantic and the Modernist, although I write in situations: certainly I stress the image and organic form.

Hence my instinctive opposition to Tuohy, whose view of art as a proposition is in the Winters tradition; in fact a month ago he said I should read Winters again. Tuohy is pre-eminently a rationalist, and his attitudes to art are rationalist. Significantly he is a protegé of Snow's.

As regards Eliot, I think anyone in the Winters camp will have mixed feelings about Eliot, whereas anyone in the Kermode camp – e.g. Read – will defend Eliot; Leavis is also in this camp. My self-division between rational and irrational/Romantic reflects itself in every way, even in my critical attitudes, and the balance is always in favour of the Romantic.

9 p.m. typhoon coming right overhead.

23rd August. The feeble typhoon after extensive preparations. Worked in an enervating heat on my article, until Tuohy came. Drank, talking about Zen and the reason why the Russians have things to say and the Irish do not (i.e. Yeats, Joyce, Tuohy) and then went and ate at the Indonesian restaurant. Tuohy: "I don't know which are Indonesians, all wogs look the same." After went to a Polish film *Repulsion*, a subjective study of a psychotic with dementia praecox.

Tuohy's strange agreement when I attacked the reason afterwards, saying the abyss which the reason suddenly sees is a real state of mind, and that most English people are unreal in feeling falsely "secure"; and that the illuminations of Wordsworth and Eliot were worth a hundred articles. Tuohy wants to go into Zen to observe further the limitations of his reason.

On the image; what is the difference between Yeats's beast and Pound's "petals on a wet black bough"? One is a symbol, the other a metaphor. Tuohy: "Yeats uses a rose in a different way from Eliot." I: "But it is the method I am talking about, not individual meaning."

24th August. Fiddled around on my essay, after going to the Prince for three hours. Apart from the heat (mid 90s) the main trouble is that I have not got an argument and cannot really get one for Eliot's technical side. What I want to say is that those who accuse Eliot of being a bad influence belong to a different and hostile critical tradition based on the reason, and that Eliot's technical innovations are effective in fulfilling his intentions as regards the states of mind he is trying to express, and that the Image is no less valid a method than statement today and can be used to reveal not another world nor the surface of things (Imagist positivism) but the abyss, the human condition, human beings trapped in history and so on. This would mean writing about critics, Eliot's intentions and my use of the Image. One point I must think carefully about: what are the illuminations illuminations of? "Unknown modes of being"? The insecurity of the reason in the world, the wholeness of the self, the finality of death – what do these add up to? What am I trying to reveal through the Image?

25th August. I must find an image for the relationship between the reason and the irrational – something more than the child, something heraldic which will serve as the cross serves, as a permanent reminder, something that will not grow up.

26th August. Wrote, or rather tried to write, on the centre until it was time to go to the Bank of Japan.

27th August. Buchanan; his war-history, his part in the capture of Hess ("Please sir, I think we've got the Fuhrer's number 2") and his night-entry into Tunis (like T. E. Lawrence into Deraa) for which he was not given the MC.

With a copy of Yeats's letters to Lady Wellesley on the table he talked of his meeting with the Duke of Wellesley, security chief during the war. I brought up Marlowe some time later, but we only discussed the whereabouts of Deptford. The Takara beer – 4 bottles and you get a free glass – and the pile of *Playboys*; the 3 line association poems, obscene ones unashamedly on the front of the pad. The way to tell that fish are fresh: they should be firm to the touch and have fresh eyeballs.

THE IRRATIONAL, THE STONE GARDEN AND WHITE LIGHT (1965)

28th August. Returned to Tokyo. Thought about the image. Different kinds of image: (1) the snapshot – a particular object that exists by itself without the need for meaning, e.g. "petals on a wet black bough"; (2) a metaphor/figure of speech; (3) an object which is particular but which represents something particular. This additional meaning if simple (e.g. Fräulein von Kulp = decay) can refer to an image, but if inexpressible – if representing itself or something general – can make it a symbol. Reflect on this: an image is an object which represents another particular; a symbol is an object which represents another general. So the difference between image and symbol is the difference between particular and general. Reflect on the relation between the symbol and magic and on Pound's definition, "an intellectual and emotional complex"; and on the part that opposites play, cf Johnson's "heterogeneous ideas".

A line should ring like a coin.

29th August. Wrote part of my essay. Then took C to see *Lawrence of Arabia* at the Korakuen Cinema. The appalling changes of the story: Tafas was not killed; Nasir was the real Lawrence's friend, not Ali; Gasin got left behind and Hamed the Moor was executed – in the film these were combined; Akaba fell without a fight, by negotiation; Daud died of the cold off stage, not in a quagmire, and anyway eight crossed Sinai, not three; Faraj was hit by a bullet and not blown up by dynamite; Feisal was hot-tempered, not cool and he wore white, not black; Allenby's hobby was ornithology, not fish; Lawrence asked Allenby if he could leave Damascus and Allenby opposed his going – Allenby certainly was not as ruthless as in the film; the counting of the corpses and the midnight sermon were both missed completely and the old man in the Damascus hospital who murmured "Aman, aman" was not shown. And one could go on endlessly in this vein. It would have been better to have renamed the character and to have used the word Lawrence figuratively. Afterwards looked in on baseball, and saw the Whales beat the Giants 12-4.

30th August. Wrote 2,000 words.

31st August. Wrote my article and defined my literary situation. I am now anti-realist. I assert: that poetry should be intense, compressed, concentrated; that the business of the symbol/image is to reveal the irrational mystery of life, the purpose and meaning of existence – in short to strive for the illumination like the illumination on the lake or in the rose-garden; and that the abstract should always be presented in a concrete way – that one definition of the image is "a particular object representing something else which is general and universal".

On the subject of personality or impersonality, it does not matter which the poet uses so long as the result is universal. I cite Eliot: "The second impersonality is that of the poet who, out of intense and personal experience,

189

is able to express a general truth: retaining all the particularity of his experience, to make of it a general symbol."

I further assert: of all the experiments and so on in the 20th century, the most rewarding one for me is Eliot's device of emotional sequence; structure to be taken not from mythology, but from the novel – the scheme of relevance being, as for a novel, "Do the situations relate to the whole and the theme?"

1st September. Lunch with Tuohy, in the place of someone else. The talk was mainly about the image and symbol, the distinction being a question of degree. On Eliot, Tuohy: "He had emotions no one wants to know about and Fräulein von Kulp is like name-dropping." I: "He had the emotions of an outsider, of an isolated exile. When he sat on Margate Sands among the English, he felt as I do sitting on Nobe beach among the Japanese."

I, on my self-division: "This division between reason and the irrational, it goes through history, it goes through England today – analysis and intuition, logical positivism and Existentialism, and goes right through me. Ivan and Alyosha. I am going to stop writing articles, intellectual (i.e. rational) words are unclean."

Tuohy on form. "It is physiological. A sonnet is a belch and a gulp." I on Winters, "I shall define a poem as an orgasm and exclude Winters' theory." I on my view of art: "Art makes us see old things in new ways, and if distortion can do that, then it is valuable." I argued that subject matter was more important than form, that if a subject takes only 11 lines, to pad another 3 to make it a sonnet is utterly wrong.

Earlier, heard that the British Council will finance me to stay another year.

Tuohy on my position in the palace: "You are like a psychiatrist, you are the court fool."

2nd September. From last night. Tomlin's cocktail party for the IAU British delegates: 18 mathematicians and zoologists. Narita, Irie, Kuriyagawa, Oshima and the Keio P.E.N. secretary. The Toshi Centre where it took place. Oh, and Nishiwaki's dual insult, turning away from both Tuohy and myself at different times.

Later, dinner with Tuohy in Shinjuku. Nagasaki/Dutch things on the wall; sticks and fried fish and onions and chicken. Talk on journalism, I saying it was no good to an artist, he saying it could be a substitute art. Then he said that poetry and argument were both a game, and when I strongly disagreed brought out his age. His drunken logic: in poetry and games you talk about the past, therefore poetry is a game.

Later, drinking in my house, he admitted to being dead because he had no desire to make a pattern of his past. "It's all compost from childhood." A lot of talk about the writer's importance to yet neglect by society – raised by me; "they should bow down." Tuohy on his severe face, and his assumed indifference of everyone to him, a kind of independence. He was very drunk when he left: dropped his pencil in the lavatory by mistake and kept stopping on the way down to Edogawa Bridge to deliver reflective harangues about this and that.

3rd September. From yesterday. The Bank of Japan's "agreement" to pay my return fare (for a visit to Britain). Buchanan's surprise and pleasure when I told him in Nobe, his dissuasion when I said I should become a PA (personal assistant); his citing of Donne, Marvell and others who did what I do for the Bank of Japan and Hitachi, in their own ways. C's love of order, and her terror when she woke at dawn and thought I had died.

The harvesting of the rice. A pole, sheaves on either side strung together at the top, ears down. Tunnels. The revolving drum to separate the rice from the stalks. The straw hat of stalks. On the beach the shoal of dead sharks, baby ones, and the furry-legged hermit crabs.

4th September. Yeats's words, "Man can embody truth, but he cannot know it" – these are central to my idea of a poem. A poem embodies truth, i.e. a poem is a symbol, like man's life. It is also an image of man's journey and of the author, and if done with Pound's complexity, a moveable image, for different parts of the poem interrelate and mean different things in different lights. Life and work can be an image or a symbol, composed of images, and the truth revealed is like the wind, invisible but present. One complex, changing moving image, which, when it represents something, becomes a symbol. N.B. A poem cannot be an image of itself.

Does the poet begin with image and then proceed to a theme? Is a poet who omits the "theme" therefore omitting organisation? C. Day Lewis believes he is, but I think a poet can have a number of images on a theme without poetic reason connecting them. Also, the question of being and meaning: "What is the meaning of the picture?"

The verse I want to write is "spoudaiotic" verse: intense, compressed verse.

5th September. To Sanseido. Got C. Day Lewis.

6th-8th September. Article.

9th September. *Encounter* came with a story by Tuohy: *A Special Relationship*. A typical Tuohy story: everything a drag and a failure, it all being hell, the prose fagged out so that you can almost hear the grunts and the sighs. The patient whose wife is an old bag, the play with a hero whose first line mentions the menopause, the nurse who was married – they are types. "People don't change much." This is Tuohy's strength and weakness. He gets across the general, but it is not very particular. Two good uses of "theatre" and "gone", with their ambiguities.

191

10th September. Typhoon Shirley crossed Japan. We got a wing. Wrote my article. Thoughts on narrative. Can emotional sequence be combined with narrative? i.e. Have ordinary narrative by compression. I don't see why not.

11th September. Worked on the article. Late at night, insomniac, I looked in on my inner life. Suspending reason I saw first of all scrivenings, like Arabic or Hebrew, in yellow and blue. Then the images began to rise. First a puddle and an orb of fire in it. The puddle turned into the smooth swell of an ocean. Then, very vividly, some four or five green cornstalks with many ears: so vivid was this that I thrilled when I saw it. Next some husks and weird cacti. Then a whirlpool; spinning waters and the central suction. Then I was going down a well and I could see the white orb of the sky getting smaller and smaller as I descended deeper and deeper. The images stopped there, because I turned over in bed: they might otherwise have continued. If it were not for my article I would write a poem interpreting them in images of rebirth and spiritual descent. I would then have to underline the potentialities of the irrational; I often see the most fantastically surreal images just before sleeping (circles with heads in them and stark dusks) but forget most of them before I can record them. I must now start listening in regularly, waiting patiently regularly, and get a hood to shut out the daylight.

12th September. Continued section 3 (of the article) and went to the bookshops. Bought Davie on Pound. So Rémy de Gourmont is behind the entire Modernist movement. His theory of Impersonality (1902) Eliot took over in *Tradition and the Individual Talent* and his realistic theory of the images as a scrupulously scientific observed object Pound took over. I must confess, I am in many ways more attracted by Pound's version than Eliot's: the "imaged experience" is halfway between the two, but it is nearer Pound than Eliot. Eliot is purely subjective; Pound is objective.

The festival at the shrine on the hill. Barrows with candy floss, tiddlers in tanks, windmills and balloons on sticks, lanterns, music. Clanging for the God. It all seemed like a Methodist bazaar, only it was Shinto.

13th September. A wearisome day spent toiling through IMF speeches and going through them with Tsuchigane in the evening. Prince for two and a half hours in the afternoon. (The workers' demonstration the other side of the high wall.)

Late at night, more images. Gold heads, a sequence of them drawn past my closed eyes as if they were on a conveyor belt. Some were Egyptian, some Negroid, some Babylonian. Animal heads of gold as well as human heads. After that the most incredibly intricate diamond patterns round egg-like diamonds, and exquisite patterns in green and mauve. The powerlessness of my reason: I remember thinking, "I want to see red patterns", but there was no change, and as much as 30 seconds later they were still mauve and green. Both the heads and the diamond presumably symbolise the Self.

An illustration to prove what I always contend with Tuohy, that we recall quotations by the situations they refer to: I sighed loudly, and then murmured, "Sighs were exhaled."

14th September. My dream. The violent earthquake while I sat in a 2nd floor Turkish-Byzantine cafe. I was alone, Tuohy having gone downstairs with C and Nan (and having paid £16 for lunch); the falling masonry as I dashed down the stairs and out into the courtyard. All Tokyo was in ruins: all foundations crumbled. Later with Ricky and others, I went into a large room with white futons on the floor in rows. Only when I was about to lie down on one (and saw) it had a corpse under veils did I realise that I was in a morgue. This did not disturb me. I sat down on a vacant bier and then all the corpses sat up and began to shake and jingle in a communal dance, rattling their bones. The dead looked peaceful, and their clumsy dance was undignified; I wished they would stop. Ruin and the dance.

15th September. Article, then the Prince. His torpor, my torpor in the heavy atmosphere. The crackle of the lightning between us and the weight that seemed to drop on bare boards above.

16th September. Worked until 4 a.m. on the article, cutting out parts which were new to me when I wrote them but which I now take for granted, toiling up to the summit. A definition of self-surmounting. Awoke at 8 a.m. and did the same until 1 p.m. Then went to the Bank of Japan and after two hours teaching toiled from 4 p.m. to 8 p.m. on the Governor's IMF speech. The nationalism; the sentence they would not modify because it had been carefully approved by some 10 people: "We will achieve stable growth, and we will raise the standard of living in Asia, for it is our responsibility." Returned home, dined, prepared for my lectures, attended to C's depression, thought the implications of the distinction between emotion and feeling – the distinction between the transient and the more permanent – and dropped, hollow, into bed. A day of grinding reality and growing exhaustion.

I am the Bank's scapegoat. I am the last to see any speech or letter of importance, and the entire foreign department is therefore touching me, getting rid of its responsibility. I am the bearer of others' responsibility. My three roles are: Bank scapegoat; court fool; and university status symbol.

17th September. To the Tokyo University of Education at the crack of dawn, through torrential rain. Too tired to teach only 10 at the first lecture, so cancelled the lecture on the grounds of the typhoon. Dozed until 10.30. Taught until 2.30, lunch-time being given to sprightly Narita and Toyama, who was clearly offended by my silence throughout the vacation. Returned home. 3-5.30, more refining of the Governor's speech and two recordings at different speeds. Putting in the accents. Typhoon Trix, the second largest since the war, is approaching, and I am too weary to think of anything other than the most vacant and moronic things. My mind is now the mind of an average English banker.

18th September. Any recreational arrangement is an attempt to escape one's loneliness – of the question as to whether we should ask anyone to accompany us to the British Trade Fair. The three halls out of a possible ten. Atomic patterns of the girders of the ceiling. Many cars and machines, a decently presented exhibition of British history with one or two inaccuracies.

Nietzsche's syphilis; Nijinsky's inherited syphilis; van Gogh's nervous irritability and inherited syphilis.

19th September. Exhausted. Wrote in the morning, hunted for pearls in the afternoon, then went to dinner with Tuohy to inspect his "baroque" ("flawed") pearls, which, incidentally, he lent C for Wednesday. Tuohy's careful preparation of paté, which must have taken a long time to cook, and his wine cupboard. His anxiety to refer to sex, e.g. "it's a lamp you make love by". On writers: Logue, Desmond Stewart. His observation of us: leaving us alone to listen in and so on. The conversation was mainly about how to communicate the irrational, he arguing that the elusive could only be communicated emotively and that he was a rationalist because he believed in organisation (I: you can organise without being a rationalist); and about the will, I saying that you have to make a vow and then get on and do it.

20th September. A wearying day. Considered T. E. Lawrence's character at the Tokyo University of Education, argued that his "personal" motive for involving himself in the Arab revolt was desire for fame and self-expression, and that one reason for his "mind-suicide" and entry into the RAF was his feeling of guilt about this motive, this being connected with his feeling that he had defrauded the Arabs; another reason of course being his "longings for a master" which he failed to satisfy in Allenby. The main thing about Lawrence, though, was his contempt for the body, which he either denied masochistically or degraded. It was completely subjugated by his will – was a part of his will as will and body were not antithetical to him. (Colin) Wilson's theory that the Outsider is the embryonic prophet who begins with a negative message founded on disgust at spiritual laxity. Withdrawal into the desert and return should have turned Lawrence into a prophet. It didn't because he could not locate the self he liked.

Debunked C. Day Lewis's "image first, order second" idea, arguing that Eliot got the title before each fragment. The Prince's visit is "semi-formal", and he will be the guest of the English government.

21st September. Wrote another page, then double Keio, then went to the British Council to interview for my class.

22nd September. Went to the Prince. He is going to England as the guest of England. Then returned, changed and went with C and Tuohy to a large reception for Princess Alexandra and Ogilvy. A very long room, a table with an ice-lion in the centre, band at the far end, sailors lining the approach. Saw (Prime Minister) Sato, met Kosaka. Avoided hundreds of British businessmen. Met Tuohy's cousin, Mrs. Barron, whose husband earns £50,000 a year. While I looked for the Vice-Governor, Tuohy got to work on C for the pearl-buying expedition next week…, suggesting a visit (with Mrs. Barron) to a print-shop.

23rd September. A holiday I was too tired to take advantage of. Ideas for paintings. The world seen subjectively through feverish eyes like van Gogh's, with houses in the air; my Christ stumbling from the Cathedral porch, his emotion communicated through his actions.

Tuohy as the arch-insider: pretending to be disinterested in domesticity but going on shopping expeditions to Kinokuniya, being the "ideal man-shopper" according to his cousin; making his own paté and (unless the newsprint has lied) even being photographed eating at the British Food Exhibition.

24th September. Woken at 3 a.m. by the dog, and tossed for a further three hours. Got up at 7.15, went to the Tokyo University of Education. No Buchanan, who had cut his thumb. Consequently I could not open my large bottle of beer, to drink all of which, alone, would have left me with a very unclear head. Got through my classes, then went with C to the bookshops. Returned after dark, and was too weary to do more than sink into the couch and watch Elizabeth Taylor pass herself off as a cultural intellectual whose sex-image is false.

25th September. Worn out. Tried to return to my article. Wrote letters. Then went to see *Zorba the Greek*. Kazantzakis, the scholar and writer of a book on Buddha, was shown as a gormless Englishman who could not have written a letter.

26th September. Took Nan to the zoo. Began typing.

General points left over from the article: Why write in images at all? Is it a physiological thing (lack of alpha rhythms) or, as with C. Day Lewis, a condition of creation, or, as with Pound, a point of technique, or all? What does an image reveal? i.e. Is it purely a matter of technique? I do not think so. I think it reveals something that cannot be expressed as a statement: you cannot state a journey, you can only say "The journey is valuable" and expect agreement or disagreement. An "image of truth" – that is what the image is an image of, truth about living as the artist sees it, in all its complexity. An artist is saying "This is the truth" in an image-poem, and the reader can agree with the truth or disagree from the image of it.

27th September. Cf August 31st. I assert:

1. All experiments depend on the intractability of the subject matter and on the poet's aims.
2. Subject matter should be concerned with the untrivial aim of "seeking a pattern and purpose in self and contemporary history and the universe".
3. The best way of recreating such a pattern is abbreviated narrative structure, with emotional linking between intense moments.
4. The best way of revealing pattern and relationship is through the image, using the "imaged experience".
5. Verse should be libéré – free, loosening and tightening across the invisible norm.
6. Rhythms should not interfere.
7. Fugal interweavings can convey pattern.
8. The essence of communication is generalisation.

An image for abbreviated narrative: a necklace, a rosary. "A story told bead by bead." "A story told through a set of coloured beads."

29th September. Article nearly finished. Looked at my poems and saw that they should be one poem: abbreviated narrative in emotionally linked imaged experiences. One poem in 5 parts with the lines numbered, eliminating everything that is not generalised. The poem is a "seen meditation", but what is it an image of? Not just of a journey, but of a growing up, a striving for command over experience, a self-transcendence. "An existential or spiritual quest."

An elusive experience on my way to the Prince's. Six cars abreast of each other, the drivers sitting impassively, heat radiating upwards, and I suddenly thought we were queuing for entry into Hell.

30th September. Finished the article. I have written no poems since August 19th (except for one session on August 26th), exactly six weeks ago. I feel worn out but triumphant, for I have vindicated my position six weeks ago, have succeeded in combining the image-poem with experience. The article means nothing to me now, for I have outgrown it. It records a self-surpassal, and looking down on it from a superior height I see what is wrong with it, although while I was writing it and striving for clarity, it meant a great deal. My present knowledge/vindication, the uselessness of the article: compare all art – the struggle of the artist and then his indifference to his creation because it is behind him, he has surpassed himself and is moving forward.

Art is a means to self-surpassal, which can only be measured by expression.

1st October. At the Tokyo University of Education, a visit to the officials to discuss the building of a room for Nan. The large room, many desks, a

196

sofa backed by an olive steel cabinet. The plans and slide-rules and the Japanese concept of the gentleman, "How gentle the Professor is, he could not be an American." Afterwards in the exam: the four palm trees, ringed and sealed in their trunks, swelling out into prepuces like cotton-wool ear-cleaners, and then joyously sprouting with palm-fans. The hot summer and my fragmentation are over and energy is returning to the baked land.

After took C to Maruzen. The exhibition of British books and above, a portrait gallery of the literary immortals, beginning with Chaucer and ending with: Tuohy. A large, younger Tuohy. My vow: "There is a vacancy among the immortals, go out and occupy it."

2nd October. In the afternoon (after seeing Patterson) to the Cathedral. The restful choral music, the priest's boots under the red curtain of the confessional and the hesitations of the fat woman with the white veil. The atmosphere of the eternal. Self-expression. I have this energy and express it in art; I have this intimation of the eternal which the particular embodies and symbolises but I cannot express it, for I have no form through which I can give it expression. Symbols which trap the eternal and make expression of it possible.

3rd October. Reflections on Japan. I like the East, I prefer it to the West which is always in a hurry, getting and spending. Perhaps it is because, like Tuohy and Buchanan, I am to some extent physically lazy, although I can drive myself when I want to. I am not afraid of the slow-moving seediness that overtakes most people who have been too long in the East. The East has got into my soul but I find it very difficult to define exactly what is in my soul. Perhaps it is the gentleness and the sensitivity; perhaps it is the secret, almost instinctive feeling that one is in the presence of a long tradition of wisdom that has somehow shaped those one meets, a tradition of contemplation and meditation that is quite alien to the West, a tradition that is something of a paradox as the East is in many ways more materialistic than the West.

The ceremony is founded on inner aloneness and strength, and marks a "coming out" of solitude.

4th October. Two posts, and two aching cries from the past: a colour photograph of the pond on the brow of Robin Hood Lane, which, together with the neighbouring pond, is the geographical centre of my memories; and a grave, grey and black reproduction of a painting in Warsaw from Ricky, who is now in Warsaw.

5th October. Premonitions of assassination. C's dream that I had died, my preoccupation with death before breakfast and afterwards. Unfounded, in spite of the fact that I gave 165 students at Keio their grades. Afterwards I went with Ando to a small and dirty café near Keio. His Englishness:

ostentatious sports jacket, refusing beer because there was no Guinness.

At which point Nishiwaki came in with a graduate student. I had not seen him since (see 2nd September) he cut both Tuohy and me, and at first I thought he was going to insult me by talking in Japanese and pointedly remarking on trifles like the weak beer, but after I was cold towards him he softened and soon we were talking about Eliot. First he was anti-Eliot (later the reason emerged – Eliot had too much unity) and then pro-Eliot when I raised Winters. "The English are good, né? Please stay as long as you can with Keio." "Not logic – witty combinations." He ended by writing his formula for the absolute on a card of mine: $(+A) + (-A) = 0$: "The absolute is where there is no difference." No difference being when the way up and down are the same. All this being "algebraic thinking".

When I got back home it was the unreality of life that impressed me. Life is a dream: we are born alone, and we die alone, and in between is a dream.

6th October. Corrected 50 Tokyo University of Education exam papers, then went to the Prince. The final revision class. His invitation to see him off on Tuesday, which Higashizono got absurdly wrong: "we shall be very glad to have you and Mrs. Hagger to dinner on Tuesday." Then the conference, the apologies.

Adrian's visit. He was withdrawn. Embassy life is unreal because development comes through concentration and Embassy life is full of distractions and dissipations in all directions. Otherwise I had to bear the brunt of the whole evening and as a result overtired myself and worked myself up so that my mind raced and could not sleep at all, although, after drinking some liver salts at 5.30 a.m., I managed to doze a little.

As dawn broke I thought I understood the Absolute in terms of the Stone Garden: "the absolute is where there is no difference", and there is no difference between pebble and mountain – the Absolute is unity.

7th October. Corrected exam papers for Tokyo University of Education, then, after keeping myself awake with coffee and optrex, went to the Bank of Japan. Began *Anatomy of Britain Today* with the Vice-Governor.

English Literature is a cripple divided between soul and body.

8th October. To the Tutankhamun exhibition, which was a disappointment: queuing and then only two shawabtis and the actual mask, all the other items being rings, etc.

From a letter to Ezard: "Although the Japanese are less formally religious than the English, there is a fund of irrational, meditative and contemplative experience in all of them, which is, to each one, a prime value. I have, in some way, begun to live beneath my reason.... I mean that the reason is no longer so important and often seems pretty unreal."

From a letter to Ricky: "I have confirmed my rejection of everything I previously rejected and feel now more justified in my role as outsider."

THE IRRATIONAL, THE STONE GARDEN AND WHITE LIGHT (1965)

On my marriage. Many men marry to increase their energy, e.g. a good hostess; I have married to reduce my energy: if I lived as energetically as I do in my study all the time, I would go mad.

9th October. To Nobe to tell the Hishinoumas (our landlords) we are leaving. The blue sky and autumnal tone of the trees; the stubs of rice in the paddy-fields, and the dry yellow rice like straw hanging from poles; the typhoon swell of the waves and the foam; no snakes, only a few flowers. It got dark about 5.30, and just before then it was chilly. Our train left at 5.28, and there was a large yellow full moon in the sky.

10th October. Wrote on the Stone Garden. After dinner went for a drink with Tuohy, who invited me to go to China with him next February or March. He is fixing up various articles for *AP* and thinks I would get the fare back. On the message of the Stone Garden and Nishiwaki on the Absolute: "You must not see it in Western terms – to a Japanese aesthetics have no meanings attached to them; rather than talk about intuition you must put it into a poem."

My dream about Tuohy. I asked him if I was an introvert or an extrovert and his reply took a long time: "Your energy is outgoing in one direction like a stream or an unimpeded shoot, it is not turned in upon itself; yet you have disciplined yourself like Thomas Mann. It is difficult to say."

11th October. Continued poems until 4 p.m., then read Dylan Thomas's *Winter's Tale* which is awfully wet. In the evening watched the Prince on TV, slow and dignified to the casual eye but terribly shaky and shifty to my scrutinising eye; I felt the kind of hot-and-cold shame that I would feel if I saw myself in the same circumstances.

After, coming from my dark bedroom into the bathroom and turning on the light, I was flooded with golden light behind my closed eyes and the pattern was of rings, each linked together into a golden net, the stone being of gold. I was able to look at each one in detail before opening my eyes and having my pee.

12th October. Rewrote "red viscera and black" and went to Keio.

In the evening took a taxi to the Prince's palace. The Japanese-Korean treaty demonstration on the way, the small gathering of well-wishers with Japanese flags outside the palace. I was ushered into the "lounge": the two rooms where I first met the Prince; there some 40 people, mainly old men, obsequiously lined the wall, waiting for the Imperial presence. Professor Fujii of Hongo, whose glasses seemed upside down and who looked very wise; Arai, bouncy and planning to do an Emlyn Williams-like one night one man poetry "recital". No drinks, no cameras, no Cabinet, no other members of the Imperial Family. The Prince walked round bowing, and shook hands with me; then stood and killed a quarter of an hour; then left, while the guests crowded to the front door and bowed in unison. With her nosegay, the Princess looked as if she were going off on her honeymoon.

In the subway we were all isolated from each other and might have been in a graveyard.

14th October. Spent the entire morning in dragging up an image of three lines ("Through the cracked glass") and when I had got it up I was not at all sure that the associations with accident belonged there. Went to the Bank of Japan, wrote out English sentences for Fukuchi's Asian tour and corrected letters, then returned and corrected the English programmes for NHK for February to March. Read the *Observer*.

15th October. Wrote a great deal – bridged the child and "On Edogawa Bridge" – and then went to the bookshops and bought C some art books to inspire her painting. Then to Adrian's. R-W was there, a quiet, unflustered being from another world altogether in which Adrian has one foot. C: "Adrian talks more easily to R-W, but you unsettle them because you're different, and Adrian yearns to talk to you." R-W's values revolve round small talk e.g. "Ogilvy did not manage the small talk very well" and "I could only judge Walston on his social performance, I did not see him at work." As C put it, there is a time for being nice and stupid and another time for being intelligent and serious, to such people. I am bored by small talk and find it an awful waste of time unless I am asking questions about people or learning about them. R-W's shudder when I said Tuohy could quote you back five months later and that he was interested in human material. "That is very bald" was his reply to me of my questions, and he was shocked when I asked him if he liked the FO; I felt I had peed on the floor. C's accurate assertion of their way of dealing with my seriousness: to make a joke to lighten the atmosphere and then secretly think about what I had said.

16th October. Spent the morning in writing two further lines on the child and one word in the "Poet of the Self" passage. In the late afternoon corrected 16 Bank of Japan letters and after thinking about Pt. 4, got a good title for it "The Death of a Stoic", which leads me to wonder to what extent the ambiguity as regards myself is true. Seeking within self and stoicism are, I should have thought, incompatible, and certainly a notion of self-development does not go well with endurance; I should have thought, furthermore, that stoicism admired the rational virtues and did not dwell mid-way between the rational and the irrational.

Is the Japanese honesty candour or malice?

17th October. Tried to write and couldn't. Was so tired that I slept. I seemed to sink deep down within myself and when I awoke at 4.30 p.m. I looked out at the growing dusk and felt my being in a new place: I was on the 1st floor (in the English way) and my thoughts were a floor higher.

THE IRRATIONAL, THE STONE GARDEN AND WHITE LIGHT (1965)

I then began to think about the problem of the self-centre and whether it is reflected in the cosmos: whether the two obey common laws and all is one, whether the message of the Stone Garden is correct. Sainthood suddenly came within my grasp – I understood Tao, that just as my self-centre unites me, so Tao could unite life and death and all cosmic opposites and pluralities, so that all men are brothers. I still cannot say that I disbelieve it – even though this must be what Christians think of as God – but I was glad to read afterwards of Jung's irreverence to the metaphysics of the Chinese philosophers in *The Secret of the Golden Flower*.

Now the question remains open: did the Stoic die (i.e. have I outgrown Stoicism)? How am I going to end my poems, by accepting or rejecting the message of the Stone Garden? I want to reject it and return to my old view – man finite and dying and the existential truths that relate to his death – but the trouble is at present I almost feel I cannot reject it. This is absurd, for I am only projecting my unity outwards, surely. I must wait and see if the feeling wears off, how much I have put myself in danger.

18th October. All morning I have been filled with a round white light: I cannot see it, except occasionally when I glimpse it and am dazzled, but I know it is there. It is like a white sun.

This is, I suppose, what Christians refer to as the soul in the centre of self. And the mystical experience is given meaning by the relation between the centre and the sun, so that everything is One. I am sure that the harmony I now feel in the universe is an illusion, projected out by my inner unity. I have no means of verifying my feeling, so I do not propose to accept it, but just let it be: my white sun is not to me eternal – I shall not be unfaithful to my fellow men who have not uncovered it, death is still the end, but I shall certainly cultivate the feeling of kinship with the whole world that it gives me. And self-unification is the first stage in coming to terms with existence, for the road to the universe is through the self, and perception of the universe depends on the perceiver.

To formulate, then, it is not the universe that has changed, but my self and my perception of it, so that it now seems more harmonious and my sense of kinship with mankind is stronger. It would be easy to follow a path of sainthood, feeling as I do now, but it would be equally easy to concentrate this white sun into a smaller and smaller disc and explode with energy, go completely insane.

19th October. Tried to rewrite the Stone Garden and fell into a reverie and imagined the world's suffering and downtrodden in a procession, all those to whom one must be faithful. As a result when, on my way to Keio, I saw an untouchable and filthy tramp rummaging for food in a litter bin and stopped and gazed and was accosted for money, I gave him the only change I had, ¥10, and hurried away, conscious of everyone's gaze but wishing I had given him more.

Suffering is futile and totally unnecessary: *therefore* one must alleviate it wherever possible – the intellectual formulation of a cry from the heart.

20th October. A day of chores. Went with Tuohy and C to buy two strings of baroque pearls for ¥3,600, including the box which enables him to escape tax. The patter of Meiras the Jew, which changes every time and therefore interests Tuohy. His sensual eyes. His honesty, admitting his price depends on the pocket and character of the person he is dealing with. Black pearls dyed in ink; pearls soaked in too strong an acid come out in spots after six months to a year. All this emerged after Tuohy had rushed away to cash a cheque at the (British) Council (and, it later emerged, to talk to Tomlin about China).

Then went to Kaigado to buy Christmas cards. In the afternoon to Seibus to buy Christmas presents; dragged round several floors, shielding my eyes from the fragmentary white lights with darks: "like broken glass in a forest glade." In the evening went through my letters, tearing up and filing.

21st October. My two roles: fixed socialiser and developing poet; my age-group will not accept me as the second, or will not acknowledge my difference.

22nd October. With Tuohy and C to *Il Deserto Rosso*. Dinner with Tuohy after, conversation about stressing the individual as opposed to a relationship. Tuohy: self-regarders cannot create because they cannot escape themselves. I: you must see to the end of yourself before you can see to the bottom of others. His generation and stereotypes: Anglo-Irish, big houses, public school and so on, so that he is a stereotype. On the Existentialists: "I don't trust the witnesses." Thinginess (e.g. smell of toes) O.K., but "authenticity is impossible for an alcoholic". I: "It is other people who prevent one from being authentic and who impose masks." On grizzly Garry, "He is very conceited and knowing and is trying to impress."

24th October. To Nobe, with Adrian, to negotiate over the house. We met on the platform. Suspecting that normally I pour my energy into him and get nothing back, that we converse through me saying something, he disagreeing, my justifying and he agreeing, I resolved to say nothing more than he did. The result: total silence, except for a few banalities. This I welcomed: it left me free to think, to look at the light on the water and imagine my death and love the blue sky and the slightly purple and greying hills. The artist can have no friends. Little was achieved: the Hishinoumas would not agree to buy the furniture for £20, and it will have to remain there until they find a new tenant.

25th October. At the Tokyo University of Education traced in brief the progression of the sick soul towards sainthood in William James's *The*

THE IRRATIONAL, THE STONE GARDEN AND WHITE LIGHT (1965)

Varieties of Religious Experience; from the Waste Land to conversion, from the Outsider to the prophet, from the divided man to the unity, there is one and the same path.

29th October. After three long lectures at the Tokyo University of Education, to Tomlin's house-warming party where I played the real-life dramatist in the garden, introducing Adrian to Hijikata for his Soka Gakkai contact, Hijikata and Narita to Tuohy and so on and observed the consequences. Emerelda de Wooters, the Belgian Ambassador's secretary, who said "I sat down by you at *Zorba*"; her bold judgement, "It wasn't warm enough, it should have been in colour", and the undercurrent of double entendre.

Tomlin's speech and presentation of £160 to some Christian charity, represented by a grimacing and camping priest.

On with Baker and Tuohy to Antonio's; red-checked table-cloth, anchovy pizza and Chianti and talk about the (British) Council and this and that. On to Baker's for coffee and crème de menthe. Tuohy's judgement on Baker in the taxi home, "He'll never be Representative because of his wife, reports get back on that sort of thing. But he isn't too concerned." Earlier his judgement on my questioning Baker, "You're making Virginia Woolf's mistake, you can't know what it's like being someone else." I: "You can get the framework of pressures and imagine the rest."

30th October. C on how tired and broken all who live abroad a long time look, e.g. Taylor, Baker. The seediness after about 40, a giving up and aimlessness. In the evening the Emerys' and Stokes's Hallowe'en "kerfuffle" which was a bore: a beat group, no one really wanting to dance, a pointless preparation for an orgy that never happened. Sato's private secretary.

Buchanan saying I work too hard and I saying, "I can only write the way I do, and if I die at 30 in the process of getting things done, then it doesn't matter." I repeated this to C later. I felt I had regressed into the land of the dead. And for all my visions of order in the more boring moments, the sad thing was that, so far from my being immune to chaos, chaos can overthrow me into Swiftian misanthropy, even now.

31st October. After my fourth late night in five days I spent all day reading, first Nietzsche, then William James. The similarity of their vision. The justice of horrid rationalist Russell's judgement on James, "an attempt to build a superstructure of belief upon a foundation of scepticism"; "subjective madness" being too extreme. Two Jameses, the pragmatist, to whom I am indifferent, and the empiricist, whom I admire. The narrowness of the "conversion" chapters, cf p251 with the white light on 18th October; there is something else, self-unification, which can take the place of conversion, and which leads on to the "superhuman" ideal of sainthood. The Superman is not "an unpleasant piece of Romantic nonsense" but a symbol for an unrealisable degree of consciousness, towards which one must strive.

1st November. At Tokyo University of Education stated my attitude to existence: the growth of the child into the hero who unites himself, creates his own purpose, and then faces the final defeat of death, knowing all along that it has all been futile, but passing on his discoveries to his fellow men, those he has remained faithful to by rejecting the illusion of eternity that self-unification brings. Behind all the absurd development and self-creation there is sadness, a deeply pagan sorrow, and the hero is a hero because he does not succumb to it, because he resists although his defeat is inevitable, because, like Leonidas, he has courage and style, and the hero reaches his highest triumph in the moment of affirmation in full knowledge, knowing his death yet affirming.

Is it stoicism – this absurd development? Or does stoicism suggest endurance and resignation and hopelessness rather than defiance? Anyhow, the giant will become cinders, and because of this fact the hero needs some force by which to live; otherwise he will be too adrift or too wretched to feel the full vitality of existence, the true warmth of life; and the stoic has no force, no purpose, just static resignation.

2nd November. Late last night, the two BBC men, Tony de Lotbinière and Peter Jenkins, at Tuohy's. The air of decadence and seediness, but the brilliant analysis of Japan that Jenkins gave. Tuohy subdued but making points, e.g. the 18th century craftsmanship leads to technological prowess. The main question: how is Japan booming, having combined paternalism and competition, when Britain is declining? And what can be learned from Japan? Answer: nothing. Because everything is based on a scheme of giri in personal relationships. An answer which Jenkins denied but which Tuohy supported. On the contradictory nature of the Japanese, the optimism born of fatalism, the division between public and private life. At the end I climbed over the barred gate, after letting the other two through, and de Lotbinière said "How elegantly you climb" and this morning when I rang him "How sweet of you to do this."

3rd November. Too tired to write much. Got stuck, then wrote outstanding letters, read the *Observer, Anatomy of Britain*, William James, erotica and so on. C's paintings: the red figure under a yellow moon, by a church – my criticism being that she has not succeeded in blending two different styles – and her picture of me against a background of art and spirit, i.e. writers and a mandala, me looking down; will she balance and unify everything?

4th November. Spent the morning thinking about the sequence. Got the idea for the final defeat of the priests; still not enough on the irrational; the "exorcised ghosts" to go before "On Edogawa Bridge", where they went originally; "Poet of the Self" to go with the maturity passage, which is to be preceded by rational psychology; somewhere there should be something on wholeness being contradictions in terms of a centre, so that the erotic and mystical are both relevant. Later went to the Bank of Japan. Oshima has been transferred. Our brittle emotional farewell, he saying "The first thing my wife said when I told her I am to be transferred was, 'You won't be able to see Mr Hagger, what a pity.'" On the way back bought *Nietzsche* by Hollingdale.

My bitterness towards my body. C said "You're tired" and I said gruffly, "I am not, I could work all night if I want to and all tomorrow. I am never tired unless I want to be tired." Which is of course not true. But I have the most terrific energy. Sometimes I feel I could run 50 miles in lieu of my afternoon walk. "Too tired to write" but with a raging energy in my body. And my savage indulgence of it shortly after my contempt for it.

5th November. After sleeping only six hours because it took one and a half hours for one and a half strong sleeping pills to undermine my energy, and after teaching from 8.30 a.m. until 3 p.m., I sat down at my desk at 3.30 p.m. and until 11.15 (with a short break for dinner) made an exhaustive study of Nietzsche, tracing the history of his concepts "God is dead", "amor fati", "yea-saying and joyful wisdom", "live dangerously", and the big three: "will to power", "Superman" and "eternal recurrence".

Nietzsche's salvation from nihilism is eternal recurrence. To me, God is dead, I create my own values without being able to "will an eternal return" along with "willing my Naught", and there is no eternal return (eternity being present *now*) to overcome the ensuing nihilism; nor do I believe in the will to power and the overcoming of oneself being the greatest power.

Nonetheless I do affirm the concept of the Superman, he who has conquered himself and transcended himself, who takes the place of God. I do not believe that the Superman has the joyful wisdom to will the eternal return – my Superman is not redeemed by any Deus ex Machina – but I affirm his will and his duty (in terms of his code) to achieve mastery over himself; the motive being not power but curiosity, a desire to know what the meaning of life is. (I was born I know not why, but I shall do my utmost to find out before I die.)

The trouble is, at the end of it all you discover it (life) just is and that all the meanings are rational impositions. But mastery is achieved.

6th November. Perhaps I have unwittingly articulated what I experienced at dawn in the Zen temple: the sense that life just is and that all the meanings are rational impositions; in spite of the terrific charge in that silence and the unreality of living forms. At any rate, perhaps that was one of the things I experienced. My view of the Superman is of a code with which one can face defeat, the nihilistic triumph of death: inner unity can face it better than inner chaos. I must reiterate the motive for the Superman, the answer to the question "Why strive, if death is the end of everything and life has no meaning?" At one's awakening one is baffled, one wants to know everything about one's situation, and that means absorbing everything that everyone has ever thought or felt about the meaning of life and everything that one knows about oneself. If there is no bewilderment, there can be no Superman.

And it is only out of this absorbing that one's own contribution begins to reveal itself: one's own position is always being challenged and modified by what one reads, but slowly it gathers substance and resists the challenges and modifications more and more. This I know from my own experience. The end of the quest, involving those concerned with the meaning and oneself, is self-unification and mastery, and although one has learnt nothing about the universe, it is therefore less baffling and chaotic, for the universe depends on our way of looking at it. From this point, all that remains is to carve one's discoveries and die.

7th November. Completely exhausted after not sleeping until 2 again. A sort of temporary nervous breakdown. Stayed in bed until 12, then spent most of the afternoon walking and relaxing, and after writing 9 lines on the silence beneath the reason went to sleep about 9.30 p.m.

Noted the complete untenability of "Eternal Recurrence". "What if" Nietzsche writes in *Joyful Wisdom*, 341, "thou must live (thy present life) once more...and there will be nothing new in it" and in *Zarathustra*, p196: "I come again...not to a new life or to a better life, or to a similar life – I come again eternally to this self-same life...." If I am now leading exactly the same life, and "this slow spider" and "the moonlight" has all been before (*Zarathustra*, p142) then I now have no free will; I am just repeating my past life; and what of actions and history, e.g. the lighting of cigarettes and so on? It is logically impossible, yet to say that it is only a metaphor is to destroy Nietzsche's philosophy: you cannot be a yea-sayer and have "amor fati" if death is the end.

How to transcend nihilism remains the problem for philosophy, and Camus's answer, by loving life in spite of its logic, is one solution. Mine is self-surmountal in the quest for the meaning of life, surmountal to the image one has of oneself in the future. I am still open to the question "Why bother to surmount oneself if death is the end and there is no immortality or eternal return?"

8th November. To look at it that way is a mistake, I believe. The fact is one does surmount oneself, although death is the end, and one does it with the trapped diligence of a prisoner exploring every niche and cranny in his prison. "If a god be lacking to mankind, is not mankind itself lacking?" (*Zarathustra*, p51.) My goal is to achieve a future self who will be in command of all the evidence, who will know all that can be known about the attempts of all history to impose a meaning on life. The qualities I endow that future self with are wisdom, profound understanding of life and the human condition and so on. But I cannot justify him with any biological scheme or any hypothetical ideas about eternity. Only the quality of his living can justify him: the intensity and authenticity of living which increases the higher one goes; which is a restatement of the idea "virtue is its own reward". In other words one seeks to intensify life in spite of death, one releases the maximum life in one in the teeth of death.

This attitude involves rejecting the idea that the phenomenal world is a symbol for an invisible Reality (cf Blake, Watkins, Barker, Gascoyne): with Nietzsche, one must affirm only the phenomenal. Do I want to do this? My doubts about this were responsible for my confusion over the image. To the "metaphysical" poets, the image reveals the unknown, the invisible; to me it should reveal the known. Write a book on the Superman and society's need of him.

9th November. After reading on the conflict between provincialism's sincerity of feeling and unique inner voice and traditionalism's insistence on the objectivity of the artefact and on foreign cultures, I cannot help feeling that I am a provincial abroad, or at any rate, a rootless cosmopolitan who is provincial at heart and who, like Robert Graves, has "taken some trouble to investigate the literature of cultures historically associated with (my) own, and been at pains to refine, by contrast, what is peculiarly and metropolitanly English". No, that is not right: I never really belonged in England and I am not really English; nonetheless I am sufficiently untraditional as to show little interest in Japanese literature, or only that interest that will help me in what I want to write. The truth is, I am neither one nor the other, not as provincial as Ezard nor as traditional as Eliot, though I incline to the traditional side in my opinions, e.g. over Europe.

10th November. Last night's conversation with C on the necessity of inner strength. The artist must be capable of being completely solitary, without (like Niels, whom Rilke learnt from) turning to people and "shallow ideals". I have this quality, but pay a price for it: my sensitivity, what some call patronisingly my "persecution complex". How right Nietzsche was about that: all the artist's energies go into his art, among them the average man's defence-mechanisms, so that what would be a pinprick to the average man is to the artist, with his superior sensibility, a gaping wound. Moved the prophetic passage to the end of the poem, this morning, thereby creating three temptations, those away from self-belief, unity and mortality, and should now add a fourth, self-deception.

My hay fever and ear fungus (which I now have again) are probably caused by the fact that I am short in white corpuscles, i.e. I have an "allergic diathesis". The scaffoldings on the way back from Morton's, rusty iron girders and steel poles and an incredible composition against the twilit sky, like an incomplete Self.

11th November. Did not sleep until 1.30 a.m. This morning thought about the self-surmounter and the importance of his going beyond psychology to the irrational ground of his being and feeling at one with all life. Then read on Beckett and discovered he is saying the same in Hamm and Clov, the relation between the essential self (which is virtually immortal) and the "I" who suffers and will die.

What evidence has Beckett of the immortality of this essential self beyond the experience of the irrational? Or is he seeking it: "it must be there like $\sqrt{2}$"? Have I an essential self? And what has my past self to do with my present self now? I can predict my future from my past, Sartre would say I am the sum of my actions ("existence before essence" – I exist and then define myself), but is there an abstract essence, "me", which is unaffected by my past ("essence before existence")? Or is this a regressive longing, this longing to escape cause and effect? This longing for existence in timelessness? I am inclined to believe it is: there will be nothing left of me after I die; nonetheless I am a unity and irrational and I have a centre which is geographical rather than extra-temporal. Go into Beckett and Zeno and get some sense out of these confused gropings. Cf the Christian vision, "I", the intellect, will die, but the "soul", the ground of my being, the "essential self", will survive. No. And yet.

12th November. Tuohy to dinner, after I had been told by Morton that I shall go deaf. See April 1964. Tuohy got very drunk and fell on the floor and crawled on his hands and knees. Before that he revealed his preoccupation with death and loneliness, e.g. "You must realise that security and a warm fire are the most important things." On the way home I tried to persuade him to continue writing in spite of a letter he had written his agent that afternoon: "Your prize puts you first out of 400." His sick reply: "It's all cod". He said he would invite us to stay with him in Somerset. He asked, "Is that a planet by the moon?" "The people like you I knew in Poland…."

Earlier conversation about "saying" and "feeling" in art – he believes that Blake, Beckett, Rilke and Nietzsche can have nothing important to say and said "You're lucky if you believe they have"; and about life and death, I saying that our defeat is inevitable and the question is how do we die and "if Aunt Maud can do it well, then so can I" and that although I may not know a Viet Cong as an individual, he dies my death and he is my brother before death and you don't have to be responsible for him to believe "If one man is damned, I am to be damned too," which Tuohy said came from Péguy. The main point that Tuohy kept on making was that I should not verbalise my feelings too much. I must write from underneath not from the top, and confine myself to what I can feel or experience and ask "But what are you making?" The irrational.

13th November. Spent a weary day reading a biography of Rilke and the *Duino Elegies*. The Angels which can be traced back to the Tuscan vision of 1898 and the view of the artist as being self-sufficient, giving and receiving within himself and therefore not subject to the transient external world, interiorising the external world and therefore escaping time. Man can share the intensity of being of the Angels if, by effort, he transcends himself, e.g. in art. The dubious derivative notions: Rilke's narcissistic notion of love, "love without possession", which was merely a justification for his own Don Juanism, which was inspired by Rodin; and (compare 17th October) his notion of the Whole and of death being the other, unillumined side of life: both of which should be rejected.

What of the Angels? As "supermen", i.e. symbols for men who have struggled and transcended themselves and achieved an intensity of consciousness – or rather, as the states of mind of such men, states of mind I can experience – they are wholly convincing; but the theorising which cannot be experienced, the escape from transience and time and the narcissism – this is verbiage, and should be rejected and with it the theorising about Inwardness: "we are the bees of the Invisible" (= inward). Inwardness is not an end but a way and "transformation" rings hollow. I note however Rilke's insistence on intense moments as the poet's subject in the First Elegy, and wonder if I could not write Meditation 2 under the inspiration of the *Duino Elegies*.

14th November. Another day on Rilke, mainly *Malte*, interrupted by a visit from Tuohy who came to watch a bad prize-winning TV film on "Araby" (al-Arabi?) and who was low and was inevitably going shopping. A brief half-hearted conversation about aesthetic emotion in art, symbolised by the pleasure I get from a balanced sentence, and the similarity of people's more human emotions; and on what posterity will learn about him from his ten letters a week: the way he verbalises everything. He seemed sick of being alone but did not seem to want to be with anyone else. And there was the defiant insistence on being a professional writer in his letter-writing which he uses as a consolation. There will be a great bursting out soon, like my sudden creativity early this year after a year's dryness and quiet desperation. He must be patient.

As to *Malte* I especially enjoyed the passage about fame ("profit from the fact that no one knows you") and the passage about the "third person". The externalisation of the interior in the two Nikolai Kusmitches. Does the "Is it possible" sequence apply to "one" (Rilke) or to "mankind"? Rilke's juxtaposition, which anticipates Joyce's *Portrait* and Pound, requiring one to "deduce a whole existence" and "what this imaginary young man universally underwent" from incomplete "disordered papers". Can I draw on this Picasso-type of form, or is narrative indispensable?

15th November. On Rilke at Tokyo University of Education, refuting my graduates who felt the Angel is transcendental, insisting that it is an Ideal that can be striven for and lived. And how that question racks me,

"Why should one strive if death is the end?" Out of natural instinct? Of necessity? Out of curiosity? I still think mostly the latter, and, considering the long history from ape to man and of its struggle and therefore my struggle against the towering night, I want to propose a "will to meaning": baffled, man yearns to know about the human condition – he wants to know how he came to be born to this life he did not choose and why he is going to have to die, he wants to know what it's all for, what the meaning of it all is, and in the course of seeking he surpasses himself, assimilates all culture and history, becomes a great writer or scientist. In the end he is still a seeker, having found nothing – that is the final absurdity – and he has not even the satisfaction of knowing that his "discoveries" can be transmitted through the genes as acquired characteristics. But he has transcended himself. Shadow, I shall never become you because you are the final, ultimate knowledge and wisdom: that is why I strive towards you, strive so mercilessly to bring you into being.

16th November. And any dumb painter can tell you that life has no meaning apart from the fact that it is. Shape, shadow, angles, shade, balance and geometric intersections – they are what appeal to a painter, and, in the case of a poet-painter like Tomlinson, one must not forget the feelings in words and scenes, the bleak and the barbed, the warm and ruddy by the fire, so why can we not just be? Why do we spend our lives in a futile quest for a meaning that can never be? And why, recognising that it can never be, do I not abandon my quest, now, instead of reviewing my books and telling myself "Perhaps after reading these twenty I shall have a new angle on it all"?

The answer is, because I could not live on the assumptions that life just is and we must just be. I could not bear to admit that the lazy are right and that I, who have rejected laziness and with it a good deal of sensual pleasure, am wrong. Laziness does not affect the facts about the human condition, the uncomfortable facts and the knowledge that life is something the condemned man implores. And so the vicious circle goes on, and my quest for meaning becomes my quest for self-mastery and understanding of my situation and my quest for what is, as an artist. Perhaps that is the pattern: the quest for meaning ends as a rejection of all meanings and a striving for what is, which is the greatest meaning of all.

17th November. Wrote well: jubilation and second temptation. Collected money from the Tokyo University of Education: a bracing walk with images, e.g. winter trees like neurons or veins in a dying brain. Late at night was intensely irritated by a review in the *Observer* of (Colin) Wilson's latest book *Eagle and Earwig* by Hugh Gordon Porteus, whoever he is. Wilson was called an adolescent intellectual and his enthusiasm for Eliot and Shaw, Hulme, T. E. and D. H. Lawrence, Nietzsche and Dostoevsky was sneered at. And who is Porteus that he can look down on those writers?

THE IRRATIONAL, THE STONE GARDEN AND WHITE LIGHT (1965)

What masterpiece has Porteus written? And how many times has Porteus been sentenced to death, how many revolts in how many deserts has he had, how many wars has he fought in and how often has he been an exile? And how often has he slept on Hampstead Heath? All these patronisers make their smug, snide remarks on no basis whatsoever and, to boot, from the smug security of an expensive room; they are nobodies, they have no vision, which is why their view of man is so static; and I must pay heed to Pound's advice "Pay no attention to those who have not written a great work" or some such sentiment.

18th November. A lot of writing again: expanded the station passage. Then worked for Tokyo University of Education and after that began reading on Dostoevsky. Compare *Notes from Underground* and *Concluding Unscientific Postscript* and make the theme of the lecture anti-rationalism. Bring in the Hegelian whole, bearing in mind my temptation and Rilke's succumbing to the temptation – an odd thing, that. The Underground man does nothing because he is opposed to the normal man's systems, (to) his belief in the rule of reason and in prosperity as a goal – in short, to assert his will, e.g. p41: "what I most stand for is my personal freewill"; and p43: "meanwhile I go on living and exercising my volition."

To the Underground man, the will is independent of the reason because it represents man's whole being, and it is the will that shatters all systems and rational formulae about man's living, and man prefers to strive than arrive (cf Lessing, quoted by Kierkegaard). The Underground man knows that doing nothing is a second best to "something for which he is hungry but will never find" (p44), but this basic motive – wilful revolt – is important: the psychological quirks, which to Ricky were his motive, are relatively incidental, his inability to be really bad-tempered or vindictive, his enjoyment of degradation out of ennui, his lack of any positive quality, his acting against his own interests – one might almost say they were consequences of his revolt against the normal man. And Ricky was wrong to make section I-VI the centre. The truly central sections are VII-X.

20th November. Tried to write in muggy weather, but could not really. Then went to the bookshops and could not get what I wanted to get. Reflections on values, the challenge of nothingness (see 24th June) and man carving out values against the nothingness, values by which he can be judged. This is the context for my preoccupation with the question "why bother to strive to one's Shadow if death is the end?" (See 7th November, 8th November, and 15th November.) It is part of the code, in other words, a self-created code. Compare the Underground man and Lessing as quoted by Kierkegaard (see 18th November): man prefers striving to the truth – he is a creature destined to strive but has a "dread of completely attaining his end", especially as the end is a "static formula of the same kind as 2+2=4" and if he came on the formula he would have nothing left to look for.

So the Shadow is a notion sufficiently precise to attract man's energies (see 7th August) and to permit him to fulfil himself by striving, but sufficiently vague to make sure that he will never attain the end. Striving is instinctive in man, it is bound up with curiosity, and the point is that man fulfils himself in striving – in the "how" – and not in attaining the goal, "the what". I must measure man in terms of his striving and I now affirm, man never arrives – that is his glory and his relief (and the static-staters should feel nothing but shame) and is a part of the human condition.

21st November. Did not sleep last night until past 1 a.m. Consequently wrote little this morning, but got one good image: the irrational as smoke. Took Nan to the zoo in the afternoon. In the evening read Kierkegaard's *Concluding Unscientific Postscript*. Although I take the insistence on "persistent striving" from Kierkegaard, I reject his end for the striving (which is never attained because systematic finality is only achieved in death), that is, one should "strive to become what one already is". This assumes a static notion of man: did Kierkegaard have nothing to say about transcendence, and is his view of man not a view of a being in transit? One should become what one is, and then strive to take that self towards the Shadow. No, Kierkegaard's "subjectivity" concerns the relationship with an object, i.e. I must measure myself by my relationship with the Shadow which attracts my energy and pulls me up.

The poet worries about getting rid of the wrong word, not choosing the right one.

22nd November. At Tokyo University of Education. There are two views of man, two traditions: one, the social-rationalist (e.g. Amis and Co), and the other the "individualist" tradition, which regards man as a being in transit, a "half-way house". Compare 22nd August for another statement of the same idea in terms of rationalism and Romanticism. The main point is that the literary world is at present dominated by the social-rationalist tradition and regards man as a static, social unit, and hence opposes writers like Rilke and (Colin) Wilson and would oppose me. To the rationalist like Larkin man's nature determines everything, e.g. *Mr Bleaney* and *Toads*, whereas to me, man is constantly modifying, if not recreating, his nature by his free actions. Compare Chernyshevsky's *What is to be Done* and (Dostoevsky's) *Notes from Underground*, which is a kind of *Shamela*.

I should do a *Notes* on the simplifications of the social-rationalist tradition, i.e. I should demonstrate in a novel (1) the inadequacy of the social and rationalistic views of man, and (2) the inadequacy of the view that man is determined by his own nature, i.e. I should affirm that man's free choices create his nature and not the other way round. This novel would be a tirade against the rational humanism of someone like Tuohy and would be about a man who was not "a part of other people", as Tuohy has admitted he is. (Cf 17th November.)

THE IRRATIONAL, THE STONE GARDEN AND WHITE LIGHT (1965)

23rd November. A muggy day, a holiday from Keio. Tried to write but could not. Toyama came to tea at 4. Buchanan came in, unexpected, and for the next hour the conversation had to be on political matters, Buchanan having declared himself opposed to any idea of "values", by which he meant beliefs.

Is there a parallel between inter-war Germany and present Japan: have all the old values crumbled and are Spengler's symptoms present and are artists driven back into themselves by not having a culture they can share? I think this is too social-rationalist a way of considering the problem of the artist as individualist, although undoubtedly it is part of the truth, just as regarding the Outsider as a social problem is part of the truth.

24th November. Not a very interesting day: (re)writing the beginning of the rejection of the Absolute in rainy weather, then working. My theme in poetry is the isolation of the artist in (1) a mechanistic society (hence all the girders and so on which come into my poems) and (2) a declining civilisation with a broken culture and no shared values of the kind that Christianity might provide. Individualism is the only possible way in such a setting, that and an isolated man's feeling for his fellow human beings. In a healthy civilisation, man can connect his view of himself as a being in transit to some shared means of expression, but today this is no longer possible, and so he is more than ever aware of his freedom, not being able to share his spiritual life. (Tuohy and I share a literary "culture", but this is not the same.)

My exile as withdrawal-and-return; an exile I did not understand when I embarked on it.

25th November. A stray typhoon. Wrote the final refusal, et seq, and then went to the Bank of Japan. Later drove to Meguro for the Keio play *Othello*, which was appalling. Othello was rhetorical and made no attempt to connect his lines to any human emotion, Iago gabbled and missed all the innuendo, and was quite inaudible, Cassio tripped over a box, Emilia knocked a candlestick over and the final chaos came when the curtain rose to disclose ten stagehands struggling with the bed and towering curtains, waited 40 seconds, during which time the director appeared and hastily recoiled, and then discreetly "drew a veil" while the audience (some 50 or so scattered throughout a vast theatre) hooted with merriment. Why should it be so funny when a deliberate illusion cracks and we see behind?

Judgement on the play: Desdemona was stupid not to see that Othello was jealous and to go on talking to Cassio, and Othello would never confront her in front of others without confronting her alone first, on hearsay evidence.

26th November. On Toynbee after Tokyo University of Education and cholera. The title of my poems must include the idea of a broken down and

213

disintegrating civilisation, which provides the background to the Shadow (see 24th November). The split between uncreative rulers and unco-operative ruled (internal and external, i.e. educated and uneducated); Freeman's self-division can be related to Part 2, which is full of abandon, truancy, drift, promiscuity. As he moves from macrocosm to microcosm, he achieves self-control, "martyrdom", a sense of sin, unity, detachment and, almost, transfiguration: the spiritual opposites of barbaric behaviour in a classic pattern. Is my energy more suited to a growing phase of a civilisation like Japan than a disintegrating one like the British? The élan and differentiation and creativity and more co-operative mimesis in Japan which, at least in the case of élan, may have had an effect on me, and perhaps I should think of abandoning the tired and weary for the vital and energetic. I could go on from my poems to become the preacher-"creative genius" who stands up in a disintegrating civilisation and shouts "Beware, your spiritual lethargy will be the ruin of Western civilisation", but no one would listen, not now that educational standards are so high. Cf the *Old Testament* prophets, e.g. Ezekiel's Jerusalem the harlot, and Nietzsche on the prophet in *Beyond Good and Evil*.

27th November. Took Nan to see Sister St. John at the Cours St Louis French school: the frightening nun's habit in the oak-panelled waiting-room, Nan's terror, the form which stated "Religion"; the classroom.

Afterwards worked on Dostoevsky, *Crime and Punishment*. Raskolnikov is free and beyond good and evil and commits a crime to which he has a right, but on having his weakness proved to him instead of his strength he begins to seek his punishment, hoping that he will confirm his strength by bearing it (e.g. the mock-confession to Zamyotov, the return to the scene, his terror when Porfyry pronounces him innocent and his unhappiness when Svidrigailov dies, leaving him without fear).

Dostoevsky's attitude must be seen in the context of his dialectic: Raskolnikov is right to argue as he does, but wrong not to seek for some solution that will limit the horror of self-will but preserve his freedom, i.e. God. In short, Dostoevsky is opposed to Raskolnikov, but given Raskolnikov's premises (which Dostoevsky denies) Raskolnikov is right, just as society is right to punish him.

My attitude is that although, from the point of view of logic and theory, Raskolnikov is right, human feeling creates arbitrary values founded on the idea of brotherhood before death. I suppose that is what Camus was trying to say in *The Rebel*. I reject all values which are "beyond good and evil", although I have created, or recreated for myself, the values of good and evil.

28th November. Worked on *The Devils*. Stavrogin as the centre of the novel, whose inner world is given physical expression by his ape Verhovensky, so that Stavrogin's two creations, Kirilov and Shatov, are both destroyed by Verhovensky in a conclusion that also destroys Stavrogin.

THE IRRATIONAL, THE STONE GARDEN AND WHITE LIGHT (1965)

The myth of creating the monster which gets out of hand and destroys you. Verhovensky idolises Stavrogin because he represents the will (e.g. in his revolt against his own nature and his "motiveless" acts, in controlling himself after Shatov's blow, and probably in marrying Mary the cripple, though according to his confession he is punishing himself for raping the child). The outline of the plot is simple: Verhovensky wants Stavrogin to be Ivan the Crown Prince and offers in return to kill Mary and bring Lisa for his "impossible sincerity". The depth is achieved by strength of accumulated situations, so that there are situations within situations. Take Shatov's death: the return of his wife and the birth and his death all have to be seen within the context of Verhovensky's resolution, which in turn has to be seen within the context of Verhovensky's promise to Stavrogin. Likewise, the suicide of Kirilov has to be seen within the context of Shatov's death, Kirilov and Shatov having been friends. The art involves a resolution or decision, then a contradiction or frustration, and the tension that leads to a synthesis.

29th November. At Tokyo University of Education, on "beyond good and evil" and the "master/slave" morality (Nietzsche) and the "extraordinary/ ordinary" morality (Raskolnikov): to Dostoevsky, there is something else, some other force which prevents everything from being permitted, i.e. to Dostoevsky, Nietzsche would have been one side of the dialectic; nihilism being "everything is permitted", the something else being Shatov's principle. (To Camus, brotherhood.) The notion "If God does not exist everything is permitted" has been attacked on the grounds that man is subordinate to society, but the whole point is that man's freedom is established in relation to God, and this freedom overrules society (e.g. in the case of the "extraordinary") unless there is some motive like compassion and human feeling that accepts social obligations.

30th November. A morning of complications, with Adrian's invitation for 10th December and Kenichi Yoshida's for 18th December; both involving Tuohy. Then worked on our historical context.

It is clear that my true role is that of prophet, and that if Toynbee is right and we are about to enter a universal state, I should do my utmost to prevent a U.S. take-over of England and should be reactionary and should whip up as much spiritual energy as possible in terms of some definite outlet rather than eternity: the new conception of man, existential possibility and a vision of England's place in the modern world being the positive message and the 8th century BC prophets' warning against material luxury and idleness being the negative message. Politically I should be anti-progressive, the progressives like Tynan lacking vision in (1) being too pro-American and (2) being too anti-spirit in the pernicious tradition of the Enlightenment which began the rot of today, just as the Renaissance began our Time of Troubles in the 16th century c1550.

Nothing can be done in the long run, however, as Isaiah must have known secretly; the decline of Western civilisation is inevitable, now that growth has stopped and our society has cracked, and nationalism and striving for a third force cannot really help. England to rival Japan and France as a third force neither Communist nor capitalist....Not a hope? Cf Toynbee volume 12: "Our problem is how to climb down to a normal level of equality without having a great fall" (p629 n2), i.e. how to become Little England. Prophecy is useless?

1st December. Second thoughts on yesterday. Ostensibly, our age needs some great idea, an idea which can attract the force that moves men and nations, an idea which can be lived by men and nations. Traditionally, this great idea has been presented in terms of eternity, in terms of a view of life in which death is not the end, e.g. the 8th century prophets. Today this great idea must involve a view of life in which death would seem to be the end. This is a necessary consequence of the collapse of Christianity.

The content of this great idea must be the traditional one of increasing spiritual energy and mastery over one's own complexity. In short, self-unification and transcendence. The argument for such an idea is that the truth is never certain, but persistent striving for the truth fulfils man, enables him to live a real life. The means of persuasion would be the present unreality of people's lives. The practical progress towards reality: keeping a diary, exploring the pattern of one's past, mastering the offerings of Western civilisation to date in relevant books, recognising the irrational ground of oneself and freedom, which are beyond psychology. In short, embarking on a quest, which is one's purpose. The assurance is that at the end the world will seem more orderly, and there will be great depth in wholeness. Social drill through meetings and lectures, to seek the Shadow. How would this new energy get into the leadership, how could one influence the leadership?

The West is declining because there is no spiritual striving. This striving must be restored.

2nd December. The first teaching: "Strive to surmount yourself and you will feel a closer bond with mankind. You cannot love your neighbour properly until you have united yourself." The second teaching: "The will can do anything – anything." Further thoughts on the practical side of this new movement: cells of 10, the Soka Gakkai principle of each one making a new convert: a corporate quest, not worship. The presentation of the great idea: "There are two problems, first to energise the people, and second to produce a leadership which will make use of this energy." (See December 17th, Neo-Cromwellianism.) The third teaching: "Project an image into your future and your energy will be attracted to it."

A leader cannot impose a new religion on his people. The movement must be the other way round. So first the cells, then a kind of revolutionary movement designed at wresting the government from the hands of the dead and soggy, that will release as much spiritual energy as possible in society. How can this be done? Accompanying land reform and overhaul of British society. Repeat: the main question is, how can spiritual energy be released in society in such a way that it will avert the decline of the West? Neo-Cromwellianism. The leaders must use this new energy to create solutions to problems which have defeated us hitherto, e.g. Britain's place in the world. This must surely be a religious-political movement, in response to the challenge of a disintegrating civilisation.

3rd December. Meditation 2 should combine the poem after *Duino* (see 13th November) with a prophetic denunciation of Western civilisation in England.

On the negative side: images of decay, disintegration, comparison with the past, examples of unreal, inauthentic living, snatches of superficial conversation and shallow attitudes, instances of what materialism has done to our spiritual energy, e.g. radios, motorbikes, refrigerators but people alienated from themselves and living unreal lives. A warning, in short, in the manner of the 8th century prophets and Wulfstan, establishing the connection between spiritual decay and decline in terms of energyless, uncreative leadership and apathetic, indifferent and unco-operative electors.

On the positive side: the great idea (1st December), visions of what the English could do, contrasting Mrs. X as she is with Mrs. X as she might be, men fulfilled in striving living real lives, transcending themselves and rising to heroic heights, banners inscribed with the force that moves men and thrills them and cells exploring spiritual problems and fulfilling themselves. Stress that we must live with modern industrial society – there can be no going back, there must be no Ludditism – and that a mass effort at spiritual energy is the only thing that will stop the rot.

This poem will include the poem after *Geronion* about England as an old lady (a dying whore, cf *Ezekiel* 16; and *Amos* v 2 for Jerusalem at an earlier stage, fallen virgin) and the journey of Christ through England, i.e. an analysis of Britain, dying of exhaustion and boredom, proudly refusing help from her wealthy son?

4th December. From Thursday evening (2nd December), after seeing *Moll Flanders*; my being so firmly convinced that I am an Eliot or a Rilke: I now talk as if I were and seem to lecture.

5th December. Read *The Brothers Karamazov*. The point is that Ivan is not solely an intellectual, nor is he to be contrasted with Alyosha or Zossima purely and simply. He is a dialectic himself, struggling to choose between self-interest and virtue: "everything is permitted" and the views he expresses in his article. He reconciles the two in *The Grand Inquisitor*, which is a socialist rejection of God's world and of Christ, who should have relieved

217

suffering by solving social problems, saying how little was permitted and unifying mankind under earthly rule. This attitude is based "on the belly", not on the rationalist Euclidean mind.

This "reconciliation" does not eliminate the dialectic, however. Smerdyakov enacts his "everything is permitted" (p743) and his other side is in Christ's kiss, cf Zossima's "All are responsible for all", Alyosha's vision, Mitya's dream. After Smerdyakov dies, Ivan confesses: compare Svidrigailov and Raskolnikov. He gives evidence against himself, i.e. chooses virtue against self-interest, but he does not understand why: "truth had gained a hold over his heart, which still refused to give in."

The question is, whose side is one on: the Grand Inquisitor's-Devil's, or Christ's? The leftist concerned with the many would be on the Grand Inquisitor's side; the prophet, concerned with man's freedom and striving, is on Christ's. Did I on 30th November and 1st-2nd December make Christ's mistake of overestimating man, of failing to distinguish the few from the many?

6th December. At Tokyo University of Education, on the basis of values. Virtue does not depend on God, nor for me does it depend on any rational scheme. Although there have been rational attempts to erect a scheme of values in terms of social obligations, an irrational basis like love, sympathy, understanding, sensitivity, feeling, brotherhood, etc. is more attractive to me. In relation to God, man's will is supreme and logically everything is permitted, but in relation to man there is some restraining principle based on love. My attempt to convince C that "all are responsible for all" because all existence is a unity: "no man is an island" (Donne) and so on and how understandable that the rationalist Arnold could never understand that, "Yet in this sea of life enisl'd." Christ would be against the Grand Inquisitor for taking the freedom of the many, for his dictatorial implications and the dictatorial implications of Socialism and Communism, but how much he would want to see established on earth what the Grand Inquisitor gave in return: solution of social problems and unity and peace.

Our attitude to Ivan, then, is that his choice is not our choice because virtue for us does not depend on God (or is my "irrational restraining principle" a God which is freely chosen?) and that Christ's view of the few is right just as the Grand Inquisitor's view of the needs of the many is right (but not his means of implementing them) and that the two are not antithetical but are different ways which can be assimilated in one Weltanshauung.

7th December. At Keio, on the Movement. Davie is technically very advanced, but his themes are far too slight and express an attitude no more. Wain's imagery is terribly intellectualised (i.e. rationalised) and is not felt; it is a substitute for statement. Thom Gunn is far more interesting than either from the point of view of his subjects; he is worth reading for the words rather than for the technique, which you cannot say of the other two. After the class was assailed by the student Morita, sat in front of his wretched thesis, and half an hour later escorted to the parcel-office of Yamachi station and handed a ton-weight parcel of canned food, the carrying of which (gift) has caused all my arm muscles to ache most foully.

8th December. All morning working on versions of the first few lines of the poem, and in the end getting just one image, I think just the one I want: society* as a tree and the breakdown of values seen in terms of apples, the whole idea working in terms of iron and concrete.

In the afternoon went to Isetan to buy a coat and longjohns, and in the evening had dinner with Tuohy. "This will be the first visit to China by a really good writer since Auden and Isherwood." The conversation was rather nerveless until after dinner – I was tired and he was preoccupied with serving dinner, a thing he does with great hospitality – but we got warmed up over brandy, I defending and he attacking writers like Dostoevsky and especially (Colin) Wilson. I said that he was a writer of my generation and that although I conceded all the usual things said about him the attempt to correlate states of mind, taking writers as case-histories, was worthwhile. Tuohy's objections: William James was educated and Wilson hasn't been; Meursault and Kurtz are odd cases; the quotations are all wrong; the linking thesis is too vague; there is not enough of him; "You say he passes from hell to heaven, but he doesn't believe in either" – this very noisily. (I using the two concepts for despair and affirmation.) In short, the rationalist's answer: "I like my polymaths to be educated." Home drunk reflecting that Tuohy's practice stresses experience, as does mine, yet our theories are so completely different. Will we quarrel in Peking?

* 12th January 1966. No: European Christianity.

9th December. Spent the morning on the first few lines, cutting, stripping to the bone, and got the line "a city like a cemetery". Went to the Bank of Japan and returned to *Heart of Darkness* and lo and behold there was the "sepulchral city". Was Conrad thinking of the Sacré Coeur rather than of slabs and tombstones in cubist blocks?

12th January 1966. No, of Brussels.

10th December. At Tokyo University of Education conversation on anarchism and Read. Back to an embarrassing telephone call from the Prince, full of silences caused by his fumbling in English, and an invitation to dinner; and to reflection on anarchism in Camus's *Rebel*. Then to dinner with Adrian.

Emery and I were supposed to draw the F.O. man, Adrian and R-W were to listen, which was what happened. After which I sat back with my brandy and did not contribute and felt, as I had from the beginning, a complete stranger to all of them. As the F.O. man had intonated when he said

"Judging by appearances you're an artist" I did not belong; their interest in the Diet riots and so on was unreal to me – what was to them a matter of crucial importance was to me just a game which did not mean a thing, not a thing. Came away feeling like Vladimir or Kurtz, aware of noise, cackling noise, filling a vast silence.

11th December. On Camus's *Rebel* and the background of Russian history. The troubles after December 1825. The anarchism of Proudhon, following William Godwin and Max Stirner and leading on to Herbert Read today; the nihilism of Proudhon's opponent Bakunin leading on to Herzen and Belinsky, to Pisarev and Nechayev, to Bazarov. Over 90 years prepared the October revolution.

Today in Britain there is not the faintest inkling of such a sustained revolutionary struggle (see 17th December), and the heirs to the anarchists are the ND pacifist-anarchists like Comfort and Kirkup and the heirs to the nihilists are the anti-Establishment Angries (the heirs of the Puritans?) and the principle-rejecting Beatniks. These groups are, because of the lack of social point to their rejections, probably symptoms of decay: they cannot lead to anything and are often "insurrections" in Stirner's sense, men standing up at a meeting without any intention that their action should lead to anything. Will there be a movement towards action, as there was in Russia in the 1860s?

Will England see a Kalyaeev or a Sazarov? If so, then I think the quarrel with our present rulers has yet to be fully articulated. At present it is only in the stage of anti-Establishment feeling. And what weakens the possibility is that to a great extent we already have justice – it is certainly not possible to feel the 19th century Russian revolt against injustice in post-Welfare State England. (Camus: "The spirit of revolt can only exist in a society where a theoretic equality conceals great factual inequalities." Hence the disbanding of the Sparticans after sterile discussion.) To be utterly cynical, the more justice, the nearer to disintegration we are (by Toynbee's law). No, it is not more justice we need, but more energy: perhaps a New Right.

12th December. Perhaps the logical movement should be a political-religious movement like Soka Gakkai, drawing on the Angries' insights that the Establishment is dead, and working for the spiritual (rather than class-) regeneration of England initially and the world ultimately, and directing the dissent of the anarchists and the Beats. Such a movement would have to be anti-Parliamentarian to succeed: would that not destroy us?

On Camus's *Rebel*. The rebel against injustice affirms "We are"; killing denies it. So limits are necessary, and the moderation of Kalyaeev is the ideal: "murder is necessary but unjustifiable". This position suggests harmony with the world ("we are"), whereas both *The Myth of Sisyphus* and *L'Etranger* present a contradiction between man and the world, between man's desire for unity and the fragmented universe which disappoints it, the Absurdist contradiction which can be traced back to Camus's thesis at university: Greek consent to the world, Christian dissatisfaction with the condition of man, i.e. the world as a kingdom in which man is happy, and man as an exile in an indifferent universe.

I feel this contradiction and division, though I blame man for expecting the world to be a unity. (See 14th June which I have perhaps betrayed subsequently by projecting my unity outwards.) I must, however, think more carefully about man in the world.

13th December. At Tokyo University of Education tied together "beyond good and evil" (see 29th November, 6th December). The main thing is that men are like trees in a common soil: they have the same roots although each trunk is different. Will and reason separate, the feelings unify. The social-rationalist, asking "Who am I in a relationship with?" does not feel brotherhood and finds the concept unreal because you cannot think it.

Camus is split: in spite of his terrifically powerful feelings, he tries to argue and think brotherhood, perhaps to curb or to clarify his feelings. Anyone who cannot feel this brotherhood is lacking, is not fully developed in his irrational feelings. The saint can understand it and feel it more than the petty average man. The Nietzschean Superman is, ideally, the saint who transcends himself, and feels unity with all men, although he despises man's laziness (Zarathustra spent ten years alone) and his "beyond good and evil" – the morality of the conqueror rather than of the Christian conquered – is to help him transcend himself and carries no connotations whatsoever of "everything is permitted" or the Raskolnikovian view of the extraordinary. Raskolnikov is one of those who are lacking.

As regards the many and the few, the best view is Hesse's – the few go ahead on the march through the jungle and report back to the many, i.e. the few are the eyes of the many. Ivan's feeling that "it was no great moral blessedness to achieve perfection" if the many cannot is answered by Christ's kiss and Alyosha's vision: the many may not be able to quest but they can, or should be able to, love.

14th December. Picked up where I left off on Thursday (9th December), the first lines. The vital force that created the English (and European) side of Western civilisation has died; society is consequently declining and decaying, institutions are decaying in a life where Nature has been mechanised. So far so good. But then I want to say why "I" refuse to take a social view of man, why "I" refuse to define "myself" in terms of an unhealthy society, why "I" am isolated – because there is no "unifying idea" and nothing to share and "I" have no fixed place in society – or at any rate, to justify my individual view of Freeman.

Perhaps I should contrast self-definition in terms of death with self-definition in terms of society but I must lead on to "my" occupation of experience, which will ultimately be held up as a kind of answer if not to death (which is unanswerable), at any rate to the decay. See 16th and 17th December, I oppose society because I oppose decay; I oppose all English social unifying ideas because all such ideas have decayed; I am isolated because everything that might unite me with others has decayed.

15th December. Read from the *Old Testament* prophets of the 8th century and 6th century BC. Their theme, that internal canker leads to a loss of national independence, that the fair prosperity without is a rotting mess within, like a whore. To Amos in the 8th century, Jerusalem is a fallen virgin (5.2), to Ezekiel in the 6th century Jerusalem is a harlot who allows all races to enter her (ch. 16). The bones of the house of Europe have yet to scatter (cf Ivan on Europe as a graveyard) and there is no question of restoration today; we are concerned with keeping together broken limbs.

Has Britannia become a whore, has she got syphylis yet? Is she contaminated by foreign vice? For meditation 2, perhaps a syphilitic old whore who must be denounced: "stop prostituting yourself, isolate yourself, recover in independence, become great again…." A dream. Wrote an image for society in terms of bones but was dissatisfied with it and will change it: society is sick because its vital force has gone and there is no cohesive national purpose.

16th December. To Meiras's office near Aoyama 1-chome to buy C three pearl necklaces of two strands each, price $2 each. Total ¥4,300 and in England £43.

After the Bank of Japan, reflected on Freeman's relation to society, which is sick and decaying. Is it true that a sick society tends to make one sick, that an unreal civilisation produces states of mind which are unreal? Unless there is an opposition? So Freeman's choice in Pt 1 is a choice to oppose, not merely a choice of his destiny as a writer; or rather the two cannot be disentangled: it is by writing that he will oppose. And this choice takes him outside society: from now on he is in rebellion against the lack of spiritual tension in modern England.

But his problem cannot be solved by a simple ascent to union with the Shadow. There is another side of himself, bound up with his mother perhaps, which forces him down to a descent into the dark world. As he comes to realise, these two opposite movements are complementary: to ascend to the Shadow he must throw off all claims on him, and to throw off all claims on him there must be a descent into the underworld, a complete rebellion against superficial order, expressed as ultimate chaos, and leading to real order.

12th January 1966, cf roots (downward) and shoot (upward); the shoot comes out of the roots.

17th December. At Tokyo University of Education, on my Quaker-Methodist background. If Eliot is right and the civil war is still being fought, then the Puritan tradition is being carried on by dissenters like Osborne, the anti-royalist rebels against the established C of E, and my dissent must be seen within the same energising context: I dissent in relation to an Establishment which has begun to decay; like Carlyle I believe that men's energy vitalises institutions, and these institutions (which according to T. E. Hulme and Eliot bring out the highest qualities in men) are now decaying for lack of vital energy among men.

I dissent because I want to improve. Believing, like Toynbee, that England has plunged into a decline from which perhaps she will never recover, and wanting to arrest this decline, I have withdrawn my support of those in power and the Establishment and take the side of the rebels, because energy is created by the rebels. Therefore I can never really sympathise with Eliot's Cavalier view of tradition: Eliot lent his support to the decay. Fox and Wesley had a better idea of things than Eliot; they had more vision.

In a time of decay, any energiser is inevitably opposed to his society, just as is any revitaliser in the modern industrial and commercial city. I am not really a Parliamentarian to the extent that the Roundheads were, for Parliament too has decayed, and it is as idle to hope for regeneration through Parliament as it is to hope for regeneration through being royalist and traditionalist.

18th December. Tuohy and I went to dinner with Kenichi Yoshida. Two gins in the Garden Bar of the Imperial Hotel, then to his home which seemed to be one of several blocks on a housing estate. The woman he passed off as his wife was not the same as the woman who bowed to me at the Queen's birthday and who wore a kimono and who wore glasses and who disapproved of his drinking.

19th December. On progress. In the spiritual world there is no such thing collectively; in fact there is only the reverse, a holding of ground that others have gained through forms which have since been lost. In the world of humanitarian ideals, democratic progress is desirable but disastrous to a civilisation. One must be on the side of justice, but the franchise and a Welfare State is the beginning of an irresistible national decay. I can see no way out of this dilemma.

In the materialistic world, doubtless there is such a thing as progress, though it generally breeds its own destruction like the H-bomb or kills vitality like the Industrial Revolution, and discoveries like writing and steam probably survive the fall of the civilisations that produce them. In the biological world there is undoubtedly progress, if man be progress in relation to ape, if genius be progress in relation to man.

The pessimism of Eliot and Spengler was largely a reaction against 19th century optimism, but I think I can say that biological progress is a fact, materialistic progress a doubtful asset; humanitarian progress a two-edged sword; and spiritual progress an illusion.

223

I, at any rate, place little trust in progress. Although, as Camus points out, this can be a dangerous reactionary creed, what use is progress if death is the end, or decay? The point is, I do not deny progress, but neither do I make a creed of it, for it can be a mixed blessing. Write a play showing progress leading to decay over the years, set in the Roman Empire, or late Greek.

20th December. Recast Pts 1 and 2 of the poems, making Pt 1 purely the decayed social background and Freeman's opposition to it, and Pt 2 the need to break out and throw off all chains before the ascent to the Shadow.

Why did I have to do this – why did my ascent have to be preceded by a "rebellion downwards"? I think because I am middle class, I could not effectively rebel against church-going parents and throw them off by ascent; it could only be by descent, by choosing something to which I knew they would be opposed. In other words I had to free myself from my background, which would have hampered me. This meant uprooting myself, for the life in Loughton was much too provincial for the task I had in mind, and the emotional world was too stifling with its taboos and its refusal to recognise the purpose of life as a question of any importance. Also because, for various reasons, I was completely isolated. So in Pt 2 I must show Freeman against this background, not just against the background of social decay, to which he is opposed.

21st December. After lunch with Buchanan, and splitting four bottles of Kirin beer, prepared to go to dinner with Their Highnesses. The usual inexpert display from me: said "Good evening Your Highnesses, may I present my wife Caroline" without looking at them, was caught with a cocktail biscuit in my mouth when dinner was called, couldn't think of anything to say while discreetly munching on the way downstairs, couldn't think of anything to say after I had exhausted their visit, China, dogs, riding, etc. C's surprising ease and fluency; she fairly chattered away with the Princess while I scraped the barrel with the Prince. The Princess is ill at ease when asked personal questions, e.g. "Was your privacy interfered with in London?" or "Can you see any film you want in your palace?" and she very rarely gives a straight reply, the question somehow evaporating. Consequently most subjects of conversation are, one feels, improper; Rhodesia, religion, politics being anyway inappropriate.

The dining-room, four candles in pairs which spluttered, no other lighting, a long wooden table, the Prince and C opposite me and Haneko and the four ladies-in-waiting kimonoed and waiting obedient in the shadows to one side of the screen in front of the door. The six course meal. The 18 carat gold tie pin from Bangkok which the Prince gave me. C's stomach-rumbles and the rug placed over our knees in the car. My refusing English apple-wine for Cognac, the apple-wine being specially chosen. My overpowering urge to touch Haneko, simply because she was a Princess and I had to observe the proprieties while sitting or walking with her.

22nd December. A call from Tuohy saying that the *Sunday Telegraph* will finance our visit to China. It will pay £750 for two articles of 2,000 words each. Then Nan's swing arrived and I cut my thumb in trying to unscrew a nut before hiding it.

Tuohy took me to the Fuji International Travel Service at 1.30 and we handed over our visa forms. His panicky nature: "I shan't be able to do the articles." The party for him "in the middle of the Kanto plain, among garages and cabbage fields". Then on to the Japan Travel Bureau opposite Tokyo station to discuss the visit to London via Moscow, tentative date being June 5th departure, Nan going for 25%. A day of arrangements.

On re-reading C's dream of 25th March 1961: C is divided into two, bride and devil. The devil is revived by the monk's fire – did she think of me as a monk? An ascetic-hermit?

23rd December. Reworking Pt 3. The point is, all the women are one woman: one obsessive image of the maternal whore. This woman, the maternal whore, is also, strangely enough, a symbol for some kind of spiritual fulfilment. She is a kind of Madonna whose physical satisfaction leads me on and redeems me, like Inanna. How well I can understand Demian and also Graves's *White Goddess*, where the woman has a spiritual value. I suppose Jung would call her the anima, but I am not concerned with any theory; I do not want to depart from Freeman's experience, and although stringing experiences together inevitably results in some form of a theory I do not want such a stringing to be dependent on any preconceived theory.

24th December. Last night's dream. I was given a scholarship by the United Nations, this emerging when Buchanan took me to look at the names carved on high, one of which was mine. Tuohy's and Tomlin's were there also.

25th December. A swing for Nan. A walk to the Cathedral in the afternoon and images: insect priests caught in barbed-wire webs, execution squads behind the confessionals; the city looked like a slagheap from the Fishers' house. Buchanan came to an unsatisfactory dinner, unsatisfactory because he was not well.

26th December. Wrote the second draft for 65 lines of Pt 4. Then Tuohy came to dinner. A long conversation throughout dinner on the subject of decay, of what is observable and what isn't. Elan and drift. The main point that emerged was that there are two ways of looking at people, as individual human beings and as individuals in a civilisation. No one should ask human beings to suffer so that the civilisation shall prosper (see 19th December). Justice must be done, and one would always choose the life of one human being before the vitality of a civilisation.

Nonetheless, one can demand that human beings increase their command of their complexity, i.e. one can pity them and make demands of them. Progressivism is wrong-headed if civilisations smash, but meliorism can apply. The importance of ambivalence: contempt for vulgarity, admiration for generosity. Complexity a feature of a civilisation that has reached the top, best expressed by a dialectic and especially a dialectic of self-division and torn attitudes to people (eg meliorist-pessimist).

Poetic devices: contradiction of Romantic by anti-Romantic, surprising by word-choice (i.e. not fulfilling verbal expectations), paradox, cadence and rhetoric – running on – and development of imagery. On the congenital syphilitics – Churchill, Lenin e.g. – and the consumptives, e.g. Keats: "They know they're going to die so they burn brilliant." Barely slept.

27th December. A day on all parts in my tiredness, interrupted by visits to the dentist and to Maruzen. Decided to combine all parts so that the poem goes from beginning to end without a break. Any one passage or line can then be seen within the context of any other passage or line and will not be chopped apart; also, I overcome the aesthetic ugliness of having Pt 5 as 450 lines and all the other parts amounting to little more; also, the decay and the hell-vision can last throughout; also, I can include more as the relevance to the whole will be wider than relevance to each part.

Ambivalence, I have decided, is the logical expression for my "philosophy", that (among other things) everything has two sides and there is always a dialectic and one cannot assert anything without suggesting its antithesis. I am by no means certain that there is always a synthesis; in fact, very often there isn't. Is this Manichaeism? Yin and Yang, "golden and black."

Anyhow, my statement about life must be in terms of opposites, just as my attitude to anything suggests its opposite, and in feelings both opposites are often felt simultaneously or near-simultaneously, and it is this which makes "modern" feeling more complex than Victorian feeling. April 1966: this is Chairman Maoism.

28th December. Worked on Pt 5, getting together repetition and the priests. The long acting image. Three pairs of incompatible and insubstantial dreamers – Shadow and fatalist, priest and fallen father, Jeanie and protecting bride – have dominated my relationships. The first pair I am prepared to continue – I do not mind projecting my Shadow, and choosing an intellectual to rise above, a fatalist to out-will, is harmless. The others, however, could be more serious in their consequences and I must beware of them. I cannot decide how lasting their hold is over me; this is anyway beyond experience and I must avoid theorising and merely present experience.

THE IRRATIONAL, THE STONE GARDEN AND WHITE LIGHT (1965)

31st December. This last year has been a year of great progress, a year of great rebuilding of myself, and how lucky I am to have had as fine an artistic mind as Tuohy's to help me. What I have achieved is: (1) I have discovered myself as a poet; (2) I have got to know myself perhaps as far as I ever shall; (3) while not rejecting psychology, I have gone beyond psychology and have got myself out of the "religion v science" impasse (cf e.g. 30th December 1964), this through the Shadow; (4) I have absorbed "Modern Britain" and its sociological background; (5) I have overhauled all the books that made an impression on me when I was an adolescent and have now a maturer attitude to some influences which had perniciously and cancerously taken root; (6) I have got my art technique sorted out: "abbreviated narrative in emotionally linked imaged experiences" and the technique of dialectic; (7) I have, I think, become a nicer person and through being more at ease with myself, perhaps slightly less divided.

I am however chronically nervous in society, and as my writing energy depends on this (I believe) I am reluctant to do anything about it. Perhaps the fact that this year everything has been in question has had something to do with it; all my defences have slipped. Ah well, one can't have it all ways. The most productive year of my life.

What I must remember in 1966:

(1) Unless there is some thesis that connects Freeman's own life to society all the time, then he will come across not as a symptom of our time but as the victim of an infallible upbringing, i.e. I must measure Freeman as a social type who is a symptom of our time, not as a neurotic, and what is symptomatic is the rebellion, the guilt and the self-division and so on. Our time has created, or thrown up, a mind with certain features, and I must define those features.

(2) I must acquire a sense of European history, and must steep myself in the entire history of Europe.

227

6.

THE INDIVIDUAL SOUL AND CHINESE MATERIALISM
January – March 1966

1966

1st January. Rewrote Pt 1, lines 1-23 (of *The Silence*). Freeman must be a social symptom, a potentially healthy man who opposes a sick society in which the religion has gone dead, and who, through self-discovery, creates his own substitute for that religion. The main doubt he experiences is, therefore, the psychological, static, dead-end view of himself, which (despite the truth of psychological insights into projections) is not true: he can define himself in terms of his Shadow as well as in terms of his "eternal face". *

This Shadow is, I think, a redefinition of God, in so far as I am in it and it is above and beyond me as my future self calling me into future being. Compare Whitehead's "Religion is the reaction of human nature to its search for God". I do not think of it as God, and to do so would be to destroy it, but although it is only a part of me and will die with me, I am in a relationship with it and my vitality and purpose is connected to it, depends on it even. This surely is one aspect of a God-relationship. Cf 4th January 1964, religion does not depend on eternity.

* 12th January 1966. Man is composed of two incompatible processes: static, habitual repetition – "spectre" – which is the business of psychology, and forward development and transcendence, which is the business of religion. Ideally a man's forward movement should not be arrested by the habitual side of himself.

2nd January. Went for a walk with Nan to the Cathedral. The pregnant silence, the white table bathed in white light on pebbles surrounded by white flags, white lilies in the vase. The peace and intensity, like being inside one's own brain. Nan and the moon: "Bo, I see you."

See 14th December 1965. Write a play on the whole of Western civilisation, showing the growth of the Empire and the feeling of decay today; also the feeling in the Middle Ages, the Renaissance and Cromwell's time. Include the play about Christ in this scheme. It is for this that I need to absorb the history of Europe. The theme: anti-progress; also the conflict between Establishment and dissenters, there being no dissenters before the 14th century.

24th March 1966. Link this play to the law of unreality.

3rd January. On Pt. 1. See 14th December 1964, I want to say that there is nothing the social classes can share, i.e. that no Christianity holds them together, and I am adding this as evidence of the failure of creative power in terms of branches and sap. After that I want to express my rebellion against and isolation from all lack of spiritual intensity, without making theoretical generalisations about society, i.e. by founding what I am saying on observation and experience.

One difficulty: have not the many been the same in every age, and is it not the few and their relationship to the Establishment that I should consider? After that I must face the question, is Western civilisation sick or is it old? If the first it can be cured; if the second, it is incurable and we must look to the saplings. The key is in Christianity, which, I am convinced, is old. "Sick" imagery can be included however.

Got so worked up inside with questions I could not answer that I had to get out of bed at 2 a.m. and go for a long walk to calm my brain.

4th January. Worn out after two nights' total insomnia. Tried to write Freeman's denunciation of a sick society. There are two aspects of any such denunciation. (1) The denouncer's "saeva indignatio" and disgust. (2) The lethargy and idleness of those he is denouncing and whom he wants to change. Should Freeman act for himself or should he try to transform society? Such a transformation is the logical outcome of his opposition, but I am not concerned with it yet.

In the evening to *Thunderball* to try and get relaxed, to try and sleep.

5th January. The theme of the poems is not a conflict between spirit and art, but the artist's role as rediscoverer of spiritual vitality. The Church has failed to provide this spiritual vitality, so Freeman is on his own and has to fumble his way towards such a vitality through art, and he becomes what Rank would call the traditional artist-hero, the bearer of a message about the spirit.

His self-discovery is therefore important in so far as it throws up an alternative spiritual form to the Church, the concept of the Shadow, which is one of the seeds that have fallen from the decayed tree. Whether it can be used socially or applied to the future of man is at this stage not a question I should consider. I am not sure how relevant Freeman's needs are to the mass of mankind – he is one of the few and should not waste time thinking about the many at this stage – and the important thing is that Freeman has solved his problem to his own satisfaction; although in a sense his problem has only just begun, for he has a life-time's struggle ahead of him.

6th January. A weary day. I am so tired, so tired. Could not write anything very much and messed around deciding that the body-blood imagery should wait until Meditation 2, which will be about old whore Britannia's syphilitic decline in a sick-bed. Anxious to write Meditation 2 now, doubtful about my ability – something I have taken to questioning which is all against the rules, for how can I question something that is not yet done? This unseasonally warm weather, clouding the brain, numbing the finger-tips. No energy, sick despair lurking round the surface of my unconscious, like an evening mist.

7th January. Another day of not being able to write. There is so much I could do if I left this one passage and I feel exhausted, ready to lie fallow: two contradictory states.

In the evening to Buchanan's party "same time same place" as last year. All the men up my end, and no Miss Arai (Buchanan's mistress) to sit next to me, and all the women up C's end. Talked Vietnam and China with a Japanese trader. Was asked whether I was 26 or 27 and hit on the best reply: I winked at Hardie (Edmund Blunden's ward) who sat opposite and said "I wish I could remain nearly 27 for the next 5 years as I have for the last 5", which created a laugh. Yamashita, (Prime Minister) Sato's former private secretary, who has gone up and is now Chief of Trade Policy and is responsible for deciding on the China problem. His wife from whom he is unofficially estranged – he shook hands with (Fred) Emery and then rather ironically with her, saying "How do you do." Buchanan: "Of course, she's very influential, even more so than he is. She knows all the Government. That's why Emery's pumping her for all he's worth." Penson could not come because he has moved to Yokohama and his maid won't let him go out in the evenings, presumably playing on his ill-health. Everyone left early, with "arranged telephone calls" (C) and no one was very drunk, not even Buchanan. Many, like me, forgot their presents, toy horses which sat on the table in the empty spaces among the debris.

8th January. A consideration of the causes of World War I before going to see a documentary, *The Guns of August*. The Austro-Hungarian quarrel with Serbia over Bosnia, the 1908 declaration and the Sarajevo incident, which followed the Balkan Wars; Germany's fear of Russia's military measures strengthening her support for her ally and leading to the invasion of Belgium and the push for Paris. What stands out is the fact that the U.K. began to decline in the 1890s, if not before, and that by the end of World War I our three bastions, agriculture, trade and the navy were all by no means supreme and that by the end of World War II we had begun an economic crisis from which we have never recovered. In other words, our present economic and international position is to be seen in terms of a trend that clearly runs through the 20th century.

This leads me back to the question that constantly racks me these days: what force governs history? If such a fine leader as Churchill could do nothing to alter a pattern of 75 years, then surely the existentialist view of history is wrong: history may be immediately affected by the will of a Napoleon, but in the long-run there is some force at work which is beyond man's control as it were, a force expressed through a people. Elan and absence of élan – these are the two extreme conditions of history and whether the absence is due to sickness or age or both is something we can never finally know. I am a Toynbeean as regards such an élan, but not otherwise – I am sure that higher religions are products rather than goals of civilisations – and although I do not expect the masses to be anything other than dependent on the leaders, there is a condition of decay that even a vital leader can do nothing about.

9th January. Went to Nobe for three hours to clear out two and a half months' smoke and grime (I have not left Tokyo since October 24th). The causeway of white-hot sunlight across the bay, the exploding waves, the alien trees with autumn tints in the horseshoes, the cicada/frog-free silence and the clear stream.

On the train read Blake and thought about the contemplative ideal: how much is it a daily thing, and how much does it depend on development towards a future thing, like the Shadow? "To contemplate the world in the light of the Shadow." This diary or journal is the expression of my contemplation, each passage being written after contemplation, except the passages when I am so tired that I can hardly put two words together, which seem to be most passages; so I think contemplation must be a contemplation of a trend, the day having a contribution to the progress from naive schoolboy to sage. What did Blake mean by Urizen (e.g.): is his meaning as simple as (Colin) Wilson would like it to be, as complex as Sloss and Wallis would have it? Take note of the Spectre, the static self of habit which arrests becoming. On becoming and the Shadow: being is a static state and only the Shadow could be; I am in a perpetual state of becoming which is a progression towards a being I never reach; being is impossible for human "beings".

10th January. At Tokyo University of Education on (George) Fox. To what extent did Fox literally mean the "law of God" and "the Lord the creator and his son Jesus", and to what extent was he using them as metaphors for greater needs and inner self (as Wilson claims)?

The main feature of *The Outsider* is, I think, that (Colin) Wilson's argument is basically sound while his illustrations distort the authors. So, I agree that one must progress from the trivial to the visionary – in the sense of "the more positive" – by recognising the self as an enemy, but I am by no means convinced that Fox thought so too, nor am I convinced that Blake was such a visionary rather than a "seer of visions": he was, after all, a Christian after about 1797 and perhaps Christ is not purely a symbol for Los in the long prophetic poems after 1797. Nonetheless even if one discounts all the illustrations, the basic idea of a William Jamesian progress to visionary affirmation is sound, and the book deserves to be read for that alone.

To the Prince. The usual tangle at greeting. He knocked on the door and did not come in. I went to open the door and nearly got hit on the head as he came in. He extended a hand and took it away. My extended hand found nothing to shake. We shook. I closed the door while he just stood. Exaggerated somewhat of course. His acceptance of my proposal that we should read the entire history of Western civilisation, which he has never studied. We begin next week with Egypt.

11th January. Wrote Freeman's rebellion, and in the evening, the end of Part 1. On the Shadow. Each man creates his Shadow yet in a sense each man is born with a Shadow: it is potentially there for every man, and each one is presumably different, though its "eternal face" makes it impossible to say this with certainty. This God we project from ourselves and feel in a relationship with – it is created by man and does not survive him, merely providing the motive force which attracts his energy and hauls him forward. Each man therefore creates God, and God is created by each man. Each man is therefore free, for there is no God to limit his freedom before he creates God. In fact, God comes into being for each man as an expression of his freedom.

12th January. A man is like a seed. He must first put down roots into darkness, descend into the chaos of the underworld; only then is it possible for his shoot to sprout upwards into light, ascend into the order of the spirit. The two processes form a totality, and a man is both roots and shoot (Yin and Yang), and without these "irrational" roots there can be no "upward thrust of the sap". This growth of the spirit, the thrusting up of the sap, is what all religions try to achieve; to cause an arrested growth to continue growing is the business of psychology, and such a static, dead-end state is a condition of sickness. Habit is static. All the time energy must win command over habit and grow.

Growth is greatly facilitated by – is dependent on, even – an "image" that the seed has, and the sick soul is usually one that has no such image. This is why the Shadow is so important. It fulfils the function of such an "image" and therefore of God, for traditionally it is God that has enabled the spirit to grow. The Shadow is what causes energy to grow; there is nothing in it to suggest a conscience – that quality is a projection, like my projection onto priests. The Shadow is created by my vital energy so that my vital energy can be further created by it: that is the paradox. The Shadow is the force by which I live. Could this force be applied to a nation? To a decaying nation? What image would attract the dead energies of the English?

13th January. Wrote 10 lines that have eluded me since last month, "the vertical vision": tried to begin them as usual and suddenly all went right. On to 4 hours at the Bank of Japan. The possibility that Shastri may have been poisoned by a Chinese or a Russian Chinese sympathiser, or by an anti-Pakistani fanatic on his own staff or by a Chinese sympathiser even: is not choking and coughing a symptom of poison rather than of a heart attack? Perhaps not. And why no autopsy?

THE INDIVIDUAL SOUL AND CHINESE MATERIALISM (1966)

In the evening worked on Conrad's *Heart of Darkness*. Marlow's slowly increasing interest in Kurtz, the helmsman Palinurus. Depressed by *The Observer*, a review of Kazantzakis on the lines of the review which depressed me on 17th November 1965. Full of knowing condescension about Nietzsche, Bergson, Kierkegaard, asking what the point of unfashionable spiritual autobiography was, why it didn't prefer "ordinary human relationships", and calling Kazantzakis a megalomaniac who flirted to no end with the Superman and sainthood and so on. Why should one write about "ordinary human relationships" – why should one not have a spiritual autobiography? Because a relationship measures a social contact and a spiritual autobiography is too concerned with the individual, too "Romantic"? "All Europe contributed to the making of Kurtz."

14th January. After Tokyo University of Education, on Blake's prophetic writings. The main complication, the 1797 development and *Four Zoas* which are the transition between the Lambeth books and *Milton* and *Jerusalem* and which are confused.

Creation myth: the recalcitrant Eternal who emanates the material form from the unity of Eternity is 1. Urizen 2. Albion (*Four Zoas*) – Albion's elements (Urizen, Luvah, Tharmas and Los/Urthona), trying to master him, destroying the harmony – and 3. Urizen/Luvah who is opposed to Los-Providence in a final dualistic scheme.

Reality: the Daughters of Albion determine the senses and therefore errors – also the intellectual processes Urizen, Satan, Spectre – and must be overcome through spiritual perceptions or intuitions i.e. Emanations. So after (1) single vision there is (2) the phenomenal as a symbol of the real and (3) supersensuous apprehension of the real, the infinite being in everything; (4) the fourfold vision is for Eternals.

Knowledge: the unity of the world is seen in terms of man: Eternal Man, Albion, Eternal Being, an Eternal who manifests the highest unity, which is that of the unity of the Absolute, Jesus, the real.

Moral ideas: Heaven is composed of passive Reason, Hell of self-expression and active Energy, the contraries being irreconcilable, the one depending on the other. These are in Urizen = restraint, and Orc/Oothoon=passion. Later, after *Four Zoas*, there is dualism between Rahab/Vala – natural religion and the religion of Jesus with energy controlled by brotherhood and anti-selfishness (i.e. Spectre = selfhood) and forgiveness and the regeneration of Los in Golgonooza, the spiritual city.

Blake's unorthodox Christianity: letter to Butts (22nd November 1802), "I still, and shall to eternity, embrace Christianity, and adore him who is the express image of God." In the *Book of Urizen* the Eternals are not the unity and Providence they are in the *Four Zoas*.

15th January. To Nobe with Buchanan. On Blake still. How much of his mythology did he believe? Quite literally all of it. The daemonic interference from the Daughters of Albion and the Emanations are to be read in terms of: "We who dwell on Earth can do nothing of ourselves; everything is conducted by Spirits, no less than Digestion or Sleep" (*Jerusalem*, beginning). Presumably the same goes for the Angels and the unity of Eternals too.

If Blake were using "Spirits" to symbolise emotional forces, we would go along with him, and I think that what we can get from him has to be de-transcendentalised: a man should be a unity, the senses should be clean, some marriage must be found between reason and energy, we should follow Los's path.

The stumbling-block with Blake is the twofold vision and upwards; does the phenomenal conceal the real (cf Vernon Watkins) or does it alone exist, as Nietzsche and even Rilke claimed? The only such real I can know empirically through Newton's sleep is "the force that through the green fuse drives the flower...."

Compare my intuitive vision in the Stone Garden, a vision I later rejected. The question is, is the world One or many? Is the universe One or many? If One then I believe in some real, some mind to which the universe is One, as the Stone Garden was One and many to my mind as I contemplated. Retrace the rejection of the Stone Garden and the white light, and thoughts about Nietzsche and my place in the universe. See 17th October 1965.

16th January. Nobe. After drinking saké and taking a walk to look at the brilliant stars, for there was no mist and there were no street-lights, we went to bed at 10 last night.

I did not so much as doze until about 4 a.m. It was cold, C was periodically sick out of the window of our room, and I was too interested in the stars which shone through the topmost glass of the sliding doors; (underneath the glass was frosted;) I felt a cold terror, lying awake in silence, alone. I was alone under the stars, companionship and love helped to make it more endurable but I was utterly alone with only myself to rely on. I was waiting to die; with horrible loathing I was breathing the last breath and being burnt in a crematorium, and the cinders contained my mind, the charred white folds of my brain-cells, and I had become an element, I was not. The stars reminded me I would be nothing. What place in a unity did I have, do I have, and what place do my fellow-men? The broken machinery and bones of my etching – what place did they have, and the mirrors of eyes and the trident of a hand?

No, there is nothing real behind the phenomenal save a force, a force which works on the same lines as my life but which is otherwise in no way intrinsically like my life: it is not "spiritual", self-realisational. In a sense the world is a unity (the paling sky over the patched sea like drying distemper) and all contraries are reconciled, but there is no *spiritual* reality in the world or the universe or behind the phenomenal.

17th January. At TUE (Tokyo University of Education). More thoughts on the problem behind Blake, which is: "Do I believe in eternity?" For the world of eternity is what we would understand by the eternals, and it lies behind Blake's entire theory, creation myths, reality, theory of knowledge and moral code.

If by eternity I mean "unity", I think the answer is "Yes", in spite of my belief last October 17th and 18th that I was projecting the unity of the world. I can see eternity in a grain of sand, in the sense that just as it (i.e. the grain) is a unity, so is the world. The manifold contradictions of the world are all a unity like a mandala, perhaps, and this is something I perceive irrationally, i.e. intuit. Compare the Zossima vision of brotherhood. To see changing things as belonging to a unity is to see their eternity, and in this sense Watkins's line in *The Turning of the Leaves* about breaking the disguise with your eyes is misleadingly Neo-Platonic.

The whole point, however, is that Blake probably did not mean eternity and unity and probably was thinking of the grain of sand in a Neo-Platonic context – the Idea behind the form – in which case I cannot go along with him: is there an Idea behind artificially natural forms like a table, a desk? My intuitions of the unity of the world are unprovable, as I discovered at the time of the Stone Garden. And what's the position in relation to change? E.g. if I acknowledge the unity, is there any change between life and death? My reason cries out that there is.

18th January. Took Nan to the doctor's to have her ears examined, had my ears examined as an incentive to her and ended up visiting Dr. Ozenberger the ear specialist after Keio. His diagnosis confirmed that made by the Japanese specialist in April 1964: the infection around and inside the middle ear conceals a basic nerve-deafness – this he established by trying the Weber test and then, I presume, the Rinne test – and he does not know what caused this and proposes taking X-rays for mastoids, which is what Keogh feared when I was seven. A week's streptomycene in April 1964 would not cause it – streptomycene being now prohibited as being harmful. I wonder, could that pain in the ambulance have been meningitis after all (see October 23rd 1965)?

Ozenberger advised me to start lip-reading and said he could not tell me how long it would take for me to go deaf until he had checked me on an audiogram to see how many decibels I have lost (he estimated 30), and this he cannot do until he has cleared up the infection of the ear-drum. He also said I would probably have to use a deaf-aid. If Beethoven could write the *Late Quartets* when deaf, I can certainly go on writing, and I wonder if I have always instinctively known – whether the self-remaking of the last year has been an instinctive preparation for the solitude of deafness.

19th January. An argument with C about Britain's future. My position: economic health is certainly the primary objective, but to get everyone to work hard Wilson must be able to offer some dream for the future, some dream relating to Britain's international position. Whereas the U.S.A. is no. 1 champion of the free world against Communism, and France can become no. 1 in Europe, and Japan can become no. 1 of an Asian Empire, the most that Britain can hope for is to get an equal partnership in Europe; short of doing a Hitler on Europe, that is, a prospect unimaginable. On these terms even if the U.S.A. and Russia wiped each other out, it would be France and Europe that would stand to gain, not Britain.

Some historical nemesis has caught up with us and we are paying for the exploitation of our ancestors in a dwindling empire and Commonwealth, and there is nothing to be done unless we adopt a nationalistic foreign policy and perhaps a right-wing dictatorship at home, and even then we might be unable to do more than hold our present contracting position. And these policies would probably be very undesirable. No, we have had it, and that's that. And this could have been predicted in the 1890s, and two defensive wars have concealed the truth from us: we were struggling to maintain the status quo, but we had the illusion, perhaps, that we were expanding, conquering. Élan senile, vigour from tired loins, and an indomitable spirit. "But there will come a time when we shall rise again; there will come a time when there is a dream." In this age of communications this may be wishful-thinking.

20th January. How to justify the vertical vision? Surely it is the oldest of ways, a way advocated by every higher religion, the striving and growth of the individual, alone. When I measure myself in terms of the stars and recognise my nothingness, I feel terror in the pit of my stomach, I dread my being nothing, dead. When I imagine my Shadow and resolve to strive forward to complete awareness, "objective consciousness" (Gurdjieff) and total knowledge of the meaning of life, I am alone, and I am not measuring myself in any social context.

I am both vertical and horizontal, and to neglect one is to limit my experience, to say that one does not exist is to deny experience I know I have had. The social-rationalist is a half-man, a man in a waking sleep. He has neglected a half of himself. He has refused to face chaos, he has refused Gurdjieff's conclusion, "Everyone should sense...the inevitability of his own death, as well as the death of everyone upon whom his eyes or attention rest." One must not, however, go to the other extreme and be anti-humanist in the sense of misanthropic. One is a part of all mankind, and one is born no different from anybody else; everyone can potentially achieve complete consciousness, and to grow each should; otherwise each remains an undeveloped, unhealthy, arrested growth.

21st January. After three lectures at Tokyo University of Education, a visit to Morton with Nadi, a letter home, and Tuohy came to dinner.

Discussion on history, his parallel between post-war U.K. and France 1870-1930 during the Third Republic, France having then no international

236

role but being creative in art, in spite of being exhausted too. Speculation as to when "Western civilisation" might have broken down: c1375 on Greek parallels, Napoleon forming a short lived universal state – but, Toynbee argues that the city-state system of Europe is a side-issue in Western civilisation.

Is Toynbee right in lumping the U.S.A. with Europe? I think not. The U.S.A. is growing and Europe is ready for unity, and they bear the relation to each other of Rome and Greece; and we must remember that Rome only took over after Alexander's conquest. See England in terms of Europe rather than in terms of the U.S.A. The Second British Empire was a "flourishing child" (Trevelyan) at the end of the Napoleonic Wars, and it did not begin to decline in the 1890s (see 8th January) – it was only really completed about 1880: what happened was that in the 1890s others rivalled us. The decline of the empire is post-World War II, although it was not unprepared for. See the decline of England as beginning about 1910 in some respects and after 1945 in all respects.

On the way home: "All civilised people worry about relationships, not stars" and "You haven't proved your vertical vision." Individual growth, alone. "I spend my time alone thinking about human beings." On "narcissistic" writers who were not interested in others: Bellow, Hemingway.

22nd January. Further thoughts on history. Considering the U.K. alone, there are two alternative Toynbee theses: (1) that a Time of Troubles began with the 16th century wars of religion, and that a Universal State is in the offing in the late 1960s or 1970s, a state to be imposed by agreement and not by force, in view of the atomic bomb; (2) that the U.K. began growing about 1215 and Magna Carta, and ended her traditional period of growth about 1910, by which time the accumulation of the Second British Empire was complete; in which case there is a long Time of Troubles ahead. The first theory sees the breakdown as a consequence of the Reformation, the second sees the U.K.'s growth as beginning with emergence from feudalism, and the wars of religion and Reformation as differentiations, a sign of growth.

Which theory fits in best with European Christianity? On the first theory the growth of European Christianity is 675-1375, and the breakdown the war between Venice and Genoa 1378-81 and the decline of the medieval church (the Schism etc.) in the Renaissance, there being a gap until the wars of religion, and the history of Europe since the 16th century – the expansive growth and the empire-building – is all to be seen in terms of one loss of élan, which is unimaginable. I am inclined to believe that the breakdown occurred in 1910, following growth in both the medieval spring and the early modern summer, and that Toynbee's dating is far too rigid; although a United States of Europe might prove me wrong. This analysis excludes the U.S.A. altogether and does not take account of the energy and vitality of Europe. In any event the U.K. is in decay and Europe has lost the leadership of the world.

23rd January. History continued. And yet, when one considers the troubles in the last 500 years, one is tempted to think of Britain as being an exception to the European pattern in having preserved its social order until 1910 whereas the French lost theirs in 1792. Possibly it was the end of the troubles that smashed us – the end of a troubled summer when we were ripening – and the only way Europe can recover world-leadership is either to become a third force, i.e. a U.S.E. (United States of Europe) as a universal state in its own right, or to enter the American hegemony. This pattern is, on second thoughts, more satisfactory in so far as it sees the 18th century Age of Enlightenment as an unproductive, spiritually barren rally. There is a parallel between the Hannibalic wars of 218B.C. and today, perhaps. Was Cromwell the cause of a schism in the body social?

Read from Ouspensky's *In Search of the Miraculous* and was transported back to those 12 weeks in autumn 1957 when I was initiated into Gurdjieff's system off Haymarket. All that I have "discovered" since then has been a kind of forgetting and gloss on what I then knew: the need to awake from sleep, the conception of objective consciousness as perception of unity (see p279) and the need to die from attachment to be born into the inner growth that takes me to this "intuitive" consciousness. The "I" behind the false Hagger: compare Beckett's "essential self" (Estragon – the self of "self-remembering") and Eliot's consciousness between time past and time future and Blake's "fourfold vision" of unity and Husserl's phenomenology.

24th January. At the Tokyo University of Education: does self-remembering lead to the part of ourselves that is really ours? That is the main question. I think the exercise I did in 1957 gives sufficient evidence that it does – it awakens and points to an "I" behind the dream, an "I" which the brain physiologist would put in the thalamus, the cortex being the "personality" which is what others have put there (teachers, parents etc.). And the sense of growth I feel (see January 12th, 20th) has nothing to do with what I have learned up to last year, until the intuitive experience in the Stone Garden, in fact. This, then is the diagram: ↑→; the vertical leading to awareness of unity (Blake's threefold vision of the real without the Neo-Platonic drawbacks of the twofold vision), and the horizontal of social relationships perceiving difference and plurality, and being the soil in which the seed must grow. The nut and the shell, the shell must become passive so that the "essence" can be active. Cf Jung's "Self" and Husserl's grasping consciousness after awakening from sleep.

The Shadow is to be seen in terms of this "part of ourselves". The completed growth of my inner unity, a goal I will probably never reach but nonetheless a dream or image which is necessary to making my vital powers grow. The Shadow can also be a future in my living, in so far as the inner affects the outer. I have understood the meaning of the mandala on my wall: the small circle is the personality, the large inner circle behind it is the "essence" – or vice versa. Cf. Zen, Zossima. The aim behind all this struggle is to see things as they are.

25th January. See August 9th and 17th 1965: I was enfolded by the irrational. There was silence under the reason, and I did not know what it was, nor did I know where I was when I was beneath my reason. The answer is, I was in myself, in the indivisible self I was seeking, achieving glimpses of "objective consciousness" like the round white light which I ignorantly tried not to recognise. The whole of Western civilisation is founded on the personality outside this indivisible self – only the East has knowledge of this self – and consequently the values of Tuohy are unreal: he stresses education, which is the part of ourselves that belongs to others, and all his values, as he often admits, are bound up with others. This is a way of shirking the hard work that has to be done on oneself to prise out the seed in oneself and then water it to make it grow.

Went to Keio and was absurdly moved when bidding the 4th year farewell. With a part of myself I was detached; it was the other part that was moved. The singing in my ear continued all day: a cross between a high pitch of a tuning fork and a tuning signal for a radio.

Made posthumous arrangements with C in the event of my being killed in China.

26th January. Wrote up the passage on the Establishment. Sleepwalkers imagery, the unreality of normality, the decay seen through a mind crying out for purpose; the bourgeois judged in terms of chaos, death and nothingness, striving and growth, unity, "objective consciousness". Then to the Prince. On the way, the fireman in the tramwires, like a spider.

The Prince's poem: "The Queen slept in the dark called loneliness/And walked in the valley of brilliance/Basking in false flattery/Waiting to be torn on the wheel of history." On Marie-Antoinette at Versailles. Does he see himself as waiting for a revolution, surrounded by flatterers and feeling lonely? He was very reluctant to let me go this evening, and I saw him as a desperately lonely man – compare his telephone call on Monday evening – unable to make any real contact with anybody except perhaps the Princess. And my disapproval of his status melted into sympathy. Compare Tuohy's self-revelation yesterday on the way to the travel agency. We were discussing the new memory-drug and comparing it with mescalin: "It's no good for those who torment themselves." Is the self-torment connected with his inability to write in Japan?

This singing in my ear has continued uninterrupted all day like a cicada, and I can hardly hear my watch tick even at low pitch. Undoubtedly I am going deaf.

27th January. Rewrote the passage on the Establishment. Then to the Bank of Japan. Saw Ozenberger. Told him about the suspected mastoid and responding to penicillin. He confessed he had no idea what caused my nerve deafness. He got awfully flustered and was sweating in the end: washed my ear out with pure alchohol to get rid of the dead matter and the membrane, then opened my left flapper by pinching my nose, asking me to swallow and then blowing air up from a rubber ball. Audiogram and blood test ordered.

Worked and went to bed at 11, but could not sleep until 3.30: the nightmare of dying, alternating between "the horror, the horror" and Marlow's vision of greyness, sent a tremendous energy racing up my blood and nothing I did could subdue it for it came in wave after wave; the stronger the idea of my death possessed me, the more energy I had.

The coal black French West African and the albino American at the clinic; the half-caste "West Indian" girl of three who spoke three languages, French, Japanese and English. The albino's contempt for her husband: built up hair that flowed to her buttocks, six inch heels, and sitting the other side of the room from him.

28th January. How much of myself can I explain in social terms? I am for example a first-generation university student, and did not have the advantage of books and academic conversation at home, an advantage that may be reflected in the confidence of second and third generation students. I have also cut myself off from my roots in "getting educated" – hence my socially rootless life now, although individually I have roots in so far as I am growing, isolated, alone. The anti-individualist pities anyone who cannot adjust himself even to a floating social background, but he is wrong not to recognise the importance of individual self-remaking, and he is wrong not to recognise that there is a part in us which is capable of individual self-remaking. "I am full of parts of others" Tuohy says, and he is right of the cortex: I have caught myself echoing other people's ideas, tones, mannerisms, even laughs, and even Tuohy repeated word for word something I told him a month previously, having forgotten I said it.

What I wonder is, to what extent is the part that is me unaffected by other people, so that one can distinguish what others have put in my brain from what is mine? That would be Tuohy's objection, and from his point of view the interlockingness of human beings is the only possible belief, each being "a part" of others they have come into contact with. I affirm this and something more: growth, and the individual nature of the growth is not an escape from the real environment.

29th January. On T. E. Hulme, who caused me a lot of trouble in the last months of 1964. What are we to think of him? One must distinguish the mechanistic period, the vitalistic period (1907-13) and then the religious period (1914-1917), which form the 3 regions of reality in *Humanism and the Religious Attitude* (1915-16); cf "belief in mechanism constitutes the obstacle which the saint must surmount" (*New Age,* 1911) as evidence of his earliest phase. There was no radical change between 1907-17. He really has to be approached after 1914, in which case we ask "Is perfection really not on the human plane?" "Is classicism not something more than fixity and tradition and organisation – is it not Deism and Enlightenment and the idea of man subordinated to social, rational values?" "Does Romanticism really only begin from one root, the Renaissance? Rousseau?" "Is Humanism not something more than the innate perfection of man, e.g. respect for human life and so on?" and "Is not the Religious Attitude more than a belief in Original Sin and the other plane and in a radically imperfect man?" I am inclined to think he was better before 1914 – provided the idea about the Life-Force is regarded as a metaphor.

My attitude to Hulme is as follows: there is a process of "spiritual growth" that depends on regarding man as imperfect in relation to the Shadow; whether the Shadow constitutes an absolute value or not is to me irrelevant – it is the striving, the existential striving, that is important for one never reaches the Shadow, one never reaches the Perfection. To talk of planes and "fixed and limited man" and "regions of reality" and to give labels "romanticism-humanism" and "classicism-religion" and to work out theories of art in terms of them is to me to blur this main point.

30th January. Worked on the vertical vision and the shoot breaking the crown, an organic image (pace Kermode), and then visited Tuohy with the two forms 1B: "application for approval/licence on foreign payment required for foreign travel." Conversation on China topics. A typically Tuohian observation: "NHK are always talking about people like Smetana, but the illustrations are always Mozart." (The operative word: "always".)

Returned and thought more about T. E. Hulme. The best thing about him after 1914 was his insistence that man is not perfect, i.e. not conscious enough, and that there may be a revival of the "anti-humanist attitude", i.e. (interpreting him literally) poets may write about man the sleepwalker rather than man the social-rationalist. His theory about the Renaissance is no less simplified than Eliot's or Yeats's theories, but it is still an oversimplification, and the worst thing about him is his Christian and militant Toryism, and his wrongly Christian sense of "the subordination of man to absolute values" (p57), for "absolute" introduces an idea I cannot live and suggests a God I have not created; the notion of Perfection must touch my life if it is to matter, and I am indifferent to it if it is on another plane. God can be defined in terms of "life" and "progress"; the trouble is, there is no progress, and the striven-for perfection is, like Rilke's Angels, never achieved.

P.S. Perhaps this is unreasonable: I do acknowledge something greater than man, some unattainable Perfection beyond his grasp, and it is the terminology I disagree with.

31st January. At Tokyo University of Education, on T. E. Hulme, getting my ideas straight. What is wrong with Hulme is: (1) the three

241

categories he separates are too intellectual and unless the absolute values are my Shadow, they do not relate to my living; and if they are the Shadow, I would say they were not "on a separate plane"; (2) he should have linked the religious attitude with what he calls Romanticism, not Classicism, for man is imperfect and can strive towards perfection and change himself by awareness of his possibilities, and this striving is better than statically doing nothing in the name of original sin and "the constancy of man", i.e. being "fixed and limited".

Perhaps I have not understood his terminology – perhaps "limited" means "in relation to the infinite" and "fixed" "with a fixed belief but without change" – in which case perhaps we are not so far apart ("the constancy of man" is true, despite 2,000 years of striving, perhaps – a more pessimistic view than optimistic evolutionary humanism) but Hulme does seem to approve of lack of striving: "tradition and organisation" are not enough. Such a classicism goes better with humanism, the humanist belief that man is complete and that there is no need to strive being much the same as the Spectre-ruled, static "fixed and limited" view of the social-rationalist. Hulme was closer to striving in his vitalist period – the "current of consciousness" that traverses matter in *Intensive Manifolds* (1913), and it is this that is right about Hulme (despite Pound's remark "Bergsonian crap") together with his "anti-humanistic" message: not "anti-human beings" but anti-the notion that man can sit back with complacent pride. Think further: are values above life, and is there something greater than man?

1st February. Rewrote "the vertical vision", inserting one or two lines, then, at 4 p.m., received Fujii and heard him through on England. Facts about where he went and how much it cost. At 5.45 Tuohy rang and asked us to dinner. Filled in two copies of the re-entry forms and a questionnaire, then talked about Rhodesia – his cousin who was killed by a cow, it emerging later that he had begun divorce proceedings against his nymphomaniac wife – and abstract art and photography and executions and self-sacrifice for an idea. Tuohy: "I could die for a human being, especially a child, but if I were to be shot I should kick and scream and would not give a damn about courage." I disagreed, saying that although my feelings are cowardly I would hope that I would force myself to die with dignity even if no one was watching. We talked suprisingly little literature.

Returned home by 11.30. I could not sleep at all: began by contemplating my increasing withdrawal from the world – I shall be a quiet-voiced elder at this rate – and ended by determining to be more aggressive, more outgoing, by which time it was 7 a.m., and I now write and watch the sun rise through the early morning mist.

2nd February. Wrote and then went to the Prince. His refusal to come downstairs at the end, my stubborn insistence by waiting, his reluctant descent at the end. I excused him just before the turn in the staircase, whereupon he bowed and went back upstairs to change.

Buchanan's phone call about China: afraid that I shall be arrested as a spy in the context of the Hong Kong affair (China demanding that Britain refuse Hong Kong as "a base" to the Americans) or that the visa authorities will not renew my visa. This after a call from Tuohy saying that the Immigration Office had refused to consider his application for a re-entry permit as "no one could go to China." Rang Yamashita, to use a personal contact, but could not get through to him.

3rd February. Yamashita telephoned about China, saying he had a friend in the Gaimusho (Foreign Office), the Chief of Passports Section, a Mr Naito, if Tuohy liked to mention his name at the Shinagawa local office to help get a re-entry permit from China and get everything speeded up so that we do not have to rely on the letter of invitation, which, according to the regulations, has to be produced before a re-entry permit can even be contemplated.

After four telephone calls to Tuohy, decided that in view of Naito's position and my going back this summer and Buchanan's worries I would go and see him. Went with Tuohy. In the car talked about morphology – endomorph, ectomorph and mesomorph. Novelists are mesomorphs, poets are tall and nervous, "aesthenic". Pamela Hansford Johnson, on meeting Tuohy, to Snow: "It's a good sign, he's a mesomorph like Proust." Are the mesomorphs the humanists – the comfort-loving static "plodders" – and are the "lean and ascetic" ones the men of energy and vitality? Does everything depend on pyknics?

Naito and his secretary Tanaka in Room 212 solved all our problems, substituting a certificate of service and statement of reasons for travel for the letter of invitation. Later at the Bank of Japan, quiet-voiced Mr Ichiki made indirect enquiries about my trip back to England and about the British Council. Altogether a day of arrangements and other-direction.

4th February. At the Tokyo University of Education, three lectures, then a recording for Sakuraba, the entrance examination dictation which had to be done twice as Shimaoka's speed was too slow. On to haircut, during which time a Boeing 727 went down in Tokyo Bay, killing 133. A day of chores.

On my energy. There are times, as I told Tuohy yesterday, when I am filled with a terrific energy that prevents me from sleeping and which cannot be fought, and when it comes I feel master of the world, so confident of being able to do anything that I feel as if I could sit down and finish a novel straight off. What is this energy? Is it manic? Is it a kind of madness? Is it connected with my nervous energy in my fingers – my finger-clicking being an expression of it – and can I draw mentally on this neurophysical energy? Could I control it – switch it on and off at will instead of praying for it to rise and then praying that it will not depart too soon, that it will stay as long as possible?

5th February. A talk with C about the future. Basically now that we have a maid she has too little to do and should get a job; but what about Nan? She would also like to see her friends, which means she should stay in England, whereas I must return to Tokyo. A job and friends – she needs these because at present she sees nobody, whereas I go out to work and then return to solitary writing. My suggestion, for the immediate future of this year, that she should go home early and return three months late, by sea both ways, if ship is cheaper than plane, or by ship one way if ship is much more expensive than the Russian route, and to wait and go with me. I would have a morning maid to iron shirts, to clean and do the shopping, and Nan could go to school next January.

On the Japanese. All their behaviour is founded on a silence, an aloneness. They live in the back room and go into the front room to receive guests, whereas Westerners live in the front room all the time, and do not know about the silence.

6th February. Rewrote the early part of Part 3. Then reviewed *The Outsider* from the point of view of the thesis rather than the justice (or injustice) of the illustrations. Briefly, (Colin) Wilson is saying that the solitary, as I would rather call him, has awakened to chaos, and that to him the bourgeois values and those of rational humanism are consequently unreal; there is release from the unreality in intense moments of self-expression, and the Romantic's desire for intensity (which the world disappoints) must be seen in terms of them; self-knowledge is knowing one's intense powers – this will help one escape one's acute sensitivity to pain by passing on to a "single, undivided Will" which can perceive the mystical "everything is infinite", which is not accessible to reason: i.e. Ultimate Yes, the visionary faulty seeing wholeness and disciplining the automatism to do so.

The main point is that man is, or can be, in transit, between "Outsider" and prophet, between unreality and intensity. This is so true of my own experience that I cannot begin to ask the sort of questions I asked of Hulme; the intense moments being connected with the stars and the forest and the sea (e.g. the wind flapping my trousers on Nobe beach, whirling through me, and the "jumping of exploding diamonds"). This is one book I shall never succeed in getting out of my system, because it corresponds so much to my own way of looking at things, and justifies it. All the errors and mistaken interpretations are forgiven him. This is how Eliot must have felt about Hulme.

7th February. After a long day, two classes at Tokyo University of Education including lunch with Sakuraba and Saito and O'Neill – Saito's

244

experiences in Mao's war-time China, O'Neill's prosaic, rather Mancunian ordinariness – and two hours with (Prince) Hitachi, I am still thinking about (Colin) Wilson. The objections to him are (1) that he is "muddle-headed and uneducated" (e.g. Tynan, Tuohy): often true; (2) that Holroyd's arrangement is better and his distinctions more intelligent: true; (3) that "too much reason is better than too little reason" (Amis): a narrow-minded example of rational humanism's indignation at being attacked by another tradition; (4) that his admiration of "brutality of intellect" is fascist: rubbish; (5) "I hate intensity" (Tuohy of Bergman): well; (6) "what has he got to offer – he has no historical sense" etc: he has an anti-humanist vision of intensity; (7) that his literary likes are an assortment of saints etc: humanist rot; (8) that he confesses humanism and the religious attitude by "knocking the fungus off old values": he starts off with a notion that man is, imperfect. No, one day all the sneerers will be proved wrong and *The Outsider* will be more widely read than *Speculations*, even though it has nothing new to say and is more derivative.

On the irrational, in reply to the objection "Is it a pleasure, is it a higher hedonism?": "No, it fertilises the whole being, and is the fertilising of land to be regarded as a higher hedonism?"

9th February. To (Prince) Hitachi. Read Keats's *Ode on a Grecian Urn*. The Prince's stirring emotion as he read it aloud, and his unwillingness to discuss the poem. Read up on China. The conflict between the two factions in Sun's Kuomintang after 1925 – Chiang being pro-left until 1926 and then turning pro-right, Mao and his followers growing out of the survivors of the left.

10th February. Corrected a Bank of Japan speech for the America-Japan society all morning, went to the Bank with it, and then went on to Masonic Building to see Ozenberger. ....His news that there is nothing wrong with my ear at all: my nerve deafness (20-30 decibels) is for low frequencies only, my flap is opening and the otitis externa is O.K. If I get any trouble, e.g. wetness, itching, I should take alchohol drops. Otherwise I am O.K., I will not go deaf, need not learn lip-reading. He ended up by talking about himself, telling me how he is leaving the Navy in May to go to Connecticut University and teach, which is what he always wanted to do.

11th February. After a completely sleepless night went to Tokyo University of Education to supervise three exams, at which I wrote well – three or four transitional passages from marriage to the first stroke. Returned and corrected two of the exams, and then slept on a futon in the sitting-room, C having bought it at my insistence after the wretched sleepless night; a simple solution to all problems which I've refused to consider, with the result that the new room has still to be built.

From Saturday, Tuohy's hatred of "long disquisitions on life" which mess up the aesthetic effect of what is hinted and suggested in art. On actresses and actors, "They don't have souls – that's why they're buried outside churchyards." Tuohy's moods, which range from the aggressive mask of the waistcoat and glasses ("the businessman and journalist") to the quiet, passive, sensitive, rather wretched and deeply likeable reflective artist: the genuine "soul". And one puts up with the puffed-up self-importance (which is not often anyway) and the rather abrupt and annihilating "what do you mean" because one knows it's a pose – not a conscious pose – and because the other Tuohy is better company than anyone else. In China I shall observe the tides of the moods, and will try to observe mine: from "manic" expansiveness, when I dominate the conversation, to impotent withdrawal, when I am too nervous to do so much as open my mouth. (All caused by something?)

12th February. After correcting a Bank of Japan speech with Tsuchigane all afternoon, went to the Tosho Hall to see Seymour's *The One Day of the Year*. Criticisms: lack of resonance, no dialectic – the Chekhovian situation within a situation and too little was left unsaid for us to imagine, this to me being an important part of the theatre: undistracted, we can concern ourselves with others and try to imagine what others are feeling; also a fault in architecture (two beginnings to Act 2) and lack of purity of theme, the class theme being only marginally related to the ANZAC theme; also the boy was imperfectly rounded (1) because he was in two halves (insufficiently resentful at first, too vehement later) and (2) because he was not independent of the author. As Tuohy said in the interval, *Coronation Street* was behind it somewhere. Nonetheless, it was very enjoyable.

The large gaijin, paying cash rather than tickets at the bar, laughing to say "I agree" in the auditorium; Bunny Brook, the actress, lined and hard, and Tuohy, who kissed her and said "It was magnificent and I wept buckets," and who was at first slightly indignant when I said "If I hadn't been watching I'd have thought it spontaneous." Tuohy came back to dinner and told me about his "skoshi ("little") affair" with M's black wife, he being an erotomaniac, and about Tomlin's mistress, who is the daughter of the Canadian Ambassador (Tomlin having been a co-respondent). His two "interesting" remarks – in the sense that they confirmed opinions I hold: (1) holding on to an image is good; (2) all great discoveries are made reluctantly (in Koestler's *Sleepwalkers*), cf Zabov. He got into a taxi at 1.30 saying "I'll ring you from Hong Kong."

13th February. Rewrote Pt 2, and then, after a walk in Chinzanso, put my papers in order in case of the unlikely event of my being killed in an air crash in China. Then went to Tuohy's to pump the Healeys and Lucas on China. Lucas, a quiet-voiced, greying man with a slightly Roman hair-cut and a sun-tanned complexion, foreign correspondent for the *Daily Mail* for 10 years, had an American wife for a short time, and is now teaching in Japan at the British Council and Hitotsubashi University and reviewing films in

THE INDIVIDUAL SOUL AND CHINESE MATERIALISM (1966)

Donald Richie's absence. He was a contemporary of Desmond Stewart's at Oxford – would he be in his 40s? He drove me home and we all sat round the futons until 2 a.m. drinking whisky and wasting time talking imperceptively. I was sick, and am now terribly unsteady, stagger slightly when I walk. I must stop drinking. I don't like drink, and only drink because it's something to do while talking, and because it loosens my tongue.

Is Lucas "Lukács"? He said his father was Italian, could he have entered Italy from the Austro-Hungarian Empire? Find out. The accent is, anyway, rather strange.

14th February. My poetry exam. My love-hate relationship with the Prince. His little rebellions: not turning to the right page and sitting back in his chair when I lean across to point to the page with my pencil; my suppressions, asking him to read and not looking up until he leans over. Also my ironic use of "Sir" and forcing him to read "Bold lover, never, never canst thou kiss" and (with relish) "Ozymandias, king of kings". And his refusal to come downstairs and my insistence. His insistence on 22nd March, my refusal on the grounds that I shall be in Hong Kong. And my deliberate embarrassment of him by asking him if he has a Gaimusho (Foreign Office) adviser for the Nicaraguan Embassy, which he does.

15th February. Went off to Keio to hold two exams and en route went to the Post Office and the Bank about deposit certificates. Because of the arrangement of times, five 4th year students came at 1 p.m. instead of 10.45. Caught Mr Taki cheating and confiscated his crib, making him sit in agony for three quarters of an hour, not knowing what I would do. At the end of the exam I handed him back his crib without a word and did no more. A long talk with Ando about China and this and that, and a visit to the Keio tax office to get my refund. Then came home and corrected Tokyo University of Education papers.

16th February. Corrected Keio 4th year papers and then went to see Tuohy to collect books and A1 questions. Returned, then went to the Prince. Corrected his poem about birds at different hours of the day. In the evening corrected Keio papers and rang Irie about not having the bedroom partitioned.

After this subject was dealt with, Irie told me that the regulations made no provision for a foreign Professor to be paid while off Japanese soil, and that he would go to a higher official. I phoned Buchanan and asked if I would be entitled to threaten to resign. He agreed. So I rang Irie back and threatened to resign on the grounds that I could not possibly return from England if there was no salary in the meantime. China will be a test-case. Irie: "Please take it easy, Mr Hagger." And "You are only the second invited foreign Professor at our University, the first being Professor William Empson in the 1920s, so we are not certain of the regulations." And so on.

Rang Tuohy; who said that China is not going down well with Waseda and that he has had to write an official letter to the President of Waseda, after he was told one would not be necessary.

17th February. Corrected Keio papers. Mrs. Patterson came, snow-tanned, and full of her "wonderful holiday". The main question from her point of view as I put on my shoes: "Will you be seeing the Barrons?" I: "I don't know – there's a possibility." Mrs. P, perennially rather scared of her boss's wife. Went to the Tokyo University of Education to get my salary and see Irie about not having the bedroom partitioned. Said nothing about my threat last night beyond emphasising that "Quite frankly" I had not taken the possibility of my not getting paid into account. The dispute as to whether futons are personal effects, like a tiepin, or not. I: "I would plead that the purpose for which they are used should be taken into account. This would put them in the same category as an irremovable bed." This argument clinched it. The regulations (which provide for a foreign Professor's bed but not for futons) were defeated.

Went to the Bank of Japan with my tax papers….At the end Tsuchigane showed me the Governor's office: the six white buzzers for each secretary; the round lights on the black panel to indicate which directors are in; the three rooms, from intimate to official.

After dinner corrected Keio papers. C's feeling that she is wasting her life on inessentials and my long harangue, urging her to believe in a future self and get on and paint. She: "I can't lead your life. You're different from everyone else."

18th February. A terribly rushed day. Tuohy rang at 8.15, believing it was 9.15, to say that the letter of invitation has arrived. After five telephone calls from the Tokyo University of Education about repayment for futons, went with Tuohy to Fuji I.T.S. and learnt (two hours before Tuohy's departure for Hong Kong) that the trip must be paid for in Hong Kong and not in Tokyo as we had been led to believe. A dash to the Hong Kong and Shanghai Bank for $500 for Tuohy. The slow-witted taxi-driver who did not respond to Tuohy's direction "Koko migi" ("here right"). Tuohy's panic: "F— you, f— you." Then Tuohy went off to Haneda.

Returned home to be rung by Yamashita: the letter of introduction is completed. Finished Keio papers, rerecorded the Bank of Japan speech for Tsuchigane (who brought 24 large bottles of beer as a present) and then talked. Tsuchigane's opinion that Japan is nearly lost to the U.S.; my question as to whether an economic thing like increasing trade with China might not have a political significance to the U.S. especially as they always get things wrong. Tsuchigane: "I have never thought of that, I must think about it."

19th February. After a week of arrangements, caught up on letters, China cuttings, poems. In the evening went to see the film of Ann

Jellicoe's *Knack*. Like Godard, no feeling; and at times an improbable mixture of realism and surrealism e.g. the painting of the room by the new tenant, which would have been O.K. as a fantasy but was not O.K. as one of the main threads. The former schoolmate of C's who was acting in character.

On my stay in Japan and way of life generally: I am the last of the amateurs in a world of professionals, combining poetry, teaching, journalism, banking, private secretary – in short anything I am asked to do – without really having the specialised, professional knowledge. I get by without trouble because I do not mind taking responsibility in a country where even the most professional experts are reluctant to assume the slightest responsibility.

20th February. Wrote my poems and made a discovery about my obsession with the Leader in Iraq (Kaseem). He symbolised the censor in myself, the conscious will which keeps a tyrannical order over my chaotic unconscious. He is the Urizen, the dictator who has imprisoned the Los. Hence my unusual interest in his deposition, and his sole journey unrecognised through the mud-huts. This was an unconscious allegory for the death of the personality – "the mad dictator". The priest, on the other hand, is a symbol (partly at least) of my "single face". Leader v priest, and the leader must die: the same formula applied to Zabov v priest, with the death of Zabov required. Hence the death-rebirth image of the buried "god" Te Deum which has found its repetition in the "risen god" imagery of the Tammuz and Inanna legend in the poems: "ziggurats and fir trees". The Leader must die and what is to be born?

21st February. After virtually no sleep and after writing up the priest and the moon on the water, received K and gave him two dictations and made him write a paragraph on England. Toyama came and drank. His diary with 70 points for some days; 12,000 points last year and 2,460 so far this year. The policeman who observes him under streetlamps at midnight. His point about Japanese culture being pro-unity and now seeking the distinctions of rational Western culture, whereas Western culture is now seeking the unity of the East. West v East – those are the two traditions I have frequently catalogued. His reluctance to go to England because he wants to help those Japanese who cannot go abroad, and because he fears he will not be able to interpret Japan well enough to foreigners.

22nd February. Tried to rewrite the speech in the Holly Bush and the rechoice of self against a background of telephone calls from Hashimoto (tax), Irie (advice on English – "a textual study of some Chinese classics") and a visit from Buchanan and so on. When I was thoroughly exasperated I went off to the bookshops under the pretext of looking for a book on Hong Kong.

23rd February. Rewrote a great deal, from the dead god to the despair in Hinksey, some four pages, which must be a record. The pattern of my rebellion: discovery of the will, which led to a kind of madness, then meaninglessness, until I groped back to the microcosm of my self…through the saviour, and wound up seeking "the single face". My messy search for truth which embodies truth – the untidy seeking and not finding but getting nearer and yet not knowing one is nearer unless one can measure it with art. Perhaps that is my justification for my poems: that without them, I would not be able to measure/ to have measured my spiritual progress; although, of course, the independent "making" that Tuohy often brings up is equally important. The yardstick idea is what gives my poems pressure. Perhaps only a seeker can be a great poet.

24th February. Wrote poems, then went off to the Palace Hotel Crown Lounge to have lunch with the Bank of Japan secretaries, Gengo, Ichiki, Tsuchigane and Saito. As I had suspected, the lunch was a monologue on China by me, the others all being embarrassed at asking questions in English before each other. Mr Ichiki's questions about Mao and about the real nature of my purpose in visiting China. The "Oh come off it" sceptical attitude when I said that, articles aside, I was interested in China's past; my documentation of Greek and Roman coins and Tutankhamun. The question as to why the Chinese accept Communism, do they obey or do they believe? Returned to poems to try and bridge science and law.

A letter from Tuohy. In the evening, a film of the Nuremburg Trials on TV: nightmarishly slow marches between ropes to scaffolds or to thick blocks of wood; voluntary takings up of positions, the black hood, and the shot which didn't hit where it should, the slow, living dying, resisting the final slump into the ropes. The morning mist and the wretched procession to the scaffold and the tugging on the rope beneath the floor, signalling life.

25th February. For a new "hobby" compile a film of all the atrocities committed in the 20th century in the name of justice and freedom and other abstract ideas. Include every hanging and shooting on documentary record, the slaughter of World War I, Auschwitz, Hiroshima, and the reprisals for coups d'états everywhere, the torture of Vietnamese, Koreans and the executions in Peking. This would be my "file" of human cruelty, like Ivan Karamazov's file on children. The theme: brotherhood, irrespective of race. And the human condition. Begin with a pure dawn and then show the contamination. I told C of this idea before we slept last night, and this possibly accounts for the black cloth in her dream. How to get the films?

27th June 1966. This should be a poem: pictures from a scrapbook, collaged into a Last Judgement and Indictment of 20th century man and his wrong-headed values.

26th February. Worked on China. One point about East-West: the notion of competitive individualism, with the individual fighting to subdue

THE INDIVIDUAL SOUL AND CHINESE MATERIALISM (1966)

Nature and progress and seek his own salvation, is quite alien to the East, where the individual is subordinated to the group and man must co-operate with man and live in harmony with Nature and therefore curtail his ambition in the interests of a satisfactory social state. My poems reflect a failure in the scheme of competitive individualism, and Freeman the non-competer is much more at home in the East, where competition is considered rather vulgar in the best circles. In the West, we admire the man of ambition who has forced his way to the top – we say he has a powerful "personality" – whereas the East is more cultivated and self-knowledgeable in despising aggressiveness and the hollowness of "personality", which is really only egotism, and in preferring subtlety to drive and confident initiative.

27th February. A miserably wet and squally day destroyed our plan to go to Kamakura, and so I read on China and took notes on the headlines in a pile of *Gazettes*, a combination which sent me back to a poem, a part 2 to the sickness of Britannia, the theme being decay and pettiness.

1st March. Two examples of Japanese idiocy: (1) Irie telephoned yesterday evening to clear up doubts about the salary business: Sato says I cannot be paid because 1. I will need an entry visa into China; 2. I will need a re-entry visa into Japan, and I will get neither of these because I have no letter from the President. Irie's astonishment when I told him I had got both three weeks ago. He honestly thought I was going to try to leave Japan without making any preparations at all. (2) S would not take a cheque for ¥106,350 today, because "foreigners cannot have Yen accounts in Japan." My two calls to the Bank: first they refused to tell S how much I have in my account (under "Clayton's law"), which made him all the more suspicious, then they said merely that I was resident in Tokyo, which proved to be enough. Also, went to Tokyo University of Education to sign forms to exempt C for tax and to entitle C to collect my salary in my absence; collected $500 from the Bank; and had a haircut at the Oriental in the Nikkatsu Arcade.

I have been soaking in intellectual facts about China, and so my language is dead and intellectual, and I have seen nothing and recorded nothing freshly.

2nd March. Wrote in a gap in the poems, the revolution, and before and after going to the Prince (where I tripped on the wooden ledge in his hall and nearly lost my balance) I arranged the poems so that in rough outline they are in the form I want. Of course much remains to be done in the way of publishing and abridging, but I am happier about them than I have ever been, for I can see now that I have opened up poetry to life and have opened up untold possibilities. I am also happy because if my premonition that I shall have a fatal accident is correct, the poems could be published. This premonition seemed to be strengthened slightly by a call from Adrian, which I have been predicting on this evening for some time. His suspect beginning: "I am not ringing for any particular reason, but just to find out how you're getting on and whether you're still in Japan." Compare Nadi: "I didn't take three sweeties this morning."

3rd March. Tokyo-Kowloon. After a rushed day – packing, laying last minute plans, going to the Bank of Japan, getting my poems in final order – I got myself off to Hong Kong. C and Nan come to the airport. Nan only interested in whether I would say she has been a good girl and if I would bring her a present, and C clearly very unhappy to see me go. Our conversation yesterday evening after her one and only depression this last week; "I'd rather you weren't going, that's all"; which ended with me saying that I am different from everyone else and cannot get on with people who will not regard me primarily as a poet: in short, "I am seeking my role."

After a terrible flight – a cloudbank like an iceberg, and the lightning – and after I had been driven from the airport to the Grand Hotel and had met Tuohy and had gone out into this decaying town of Kowloon, I said something rather similar on being asked my name: "If I had a name I would have an identity." This came out quite spontaneously in a semi-humorous context. Tuohy had returned from Macao by hydrofoil that morning and did not meet me because of one of his many dinner engagements; though the Snowdens forced him to eat near the Hotel and not across the water. He seemed pleased to see me, and then tore up my letter and the typed *Newsweek* questions I sent him, a gesture that surprised me as being unnecessarily rude. The old love-hate again.

After Tuohy went to bed I went out for a stroll, and without a doubt, this town is falling apart, from tenements to buses. It is rotting, and all the walls are blistered. The pickpockets.

4th March. Kowloon. Got up at 8 after little sleep and went over the ferry into Hong Kong to the China Travel Service. Encountered Princess Margaret in a shopping centre and then again, later, when we tried to have breakfast at 12 noon. After lunch – beer at the terribly confident and snobbish English Whitbread pub – we went shopping and I bought two perfumes ("Je reviens" and Worth), and black silk shantung and silk thread in gold, this with some difficulty from some Indians who took our money without handing over the goods.

When I returned to my hotel I was pitching and swaying with tiredness and from the bad flight. Nonetheless, struggled out...to the Ambassadors and Nguyen (= "Nian") M and Mrs. K, whose sister's husband teaches architecture in Shanghai. The clothes. NM's fluency, which was tiring. Her background: an uncle and a brother in the Viet Cong, and a cousin helping, she having twice turned down CIA offers of 5,000HK$ a day for an hour's broadcast and to be silenced as an anti-American journalist in English. Her godfather is Angier, Kennedy's aide, and she travels to Vietnam three times a year. On the way back to the hotel I said she was up to something and this led to disagreement with Tuohy, who accused me of being too suspicious (e.g. of the hotel being wired, I having found the wooden blocks) and said "Life's impossible if you go on like that." The crystal snuff-bottle, and her husband, who had that day been diagnosed as having a bone disease which is incurable. The earlier episode of Miss Lau's telephone call and of the man who eavesdropped when I left a message. The crowded bookshop which turned out to be a cocktail party given by Ron Heapy, a contemporary of mine at Oxford.

5th March. Kowloon-Canton. Left the Grand Hotel at 7.55 for Kowloon station where I read in the paper that my DC8 crashed at Tokyo airport yesterday, killing 60-70, including the crew and two air hostesses I had, Miss Ho and the Japanese Miss Himaguchi (?). This depressed me. The train journey to the border: hills, yellow soil, water pipes from China, squatters, a missionary school, peeling buildings. The wait from 10.30 to 12.40 at the border. "Will our bags be all right?" "Everything is all right in our country."

China: red sandstone (later yellow-brown), firs, tombs in hills, bright green rice, green-brown water in the flooded paddies; empty spaces in the streets like a 19th century painting; few telegraph poles leading to villages, houses in same direction (geomancy); watchtowers. A country of open spaces and blue hills in the distance. Barefooted children and peasants among hens and dogs; the booted army and police. (This at Zhangmutou). A cattle market, bananas and sugar-cane, tea with leaves and blossom that are supposed to sink. Buffalo, ducks. Farm encampment, white walls and outhouses, rather patched. Flies in the train. Junks with sails like fans. Pigs in the truck. Clover? The dormitories and factories outside Canton; no tractors. Coke?

In Canton, the drive to the hotel in an old Humber Hawk. The poster of the U.S. soldier being strangled by a Chinese. The walk while Ho (our guide) got the permits. The goat, then the squalid, ill-lit department store, then the dynamic but oversimplified opera *The East is Red* in the Sun Yat-sen Memorial Hall; the words on screens on either side; the Thai dance; the applauding of "Chairman Mao". Not allowed to drink outside the hotel afterwards so sat with Tuohy on the 7th floor lobby and talked unbugged and saw the Ceylonese (?) who sat behind us at the opera.

6th March. Canton. Off at 8.30 to a People's Commune, Dai Li, between Canton and Fushan. The long talk with Mr Lin the Chairman, in the hall. (Red star, whitewash and Chairman Mao.) The system of troop-brigade-team; pay according to efforts (and abilities, in the case of the old) in cash; incentive for the intelligent to leave; own plots, decided by the brigade. No war expected, and no real intention to help North Vietnam yet. The whitewashed stone and brick homes like an encampment of farm outhouses with narrow streets, or like Herculaneum. Architecture 100 years old. The human hair spun by the children, who broke into spontaneous applause, assuming we are friends. The two selected houses, the first of which had food on the table and the second of which had a man who coyly told me that he was saving for daily needs and not luxuries. Meetings in the evening at the brigade office. The shops: the collective of 10, so private ownership is not abolished. The hospital, the children's reading room. Fushan pottery, political subjects including Castro. The soccer, Shanghai v Liaoning.

On the way back from Fushan (to Canton) saw a searchlight and was told a pilotless plane had crashed in South China the day before. A walk on the foreigner's island near the Pearl River, and the French houses and the fear of cholera in the 19th century.

After dinner to a gymnastic display, which was full of errors, and a table tennis contest. Not up to Olympic standard? On the way back saw a picture of U.S. buses for students' and workers' protest. Tuohy on security and boredom and its two causes, education and envy. Also on the need for a writer to have vision and a "sharp, not blunt instrument". Tuohy: "Canton is very southern."

7th March. Canton. Went to a teachers' training college. (28th September, later the Red Guards' Centre for South China.) The campus: green grass, bohemia and hibiscus trees. The talk with Mr Pan, then the tour, orienting slowly upon the English division of the foreign language faculty, which mobbed us in a deserted classroom. As Tuohy said later, their joyous faces almost defied analysis; they were very like the faces in the opera; conditioned as in Huxley rather than compelled as in Orwell. Later, the musty, pre-1949 library.

Then to the Pearl River to see the sampans and the rehousing. After, to the boat primary school and the pioneers. Always when we left: "Have you any criticism?" Which led to a lunch-time discussion with our guide on self-criticism, a discussion which was continued after lunch and which stopped short of brainwashing. Mrs. Ho's sadness and eagerness to convince herself by convincing us. Thence back to the hotel. The photo of the students' protests in the U.S. – a map and bases with the torch of freedom, which I photographed quite openly. To the airport, not past the poster of the soldier being strangled. The British Viscount, Mrs. Ho's sadness about my pamphlet *Traitorous Revisionists Support U.S. Imperialists on Vietnam Aggression* – the sadness of a Christian who does not believe in original sin.

Dick Wills, who is shy and rude, a failed saint who wanted to go into a monastery, "badly smashed" (Tuohy), a cross between Greene and Corvo. His book *The Orthodox Church*. Heard from him that the pilotless U.S. plane was shot down, also that a BOAC 727 has crashed on Fuji. Our flight. The clouds like slush and melting snow-drifts.

THE INDIVIDUAL SOUL AND CHINESE MATERIALISM (1966)

Met at Hangchow by Mr Wi ("missed a wee"). Tuohy's childish giggles, and mine too. The beauty of Hangchow. Decided to go to Shanghai a day early as this place is awfully dead: Mr Wi showing some panic.

8th March. Hangchow. Mountains in the distance, a lake with a causeway and bridge, an island, trees. In the morning went to a middle school, where there was a poster about the militia, and then to Lingyin Ssu and Yueh Fei temple and tomb. Then for a walk till lunch. Quite a few couples.

Over a lunch of lake herring and shrimps in tea, outlined a plan for revitalising Britain on Chinese lines: a system of townships, each one self-reliant in industry and agriculture, with education for all and an assault on inarticulacy, reconnecting old ladies with a symbol of the nation more vital than the Queen. Hold this up in Poem 2 (later *Old Man in a Circle*), contrast Chiang and now with Britain now and in the future. The dream which the Shadow will become: an industrial version of Chinese energy, and a more cultured (because more advanced) bias. The U.S. as the enemy. Cromwell is the hero. Tuohy: "I like my English mad, private and eccentric." "The English are so awful in groups." "You'd never get rid of the class system." Land reform and one-way visas to the Mediterranean for the upper classes who would not co-operate. Persuasion, not terror. The new problem: revitalisation of an advanced and technological nation. Giving the worker a share of the country's destiny. Nationalism.

After lunch visited a tea commune. The brigade office is the landlord's former house and determined Mrs. Ching, his former peasant. The primary school: the joyous children aged 4, who did a tea dance and came to shake hands and shouted "Susu nin ha" ("how are you uncle?"). The important plan each year. Tuohy's mistake about the film, which got jammed near the end.

On to Shanghai on a freezing train (42°F). Met by a suspicious Mr Chung: the mess-up over Lee/Li. A talk with Tuohy about prose style (his ideal of translucency) which ended with a joke by me: "The loop costs eight guineas, because if a gynaecologist says 'Say Ah' it costs eight guineas."

9th March. Shanghai. Disenchantment with China beginning, possibly because today we did things against our will with two guides, both Chungs. We did not ask to go to Shanghai Mansion or the Worker's Community, nor did we ask to be dragged round tool and thresher factories and cows on the Ma Lo Commune and so miss the antique shop. I still believe that there is a new kind of man in China: the joyous welcome we received from the workers, and the young children, and the peasants who occupied the former landlord's house (he living in a kind of stable) confirm that. They have showpiece-communes, but they are sincerely happy.

It was the conversation with our guides on art that unsettled me. The two views of art, one emphasising a political judgement, the other the aesthetic qualities of complexity, subtlety and depth and discovery (and as Tuohy put

255

it, no one can discover the Liberation as everyone knows it). I just do not agree with their view of art, and I do not like their lies (regarding Beryl Grey) and their distortions. For example, "Let a hundred flowers bloom through weeding out the past", seems to me to be very different from "Let a hundred flowers bloom and a hundred schools of thought contend". Perhaps Mao did say them at the same time; I suspect rather that the first is the slogan that transported Ting Ling to Sinkiang, and that it succeeded the second, which marked the opening of free criticism in 1957. The security for the children is good, the security for the peasants is good, but you cannot drag everything down to the opinion of a group of workers and peasants and soldiers.

Later, to a social realist film *Valley Sisters*, which did not engage my feelings and bored me to death with its black and white simplifications.

10th March. Shanghai. My disenchantment has turned into repulsion after: (1) a visit to Mr Liu, national capitalist and son of the former match king of Shanghai, in the course of which it emerged that he had been brainwashed, what he called "remoulding" – "these Americans call it brainwashing" – "the process of seeing things in their right perspectives", a process demanding "time, patience and forbearance"; witness the lesioned thoughts and Party clichés over iced cake and tea and coffee and beer and biscuits in his bright, compounded and guarded house; (2) I found a tear in my luggage which could only have been caused between 9 and 12 (when I saw it) and was presumably caused by someone sticking a finger under the lock to see inside; and which might be related to the fact that we were observed going out alone early this morning: the guide's question, "Have you taken any photographs of junks?"; (3) most of all, a visit to a children's district palace: an assault course based on the Long March, an amusement centre with targets of Americans, singing and dancing to Chairman Mao, models of U.S. planes that have been shot down.

My sadness during the dance "Embroidering the portrait of Chairman Mao", for the Party has captured the minds of these children, the Party has put the smiles on their faces, and when 800 pioneers in blue shirts and red scarves applauded us, I knew it was the Party that had put their spontaneity there, just as it had remoulded Mr Lui. What we have seen is not Communism but energy, organisation, security and Western medicine, and the joyousness and the love of labour have been put into those children's minds by the Party, but one cannot say it is insincere, just as one cannot call a conditioned reflex insincere. But is their conditioned gratitude not better than the starvation of the 1940s, and can one honestly prefer starvation to freedom of mind? In the face of that though one feels repulsion and admiration at the same time.

11th March. Shanghai. It is the suppression of criticism I do not like now, what Mrs. Li was afraid of acknowledging yesterday evening after

THE INDIVIDUAL SOUL AND CHINESE MATERIALISM (1966)

Tuohy handed over the smuggled clothes and she belied her sister's impression of her by not being frank: "We are different people; she does not know me. She does not understand that clothes are cheap here. There is a gulf between us." She would not talk objectively about the "spontaneity", and this morning, in spite of an immensely frank talk at Futan University, we were told that intellectuals who despise labour have been influenced (1) by capitalists and landlords (like Mr Liu who has "confessed"? and where are the others?); (2) by living before the Liberation (in 1949 students would have been two years old); (3) films and plays (why did they get produced?); (4) by bourgeois teachers (like the Professor in the room). What nonsense, especially as only 40% are of worker-peasant origin at that university.

So in spite of the closure of the hundred flowers, criticism "does not exist" and the bourgeois reactionaries are unsettling intellectuals. So intellectuals must be encouraged to love labour, in the case of (1) full-time student-intellectuals by working in the countryside for three months a year in two stretches, and in the case of (2) work-study student-intellectuals, obviously by working in factories but also by going to the country for three weeks in the last two years.

The final vision is to break down the division between peasant-worker-intellectual, between country and town, peasant and worker, and manual and mental labour, and in fact a new school has been devised for uniting these three and is being experimented with, and in the final Communist vision there will be no criticism for the intellectual will love labour; but in the meantime the intellectual must suspend disbelief and struggle and "criticise" his own bourgeois tendencies and if he is an artist, alter his art in accordance with the judgement of the people; and under transitional socialism he must sacrifice his freedom to think and voluntarily accept the degradation of his own intellect. No thank you.

12th March. Nanking. Having arrived by train at 12.53 a.m. this morning. A day of great suspicion i.e. watchful silence from our guide during our visit to Nanking University and to the Ming founder's square wall and tomb and in the Department store.

Two threads could be responsible for this, and all or some of the situations in one or the other or both. (1) Tuohy. In Kowloon he inadvertently telephoned the U.S. consulate about a book, which he went to collect, and he may have been watched by the manager of the Grand; in Shanghai there was the business of Mrs. Li and his walk to photograph the "junks" and his strong pressure on Futan University; and this morning he inadvertently photographed work on a shelter, which is being put up in the grounds of the hotel; and they may have found out that he is a writer, hence Mrs. Chung's lead: "Are you going to write about this when you get back? It's only natural." Admittedly addressed to me. Lucas said they would have found out through reference books by the time he reached Peking. (2) Me. Yamashita's letter to Soma may have been intercepted in the post, resulting

257

in the search through my luggage in Shanghai and the scratches on my lock and the turning upside down of my medical box and the stuffing away of Yamashita's letter of introduction in the outside pocket when the searcher thought he heard me coming back; I too went for a walk in Shanghai; I raised the question of bourgeois reactionaries again this morning – "Are there any bourgeois influences on the campus?" – and have taken photographs and notes and asked questions, all in the name of Chairman Mao's call for discussing differences and criticising to resolve ignorance.

Furthermore, we may have aroused suspicions by changing our itinerary, going to Shanghai early and coming here to Nanking, and they may feel that there is some ulterior motive, quite wrongly of course.

13th March. Nanking. Abdication in favour of God is a well-trodden path, but abdication in favour of the State is a 20th century problem, and its weakness is in its treatment of children. At the Youth Hall this morning, being applauded by 400 young pioneers and listening to children singing songs about war and oppression and the old society and Chairman Mao, I understood why the children are so important, for they are the future in whose name the intellectuals are now being suffocated, and it is for them that the past must constantly be revived, for the Party has them so long as it can keep the dimension of the past alive. Hence the mythical outside enemy and the mythical inside enemy, the U.S.-Chiang, the Japanese-Kuomintang alliance in the film last night, *Tunnel Warfare*: the children must be kept vigilant in terms of the past – the activities of the militia are secondary to this end – and then they will present no problem and the Party will survive. It is indeed the kind of power for power's sake that was Big Brother's policy.

This conclusion is also the conclusion of the view that it is the bourgeois intellectuals that the Party is afraid of, a view which must be connected with the children to be understood. In a revitalised Britain there can be townships and a land reform, yes – these things would be great – but the future of the revolution must not depend on the conditioning of the children, and it must not therefore suffocate the intellectuals and individual creativity, for a nation that cannot create cannot survive. In that respect, the prospects for China are grim, judging by the art of their children, and can one predict that for this reason Communism must fail? The principle of revitalisation has overthrown all my Toynbeean ideas about the pattern of disintegration in a civilisation, but in that case one can say that Mao is not the new Christ.

14th March. Nanking-Peking. A day spent in the train between Nanking (left 9.20 p.m. Sunday) and Peking (arrived 6.44 p.m. Monday). The situation between Tuohy and myself largely depended on a conversation yesterday, over dinner. I began it by saying that R-W in the Embassy cannot have seen much in China as he did not even remark on the blueness. Tuohy: "I could dine out on my impressions here for the rest of my life, whereas yours wouldn't last a week."

THE INDIVIDUAL SOUL AND CHINESE MATERIALISM (1966)

This completely unprovoked attack drew me out. I immediately said that there are two kinds of sensibility, that which feeds off the outside world and that which wells up from within, and after distinguishing the Greene-Eliot sensibility from Angus Wilson's, said: "Anyway, would you want to dine out for the rest of your life?" And "I would rather stay in China than get caught up in that world." Tuohy withdrew and after that we went on about sensibility, he rather reluctantly, and I not saying that observations are superficial when compared to the fertile silence on which my sensibility depends. Tuohy: "I was always an observant child" and "when I was in my 20s I had an anxiety neurosis and saw a psychiatrist and tried to get outside myself." I: "Do you attribute your present style to an attempt to get outside yourself?" Not really any answer.

In the train we kept off it. But having met our guide Mr Tsu on Peking platform, he was again awfully curt: "Hagger, tickets." Which I ignored. After wrecking relations with the guide by his aggressiveness we went to the 6th floor bar of this, the Hsin Chiao Hotel and drank in a room of billiard tables and many nationalities and lonely wreckage and the next morning at breakfast he said: "You handle orientals better than I do. I'm sick of orientals. There was so much more to the chief of Police in Macao than there has been to anyone else I've met for a long time." A comment I ignored.

15th March. Peking. The brown mud, the maize screens against the dust. A day of thinking about energy and decay. The determination and guts that built the Great Wall in a flinty surrounding: where people are more dour, grim, individual than in Nanking, more aggressive and less joyous, more arrogant. And the decline in Wan-li's tomb: no preparations against pulverisation, no sealed chambers within the sealed brick. Did this late Ming emperor come to doubt his divinity after his 20s, when his tomb was completed? In the early evening, the film *Red Woman's Detachment*.

The trouble with China is that the struggle's over and is moving into the boredom of establishment, but Mao cannot afford to admit this; and so there have to be trumped up struggles today: "the class struggle is not over", and the struggle of the militia to defend the revolution against its mythical enemy, and China's sympathy with the struggle in Vietnam. Since I came to China, my attitude towards Vietnam has changed, for I believe that China genuinely believes (1) that, like the Kuomintang, Ky does not represent his country, and (2) that (contrary to Dean Rusk's view that China is using "liberation" as a pretext for aggression) there is genuinely a war of liberation going on against a corrupt government. I don't say China is right, but I do think her position is understandable.

The energy that goes into the initial struggle, and the decay that follows the establishment of its cause, after which there must be a new struggle. Apply this to Britain. There must be a new struggle in Britain, the decay must be energised.

259

AWAKENING TO THE LIGHT

16th March. Peking. An all day visit to Peking University which seemed to confirm that the 3rd and 4th year were being punitively remoulded in Sinkiang.

The morning's evidence was scanty: there was nobody on the campus, and when, after visiting a 2nd year class, we asked to visit a 3rd or 4th year class, we were told they were "in the country", that they went in August and would be back some time soon. After the unsatisfactory, frightened talk in the U.S. house, Prof. Chao, said it was "socialist education". Tuohy had earlier heard "re-education" – I think misheard – and over lunch there was a slight disagreement, I saying there was as yet insufficient evidence.

In the afternoon we visited a student's dormitory and talked through a 5th year student and established: the 3rd and 4th year are sent individually to Sinkiang, they live and eat and work and talk with the peasants, one or more in the same village, have no books or study for six months, and are supervised by the peasants. We also learned from the Secretary to Administration (1) that there is discontent with the 5th year course (abolish this six months labour and it could come down to 4 years), and (2) that history and philosophy subjects are being remoulded to get rid of bourgeois ideology, and that history and philosophy have been moved permanently to the countryside. I asked a student, "Why aren't you in Sinkiang?" and he replied, "Because I've got a medical certificate."

In other words attendance in the countryside is compulsory unless there is a reason for exemption. One can object "What went before to cause this 'purge'?" and "Why aren't they brainwashed more actively, with Marxist thought?" but the interruption of a five year course for a period of labour without books does suggest punishment and remoulding on a much more serious scale than the one and a half months a year maximum labour elsewhere. As Tuohy said: "When they come back they will be asked 'Do you want to go there again?'"

We decided to make a stand and after a boring, feeling-free film about the creation of a commune, we raised the whole thing with our guide, and learnt that the socialist education movement began in 1964 (in fact 1962), and demanded to return to Peking University or to visit the Ministry of Education on behalf of the Ting Lings, and who are we to interfere?

14th September 1966. This is the first glimpse by any non-Chinese of what was later to be called "the Cultural Revolution" and the Red Guards.

17th March. Peking. An icy cold day. Visited the Forbidden City in the morning, including the tree on Coal Hill where the last Ming emperor hanged himself, and a prison in the afternoon, in a grey-fawn monochrome part of Peking, the sky, like the road, being a leaden white. The counter-revolutionaries included spies sent by the Kuomintang and the U.S., reactionaries and saboteurs. The broken dignity of these as they made gloves, the coarser faces of the "evil-doers". The electric fence, the

260

whitewash below window-level on the walls. The searchlight.

In the evening, a play about Yuan Wan Tsé, the Viet Cong executed by the U.S. His pleased smile, the caricature of a U.S. Captain who would not negotiate with revolutionaries; the affectionate wife.

The thread throughout the day was the stand (see yesterday). I argued with (our guide) Mr Tsu (pronounced Chou) on Coal Hill, he lying and saying that the 5th year student had (1) wrongly said "yes", (2) wrongly said "supervise". I corrected him. "I asked 'Who supervises the students?' and he said 'The peasants'." Tsu got rattled, and sulked in the car on the way to the prison. In the interval of the play I told him about the imprisoned students in Iraq, and he said he would arrange for me to see the Vice-Dean at Peking University.

Earlier, at dinner, Tuohy said (after telling me he would not go to the play): "Go easy with Tsu." I: "He lied to me and underestimated my intelligence by believing I would swallow it."

18th March. Peking. Dreamt I was beating coalminers on the head and did not want to split their skulls. Presumably repressions. Woke to a duststorm.

Went through monochrome scenery to a work-study, then to the refreshing Temple of Heaven. The causeway path from the sun-wheel to the distant gate of death, and the duststorm that blew across and concealed the god and I had been there in my dreams. Square earth, circular heaven; did the Ming emperors believe themselves divine, and did they also reconcile their contradictions?

On to lunch with Donald in an old-style Peking house that looked like a fire station. The information about the purge and socialist education, the turning on of the screws. After, went to the military museum – nothing modern – and the People's Hall, which was full of vulgar art, external details and no inner flow.

After acrobatics drank with Tuohy and discussed futility. Tuohy was very much against suicide, because he is an experiencing human being who likes food and drink, and lack of appetite is "an illness". He does not kill himself to save himself the sweat because "it's fun". On the acorn's dream of the oak: "An acorn is not affected by external experience." He is still growing, i.e. understanding. He believes in a left wing resistance to, and denial of, pain, and a right wing acceptance of, and understanding of, pain. "I shall be staunchly right wing after this." I: "The executed man and the suicide are heroes in a tragic ritual, and in watching their living and dying we can relive the deaths of all men. We need kaleidoscoped myths that relate to our needs and illuminate them, witness the play about Yuan Wan Tsé."...

Tuohy left me, and dreamt that he and I went to visit (James) Joyce, who showed us a hitherto unpublished work: an indication that he thinks of me as a writer?

19th March. Peking. A day attacking the Party line. Made our stand at Peking University with Professor Hwang, the Vice-President (see 16th March) and learnt that the students are following a Party, not a university line, that their courses are interrupted, that they "write histories for the peasants even though they are unreliable". They are being indoctrinated, that seems clear.

Later, saw a list of candidates on the campus, and this led to an attack on Mr Tsu (Chou) in the Summer Palace restaurant, I saying (1) that the people of China are not masters of the Central committee, because they have no power to sack, and (2) that if Chinese history books say the concessions were seized by Mao in 1949 rather than that they were given back voluntarily in 1945, then history is being rewritten and Mao has lied. "You must doubt", I said, "as we doubted the British figures in the war and as we doubt the American figures now. What guarantee have you that the North Vietnamese figures are right?" The rest of the afternoon we spent in an angry but compassionate silence, with a great gulf between us, and walking among the ruins of the sack of 1860 and the plundering of 1900 and then in the Garden of Delight in Harmony with its green lake like a meditating mind on which the world is an unreal reflection.

After walking down an old Peking street we went out to eat Peking duck with two old ladies from Australia, and again I got at Tsu over the children and over creativity, and asked him if he doubted the story about the pigs in the stream or the 1949 figures in the Commune, and when he said "No" I gave him a resumé of *1984*, ending with the question "If the Party asked you to believe that 2+2=5, would you believe it? If the Party told you that Chairman Mao has been wrong, would you believe it?" The answer: "Impossible". And I had defended the Western value of freedom of thought, the right to vote out, the truth of history and the individual criterion of the truth.

20th March. Peking. Last night Tuohy dreamt that he and I crossed the bottom of a gorge while a voice echoed messages of hate to a group of pioneers; the owner of the voice, a scoutmaster, was knocked down by a lorry, which turned out to be driven by two American G.I.s.

This has been the theme of today, knocking down the messages of hate. The Children's Palace, in part of the old Imperial Palace, was full of clean, bright, happy pioneers, playing their games, firing machine-guns and knocking down a cardboard G.I. Their eyes shone to military music like "People of the world, unite". They joyously waved their flags under the Ching arch. But there was not a soul among them, not a soul, and I felt how unwanted Christ would have been, treating them as beings with individual importance rather than as material for remoulding.

After lunch we went to a church. We had tried to go after breakfast but we had been told "Today is Sunday and the churches are closed" and "You can go to the Lama temple instead." Outside the barred doors, and under the cross, sat the hopeless, old men who had nothing else to do, the individuals commemorating the spirit. We went past this hell into the courtyard and into the church. An old woman knelt in prayer. Otherwise no one was about. There were 14 framed pictures of the suffering servant. The cross was too much for him, and he was crushed under the feet of the people: workers, peasants, soldiers. Here men were defined in terms of pain and were of individual importance. Tuohy must have been as moved as I was, for he put 5 yuan in the box, much to the guide's disapproval.

Afterwards we went to the two museums on the history of China, where the Red Army was being taught the origins of the Revolution, and we walked among the dozens of groups in the vast People's Square, and I knew that this bright, happy world of theirs is shallow, unreal and rootless, for I knew the soul, I was on Christ's side against this Chairman Grand Inquisitor, and I knew that I, too, had crossed a gorge.

21st March. Peking-Hangchow. And yet I have always been on Christ's side. No, rather I crossed over to have a look and then returned, as I crossed the Yangtse River. And I have brought back with me a real knowledge of how the Grand Inquisitor (in Dostoevsky's *Brothers Karamazov*) enslaves, and I have thereby come to respect still more the values of freedom and responsibility.

All through a miserable day, being delayed first in Shanghai and then finally and for the rest of the day in Hangchow, because "the weather is not up to our flying standards", I contemplated the revolution in store for Britain. It will surely be based on the individual, for Christ is our Confucius, and the Renaissance tradition has not conflicted with the importance he gave to the individual. And it will surely not deny freedom or responsibility. It is not that the Grand Inquisitor was wrong, or that times have changed; we in Europe have no need of him, not only because we are not starving, but also because we prize our individual responsibility too much. In economic terms, this responsibility is rather unpleasant (see 26th February) and in terms of high society, it is unreal – the depth of Japan is infinitely superior to that – but in terms of the State it is much superior to the collective soullessness of the Grand Inquisitor's subject-slaves.

Our revolution must be both religious and social, without considering men as material for remoulding and without corrupting the children. Its aims will be to raise the soul-level of the nation, and to equalise and release the energies of men by reorganising society. This is a message in a time of decay, and it needs a soldier-Christ, not a Lenin or Mao, for the national cause is secondary to the spiritual. It is the deadness rather than the ogres (the ruling class, the landlords) that must be overthrown. A new religion is needed, not a new workers' and peasants' movement. The Christian way of life must be redefined, as Christ redefined Judaism, and the result will pervade wider, deeper and longer than any social movement that loses its raison d'être when society is changed.

22nd March. Hangchow-Canton. And yet a social change very often releases religious energy, and after leaving gloomy Hangchow at 12.20 and flying to Canton, which is darker in its greens, where people are barefooted and noisy and walking in groups, for it is hotter, I noted down what needs changing.

The distinction between worker and bourgeois should be removed, automation doing much of the worker's former work; the ruling class should be expelled peacefully, the Queen exiled, Parliament replaced by a more modern assembly; Britain should be reorganised in a scheme of self-reliant townships, but after the initial direction of labour, there should be as little interference with the individual as possible; women should work; every citizen should plant one tree a year; Christianity should be abolished in practice, though one church should be left open in each township; Buckingham Palace should be a children's centre; above all, all land should be seized and owned by the State.

In one generation, there would be a complete change in our social structure, and all this can be achieved by cells of ten. Energy would then not depend on birth, on class, and with a crash programme in education, again the principle being cells of ten, in one generation every worker and peasant in Britain would be reasonably cultured. So much for the background to a new religion. The religion itself should work through cells of ten – "families" – each new cell recruiting another on Soka Gakkai lines.

The aim of each cell is self-discovery and self-knowledge and the first task should be to recognise the truth about the human condition, to understand the silence of eternity and to feel the triviality of unreal living against it: that triviality bred of time, luxury and lack of anything vital or creative to do. The end of the cell is to produce fine and responsible fully-grown individuals, and therefore a nation of existentially authentic contemplatives and seekers. Then, when the State shall be a part of the "Church" – then there will be energy and purpose. That is the great Idea.

23rd March. Canton-Hong Kong-Tokyo. Left the world of the collective for the world of the individual. Our Volga broke down at 7.20 on the way to Canton station. There were pioneers waving good-bye to others on the platform. In the train the radio reminded us of their Revolution: the cracking of whips, and the triumph of Chairman Mao. And I would rather have been a slave to any Mitsubishi than a slave to Chairman Mao.

At Kowloon station 15 tubercular porters stood like vultures and then flapped around our luggage; and later a newsvendor demanded a 10 cents tip, the two barmen disappeared without returning our change. Here the individualism was wretched, but I preferred it, and would rather live here among the split skirts and decay than in China. And yet Hong Kong was a trivial place, and one felt one had left behind the fundamentals, the violent attitudes and the quarrel with Mr Tsu, the vitality and tension that spring from a meeting between East and West. In Hong Kong, one got one's ticket endorsed over to Pan American, one shopped for a child's doll in Lane and Crawfords, one packed and stood in a queue of American trippers at the airport and listened to their anxiety: "You know we never fly together. We've got a boy and we never fly together."

In the large Boeing, the other world was already behind: the world of Tuohy smuggling his films in his socks and of Mr Wu our guide saying "I study Chairman Mao's works three evenings and two afternoons a week." I had regretted leaving Hong Kong for I recognised the decay and knew I could be at home there for a time, but when I saw C and Nan at Tokyo airport, against all conceivable possibilities, I was happy, I was at home, I had come home, and I had resumed my existence of anti-bourgeois individualism among bourgeois people and capitalist chauffeurs.

SPIRITUAL DEPTH: SILENCE, EXISTENCE, ISNESS
March – June 1966

24th March. But throughout a day of catching up – taking 18 rolls of film to Mikami and giving an account of my mixed feelings about China at the Bank of Japan, for example – I felt as though I had, for the first time, really heard the call from my future destiny. I am not primarily a teacher, I felt that throughout China, nor is my Shadow purely that of a writer. I shall be a writer not for unity's sake alone, but to express the real, and now that my notion of what is real is beginning to unfold, I must be prepared to accept the responsibilities that go with it, the responsibilities of action, just as I was prepared to accept myself as a poet last year.

I must be prepared to choose myself as a teacher of the real. I must contemplate this for another two years, but I am at present sure of the unreality of my English background and of fragments of my message: never forget you will die; experience the silence that exists before your birth and after your death; measure the triviality of much living against this silence; understand that some men have never grown spiritually; understand that one can live at different levels and that the deepest is the most real; understand that at this level, all men are your brothers, and that every man has feelings and is a person and must be treated as such; you can reach this level by long discipline through keeping a diary and shedding your unreal onion skins; you will then have a centre and be you; you will be aware and will not live in a dream; your existence will be genuine, not dud; quality of existence is more important than quality of intellect, so this is open to all; the right social attitudes depend on reaching this real, genuine, deep existence, and once you have reached it, you will see society not in terms of class – workers and peasants and so on – but in terms of spiritual growth from unreality; in other words, just being a worker is not enough, for besides justice there must be reality throughout our society, and the more unreality there is, the more it is in decay.

25th March. And this is a universal law: the law of unreality. The more society – static ego (a symptom or a cause?) – suffers from unreal living, the more it is in decay. The criterion of unreality is triviality, shallowness, being concerned with inessentials, not living from the deep, central self. Exactly what is essential depends on what the deep, central self regards as essential and pursues with dedication, passion, conviction. This will vary from age to age, and from civilisation to civilisation. It can even be dedication to production, for a time, but only for a time, for the deep, central self will cease to find production a satisfying outlet for its energy when production has achieved its aims. It is usually some kind of religion. And it is not the external beliefs of a religion that provide the dedication, but rather the life from the deep, central self which can find an outlet through symbols. This has generally not been understood in Western civilisation; it has been understood in the East. Religion is a daily attempt to escape the unreal for the deep, central self. And the symbols that assist this daily attempt are the guides, and they have no reality in themselves in so far as they do not point the way towards the deep, central self. Christ, Buddha, Mohammed – they are all pointers of the way, escorts to the temenos gates.

Coffee-mornings, hair-dos, clothes, holidays: all are opiates and emptiness. The converse law states: the more a society has real living (and growth), the more vital it is. And there is no inevitable decline, as Spengler believed. Decline is rather a seasonal thing. There is always a new year, and unreal living can turn into real. This depends on the people. If they improve the quality of their living, then the quality of their society must necessarily improve. Ultimately, all societies depend on the reality or otherwise of the living of its citizens.

26th March. In spite of the fact that most of the day was spent in dictating 19 typed pages for *Newsweek* and sorting through photographs with Tuohy in the evening, I tried to see the law of unreality more concretely, in terms of Britain. The contrast between Hong Kong is revealing, and although the "real living" in China would not satisfy me, it is still real living, whereas the whores, the rickshaw-driving pimps, the begging tradesmen in Hong Kong, and their hopelessness, all explain the black and peeling walls. That was why I recognised it all: my feeling for the real is enhanced in an unreal environment, I can define my ideal by contrast.

Britain is not as far gone as Hong Kong, but it too is hopelessly unreal. The loudmouth laughter in the pub, the smashed telephone kiosk, the shrieks at Michael Miles and Hughie Green (TV presenters) – these are earthy but from a level of living that has never known the deep, central self which is the source of all greatness in civilisations; the artificial niceness, and avoidance of fundamentals, and respectability of the bourgeois – the affluent ignorance in a good accent, the lack of charity towards others at the church bazaar – these attitudes are unreal, these are artificial and shallow and are undeepened by the central self, whose springs have never been tapped; and the bored cynical indolence of the ruling class, the insistence on small talk and the offence at ill-bred passion, the taking for granted of land and wealth and the scorn for the lower orders, and the insincere politeness – these attitudes are unreal. There is a connection between unreality and money, of course, but money is not at the root of unreality; lack of awareness of death has as great a claim. What is needed in Britain is not a denial of the body but a denial of the shallowness for an affirmation of the deep, central self.

27th March. I must connect the deep, central self with the vitality of institutions. I believe that men create, and are not merely created by, their institutions. In a time of decay, the institutions decay because the deep central self is withdrawn. Is this true of Greece and Rome, as well as Britain? There is certainly a connection between comfort and luxury and shallowness. In that respect, a materialistic age must necessarily have lost all touch with the spirit. If it hadn't, it wouldn't be a materialist age, i.e. a spiritual age does not use material things to promote comfort and luxury, and an age that has not lost touch with the spirit has control over its comforts as we in the West have not. A new religion must be against excessive comfort, but it must not be anti-body, anti-sex, any more than the *Old Testament* prophets were.

And why am I so eager to get a new religion going, when I am far from certain that I believe in progress as opposed to change, and have no certainty that a spiritually healthy society would progress mankind? The answer is, I think, "because I believe it will benefit man". Man may be little better now than he was 2,000 years ago, morally, and he may show few signs of having benefited from those who have discovered the self, but the few have managed to raise themselves as high as they can go, and man's only hope is that they can take charge of the many, spiritually, and lead them up. I say it again: the institutions of Britain will be regenerated, and changed, when the few wage war on the present comfort and unearth man's creative spring.

28th March. As yesterday, went round and wrote an *AP* article with Tuohy. He was exceptionally moody today and vetoed all my words, disagreed with my parody-title "The War Hoax" and pooh-poohed sensitivity about pain: "Ivan was kinky", and "It's only those who haven't experienced it who find it terrible" and "To say it's horrible is very bourgeois" and so on. All false toughness, very like the Group Captain. C: "He feels threatened, he's protecting himself because you're on his level and you're young." Is this true?

I have much to be grateful for. He has taught me a lot about style, e.g.: (1) a sentence must connect with the one before and the one after, and it must have a physiological rhythm in terms of a breathing diaphragm; (2) put a full-stop before "but" to make it more punchy; (3) omit adverbs and relatives; (4) form is physiological and goes with a grunt, or sigh, then another grunt; (5) it must all be "thingy"; (6) there must be timing – there must be a delay, a holding back; (7) never draw conclusions, "only unintelligent people draw conclusions"; (8) "don't be too upbeat or too downbeat"; (9) avoid weak words, try every word out for size"; (10) be succinct; (11) forget all books and concentrate on *you*; (12) be personal. Learning these points has justified China. Writing while Tuohy accepts or rejects suggestions and dictates, is like a playwright learning how to write plays by working in the theatre. One drawback is his privacy: not wanting to read me his *Sunday Telegraph* article....His grunting. In Hong Kong, two waiters rushed into his room to find him make the noise he made on his pot. What Tuohy has really taught me: to do without books ("It's not me – it must be me") and to find concrete equivalents for abstract ideas.

29th March. To lunch with K (with a view to selling some China photos)....When I met him it was his fullness that first struck me. Unlike C's dream, he was not thin, he did not look like Hardy or have a red tie. Later I thought he was rather like Venn at school. He had the same soft eyes. The same shyness. The questions he asked were all archetypal: I seem to have scooped the entire Intelligence Service over Peita (Peking University), so when would I go again and would I go with my wife? And how much did I earn and how much was I getting from *Newsweek*? And did C like Tokyo? And so on. Over lunch I gave my impressions of China. From my point of view the most surprising thing was his insistence "When could you go again? And could you go before December?" Last night C dreamt I had written a report on China called "An exercise of innocence." The pally Christian names.

30th March. K came and stayed for an awkward quarter of an hour and made small talk with C while I smirked to myself; and when he left he nearly fell down the steps and into the roses. The sum total of all I learned was that he knows Buchanan and has been here for "many years" and that he goes away for week-ends. C: "He is terribly difficult to talk to." It is a terrific paradox: I, the angry poet of the decay in Britain, plotting revolution against the Establishment, actually "serving" the Establishment. I suppose one answer is, although I hate the ruling class in Britain, I hate the Chinese Party more – especially what it is doing to intellectuals and children. It was good that the old order was overthrown, but what has replaced it is terrible. Perhaps K is Marlowe's Mephistopheles (or Mephostophilis).

31st March. A day coloured by the frustration of "doing business". I rang *Newsweek* on Saturday, after lunch, and was told that both Krisler and Truitt are out of the country, Krisler in Djakarta, and Truitt in the U.S. I said my name is Hagger and I have 19 pages answering all questions: would the girl send a cable to New York saying that my expenses were $1,100, that I probably can't go back to China because of my important interview with the Vice-President, and that this interview is exclusive, i.e. Tuohy will stay off it. Yesterday it appeared that New York did not know I'd replaced Tuohy on the job, and that even the girls here did not know. I sent an immediate cable asking for a guarantee: "Hagger acting for Tuohy has answers to all questions plus exclusive interview with Vice-President Peking University on question of recent purge of student-intellectuals" (i.e. world scoop on the Cultural Revolution which broke in August). A second cable went: "Difficulties owing to delay and other newspaper commitments. Suggest immediate offer plus expenses exclusive rights Peking University Vice-President interview. Tuohy-Hagger."

1st April. The election result came through while I was with Tuohy and Roderick. It was of course a foregone conclusion, and should put the Labour Party in the same sort of position as it occupied in 1945. Then it could have conducted a revolution, and did not. Will it now? If it does what it should do, the social side of what I wrote on March 22nd should not be necessary. Wilson is not that extremist, however, and the ruling class will survive.

What I have to prove is the religious side and the following two hypotheses: (1) "that Britain is declining because there is no spiritual striving", and that if spiritual striving could enter the leadership, the decline would cease, because our small island would find a response to this present challenge (see 1st December 1965); (2) "that the more society suffers from unreal living, the more it is in decay" (see 25th March 1966). What I need to illustrate is decline in terms of what? Decay in terms of what? And why is the change not progress?

The answer is of course decline in health, creativity and influence, direction – above all direction – and decay in terms of vitality, independence, greatness. And a change from health to sickness is not a progress. There must be a Messianic ideal, a great idea on a world-wide basis, the kind of idea that rules a Chinese Communist, that Communism will spread throughout the world and will be for the benefit of the whole world. And this ideal must carry some social obligations. That is the response to the challenge: spiritual striving and real living and health as a world-wide ideal to be fought for, as a way of life to rule the average day of whole nations. Get this in Britain and Britain will be really new.

2nd April. Spent all morning at the Japan-Soviet Tourist Bureau next to Kamiyacho station. Fixed my itinerary for England. June 5th Yokohama depart at 11. June 7th Nakhodka arrive 6 p.m., June 8th Khabarovsk arrive 12.35, and Moscow arrive 6.30. June 9th Moscow depart 6.15 p.m., June 11th London arrive 20.35. Fare, about ¥132,399. Return: August 20th London, depart, August 25th arrive Leningrad (via Copenhagen, Stockholm, Helsinki) 8 p.m., August 26th Leningrad – Moscow arrive 2.05 p.m., depart 8.20 p.m., August 27th arrive Khabarovsk, August 28th arrive Nakhodka, August 30th arrive Yokohama 4 p.m. Fare, about ¥140,839.

I shall be travelling through Russia twice, and, following my visit to China, should be able to test the truth of the following hypothesis, which is the ultimate answer against Communism: that in all Communist movements, the Revolution is glorious, but the Party which follows terrible. A Messianic ideal depending on the release of physical energies for material ends cannot last (see 25th March, disagreeing), just as social conditions cannot last. Tyranny is no substitute for creativity, and brainwashing slaves into thinking themselves free and happy is no substitute for the spiritual health of striving and real living. The war of the free world should not be against Revolutions but against the Parties which follow them, and the West is making no progress because it has no spiritual alternative to offer, no superior spiritual way of life, beyond a bankrupt half-belief in a collapsed Christianity.

When the West has transformed the great idea into a way of life, then it will recover its leadership and moral superiority without the taints of colonialism and imperialism and all the rest.

3rd April. A day on the contrast between Jeanie and Mrs. Farr – sex in terms of machines and in terms of property.

4th April. A rushed day for other people: getting the Peking University articles off for Tuohy, talking about China for a completely incurious Prince and the only question he asked was "Is it true there are no flies in China?" – and then, in the evening, talking about China and sumo for Ando.

In my only spare moments, in the car and to the station I wondered (see April 2nd) exactly how the great idea could be transformed into a way of life. The main point is that everyone should be able to do the equivalent of going to chapel for two half an hours a day and two one hours on Sunday; and that instead of wasting time on meaningless hymns and chanting mechanical prayers, each should spend the time striving. The group of 10 would seem to be the best way of achieving this; there could be a discussion on a particular aspect of striving, to be followed by individual reflection, i.e. each of the 10 sitting alone. You only get out what you put in, that which you sow you reap, so, like all exercises, this may not seem to benefit the man who will not bring something to it. And yet, even the thickest dullard will not be completely untouched by the drill.

Self-realisation has been completely overlooked by our educational system. We are taught about God, and we are taught to think, but we are not taught to find the deep parts of ourselves, and if the double-barrelled R-Ws tried to find these parts for just one hour a day, I am sure they would not be so self-centred. The dullard who becomes aware of his life as a series of existential strivings towards self-realisation has made great progress, and this perception may lead him to bring something to the struggle.

5th April. During another rushed day – buying a typewriter and a watch, visiting the Japan-Soviet Travel Bureau, getting a haircut, rewriting *China and the U.S.* with Tuohy, sticking up all the *AP* articles with Tuohy – I thought more about the way of life that should embody the great idea. It is a way of preparing people for living at the deepest and most mature level, for unearthing the spiritual potential in each and mastering experience, so that the social norm is the detached mystic and contemplative, and the vulgar and bourgeois are those who have fallen short. This transformation of society would mean a transformation from the ideal of economic and social individualism to the ideal of spiritual individualism.

Such a transformation is possible because of the individualistic root which has run through Western civilisation since Christ and the Renaissance, and it is today absolutely necessary because our social system in the West contains nothing to release the most important part of man's creativity. The Communists are right: capitalism is pernicious in its effects on the individual and in the warped view it gives him of his fellow man. But Communism is equally pernicious in its effects on the individual, treating him as material for remoulding. Spiritual individualism founded on individual striving for self-realisation, which is never achieved, and the idea that one's view of the world depends on one's wisdom which depends on the amount of striving one has done – these are the basic ideas behind the new way of life. Each life is a progress, each life is important, not in terms of a God, but in terms of death. For man is like a pool of water, and death like a strong sun drying it up, drop by drop.

6th April. How can one fail to be pessimistic if Man, the repository of all achievement in the struggle against death, is doomed to ultimate extinction? And what am I doing, worrying about transforming my great idea into a way of life? And yet in a day given over to MITI and Yamashita and seven of the top men I have to grade in the next year, and to Prince Hitachi, I have reconsidered the last two sentences of April 5th and vindicate them. The point is, if death has replaced the idea of God, then every individual's life is of the most vital importance, as it is the only thing he has.

How could so basic a truth go for the most part unproclaimed? The murderer, the firing squad, these are the most terrible of criminals, for they deprive of life, and it is life – living, existence, call it what you will – that is of fundamental importance: no just values can justify the taking of life. Just as each life is important in terms of death, so is each life a progress in terms of death, a progress towards the richest and deepest experience of fugitive life. And, leaving aside all the considerations of the ideal society, that is why a new way of life based on "spiritual individualism" is necessary: a stupid bourgeois has never known what it is to live, and in terms of the highest and deepest experience of life, he might as well be dead.

"Why worry about the new way of life?" Because living at the end of it is totally different, and one's understanding and experience of existence is quite different. And the compassion and vitality which arise from this are much better than the more indifferent and nihilistic attitudes towards life in terms of death. "Better?" In terms of my understanding and experience; better reactions. Ultimately, all my values are founded on death, on that silence like the silence around Canton; i.e. on life, on staking all on life.

7th April. A day in which six hours were swallowed by the Bank of Japan – talk about China and the "treacherous British" who work in "a hidden way and maintain their influence, guiding the U.S. and France".

Reviewed yesterday's entry. What I tried to say was: if death is the end, existence is all; there is existence and existence – bourgeois existence and artist's existence. And experience of existence is absolute, for existence is, in its purest sense, the most complete opposite of death. One must strive for the purest existence – the cleanest consciousness – because one is fulfilled in the striving, and because one's world-view changes in the course of it. As death is the end, existence is holy. And all values must help preserve existence and eliminate suffering and create the best possible condition for the purest and deepest level of existence.

Seen in these terms, Chairman Mao has failed abysmally. Hence I oppose him and work for his downfall. Hence too, my vow today to dedicate myself to the British Revolution, which is dedicated to "creating the best possible conditions for the purest and deepest existence." I vow that within 20 years from now, by Easter 1986, I will have transformed my great idea into a way of life, and that I will have found the right social conditions for it, and that I will have promoted this and succeeded. This is my destiny, my self-definition, my answer to the question "Who am I?" I am not just a Professor, or a tutor to a Prince, or a Central Banker, or even a poet; I am a religious teacher of the real, and all the other parts of me must serve that end, for that is how I will express myself.

11th April. Revised Part 1 of the poems like yesterday, and rewrote the second block about the two agonies. C began typing the first typed draft after which there will be just a final draft; in ink there have been at least two drafts so far, and in the case of several sheets more.

I have been thinking about the sequel I am to write this summer. I think it must connect British society with the law of unreality (see 24th and 25th March) and it must propose the two hypotheses about spiritual living and unreal living (see 1st April) and therefore define decline and decay in terms infinitely more concrete than Toynbee or Spengler. This poem will draw on the theme of the play I proposed on Western civilisation (see 2nd January).

You can judge the health of a society or civilisation by the quality of its living – that is what I want to say. And so I must examine the great periods of Western civilisation (e.g. Roman, Greek, Byzantine) in terms of the real or unreal living – i.e. the being or not being in vital touch with the deep central self – of the greater part of the people. These periods will form memories in the long life of the dying old lady, and her present sickness will be related to the unreal states of mind of the people. To connect these periods with the living and the people will be impossible unless I take certain things as indications, e.g. attitudes to certain events, attitudes revealed physically, and I must place the health of the people and society within a context of decline, so that I am saying something about the future prospects of Western civilisation. What part will China play in all this – how real is the Grand Inquisitor's subjects' living?

12th April. After grading two MITI (Ministry of International Trade and Industry) chiefs while various men dropped in and listened, under the pretext of going through filing-cabinets and ransacking desk-drawers, I went to the Shinjuku Bunka. There I saw Mishima slit his belly open and die in a pool of blood, then, in the latest Bunuel, a goose-b——r rape a child, and finally, Isak in *Wild Strawberries* touch No-Face on the shoulder and see his head split open and pour blood into the gutter. On the way home our taxi turned left to cross the Edogawa and knocked an errand boy off his bike. He went over his handlebars, over our left wing, and his knuckles took the taxi's left mirror with them. He got up bleeding profusely from two fingers but with perfect self-control and would not hear of coming back with us. Nor would he go to the police-box. He was scared, he didn't want to pay for the broken mirror or lose his job as errand boy and so after several "dormor sumimasens" ("thank you, I am very sorry") and with blood splashing all over the road, he got on his bike and beat it.

Discussing the day's blood in the kitchen, C said she felt sick. I said: "Seeing it is no more terrifying than imagining a shooting." She: "Oh no, you're wrong there." Which made me wonder whether my imagination is exceptionally powerful, for someone only has to mention the word execution and I can *see* the wounds on the body; someone only has to mention the word "hara-kiri" and I can *see* the slit across the belly and the contorted face. In fact, my imagination is more terrifying than any film, when it comes to man's suffering.

13th April. At the Prince's taught the rival Muslim factions, the followers of Mohammed's father-in-law Abu Bakr (the Syrian-based Ummayad or Ommayed Sunnites) and son-in-law Ali (the Persian-based Abbasid Shi'ites). On the way back, thought about Baghdad, and decided I need to live in a decayed place. Hence my nostalgia for Kowloon (see March 23rd). Soho-Jericho-Smallpox Alley (Baghdad)-Nichigeki (Tokyo)-Kowloon: they are all one place.

I derive nourishment from decayed places and feel stifled in dynamic places like China, so why am I planning a re-creation of Britain? I can't hope to answer that question: it is a paradox in me, my preference for the rotten while advocating the healthiest and being prepared to sacrifice myself for it. Perhaps these decayed places represent the chaos in myself, which I project. Certainly a Revolution would call into being all my existential motives: I would be creating myself as well as a country, like Ivan the Terrible. Order without creates an order within, and, above all, gives it expression.

Images: a cluster of red balloons, like atoms; a crowd speeded up like an old film (China); a queue like a row of sunflowers in stony ground; people like caged mice under a wire net, peering through to a leaden sky.

14th April. Finished Part 1 of my poem, which C typed while I was at the Bank of Japan. Reading it through on my return I was surprised at the connections I had not seen: for example "ascend" is followed by a working up from working to ruling class, and then by "the sun rose", and then by "On the top of a London bus," so that there is an ascending movement until the falling melanistic smoke; and "dinner", "before dinner" in the second block being wrong for "after dinner" to connect with "on after dinner" in the first block.

These connections are the fortuitous results of deep "subterranean" creativity activity. Undoubtedly I had understood the relationship between the parts in my subconscious long before I "discovered" the connection in my conscious. Ever since I made that awful mistake about Zabov, I have trusted my subconscious more than my conscious when it comes to aesthetic criticism, and so far, I can say I know what is right before I have seen why. I am afraid that Parts 2 & 3 are not as good as Part 1, but so far my judgement tells me that I have written the most complex poem since *The Waste Land*. Although I know this, I am still diffident, and I am still afraid that when I show the completed first draft to Tuohy he will say "It's not poetry" or "It's nonsense" or something like that. I would contest his judgement, but I would be bitterly hurt if he did; if in one minute he could pass judgement on 16 months' work by me and find me wanting. "Weighed in the balance."

15th April. After a weary day rewriting the beginning of Part 2 and not really getting it right because I was not sure of the theme, or of the connection with Part 1, I went to Sanseidos to sort out books for classes, and then went to Ann Gegg's cocktail party with Tuohy. I felt tired and depressed, and was glad the car lost its way and made us arrive one and a half hours late. Spoke to Tomlin, about China and Narita. Spoke to Baker, was flattered by the greasy poet with glasses and saw Miss Arai. Otherwise I was landed with the two OUP representatives, one Japanese and the other English. Both were equally patronising, but the Englishman assumed I knew nothing about 20th century poetry until I was riled and gave him Gunn and Hughes and Conquest and Eliot and so on.

Ate at Nicola's with C and Tuohy, feeling discontented: as Tuohy put it, it was all "an expense of spirit in a waste of shame". I overheard the OUP Englishman asking Tuohy: "Are you writing a novel now" and Tuohy's trapped "Er...." One should not have to discuss one's writing with patronising strangers. For the rest, heard C on Grisdale's conceit and on Mrs. G's fatuous remark "on the middle classes"; and Tuohy on Toff: "He was a Whitechapel tailor after leaving school at 16; he's done it all himself. I rather admire him."

16th April. On a very hot morning rewrote the giving up of Law to connect with Pt. 1. The thread has emerged. In Pt. 1 Freeman rebels against spiritual laziness and is opposed to society and has glimpsed the future idea. The question that confronts him is "where now?"

Answer: He must build the Shadow, bring it into being with his will. This he tries to do in Pt. 2, but the point is, he misuses his will, with the result that, instead of creating himself as a "sage", he creates coldness between himself and Jeanie and then, in the nightmare, abandons discipline altogether and ends up spiritually bankrupt and paralysed in a land of the dead. But this paralysis, this chaos and unreality, are necessary to his growth, and he begins to grow as soon as he learns to die away from self-will – the assertive will – and rediscipline himself. Then the escape from the land of the dead is possible, and the god ascends and his will is flowing in the right direction.

17th April. Undoubtedly, the experience in Nan's life which the hypnotists will try to extract is the incident concerning John: when she was hit and came home crying. Ever since then, as C says, Nan has had a kind of inferiority complex and thinks no one likes her, save for Aikosan and us and the animals and "Uncle Brian" (Buchanan): hence her daily demand "I want to go to Nobe". She is afraid of "Auntie Bank" (Frank Tuohy) – witness her reluctance to enter his flat – and she is ambivalent about "Auntie Frances": sometimes she wants to return to England to see her, other times she does not. My going away to China did not help. "I couldn't find you", she has often said since then, and she has not been so confident of me since then.

I think Nan must be given as many opportunities to meet people as possible, and should possibly be encouraged to like John; and that she should say her prayers for her friends; though she must not be forced. Meanwhile she loves to come and sit by me in the morning, long before I get up, and tell me physical things, e.g. "I didn't make my bed wet" and "I didn't have my hair washed tomorrow did I?" And then "Shave, Nick, shave."

18th April. A full day. Prepared pages for C to type, went to Tokyo University of Education, had two classes and was not allowed to eat my lunch because of disturbances like Enozawa's and Hashimoto's; then went to the Prince and wrote a letter to the Sultan of some Malaysian territory and taught the conditional ("I will ask her to marry me if she likes me") and read enviously about the Lady of Shalott in her mirrored room – there's much to be said for what Tennyson was attacking, the artist's complete withdrawal from reality – and then came home and struggled with the next part of the poem after reading to Nan.

And I am weary, weary. I think if I go on like this, I shall kill myself: in that respect, Buchanan is right. Revising a poem of my poem's length, after China and all those articles, and on top of my five jobs: it is asking for a heart attack or some great burning out and dying – yet I have always known this would be in store. Hence my preparations before flying on the doomed DC8 I only pray I can complete the second poem, apply the Shadow, nationally, to our society.

Sometimes, however, I long for death. I long for the peace of just lying still and doing nothing. I long to lie down and yet I never do: I must flog myself on, for that is how I work. And what was the meaning of it all, of that unsparing effort, while other living beings took things more easily?

SPIRITUAL DEPTH: SILENCE, EXISTENCE, ISNESS (1966)

20th April. Spent the morning at the Tokyo Immigration Bureau, getting my re-entry visa before going on to the Japan-Soviet Travel Bureau and, later, the Prince. Wound up at the Customs House, Shinagawa first. The *Deserto Rosso* scenery: waste land, earth mounds, dandelions; stacks of lead piping (thin and thick gauge) mostly rusty; decaying stacks of asbestos and corrugated iron; large grey balls, and connecting windows which seemed to be some kind of a refinery; an enormous plant in the distance which looked like cans chucked on a heap with a few arbitrary planks of wood. The channels of oily sea had dredgers on them (as in *Deserto Rosso*) – great flat-bottomed things with enormous funnels and cranes – and, on either bank, the sloping masts and rigging of worn-out ships and patient cranes, like herons angling for fish, amid piles and dumps of inconceivable refuse, mostly rust or grey. I went by in the Bank of Japan car at 40 mph; I would like to return, and wander, for all round the Customs House is the most fantastic industrial decay, an amalgam of Conrad, Eliot and Antonioni but on a scale that none, perhaps, have succeeded in communicating.

How much the Prince misses. He had not heard of income tax – I really had to explain it to him – and he would not know about scenery like this, and so his poems are about seagulls and views from hotel windows and ravens "who know the hearts of Kings and Queens." Anti-monarchism aside, I would rather be me, because I see more of the truth than he is allowed to see.

21st April. Finished typing up Part 2 section 2 and reflected on how I differ from Tuohy. Tuohy is striving for clarity and translucency – i.e. he is trying to exclude other meanings; hence his frequent attacks on ambiguity, which is my forte. I am trying to include as many meanings as possible within the framework of one meaning. This ambiguity is as natural to me as breathing. I know this from reading the proofs of *In Defense of the Sequence of Images*, much of which I could hardly understand because of the ambiguities. What is to me a strength in poetry is a weakness in prose of this kind, and so I shall not write critical prose any more.

"Abbreviated narrative" still seems a new idea in poetry. I was wondering whether it could be applied to plays, and opened *The Entertainer* purely by chance. In a way Brecht and Osborne have done it: I would abbreviate situations more, and try to blend the realism and the distancing more satisfactorily than Osborne does. As to the subject matter of *The Entertainer*, Osborne is depressingly right. The music-hall decaying into "Rock'n Roll New'd look", the "drab equality" under the Welfare State and Archie's going to prison for evading tax and Mick's dying for the remaining "bits of red on the map" – all these are images on my theme, and Osborne got there ten years earlier. In fairness to myself I should say that I am treating it all from a different point of view, and have at least attempted a solution, whereas Osborne and Archie and Bill Maitland despair; nonetheless when *The Entertainer* appeared Osborne was only 25.

22nd April. And what attitude do I have towards the past? Osborne's admiration for the Edwardian age is guarded – "there must have been something phoney about it" Jimmy says – and he is only half a romantic, although he clearly does prefer the past to the present. I have a little admiration for the Edwardian age too, but I am not so nostalgic as Osborne, and look rather towards the future. "Well," I should like to think I feel, "we had it good then, but the upper classes and Empire-builders were intolerable, and it is a good thing it's all over."

Certainly we are in decay, in terms of the past greatness, and certainly Little England is no substitute for Great Britain, but looking back with nostalgia will not set things right, and we must try and rebuild ourselves. Osborne says we are all "dead behind the eyes": perhaps he is right – for decadent periods of history produce decadent feelings – but the problem is to try and do something to bring our feelings alive and prevent such "Raskolnikovian" indifference as Brady's from catching on in our society. Spiritual individualism – we come back to it, and reading *The Observer* obituary on Waugh's senseless nostalgia for landed Catholics has reconvinced me of its urgency. I am still not certain about "progress"; I think "progress" is often a decline into a uniformity which inevitably breaks up; but I must not be so right-wing as I have been about the past, for there is a lot in the past that I loathe, and even if history shows that every change spreads further decay, we must still fight for the changes, in the hope that, just for once the historical laws will be defeated, and an individual will be able to arrest the decay.

23rd April. But perhaps this is unrealistic, and nothing can in the long run arrest the decay; for the decay is in the body of the old aristocratic order, and no individual can restore the aristocratic order in Britain; and to abolish it altogether would be to aggravate the decay from a long-term point of view. No, perhaps we should regard the old order as finished, and in the interests of regeneration (1) make changes with a short-term end in view and (2) work for our entry into the Universal State of Europe (see January 22nd): our ideal being a power-block from Scotland to Sicily, from which the U.S. would be excluded, and a release of energy among "national minorities". This is historically on the cards: objections like language, currency, de Gaulle are only short-term ones that can be overcome.

If the conception of the Universal State could be based on a regenerated Britain ((1)), so much the better. I am aware of the paradoxes of my position. First, I, who have been so anxious to preserve and restore, am now advocating dissolution of our national independence, thereby contradicting everything I wrote on 30th November 1965. Second, a Universal State, and the regeneration that went with it, would be one (admittedly vital) additional step towards the extinction of Western civilisation, so why am I getting so excited about it, for there will be no progress, and a regeneration would not last. There will come a time when Western civilisation is as extinct as the old Egyptian civilisation. What will it all have meant then?

Carry the insight further. There will come a time when no man walks the earth, and in the silence of that new ice-age or desert, what will it all have meant? And why should I so much as lift a finger to help regenerate Britain or work for a United Europe?

24th April. There are two answers: (1) because, in doing so, I should express myself and fulfil myself and (2) because, in doing so, I should help other people and save them from suffering: there have been queues outside gas-chambers, and even though that icy night will come, and history will be proved meaningless, anything I can do for my brother men, to give them peace and make their lives more real, will be valuable.

Going down to Nobe yesterday, a woman opened a heart-shaped musical box to Nan and began, in her loneliness, a monologue: she lived at Yokosuka, she had three children aged 9 or so, her husband was a neurosurgeon on the U.S. base. My reaction was to keep on my glasses, to try to go on reading, and, feeling awkward about talking to a stranger in C's presence, I even blushed a little, almost as much as Nan. We parted on Yokosuka platform without a word of goodbye. Later Buchanan, in his loneliness, talked about the time he went off with a geisha, and was helped by Keikosan's brother, and when he died of a penicillin shot and his wife died a year later of a heart attack (both in their 30s) he took in the delinquent children. He also talked about Keikosan's hard life, her parents died when she was young – her mother when she was born and her father in a mining accident; and said she is sick of dogs and books which fall down from the rail over their double bed. And he said he did not want to live much more: "the consolation for getting old is that one doesn't want to live in one's time." (Judging by his coughing and the frequency of his wind-breaking, he will not live too long; also his slum habits with his dogs.)

These two lonely people are two of millions, with greater spiritual depth they would not, perhaps, be so lonely. Though the spirit of course is not the only cure.

25th April. After the frogs like factory-saws yesterday, and the rain, back to work and a discussion with my graduates on "isness". Distinguished the poetic response to "isness" in the poetic image from attempts to interpret it and give it a meaning: (1) the pessimistic view that history is meaninglessness because of the silence for which our swelling universe is heading – our earth getting one second older every 31.7 million years (Dicke) and so on; (2) the false optimism of evolutionary humanism with its false Wellsian belief in "the underlying life of man", and the false Christian view that "isness" is meaningful. Godless Sartre and God-fearing Alyosha both approach "isness" and experience the same thing in terms of disgust and ecstasy, and define it in terms of God or the absence of God, but the poet is not concerned with giving the root, the stone, the earth "a meaning".

279

Isness just is. All meaning involves interpreting A in terms of B. (According to Fitzsimmons, A-B in terms of C.) A life is valuable in terms of itself, and not in terms of history. If existence is seen in terms of history, it will seem meaningless on the pessimistic view that history is leading to a silence, or meaningful on the optimistic view that the life of man will never die. The historical dimension involves thinking, and isness cannot be responded to by thought, and so the thinker misses the mystical beauty of a sunset or any other naked example of "isness".

There is a non-thinking way of seeing isness that gives it clarity. Why should I strive, if death is the end and history is meaningless? Because existence is all I have and I must live as fully as possible, at as intense a level of awareness of "isness" as possible. This is not really a reason, just an affirmation of the instinct to live to the full. You cannot impose any rational meaning on my existence any more than you can impose any meaning on the sawing of the frogs, and the same goes for meaninglessness.

26th April. Had a holiday from Keio because of the rail strike and worked all day and got my work typed. Was pleased with the view of man as "nothing and all" at the same time; the ambiguity catches the ambiguity about man in my mind, and every day I seem to waver between regarding him as nothing in view of the ultimate silence, and regarding him as all from the point of view of existence, which is all we have.

What I was trying to say yesterday was that man is all; in other words, that one should discount the historical view of him. Perhaps today's formulation is more satisfactory, and the halves of the paradox must be retained in the mind simultaneously, all the time, although perhaps more weight should be given to the "all", without upsetting the paradox.

Looking back over Pt. 2, I have mixed feelings. Some parts are good, others not so good. The general theme is the search for a single self. In Pt. 1 (see April 16th), Freeman has discovered what he must do. In Pt. 2 he misuses his will and enters the land of the dead. What he must do is uncover his "single face", which is identified with both Shadow and Woman-guide. His marriage brings him near to this, but not near enough for he is still dominated by his will (= the Leader) and after glimpsing his unborn wholeness in the priest he must overcome the bogey of mechanism and his father's death before he realises that his progress is being impeded by Western civilisation and that he must remember the "priceless" value of existence, so Pt 3 grows out of the depth he has achieved in experiencing his father's death?

27th April. Worked on the first 100 lines of what is now Pt 3 and got them typed. The theme so far: peace – the significance art gives to life – spirit and intellect (i.e. reason). Also wrote the dedication: "To Mr F.T./This string of baroque pearls/To be told like a rosary." This after coming by chance on the entry for 27th September 1965. (How

dependent the creative process is on accident and chance encounter.)
Went to the Prince.

28th April. A morning of little writing but much thinking about the title.
I really want a title that will be an image of a search in terms of growth
against a background of decay; some concept of a journey towards some
concept of a shrine. But I think I can go deeper than that and have a title
which explains the search and the need to grow in decay: *The Silence*.

For the last nine months I have been obsessed by the way human activity
is all noise on silence, and also the way that any form of search or quest is
a response to the silence of the universe. The silence at Adrian's party on
9th December and the silence round Canton were one and the same. I think
this a suitably ambiguous title too, for the word "silence" is used in the poem
to suggest the meaninglessness of history ("ice and silence"); the imminence
of death ("bones and dread"); the response to it ("silent room"); the
nourishing quality it possesses ("let Eastern silence"); the fact that it is
under the personality and the reason ("empty seekers"). It suggests therefore
mandalas, and is to be connected with the Shadow, and escape from
unreality.

In my poem, it is a purely positive concept, unlike the negative concept
in Bergman's film, where silence = lack of communication with men and
the absence of God. In my poem it symbolises the spiritual life, and it is a
purely existential concept, one that can only be felt and experienced and
responded to. It is, in fact, my main contribution to Existentialist categories,
and I think it is an important contribution for it connects atheistic
Existentialism to a life of reality and authenticity without the need for any
abstraction.

29th April. A national holiday. Rewrote and got typed, on to about line
1100, then prepared to dine at Tuohy's. The fire in the printing works
between Edogawa Bashi (bridge) and Waseda: first it was a column of black
smoke, then (as I watched from our hill, with my left hand on a house wall)
in a green flash, flickering twice and three times, the electricity went up;
after that there was a red glow in the smoke, and sparks, and another
explosion, like sheet lightning, white in the vault of the night. The gutted
building and the standing crowd, later; people wanting to pass, waiting to
see what would be brought out to the ambulance; police, whistling, and
flash cameras like miniature explosions, and the four on the roof, and the
feeling of anti-climax rather than relief that the fire had not got out of
control and spread, as the radio feared.

The first cicadas of the year, like a dripping cistern, and my strange
happiness. Tuohy's gentleness towards me: showing me a passage Graham
Greene may have plagiarised from *The Ice Saints*, and, after dinner, asking
about my poem, asking who I want to read it. My answer: Wain or Kermode,
preferably Kermode, although he is not a practising poet, as Wain might be

too Movement. Later included Spender, for his interpretive interest. I have no idea how good a poet I am, (1) because I can no longer judge the work I am writing, (2) because I do not know whether it works for anyone else, and (3) because, compared with even minor poets of the 1930s in anthology (admittedly poems I am seeing the first time) I am not at all happy about my images. It's not that I think them bad: I am worried about the amount of imagination they contain. Left at 1 a.m., drunk, and walked through a handful of snake-dancing, rioting students.

30th April. Got some 250 lines typed: a lot. Am now tired from my late night, and will record my reaction to Brady. Earlier this week C said "He can't have a point of view", whereupon I tried to find one. Read the report on the tape-recording, the dialogue contained lines like "I can't breathe" (Ann) and "If you don't put your head down I'll slit your throat" (Brady), and made it quite clear that it was fellatio, with Myra Hindley photographing. Why she should do this I saw yesterday from a photo in *Time*: she is much less attractive than he, and was lucky to have as strong a man as Brady.

So what of Brady? Is he a cynic, a bored uneducated intellectual, a non-upper class Stavrogin (who also raped a little girl)? This evening I read that he claims Smith has framed him and that he killed Evans in the course of robbing him and picked a queer because he wouldn't go to the police. Do we believe this of a man who was addicted to De Sade and who would have been bisexual? What sort of a man is he, and above all, what does he lack? A constant theme this week on my part has been that if you put in effort, you come to realise that all men are your brothers before death; anyhow existence is all we have, and even the slightest sensibility has enough feeling to value the existence of others. Did Brady deliberately flout this value, like some wilfully misguided Stavrogin, or did he never have a chance, like the kids on the streets? Why didn't he feel?

1st May. Finished the first typed draft of the poem. It is now over 1,330 lines long, which is perhaps too long, and the typing has taken exactly three weeks. I am not sure what my reaction to it is. When I consider it as a whole, it seems a tour de force; when I consider individual lines I am not so sure. I do know that the feeling is fresh and my own, and that whether or not it is poetry depends on whether or not you accept the "necklace" analogy. If you do, then I have undoubtedly done something exciting and new, and have liberated poetry from the neo-Georgian Movement both technically and existentially, and have given the poem significance again, raised its kudos as a form for art relating to the struggle of living in contemporary history. These things in themselves should make it possible for other poets to write on "the grander themes".

I am, however, no judge. Compare Arnold's "destruction" of *Empedocles on Etna* and Kermode's praise of that poem. I can only judge *The Silence* by how far it fell short of what I was trying to do, whereas somebody else will say "This works" or "It does not work". When I think I may be on the verge of fame, however, I tremble, and remember Rilke's words "Young man everywhere, profit from the fact that nobody knows you." Subconsciously I am ready for fame. I dreamt last week that Wilkie-Murray from school took me to a 6-tiered circus; he had forgotten to get me a ticket and I was on the ground floor, watching cars driving round the ring. I climbed up on my own and met Tuohy and Waugh. Waugh commented on my appearance. I defeated him by quoting his own works against him. Waugh said: "If the younger generation are as bright as this, we haven't much to fear." Coming from a noted Tory and opponent of the present, this was a compliment, and Tuohy was pleased.

2nd May. On values at Tokyo University of Education. I am anti-Absolute – both the idea that values existed before humans and the idea that "the undying life of man" makes values "more than relative". I think a lot of people's values are relative in the sense that they do what is approved of by society (which is arbitrary), but in my view a much sounder basis for values is individual choice. Men come and will go, and death is the end, and we must choose what to value, and as our existence is the only thing we have, the most basic value to profound people is the preciousness of existence. This value is felt and based on sympathy: we are all in the same position. Values chosen individually and intellectually always lead to danger: note Brady, Raskolnikov, Hitler.

Never depart from feelings and sympathy – never, never, never. The film to be made of all the murders and violations of existence in the 20th century in the name of ideas, arguments, the intellect. Camus's "we exist", felt and not rationalised, is the basis of all values, and anyone who has not felt this is not mature in his values or as a person: note Brady, Raskolnikov, de Sade. Feeling should regulate one's "free acts", and feeling and sympathy should form the basis of the existentialist ethic that Sartre is supposed to be producing. Raskolnikov thought values were approved of by society until he came to realise the part played by feeling. Some time write a novel about the modern Raskolnikov who discovers the brotherhood of man before death, discovers it as sympathy, feeling, not as an idea or an argument or what have you. His image: men waiting to die.

3rd May. A holiday for Constitution Day. Handed over the poem (*The Silence*) to Tuohy and came away plunged into a depression, the cause of which was (1) now that my purpose over the last 16 months has come to an end, I am futile, and (2) Tuohy was in an odd mood, talked of sending the poem to the BBC, and seeing it through his eyes I felt full of doubt about its merit. When I look at it alone I have no doubt: it is good, it is much better than anything written in the 1950s. But I am judging it by Eliotian criteria and in terms of the pressure, whereas Tuohy judges by language, by Wittgensteinian positivism. I can stand the test, I think, but he is the last

283

person who should read the poem: he is not a contemplative or reflective. Perhaps it was a mistake to show him, perhaps I should have done it through Tomlin or handed over the final draft to him.

I was feeling this when I took down Gabriel Marcel from my bookshelf this evening. In the introduction by the translator (an Aberdeen don) I read words to the effect: "Marcel has meant more to me than any other writer." Marcel will lecture in Tokyo on May 12th, and I suddenly had a nightmarish "vision": an artist toiled for two years on a masterpiece and killed himself in despair at the end of it, and a reader, reading it a year later, had a mystical experience which took him to the meaning of life. This "realisation" brought me joy, and I put back Marcel and went through to the kitchen and got myself another beer and returned to my room and began to write this, and I knew that nothing Tuohy said about my poem could shake my faith in it: just as nothing derogatory Tuohy says about Marcel can shake my interest in him as a writer. This is what Yeats would call a "victory".

4th May. A weary, unproductive day browsing through the poem, doing little to it and renewing my faith in it. Again I asked: "Why am I so anxious?" And a passage C found in a book called *Children Growing Up* was of help. It was on Sheldon. The fat man is "endomorphic" with a visceratonic temperament (digestive); the middle-size is "mesomorphic" with a somatotonic temperament (muscular); the thin man is "ectomorphic" with a cerebrotonic temperament (sensory), i.e. he tends to move away from people, not towards (endomorphic) or against (to be at ease with and aggressive towards) people (mesomorphic). In short, the ectomorph is always "itching to retire and contemplate" and he, alone of the three, is an introvert, being "restrained, inhibited, hypersensitive" and "keeping himself emotionally and socially at a distance". The scale is 7 for each, so an extreme ectomorph is rated as $1 + 1 - 7$.

I do not know how Sheldon would have rated me, but it seems clear that my body and physiological make-up has largely determined my personality, and has possibly disqualified me from business – a competitive, mesomorphic occupation – and made me a poet. As teacher-poet I am divided between the social and the individual, and it is possibly my ectomorphic structure which leads me to incline towards the individual. It certainly contributes to my anxiety. There are other reasons however, for anxiety. The war may have had something to do with it: for example, the string of bombs that lit up the sky as I went through the gate in Brooklyn Avenue.

5th May. Another holiday, the last in Golden Week. Sat around in a torpor, trying, for the third consecutive day to rewrite "nothing and all" and vaguely preparing my lectures for tomorrow, utterly worn out.

Nothing and all: the point is that in terms of history, man is nothing, but in terms of himself and his existence, man is all, yet, paradoxically, that one needs the silence – the historical silence – to realise this. The silence is the measure of the genuineness of an existence, of the extent to which I realise its preciousness. All idea of its preciousness is based on the silence, and to live without realising how precious existence is is to live in a dream, to half-live. In contemplation, I become aware of this "I" on the silence, and other sounds – voices, passing cars and city sounds – sound unreal; and in becoming aware of the unreal on the one hand, and of death on the other hand, I feel my existence more nakedly, I feel that to exist is precious and all. I cannot argue this or think this, I can only feel it. It is a felt value (see May 2nd). And it has no "meaning" (see April 25th).

This feeling of the preciousness of existence, and my artistic purpose and approach to my Shadow, combined, are what help me to live, are what motivate my life. My greatest horror is the idea of a wretched suicide and complete loss of artistic purpose, both of which I felt yesterday and the day before. Yesterday I lay on my futon on the floor and imagined myself a failure as a poet, and having to go through with "my desperate vow"; I would do it, but the idea was terrible, it sickened me, and I felt I would rather live on as a failure than make myself nothing.

6th May. Went to the Tokyo University of Education to lecture at 8.30, returned home about 2.30, went off to the Bank of Japan, and stayed from 4 to 6.30 talking about Japan's future Empire ("we despise the Asians but we will be a teacher to them") and about China ("are they preparing for war?"). But the theme of the day has been London, since Buchanan gave me the *Time* article this morning and I discussed it with Tsuchigane this evening.

London may be a "swinging city", but I think *Time* have misunderstood the "new vitality". It is not the positive effect of lightening a pound after losing an Empire, it is rather what happens when "an old seasoned culture (has) lost... its drive", ingenuity and indulgence having replaced fortitude and devotion (Ruskin on Venice). This "vitality" is a reaction to futility and aimlessness, and any such reaction is far removed from vitality. As Tsuchigane put it: "In the last days of the Roman Empire, morals declined too," and the result is *La Dolca Vita*.

The main question is "Does one want Little England?" Whether we like it or not, we have got it; that has been clear ever since Suez. Slogans like "Isolationism" may sound grand, but they are still symptoms of decay, however much one abhors all the Empire-builders. Our interest in Africa is really discharging old responsibilities. Asia is far more important than Africa, and we cannot hope for influence in Asia. Perhaps isolationist Little England is making the best of a bad job, "choosing" one's lot. I do not like parties and provincial life, so I am instinctively against the idea of Little England, though I am also against Great Britain, and rather welcome the decay of the old order. I am divided about the new: anything is better than the old, but the new is not good enough.

7th May. Tuohy came and criticised my poem. His review made three points: (1) there are too many reminiscences of Eliot; (2) my "rosary" method is objective and I am too little detached from Freeman for it, i.e. there is too little irony (cf. the "passionate" statements at the end) and I am too subjective and express opinions (e.g. "bourgeois", "land reform" and so on); (3) I do not say where we are, i.e. by not saying what two brown rivers, I am not giving the full experience and so there is no emotional response – I must be more precise and so on, à la Winters. I said it was my intention to be detached, and disputed the third on the grounds that my method is to purge place of its particularity. He: "Universals are always presented in particulars", and so on. I am still not sure about this, although I cannot cite others as he demands. Conversation threw up also: (4) my rhythms tug the reader forward past the meaning, so I must make the images longer or break the poem up with numbers; I think I agree; (5) it is all too private, I am not presenting and communicating, it is not discourse to a person. This is another aspect of (3) above, and I am not sure that clarity – subtitles or glosses e.g. – are a good idea. I want to present an image and leave the reader to make the effort and relate it to the parts. And (6) my language is too private which he later retracted, praising all the technical side – the rhythms, cadences, the language, the dominated style. (Though he did take issue with my ambiguity.)

I am grateful to Tuohy for giving the poem so much thought and for being honest, but I was rather depressed by his aggressiveness and total lack of encouragement – he has never given me a word of encouragement – and attributed this to drink, pills, "mesomorphic" weight-throwing and possibly a little feeling of being threatened.

8th May. Tuohy rang this morning to apologise for being so aggressive, and blamed the pills. I said his criticisms were stimulating and helpful, and over the telephone we discussed: (1) glosses, which I now think a good idea (and they could always be left out in the future); (2) abbreviated narrative, which he described as "a strategy rather than tactics"; (3) the two rivers – if they could be repeated once they would have more reality; (4) the long five and a half rhythm, which he feels is better suited to conversational than to meditative poetry, on the grounds that you hurry through long lines and dwell on slow gnomic lines (the long being my forte); (5) gaps, "to check the flood, to break up the flow"; (6) typography, to get an abstract idea. He touched on things I did not record yesterday: I should read earlier poets than 20th century poets to find/preserve a voice; "a work of art is to discover what a work of art is" – which I disagree with. Nothing on the theme: "there are plenty of long poems and they don't get published because the mood isn't right." "You have a better rhythm and cadence than any of the Movement poets."

After all this he invited me round this afternoon. He was in a mood again, rather monosyllabic, perhaps hoping I would reveal myself. We talked about China, about ectomorphs and so on, strolling among the Waseda azaleas. He: "Orwell was an ecto." (Out of a silence). I took back the corkscrew he forgot to bring yesterday and left him to worry about his difficult class tomorrow and Kyoto on Thursday, returned and took C and Nan for a walk. C was more cheerful, after a morning's despondency because effort is not rewarded.

9th May. Had no lecture in the morning, so wrote most of the glosses and brooded on the artist as self and type, wondered whether I will ever get my own voice (if I have not got it already) and on why I am an artist. Decided Tuohy is in the (Henry) James tradition whereas I, without being extremely Wellsian, am rather pro-life; so Tuohy's problems are all about art – form, structure and so on, the traditional things – and mine are concerned with my quest. (Cf what he said on Saturday: "You have solved your technical problems by accident." To which I retorted: "It is a question of pressure; genuine feeling presses language and rhythm into freshness.")

In the afternoon, lectured on the truth the artist has access to: Kermode's "joy" or "the Image"; Joyce's wading girl, Wordsworth's girl with the pitcher, Yeats's "victories", Keats's melancholy being the pip of the grape which is Joy, Pater's Cyrenaic visions, Arnold's Callicles. This joy being a joy that must be paid for by suffering or melancholy.

I am different from these people, if Kermode's view of them is right. I too love and record the all too rare joyful Image, but I am aware of self-discovery and the quest for the Shadow, as they are not. They drift for the moment; I drift through such moments and, I like to think, towards. Or is that an illusion? The truth they have access to, therefore, is another world, which is momentarily unveiled. The truth that I have access to, and which justifies my healing, therapeutic place in society, is a truth connected with my existence, which is in progress, and my "Isness-Image" is therefore different from theirs.

21st October 1991. I now regard the Image as revealing Being, the metaphysical reality behind "isness", the invisible behind the visible (or unseen behind the seen).

11th May. Spent the morning writing glosses to my poem, went to the Prince, then got them typed on the the top copy in the evening and wondered whether they are an improvement after all. They made the poem more muscular; that is certainly true.

But do they not also detract from the revelation of the image – has not Tuohy failed to understand what I am trying to do, in that respect? Perhaps I am wrong. On the other hand, I feel the images are not so satisfying after the rational explanation: the images are one side of an equation, and the other side is what the reader has to "get", and by being given it to begin with, he now has very little to do; in spite of what Tuohy said about the "active" reader, his method is more "passive" than mine. I think I shall leave them in and see what happens.

For the rest, I must rewrite some passages: the "ailing knight" passage, which is too much of an opinion and too little of an observation; the rebellion against the environment and background, which seems all wrong; and the death and discovery of the preciousness of existence. I also have to decide whether the glosses really do reflect what the passages are saying and vice versa: for example there is not much about discipline; that must be inserted. After that I must try to decide whether the glosses will serve instead of more gaps to preserve the separation of each rosary bead and think again about my detachment from Freeman, i.e. I must see him objectively and not see through him.

12th May. I have been thinking again about my relationship to the traditional Romantic (see 9th May). I feel an opposition between myself and the world, I feel the isolation and go for the Image, but there is an active streak in me as well as a contemplative one.

Of course, it might be argued that this is what will destroy me as a poet, as it destroyed Rimbaud and Arnold, and I know deep down, that the whole thing is hopeless, just as much as they did: nothing conquers death, and to stake all on existence requires a deliberate and rather perverse blindness, or anyway a deliberate attempt to see life in categories one has chosen. Nonetheless, I have staked all on existence, as, perhaps, they did not. Existence is my absolute, not any Platonic idea or Tomlinesque category or Christian God. And this is the truth I try to reveal in my Image. I try to say "Look, this is, and you can't explain it; its basis is quite irrational, you can't give it a meaning, it *is*, and that is its glory."

"'Heavenly God' cried Stephen in profane joy": yes, but there is no Platonic or Thomist "other world" that is being revealed. The wading girl just *is*, like the girl in the wind, and that is a great mystery, it is truly wonderful and exciting. And to reach this vision one must make great efforts, embark on a quest like Freeman, and die away from the rational part of oneself.

I am an actor in progress to my Shadow, and I have staked all on existence against death. I will surely lose, but I have chosen my values. What is that? Callicles, the ignorant Callicles; or Marsyas, that arrogant fool? Is the mature melancholy of Empedocles in store, and the shot in the head, that perennial leap into the crater?

13th May. Yesterday discussed the economic situation – the Selective Employment tax and the future of our balance of payments – with the Bank of Japan; today read the attack on British right-wing attitudes in Archie's song "Number One" – the anti-democratic selfishness and lack of charity, the opposition to the National Health, the belief in force to hang on to the Empire and so on. Just what has happened? Is it those 1956 right-wingers who have got us into this hopeless mess as regards exports? Or is it, on the contrary, the Osborne protest, for example, that is responsible? Or is this protest a symptom of something much deeper, which not even the right-wingers could check?

I think the latter – perhaps what is called the tide on anti-imperialism. There was some idea, floating about like a germ, which was fatal to empires, and nothing the Osbornes and the 15,000 who went to the Rally in Trafalgar Square did really changed things. And so one cannot blame their isolationist, Little Englandism, or the right-wingers, for a balance of payments situation which has arisen because all the props have been taken away: the colonies. Who was right?

Again, it is difficult to say; should one be in principle pro-Empire, or anti-Empire? I personally find it difficult to distinguish my hatred for the upper class Empire-builders from the national interest and image, which is rather pro-Empire. I am all mixed up on this point, like most Britons. I have Osborne's hatred of the right-winger and the right-wingers' dream of British influence abroad.

14th May. More thoughts on the artist, after reading Kermode's account of action in the artist as being an escape from the painful art. Is that what my dream for revolution amounts to, an escape from the gruelling ascent? Is that what sensuality would amount to, if C left me?

15th May. An account by Peggy Kennet in the *Japan Times* of her experiences in Zen. Her conclusion is that she has obtained peace of mind and a knowledge of her "immaculacy" (i.e. spotlessness), and that under Zen she has taken up a position that is detached from existence; she can view the dark and the light, night and day, as if she were an astronaut looking at both sides of the moon. She will not return to the U.K.: she will bury herself in the country here in Japan, and just live, having renounced all right to teach the unteachable.

I was very affected by the account. Her conclusions are more or less mine in the poem: the calm, the "white sun", and the black and white of the Stone Garden. I have not gone as far as her, I have not seen myself as being outside life and death, both of which are unreal; I see myself as within both of them, but being still and detached from them. I also, therefore, rejected immortality, whereas she seems to accept it. My stillness is, however, as positive as hers, I believe, from the point of view of the mind; it can take one to eternity, in the sense that I can see the whole history of the universe as being one mere flicker on the slumbering retina of an eternal eye.

It is this dimension of the eternity of silence that I need in Pt 2 of the poem, for it is this that Western culture has overlooked: the eternity of silence *and* the preciousness of existence combined, these are black and white, night and day. I am within both of them but can be detached from them and yet love existence; this is what Freeman learns from the death.

16th May. At Tokyo University of Education, I asserted that man lives in an indifferent universe – Camus, Beckett, Hemingway and so on are right about that – but that this does not prevent him from creating values against that indifference, or raising his vitality to its highest extent. These things should depend on reverence for existence at its fullest and not on any Wellsian notion of the "underlying life of man", which is a swindle because of the final nothingness. "Wake up and live to the fullest" – that is the justification for Rimbaud's concern with consciousness, and it justifies because one cannot exist until one has lived to the full.

This insistence on vitality (i.e. growth) is one of the things I demand of a healthy culture, and of a healthy society, and in my poem it is what Freeman has to leave the West and come East to find. There is no silence in contemporary Western culture, and little notion of growth; death is the end, but existence is precious. Existence is not precious in the East, because of the system of duty (the kamikaze) and the traditional "nirvana", but there is this nourishing silence. I, a divided man, have joined the Western ideal of the preciousness of existence and the Eastern ideal of the detached calm. I have done this by rejecting immortality. Detachment and preciousness are an improbable combination, but they are not alternatives, and detachment is certainly not indifference.

I have still to decide what Freeman discovers during the death, which leads him on to his rejection of Western culture and acceptance of Eastern silence. The absence of silence has led only to despair and lack of growth for it is all rational. The Western private experience; there is nothing underneath, nothing to create a dynamic urge. Is this what Freeman sees while his father despairs – lack of growth and despair?

17th May. And so it seems as though I shall return to England concerned with the same problem that concerned me when I left it: East-West differences, what Ezard said to me on 11th November 1963. I have not become completely Easternised – I do not hold life to be an illusion and I have no total scorn for the body, like a Buddhist fire-martyr, but I do not value the reason much, not any longer, nor do I value bodily indulgence. I am still a Westerner, but I am more Eastern than most Westerners.

18th May. A rather fruitful day on the poem, Part 2, which is to be seen in terms of the irrational, or rather the infra-rational; this being symbolised by art and the Rescuing Woman. So the failure to grow in Part 2 is a failure to come to terms with the irrational, i.e. living too rationally; the silence being the irrational which makes one grow in the vital culture of Japan. Refinements: the reason is connected with promiscuity, the irrational (in spite of the dream about "the whore", which is to be changed) being connected with one woman only. Perhaps I am trying to die away from the reason and the aggressive world, and hence, all the things I have done against my own interest. And perhaps I secretly knew this all along, which is why I devised the type of the Sufferer, an actively co-operating "Sufferer" who worked things out against his own interests, "mine own Executioner".

19th May. Thoughts on eternity. Eternity is quite different from immortality; I can experience eternity, but I am not immortal, nor do I experience my eternity. Eternity is the long reach of "time" that stretches before the creation of the universe and after it is reduced to cinders, and spiritual life is a response to it, that long, silent reach of timelessness. I can understand what Blake meant when he wrote "Eternity is in love with the productions of time." Of course it is; for eternity is nothingness, timeless nothingness, and nothing is in love with being because it is expressed in being. Blake believed in a spiritual world of eternals, so this should not be pressed.

I say spiritual life is a response to this eternity. What I mean is that there is a point of contact in the infra-rational. The silence which is one's fertile depths is also the silence of eternity, and by making the infra-rational grow, one can enter into this silence of eternity, on which traffic sounds are transient and unreal. Perhaps this is the end of the agonising part of my quest, for perhaps this is what all Christians understand by God and the soul, this infra-rational of mine and the Great Nothing, the Great Infra-Rational. If this is what Christians know, I am glad I am not a Christian, for it has nothing to do with Christian concepts, and I am all the more convinced of the need to redefine Christianity completely, scrap the churches and concentrate on real spiritual development.

So far as I am concerned, it is feeling silence underneath one's reason, a silence which stretches for longer than the existence of the earth; nothing more and nothing less – no faith, no immortality, no "being" unless you can call awareness of silence "being", and certainly no One to talk to, to confess to, to be moral before.

20th May. But this infra-rational silence which is a part of this silence of eternity, or which is rooted in it – is it not also the silence of one's own existence when it is emptied of reason? If it is, there must be a distinction between negative and positive existence, for I think one's existence can be fertilised into fertility, i.e. one is not born with this infra-rational fertility, one has to cultivate it and make it fertile, positive. Most people's existence is just rather negative.

Perhaps I am aware of Being, in the sense of "positive existence", and perhaps I am not sure whether eternity is Being or absence. I do not know, and do not want to get metaphysical about it. So back to a real situation: last night, driving by the river in a silent taxi, with Fujii sitting in the front; and later Fujii saying "It is very nice to drink surrounded by one's sons" (he has four) and I glimpsing his loneliness, his craving for company, his turning away from the wall of death and pretending it is not there.

I must confess, I am still divided, for that is to me the truth, and eternity is a long reach of timelessness devoid of Being. And yet this silence teases me out of thought: it is so positive and charged, and I am so conscious of what is an illusion and what isn't. The issue is important because it is the goal, this silence, and I cannot interpret it. Perhaps that is my great mistake, trying. Perhaps I should say, "This is the ground/height of one's 'isness', and all interpretations are unreliable. Just experience this and you will be creative, your existence will be real." Yes, I think I must stop there. There, on that frontier, reason must recognise its limits.

21st May. Tuohy came at 9 and stayed to 1.30 a.m., drinking. On my poem he made one main point, that there still is not enough distancing, and that some of the poetry should be taken out and put in the "meaning", i.e. narration. On the relation between poetry and meaning he adopted a strangely Eliotian viewpoint: the meaning is the sop to the dog while the burglar's rifling the kitchen (I having raised this). When I said I agreed, and showed him a passage whose meaning I had changed for the sake of the poetry ("In a graveyard of uniform stones") he said "Hmm, and so you bloody ought." Also: "People are asking you for poetry, not meaning." On distancing, he objected to "comprehensive". I said I was trying to be contemporary. He retracted and objected to "slumped" and "numb" on the grounds that it was a gesture and suggested self-pity. I said I saw the first but not the second. He: "The objection I have against you is the objection I have against Joyce. Stephen is a pain in the arse." I: "Distancing matters more in novels that it does in poetry," and "I have never been a woman in an orgy." And so on – he taking back his objection to "afternoon tea", but saying "under a moon" is a cliché. I fought all the way and it was all very friendly because he was not in a mood. Again and again I asked him to identify undistanced passages, the "line a page", emphasising that the particular poetry was an image of the general meaning, i.e. one side of an equation. He was doubtful about this but could not refute it, and did not identify any more passages (i.e. those he regards as being there only for self-expression).

22nd May. A birthday. It poured all day, as the result of typhoon no. 2, and Nan sweated and got delirious, as the result of complications on the 8th and 9th days of her smallpox vaccination: her arm was inflamed, she had a temperature of 38.4C (= over 100F) and there were spots on her buttocks and arms. This came on yesterday afternoon, and although I know about the dangers of encephalitis, I kept quiet and C did not find out until 6.30 p.m. in the evening; whereupon I "dissuaded" her from being worried.

23rd May. At Tokyo University of Education, on the individual in society. Does unreal living (i.e. being concerned with trivialities) depend on a materially prosperous society which values bingo, Beatles, TV, adverts, etc.; or is it the other way round, does the unreal, i.e. sick, society depend on the unreality, i.e. sickness, of its individuals? I want to believe the second: without their "demand", the society would never have fallen sick in the first place. Although by now the first is true in Britain, and the younger generation now has not had a chance. By now it is a vicious circle.

So where does the cure lie, with society or the individual? I think with the individual, for a cure cannot be imposed from above. A healthy society depends on the real living of its members as individuals, and the criterion of "real" is bound up with self-knowledge or command of the inner life in some way. This is evident in China, even, which has got hold of the wrong reality; there is self-criticism and little material prosperity. In Japan there is self-reflection, but Japanese society is to some extent sick, and has become ill since the war. Consider the relation between the philosophers and Golden Athens in the 5th century BC and between the poets and Augustan Rome, and between Sidney and Shakespeare and Elizabethan Britain. Perhaps this last parallel is bad.

Anyhow I posit a law: the more self-knowledge and depth in the majority of individuals in a society, the more creative that society will be, the more readily it will solve its problems, and the more healthy and growing the society will be. The antecedents for this idea are Iran (State within Church) and Eliot's Idea of a Christian Society. What about the U.S.A., which has physical rather than spiritual power. Does the U.S.A. prove my law wrong?

24th May. Perhaps I am seeing the problem in the wrong terms. The point is, self-discovery and cells of 10 teach one the value of existence and the preciousness of the existence of others. If the majority in a society could achieve this vision, the society would be a good environment for the young. British society is far from such a "good" environment and is therefore to be condemned. In fact the atmosphere is sterile, the country falling apart – witness the State of National Emergency and our ruined exports drive.

The point is, a society should make seeing through self-discovery as readily available as possible; a society should create conditions which promote values based on understanding – deep understanding – and not ignorance. A society should help one command one's experience and not fragment it. It is the values, the vision, the quality of the existence, that are important, not the standing of the nation. Nonetheless, national decay is a symptom of spiritual decay, and the standing of the nation is important in preserving the values, so the fact that the values incidentally affect the nation's standing is not one to be overlooked.

So my role as an artist is to bear a truth from the infra-rational depths of our natures, a truth which determines our values, our vision, our living; and to pass this on to our society in the interests of the health of the individuals, and not in the interests of our nation, though these will be served as well. As an artist, I bear a truth that can heal; as an artist, I am a healer in a sick society.

25th May. The Tokyo University of Education party at the Mikasa Kaikhan, at which I was a guest of honour, along with Meyer.

The whole evening was a disaster. To begin with, I was told at Hitachi's at 5.45 that the party had been postponed from 6 to 7, between which time I had a beer downstairs with Saito, Ruth Witt-Diamant (who offered to get me a job in San Francisco) and, later, Narita, who was rather disapproving. At 7 we went upstairs, but no one really turned up until 7.30, during which time Mrs. Witt-Diamant attacked Meyer's precious linguistics. I joined in and between us we demolished him with statements like "How would you analyse 'Careful – I got fragile mementos?' and 'Whereof one cannot speak, thereof one must be silent'?" The others arrived and Fujii (opposite me) opened proceedings, treating the guests in alphabetical order and putting me first. Narita was then very rude: praised Meyer, said nice things about his wife, whom he had never met, and then treated me at disproportionately short length, and purely in terms of family-visiting, made no mention of C, and deliberately forgot Nan's name 3 times; and presumably his opening "Nicholas" was intended to convey his lack of respect rather than his friendship. Irie said some nice things, but no one said they were glad I was coming back, not even Kuroda, who had called out "Please stay" last summer.

After the first round of speeches I had had enough, and it was late. So taking advantage of something inaudible down the end of the table I stood up, said "I understand I have been asked to speak" and said at the end "I'd like to thank you for the kind things that some of you have said." Mrs. Witt-Diamant followed with a long speech about Japanese kindness: "They are so warm, so kind, so generous, so gracious; they make you feel so much at home", etc. All clearly ironical. Saito was kind to me. But Ohta vitriolic through misunderstanding, e.g. saying Mrs. Witt-Diamant did not like linguists (as opposed to linguistics), saying "I hope Dr. Meyer will like New York more than London."

As Mrs. Witt-Diamant would say, "It's funny rather than terrible." I think Hashimoto understood my emphasis on "some". He said: "English intuition is to be valued."

27th May. After four hours at the Bank of Japan – saying "Goodbye" to Tsuchigane included – went to dinner with Prince and Princess Hitachi. The pathetically short list of conversation subjects, and, in contrast, the very pleasant and positively delightful evening we had. The Prince talked much more fluently than usual, the Princess was, as usual, at ease, and not trying to be a Princess like Michiko.

The only awkwardness there, in fact, was me: at dinner first my voice went husky (so husky that it would need a lot more than a cleared throat or a drink of water to clear it) because I was tired and had strained it; then I chop-sticked some cormorant-gulleted fish on to the imperial lacquered tray; then an eye-lash threatened my left eye, and in addition to being reduced to silence, I could not see properly; and finally my stomach began to rumble, as I had missed lunch that afternoon – an acidulous rumble, like the swirl of bathwater down a plug. This I tried to cover up with words, and consequently I talked some rubbish for my conversation was dominated by my belly.

After an awful ten minutes I recovered my composure, and did not lose it again until after I had shown Their Highnesses the photos of China: "This was once the Imperial Palace, and now it is a centre for children." The Prince's reaction was to sit back; the Princess's to look through with great interest and comment only on the magnolia blossoms, ask if this was a fishing-boat, and so on: all the polite things. The Prince: "If we Japanese do not like the U.S., we do not learn English," and I realised that he was proudly defending his father. (Hence English was cancelled in 1939).

Earlier the quarrel over a word, the Prince saying "syllable", Haneko "letter". Both turned to me for arbitration, and I said "I hesitate", but I knew she would not let him get away with things because he is a Prince.

28th May. A day on the poem, checking my attitude to Freeman. To be detached from him, I must see all sides of his situations and comment on, e.g., his lack of feeling, his moral blindness, his narcissism, his guilt. I must deflate him if he is too pretentious, perhaps satirise the earnestness and seriousness of his quest, call him a prig, show that I disapprove a little. Thus I shall be able to undermine what Freeman is saying. It is important that he should be doing the saying and I the undermining; thereby I shall present a distanced, understood experience.

All this sounds rather like Hamlet's advice to the players, which I heard yesterday at Tokyo University of Education; I advised my students then to concentrate on emphasising the meaning at the expense of the poetry, i.e. emphasise lines which establish the situation and hurry over Herod and the image and so on; perhaps I should apply my own advice to my poetry. I think I can retain the "baroque pearls" idea. Having spent two hours with Meiras, learning about the 800% profit yesterday, and having explained my whole poetic theory to Princess Haneko in one sentence – that one image – I think it is too good to jettison. Tuohy is right: it is a style of detachment. And the next thing I do must be very detached: on the one hand British self-pity and illusions, which are to be criticised (in terms of the silence?) and on the other hand a true exposure of what the British are like.

29th May. Tuohy came round at 11 a.m. to take back the photographs. We drank beer until 12, after which I could not write. I suggested he came to the Kenkyusha Party, even though he had not been invited. When we arrived at the Akasaka Prince Hotel 6th floor at 5.30 we discovered a tray of rosettes. Tuohy: "Shall I retreat?" and "You'll have to introduce me." He was given the yellow rosette of a gatecrasher, against my pink one. In the next two hours met Kuriyagawa and Ando, Toyama and Fubara, Fukuda, Prof. Ichiro Ando the poet, Shumoto, Collcutt, Fathers Milward and Johnstone. Learnt from Milward that Enozawa is a Catholic.

The sadness of Ando and Takahashi. Ando has wanted to thank Tomlin for a letter of recommendation since 1963, and mentioned some person; Tomlin, "Oh was this a few days ago?" Tomlin has no recollection of the kindness Ando had remembered so gratefully, and Ando's eyes glinted. Takahashi sent his Coleridge paper to Hough, "Dear Mr H, you may not remember me...." Hough's reply: "Dear Miss Takahashi, Of course I remember you." Tomlin's insincerity "You must come for some drinks before you leave," and so on. Tuohy, on the way to eat in Shinjuku: "He's a hanger on to the Eliot crowd: 'may I eat with you so I can say I knew you when you're dead?' He hasn't got a reputation in England."

Talked about the idea of the apprentice-writer, or articled writer, learning by word of mouth, and Brady. Tuohy thought his illegitimacy and desire to be different were responsible; also the desire to do the wickedest thing possible. I thought he was trying to feel de Sade's pleasure.

30th May. Tried to write and went to MITI, where one of the candidates was Chief of the Osaka Fair Office, and responsible for the planning of the Fair.

Letter from Mrs. N saying the Group Captain has had a very slight stroke; very sorry, in spite of his lack of sympathy as regards father. He will have to be very careful for the next few years.

31st May. Last day at Keio. Reflections on Tuohy. He has been very kind to me, and I must be really grateful for the time he has given me, but I do believe he was the last person I should have shown my poems to. "Poetry is discourse," he said on Sunday. To which I replied "That is only one theory; poetry is also image." And I wrote in all the glosses in accordance with his theory and not mine, which I know to be right. "The logical positivists are really right about language," he said on Sunday. I have never heard anyone defend Ayer before, and was at a loss: I didn't know the arguments, and anyway, I am sufficiently in favour of writers attending to language as to be here in Tokyo where English is regarded as a foreign language. "People won't read you for the meaning, only for the rhythms," he said two weeks ago, "so you needn't worry about what you are saying." This is balls: my students are lost without meaning, and this goes for most readers of poetry; although I can stand the test on rhythms.

He was the last person, but his standards are the same as those of (e.g.) *The Observer* critics, so I must listen to what he says; do the first one their way, the second one my way. Later I chanced on a page in *The Angry Decade* which excluded Tuohy from the mood of the 1950s. He would agree and say "With-it writers never last" and so on. Perhaps he's right, but there is another side, which has little to do with technique: Eliot is not solely interested with technique in the *Four Quartets*, nor is Rilke in the *Duino Elegies*, and it is to their tradition, ultimately, that I belong, and I must bear this in mind when I listen to Tuohy.

1st June. A wet day spent in making corrections to my poems and typing them in. Then went to the OUP party given by Kawawaki, with Tuohy. As usual, did my utmost to destroy myself, or undermine myself: in producing my right hand from behind my back, I sent someone's whisky glass spinning out of his hand and crashing to the floor. As our two groups were being photographed, I could not turn round and apologise and take the blame; so I pretended I had not noticed, shook hands as I had intended, and got on to China photographs. Met Bonas....Baker and Corbett on their dismal futures with the British Council. (Corbett: "I do just administrative work.") Mrs. Baker is playing Portia to FT's Antony. Saw Toff: "In Russia you can't even have a piss if it's not on your schedule." Then met a Heinemann's publisher who said he saw me at a party in Hong Kong in March – I having walked into one with Tuohy, by accident. It was given by Ron Heapey, whom I knew at Oxford, I believe.

On the way back with Tuohy I said: "Self-destructive people never enjoy anything" and "If I really wanted to go back to England, somehow I would make sure that I wouldn't." Is this true, or was I trying on a mask to see if it fitted? A depressed, scratch-dinner of spaghetti with Tuohy, talking about reputations; he saying that approval from the inner few does not necessarily grow into a reputation, and that he wanted a reputation now rather than in 2016, because he wanted the money.

2nd June. Went to the Bank in the morning to get over £300 of travellers cheques. British bank clerk was talking to a Filipino (?), and called to another clerk: "Lesley, would you like a drink this evening?" Lesley's reaction was to giggle. This clerk was small, very clean and rosy-cheeked, with thin lips and fuzzy fair hair and unflinching eyes; he wore a blue and white striped shirt. I hated him. Why? For one thing, I was slightly intimidated by his confidence, for I was standing by C, waiting, and felt awkward. For another thing I feared his air of being with-it.

3rd June. A day of negative emotion. At Tokyo University of Education went (reluctantly) into the staff room to be greeted warmly by Narita. Sat down coldly, reacted to his questions and addressed myself otherwise to Fubara and Toyama. On the subject of Waugh, I said, almost before "I" had seen the opportunity: "He was very right wing and intolerant, he deliberately got people's names wrong: he called Kingsley Amis 'Kingsley Ames'." There was a terrific silence. All took the point, I am sure of it, and when Narita spoke next time, it was in a subdued and guilty whisper.

Then Adrian telephoned, presumably having met Field (or possibly Tomlin). He irritated me by saying, very sillily, at the end: "You seem to be building a wall between yourself and the world." I: "Not really." I rang off soon after and was depressed. Why? Because he had judged me in terms of his values which approve of parties and senseless chatter, and disapprove of serious writing, of solitude. I will not have art reduced to an after-dinner joke, nor will I laugh and agree that the artist should give his full attention to dining out. Nonetheless, he judged me. I should have replied: "Between myself, your world, and the world of your values maybe, but not against my world." But what would have been the point? Just after Tomlin rang to ask us, phonily, "in for drinks". He wanted to offer, he did not want me to accept. He knew I was going (to Hong Kong) on Sunday morning, but he suggested Sunday evening and simulated his surprise, pretty well, on discovering he had "got it wrong". This is the world that Adrian sets up as a standard.

Dinner with Frank (Tuohy). Discussed Hardy's mistress (Tryphena Sparks) and a *Time* edition 1922 which said De La Mare, Housman and Masefield were the three greatest contemporary poets; and tried to think of someone who would read my poem sympathetically. Tuohy was against Wain, Amis & Co. on the grounds that they are too "selfish". Does he mean they wouldn't like it? Probably. Or is he (being) genuinely instable, getting a different slant on things? On Saturday morning Buchanan came round and suggested Blunden, who is willing to help rather than judge.

4th June. My last day in Tokyo for a while. Packed, had a haircut, and turned my thoughts to history. Once again, is history just wave upon wave, or has it a pattern? Is freedom the key concept, or is there a determining pattern connected with the spirit, for example? I am very self-divided about this and would like to believe the best of both. I would like to believe in Britain's freedom to emerge (strange, my stubborn nationalism, which I "destroy" in my teaching by emphasising "Little England") but deep down feel there is a decline ahead, a decline into a U.S.E. (United States of Europe) or a U.S.A., and that the decline cannot at all be dressed up as a progress. Perhaps both are true; there is no rigid law – rather a tendency – and freedom can always shatter laws, although there are odds against this happening.

This ambiguity is at the heart of my next poem. The dying whore is Britain, at one level, but is her decline inevitably (and syphilitically) determined (cf Spengler) or is there some hope of a total recovery (cf Toynbee)? I think the first, discounting the U.S.E. as a total recovery although all my revolutionary ideas are based on the second, on the concept of hope. Perhaps I should be completely pessimistic, and abandon the false escape/revolution, and accept myself as an artist, totally. At the other level, the dying whore is a mad visionary, who feels the divisions of her country in her own body, and who is to be certified syphilitically insane and finished. Again, the pessimistic, deterministic interpretation of history. Perhaps this is the paradox: that the individual is free and above all laws, whereas history obeys a law and determines the individual; and that the individual's freedom is at its most acute in his struggles with the determining law of history.

8

BRITAIN, FEELINGS AND SPIRITUAL REFORM
June – August 1966

5th June. Tokyo-Nakhodka. Got off to Yokohama. The formalities: Immigration, Customs and Quarantine. Then the crowds round the gangway, where Kuramochi stepped forward to discharge his "on". On to the Baikal, straight to the Purser's office, where I left our passports and health certificates; then to the Intourist lounge to surrender travel vouchers. After that watched the boat depart at 11. The streamers, the cheering and clapping from the quay: leavers and left clutching streamers.

Up and down movement but little swaying until about 7 p.m. Read Greene's *Comedians*: is there spray from the port side? Otherwise, walked on the first class deck, looked in on the lounge: few hand-outs as in China. Strapping Russian peroxide-blondes, more co-operative than in China. French classes over the loudspeaker because of De Gaulle's anti-Americanism.

Thought more about Britain: we are leaving ELDO, but are building the Chunnel. There is a distinction to be drawn between our national position in relation to the rest of the world – here our decline is inevitable – and the possibility of a spiritual revival. This distinction is not in Soka Gakkai; how is my "law of unreality" affected?

Anyhow the situation in my poem is now: a bankrupt whore is in a labyrinthine hospital suffering from cancer; she thinks it is a syphilitic decline imitating cancer – a decline connected with abandoning religion and becoming a whore (?) – and she dreams of a recovery she fears impossible; this physical recovery being seen (1) nationally (2) spiritually. So she is preoccupied with the question "What is my disease?" There should be a separate poem on China about the individual and the collective soullessness. All this overcomes the freedom/law difficulty (see June 4th) but I must think more about the connection between a spiritual revival and national resurgence and (in the whore's case) consequent physical recovery.

6th June. Tokyo-Nakhodka. The boat ploughed on through first sun, then mist, and passed Hokkaido about 8 p.m.

Spoke to the Russian Purser's assistant, a graduate in English language and literature and history from Vladivostok. Her eagerness to talk masking uncertainty, her fear and frown when I went too far. "I don't feel I am living in a country which is not free" – this after Sinyavsky and Tarsis and Pasternak had come up, and the Hangchow classroom and the Hungarian refugees. "Englishmen are not arrogant, they are shy." She made no attempt to go; was she vetting us? She spoke of her mother-in-law; her job is a strange one for a married woman.

Otherwise the day was spent in waiting for the scanty and greasy meals, at 8.30, 12.30, 4.30, and 7 (1st shift); and avoiding the Todai (Tokyo University) Economics students, and observing the Armenian (?) who had difficulty with his Russian but who behaved like a spy, loitering in the passage and eavesdropping on the back desk. I was too tired to think much about my writing.

The meaning of what I wrote yesterday, however, regarding Britain, is: Britain has got some cancerous disease and is physically declining. Exactly what caused this is uncertain, but it seems it could be (1) seasonal, i.e. connected with old age; (2) some internal "cancer of the spirit" (the hooligans, the results of democracy); (3) the result of a riotous youth (i.e. a disease following from mixing with so many nations). The cure is first, restoration to health negatively, and secondly, a recovery of the former position. This second and positive possibility can be discounted; she is too old. The most she can hope for is recovery of health i.e. a recovery of spiritual power. The former position has been lost for good.

7th June. Tokyo-Nakhodka-Khabarovsk. We arrived in Nakhodka early, about 4.15. We were taken by surprise, sighted land during early tea. Earlier, you could see your breath, but on the land it was not very Siberian, and much lighter. Customs clearance (i.e. declaration of money – $, £, ¥ – and jewellery) was done in the cabin, health certificates and passports were returned, and after a long wait we did a tour of Nakhodka on a bus with two New York Jews and a Fulbright Chemical Engineering Professor and his wife.

This was really just a visit to the Seamen's Building, where we were given tea and propaganda and Chinese-type friendship. The posters, the Lowry-like trafficless streets with individuals and groups; the peroxided hair and tight skirts and quaint, high 19th century buildings being very unChinese. The cost $1.50.

Shortly after came more or less the same way to Nakhodka station. Got in car 5, berths 9 and 10, of a Victorian style of train. It must be pre-1917; the notice on the lavatory door is in Russian and German, suggesting August 1939 as a date for overhaul. In the restaurant, i.e. dining-car, discovered that Katakura has given me only two sets of vouchers. The Intourist guide's cheerful lack of concern for Nan. The New York Jewess and her granddaughters: the small photo album, the polite interest from the Japanese. Throughout the day, Nan's shyness. She takes after me, and cannot be expected to move towards others when I move away from them, and, as at lunchtime, prefer hostile silence to small talk with a Japanese student.

The frogs two hours outside Nakhodka, sawing as at Nobe.

8th June. Nakhodka-Khabarovsk-Moscow. A long wearying day. Slept little on a precarious 8ft high bunk, one arm through an improvised strap, a towel, to prevent me from rolling off when the train jolted.

Arrived Khabarovsk 12.30 p.m. The heat, the long wait in the bus, the drive to the airport; lunch and the long wait until 4.20, when the Aeroflot at last took off. This was 9.20 a.m. Moscow time, so therefore the day began all over again.

The heat, the roar of the four turbo-props: like a wartime bomber or an electric drill, for 9 hours non-stop. The cotton-wool snowfield clouds, Nan's friend Elma, the Japanese-Austrian, and her dolls.

Arrived Moscow at 6.30, Moscow time. The Professor was met by his Academy: his literary wife's pride. The inefficient guide, Mr Roberts. Got my own luggage 10 minutes after identifying it. Drove 20-30 kms into Moscow: spaces, trees, flats, then the quaint charm of the 19th century terraces and their varied, fading beauty. Stayed at the Hotel Minsk in Gorky Street.

The struggle with Intourist and the hotel's Service Bureau. "It's late and I'm not working tomorrow – you get your tickets and ask about your car then." A telephone call: "You have asked for sheets for your daughter? Look here, you must pay 150 kopeks a night." (£1 = 2.52 roubles.) On bedding, I won; and succeeded in taking the Minsk coupons to the second floor restaurant, attracting attention, and taking two beers and an appleade up to our room (740 on the 7th floor) in the clanking Edwardian lift. (Open gates.) Otherwise I surrendered; being too tired to battle. Like the English girl married to the U.S. G.I. who had been booked on a flight that was full. The Russians' rude front, yet their kindness when you get through; something which is typically working-class; surly, barging manners, and kindness. The hot room. To sleep at 10.30 p.m., i.e. 5.30 a.m.

9th June. Moscow. In Russia you need for every half day of sightseeing another half day of pushing. Woke at 6.30 a.m., got breakfast after waiting only a quarter of an hour, and was first at the Intourist counter at 8.50. Was referred on to Service Bureau at 9.10; no car before 11, must take a taxi to the E. German Consulate for a double visa (waited 10-10.30). Arrived at the National Hotel Service Bureau at 10.45 for the 11 tour of the Kremlin, to be told: "It is in French; return at 12 for an English interpreter. Pay $3.21" (If you don't pay for excursions outside Russia, you must pay in dollars: the Cold War.) At 12: "That girl was new, you should have come at 11. Pay 8 dollars and come again at 2."

I paid, but blew up about the time ("Niet") and we set off at 12.20 for a tour on foot of the Kremlin, Red Square, etc. The Archangel Cathedral, the icons (5+5), the murals on the pillars (3x6+6), as in the Annunciation Cathedral to the left. I got the idea for a "new" poetic form, the pictures on the wall. The Grand Dukes and episodes from the *Bible*. The name from the second icon from the right. Ivan the Terrible's tomb. The Armoury. St.

Basel's Cathedral, 9 in 1, 1 in the middle and (4+4) round. The invigorating cobbles. The brilliant light on Lenin's face in the dank air; the bayonet-carrying soldiers; the boy who was anxious about his behaviour in the square, and who fell down the steps as we left. The Gorm Departo, Revolution Square, Kiubashov Street, 25 October Street.

C and Nan left at 2.30, I joined them at the Minsk at 3.30. "Your train will leave at 7, not 6.15, so the car will come at 6, not 5, and your tickets will be ready at 5 and not before." Tea: waited 20 minutes. Got the idea of going from Warsaw to Leningrad. At 5, at the Service Bureau, "Intourist are out, come back at 6." And: "There is no train from Warsaw to Leningrad." At 5.50, I discovered I had been given no meal vouchers for the train, and having only 40 kopeks after paying out another 2.31 roubles on the tickets requested to be driven to a bank that was open. The driver drove instead to the station, where the Intourist rep spoke no English at all.

10th June. Moscow-Berlin. These last events (the tickets not being ready, the train being "changed" in spite of the blue train on the platform, the extra payment and absence of meal vouchers, the fact that in spite of the note there was no Bank and the Intourist man spoke no English) began a very "fishy" journey. The two guards gave me 13.04 roubles at 2.52 a £, i.e. on the black market, the £5 to be given to them after the currency declarations in the Iron Curtain countries.

At Brest, the exit station, one of these two told us several times to take a walk, and when we did our train disappeared for an hour, to return on another platform very incomplete. Although we were the only English on the station, an announcement was made in English, and we got back escaping Soviet customs and currency interrogation, as we were later to escape the Polish interrogation. Also the restaurant car disappeared, leaving us without lunch and dinner. The guide tried to hide or atone for this by bringing us some biscuits for lunch and making us dinner (after I had paid 3 roubles for two bars of chocolate).

At Warsaw he seemed to be in trouble for encouraging people to leave the carriage. When we restarted the train braked and some latecomers got on and he was ticked off. He had encouraged us to walk – I said I was tired – and he talked on the platform with a curly haired middle-aged man. At Warsaw too, we lost the rest of our train, and our carriage seemed to be filled with Arabs in track suits who stood in the corridor. Quite clearly we should be on the train with the restaurant car, and the guards are hiding this from the English. The East German farmer at dinner, the Russian pensioner who had visited his daughter, who was in a concentration camp in Berlin for four years.

11th June. Berlin-London. At Brest, the carriages are lifted onto wheels with a narrower gauge. The restaurant car came on in Belgium.

Earlier, last night after midnight, Berlin. The dark approach from the East, the ruined buildings and dim lights. The searchlights and the river, and then, over the wall. The blaze of neon in W. Berlin. Yesterday I began the poem on China and Russia (later called *Archangel*); today I wrote up to 150 lines. It is a general reflection on Communism and the West, on the basis of values and the ideal the West should pursue to maintain its moral superiority. It will make a good foundation for the one on Blighty, the dying whore, suffering under the consequences of syphilitic imperialism and colonialism.

Belgium: the terraces like those in Moscow, Flanders barley fields. Ostend.

The awful English. The shoving to get off at Dover. On the train I loved the green fields but hated what they represented, and dreaded my return: I would have nothing to say to any of them, I thought, because they would think me someone else. Japan was my home, whereas, to them, I would be coming home. I was a stranger. To C I said at Victoria "Shall I pretend or be myself and disappoint?" Yet, to my surprise, I managed to be very "spontaneous". Chattered to the Group Captain and Mrs. N in the car about modern Britain. The Group Captain's stutter after his stroke, his insistence on carrying my bags, though I had my way.

At 55 High Beech Road, greeted my family: mother & R first, J & F later. Mother organised, and pointed everything out, and when I drank Mrs. Nixon's coffee by mistake, she made me some. I used objects: the atlas, the China photos, presents. R was at ease; J & F were unrecognisable.

12th June. After tea went with Rob to see the cricket.

14th June. Monday 13th. Changed $830 travellers cheques at $2.78 $3/4$? (just before the lift in the £) and rerouted my return trip via Berlin-Leningrad. Drove up to the Forest, which I first visited on Sunday morning: the pale water-lilies like lotuses, the golden irises, the purple pond plant; the dark, sodden Forest floor, the Alsatian in Truffer's drive. The children sitting on the fallen beech.

In the evening Rob and J came. Talked with R about revolution. His objections, based on legal knowledge and locality and what is right for Britain. His agreement with my analysis of the situation: a breakdown in 1910, the old order gone and nostalgia being senseless, and only material (economic) and territorial (geographical) decline ahead, and nothing to choose politically between Wilson or a "new Cromwell" (Donnelly M.P.).

Spiritual regeneration is all that can be hoped for. Do not mix spirit and politics. Loss of national independence aside, why, then, do I want to act, if I believe the decline is inevitable? Perhaps I am embracing the fate which terrifies me the most: execution by hanging or shooting. Perhaps, one way or another. That is how at Oxford, I knew the sufferer so well. Last night until 3 a.m., lay awake contemplating my self-destructiveness.

15th June. Tue. And in "Palmerston's lounge" I carried my self-destruction a stage further after a very red-faced, grey-haired, black-suited

P—had passed me on to D. S. Was offered help to rush down, like the swine, into a deep abyss. The crest on the fireplace, the crowns on the lampposts by the river, the statues from an old world: Curzon, Burgoyne, Franklin, Frederick Duke of York, John First Lord Lawrence, Clyde, Scott, Florence Nightingale. And later too, in Peter Street I tried to smash, among the 15 (doss-house) men....

After I changed worlds and arrived late for dinner at home, and mother saying that eggs are one and sixpence a dozen at another shop and F laughing innocently. Later, went through old papers: drawings I did in 1944 and 1945, all of the Battle of Britain. The nationalism of the Union Jacks. Learnt that mother had a miscarriage in 1941 April, R (born) in March 1942 prematurely, the twins on April 12th 1945 (one lasted three, the other six weeks); then Janet in 1946 (October 14th) – died after 18 months. Then J in February 1949 and F in March 1952 (together with one stillborn brother). Father born 12th September 1906; mother born 7th October 1910.

16th June. My infancy, reinforced by going through old papers. Got my memories into context. The marriage was on August 28th 1937. I lived in Fairview Road, Norbury, May-September 1939; with Grannie in East Grinstead September-December 1939; at Caterham December 1939-September 1940; with Grannie at East Grinstead May 1940-1941; at Beechholme East Grinstead 1941-March 1943 – Dad living in digs November 1942-March 1943: from this stay I remember the pine in the garden and the toads in the cellar. I moved to 52 Brooklyn Avenue, Loughton in March 1943 and did not like it because, suddenly, I knew nobody: "Could we meet somebody to smile at?" I once asked, walking out of the gate with Rob in the pram. I went to Essex House May 1943, (the old) Oaklands over the road, May 1944. After one term in September 1944 Oaklands moved up Albion Hill. My memory of Ilfracombe – Dad swimming in a cove – is to be dated to August 1944, when the V-bombs began....The South Coast was prohibited, and the beach toll was 1d. per person. The weather was rotten, and the wind blew the coffee as it left the thermos.

Perhaps my anxiety is connected with this time: no father, then knowing nobody, changing schools, and the war. We moved to Journey's End in July 1945, so what about the string of bombs in Loughton, and Grandpa lost in the fog?

17th June. On provincial life and ambition. After going to London on Thursday and looking at the sand-baked mummy in the Upper Egyptian Room of the British Museum and buying a book on the Kremlin and walking through a blistered, peeling Soho, I was able to observe Rob against the provincial background. Earlier, he had asked me: "Will you go into politics?" and I had said "I doubt it. My temperament is, like T. E. Lawrence's, suited to empire-building or destroying, but unsuited to committees."

BRITAIN, FEELINGS AND SPIRITUAL REFORM (1966)

We went to the local Conservative sherry-tasting: a lecture from Derek Balls, and tastes of Fino, Amontillado and Oloroso. When it was over Rob got up and talked to everyone he could. I sat in the corner and asked people why Britain was in decay, and although I would sooner have been me, I could not help envying Rob his inability to see that, committees or no committees, councillors and M.P.s or none, Britain is inevitably in decline and that political ambition is (social status apart) an awful waste of energy.

18th June. Went back to Chigwell for Speech Day and was transported back to the environment in which I first became a writer. The car-park in Lower Field, the ropes on Top Field, the talk with Dutchman from behind darks – all had an unreal quality, as though people were all actors at a fancy-dress ball. Then the search for the decay: the noticeboard outside the dining-hall with its lists of labour squads, the Honours boards in BS1 round a whitewashed Harsnett, the gym with its battered changing room and broken pegs, and its scratched and holed upper door, the broken desk and lockers, and the gulleys in the red brick "cave" (KV) window; and the drying room, still sinister, with the hole in the plaster ceiling. I felt I was dancing, and repeating a dance after a long interval. The science labs.

Sitting in the chapel I remembered old influences (the eagle-lectern, the tattered hassocks) and was aware of history repeating itself: my choice and Jonny's. The "comic" meeting with Auton in the aisle, Auton encouraging Jonny for an organ scholarship. Whereupon Nan walked in sucking an iced lolly; could I have foreseen that in the early 1950s?

After this the walk past the Under15 to the 1st XI cricket. The meeting with Mrs. Thompson, then Thompson. "Where are you back from?" and, in reply to "China is very misunderstood": "Oh that's nice isn't it." Perhaps, after all, it is not deliberate, but rather just inadequate, his failure with conversation. Anyhow, as in 1963, I felt I was talking to a wall, unlike Salmon, who showed a very intelligent interest in the foreign cities I have been in, and said rather sadly "I would have nothing to offer them" when I asked him why he did not go abroad. Old influences I have resisted and deadly provincialism.

19th June. Went to Loughton cricket ground with C and saw the Corpus Christi procession from the local Catholic church, high cross in front and the priest who paid in a bag full of silver last Monday carrying a golden star under a canopy while the faithful knelt. They went up to the convent, did the Benedicte in English ("Blessed is the Sacred Heart of Jesus", etc.) and then returned to crown the statue of Our Lady in the church. It was all an image of something: the virgins in white and blue, the friar, the people singing behind the canopy, the materialist shops in the background.

20th June. A day spent writing up 50 lines of the poem on Communism; reflecting on De Gaulle's Europe from the Atlantic to the Urals – could Russia be split again, and could both Russia and the U.S.A. be made to withdraw from Europe so that partition ceases? And reading through old correspondence and realising how blind I was at the time to what others thought of me: how they loved me.

21st June. After another morning on the poem, and an afternoon sorting through old papers and redreaming the past and thinking of unfulfilled possibilities while C was at Dulwich, I had dinner at Journey's End and lectured Jonny and Frances. I quoted Hamlet: "There is something rotten in the state of England," and said it was an infectious disease, like smallpox. I then appealed to them not to be like sheep and follow their trends. "In five years time you may wish you'd tried to be different" and "The only way to do anything today is to be different." I went on: "You should have a thirst for knowledge. You should want to know the answer to the meaning of life, to man's place in the universe." And: "You should read all philosophy, religion, psychology." This took us on to Existentialism, to freedom, possibilities and authentic living. Finally to Toynbee and the future.

Over lunch mother told me that Dad bought the TV in April 1956 to cheer Rob up after he returned from hospital, a diabetic.

22nd June. Lunched with D.S. in the Fontainebleau, Northumberland Ave. Walked back down the Mall and through St. James's Park (earlier, Big Ben peeping over the trees and Nelson raising his arm) and met K.D., who was in a fluster, being in the process of moving to Millbank. D.S.'s wife lives in Winchester, he living alone in London. Left him near the Crimea monument.

24th June. In the afternoon I drove over to see Mrs. Riley in Mott Street, High Beach; her alms house and cat. Afterwards I drove in the rain down Church Hill to Fairmead and on to Lippitt's Hill Lodge, which Clare knew. Should I bring Blunden here and take him on to the Owl for lunch?

25th June. At the St. Mary's Fête, as I watched the Oaklands girls dancing in the rain on the Vicarage lawn, I could see mother was reliving old patterns, as she held Nan's hand and showed her off. And in the Owl with J that evening, hearing his fear of leaving friends and his dislike of London, I was taken back to 1956 and relived my fears.

26th June. A day on Britain. After Nan returned from church with mother I drove over to Dulwich and discussed revolution and Quintin Hogg's recent speech with the Group Captain. The main points: we have weakened in all that has made us great, we are destroying ourselves, there is too much enjoyment without responsibility, "fantasy without facts", we are going bankrupt, and ability is considered undemocratic. After an afternoon revisiting the scenes of my despair in Dulwich Park we visited Mary and Celia. Lily: "The country's going down the drain isn't it; the loss of empire."

Returned to converse with the Group Captain and formulated the question "Are we sick or dying?" That is: will (the U.K.) shrink to Great Britain and be absorbed into Europe, inevitably, in which case revolution is a waste of time, or will Britain recover and be able to become no. 1 in Europe? I thought the first: Britain's illness is fatal, we are dying, and revolution is a waste of time, although I would like to believe the reverse. M's dogmatic complacency and ignorance: "History is a succession of waves, that was what I was taught at school; Britain is only in a bad phase – we'll go up again; our culture is not decayed, and is better off than the Japanese." She knowing more about Japan than me, of course. Mrs. Nixon disagreeing and siding with me.

27th June. A day writing my poem and walking in the Forest and then visiting the two pubs in the High Road, the Holly Bush and the Royal Standard, where I felt a stranger, as no one else spoke English like mine. Lower-middle or regional accents were the norm, and all my study seemed merely to have alienated me from normal people.

28th June. Mother brought lunch as she felt C would be busy and talked a lot.

30th June. Went out to ask the Travel Agent about Dublin and to get a book on Yeatsian and Joycean topography from the library. Called home to look for material on Dostoevskian topography.

After lunch, drove to Waltham Abbey. Harold's tomb which symbolises the loss of national independence and foreign conquest. The three stained glass windows of a tree and, instead of apples, prophets and saints; the 7-petalled flower telling the creation story. The stream winding through the meadows and covered with lilies, as still as a pond, yet, under the humped bridge it suddenly moves and, revealing current, plunges down and is lost underground. There is an image in that stillness and final death.

Was giddy with sunstroke when I got back, and C had a sore throat.

1st July. Human beings and material. C and Nan went to Dulwich to take Mrs. N to the doctor, I went with them to Gieves, and then on my own to Intourist, where I learned Leningrad would be impossible. Came home and went round to mother for dinner. Here, once again, was a different world, a world of golf on the lawn and of talking about Cromwell (in connection with Ricks's TV lecture last night on Milton) and Rasputin.

Then Argie brought South African David Brink round and we talked about British decadence. He: "It's connected with your Welfare State and scuttling, throwing aside private enterprise and settling, the things that made you great." I: "Imperialism is a dirty word in the 20th century, because we recognise all men as human beings with the right to self-determination. We withdrew in the face of world opinion to preserve our self-respect." He:

"Self-respect comes through opposing the world." And so on to the 180 day law and Ruth First and Sharpeville. "If the Africans win, there will be economic chaos, starvation and military dictatorship." I: "There are two ways of looking at the Africans: one, as human beings, the other as economic units. We prefer the first, you prefer the second. The African is not material, he is entitled to self-determination and to believe that whites should be resettled in white countries." And I pleaded for men as humans.

2nd July. Rang Ezard's mother and found out that he is working on the *Oxford Mail* and living at 324 Cowley Road. Hence his postcard last summer: "There are many situations which call you to mind."

Later, over dinner at home, learnt the background to...Aunt Lucy's dislike of me. Uncle G married Lucy (Harold's girl-friend) in 1927, one year after his father's death. Grannie opposed the wedding because she was only a typist. His father's money went into the business and Grannie was to be paid a high rate of interest. At Lucy's insistence George persuaded Grannie to sell out and reinvest elsewhere at a lower rate of interest. The business was thus taken out of the family, and George had sole ownership. Grannie was sore about this and used to attack Lucy, and I was a weapon in her war. As I lived in EG (East Grinstead) 1940-2, Grannie saw a lot of me and speculated on my progress and how bright I was, and, being rammed down Hove's throat, I was not very popular. After that, I did better than John and Tom, and went to Oxford, and this intensified the dislike. Argie to Lucy in Jersey March 1966: "George tied up his money so that T & J couldn't do to you what he did to Grannie." Lucy: "Oh no – he was a wonderful man." So the Hove snobbishness was all based on a dubious deal, as a result of which Tom and John have been able to live extravagantly at Grannie's expense.

3rd July. Houses. In connection with mother's two houses and the Hammertons and the Hoathers, I learnt the effect of the 1964 Rent Act: a widow who wants to sell her house and buy another to live near her son can't because the present tenant is protected under the rent tribunal, i.e. cannot be evicted until the rent tribunal approves, which takes about 6 months.

4th July. Fixed up a meeting with Hogan on Thursday. He was spoken of as the king before I could get through: "I think I heard his car pull away, but I'm not sure" and "I'll see if there's a reply from his office." Hogan: "Two and a half years. A lot of water has passed under the bridge in two and a half years. I've been divorced and have since remarried." Thoughts on the novel I shall write about him. It would be a novel about a materialist and his monument. This economic man builds a palace and fills it with material objects which are a hollow substitute (sop?) for the feelings and companionship his wife and children need. "The cars got bigger and bigger and he got later and later." Because of his hollowness, the monument is hollow to his wife: she never wanted it. And his own blindness prevented him from seeing this. In fact he got her wrong: "She's a materialist and I am an artist" whereas in fact the slave to the arms trade is the materialist, and his wife paints pictures of goldfinches and blue tits. He is the child of an age which values vulgar objects at the expense of people, and which admires the man who gets what he wants. "Johnny's always got what he wants. Johnny sees something, Johnny gets it."

I must try to say something about contemporary British society and our age, and about the false values it can give to an intelligent man.

5th July. I have not recorded J's attitude on England, which is very logical Little England: "Let's cast off all our obligations East of Suez and put the money towards getting our balance of payments straight and stopping ourselves from going any more rotten." He came round for the figures: in 1965/6, defence took 31.3% of the total budget, and in 1961 there were 2.1 million foreigners in Britain: one third Commonwealth, one third Irish, one third others. Add 388,000 1960-2 and an average of 70,000 a year since then. Taking into consideration the fact that we never wanted the Empire until the 1890s ("those wretched colonies will all be independent in a few years and are millstones round our necks" Disraeli said in 1851), I begin to think I have been partly wrong about Britain: perhaps influence abroad is of no particular value, just as there is nothing wrong in not leading a dazzling social life.

The thing is, is the "stay-at-home" healthy or not, solvent or not, and certainly an insolvent, sick stay-at-home has no chance of expensive socializing. In a day given to *Blighty* on the last day of the Test Match, I wondered too, about history. So what if nations rise and fall? It all suddenly seems so unimportant. That, too, I learned in China: the unimportance of whether or not a nation is vital. (This is Cromwell's disease. Does one not care for one's fellow men?)

Another thing: Blighty is no whore, like South Vietnam. ("All Saigon is a brothel.") Blighty is not occupied by foreigners in return for their money, or is she? Are the 2.1 million equivalent to the foreigners in Isaiah's Jerusalem? Blighty has lost her fortune and her social position, and she is too lazy to work for a living, feeling she has a right to live off her former position, which she dreams of recovering. She also feels sick and imagines she is falling apart, along with her house, and attributes this to a disease connected with her position which may or may not be syphilis, for that could be just an image. She imagines herself becoming a whore and being occupied. But she is no whore at present. Though she has always been a charmer and has always got her way.

6th July. In the evening Richard came with Argie. Our trip to the Duke of Wellington, via Beech Hill House, where Tennyson lived 1837-1840; it was pulled down eight years ago and there is only a cobbled arc left. R's indifference when told by his boss that he was in the wrong job and when given six weeks to leave. Compare Meursault. Richard is a rejector, like me and like Tom (who signed on for the RFC when under age and got killed (in 1918) because of a "burning desire to do something unusual." Rob the acceptor, like George (my uncle). I: "It's the rejectors who do things." R: "The rejectors are unpopular on the whole, save among the few who understand them." A perceptive comment....All this arose out of my expressing interest in his indifference, which, he admitted, was "unconventional" and not what a "sound" person would feel, and out of his saying that farming would be his RFC or his poems.

When I got home Ezard rang, and I visited him. "No more lines" he said under the light, and he looked the same. His hope that we could pick up where we left off, and his praise for everything I have written, which was of higher standard, he said, than the 20 novels he has had to review for the *Oxford Mail*. His walk home along Staples Pond. To what extent is he a rejector?

7th July. A visit to Hogan while C went to see *Let's Get a Divorce* with Celia. I went to Liverpool Street, walked down Houndsditch to Aldgate, got a 42 to Albany Road. The dreadful area. "The 24 hour export packers" the sign said: black brick, broken glass and boarded windows, barbed wire; the brick yard next door; the corrugated iron. The beaten-up laundry opposite, and an abandoned block next door. The large car outside. The factory: the crated boxes to Ostend, Kuwait, etc: fire engines, arms, electronics equipment, antique furniture: "you say it, we do it." In this junk yard of material goods Hogan said: "I built this up from nothing, these roofs, all; it was cobbles when I bought it." The tropical bags for the Ministry of Health done by one of his five companies. "I have so much money, it's meaningless."

We went to his flat. S dandled his son in the window and greeted John: "I'm sick and tired of looking after this child, and wiping him at both ends." Her terrible accent, her hooked nose and black hair in a beehive, but her untutored intelligence. J: "She's taught me to think", i.e. practically. The situation was V, and...I talked about the need to feel. J: "I haven't time to feel." "I have executed V and I have executed myself." His self-deception, blaming "life" and not himself, contradicting: "We make our bed...."

At the door she winked, in the car Hogan talked of V's laziness, her sharp tongue, her prudishness, but: "Did you think her lonely?" shows he feels for her, or tried to show me she does. To S: "I would like you and V to meet and become friends." I got at him in his weakest spot, and this man who lives from day to day – this "24 hour" man who lives for himself – will now try to demonstrate his feeling for V, out of ego, so that he will get my good opinion.

8th July. Did three speeches for the Governor in the morning, got them off express air mail, lunched at Journey's End, then went up for two suits to be fitted. On to Whitehall, the Banqueting House. Charles I's route to his execution: Westminster Hall, St. James's Palace, round along the covered walk, up through one of the (Whitehall Palace) doors, under the Reubens (which are all about James I, not Charles – the guide books are wrong about this), up some zigzag stairs, and out through a window in the North wall to a platform above what is now Whitehall. The sandy square.

Decided to write a poem about the Civil War and "new Cromwell": the Banqueting House and Downing Street, Big Ben and Nelson's sword. The Regicides, my Puritan roots. Prince Hitachi. I want to do one on Ireland too.

In the evening met Ezard. In the background was what he said (and no longer believes) before I went: "When you return we will be out of shouting distance." West v East. I said I belong to the East, though I shall never escape my spiritual home, the village of Loughton. I have moved away from seeing plays to meditating in poetry, and this is all bound up with Eastern silence and denial of humanist purpose. J was reluctant to say anything about himself. "I live in a world of feelings, and I don't build them on ideas." He is very much against theories, critical simplifications or theories of history, Movement and Group and Kermode or Toynbee. He felt ashamed of advancing a theory about Samuel Palmer, that his marriage ruined his art, and is not interested in how he came to be in the universe.

9th July. In the afternoon, had a polite tea with Miss Reid at Elm Cottage, on the old Pollards estate. The estate walls, the orchard. The ivy on the Balls' house. (Compare 17th June). "I am glad I am retiring, I want a life of my own."

10th July. Lunch with Lucy at Brook Road. After the experience of the business, should I really shed tears because probate is still not through, as she wanted me to after (pulling down her skirt and hiding her petticoat) she got out of Argie's car at the garage. When she took the side of business against art in my case, and was offended when, in Jan 1963, I told her and George in father's room that I was not going to get a money-making job because art came first, should I refrain from refighting the battle when she asked over lunch: "Will J do accountancy – do you think he's suited for that?" She has quietened down, but she still wants her way all the time. The episode of the Yorkshire pudding, which, following Lucy's recipe, stuck to the tin and failed to rise, while Argie said in effect "I told you so", was proof of that.

11th July. More on Lucy. Lucy spent a sleepless night worrying about things I had said – the possibility of a 10% Bank rate e.g. and a crash in shares and "real values". She went round to Journey's End and gave mother £1 for Nan, this to cover Nan's birthday and Christmas for 2 years. Grannie was angry that G & L never remembered Nan. L's insomniac night was over a new shop-front in the business, which had taken all the profits. Argie said menacingly, "What's been spent can't be changed", and possibly this was ambiguous, Argie referring to the take-over of the family business. Argie trying to get any of it back? I probed when we discussed the genealogy at Journey's End. After asking about all the Jewish Christian names in the early 19th century, and being told they were Nonconformist, I said (when Argie asked "Can I be of any more help?") "I'd like to know how L got the houses she gave Tom and John as wedding presents." Argie just looked shrewd and said "She bought them." She did not say with what. Presumably with the business profits.

12th July. Raised my poem in the context of Blunden's visit on August 18th. "It won't be finished when he comes; it will be my unfinished symphony."

Last week on Wednesday Jill Bradbury telephoned and I spoke to her. She complained of being "bored to death" and said she wanted some practical advice. I rang back on Friday. I left a message for Jill to meet me and C in the Helvetia at 5.30 tonight. Mrs. B. telephoned to say that Jill was "ill". So C and I went up to the first house of *Who's Afraid of Virginia Woolf* at the Curzon.

Afterwards walked through Soho with C. Visited 15 Poland Street (Shelley) but 74 Broadwick Street and 61 Greek Street – Blake's house and De Quincey's house – had both been pulled down for offices. For the last month I have been living an extrovert tourist's life, meeting people, gathering material. I have lost the silence I knew in Japan – the West is more shallow than the East and I shall recover it.

13th July. What is the sickness and decay of British society?

Went to the Soviet Consulate to confirm that no addition need be made to my visa. The chaotic waiting room in 5 Kensington Palace Gardens near Queensway. Then, past a bombed-out cellar with purple flowers, like the subconscious, to Notting Hill Gate and on to Westminster Hall. The dank light as in a slumbering mind, the niches and 14th century statues of kings on either side of where Charles I stood.

Thence to Westminster Abbey, which is a forum and baroque heaven in one; Britannia's heroic images, and splendid gilt. On to St. James's Palace and the chapel Charles I visited on that fatal Tuesday morning. Could not go inside. The arched gate. Walked back and made firm the vow I made in Poets' Corner: one day my bust or statue will be there. The newspapers screamed "£105m. trade gap record."

14th July. To Dulwich, after writing the first 7 lines. Visited the Park and learned that Gordon is in Peckham. The ducks, the widgeon, the quail chicks. When I returned there was an accident, and a woman lying on the pavement. M phoned the ambulance station with irritating calm and authority.

Largely to avoid her, I went up to the library. Mrs. Crossingham was off, sick, having been away a lot recently, so Bob, the one-eyed cleaner, told me. While he talked in his pathetically creepy servile way about my car and Japan, I could not help remembering the dirty pictures I once caught him looking at near the top of the cellar stairs. The warden came down and told me an experience to correspond to mine in Japan: the Canadian lakes in 1926, iced over, and the cherries over the hills. Drove home in a clear dusk of chimney pots like ships' funnels and aerials like masts.

15th July. Late last night I got a new idea for prose-writing: 100 short prose-poems of about a paragraph each, to be collected under the title "100 people". Today I wrote the first two, *Limey* and *Tunnel*. These prose-poems are to concentrate on intense or extreme experiences which have shaped people's lives, and which therefore reveal the essence of the person. The advantage is that I can write up straightaway stories I hear and want to record, but never seem to be able to use.

These prose-poems will be about people, my poems concentrating on the quest for the self or meditations on the values of society. I have planned at least 7 poem-meditations after the one I am now on: *Blighty*. And I am confident that I shall be able to show Blunden four on August 17th: the *Expatriate*, the *Silence*, the one on Communism (*Archangel*) and *A Lingering Death* (*Blighty*).

In the afternoon drove to the Owl to confirm that Blunden and I can get lunch there, and on the way back found the "brook without a bridge" (Clare). First asked permission at Fairmead, and was taken by the nurse, to a cripple in a two-wheeled bathchair; a once very attractive woman of about 45 whose legs seemed to be missing beneath the rug. On the way back (via Turpin's Cave) I called in at High Beach church and saw the name "Mrs. Darby" on the flower roster, and this tallied with what the next-door neighbour had said, "Is the name Darby?" Looked her up in the telephone directory and found two numbers, one for Mr and one for Mrs. Did she have a car-accident? I am interested because I have not seen anyone who has so evidently despaired: her smile was brief and hollow, and she was totally disinterested in my inquiry, merely saying "Clare was a very poor man, he owned nothing." She had never heard of Blunden.

In the evening corrected *The Expatriate* in the Standard.

16th July. Wrote up to about line 55 of *A Lingering Death* (now *Blighty*) and then went to lunch at Journey's End. C's baroque pearl necklace split, and the unknotted pearls scattered, resulting in 15 shillings to be spent on restringing. Nan's conversation with the man next door. "What did you have for lunch?" "I only had a cup of tea actually." "Well, you should have lunch, shouldn't you." In the evening prepared to finish the poem in the Standard.

17th July. And did (at home), having been got up early by Gengo's telephone call, and after a terrific push-through, in spite of the presence at one time of the entire family downstairs, drinking coffee and gardening and otherwise distracting. It is some 120 lines long and does not read badly. It is rather a right-wing view of things in some ways – that is, although it is not pro-Empire it is rather anti-democracy from the point of view of the good of the whole, and holds prosperity responsible for the rottenness.

Is this my view? I do not know, really. I always have great difficulty in deciding between Right and Left, so perhaps I am slightly Right of Centre with one strong proviso: although I believe in the good of the whole, I believe equally strongly in the feelings of the people, and do not want them to suffer in the cause of the whole unless they will also benefit. Anyhow, I was writing a poem about the muddle in Blighty's mind – on reflection, perhaps it is a little too unified and a little too little self-contradictory – and my political views are irrelevant. That is to say, the political views Blighty expresses can in no way be pinned on to me, though I may share some of them as a sneaking coincidence.

I think I am self-divided. On the one hand I believe progress is a decay; on the other hand, I genuinely believe in certain non-spiritual forms of progress. About differentiation, I am not so sure. Uniformity – the levelling of classes – may be a sign of decay, but what of regionalism of accents: is not this differentiation a falling apart, when the centre cannot hold – at least in the form in which it exists in Great Britain today? Equally, the levelling of classes can be considered as progress. I do not know. I am torn between Right and Left, and there might be another poem.

18th July. Got back on to the poem on Communism (now *Archangel*), and wrote in draft the bit that held me up in June. Then went round to lunch with Mrs. Baker at Journey's End. Her wooden leg was underneath darkish stockings and invisible. Went round to the library and got a history of China, then went up to the Forest. The man feeding the ducks.

In the evening took C to Harlow New Town. It was all bright and clean, like rootless China, and there was no connection with the past, save the old churchyard and pocked stone crosses. And there was "a blemish" beside the umbrella spire. Perhaps it was better than living in a slum of character – perhaps even drinking in the vulgar Avenue Bar of The Painted Lady, with its bright and monotonous wall-paper, is better than drinking in a squalid pub at the end of a row of terraces.

On to Sawbridgeworth. The old charm round the village green, the 13th century church and stained glass and reverberating bells, the echo like a tuning fork. "The most resonant in Hertfordshire." The ivy sprouting from the box tomb surrounded by rails. The old houses, like the Liells' and Vantorts Farm (which received one of Henry VIII's wives) and the Tudor chimney of the vicarage and of the house next to the Clays. The phoniness cashing in, like the Clays' large but modern beam-house. But not the William IV pub where the publican is suspicious of you in case you're from Harlow. The silence, a community which began in Loughton (the Clays, the

Liells and the Fosters) but which has been pushed out by the expanding urban life. C wants to live here, and I shall never be able to afford it.

19th July. Finished the bit on Revolutions, and formulated my present dilemma on this subject: I am against all killing, so what is my attitude towards Revolutions, since I approve of Revolutions if they cure disease? Under what circumstances is a Revolution justified, and is killing justified if it serves a noble end? Surely Revolution is justified, but killing never is, no matter what the excuse. And where does one draw the line in subordinating the individual to the State? I think on the Tory side, and all this is the foundation for a "new Tory philosophy" (Angus Maude's article in *The Observer*).

The state is a body, the individual a cell. The body comes first, but the body must not kill the cell or encroach too much upon it. On the other hand, when the cells dominate the body as under socialism, there is cancer. Just Right of Centre philosophy. "The body comes first", so under what circumstances is Revolution permitted, and what arguments did Cromwell use for his anti-democratic rule? None, as he represented Parliament. Ah well.

For the rest, corrected a Bank of Japan address, and then went up to London to meet Ann and Barry. Waited in the Shepherd's, an 1890s pub judging by the faded brocade chairs, the Regency window-bays, the miniatures, the sedan telephone kiosk; waited 45 minutes until 8.40 and then left, went to The Cheshire Cheese in Wine Office Court, saw the Rhymers' Club cellar and Goldsmith's house and Johnson's house, and walked past a floodlit St. Paul's. The Corinthian columns that no one today could begin to imitate.

20th July. Wrote on the Party, and then went round to Journey's End for lunch. Returned to have tea with the Skiltons, and there, and later in the pub, as Jonny came round to watch the World Cup, considered the problem of England with Jonny. Today was a special day, as (Harold) Wilson announced his new measures for saving the pound and as usual Jonny took up the classical Little England position: let us scrap East of Suez, cut down drastically on the 31.3% Defence: total Budget ratio, and concentrate on getting our own home in order. All very logical, and so what if we achieve the international position of Sweden or Switzerland: we are only an island, and anyway, who wants an international position? What difference will it make to Jonny whether the Russians dismiss us with respect or dismiss us with contempt? (Cf folie de grandeur.)

Of course, this is what it's coming to, and its got to be Little England, whether we like it or not, but, as a cosmopolitan rather than as a provincial, I cannot help feeling sad at the loss in our prestige. That is to say, as a provincial, Jonny's attitude is quite right. A revolution, then, cannot hope to restore Great Britain and our international position; as in the case of

315

France and Japan, this must follow from a strong domestic position, and is quite unjustifiable unless the following paradox is obeyed: the individual is to be respected as the basis for all values. Yet the body must be strong, though it cannot be strong at the expense of the lives of individuals. I am against the effects of revolution, I am against the suffering one would cause. So I must put the idea quite out of mind, certainly until a strong issue emerges, i.e. in 20-30 years time. Political action is not the answer. Spiritual action is.

21st July. And my refusal to recognise this explains much of me. My inclination to the Right (for Labour is the Little England party) and my interest in what is really the ugliest form of fascism, for the prototype is Mosley not Cromwell. Yet if either took over, I would be the first to join the democratic party.

No, what I am really trying to do is to bring about a Reformation from doctrine to experience. I am trying to say, "Don't believe in anything, and forget all doctrine. Just concentrate on your experience, and on your experience of what is real and live this kind of life." I am really in the tradition of Protestant Reformism – that is, of Puritanism, except that I am reforming God of it for the time being and am saying "Your existential apprehensions of the silence* and so on are what you need to give depth to your life." This is what I must devote my energies to, and not art, and I must study the whole process of the Reformation and visit Hampton Court and the Tower. My failure to recognise this has, too, got me mixed up in that other political action in connection with which I today visited R— House....All this is inessential to me – look what happened to Otto John whose biography was on TV last night – just as my ideas about Parliament are inessential to me.

The point is, I have still not found myself, not completely. I can see a pattern ahead, I have always known I was born to extraordinary things, but I have not sorted out whether it is connected with Politics, with Art, or with Religion. Or rather, the pattern is there, and so I get the interpretations confused. I loathe teaching, and must begin giving my energies to this Reformation as soon as possible, say in 1969. Art is a medium, an instrument.

* February 1967. Emphasis wrong: should be on the growth of the Shadow.

22nd July. The conditions are right for a Reformation – there is fantastic decay in Britain – and they are wrong for a politicial Revolution, in so far as there is no striking issue. What I have to overcome is myself, for I am still sick, I suffer from pessimistic melancholy and lack of motive. Questions, I cannot escape questions. "Why should I want to lead a Reformation, since one day there will be night everywhere?" "What greater significance is there in spiritual action than in political action?" C: "One does things because they are satisfying – it is like cleaning cars and doing the housework" – and to express oneself (cf T. E. Lawrence) and to have an influence on others, even though night will come. Cromwell had an influence on the men of his time, and that was all he could expect. He could not expect it to last for ever. "For ever" is until the end of human life. He influenced others because he wanted to help them, because he thought life would be better and his values promoted."

All this seems sane, but why should he want to promote his values or why should he want to do anything? Why should T. E. Lawrence want to express himself? Perhaps my sickness is the sickness of the chrysalis before it becomes a butterfly, and is comparable to Cromwell's sickness and melancholy between 1628 and 1636. Anyhow, I have still to make myself whole, to find the answers to certain questions that, unanswered, prevent me from acting.

Today I stayed in Loughton so that I could go to Miss Reid's. Yet when I came to it I had no inclination to go, I sat and played J chess and seemed completely will-less and reflex, responding to Argie's arrival, seeing beyond their pettiness into the universal night that makes all meaningless and yet listening, tolerantly, in detachment. "Why should I want to make people lead real lives, if death is the end and any historical answer is meaningless?" – that is the main question I must answer, and perhaps there is no rational answer, only an existential one, through action.

23rd July. Yesterday I finished *Archangel*, which seems generally very satisfying. Today I revised it before typing, went for two glorious walks in brilliant sunshine and stared at the similarity between the Witches Copse and Stonehenge, and, before watching England v Argentina, visited the Mansion. Foley was on his own ("This weekend I'm a grass widower") as Mrs. Foley was in Liverpool. He was ferrety and rather obsequious, but nice. The object of the visit was to decide whether it would be too small to live in for more than a few days at a stretch. Decided it would be.

24th July. Nan went to church via Miss Root at the ridiculously early hour of 9.40, C went off to continue F's dress about 11.15, and I revised until 1, when I went to lunch and took apart father's Edwardian fob-watch, which blew up in my face when I unscrewed the back. After lunch, went to thank Mrs. Castle for giving Nan a doll – her widow's eyes were made up to kill – and then visited Argie to meet Lady Jameson, who is also a widow. Her slight nervousnesss, her graciousness like the Queen's, while I sat in a mess with Nan and the gong on my lap, my collar up, my hair dishevelled; before I got up and turned my back and went through the bookcase.

25th July. After lunch, a typing session, a confirmation for Leningrad and a visit to Loughton camp, whose pollarded trees looked like brain-nerves rising from a deep memory covered with dead cortex cells.

26th July. Went to the Tower – the Tower green scaffold, the one way traffic round the White Tower, the one room in the Bloody Tower; and then to Hampton Court: the zodiac clock, the figured garden from the Tudor window of Wolsey's four oak-panelled rooms, the painting in Wolsey's closet uncovered during restoration and the fantastic gilt woodwork of the chapel ceiling. And on Wednesday after typing in Rob's room, and after J had returned from his driving lesson (mother taking C and Nan to Dulwich) and after playing chess and having tea, I talked about the organ. Clutterbuck is trying to make him Assistant Organist.

28th July 1966. The *Dream of Gerontius*: "Carefully I dip thee in the lake."

Went to Dulwich and arrived for tea. At 6, met (Sir Vere) Redman and his wife in the Grove; R in his blue beret and squashed up tomato face. He was detached for three minutes while he made his judgement, but having decided I was not a Thwaite, he was O.K. We talked about Britain's decline and I saw it in terms of empires and socialism. He: "Empires are built by accident, as a kind of overflow from economic prosperity. If we'd tried to be a Sweden a little earlier, we could have been a damn good Sweden. But nothing to do with Empires is ever planned."

My faux-pas: I said the BBC newscaster had, on one occasion, a Liverpudlian accent. He comes from Liverpool. Was rather drunk when I returned. Reflected on a remark of Butler's: "One must be true to one's nature and I am not that kind of man." This is rather anti-Existentialist but is true, I feel. Reformulate: "One is free to choose, but one is also bound by one's nature." So every choice is a clash between one's freedom and one's nature, and is (unless consciously otherwise) the expression of one's own nature.

29th July. A day spent revising and typing and then getting ready to go to Bognor. The visit to Hill Place impressed on me the need to settle down in a farmhouse somewhere in England, and have my books in one place, as Tuohy is doing. In my letter to Tuohy on Friday, I said: "I have warmed to England more than I anticipated and would not be sorry to live in Somerset, like you." The question rose as to how we should afford it, and C got rather depressed, saying "There is no future ahead of us" and "I wish we didn't have to live at the opposite end of the world" and "You are not going to get rich by writing".

This last remark set me thinking, and it occurred to me I should write a book about the spiritual reformation and the need for it. Headings: the need for religion and the favourable conditions that exist today; the decay of present religion and the need to redefine doctrine in terms of experience; and the need to apply it to society. I must show that the purpose of the Church is to interpret our experience through symbols, which (I must argue) have ceased to work, have gone dead; and to share in corporate praise and practical application, which can be done better through cells of 10. I must create new symbols where now there are dead clichés: the silence, in place of God – there being no reason why one should sing hymns to it or personalise the Ground of our Being. I must define brotherhood in terms of the silence and explode the Resurrection – and any "divine" basis of values other than "the silence". I must include the "law of unreality" whereby a strong spiritual life expresses itself in vitality of institutions, and I must play this off against Toynbee and those who believe in a more inevitable decline. In short my thesis must be, that the future of Britain must lie in a spiritual regeneration i.e. everyone growing to the full not just intellectually (i.e. rationally) or socially, but spiritually.

30th July. Loughton-Bognor. This was a trip through East Grinstead, and therefore through the past of most of those in the car. The first stop was (my cousin) Tom's: the cellar where the three martyrs were kept before being taken outside and burnt at the stake in 1556, and their graves in the church, "fideles usque ad mortem".

Hill Place. Aunt Gwen, less scrawny and scraggy than usual, with red-rimmed, devout eyes, and Gwen, the schoolmistress in Horsley....The awkward visit to the stocksshed, and the conversation about three week old calves. The conversation about art. The awkward coffee after the inspection of the farm building, which is reputedly 1296 in origin, but in fact mostly Elizabethan.

Later saw St. Anton; the tool-shed is still there, the high laurel wall and the arbour over the winding path and the greenhouse, though the magnolia has been cut down; then Beechholme: the pine was cut down – I saw the stump – and I felt sad, for it dominated my childhood; and there was no cellar or basement in the front. Sick Mr Gray in his pyjamas and his Australian and Scottish lodgers now that he has retired from his laundry. And finally Daledene, where a wall has been built in front, and gates removed at the back.

These places, though shabbier, mattered more than Lingfield church and the chained Bible and the Cobham tomb (the 13th century coloured knight on his back) and Bognor, for they were memories with the force of images. A cellar, a stocksshed and silage tower, a tool-shed and a pine stump – these are remembered landmarks from an innocence that's irrecoverable and unlocatable. I went over the same ground, but all the meaning had gone and I was an exile.

31st July. On the beach this morning,...over God....Quoting Graves, "I become sharp, mistrusting my broken images", I said there can be no confidence in the 20th century because values have broken – who is right, Butlin or the Archbishop of Canterbury or Graves – and that only people who cannot see this or who believe in the old 19th century values which Chigwell encourage can have confidence.

1st August. After dinner on Sunday I asked J to accompany us for a drink. We drove past Butlins – the bright lights like a thousand stations in a nightmare – and into Felpham. The Norman church. The George with its landlord, ex-RAF and rescuer with helicopter. On to Blake's cottage. The thatched eaves, the twilit interiors. The garden he chucked the soldier out of was closed. The Fox, burnt down 1946, and rebuilt.

On Monday morning I read Cromwell on the beach....The afternoon was wet and cold, so we went to Arundel castle, which is mostly 1890-1903, and very late and imitative, though some parts go back to 1801. The Fitzalan chapel and the "reminder of mortality": the marble ribs and skull and eaten arm and rotted toes and slightly closed lids of the 7th Earl who died at my age in 1435.

At 6.15 J came up and we played chess. After dinner we captured BBC TV and watched a programme on the Aztecs. When this was over at 9, I asked him if he wanted to "come out". He said "No", then changed his mind and we went to the Fox. We talked about linguistic decay and standing out against one's friends.

2nd August. We drove (via Chichester, Portsmouth and Southampton) to see L and V. Their bickering – V taking too long, L doing nothing right as the sherry pudding had not enough sherry – and the tell-tale book on the shelves: *The Well of Loneliness.*

3rd August. Because I ran down the car battery by leaving the lights on we could not go to Hove and, on a cold day, a visit at 2.45 from Tom, Judy, Lucy and three boys. We greeted them in the reception-room, then went down to the promenade, but it was too windy and icy to sit. While we stood I engaged Tom on the country's assets, in view of the latest gold reserve loss, which was stated at £25m when it was in fact more like £150m. Tom: "It's all right – there's nothing wrong. There'll be devaluation in October and a coalition. It's just Labour government. We've always been like that." After this there was a frosty silence, while we walked 200 yards up and then back via the putting-green, although I did monologue about Mao. Tom: "All governments are run by two or three men beneath the leader." Lucy: "Nadi's won D over, D was hostile but Nadi kept taking him by the hand." I had not won Tom over although I kept tugging at his mind.

We went on to the beach, after losing J and the bucket and spade (which blew away) and sat in the shelter of a beach-hut. Lucy sat on a stump, I sat at her feet and I got her talking about the family business, while Tom prowled angrily to and fro, unable to stop the flow of confidences. George bought Grannie out between 1931-1952 at £250 capital a year, bar a spell during the war. Later she told me she'd bought Tom's present house there for £1,500, which was presumably why they could not keep up with repayments for a while. Lucy said this was all in the will, and the interest rate was 7%, which was too high. Just as I was going to ask the crucial question, "How much was the business worth in 1926?" mother interfered and suggested tea.

We sat outside the café and mother organised, going round with cake-tins. We later discussed the family qualities – thrift, ecclesiastical determination and drive, obstinacy. Tom sat next to J with his chair drawn back from the circle, and did not talk or eat – he was slimming – and then went off to play with F and the boys and Nadi on the beach. I sat next to Lucy and got her to talk about her buying and the "thousands" she has to pay in income tax and the £10,000-£11,000 she had to pay for the hideous shop-fronts. And then about not liking to sleep alone because of "the silence" and not having George and "liking company". We then got up and walked down to the beach. I said to Lucy: "I don't think Tom likes talking – he'd rather play." I talked to the boys a little, especially Christopher, about cricket, and then went and peed and walked back to the Hotel.

After seeing Nan in the bath I walked downstairs with Lucy and sat in the garden with her and got her to repeat the year 1952, but could not get her to give me a figure as to the assets in 1926. She did give me her view of the coup d'état: a Bank Manager advised Grannie to invest the repayments/ legacy (?) in 100% War Loan; when it slumped to 80, George advised Grannie to sell, but she would not and lost most of it, whereas if she had reinvested in a Building Society she would have been all right. Mother, "It's true." Lucy did however feel guilty about our financial position: "Does Norah have to teach because she needs the money?" and "If she needs help, I..." to which I should have replied: "She would not accept it from you"; and again, "Did you pay for the teas, Nick?"...She kept saying Argie would be furious if she knew about our talk and she did not want to pry and "as George used to say, 'I gave my advice, and if she won't take it, there's nothing I can do.'"

At last she went to Tom's Rover 2000 and got in the front seat because of her size. Tom gave his brawny labourer's goofy grin and they drove off. Mother's sadness when I called her through to report on my findings – and also that I had said, when Lucy said: "You haven't seen John", "No, he couldn't come to our wedding and he lost his voice at my father's funeral", and she said, "Oh yes, so he did." She had organised a beach-party which, in this weather and emotional temperature, was doomed to fail, and she couldn't see why people couldn't be nice to each other, why they didn't accept her organisation.

5th August. Mother. There is a paradox in her. In spite of her organisation, there is always clutter – the untidy piles everywhere. It is as though she is endlessly sorting out her memoirs and throwing nothing away. As C put it "There is this organisation, yet there's untidiness, and this is a lack of balance."

4th-6th August. On Thursday, went to Chichester. The Cathedral, with the crumbling spire, which is in "imminent danger of collapse" as in 1861;

the Church falling apart. The verger who lost a finger in Warsaw in the war, and who showed me the chalice and the roof-gargoyles and the peep-seat; his vulgar joke about monkeys and then the solemnity of the choir-procession which he led. The peace as, imprisoned in a wrought-iron nave, the choir sang to the organ while I fingered the 1130 carvings under glass. The Market Cross, 1501, with vanes and the niche of Charles I. The King's Arms where Lumley entertained Elizabeth in 1591. *The Cherry Orchard*: all the tragedy missed because it was played for laughs, with gusto, but a striking interpretation by Tom Courtenay as Trofimov the Angry Marxist. Yasha and Lopakhin – men of our rebellious, self-made age. Which set me thinking about a novel on Brady, as a companion to the one on Hogan.

On Friday, the last day, sat on the beach, played chess and putted with J, and went into Felpham in the evening with C. Had a long talk about feeling for the existence of others, and the moral and the practical. Depriving others of their existence is always morally wrong, but is in certain circumstances practically necessary, if there is a threat from a Hitler for example. The necessity does not affect the wrongness however.

On Saturday, Bognor-Loughton via Guildford, where I walked as last Saturday among my childhood memories and revisited the place on the Downs where I felt I had lived before one warm summer day when the bees hummed in the harebells, and Newlands Corner; via Runnymede and then Windsor – the enforced prayer over the microphone in the Gothic St. George's Chapel, after which the scarlet Canon said, to me alone, "Good afternoon", as though I were a sinner. The vault containing Charles I's torso was closed, and the State Apartments were gaudy, with Verrio's hideous ceilings, like Hampton Court; and finally (home) via Eton.

7th August. After writing a bit into *Archangel* I went to lunch with Argie and on the way home, in her car, raised the subject of mother. She said mother will have a heart attack or a nervous breakdown soon if she is not careful, and pointed to her overactive thyroid, which means she is burning too much energy and needs calming down. She recommended (1) clearing the muddle, (2) phenobarbitone to calm her, (3) getting rid of WG (the Mansion could be left, she thought). C and I went straight round and did no. 1 with J, while she was in Frinton with R and F.

8th August. London-Edinburgh-Glasgow-Belfast. The beauty, squalor and decay of the U.K. – that is one outstanding impression. I got up at 4.30 a.m. to get the 5.17 train to be at Cromwell Road terminal by 6.40. Took off from London Airport at 8.10, arrived Edinburgh 9.30.

In spite of the domes and spires, Edinburgh is black and grey, and the front of the public buildings are sooty. Visited the Castle, then Holyrood and the rooms where Darnley had Rizzio stabbed and where Mary quarrelled with Knox; then Knox's house – the 1561 panelling – and St. Giles, the High

Kirk, and the Burns Museum, and wandered in and out of dozens of the crumbling closes along Royal Mile. As the taxi-driver said, "All Royal Mile is falling apart, it's all coming down."

The train for Glasgow left at 2.30 from Waverley Station. A party of drunks sat next to me and an ugly situation brewed until, when challenged, I told them in broken English that I could not understand what they said because I was a Japanese. Whereupon one of them said "Sorry pal" and later at 3.30 "This is Queen Street mate."

I came out of Queen Street station and wandered in George Square. There were the same black buildings, and Scott's column is in the centre. It began to drizzle, so I walked down to St. Enoch's Square and the air terminal and we drove past idle cranes like abandoned fishing-rods and patient one-legged flamingos, and wild purple flowers, to the new Glasgow Airport.

We took off at 5.50 and arrived in Belfast at 6.35, having flown round the hoop of a rainbow. After booking a hotel (the Hamill) I drove into Belfast and the rainbow was an arch, one side in Belfast and the other, out of sight, in Dublin, and the two opposites of partition, North and South, were reconciled in it. Belfast, like Glasgow and Edinburgh, seems to a city built on green fields, the squalor beginning suddenly. There are rows of drab terraces – door, window, door, etc. – and there are gaudy pubs (e.g. the Crown Bar) in 1890s yellow, but no sin: only the unlicensed Gala dance-hall near the large clock (no jiving). The sailors prowl in vain and curse: "not in Northern Ireland." I went to bed at 11.30 and fell asleep with the light on.

9th August. Belfast-Dublin. It is an ill wind. Advised by the Hamill Hotel, and in the absence of anything to the contrary from Diezel (the travel agent), I took not the 8.00, but the 11.30 from Great Victoria St. Station, and was therefore able to drink in one of the snugs in the Crown Bar. The green pastures of the North became the yellow wheat of the South, and passing through TV aerials like ships' masts, we arrived in Dublin at 1.40.

I got quick customs clearance and went to buy my ticket for the 2 o'clock for Sligo, to be told I was on the wrong station: this was Amiens Street, not Westland Row. I tried to get a taxi, but (although I didn't know it) there is a bus strike, and there weren't any. I hurried across Butt Bridge, and dashed into the station that faces it, to be told that this wasn't Westland Row either. Whereupon I gave up and arriving at Westland Row at 2.10, rerouted via Gort-Sligo and found this, the Grosvenor Hotel in a drizzle, and then took a taxi to Sandycove.

I was lucky: the driver was one of the 1916 rebels and he took me on a tour. After the Martello Tower and the portrait of John Joyce by Patrick Tuohy and the girl who wanted to teach "and not waste my time doing this", I passed Sandymount Strand, where the gulls were like a swarm of flies and the distant cranes like artillery, and various other places connected with

Ulysses, including 28 Eccles Street, and wound up in Kilmainham prison, where I saw the execution yard. A man with a stutter told me this was formerly a stonemason's yard, and that John Connolly was brought in through the wooden gates in an ambulance, dumped in a wheelchair, and shot.

Later I walked round the Post Office, recalling the driver's words about "the stench of corpses in the heat", and saw evidence in the shops of the 1916 hagiology: there are commemoration cards of the heroes, commemoration books, and the revolt against Dublin Corporation's modernisation plan begins by referring to the 1916 heroes. After tramping through the slums of Summerhill and drinking in Mulligans (1782) I returned, footsore, to be haunted by those towering, grey bouldered walls, the two crosses, and to the horror and shame and guilt of what our army did to them (i.e. the 1916 heroes), and wanted to do to our conscientious objectors.

10th August. Dublin-Gort-Sligo. I dreamt I was acting out a play about being one of a group of condemned men who somehow survive by playing possum; I had been through this "play" before, but there was still danger that I would be shot. The 8.40 to Attenry trundled through sun towards a rainbow and a black storm, and passed green fields, isolated farms, bridges over streams, rough hewn stone, purple heather and bronze heaths, and grass sprouting from collapsed rafters.

At Gort station (12.22) I took a taxi to Coole Park and walked in the overgrown Nursery to the copper beech. Only the Laundry remains of the noble House, a square and crumbling wall with grass knee high, and briars, and, to the left and at the back, a couple of red tiled floors and a marmoreal limestone slab. All else is grass, and fir-trees. These stretch down to the brown river which runs from Ballylea into the lake. Here was Rome and Greece in 30 years, here was the death of the old order, here, in the presence of Mrs. Gough, was the philistine.

I was in this elegiac mood when I met the Phelpses, who had never heard of Lady Gregory or Yeats, and who had strayed in by accident. My guide took them over – the wife and two daughters – and I was left with Phelps, a professional man with a chip on his shoulder, and very jealous, judging by the way he kept running Yeats down on the basis of one line I quoted and commenting on the personal associations "like pain" and on the insanity of poetry, which is "getting away from everyday reality." Yet, being an intellectual of sorts, he was trying to convince himself of the merits of "everyday reality". Having wandered through the coachhouses we drove past Robert Gregory's racecourse to the Thoor. I climbed the winding stair and surveyed the land rolling down to Galway Bay and the dividing river, and was pestered again.

Eventually they went off – a daughter was riding at some Castle – and I left the turf-hearth and the ledge and the restored "ruin" and took the 4.46

to Claremorris, and then the 6.35 coach to Sligo. I passed the trees on the Collooney Bridge, and entered Sligo (8.55) through Ballysodare bay, with the sun setting over a calm sea, and I understood why Yeats could never escape Sligo.

11th August. Sligo-Dublin-London. And yet I, with my fallen urban sensibility, could never be happy here in the rural Paradise between Ben Bulben and Knock-na-Rea. Admittedly the Ship Inn was dynamic, with the singers ("Maisie's sister") and the Irish jig. I identified with unhappy O'Hanlan, who is "don", and who feels a stranger in Sligo, and who, at the age of 71, after 40 years there, is going back to the village of his birth in the North to die. This was my sensibility, not the simple uncomplicated rustics'. And, standing in Drumcliff churchyard next morning, I wondered what Yeats's position was: had he really been happy in this rural society, hadn't London or Dublin corrupted him at all? Wasn't his return to his childhood at all like O'Hanlan's?

Passing wagtails bobbing in the rocks near a broken harbour wall I got to Rosse's Point. It was beautiful, Memory Harbour and Elsinore House and the metal man and the lighthouse and the sweep of the estuary; just as the silver-grey Lough Gill was beautiful, and Dooney Rock and Innisfree and the waterfalling spring of the ancient Holy Well. But I knew I would be bored within a week. Just as, perhaps, Yeats would have been bored with Epping Forest within a day. No, my spiritual home is essentially urban and rather ugly, and Yeats's spiritual home is a thing of the past, an ideal that no longer exists in England, an ideal for which the turf over the laundry floor of Coole House is a good symbol. Coole House: a Paradise to which one can never return and about which one must not be nostalgic.

After visiting the Abbey – the Speaker's desk – I left with my lift, Tom Downs, for Dublin, and discussed the history of Ireland from 12.30-5.30 non-stop. After drinking in Davy Byrnes I discovered the bus-strike has spread to airport buses, and after a taxi-ride to the airport with Behan's driver, Michael Breen, and paying a 10 shilling "tax", I was detained one and a half hours as the flight was delayed. As a result I flew 10-11.30 and only just caught the last train to Leytonstone, where Rob very kindly picked me up at 12.45 a.m.

12th August. Last night as we came down London was a computer brain of orange lights and looked like a vulgar star in a Butlin's park. Today, visiting the Bank and Diezel and the library and going up to Gieves, I was just one of the millions of half-conscious thoughts in this brain.

Later at the Royal Albert Hall I quivered, for what I saw was an image of something I could not otherwise express, an outer equivalent for an inner truth: under the hanging lights of the planets, and the dome, was the world, and the tiers and banking contained the classes, the structure of our society; the people were gathered in the pit, intent on the orchestra. There was nothing new in what the orchestra played, in fact the changing moods had been rehearsed, and performed, many times before, as had the solo parts. There was no room for freewill, the end was inevitably contained in the beginning – a life made into art. The controller of this deterministic, repetitive nightmare was the conductor. The audience watched itself in the orchestra, for they, like the orchestra, also rehearse and play their parts, just as the previous night's generation played their different parts, and the conductor held all together by his will. He is the unifying force in society, the centre of serenity, and the reason why we play our social parts. He was the symbol of the men we play our parts to, being eager for the applause of the audience; he was the symbol of our social follies, and of the way we play parts and are not ourselves and of the corrupting influence in society.

On Saturday (13th), driving to see Dick and Vivien and overtaking a line of cars and, on gaining the no 1. position, speeding away, while the butterflies smashed into the windscreen and spattered, I was a symbol of the brutal, gloriously free but cruel thrust to the fore, which is the opposite of the deterministic music of the orchestra.

13th August. On the way to Kimbolton, Hunts, I visited Cromwell's house in Ely and was taken inside by the present vicar and shown the office, and the stone staircase covered with oak. The house has an Elizabethan front, and there is ivy along the side, and the roofing of the old part of the "L" is very uneven, with bumps and depressions.

That afternoon I went to Little Gidding, from Stow Longa. The church is cradled in trees and faces yellow and dark green fields and open space from which a wind sweeps through the long grass. For all that, and the pond, the lane and the wooden gate and Ferrar's tomb, I was slightly disappointed by the plainness of the church: the two seated pews, the vulgar royal arms, and the crucifix. And thought Eliot must have seen things in it that weren't really there.

Cromwell and Charles: the Civil War was in my consciousness, and after lunch I had a long talk with Dick about which side one would have taken in the Civil War and again got onto the theme of the need for spiritual reform as opposed to political revolution, which is (in the case of Spain, Ireland and China) a symptom of a developing country, and which, in the case of a developed country in decline, is doomed to failure, as in the case of 411BC and Commodus. Again and again I come back to this theme of spiritual reform, and this insistence, together with my walking round churches and cathedrals whenever I have the opportunity, undoubtedly heralds a great conviction, which I expect to become more pronounced.

14th August. For the first time since 1963 I went to church (C of E). I felt awkward about entering – as if it were a brothel, I would not be sure what to do, where to go. Rob stood in the door and gave me the two books and indicated the pew. There were two hymns by George Herbert, which needed understanding, and the sermon was a direct attack on the congregation ("How many of you..."), the theme being Christians' lack of knowledge about their faith and mechanically going to Church, and the arrogance of Christian claims that Christianity can solve all problems.

Otherwise the whole service was a drama, no more mechanical and no more sincere than a routine performance of a Shakespeare play, and with the same pre-knowledge in the audience and the same wondering about the meanings of the 16th century words. This, however, was a communal drama, with a part for everyone, a ritual. None of it bore any relation to the silence, any more than one of my lectures bears any relationship to a hometask essay, beyond indicating outer symbols for inner truths, just as my lectures indicate, from the outside, possible patterns for personal effort. So in the Benedictus, the words "a Prophet of the Highest" spoke to me, as did the collect about the shades in the evening, and perhaps the man who knew all the hymns and the prayers and who did not read a book, and Rob who said and sang everything loudly – perhaps they were taken into the inner truth. But I doubted it.

I was hoping to feel depressed at the decay, but I must confess to feeling braced and even purged at the end of it. Why? Was it because I have a need for ritual, or because, so far from being dead, the form had actually taken me inside? I don't think so – I think it was elation at Vine's attack on the bourgeois. And I am sure the form is dead for all regular goers, though perhaps playing Shakespeare 1,000 times deepens one's understanding each time. This could not be said of the Catholic Mass I attended in the evening, which was entirely mechanical, depending on signs and genuflections.

Sunday still. A visit from Jill after she had rung twice, and at lunch on Sunday while Argie was there. She allowed "George" to bring her about 3.30, which he did, leaving for London, being due to pick her up at 5.30. C, Jill and I walked in the Forest until about 4.45, Jill walking in bare feet to impress. We talked about the rootlessness of the many, and the need to connect to the past, and the need to embark on a quest and the nihilism of the Randolph Set. Jill's reaction was "I come and listen to you because you think as I do." Over tea she said she had changed and was rediscovering her childhood innocence before she lost herself at Oxford by coming into contact with shallow people and her world "shattered in 1961" and I hurt her by asking if she still made telephone calls at 3 in the morning and whether she was not now more considerate. She: "I was a neurotic bore."

17th August. After going to the opticians and the doctors,...I was called out by mother because of activity at the police station. They were in fact searching for Roberts, the 3rd police murderer, in the Forest. Watching the army lorries, the ambulances, the innumerable cars and vans, and hearing the barking of the dogs, I sympathised with Roberts, and imagined him waiting to shoot himself in a thicket. This though I knew he "deserved" all he got.

18th August. At lunch C and I met Ruth Witt-Diamant ("Wise Emerald" – Kerouac) and the McAlpines in the Salisbury, St. Martin's Lane. C: "W-D is cultivating you as a poet." After drinking three and a half pints and discussing poets C and I left, did some shopping, and C went home while I went on to meet Ricky at Notting Hill Gate, where we waited at different places.

We met at 6.30. He has a limp after being knocked down by a bolting horse, but there is no trace of his cracked skull, no scar. He stammers a little more and seems happier and talks about "birds". We talked generally at first, about Jill e.g., and he said that Jill met Henrietta Guinness in Dr. Allen's mental hospital in Northampton in 1964, where H was recovering from Bebe and the accident. The irony of Sunday: I took Jill to the sister mental hospital in Epping Forest – no wonder she was silent on the way back. Furthermore, I should have taken Blunden there today (he has been ill and is convalescing in France) and Roberts was reported in the Owl next door.

Anyhow, soon Ricky asked "How is your inner life going?" and I told him about the silence. He got excited and started quoting sutras about the death of the ego, and his position was so like mine that I suggested we collaborated on cells of 10. His initial reaction was one of scepticism, (1) because he felt he lacked the authority – I: "We shall lack it at 70; the point is one is further along the road than most; (2) because he doubted whether we could establish a strong central organisation or prevent the movement from fossilising. The other possible objections – why bother, how does one set about it practically, should people have less unreal lives and so on – he dismissed: "If a thing is important enough, the way will open." Which is my view of faith.

We moved from the Notting Hill Gate pub to one in Chelsea, and after four and a half pints he drove me to Marble Arch. On the way he said he agreed with me that the Oxford nihilism was a prelude to inner unity, and wondered if unreal living is also a necessary prelude – Beatles and bingo i.e. I: "There is still a concept of a real life ahead of the unreal." He agreed. And we parted, determined to correspond after further thought to see if we could not teach "the silence" full time. To Ricky as to me, the Father is all silence, the sea; and Christ is the silence each man has, which is a drop in the sea.

I returned to Journey's End, flushed, and announced the new Reformation to mother, Richard, Rob and C, who were sitting up at 12.30 a.m. in the lounge. We fell to talking about Roberts, and again I took Roberts' side, saying that one should sympathise with the greatest sinner on his way to Hell, even though he deserves it; and later, when Rob raised Leningrad, I said he should not find out what we already know but get the Russian lawyers to admit that the Sinyavsky trial was a violation of decent human feelings. Richard took my side, and walked back with us, preferring the slightly chill autumn mist.

Later C said, on the subject of the silence: "People are all different – don't expect them to behave in the same way." Perhaps I am making the rejector's mistake of foisting my view on the acceptors also, or perhaps it is not a mistake? I am a leader of movements, not a contributor to committees; I bear a message of health from the unknown – I do not help the existing order to turn round and round. The difference of people is immaterial to the unknown.

19th August. Friday. Finished typing up *Archangel*, reflected on feeling and caring as the answer to all questions about motive and Cromwell's disease, and saw Osborne's version of Lope's *A Bond Honoured*, and so was concerned with feeling. Leonido is a challenge to all "decent" values. Incest, adultery, matricide, sadism, brutality – he breaks every law and pays for it all by refusing to be saved from death, and therefore dies true to his beliefs.

To what extent can one kill or violate others in the course of one's own self-discovery? The whole course of my work has been to say "Never", and Leonido must be ranked with Stavrogin (I have been rereading the suppressed confession, about Matryosha) and Roberts, and no intellectual or substantial argument can replace feeling. In fact, these men are living examples of emptiness, of lack of feeling. Osborne is clearly on Leonido's side – he is a Jimmy Porter to Osborne, despite Lope's theological intention, which Osborne mocks – and thereby displays his own nihilism and emptiness and despair. Osborne may mock "twice a week religious movements" but I would say, the passion with which he rejects them indicates his surest recognition of his need for them – so Tihon would speak to Stavrogin – and Osborne could do far worse than embark on a thorough overhaul of himself, for he is all ego and has never found himself, and appears to lack the most elementary values.

I should add that the severity of my reaction is based on self-recognition. Leonido is me, as I was in my pre-Oxford days, when I did not feel, when I was nihilistic and valued nothing. Now I believe that feeling and caring are the basis of everything, feeling for one's fellow man because he is not as healthy as he should be, the feeling of the spiritual doctor. And this, the basis of the new Reformation, is what the Leaders must learn – they must appreciate the value of *all* men and come instinctively to see the world as a whole, with the interests of the State subordinated to that whole, and this is impossible if a man lives in Leonido's chaos and has never united himself.

20th August. I combed the MSS of my poems for lines or half-lines that can be used in future poems and watched Loughton play cricket with Rob....In the evening I drank with J and heard him out on friends.

21st August. I met Ezard in the Standard at 12.00, and talked about Yeats, and later his idea of becoming a publisher's poetry reader. I told him about my ideas of a Reformation, and he was rather jealous – "R must have developed the same way as you; I have abandoned all ideas and no longer need to interpret experiences like walking down the street or buying a shirt, and I wouldn't buy your argument." And so on. Eventually: "I suppose we have no common language." I: "To quote what you said in this pub in 1963..." and "We have a common language, but it defines our differences, which is stimulating." He: "You are living at a deeper level than you were when you left", which is what the Group Captain said in the evening.

Earlier Guinness (the Group Captain's dog) had fallen into the pond and got covered with duckweed, and we had walked in Epping Forest and thought we'd seen Roberts in a blue shirt, and I had taken John to Loughton camp and heard that he has abandoned the idea about the house until the credit squeeze is over, if it ever is. When he said this I said "My withdrawal will soon be complete. I shall be able to return" and "Dulwich Park had a beneficial influence on my imagery."

Mother brought dinner on a tray. When they left C wept, and, feeling selfish and guilty – for she is not interested in withdrawal or exile – I went to the Standard and drank and reflected on my stay in England. I have written more than I could have imagined (see 11th June) and I have seen dozens of people, and I have come to love England as I have never loved it before, with the passion and intensity of a short affair, and I no longer felt that Japan was my home, I was no longer a stranger to my spiritual home, and I would give anything to stay in my own country.

22nd August. My last day in England, and a great sadness. After a morning of telephoning, collecting dollars, organising *The Observer* and failing to send my P.O. book up for interest because "the P.O. is understaffed and too busy", and an afternoon of packing, I went up to the Forest for my last farewell. The sky was overcast and there was a lot of litter, but I felt an aching peace, as if I were at home, and I knew it would be nice to be buried between the two ponds, among the pollarded beeches, or to spend eternity looking down on my fallen, spiky beech, and going was a hellish separation. Drank in the 480 year old Owl; the universe was more than the bubbles Nan blew this afternoon, through a ring; it seemed more permanent than their floating and exploding.

After collecting our last dinner and later taking empties back to pubs, I went round to Journey's End and helped Argie (who called to say good-bye) with her book, and then went out for a final drink with Jonny. In the Standard I put it to him, now that he has has two A levels (he heard today), he has a choice between "a bed of feathers and a bed of nails" and the second course is one of pain, aloneness and exile, with all the familiar rejected, and no guarantee of any success. I said I was not going to advise him not to choose comfort, security and a salary, and he was in favour of a compromise. He left, after returning to 55 High Beech Road.

C was tearful again. She explained her mood as guilt, because her mother has had a rough time and C's company is one of the few things she enjoys, and C is going away and would anyway go away. This after I, feeling guilty at taking her away from her mother, had said "Our marriage is a bed of nails and a feather bed – out of loneliness and pain I get into your feather bed from time to time, and you never want to come onto my nails. But if I'd married Jill, I would have bled to death."

23rd August. London-Germany. In great sorrow, I left, after going to Victoria and having to rush by taxi to Liverpool Street to catch the 10.45. When I leant out of the window to say goodbye, I felt tears coming – for the first time when leaving England – and later, in the train, after smiling at my saying to Jonny "You'll have to go on the wagon now", there was another rush of feelings which washed me through and left me purged. Was it sadness at leaving people – mother and Jonny – or sadness at leaving the Forest and England? And have my feelings been purified and intensified since I left in 1963?

In any event, my attitude towards England has changed: I now feel I belong to it, and have given myself completely to it (e.g. by visiting Hampton Court, etc.) and by bringing something to it I have discovered my roots in my past. Exile was necessary for all this, to create the love by the inevitability of separation, and there is a paradox: you don't know your own country until you have been an exile, and to know it you must become an exile. I did not really feel this love in 1963, possibly because of the rewarding but cruel time I had in Dulwich Park; anything was better than that. And my love almost carried to the ugliness, the faded parchment yellow and charcoal and black of London, as though all London had got mildew and were rotting.

In the train I could not explain my feelings – I was in C's world in this respect – and thinking of Jonny's words "I want to be happy", I could only hope that Jonny would not seek happiness through exile. And when, after the crossing from Harwich to the Hook, I found there was no sleeping-wagon on the 19.59 and that I would have to guard our first class compartment all night, I longed to settle down, to find a house somewhere and stay there, with all my books, and not lead this nomadic life any more, with its incessant pushing and shoving. I wanted to stop being a cosmopolitan, I wanted roots and a feather bed. Why do I do it?

24th August. Berlin-Brest. And through a mindless day, this resolve became a decision. It was not just the ripples from Rob's remark, "We haven't seen much of you, you've always been away, at Oxford, at Baghdad, in Dulwich." Nor was it Tuohy's letter (from Japan) which arrived yesterday morning: "Perhaps you all would be my tenants at Tumbler's Bottom some time when you are on leave in the future." It was essentially a family decision. Every time I looked on Nan, I felt I would dissolve into tears, for I wanted her to have roots, the kind she had already begun to put down. I murmured the Ancient Mariner's words: "A spring of love gushed from my heart,/And I blessed them unaware." And the question became, what could I do in England?

At dusk I felt melancholic, and three times my eyes unaccountably filled with tears. Before Warsaw the sky was golden, and there were golden angels in the trains, and the black silhouettes of trees to the last leaf. Then there was a crimson sun, and a thin knife of a cloud split it in two, and I thought this was an image for Original Sin. There were tears in C's eyes, and Nan asked "Why are you dribbling on your face?" There had been tears in Rob's eyes when he said goodbye at 8.30, and I had prided myself on my detachment in noting them and bluffing a lack of involvement. But I knew now there was nothing shameful in feeling, and barely tried to hide my wet eyes from C.

I was a new person, and all my responses were new. My hatred of myself and of the things I loved seemed to have gone. I went to sleep at peace, not cold, tired and hungry, and I had come to terms with my exile. A day in which the only action was changing from the first class to the schlafwagon on East Berlin station at 8.55 a.m., and knocking on all the locked doors from the platform, asking and pleading for admission.

25th August. Brest-Moscow. The train travelled on through a Russian mist, pine forests and steppe, and by changing sterling with the currency rogues of ten weeks ago, we were able to eat with a party of Russian women on their way back from Paris. We arrived in Moscow about 4.30 p.m., and on the platform, outside the schlafwagon with Victorian fittings, we met up with Ena Gallon, the wife of the British Judo Champion. She was travelling alone, with her daughter Catherine, and was sent off by TV; Gallon having arrived in Japan in February to get his 4th belt and thereby qualify as a National Coach in Britain.

We drove to the Hotel Ukraina, which looks like a fortress, and while C went to room 648 in what Nan remembered as "the box", I went to Intourist about Leningrad and presented my ticket. Within a minute of dexterously dealt blows, they had demolished any chance I had of going to Leningrad: first, the airport for Leningrad and the airport for Khabarovsk are "three hours apart", so I should take the flight before the 4.50, and only Leningrad could book tickets or say if there were seats; secondly Aeroflot had not informed Intourist, so no reservations had been made, and my "ticket" was merely a voucher to the effect that I had given them my money, and no seats were available on the 7.50 outward flight; finally, anyhow, the trip was not on my schedule. I admitted defeat and proposed a tour by bus of Moscow, one that is quoted in the Intourist handout. "It does not exist" came back the reply.

Ticked off, I slunk out and having broken the news to C in a vast and vulgar room, I went downstairs to a two-hour meal, there being no waiters in the section of the restaurant I had sat down in – and, in between Western cabaret songs, talked to an American couple.

26th August. Moscow-Khabarovsk. In Moscow everything takes two journeys – passports, ordering a car, exchanging vouchers, collecting tickets, tying on labels – and the Dostoevsky Museum was no exception, not opening on Fridays until 12.

I took Tanya, the student guide I had found, to the metro, and we went through Victorian stations with fruit and fern leaves on the columns in silence to Semyonovsky Square. It was autumn and the leaves were falling. Where three stakes were driven and three graves dug, where a platform was erected, is now a tarmac surface, and the Metro and a cinema and a productivity hoarding make the order to (Dostoevsky's) firing squad remote.

Back at the museum, next to the hospital, white tiles and peeling window-frames apart, I was most interested in the photo of Stariez Amvrosec, the original for Zossima, and the portrait of Spershnev, the original of Stavrogin, and in the picture of Christ that is mentioned in *The Idiot*.

The scene of Shatov's murder, the Agricultural Academy Park, was too far, so in the afternoon we went to the Revolution Museum. They had never heard of Kalyaeev and had no portrait, and were very shifty when, after bearing with them about the cruelty of the Germans, I asked what they thought of the cruelty of Stalin's purges: "He made mistakes, but people died with his name on their lips, so we cannot say he is bad." The dialectic without a synthesis.

It was impossible to get a taxi back to the Hotel Ukraina and at 5.30 it began to look as if we would not get our plane to Khabarovsk (the 20.20), when two private citizens stopped and went out of their way to take us free of charge to the Hotel. (Compare the immediate seat-giving to "foreign friends" on the metro.) When there were no porters available in the Hotel, Tanya helped us with our bags, and at the airport Rykui Leonid let Mrs. Gallon off 17 kilos of excess baggage (about £10 worth). He later told me he is desperate for modern novels, which he can only get in translation on the black market, but I still felt that a lot of the Russians are basically very kind, the few perhaps treating us like "capitalist swine".

27th August. Moscow-Khabarovsk-Nakhodka. The flight, in a converted military bomber, was as noisy as a factory with all machines pounding. I slept from 12 to 2. When I awoke there was a green dawn through the far window, way beyond the Siberian horizon. Then we flew over mountains that had been chopped into veined cubes, a barren, angular desert of the analytical mind, and a snaky yellow and black river like a Chinese dragon.

We landed about 5.15 p.m., i.e. 12.15 p.m., and while we waited in a hall of Corinthian columns and vines and icing sugar ceilings, I struck up conversation with a Baptist missionary called Williams. Later, over lunch at the airport restaurant, he told me about the experience that shaped his life, his time in a mental hospital after his father's death and his promise to God if he could be cured, and several times touched on the theme of serenity and peace of mind, which it was his mission to bring to all men.

After lunch, to kill time, we took a coach round Khabarovsk, ten of us, six Japanese and four English, and stopped at the cemetery as the Japanese wanted to honour some 1904 dead, and after he had joked about death and I had remarked on the wet mud on a gravedigger's spade, a tear rolled down his left cheek. Quite clearly his whole life was a self-deceptive escape from the pain of mental hospitals and death.

The next stop was a flower show (he thought it might be a "floor show") and I had to go and look for him as he was late back at the coach. The Japanese had agreed to wait. I told him after I'd found him that he should apologise, but for all that he just called "Sorry".

His ignorance of the Japanese, and his airy confidence about cutting the Gordian knot of Japanese Buddhism and his joky fellowship all annoyed me, and on the train that night, in a humid 2nd class compartment with a broken fan, an unopenable window and an elusive but accurate mosquito, between trips to the bog which stank of appleade and was awash from Japanese slooshing, and to a creaking like the beating of moths' wings, overtired and insomniac, I could not get him out of my mind. First of all it was his view of Christ that obsessed me. He believes in Christ living through you and therefore in the need for a personality change – for openness and complete lack of introspection. There is a Christ for the many, and a Christ for the few, and this Christ, which can enter you within a few seconds, is for the many, being the imitative way of the practical man – this is what I felt at first. Yet what of his missionary teacher's hard-won serenity, after suffering – was this not admirably the way of nails, Zossima's way, the serenity of a hard-won sense of unity?

Then I saw that what irritated me about him was not his ideal of serenity, but his (possibly admirable) desire to prevent people from suffering and to conceal the unpleasant facts of pain with a false jokiness and frivolity. "Recognise the pain and don't try to pretend that it doesn't exist" – that was what I wanted to say to him, and then and there, in the topmost bunk, I wrote a story on him (*A Spade Fresh With Mud*), and now affirm serenity is ideal, but it must come from the whole being, from the depths and through great suffering for all men, and not from the top: otherwise it is a synthetic serenity, one in which it will be difficult for the man himself to believe, the way of the Grand Inquisitor. And Williams will do well to nourish himself in this silence.

28th August. The train arrived at Nakhodka about 10. Then followed a nightmare: queuing with passports and then health certificates and then waiting for the lorry to bring the cases, struggling through a narrow door with five cases, after producing a slip inside the health certificates – as in a children's game, one had to produce the right bit of paper – going through the customs and then producing passports, tickets and passport slip to get onto the boat, then checking in at the 1st class lounge, surrendering passports.

After which I was exhausted, slept all afternoon, and wrote up my story in the evening, having nothing to do but appear for first lunch at 12.30, tea at 4.30 and dinner at 7, and stare at my fellow-passengers or sit in my cabin and listen to the steady downpour of the air-cooler, the high shudder of the engines, like the pealing of distant church bells, and the creaking of rolling timber.

29th August. Nakhodka-Tokyo. Spent the day writing up Cromwell as it got hotter and hotter. Before dusk, Japan was a black and misty silhouette, like an ink-drawing, and a black cloud obscured the sun, creating shafts of sunlight which fell all round a solitary fishing-boat on a wrinkled sea. The scene was an image for pain and evil. Later the sun was a crimson disc through mist, and it slid down behind the mountain range and the waves grew dark.

And sitting under the awning on the hind deck while Soviet scientists played chess, I thought again about my idea for a school for self-realisation. It would fulfil the prophecies of the Eternal Seeker and of the section of *The Silence* about what our age needs, and would draw together the teacher and the seeking poet and unify my life.

I often long to feel that everything I have ever done has been necessary, i.e. has contributed something essential to the whole of my life, and perhaps my teaching in Baghdad and Tokyo is but a preparation for the spiritual pursuit, through teaching, of final knowledge.

30th August. Nakhodka-Tokyo. We anchored off Yokohama about 12.15 and had to wait until 4 before docking. Before going through quarantine and immigration in the 1st class lounge I wrote home, and in the course of my letter suggested I should open a school for self-realisation, a small evening school for adults. I think it best to insist on a definite policy and ultimate aim, i.e. the self-realisation of all England, and to state that those who attend the school will in turn go out, persuade others to join the organisation – half the membership fee being sent to central funds.

Had to wait in the Customs Shed and got a taxi from Yokohama to Tokyo for ¥4,000. Faint despair all the way, and the sudden rush of joy when Aikosan (the maid) jumped for delight in the gateway and everything was spick and span in house and garden.

9

UNITY OF BEING: SELF-DISCOVERY, ACTION AND CONTEMPLATION
August – December 1966

31st August. But it was hot, and after lying awake a long time, my mind still active from the journey, when I eventually fell asleep I had a number of dreams. The early ones I can hardly remember. It was the ones about G that hurt....I was asked "How many writers do you know?" and could only lamely think of Colin Wilson, which was not good enough....G told me she did not love me any more and sent me away with tears rolling down her cheeks. After a final dream about the Russian sector of Berlin being a turnip field, on which Nan walked, deserting the dykes, and shooting across cabbages at cardboard victims of execution, and someone throwing a fake bomb, I leaping up from behind the school piano and shouting "Bang bang bang – is that realistic?" whereupon all the fake soldiers laughed, I woke up.

It was G who was in my mind. It was as though coming to a new place had lifted my trap-door, and repressed memories were coming up. In the Soviet I had dreamt of returning to my flat and opening a door to find a burglar there, whom I immediately overpowered and held firmly in a half-nelson,...but now the burglar had escaped....G was still in my soul, and I wondered what she would be like: would she be devout and detached – the result of knowing me, the curse of knowing me, or would she be a Flora?

I went to the Bank and to the Tokyo University of Education, and sorted through old poems while the cicadas revved and whirred, like a child revving up a clockwork car and then releasing it across the floor. Then Buchanan came, and the faint depression I had felt all day at not being in England began to lift. Nothing had really happened here. He talked about Keikosan's religion (Buchanan has to pray to Benten every morning) and about Penson. Otherwise we discussed Russia, the Red Guards in Peking and Sartre and de Beauvoir who are coming here. The Prince rang in the middle of all this, to welcome me back. Tuohy was still away. I went to bed late and very slightly drunk, but couldn't sleep until about 4 a.m. for the heat.

1st September. After sorting through my poems and deciding that another 10 or so are possibly redeemable, I went to the Bank of Japan and in spite of being tired, talked and talked. Returned and spent another near sleepless night. I am apparently just not tired.

2nd September. Yesterday I revised *The Oceanographer* and got it typed, and today I began the revision of *Twilight*. Tuohy would argue the revisions are wrong, that it is the first version of *The Prelude* that is the best; I would cite Tennyson. A work of art evolves.

In the course of looking through the OED I come across "selfhood": "personality; separate and conscious existence". And suddenly I knew what the Buddhists meant about dying away from self. It is recognising that one is a part of all, that every man is my brother and that his pain is my pain. It is the sense of the unity of the earth and the universe, that all are one in the silence. "No self" is therefore a way of looking which regulates behaviour, and ego is the confrontation between "I" and others that separates one from one's fellow men.

Existentialism tends to be about this confrontation, and the ego. The silence is an existential concept and the experience of unity is too, so there is no reason as to why concentrating on existence as opposed to essence should compel one to confront and freely create at others' expense. The silence modifies behaviour and forbids one to kill. This is the story of Zabov and the priest – the death of the ego. Confrontation yielding to brotherhood, to the vision which Truffer got from Japan and China, the sense of the One. Possibly it is this shift in myself from ego to silence and unity that has been responsible for my shift from novels to poetry. And perhaps I should return to my novels and edit and complete what I've got, bearing in mind the characters are symbols from my inner life and not from the social world that Tuohy is writing about. Their stage is the human mind.

3rd September. After completing the revision of *Twilight* and typing it up, I went to dinner with Tuohy, who was in a very belligerent mood. Russia and England and Ireland went harmlessly, and what he'd done in Japan. It was future plans that began it, I saying I wanted to stay in England, he saying I couldn't do anything and that he was "going back to be a journalist". I: "That's bad. Newspaper articles are worthless beside art. In 200 years' time no one will read your China pieces." He said he did not make the distinction; he did whatever was on his desk because "I write to make sentences, like pots."

We then got on to my writing (a mistake I must not allow to be repeated in the future) and he said: "It's like playing darts – you have off-days," and, in one way or another, usually fairly indirectly, suggested I was wrong to write introspectively, that no one would read me for "moral truths", for what I was trying to say; that "saying writers" are pretentious." A lot of this was backwash from (his) internal churnings round at not being able to write – he welshed on his commission to do the Penguin short story and can't see any novels ahead. I felt irritated that he should have to work it off on me. I am the one who needs encouragement, and he is too depressed to give it, or deliberately withholds it: "No novelist will embark on two years' work unless someone shows an interest." ("Writing is communication.")

Moreover, all this contradicts what he says about pain. "Be aware of the pain of others" he said several times, not knowing about my 100 people, yet he did nothing to alleviate the pain of this one other. Perhaps it is a consequence, not a contradiction – perhaps he hurts others so that he can be aware of their pain and write about it, just as he gets up and leaves the room in the middle of what another is saying to emphasise his boredom or to test persistence or to make a telling break which can later get into a story. It is good for me to be opposed by another tradition, but Tuohy does it in a very depressing way. C: "Don't pay attention to it."

4th September. And for the next two days I was depressed. To C, who was also depressed, everything was straightforward: "We had not seen Tuohy for three months and he greeted us grumpily and didn't seem interested in what we had to say and found fault with your Anglicised pronunciation (Khábarovsk) and said at dinner, quite unnecessarily, 'I can't give you the serviettes I bought today, I've got people coming to dinner tomorrow and I can't use them on you,' and then he was just very rude. It's because he can't write. Let him stew."

No doubt she is right. I was depressed by all this, and more: the problem of the two traditions. I have articulated this before as regards Colin Wilson – the social rationalist tradition on the one hand and the "private" tradition on the other hand. I have always articulated it. Now I see that my writing centres round the inner life: all my characters until the time I met Tuohy were symbols from an inner world, like Kurtz, and my poems are really only finding objects to symbolise inner states, like the People's Square and brainwashing or the 1,000 effigies. *The Expatriate* is set in a social situation, but the pressure is from the inner life. Tuohy on the other hand writes of the social world (see 2nd September) and consistently opposes anything "autobiographical" (not that *The Silence* is) or "introverted", and his prizes reflect the similiarity of his outlook to that of critics in key positions.

What is at stake is the tradition I am writing in. I am prepared to agree that "language, humour, wit and structure" are important in writing, but I refuse to agree that Brian Moore is "better" that Dostoevsky or Conrad, or that Tuohy himself is, for that matter. The truth is, Dostoevsky and Conrad had a much deeper and profounder grasp of the inner life than Tuohy. And I refuse to believe that people will only read me for my language and not for my images and what they represent. This is a self-protective view, related to the emptiness of Tuohy's social "images".

5th September. I was tired and depressed and ached all over from the journey, and Nadi had a very bad cough, so we did not go down to Nobe with Buchanan. Instead I began revising *The Silence*, tightening the structure by adding numbers. This also breaks the flow and solves the problem of grouping. The text is very much a comment on the text from *St. John*:

"Except a corn of wheat fall into the ground and die, it abideth alone: but if it die, it bringeth forth much fruit." How true this overworked text is. The will must die, the "will" in the sense of the ego that makes for confrontation between "I" and others (see 2nd September). Discipline, determination, dedication, or even the freedom to learn one's job – these are not a part of what I mean by "will". The first three are deeper and affect the whole being, and the fourth is a tool in the hands of the whole being, whereas what I mean by "the will" rules the whole being.

Only when that will has died can the silence be born. Freeman surrenders himself to the Image of the Woman in Pt 2, but his will does not die until he had defeated static rational psychology and accepted the irrational. This static self, the "repetitious bourgeois" is the will, that "gaunt tyrant" who keeps the being under strict martial law. The revolution against the tyrant is not easy to achieve. But if it isn't achieved, the land will be barren, and there will be no crops. And first one must learn to recognise the will, the "me" of the Gurdjieffian scheme.

What happens when the will has died and one lives in the silence? First, ambition and things connected with the world cease to be of great importance, though pain and suffering remains acutely important. Secondly, one is growing, one is healthy, and one's inner being will blossom and drop fruit. It will die, yes; but it will have lived in the fullest sense of "to live".

6th-7th September. So what is the Shadow? In the outer, social world, it is the image of a completed social role: the elder statesman, the distinguished teacher, the Nobel Prize-winning poet. It is the completed social role that calls the incomplete social role into being. It is an image invested with all the qualities the incomplete self needs to become complete. In the inner world, it is the image of a completed future self and within the context of the death of the will, it is the willless future self who is living almost entirely through the silence; that is, supreme fertility, wisdom, "wise passiveness". I do not move unless I have something towards which I should move, and the Shadow is that something, the final goal of my self.

Every man has a Shadow, i.e. every man is free to create his Shadow. And there are therefore as many Shadows as there are people – there is no one Shadow. Every man is free to create and be created by his Shadow; it is a mutual process, and as my Shadow is an image, a face, I can change its meaning from poet to religious teacher or vice versa, as I wish, just as what it is will have a bearing on what I am. And just as there is self-will, which is egocentric action, and Will, which is the divine force from the whole being, roots up, and the motive that carries one towards the Shadow; so there is shadow, which is unsubtle, naive ambition – the image of an ambition realised – and there is Shadow, which is the total image, the final image of the whole being, from root to crown.

It is this sense of Will that is dedication and so on (see 5th September), and it is not this but self-will that must die. This is what dying away from the world means. And to feel this, all the time, one must maintain one's vision actively and not allow it to lapse. I have rather allowed it to lapse this summer, and as it will presumably lapse when I finally leave Japan. I love England and living in England, but when I do live in England, there is no doubt that I lack the inner life I experience here. See this *Diary* from June to August.

To be fair to England, I did see a lot of new people in that time and have a lot of new impressions and perhaps if I were to live there another one and a half years, my daily entry would be as introspective as any average Japanese entry. But I doubt it. For as soon as I left Japan I could not stand the sight of the Japanese, and the same was true on the way back, and yet talking to the Prince or the Vice-Governor I am infinitely more watchful than I ever was in England at any meeting with anybody. For half an hour while the Vice-Governor confided that Miyamoto and the JCP (Japan Communist Party) had been asked to lead guerilla warfare by Peking, my eyes were glued to his, and I could hardly focus at the end, whereas there would never be the same intensity and pressure on the temples in an equivalent situation with Rob or DS.

I suppose in the last two and a half years I have gone through some sort of transformation to faith, to a faith totally devoid of belief. I wonder whether this faith will survive Japan. I hope it will but possibly Truffer was a fantastic prophecy, and I too will yearn for these days if and when I reach 60. For now I *do* understand the One. I cannot explain how or why, but, being a unity myself, I can feel the world is a unity, can feel that every man is my brother, every woman my wife; I can hate men and women as I can hate my brother and wife, but they are still to be respected.

8th September. During a day in which I revised *The Silence* (for C to type up) and went to the Bank of Japan, I wrote home and did nothing.

I have been wondering if I have changed any of my opinions since May. As regards the artist, I think I affirm my attitude of 24th May, that the artist is, like Owen, a bearer of truths rather than a detached "maker" (see 28th May), though all Tuohy's "propaganda" about the need for total detachment and no one reading anybody for the meaning has rather put me off my stroke. On the subject of revolution, I have not really gone beyond the statement of 5th and 6th June – not even in that of 20th-21st July – and still distinguish national and political from spiritual action. On the cells of 10, Reformation, the entry for 21st July was not really a departure from everything I have written since December 1965, including China (24th-26th March) (1st-7th April), I still have a choice between art and spiritual action, and wonder if my idea for a school for self-realisation is an "escape from art" (see 14th May).

The other problems that have concerned me are (1) "isness" and meaning (24th-25th April, 20th May), and (2) feeling as the basis of values (2nd, 5th May, cf 12th, 15th, 19th May), and I have not developed as regards these; that is to say, the attitudes in *Archangel* for example were an application of what I discovered before I left Japan. I do not think I shall develop much as regards these two, and having rejected political revolution, this means that there is only one crucial problem on which I am still undecided: "art or religion?" In other words, what shall I do when I return to England – shall I throw all into a school for self-realisation, or, shall I recognise this as an escape from art and shall I concentrate all (as in 1963) on writing? As yet I do not know.

9th September. To Nobe with Buchanan, in spite of a nearby typhoon, which in fact changed course and left us good weather. We lunched at the Drive-in and talked about Britain's decay, among other things, and its symptoms: no T.T. entries from Britain for the Isle of Man race; the Penguins now come apart; the smudges on the Churchill coins. Buchanan's picture of Rumichan's mother against the red and yellow cannae, which were like twisted penises. The rolling breakers, the yellow and green rice valleys, and the poles with rice hanging upside down.

In the evening I went for a walk with Buchanan. We went down to the dirty beach, where the rollers boomed, and speculated about a glow on the horizon, like a submerged midnight sun. Then we went up onto the hillside and saw it was the "reflection" from Tateyama City. And the clouds cleared to reveal the Plough. We sat on outside the hut the local fishermen keep their tackle in, while the autumn crickets tinkled like sleigh-bells, and then we went and got the owner of the vegetable shop to take us to his "house", a miserable lower flat of two rooms excluding bathroom and kitchen-hall, totally surrounded by other houses and therefore cut off from breezes, for which he asked ¥12,000 a month plus £24 deposit.

On the way back I asked Buchanan why he didn't move down as he had planned and he blamed the expense: it would cost £3,000, and he has spent money only recently on a new veranda. We got on to living in Japan as opposed to England and back to England's decline and lack of influence. I: "Which is better – happiness or influence?" Buchanan (referring to a story he had told earlier, in which Mme de Gaulle mispronounced "Happiness"): "A penis". I went back and drank more and went to sleep about 9. Returned Saturday 5 p.m.

10th September. Yesterday and today I have been thinking about freedom, after dipping into de Beauvoir's autobiographies vols. 1 and 2 and reading summaries of extracts from *She Came to Stay* and *The Mandarins*. Freedom has always been one of the main points in my credo, and there is much of Sartre I go along with – the desire not to live in one place or have possessions, the desire to choose every day and rechoose every relationship and so on. There are limits to freedom in the outer world, however. A fully developed person feels that every man is his brother, and sets a value on it, and the theoretical freedom of Mathieu's "Thou shalt not kill – bang bang bang" seems childishly nihilistic to such a man.

341

Theoretically one is free to do anything, yes, but in practice one chooses not to or is prevented by circumstance: I am free to break my contract and return to England, but I am limited by my lack of money, and in the same way I am free to kill but prefer not to. One must recognise a check on one's freedom – and that check should be based on feeling, that is the point. And if Sartre is Robert in *The Mandarins*, then he seems to be beyond feeling. Nonetheless, it is good to be aware of one's freedom and to use it within one's own limits and not egocentrically, e.g. in choosing one's outer Shadow, keeping one alive.

But one needs more: one needs to find oneself, not only in relation to other people but in relation to oneself also; and that means rediscovering one's roots in one's past and unfolding the depths of oneself. The point it, one has a self, and although I can choose to leave my job or my wife or even to stand in front of an audience I dread, I cannot change my nervousness, and that is not just because of the "nervous" choice of myself – it is because I am as I am. I may not be able to say "I am a coward" or "I am a hero", but I can speak of my nature, which is the way I behave when I am not conscious that I am choosing, my natural, automatic behaviour.

11th September. I went to round to Tuohy's to snip up the FO negatives and found him in a subdued mood, having been drunk last night and not on dexedrine, which I believe is primarily responsible for his aggressiveness. We talked about Sartre and de Beauvoir, and he predictably said he would not hear them and contemptuously gave me *Les Mots*. It is childish, his sweeping rejection of all writers with a higher reputation than his own. So, de Beauvoir "has no selectivity" and Sartre is "narcissistic". True, but even so....

Once again I attacked Sartre's notion of the self. I said I could act against my nature, but my nature is still there, and although some of it can be changed, other things can't. Neurotic fear can, but can "fear of heights"? (Tuohy's phrase, which he significantly scrawled three times on a piece of paper – "fear of heights"?) So I am always nervous before a large lecture, and Macmillan was always nervous before a speech, even though to others I may seem confident.

Later revised *The Silence*. There are two views of my old egocentricity. Either I died away from it, or I disciplined it with an interiorised will. If the latter, then the leader is that will as well as the static personality who prevents growth. If the former, what are the effects? (1) Existing in an egoless silence; (2) thence driving up with dedicated, undivided Will to the Shadow; (3) seeing the world with a visionary's intensity while doing that. If the latter, what are the effects? (1) Clamping down on the chaos with an iron rule; (2) deposing the static leader so that freedom/growth can take place; (3) thence as 2 and 3 above, or else freedom. This is the psychological explanation, that I subdued the chaotic land by a Dictator's methods and that I am now rising up against the Dictator and his mechanistic habits.

I am both dynamic and static so both are true – the psychological explanation possibly explains to some extent my nervousness – but I follow the dynamic.

12th September. A very busy day, after a totally sleepless night, I took the China photos to…the Foreign Correspondents Club, and, arriving early, met first Emery then a shuffling P who is going to give me "a tinkle". They were attending Aiichi's press conference. Waiting on in the lobby I was in advance of time. "God," I thought, "he looks like Krisher", and the same moment another door opened and another man, Krisher, came through and passed me without speaking to me, although he recognised me. There was something psychic here. Compare the plane crash in March, which I "knew about" at least three weeks before through a strong premonition of danger.

I talked to F in the bar. First of all he was very much against the idea of our moral decay, but when I said I sympathised he dropped the Embassy front and agreed and we spent an hour and a half analysing Britain's decline. I walked back with him to the Hong Kong and Shanghai bank, where I had already handed in my transfer licence, and as in a nightmare an official came out of the bank and accosted me on the pavement and said "Mr Hagger would you please step inside when you have finished your conversation?" They had given me the wrong chequebook and I had drawn two cheques on somebody else's account – that was all. But as I said to F, "I have a feeling all executions begin with a polite request to step inside."

I went back home and took the car to Hitachi's, forgetting his diary. When I returned home, the Princess having just managed to thank C (via the Prince) for the antique, the Bank of Japan appeared with a badly written English version of an important speech. Correction took two hours. Then Buchanan phoned to say Sartre, being an anti-Gaullist, will not be invited to any public reception, to placate the French Embassy. And finally I got down to preparing for Keio, breaking off to watch Hitachi on TV for a quarter of an hour.

13th September. When I slept I had a number of dreams, but really only remember the one I woke up with. I was passing through East Germany on the Moscow train. The train stopped alongside a canal and there were shots, and while the guards went to investigate, a civilian dived in, throwing up a lot of spray, and swam across. The train moved on a little and stopped again. Two men had been captured and they stood on the other side of the train, on a stretch of wasteland. One was taken away, and the other (who looked like the currency swindler who was conductor on our train) has his throat slashed with a knife. He sank to the ground. Then his guards dug a kind of grave, a very shallow trench, and they lay him in it and covered him over as if he were a sunbather on a beach, putting earth over his neck-wound but leaving his face free. He was still alive and suffering horribly. Then they took his rosary, for by now he was a priest, and put it over his head, like a

343

necklace of beads, and, laughing, set up a friction on the earth wound. The priest's eyes were sunken and contorted with agony, and I could bear it no longer. I rushed down the corridor, got off the train and stood beside the buried priest, raised my left arm and shouted "Pity, pity, pity" and then "Mercy, mercy, mercy". The guards did not hear me at first, and it seemed as if I were calling on God. When they heard me they drew away, and I thought they were going to shoot me. I turned to walk as nonchanantly as possible towards a small square and café some 50 yards away. Then I saw Nadi ahead. She was crossing the road and might be run over. I ran, and somehow the guards did not shoot. When I had rescued Nadi I ran back to the train. As I got back on the train I turned and saw inside a nearby building. The guards held C, and they flung her down so that she slid along the polished floor and out of sight. She was going to be tortured. That was all.

What does this mean? That my concern with my fellow man will get C into trouble and cause her pain? Or as in my poem, did the priest and C symbolise the irrational unconsciousness?

14th September. And were the guards those forces in myself, now unmasked, which cut me off from the irrational depths of myself, and is that why East Germany fascinated me – were the guards the agents of the inner "Leader"? And on Tuesday after Keio, too, the Albion was a dream in the great Nichigeki brain, and flesh and blood was an image. And there is all the symbolism Tuohy did not even begin to understand – the K man, the caged President, the thirsting priest. The value of all these inner images, apart from the literary value, is in the fact that people do see the world in this way without really being aware they do. We live in a dream that we have projected out into the world – that is the point. And for Tuohy to say: "You should be concerned with other people and not yourself" evades the point altogether. For my territory is the way we fail to see others as they really are. And the fact that we project as we do is evidence of the need for us to come to terms with these images.

We begin by thinking of the "sub-rational" and end by acknowledging the "irrational" – "that which defies the reason", "existence, which the reason cannot explain or reduce to a comfortable abstraction", "the depths beneath the reason which the reason knows nothing about." We need this irrational; hence the image we have of it. The dry soul lives in a dream and is blind to these images of the irrational and does not realise that it is looking for objective equivalents of inner states of mind. So the man who turns away from every social observation to subjective "blindness" is not a narcissist or an egoist. He is stating subjectively experienced objective truths in the only way he knows – in terms of his own vision. I think my vision is unique in literature, and I think I have given a new significance to the image in literature, in so far as "realistic passages" symbolise aspects of the irrational.

15th September. On my way to Keio on Tuesday I met Miss Tsuda, the plain Tokyo University of Education 4th year student. She is going to become a teacher but would rather become a hostess. Within a minute she had overthrown all my defences with a hostess's questions: "Mr Hagger, are you happy, for I know you don't believe in God, only in existence." (She does believe in God, she knows that God loves her.) And: "Mr Hagger, what is the most precious thing for you – love, your work?" Under pressure, to this I answered, to my own surprise: "Unity. Being One Self and seeing the world as One with all men as brothers. Love and work are contained in this." Then it was: "Mr Hagger, did you love your wife when you married her?" No doubt she was thinking of arranged marriages, but, sensitive to seeming remote, I did not go into the meaning of "love". It was simpler to say "Yes", so I said "Yes". "Ah" she sighed enviously, "then you must be very happy." And I did not say that happiness is something I do not think about, as I have my writing to do and do not expect to enjoy "a feather bed".

Then came the shock: "Mr Hagger has many qualities," she began, and when I modestly protested, she insisted: "Yes, he has many qualities, he has everything and he is popular with everyone, but perhaps because he is popular with everyone he is rather remote and does not treat each person separately?" "Perhaps," I said defensively, recoiling and wondering how I could use my position as Professor to ward her off, on the train. "Yes," she said, "perhaps". "When you are a hostess I will come to you," I said, "and you can teach me how to 'treat people separately'" and that saved the day: it made her giggle. This should make a story: *The Hostess*. (Who has a talent for getting to the fundamentals.) 12th April 1967. Too personal for a story.

16th September. A holiday yesterday, Tokyo University of Education and the Bank of Japan IMF work today, and in between a brief meeting with E. G., who seems to be deceiving herself about her husband. Just before she arrived he was released from prison, where he had spent 9 days. He only told her "last night", "to save you the embarrassment of not knowing why there are silences."

17th September. Spent the morning revising Pt 1 of the typing and longing to get *The Silence* out of the way so that I can get on and do more things. Thought about my old novels. On February 20th I rather misunderstood *The Eternicide*. Te Deum was the irrational silence, Zabov the ego – the scientific pride that thinks, wrongly, that everything can be explained, that certainty will follow. The priest is a kind of superego, but he is also the guardian of the silence, eternity. That is why he is so concerned with refuting Z's arguments. After Z has killed Te Deum, there is only one outcome for him: suicide. Killing Te Deum amounts to committing suicide,...for without the nourishment of the part of himself that he denies, he is lost.... I, not understanding my own creation, decided that a real man would not commit suicide; and saw it all in terms of Christian faith – and so decided that the priest was wrong and Z right, and decided that the modern "certainty" could never die. In struggling with *The Eternicide* I was struggling with myself. The priest and the Zabov in me were locked together in an image that was infinitely satisfying.

I must revise the novel in the light of what I have learnt and bear in mind *Juben*. If Juben is "ego" what is Lasco? A completely free, lawless being – the Jungian shadow? Juben was going to end in a monastery – was Solange "The Rescuing Woman", the silence? Zabov's wife, in one of the versions, was presumably the silence too, and perhaps their child was the prototype of Pt 3's child in the poems.

18th September. A wet day. Worked on knowledge and postulated (for Tokyo University of Education) that all knowledge depends on a relationship between "I" and the world. This relationship is an indivisible totality – it cannot be divided as Kant divided it, putting space and time in the mind. It can only be experienced and is not to be thought. Thus my sense of time is my reaction to change in the world – the falling of the leaves, the cooling of the stars. The theory of relativity asserts that if I travel out 30 years and back 30 years, my sense of time will be wrong, because the earth will have travelled on 50,000 years. (I am not sure if these details are right.) The principle is understandable, because my sense of time is wrong if my sense of the world's change is wrong. Similarly, my sense of space is in my relationship to the world. "I am three feet from that chair." Certainly if I have a knock on the head I can misjudge distance, but there is a norm, where my jacket hangs on the peg. Space is not in the mind, nor is time – this is the point, and only a man who has departed from experience into abstract categories could assert that they are.

For the rest, I spent part of the night and Monday morning thinking about the title to Pt. 3, trying to recall the glimpse of it I had at about 3 a.m. four days ago: a waking dream. It came to me as I walked to Tokyo University of Education: "Reflection". That gets the idea of the static self, the dead personality, and makes a good contrast with Shadow, a contrast I have already made, subconsciously. Shall I call it "A Shattered Reflection"? or "The Shattering of the Reflection"? And how can I suggest that it's the dictator of Pt. 2?

19th September. To P's. Was delayed by the Prince and a traffic jam, and missed the way for Jingumai. P came and met us, and when we arrived M had a log fire blazing. "I am cold", she said, flinging her arms about and exposing as much leg as possible, "and I don't want to put my winter clothes on." We talked about Russia while she mixed trendy martinis and poured me an enormous Scotch. She was there about 1953 "heavily pregnant" and so was he. That was the signal for him to say "I'm glad you saw Douglas er S, while you were in England." There was a terrific silence for five seconds. Then, choosing my words carefully, I talked about Peking University and the Red Guards, saying my findings had been proved right and that I was the first to discover the purge and so on and that even DS had doubted my findings in June.

Then we got onto Japan and Britain, and M who was slightly drunk started staring at me and saying "Poppet (to P) if you want me to wear a mini-skirt like this..." giving me an eyeful of pants in the demonstration. P shut his eyes in pain, and I looked at him as much as possible. On the way down the garden M took my arm and breathed heavily.

20th September. Having lectured at Keio on moments of order – Roquentin's response to the Negro singer, Meursault's happiness, Krebs's moments in the war – I went to hear Sartre and Simone de Beauvoir. There were 2,000 in the hall, and there was a mess-up when they arrived, de Beauvoir sitting at the microphoned desk on the platform, Sartre almost joining her and apparently taking fright and walking round behind an enormous vase of flowers and sitting in the front row, whence no one could persuade him to budge.

De Beauvoir spoke first, misjudging the Japanese for there was nothing about Japan at the beginning or Keio. She just switched on a flow of thought and sat like a robot and shouted stridently on the need for feminism for an hour, until her voice cracked, when, after several husky sentences and the aggravation of sympathetic coughs from the audience, she stopped. It was all so fast and aggressive that she had been difficult to follow.

Sartre came on five minutes later. He sat sideways on to the microphones and consequently his words kept fluttering to the floor. In addition he kept dropping his voice, and he was very difficult to hear. From what I heard, an intellectual was somebody who opposed the Americans in Vietnam and the French in Algeria.

How much truth is there in the idea that women and intellectuals are victims of the structure of society, whether Communist or bourgeois? Obviously, generally speaking, the women of a bourgeois society will stay at home whereas those in a Communist society will work, but there are thousands of working women in London and is there any evidence that all women in China want to work? Women are free to choose against the social norm in bourgeois societies as they are not in Communist societies – that is surely the point.

Having heard these two doctrinaire people, although as firmly "anti-bourgeois" as ever in relation to the snobbishness and complacencies of provincials, I felt I remained bourgeois. I believe in individualism – though not at the expense of others; and I believe in the inner vision; I do not believe that man is a social unit, or that the structure of society should be designed to kill incentive. I hate the worst element of the bourgeois, yes, but I am still thoroughly moderately-bourgeois at heart, and my revolution would not destroy the individual spirit.

After the lecture, while Buchanan was (unknown to me) talking to Sartre and de B at the Mitsui Club, to which we had not been invited, I stood among the bourgeois at Miss Gegg's and drank four large whiskies. Met Guest, who shocked everyone by having very long hair and wearing outrageous clothes and having very timid eyes behind thick lenses. Met Hill, a lower middle risen who said "Pleased to meet you" instead of "How do you do" (like Rainer) and who said "Ta" to me over the telephone next morning. Otherwise talked to F about Britain, having defended Britain to the Librarian of the National Diet Library. His magazine *Britain Today*, which, he insisted, is not propaganda, but is balanced. Towards the end met a Miss Woods who is teaching at Tsuda and who lives at Iidabishi; formerly of BE Commercial. "I wanted to go to the East and Japan was the only place going...." "I wasn't a very good secretary and I'd always wanted to teach, so when I met Alan Baker...."

We left in Tomlin's car. Tomlin's absurd good-byes to people. C: "He's a mess – he's nervous and he's always looking for people, as if he's thinking 'Where is everybody?'" which made me plan a story on him, to be called *The Representative*: the perfect bourgeois, defender of his own tradition and Establishment; and the way he has been moulded by the break-up of his marriage.

22nd September. The principle of gain. I reluctantly agreed to take Toff's class for him yesterday, even though I was only helping out and would probably get paid. And today, in negotiating with Irie for another tax certificate to say "Mr Hagger took up a new period of service from 1/9/66", I was motivated by gain. Of course I have good reason to think of gain, for my liabilities increase....But the point is, I am not sure that I could ever work for the good of the commune – give classes for the cause, pay tax to the cause. I am a mean bourgeois, unlike Rob who wrote to about 200 people after the C of E accountant "lit a bonfire and died", and who got nothing at all for doing so.

My art is about the only thing I serve vocationally, and I give most of my leisure to it, but then I am a bourgeois artist. What interest is it to a Chinese to read about Reflection and Shadow? Or the struggle which takes place until the Reflection serves the Shadow? And more important, my art gives me an aim: the finishing of my work is a kind of purpose. Whereas non-bourgeois art is all in the anti-bourgeois cause.

I am tired from sleeping on a futon, or carrying luggage, or rheumatism, or flux – I don't know which, but I ache, and value my comforts (beer, sex, images) and at present cannot conceive of a new society that, without denying gain and aim, works very much better than our present bourgeois society.

23rd September. A holiday. Worked on my poem, and on history and the artist. Reading Kermode on action and contemplation, and on the escape of Arnold and Empedocles and Major Robert Gregory, I felt that the unsolved question posed on 8th September, "Art or Spirit?" should not trouble me as much as it does. My ideas for a spiritual revival do seem the escape of action, from the solitary pain of writing, and perhaps I should scrap all idea of being didactic and concentrate on the wading girl and the girl in the wind and other "victories" of this kind.

On the other hand, reading up the struggle between the Holy Roman Empire and the Papacy, I am not so sure. Of course, the issues that divided Henry IV from Gregory VII, or Frederick II from Gregory IX, were, by today's standards, rather boring: appointment of clergy and power. That does not matter. History is a kind of challenge. It is there, stretching ahead, a virgin sheet, and although Britain is like the Abbasid caliphate in the 10th century, inevitably approaching the sack of Baghdad 1258, one has the feeling that one can define oneself, make one's mark, do something worthy of memory before one becomes nothing. And what is there for me is spiritual reformation.

Which is more important to me now: a Luther, a Wesley, a Knox, a Calvin: or a Blake, a Yeats, a Shelley, an Eliot? I think I would have to reply "The latter". And yet, after the fall of Acre in 1291, there was no Christian foothold in the Holy Land until T. E. Lawrence. Action or contemplation, history or art? I don't know. I am torn apart between the two and doubt whether I have the talent to do either, yet believe in myself sufficiently to know that I have.

24th September. I have been reading up on phenomenology. To what extent does it conflict with the silence? Discounting the attention from the object and trying to escape the "natural standpoint": Husserl's method is one I would favour for defeating the Reflection, just as Whitehead's second mode of perception, "causal efficiency", published 15 years later (1927) is a blow against the static passiveness of Hume. And if Brentano's "intentionality" comes down to selecting objects of consciousness, it is certainly better than Fichte's "trialism" and all its Kantian "solipsism".

The notion of an active consciousness is valuable, but man does not consist solely of an active and passion consciousness. There is also the silence beneath the reason, the depths of ourselves, and this active consciousness belongs essentially to the world of the ego, the "will", the reason, the social self, in fact, the Reflection. In other words, there is also a "wise passiveness", and the depths of oneself can teem with images – I know. Let consciousness create meaning (Whitehead) and select what it wants to see (Brentano) – I am all for that, and am against nihilistic passiveness; but let the consciousness be that of a deep contemplation, involving the whole being, and not, for example, the sharp eyes of a Tuohy which notice things but which lack a world-vision. Perhaps Whitehead would not disagree: "When...Rutherford...knocks a molecule to pieces, he does not see a molecule or an electron. What he observes is a flash of light," and "Our experiences of the apparent world are nature itself." Perhaps Tuohy would not disagree. Anyhow, there is a time for active selection of objects, and a time for contemplation. Or perhaps I do not have the phenomenologist's temperament.

25th September. And so we return to "the inner vision" – finding equivalents from the outer world for mental states, projecting, seeing other people as symbols of inner truths; when one is really only seeing oneself. Projecting and selecting are opposites, as are inner and outer, and one needs both to be whole. The image is of the boat on a lake. The man in the boat can look around him and select details from the forests of Dooney and Innisfree, but it is equally pleasant to lean over the side and gaze at the wobbling images under the surface, images whose outline is suggested by the hills. And when he perceives a condition, he feels joy and the sense of significance that makes me underline all the images in this diary.

After finishing the final corrections to *The Silence* I picked up a book by Laing called *The Divided Self*, and was startled to read of the inner self and the false personality as a pattern – pure Gurdjieff, see 23rd and 24th January and of the way the vital embodied self gets cut off from the world by a dead, embodied "false" self. Perhaps this "false self", the personality, is the Reflection – perhaps I knew this all along and have felt that joyful shock of recognising support for one's own position. Anyhow a feature of this false self is futility, meaninglessness, purposelessness, which is what Freeman feels throughout Pt. 2 and throughout Pt. 3 until he comes to terms with his "disguised" Reflection. (I cut out the word "disguised", preferring my reason, which knows nothing, to the intuitive judgement of my self.) So perhaps F subdued his inner chaos with a false mask.

The point I am trying to make is that perhaps the active consciousness comes from the self and is the self's function in relation to the world (this "false self" being what receives impressions passively), whereas I prefer the inner gaze of the self. In which case, what does the projecting? The self-in-silence – the "irrational" – trying to attract the attention of the Reflection? (See 14th September.)

26th September. Or is it a symptom of borderline schizophrenia? (Compare the deadness of Juben's language, which was a sign of the "false self" – Reflection.) Have I tried to "create relationships to persons…within my microcosmos" – is that the meaning of "the inner drama"? Rather than projecting 7 images out onto people, have I tried "to be omnipotent by enclosing within (my) own being, without recourse to a creative relationship with others, modes of relationship that repair the effective presence to (me) of other people and the outer world"?

I think not. I may have desired "safety for the true self, isolation and hence freedom from others, self-sufficiency and control" – I may desire them still – but I still maintain that my territory in *The Silence* is the "blindness" which prevents us from seeing the world as we should, the meanings we unconsciously place on others' faces, without their being aware we are doing it. I may have stared for five minutes at the White Tower, because it corresponded to something I felt inside, but I have not such a consciousness of "central citadels" that my mandalas are to be seen in schizophrenic terms. All this is a part of the Reflection's temptations. I think my contact with the outside world is not too bad, for all my insistence on "the inner vision", and I don't think I by any means shirk "creative relationships". Nonetheless, I would question the basis of the view that "creative relationships" are the interior of normality. Again, that's the Reflection's temptation.

Contact with the outside world's more complex. I can feel the agony of an executed man, and I think I could feel for Rob, who had a coma in the Russian boat and was put in the Orsett Hospital near Tilbury. To what extent could I feel for the 180 odd killed by typhoons Ida and Helen, which uprooted 4 trees in the Tokyo University of Education front quad, the only evidence I have actually seen? Perhaps not enough, not as much as I would want to feel. I reject this view of myself as schizoid, however. And cite Kermode.

27th September. After Keio met Jon Halliday and brought him back to dinner; this meeting being planned when I rang Adrian's home and found myself speaking to Jon. He has rimless glasses now and says he feels no different from the way he felt in Oxford. He is still Marxist, and resembled a narrow-minded Catholic in so far as he was not at all anxious to hear criticisms of China or listen to Peking propaganda.

We talked about Japan and China and art, but the most interesting things he said concerned the Randolph Set. After I had attacked Kingsley's dependence on psychiatrists and claimed the artist was not a schizophrenic (this being a label), J said that James Greene did 4 years under Laing and is now an analyst. He must have made the decision just after Jenny's wedding in 1961. He has also inherited £750,000. Lady Rosemary and Charles Nunn have been divorced, CN teaching economics in Canada, Joanne nursing. Quintin has given up his thesis ("having bitten off more than he could chew") and his marriage is breaking up, his Yugoslav wife having visited Albania with the *New Left Review* lot, Perry Anderson and (I believe) Peter Wollen, who is now in films. Quintin has lost his self-confidence. Herbie has moved from Aberystwyth to Colchester, where he is presumably in Davie's department. He has three daughters, and has given up the idea of writing. Perry's wife, Juliet, like Jon Halliday, is teaching at Reading University (near Ricky) and Pat Major and Erika are teaching in the same private school in London. Henrietta has completely caved in following the accident, and Glen pulled Bebe out of a river when he was about to drown, having been thrown from the car. Did she meet up with Jill in this Northants mental hospital?

It seems, then, as though the Randolph Set is now teaching, or connected with magazines or psychiatry, and all that fantastic "talent", which is a part of me and which I shall never escape, has failed to flourish or has been destroyed by its latent nihilism.

28th September. Corrected the Keio exam papers, 4th year, and then went to Baker's cocktail party, where I had about four whiskies. Spoke to Father Milward; Field and others. Left 40 mins after the end with Tuohy and went to Nicola's, it being C's birthday, and drank Chianti and got drunk and came home and drank more whisky.

Earlier I had remarked on the decay in accents to the working class Home Office Inspector – as in a nightmare, I went through with an embarrassing subject – and disgraced myself over Whitehead; Goodwin having said W was responsible for Nan's not going to school in the Embassy car. I was polite to this wire-glassed "Caligula" of *Frenzy*, until Miss Gegg came in, when I introduced her as "not a member of the British Embassy". When she indignantly disagreed I said, "But how strange, I am not a member of the British Embassy and I am a member of the Council, according to Mr Whitehead that is – where is the logic in that?" W could not say anything and I was elated in the silence that followed before Miss Gegg, tears glistening in her eyes, invited us to her second party out of sympathy. Tuohy: "You deal with Orientals better than I do, but you should know that Tomlin could fix it all up for you." I: "I would rather pay the extra £50 a year than accept charity from that b——." And this was the theme all the way to Nicola's, I feeling the party had been "an expense of spirit".

Thereafter the theme was T's desperation – not the theme of conversation, needless to say. When I had introduced Hill his reply had been "Blast you, I was talking to a Noh director and now he's slipped off to the benjo", and the established author was threatened when he met an author, a devotee of A. Huxley who has had three novels accepted by Faber, and who, like Higham, did not appear to know who T was. All T's persecution complex came out, and thereafter it was all how good he was (*"Encounter* thinks my article the best it's had") and how important his acquaintances were. So J. Halliday was "of no importance", and nor were "these people who try to smash you at parties". Nonetheless, he did betray the truth, that he has shot his bolt with *The Ice Saints* and just can't write any more: he was very scornful about "journalism", having come over to my view of journalism (see 3rd September), and so "I would not go to N. Vietnam – I am not a journalist"; and he has to get drunk every evening because he is "too tired to do anything else." He lives in desperation (cf "quiet desperation") and has been shaken by James Farmer's success after all his predictions to the contrary.

Tuohy needs me, because I am one of the few who appears to believe in him, and with whom he feels confident – with whom he can play the writer; and I need him because I am trying to catch up on him by making use of the knowledge he has gained through his 16 years start – because he is a Shadow. Hence I put up with his attempts to keep ahead of me, with his denials of what I say and his later echoing of the same principle.

30th September. Thursday. After last night had a hang-over. Nonetheless took Nan to school. Her proud, springy walk down the hill, and her disillusioned tears when we left. The nuns with "church-clothes" and the French wives in mini-skirts. Felt giddy until 11, when I threw up. Then went to the Bank of Japan for a lunch (12-2), after which I talked for a further two hours with Fukuchi and the V-G (Vice-Governor), mainly on neutralism. I said Japan should declare her neutrality from U.S. and China, hold a conference to end the Vietnam war, and then create a Neutralist Alliance throughout Asia, in the course of which Article 7 could be dropped.

Before I went into the V-G's room, I heard him talking on the telephone. It was evidently an outside call and he was doing all the talking (I heard "Kyoikudai", "Vietnam", "Hagger sensei") and I wondered if he was being asked for a reference. He was glowing and embarrassed after, and couldn't find his books and didn't know what to say, so it might be, Narita's tremendous friendliness on Friday suggested the Emperor's visit to Europe; the Crown Prince; or Sato. It is probably nothing, but if it were any of these, I would prefer Sato, simply to apply Neutralism through him and have a hand in building an Empire, which has always been a dream of mine. For (though they were not Empire-builders) there is a bit of TEL (T. E. Lawrence), or Rizzio or Rasputin (in me).

1st October. Thursday was "chu-shu no meigatsu" ("mid-autumn bright moon") and the moon was like a yellow lantern. Gave three lectures at Tokyo University of Education on Friday, then came home and wrote...and had a bath and went to Miss Gegg's (see 28th September). There were only 15 or so present:...all gaijin. The thing was, Miss Gegg sent the wrong date to the Cromwells and so had to hold another party for them....Spoke mainly to Bickley, who was short, crew-cutted, ginger-haired and red-faced and puffy-eyed. He looked very hunted....T: "He was much better when he came alone: he had more confidence." Went back with Tuohy.

Earlier, when going to Miss Gegg's in the taxi, he had apologised for his "rumbustiousness", which he attributed to drink and pills, and he said he was not on pills. This evening he was much nicer as a result. He gave me some ink-painting material and confessed "If a man comes up to me and says 'I want to be a writer', my natural reaction is to feel 'You're treading on my toes'." And, in showing me some poems and a short story by a student of his, "I feel I've given him the wrong advice, because the 2nd version's not as good as the first." C: "He feels guilty about you."

2nd October. Saturday. Yesterday I failed to record an incident at Miss Gegg's. Bickley came in on a circle of six or so, and Baker tried to bring him in on the conversation. "Frank says the *Gospel*," he began, and tailed off. Then he began again, referring to the Pasolini film: "*The Gospel According to St. Matthew* is very good." "Oh, er, yes, I'm sure it is," Bickley replied, startled, not realising Baker was talking about the film.

Today, after writing *The Man Who Wasn't There* and getting a haircut, I went. It clearly ranks with *The Seventh Seal* even though it tails off after the temptation. The thing is, it is so real. Joseph suspects Mary of adultery, Mary is afraid of the Wise Men and the Kings, Christ yells out when he is nailed to the cross. Christ's first appearance was simply stunning; he had the most dynamic look as he came to be baptised, and yet it was a joyous look. The thief in the night in a hood, perhaps. Tears actually trickled down my cheeks, for this was how I had always imagined him, glowing with self-confidence and love. Later the self-confidence became self-satisfaction at times, and I wasn't sure about his harsh, swift voice, but that long look under the hood will be with me on my deathbed. The recruiting of Peter and the entry into Jerusalem were both very moving, but there were long stretches of boredom between. Satan came up on the horizon, kicking up dust behind him, a sensualist dressed in black, and was very good. He looked rather like Peter and Judas, the two traitors who are a part of one.

The whole thing was conceived at depth and nothing was simple, not even the Angel whose hair was as long as Screaming Lord Sutch's. I may be wrong, but it seemed that Christ at first tried to flee in Gethsemane. The miracles were the only weak part: it would have been better to have been more humanistic there.

3rd October. Spent Sunday revising *The Great Pyramid* and Monday morning revising *Blighty*. After an exam at the Tokyo University of Education, went to Hitachi, who had done four bits of written work for me. Returned and then went off to Tomlin's cocktail party.

The first person I saw was P, who was not too anxious to speak. Talked to Hijikata and Aratake and Kuroda and then M and Yoshida, who did not remember her name, according to C, in spite of saying what good friends, etc. Then, H-L, who was on crutches, having had a skiing accident....Later, after talking to Amino and call-girl K and Roland and Taylor and M again (about a Belgian pendant), I talked to Toff and Brammah of OUP and Summerskill and eventually wound up back with M who was talking about mistresses and lovers, but not coming over quite as well as in her own home. P came over, slightly jealously. Then I joined Yoshida who wants to go to England next year. I told Tomlin who went off to say good-bye. (Later, Tuohy: "You should never discuss business at a party".) We left with Yoshida and I was drunk and joked about his hat and his eyes and his reputation, and we went back and had spaghetti with Tuohy, who had not had a pill: "Oh nonsense – and I haven't had a pill...."

4th October. After a 4th year class on Hemingway and a 3rd year exam at Keio, returned home and then went off by taxi to F's dinner party. The taxi did it in quarter of an hour less than we had reckoned and we were received by the maid and Dorothy, R being in the U.S. (because of a death, I believe) and F having been delayed by a large U.S. car which prevented him from driving out of the Pakistan Embassy car park. After F came Adrian, as gauche as ever, and then the Shorters, an accountant couple, and finally the Rs, to my horror.

As to the events that followed, see a short-story I wrote this morning (Wednesday) about a man called Plastick and his need to smash because of his insecurity in relation to his wife, I sitting between them at dinner and talking to her before dinner. I have not recorded the argument I had with Adrian, who denied that J.H. is a Marxist. It afterwards occurred to me that possibly A was afraid of F. As I said, "You had him for five weeks and we had him for an evening, and you say he's not a Marxist whereas he claimed to be one with us. A one-night Marxist can't be a very serious one." When I said J.H. had condoned the 1949 executions in terms of "culture patterns", A couldn't believe it and said I must have forced him into a position he didn't want to hold. He would not believe that J.H. would not listen to the radio. I was left with the feeling that although it was all an expense of spirit, I had got something out of the evening, including (besides J.H. and the story) the information that John Walker left the priesthood 6 months ago and is now in Zambia; but that nonetheless the evening was badly chosen – what writer or artist would have chosen R and me together, unless he wanted to provide material for a story?

5th October. Tears from Nan when C and I tried to leave her at school. Why? Insecurity, I think, and probably a fear we will not collect her at 11.30. ("Will you come and meet me later?") Also, fear of sister's "church-clothes" still. I connected the temper-tantrums she has been prone to in the last week with her resentment towards C for sending her to school. She has bottled up a lot of indignation which comes out when she is angry. It is a wrench for her, going to school: there is no doubt about that. She would rather be in the kitchen, playing with Aikosan's and C's undivided attention, and so she has asked C several times "Do you like me?" and has said to me: "I love you."

I suggested breaking down the barrier between home and school by converting her bedroom into a schoolroom for her pots – teddy, golly, pussy and so on; also by putting A-Z and 1-10 on the wall. Another good idea would be to invite "the little girl in the white skirt and red shoes" (who, I thought, was herself, originally) to tea, so that she would have someone to go and see every morning. And what about "Old Wobbler", the Russian boy, and "Old Scribbler", i.e. "Old Squibbler"? Another thing is to give into her over the sandwich and let her have a sandwich like Daddy instead of a biscuit every morning. Anything to make her feel important. And of course "sister's church-clothes" should be made as familiar as possible; and I should clown around with my Russian cross as much as I can.

What does Nan really think of school? I think she is primarily afraid of sister and the other children, and must just grow up and adjust, but her disillusion, after her expectation, was rather sad to watch.

6th October. I have not recorded something Jon Halliday said. He remembered three things about me: boots – i.e. the mosquito boots I used to wear at Oxford; the fact that I was going to write "the great novel", an intention he had heard about from Herbie; and finally the episode of Ricky's plunge into "the river", which was in fact a canal. What happened was that he (Ricky) and I were returning from a party as drunk as I am now as I write this, and were talking about Sartre. I said: "If he is right, then you are completely free to do anything, and you can easily prove that he is right by jumping off that bridge. Jump and you are free; don't jump and you are a slave." (He sometimes liked to refer to himself as a slave). He jumped. I was drunk and did not expect it, and remember collapsing with laughter, then coming to and peering anxiously over the bridge and seeing his shape rise out of the water like a god and stand dripping in the moonlight before wading to the bank and climbing up a straight iron-rung ladder onto the road and then walking round to me and suggesting a bath. For some reason C knows the exact bridge, which is very near Worcester. I must have pointed it out to her or someone else did. Ah, how one has changed (and how wrong Jon Halliday is to bring this forward as evidence of Ricky's insecurity).

And while on the subject of change, I should note that I have been much more settled since January 1965. No longer am I at the mercy of my moods, and no longer do I feel futile. The only despair I really feel, apart from depressions Tuohy dumps on me, is in the middle of the night when I wake and turn and wonder where I am and realise: "I am alive and I am going to die." I think about my death with a terrible sinking feeling, and go back to sleep. That has happened some three times this last week. Perhaps it's connected with sleeping on futons and I would experience nothing so devastating in an English bed. Or perhaps maturity has come at last.

7th October. Have I begun to bloom and is one of the effects a reduction in intensity? For I don't feel or seem to feel, as tight-lipped as I used to, and this *Diary* is becoming more and more of an effort to keep up, introspection takes place more seldom. Possibly I am tired after so many cocktail parties and dinners and exams, but, equally as possibly, perhaps I do not delve into myself as much as I did last year or earlier this year and 7th September is a distortion of the truth – England was part of a general tendency that had nothing to do with England and much to do with my act of self-discovery in *The Silence*. Perhaps that is part of a life-pattern that is fairly typical – the intensity of the twenties, the drive for self-discovery, and then, when the quest has succeeded, a slackening, a blossoming, an existence less impatient and impetuous, more slow, more weighty, more in the present than in the future?

Or perhaps when one is creating everything is in question, so that every day something strikes one as being of the utmost importance, whereas at present I cannot create because exams and revision and other things forbid, and so I seem duller, thicker? I do not know. But I do know that a crust is forming, and the inner fountains have been blocked, and this crust is not really broken when I revise or make corrections. Adding to or changing a line does not make one see the world in a new way. If the state I am now in is merely a question of not being able to create, then I have nothing to worry about. But if it is a part of a typical life-pattern, then maybe I will not write much good poetry again – maybe this is the beginning of the menopause at 30, and maybe it will seem a mistake, in the future that is, that I ever embarked on my self-discovery. For to discover oneself is to lose one's intensity, and one cannot be sure it is not also to lose one's creativity.

8th October. And so one's prayer should be: "O Lord, may I never discover myself." And yet self-discovery is the thing one yearns for most of all. All my life I have wanted to know who I am, probably because I have never had any place in British society, not even at school. "I have never been able to define myself socially, and so I have always rejected social definitions and wondered who I am – is there any truth in that? I do not know. All I know is that I want a place in British society as someone who is responsible for that society, and although I have discovered myself in terms of my own past and problems, perhaps my self-discovery will not be complete until I have found that social place.

What is it? Here we come back to the main outstanding question (see September 8th), artist or religious teacher? In England I felt I was destined to be a religious teacher. Now I am not so sure. Perhaps that is the escape I should dread, for perhaps that would make the menopause certain. Today I finished revising my poems, and in a tremendously energetic burst, C typed them up for the first time. Would the social position of poet do? Today I also dipped into smart poems by clever people: Thwaite; Enright; and Davie (on Eliot). Would it really be a definition, to take my place beside them? I know it wouldn't. They were clever, yes, but timid, "insiderish". And if I were asked to address a meeting, or take part in a meeting, that they would be present at, I would refuse, out of a sense of difference. No, the social position of poet would not do. And perhaps therein lies my hope as a writer – perhaps so long as I fail to discover my self socially (as Tomlin has succeeded) I will continue to cheat the menopause. Perhaps I will never discover myself socially, and that is my good fortune.

9th October. And yet what do I want to do, as a poet? I suppose, to lead the reaction against the 1950s, against Movement and Group. Their poems are timid, neo-Georgian wastes of time, from the point of view of the subject matter, all too often. I want to lead in a new significance, a new depth, the sort of newness the Romantics brought in after the Augustans, the sense of a quest after all the static cleverness. All very well, supposing I were to do it, what then? What does it all amount to? I am reminded of Ricky's scornful comment when I told him I had heard Robbe-Grillet: "Yeah, and who gives a f— about the latest objective movement in art?" For my sense of a quest involved a new subjectivism, in so far as it was "derived from the mind or consciousness as contrasted with external qualities or forces" – at any rate, in Pt. 3. The Shadow, the Reflection – these were to be seen subjectively, and no doubt everybody has experienced both in varying degrees of consciousness.

All right, supposing subjectivity is truth, what then? I cannot escape the conclusion. In so far as I have been using a technique, my work is of no interest to me as a questor, and it is as a questor rather than as an artist or maker that I regard myself. So the answer I gave on lines 1-2 is not the real answer, which is: to pursue my quest through to the end. And I can only do this by defining myself socially. Oh, vicious circle! What do I want to be as a poet? I don't know. Or rather, I know in relation to what has gone before, but that is not important. What is important is what comes after, and in relation to that I do not know, and live in doubt.

10th October. At the end of a day given over, like yesterday, to ploughing through exam papers from Tokyo University of Education (about 200 of them), C, who was reading the paper, said: "Perhaps that's my trouble: perhaps I suffer from an underactive thyroid." On closer questioning she admitted she always felt tired: "fatigue, the most frequent manifestation, begins so insidiously it may go undetected for months or years." And she admitted to other symptoms: finding it difficult to get started in the morning; feeling drowsy most of the day; lacking ambition; finding the winters progressively more severe; having a bad circulation; aches and pains and stiffness, insomnia; and of course anaemia. Nothing about sterility. She certainly does not seem to have myxedema – puffiness of face, eyelids, tongue, dry and rough skin, brittle and coarse hair. But: "as metabolism falls lower and lower, mental and physical inertia deepens. The majority of victims are apathetic and have all they can do to keep going." Thyroid extract is the remedy.

11th October. The poems before going to Keio, justifying the inclusion of *The Great Pyramid* in *A Forward Vision* on the grounds that it made a good base from which to explore the themes I have tried to explore. Theme and image are interwoven throughout the 7 pieces, and the last three lines of *Blighty* pose once again the problem of the futility of history, a problem I must try to answer anew in my poem on Cromwell and political and spiritual revolutions, a problem I stated in *The Great Pyramid*. All the main literary posts have been captured by Movement sympathisers who just want something clever, mannered, unpretentious and detached. I feel they've had long enough in office and a change would be a good thing for poetry, but "I do not think they will listen to me" (Eliot). I also think they are often wrong, just as Tuohy is often wrong: it does not matter whether I am thinking of the Tigris or the Euphrates, or the Mississipi or Ganges, just as it does not matter whether the city is London or Paris or New York. A sense of place is not absolutely important to poetry.

Nonetheless, I have gone beyond hope, I have renounced all expectation as regards the immediate future. Why am I so calm and detached about something that would once have been a matter of life and death? Possibly because I am completely confident that one day my poems will be widely read and accepted. Possibly because I have learnt that it is only by denying hope that one's not hurt – it is only by accepting defeat as inevitable that one has the courage to continue in spite of it. A very stoical attitude for a believer in the Shadow.

12th October. Began the Cromwell poem, got into difficulties, went off to Hitachi and at the end of a conventional class, redefined my relationship with him. I told him we should learn English in situations, and recommended walks in the garden and then suggested we met somewhere in Tokyo. Where? was the question. I recommended a cinema, the idea being that we should discuss something outside ourselves. "Would this be possible for you?" I asked "To be frank, you are a Prince, and I don't know if that would be allowed." "It would be allowed," he said indignantly, and I thought it was a sore point with the chamberlains. The question arose as to where we should go after, and it was quite clear he would come back here. Would he be able to leave the chamberlains outside and come without his wife? Having confided one thing he would never tell a Japanese, he might just confide again. As Tuohy would say, "He's a blurter."

The Revolution against the chamberlains took a new turn when I left his room. When we got to the foot of the stairs I noticed he was agitated, and before we'd gone half way to the door he stopped me and said, "I can have films sent here – you can come and watch James Bond here." There were three chamberlains almost within earshot and I could not incite him in their presence by saying, "Meet me in the Nichigeki Bunka incognito", so I said "We'll discuss it on Monday and I'll have a think," and left, having applied a most revealing stimulus. For he is quite clearly afraid of defying his chamberlains, he is the prisoner of his palace.

13th October. Began a poem on my "spiritual home". The original idea was that it should have some 5 or 6 stanzas of 10 lines each, beginning with my childhood and ending fairly recently. The Forest was to be realistic at first and was then to symbolise the irrational, from which I have always derived consolation and which has always given me the intensest moments I can remember.

This idea was broken up by the sudden arrival of the final proof of my Kenkyusha article, which I reread. Ah, in *Archangel* and *Blighty*, have I not departed from my principle of compression? Is compression perhaps not me? That was what I felt.

Yet looking back at my poem after I had corrected the proof, I felt it had included too much "wadge" (like that awful poem I wrote in Nara), and the thing was reduced to two stanzas, the second being the short line bit about "Waltham stream" I wrote in Loughton, the first being very incomplete.

What is it all about now? Clearly it is a contrast between forest and stream, between permanence and change, and between permanence and the illusion of permanence. The Forest is an inner forest; its geography is an inner geography; it knows the answers and gives the answers – the blazing pond, the silence – so it is the principle of "meaning" objectivised, projected out.

My growth is measured against it, so it is also the yardstick of growth – it assists my growth. I think it is these factors that make it changeless and therefore encourage the feeling in me that I change against its permanence (it is the depths of myself objectivised) but I have still failed to understand my images, and so the poem is not going well.

14th October. At MITI (the Ministry of International Trade and Industry) I had a most extraordinary experience. I had had sashimi (raw fish) for lunch, and had therefore had beer. I had little time to pee and could not find the gents while waiting to meet Hirabyashi's successor, Myamoto. I left the second candidate while he was writing to look for the gents and was unable to find it. There only seemed to be a ladies near the lifts. I was hoping to go after my second candidate left but my third candidate arrived on the hour (each candidate gets one hour) and I had to wait until 4.40 before I could try again. I went while the third candidate was writing. I was bursting, but again I couldn't find it, and I couldn't very well go back and ask my examinee "Excuse me, but do you know where the gents is?"

Taking a deep breath, I opened the door of the ladies, had a quick look round, and, seeing it was empty, belted past the basins to the cubicles and dived into the nearest. No sooner had I shut the door than two further along flushed and two women walked by to the basins, talking. When I had, most awkwardly, peed into the floor I stood up, but there were still sounds of the two women, and I could not move. I waited five minutes, and still they ran the taps and dried their hands and talked and then began all over again. My examinee by this time had had getting on for ten minutes for his writing and I was desperate. I couldn't hear any talking, but I knew the door was silent, and I knew I would just have to risk it. So I flushed, opened the door, side-stepped, peered, and, seeing there was no one at the basins, belted for the door and rushed up the passage to the lifts where I paused to straighten my tie before assuming a sensei's dignity and re-entering the examination room. The absurd thing is, I still do not know where the gents is.

Could I have foreseen all this in December 1963 when I came out of the radio station opposite with Kuriyagawa and saw the scaffolding of a new building where I later peed?

15th October. After writing a subtantial amount of *An Inner Home*, went to see *One of our Spies is Missing* at the Marunouchi Tokyo, in the bottom of the Nichigeki, where the whores hang out. It relaxed me (which was the object).

16th October. My dream last night was about Eliot. He wore a hat and a raincoat, and he spoke, looking ahead and almost thinking aloud, with Blunden's intonation: "Of course, some of these people writing today have no idea about poetry, you know." We talked in a park, and I was trying to convince him that his theories about dislocation and doing without the "wadge" were right. In the end we went into a urinal and he said, peeing, "These Winters poets aren't a bit natural either." "No," I said "they're much too mannered," and thereupon, to my annoyance, I was woken up, though I should have been relieved as I was going off to take a Latin class (gerunds) at 5 pm., much against my will. Was it in England? I suppose so.

After breakfast the two workmen arrived to redo two lights they had been told to do again less shoddily. There was no phone call to prepare me so I refused to let them into my study (and as a result finished *An Inner Home*), and as a result they rehung the dining room light off-centre in an absurdly crooked position, and then went off, as they came in, without saying anything.

On our way back from a walk to the church we met Buchanan, who had found no one at home, and we returned with him and drank saké until, by 8.15, he was completely drunk.

17th October. Another ridiculous experience, this time at Hitachi's. My car drew up as (Princess) Haneko was saying "Goodbye" in the porch to a stranger. I did not know who the stranger was and when he said, as I tried to slip past him, "I am Takemura, my name is Takemura," I reacted with a startled "My name is Hagger." "I am her teacher," said Takemura. "Oh really?" I said, feeling shifty, while Haneko clucked ineffectually. "I am very pleased to meet you," said Takemura. "I am very glad to have had this opportunity…." I began, trying to avoid a "lower middle" phrase, but could not continue, for it was all too absurd. Whereupon Haneko came forward, extended a hand which I, surrealistically, thought of kissing. "Good afternoon Professor Hagger," she said with a nice smile, and I, taking her hand, thought of wishing her the same and beating it back into the car, while Takemura babbled at me from under my elbow.

I just couldn't connect at all – I was still in my own thoughts and all this was a dream – so without any attempt at a farewell I headed for the stairs, just to regain control, and to my horror found all the chamberlains hanging on the banisters, giggling, and Hitachi muttering to himself and beaming by a table at the top of the stairs. It was all unreal – *Alice in Wonderland* – and I burst out laughing and blundered into our study rubbing my eyes, and shaking my head, for the Court had gone mad.

Sartre: "Etiquette deprives of spontaneity and yet there is more spontaneity in Japan than in France."

18th October. The smoke here is appalling. Would I be able to get a job with the Bank of Japan, London, or with the Japanese Embassy (teaching

Modern Britain), or even with a Japanese business, on the strength of my job with Hitachi? This prospect, thrown up by C, has filled me with hope that I may be able to earn what I do here in London and put in as few hours. Thought about my journey back. If C and Nan go straight back I shall go via Korea, Taiwan, Hong Kong, Philippines, Malaya, Indonesia, Thailand, Burma, India and Pakistan (Nepal?), Tanganyika (?), up to Cairo, across N. Africa (?) to Portugal and Spain and so home.

19th October. Spent a second day on *The Conductor*. As things are at present, it will be in 5 stanzas: (i) setting the scene; (ii) seeing the Conductor as the centre of society; (iii) seeing him as the falsifier of self in society; (iv) (not written yet) having a dialectical synthesis of (ii) and (iii), i.e. seeing the Conductor as Artist, falsifying to make real, the real centre of society; and (v) seeing the Conductor as Reflection and centre of self.

Hitachi was drunk this afternoon, and shook me by the hand and picked at all my books and tried to pinch Graham Greene for his cousin. I told him about Russian roulette, asking him if he'd ever played it and then got him onto the sentences he was supposed to have prepared. He smiled at the one: "My wife is less economical than yours." Later he said virtually nothing at conversation time, and, when I was about to leave, produced a dancing programme and detained me 20 minutes past leaving time explaining that one of the dances we shall see on Saturday is a popular dance from 850 odd, whereas the Imperial dances are from 834.

20th October. Just as I finished the first draft of *The Conductor* a letter arrived from Kingsley, a 5 page lament that has knocked me sideways and boosted my confidence, for on page 4 he confirms that he has now reached the position I was in when he knew me (i.e., in 1959-61), and is (after all his criticisms) embarking on the same freedom I had then. "I see now," he writes, "that you were perhaps fighting for your life at a time when most of us didn't even know there was a war on." And he recalls my "determination to make things happen, to startle other people into self-revelation or action."

The fact that I have moved on is beside the point. One longs for the approval of people we have admired, and this spontaneous admission, along with the admissions of Ezard, Jill and Ricky earlier this year, has convinced me that I was right then. May I not be right now? Perhaps Tuohy will come round in a few years' time, and I shall be able to effect a complete return from this exile from my past and "go down the mountain".

Yet, before I become too complacent I must confess to feeling uneasy still. "I am essentially a T. E. Lawrence, an Empire-destroyer or an Empire-builder." If this is true, what the hell am I doing in this backwater in Tokyo? Why aren't I *doing* something to fulfil my great idea? And Empires or spiritual regeneration, are both an escape from art? I am uneasy, for I shall never really express myself to the full until I have *built* something in history and building something in history means moving nations, and how can I possibly do that, constructively? With my nervousness it will be quite impossible to do it through committees, and how else can one build a worthwhile dream these days?

21st October. After three wearying lectures at Tokyo University of Education, Adrian came and we talked about Kingsley and his volte face. I said that in 1960 he left the way of action for the way of "subtlety", which he had now finally abandoned ("all that f—ing subtlety") because as in Jon Halliday's case, he wasn't doing anything. I said I had moved on to the way of contemplation, which is different from the way of subtlety, the way of the professional intellectual, because it is based on self-discovery.

What I did not say was that I have almost completed the way of contemplation, and must look ahead to the next way. Perhaps this is connected with the ideal of uniting action and contemplation, and lying awake this (Saturday) morning, as a result of drinking too much beer, I realised that the Conductor is the image for this ideal*: his eyes are closed, he is in a world of his own, and yet he is the supreme actor, for without him the orchestra could not play a note. He is the centre of the evening, and is also the Artist.

Artist-Actor-Contemplator: that is the new ideal. Instead of changing the image for action, I must attempt a new fusion of all sides of myself so that I can both image and act. Will this be possible? Is it not a kind of Renaissance ideal: the whole man, expressing all sides of himself, uniting all in his life? Can one not do what most others seem to have failed to do, and balance action and contemplation? And is this aching yearning to build an Empire not one aspect of my present failure to act enough – am I not too much of a contemplative?

*Is there any comparable image in Noh?

22nd October. With Tuohy and C to Gagaku (Kangen and Bugaku) in the Imperial Palace. The stage looked rather like the Globe, as Tuohy remarked: seats on three sides, a back space, behind which the orchestra sat, and a balcony above. The Kangen (= wind and string) was composed of 16 people and instruments like a piece of grass between the fingers or "a comb and lavatory paper" (Tuohy). There was a terrific rhythm, and I rather liked it.

The Bugaku was fascinating. Instantly I knew I had an image, and the red quartet that appeared from behind the left flame drum, the sun, and stood in each corner of the conscious brain, represented my opposites, dancing in a very slow unison. After the (Mongolian) Reflection had appeared alone, in a brown mask and with a knobbled stick like a bone, the four opposites danced with a Gothic shield, a sword and a spear, thereby revealing themselves, in their helmets, in their true form. They were essentially hostile to each other. The flame drums supporting a spoked sun and moon

(Chinese and Korean in origin), I think, referred to the divinity of the Emperor, who was Son of Heaven in China and I believe the same in Korea. The flame drum bears a crest, and the pattern round it may relate to the zodiac (like the clock in Hampton Court), the idea being that the Emperor holds up the sun and moon. Is this conjecture true? If so, the two drums are placed behind the conscious brain and relate to the universe. Godhead.

For the rest my impression is of seating chaos and of Americans who whirred cine-cameras and picked their noses and of menopausish women with dyed grey hair and silver fingernails.

23rd October. A plan as regards going home (see October 18th). Nadi's school is to close in June 67 we heard yesterday. It is better she should start straight in an English school, and preferably remain at the same school for some time....C could leave and Nan could go to Oakfield, possibly moving to Loughton when I return.

24th October. Worked on the "her body thought" theme in Yeats and read his words in *A Vision* about Byzantine eyes staring on a vision whereas Roman eyes stare on the world, and understood the Unity of Being and how history passes from periods of subjectivity (vision) to periods of objectivity (the world). For this is the quarrel between Tuohy and myself. I have the vision and seek a vision; he stares at the world. He would call my Byzantine "sad-eyed Saints" from the Archangel Cathedral "narcissistic".

Later, as bed-time reading, I dipped into Underhill's *Mysticism*, which I have never read, and in the chapters *Introversion: Recollection and Quiet and Contemplation*, discovered that the Silence is a well-known experience in mysticism, and that I am indeed well down the "Way of Contemplation" (see 21st October). The concentration which is "Recollection" requires "a gradual handing over of the reins from the surface intelligence to the deeper mind" until "individual activity is sunk in the great life of All" (p311), and it is this process I have struggled to outline in *The Silence*.

The main thing about that poem was that I did it all for myself, without any aid or guidance, and so I did not know where I was going. I was travelling down a completely unknown road, without the slightest idea of what was at the end. Had I had someone like Underhill to tell me what was at the end, had I had a Christian tradition I could have believed and trusted, I suppose it would have been easier, and clearer.

Anyhow, after reading these chapters I felt elated. For my "discoveries" had the full support of the saints and mystics – these were now "rediscoveries" – and I almost felt I had discovered myself: I am a contemplative and visionary who should ideally have been born in the Byzantine Age. All that remains is to act, in the name of the Silence.

25th October. More on phenomenology, from Tokyo University of Education (Monday). The point is, the phenomenologist is concerned with sense data and "modes of perception", with ways of looking at the world, whereas the contemplative shuts his eyes to the world and feels a unified view of the world, through a vision. Whitehead, Brentano, Husserl and Gestalt are all very good at making us more observant, by teaching us to grasp objects with our consciousness, but one can also respond to the world without "perceiving" it – one can respond to an image of it. And unity is in an image, for example in the image of a mandala.

How these two ways affect one's response to people can be seen in Ivan (Karamazov) and Zossima. Ivan keeps a file on children and commendably feels for their suffering, and for all suffering through these particulars. Zossima on the other hand already knows all suffering in the universal, and he has already suffered with the Ibos, the Jews, the Vietnamese. One should have both, but one should not say, as Tuohy did in China: "I am only concerned with those I know and feel responsible for – I can't know about the others." This is seeing "know" in terms of perception, and is no argument against brotherhood. One must take the world into one's soul, not to talk about it and palm oneself off as a professional intellectual, like J.H., but to feel for all suffering, everywhere, for the seven Yeminis executed yesterday and for Dr. Subandrio.

In a sense, the real solution to the problem of uniting action and contemplation is to become a Schweitzer, and work for brotherhood in some concrete way. I doubt whether I would have the courage or the ability to give up my art-form, but perhaps it is the Schweitzer, even more than the Luther, who has achieved the balance.

26th October. A wearying day in which I spent five hours getting up the final written draft from *The Conductor*, went to MITI and examined for four hours, then returned £10 the richer and wrote two short stories, *Tanaka's "On"* and *Foreigners Apart*. In fact I worked so hard that I could not possibly unwind myself and as a result did not sleep a wink all night, and now write with slight migraine-worms and blotches in the corners and centres of my eyes.

I had some interesting candidates yesterday: a consul in Pretoria, a war reparations negotiator in Indonesia, the man who liberalized Taiwan bananas in 1963 and thus set into motion the recent government scandal. But the most interesting was a UN fellow who spent 6 months in Britain in 1962/3. His observations were interesting. He thought we were in decline and remarked on the concentration of wealth and on the seeming disinclination of our working classes to want to become white-collar workers. I made an exception in the case of the universities, comparing Futan's proletariat percentage (40%) with Oxford's (60%?), but generally he is probably right, that class barriers were more rigid in Britain in 1963 than anywhere else in the West. Another comment was that we seemed to have got rich through our colonies, and so there is an elephant on a pillar in the middle of Coventry, the nearest town. Also, the disappointing lack of new buildings as compared with Japan. I: "We are very unfortunate not to have lost the war. We too might have had a chance to modernize our cities and have a land revolution."

This is the sort of picture of Britain I must present in my poems, for how we appear to perceptive foreigners now will be how we appear to ourselves in another 50 years. I must get to the heart of living in the modern age in Britain, and then my writing will have the right pressure.

27th October. At the Bank of Japan spent an hour talking with Fukuchi about Middle Eastern influences on Asia, and, in particular, the relationship between Zoroastrianism and Chinese Yin and Yang, Zoroaster's dates being variously attributed as 6000 BC and 660 BC. Yin (dark, female) and Yang (light, male, Japanese "yo") are united in Chinese thought by Tao, whereas Ahriman (dark) and Ahura Mazda (light) have no such unity, and therefore the question must be left open as to which influenced which.

Fukuchi referred me to the "Yi King", which I recognised as the *I Ching*, which I have. This contains the first mention of Yin and Yang, and much of it derives from King Wan, BC 1143/2: ⚏ (yin) and ⚌ (yang). The 64 "hsiangs" (= ideas, emblems) come from rolling out the circle of the "Great Extreme" (=Tao?) into a straight line, which was cut up into 2 lines and thence 4, 8, 16, 32, 64. But why stop at 64? The circle appears unsatisfactory, and no one is sure about the "Great Extreme".

Anyhow, all political and social and metaphysical phenomena could be related to these 64 hexagrams, and they are still used in Japanese fortune-telling with sticks and, of course, in Chinese writing. For every Chinese ideogram contains Yin and Yang. According to Fubara at Tokyo University of Education, a ghost always enters with the palms down, as the back of the hand is "yin" and in such a case symbolises death. If a ghost enters with the palms up it is funny. Moreover, the Gagaku flame drums *do* support "yin" and "yang" in a creation legend which is bound up with divinity. (See October 22nd.) Heaven seems to be involved in all this, e.g. heaven it was that created the spiritual tortoise, and the perished River Map (the river being the Yellow river) suggests that — was used for a bright O, and — — for a dark O, by King Wan: i.e. it was all originally moon and sun.

Two "I" (forms) became 4 hsiang (emblems), became 8 Kwa (trigrams, discovered by Pao-hsi, = Fu-hsi 3322BC), became 64 hexagrams.

28th October. It was announced that China has exploded a nuclear (possibly hydrogen) weapon with a guided missile delivery, and the test has been confirmed by international nuclear measurers. Although the U.S. has said China cannot assail the U.S. for 10 years, quite clearly they have underestimated China, and have been taken by surprise. When I went to China I thought the Chinese were too concerned with their own problems to be aggressive. Now I am not sure whether the Lin Piaos and so on are reliable and responsible. Would it not be better to depose the Chairman straightaway? The question of course seems absurd, but that is not the point. Would it not be in the interests of the future that the Chairman should be replaced by Chiang's deputies – would the world not be more secure in the future?

If so, what is the best way to overthrow Mao? (Or his deputies, if he is already dead.) Surely there should be a combined Anglo-American plot, with an American-sponsored invasion of Peking by Chiang Kai-shek and Co. The best way to invade is to provoke the Chinese into entering N. Vietnam, declare war (?), and push Chiang in. Various people inside China would have to know of the day – D-Day – and this is where the British would come in. My aim should be to prepare for an internal revolution against Mao. The main drawback: the bloodshed (which I am deciding would be less than the bloodshed and anxiety the present regime will cause).

29th October. Went to Nobe. On the train got the mysteries image and discussed the plan to overthrow Mao with Buchanan. Buchanan was in favour, but thought it would be extremely difficult.

The valleys were beautiful. I climbed right up to the top to get a photo of the sea. I wanted one through a spider's web (an image for senses trapped in a word-spinning intellect?) and pressed back against a steep bank to crane the camera into position, for the fat polychrome spiders prefer the shade and this was the first I had found in the sun. Behind me there was a rustle and a slither, and I yelled and leapt forward and put my face clean through the spider's web. After I had spat out the revolting gossamer with its wound-up balls of dead-matter I turned and saw a large snake (grey and green and red) withdrawing into the undergrowth on the bank.

Later, after a bath and a meat-supper, I heard Buchanan's life-story. Later we went for a walk under a moon with a Picasso face, and the sea was, in places, a white-hot, silver fire. It was as though petrol on the water had caught fire, and the flaming petrol came in on the crest of the wave and got swallowed up and doused out in the curve of the roller.

I went to sleep about 9.30 p.m. and slept well and spent all Sunday morning sitting on the beach near the boat-ramps and lying on my back under a deep blue sky in the valleys, and at 5.30, back in Tokyo, we all ate in a sushi shop among hawker-voiced, white RAF hatted chefs.

30th October. All Saturday and Sunday, on and off, I discussed Britain's destiny with Buchanan and I feel dissatisfied with all my former attitudes, and wonder whether I have been wrong to reject politics and revolutionary action. All national regenerators have had "une certaine idée" – Kamal's modernism, de Gaulle's revival of the old greatness. Kamal followed a pattern of withdrawal (abandoning all remnants of old empire), concentration (i.e. modernising) and then expanding, and the pattern is one we could adopt: withdraw (i.e. abandon Fiji and Gibraltar), concentrate (i.e. effect a complete reorganisation of Britain on the lines of 8th March and get everyone acting on the line of Roosevelt's WPA) and then expand, i.e. offer a dream of a politically united Europe with a Parliament in common, and the spiritual way of life outlined about 22nd March.

All this may seem impractical, but that does not matter. The point is, this is a great idea, and if the belief is there, the dream will come to pass. There would have to be a rightish coup d'état – that is unavoidable – but as soon as it had taken place the leader would respect the individual in everything save his right to vote for the next year or two, during which time he would be "on approval". Should he be a man with a myth, an ex-war leader like Kamal or de Gaulle, or Churchill; a Wellington or Pompey? Buchanan says he should. (Compare Mao and Cromwell.) But there is always a first time.

On July 20th I wrote: "A revolution cannot hope to restore Great Britain." What I have just written answers that. A revolution's aim should be to achieve domestic strength, and the expansion will follow later. On 5th and 6th June I distinguished political from spiritual revolution, but would not both be attempts to revive the moral strength of the nation? To the objection that all this is fascist, I would argue, "It would not be in practice – is de Gaulle a fascist? And history shows that a strong leader is a greater unifying force than a bickering democratic Parliament."

31st October. After two lectures at Tokyo University of Education and two and a half hours with the Prince, in the course of which I discussed feudalism in post-war Japan (he saying only gangsters are feudal and I disagreeing), went to P's house. The chauffeur rang the bell and would not go away. I was still trying to persuade him to go back to "Prince's house" when M appeared at the gate to let me in. The awkward talk about Hayama, Nobe. M is rather nervous and shy when alone. She derives her intensity from opposing P, whom she needs to be herself.

P was flustered when he came in: "If only I could stick a knife in somebody." M went out "to write a letter" and I put it to him, hesitantly at first, that the 4th nuclear test will endanger the peace in Asia for the rest of the century, as Mao's successor's cannot be trusted, and that rather than "waste his time" collecting information, he should be plotting to overthrow Mao. I then outlined my plan: infiltration of the mythical liberator through posters, claiming support from Red Guards; contacting and bribing disaffected Army leaders; the internal revolution and Chiang's entry at the same time, the liberator "handing over" to Chiang after 2 weeks; this being supported by the U.S., who would have provoked Mao by retaliating for a "torpedo incident". After a little banter he put forward a few objections and said "You'd be the only one trying to contact non-existent disaffected Army Officers – it would be self-immolation." Whereupon he called M in.

Not to be outdone I raised it all again, and caught fire. I put it to him again. As I had said before, there were a thousand and one objections, but this was a dream and if you believed in it enough it had to come into being. M took my side: "He's really with you," and "Don't be so wet and dispiriting." (To P.) P listened quietly and in the end said: "This is visionary." I: "Yes, it's a mystical creed, that's the whole point." Before I left he said strangely, "I promise I will write a memorandum at once and I will see it gets to the very centre in London."

1st November. In the course of my appeal to P yesterday M said: "You talk like a missionary." My defence was: "I wrote *Archangel* during the summer and discovered Mao represented the opposite of my values; one must act out one's beliefs and values, otherwise no value is worth believing in." And as I walked down to the gate to leave and M said "Your bag is heavy" I said, "It's mainly *L'Être et Le Néant*, and "Sartre believes in acting, though Mao is one of his heroes."

Is it really true that I believe one should act out one's beliefs and values? I have always maintained some such position and Kingsley remembers me "as someone determined to act out the consequences of man's absurd freedom" (or some such phrase). But to the point of dying, and for "a value"? For, in the unlikely event of my plan's being adopted, I could be caught and shot. I don't know. I know I believed what I said at the time, and that I spent 20 minutes in a coffee bar beforehand trying to convince myself that I did believe it. Anyhow, so far as P and London are concerned, whatever my private feelings are now, I do believe it. I committed myself yesterday. "Say I'm a crank if you like," I said, "but write in and tell London that you have to make dreams work." And what I said last night applies for all time, as regards London.

And how inconsistent I am still. I was so full of confidence yesterday, yet today I was reduced to a state of near-terror by a telephone call from the new Council Language Officer who wants to visit Tokyo University of Education and sit in on classes. He is a small, harmless man, and I know I can silence him on any subject but my confidence drained away, and I had awful trouble at lunch with EG (then being on holiday from Keio because of the baseball) and only put up any sort of a show by talking about the decline of Britain; which got back into the final, typed draft of *The Conductor*.

2nd November. In the afternoon went to Hitachi's and gathered that Princess Haneko saw me walking in my bum clothes yesterday afternoon near Edogawa bashi. I was composing the end of *The Conductor* and had my head up, or down, no doubt, and she had been to Arai's wedding in Chinzanso, and presumably did not like to intrude and bring me back to earth. Apparently there was a great deal of speculation over the imperial dinner table last night as to whether it could have been me, in a corduroy jacket too. Otherwise, I cleared the ground for the long poem on politics and spiritual reformation, and read through this *Diary*, picking out the relevant bits.

I assimilated on 8th September, but since then there has been a notable development: I have become increasingly torn between action and contemplation, or rather, I have been increasingly conscious of the need to act (e.g. 23rd September, 21st, 24th, 28th October and so on). This state can be traced back to 22nd July. "Why act"? But the questions on September 8th "Art or religion" and on September 23rd "History or Art" show a need to act in a religious or political context. And my development as regards political revolution (see October 30th), coupled with an inclination to defy, if not reject, the inevitability I was so sure of on 4th June, have brought the whole problem to a head.

Last summer I was sick with Cromwell's disease ("Why do anything because night will come") but now I am determined to do something for my fellow-man and, into the bargain, unite the opposite poles of action and contemplation in myself. October 28th and 31st must be seen in this light. So much for Man. And more positively, as regards Britain, could it not be Art and Religion and Revolution: a new dream to work at all levels?

Was I not wrong to renounce revolution and a clean sweep in Britain? Revolution breeds in decay. I am the poet of decay; should I not also throw up the solutions and defy all the inevitable laws of decline?

3rd November. Last night Tuohy came to dinner, having rung up on Monday to invite us. He was much more restrained when he arrived. He had only just finished teaching, and I did not think he was on pills. Nonetheless, the evening had a familiar pattern. He started off by drawing attention to his notice in the *Observer*, and we then talked about Japan and China and teaching until dinner, when it was Blake and spies, and then art. As usual, he knew it all. "Mrs. B was a spy and so is —. I nearly became one when I left school. In fact I had an interview with Trevor-Roper." And as usual he did not enthuse at all about C's paintings, especially the one about me: "Because it's you I haven't really looked."

After dinner we talked about aggression being insecurity, and the vulgarity of the working classes. I: One should be classless, but one does not like lack of respect (e.g. the new Mrs. H) and treating people as things, and these qualities are to be found very often in the working classes. T: "One judges by those who've got out." For the rest he raised objections to everything, being pro-Embassy over the Honda take-over ("they wouldn't tell you") – this switch being because of Sophie – and opposing the idea of withdrawing from Gibraltar ("what about the people there?"), and bashing down on Baker for being a...Christian, and for not finding it easy to get a job. "Trust is always misplaced" as *The Ice Saints* says. Baker has evidently got fed up with T's incessant attacks on the Council, and I can't say I blame him.

"Bleak, brilliant and often unbearably moving", the notice described *The Ice Saints*, and if moving = depressing, that is a good judgement on T. In the end, between 12 and 1 a.m. he spent a long time trying to get me to admit something totally untrue, that I got my park job through a labour exchange and not by choice – such a petty and stubbornly blind line. On the Edogawa tram stage I told him he should "sleep in doss-houses" like T.E.L.

and take the world into his soul, and even then he told me it was all very well to talk about it – I having done it, and he never having done it.

4th November. On Tuohy, the main thing is one cannot live by judging. "Judge not that ye be not judged" – one must live by feeling not as a rationalist. Today C saw him at the Tokyo Medical and Surgical and later she passed him in her taxi: he was mooning along, without purpose, a living indictment of his own creed. He; the great advocate of "respecting other people" yet he does not respect any Haggers (cf his refusal to be called "Uncle Frank" on the grounds that he would be liable for money in the future), and always puts judgement first.

My dream last night was vile. I was in a football stand with Nan and saw the left back come near the right corner flag where we were. He might have been me at 19. Nan said "He's one of the big boys at school." At half-time the teams went to the side (it could have been Walthamstow Avenue's ground) and the left back walked to the centre circle with a rotund butcher of an executioner who held a machete. He lay down on his back and the executioner chopped his head to bits with five swift blows. I was appalled....This dream haunted me throughout a terribly busy day (triple Tokyo University of Education, two hours at the Bank of Japan)....When I got home from the Bank of Japan, worn out, I wrote *A Wish and a Fear*, having had the conversation with B this morning, and I am now too tired to do more than make short notes for today.

5th November. Left at 12 a.m. for Iwasaki's wedding to Noriko Wada, former student. It was in the Gakushi Kaikhan, near Jimbocho at 12.30.

There was no one by the door, and we nearly got into the lavatories before going up to the second floor. There we nearly went to the wrong wedding. After signing our names in ink-pencil with "Congratulations and Very Best Wishes" we went through to an "oak-panelled" room where Japanese sat grimly all round the edge. We sat in the centre and spoke to Ando, Yamada, Kuriyagawa. Ando's gloomy news that he is definitely to be married in April. The line of Keio sensei I had to shake hands with. After a drink of paraffin and saké – C said there were chemicals in it – we went through and sat on top table, looking out at a two-way flyover. The parade of the stooges, the formal speech from Kuriyagawa and from various others of the 140 guests. I escaped. As the only gaijin, I would have been out of place. Or else Ando (MC) thought I would mess things up. Even so, I couldn't enjoy the six course meal because I was waiting to be asked and had to have a beginning ready. Nervous Yamada who sweated when talking to me in the foyer, but who was perfectly at ease at the microphone and who chattered away for about 10 minutes. The Japanese are at ease with monologue and cannot cope with dialogue.

Came away about 3.30 and went to Tuttles. Bought the *Pelican Atlas of Medieval History*, the one in which empires grow, swell and shrink. Later, wrote home and then wrote *A Rubber Man*, my tenth story since July 15th i.e. in three and a half months. C began typing the 10, and I wonder if I can't have a drive on these and leave poems for the time being, at least until I have settled down about revolutions and spiritual reform, or until I have time to devote to the long poem, i.e. until the Christmas vacation.

6th November. Wrote *O'Hanlan's Dream*, then worked for classes, especially on Sartre. Both Heidegger and Sartre "unveil Being", but Heidegger reveals the wonder, Sartre the nausea; Heidegger is the poet, Sartre the neurotic.

Sartre can certainly be faulted for presenting the mescalin "No" or "Hell" as a general, objective experience. Can he be faulted for having a wrong view of consciousness? For having the wrong mode of perception – "presentational immediacy" rather than "causal efficiency"? I think he can. The pour-soi, he says, is a nothingness because it cannot be touched like a table. It can therefore make itself, which is something of a contradiction, anyway, as a nothingness cannot create. Consciousness is therefore purely a reflector of objects, the "cogito" being a reflection on oneself reflecting. It is passive rather than creative, a man exists in the world and has no reality apart from the world.

I agree with Sartre's conclusions, but not with his premise. To me, man makes himself, but he has a self and his consciousness is "a something". So if I fear heights, I have to struggle against that fear (i.e. myself) when I ascend a high building. In other words, one is, constantly trying to add to or deny, to perfect or undo one's existing self. The evidence for this existing self or "nature" is in *The Silence*. There is a definite, determining thread, although the "self" is trying to make itself, and this is a much more satisfactory view than Sartre's view of Nothing making itself, single atom annihilating the entire universe or no. Making oneself, then, involves a perpetual struggle between the temporary being one is (one's existing self) and one's Shadow (one's future self), and both affect and limit the other.

7th November. More on Sartre. The thing is, his method is wrong. One cannot know oneself by reflecting on one's consciousness, but one can by looking at repetitions within one's experience (e.g. 14 divorces, fear of heights, aggressiveness, inferiority, all of which are unlikely to be caused by freedom). Sartre's rejection of Freud may be right but his rejection of an unconscious is therefore wrong. The self can be deduced from experience. Sartre might object: "Granted, but now your nature is not important – you can choose against your nature; the point is, now, in relation to your nature, you are a nothingness." I might agree, but the point is I still have a self (even if the proof of it is to see it as "being for others" through "someone else's eyes" i.e. my eyes looking back on my experience for repetitions), and life is in tension between the determining forces of my self and my future, unmade possibilities.

What I am advocating is therefore a more limited freedom than Sartre's. One is limited by what one already is (one's own nature), but one can still realise one's possibilities, and there is now a "something" to bring them into being. One is thus both determined and free, and self-knowledge is knowing one's limitations and possibilities. (To Sartre there can be no self-knowledge.)

The failure of Sartre's method is really the failure of Rationalism. Sartre denies the "I"/Self/Unconscious and puts the thinking "I" in the world. There can therefore for him be no inner purpose, with goals along the line towards the terminus, and his self cannot travel along any path of becoming. Only Marxism in the "outer" world. By denying that one's self is always becoming and that one makes one's self within, not only in the world, he has done away with all purpose, and man is a useless passion, as, when viewed in terms of the world, he must be. Sartre, one never finally makes oneself, but one does make (or arrive at) certain stations on the way.

8th November. After an exhausting day at Keio, before which I wrote on S (*Dead Skin over Bone*.) I worked on revolutions and especially the old regimes, using Brinton. What he calls revolutions are movements in the name of the majority against a minority ruling class, so 411BC is dismissed as a Rightest coup doomed to failure. Taking four revolutions (the English, the American, the French, the Russian) he finds a pattern, from the takeover by the extremists to the return of Thermidorian pleasure.

It is a pattern one already knew. One did not know that the old regimes were prosperous societies with bankrupt, inefficient governments trying to levy taxes; nor did one know that these governments all tried to reform government (i.e. that they were very far from being tyrannies), so much so that members of the ruling class actually deserted and joined the poor, a socialist fracture which helped to weaken the ruling class and open it up to revolution. Other features recall present-day England: the desertion of the intellectuals – compare the Angries with the "chorus of loyal praise for the Elizabethan ruling class – and the divided and inept ruling class of the 1950s, e.g. Profumo and the denial of careers for people like myself. (Although a lot of unknowns like Lennon have become known.)

The main question is: is (Harold) Wilson a member of the old ruling class, or is he bringing about a revolution? This is connected with the question: what class would replace him? It would have to be a non-working class, e.g. a new Puritan class, for W is surely giving proletarians a good deal. He is, furthermore, in more of a position to commit the mistake about taxation than any Tory P.M. It looks rather as though a revolution would come from a minority, and would fail like that of 411: for the middle classes are the losers under Wilson. This is, however, not certain, and it is possible that revolution will become more widely discussed.

9th November. A mess-up over Bickley. I told Irie B would like to see over Tokyo University of Education, and Irie's immediate reaction was "Please leave this to me." He raised the whole question at the Tokyo

University of Education conference on Wednesday and as a result Fujii telephoned while I was still at the Prince's, asking if B could have lunch at the Meke Kaikhan, off the campus, on Wednesday 16th from 12.30 to 2.30; after which the sensei would have to go to their conference. As I said to Tuohy: "Can I come to your university?" "Sure, see you in the Meke Kaikhan." I told Enozawa (who rang on Fujii's behalf) that B had not wanted a State visit" and that his prime aim was to see over the campus. I should ring B on Thursday a.m. and find out his wishes.

I could not contact B even on Thursday p.m. (he had been at Waseda during the morning), and at 6.30 Irie rang to say that, "owing to the Dean's resignation over the question as to whether the University should move", Tokyo University of Education would have to postpone the lunch, which was satisfactory so far as I was concerned, though the problem remains: how to get B to Tokyo University of Education on a Wednesday without agreeing to formal lunch with speeches. Trouble, too, over Aikosan...,Fumikosan "translating", saying that the doctor has "ordered" her to return to Okinawa at the end of this month.

10th November. After writing *A Shrine and Rainbow Trout* and *Breath Smelling of Violets*, went to the Bank of Japan, rather weary from insufficient sleep, and had a most interesting session with Fukuchi on the *I Ching*.

Originally the hexagram was arrived at by heating a tortoise shell until it cracked. It is now done through 50 bamboo sticks in a cup. One is put on the table (leaving 49). The rest are divided into two, 25/24. The group of 25 is divided by 8 for the bottom trigram (which is the remainder). The process is repeated for the top trigram. The next time it is divided by 6 for the change, and as the remainder is again only 1, it is the bottom line which is varied, for counting is from the bottom. Other variations are: turning the hexagram upside down and seeing it from the other point of view; making the Yang (—,= light) into Yin (— —,= dark); and taking the middle 4 and expanding to 6; there is one more Fukuchi could not remember.

You go to the fortune-teller with one specific problem, e.g. "Shall I leave Japan", and ask heaven to give an answer through the bamboo sticks. There is no one hexagram for any one person. One has to find a hexagram that fits a problem. Within a hexagram there are normally 6 stages, and these may apply to the problem e.g. war, promotion, etc. There is never an absolute answer, because Yin is always contained in Yang, and so even the Yang hexagram can be reversed. Yang (= light) = heaven (and the positive dragon is a symbol for this); Yin (= dark) = earth.

Fukuchi: "I would like to retire and master the *I Ching*. I want to do it when I retire. You should meditate on the whole book, for all problems are answered." A very pleasantly earned £2.

11th November. A long day dominated by the Tokyo Immigration office. Spent the lunch hour at Tokyo University of Education collecting forms and working on Irie for the President's seal, Irie having said there might be no letter guaranteeing my stay as the Dean has resigned and there is therefore no one to sign the letter. Eventually got off with the wrong address written out in Japanese. By sheer luck I saw and recognised the building under that awful, long railway flyover near the docks. There was no queue, but by bad luck I picked on the novice, as I did in May. I had to fill in "Nan's parents" and then a complete set of forms for her. What a waste of time....It was all hell.

After it I had a terrible nightmare, from which I finally awoke about 6 a.m. I was on a large boat staffed by armed soldiers, and the passengers included most of the "society" here in Tokyo e.g. Tomlin, Adrian and so on. I had been sentenced to death, and for two weeks these acquaintances dismissed the sentence as pure form. On the eve of my execution, however, they all took it seriously and said there was nothing for me to do but to be brave and go before the wall at 6 a.m. the next day. They all wanted to look at me in morbid curiosity. I went for a last walk the evening before, saw land nearby (East Germany) and, not seeing any guards, without hesitation jumped and swam ashore in the night and thus escaped. Except that I had no passport, no money, no identity or visa.

12th November. Is this dream about the hostility of society towards the artist, who is forced to flee civilised life?...The shooting came up later with Tuohy, after I had written *Arabia and a Mortar Shell*. I was supposed to discuss Japan for his *Sunday Telegraph* article. After looking at the Penguin *Ice Saints*, on which he is described as a lecturer, and saying no one remembers newspaper articles (Tuohy: "They do if they're by me"), and hearing that he is getting mixed up with the Rangers and Pattersons for the Waseda play, and listening to a poetry record and *Beyond the Fringe*, we got on to China and Japan. I gave him a hypothesis. He interrupted: "No, we don't want hypotheses. Look there's a power-station in a field" and so on.

We then got onto war-crimes, and Tuohy said: "The thing is, they expected it to be done back to them." And he then said something about it's being quite understandable. I said it wasn't justifiable. T: "That's quite irrelevant." I: "It's not irrelevant to the men who survived the Burma railway." T: "Oh, nonsense. No one gives a damn about them. You just accept that – that sort of thing was bound to happen." Whereupon I blew up. My voice quivering I said they were human beings, just as the 20 million Mao shot were human beings, and that it seemed that Tuohy, the so-called great respector of human beings didn't give a damn whether human beings lived or died, whereas I, the so-called rejector of human beings cared much more. "Caroline, right or wrong?"

There was a fearful quarrel after this, with everyone shouting at once. I remember Tuohy saying: "You can only care for those you know, for people you can see" – i.e. the old nepotistic fallacy; "It's quite understandable that a Japanese should walk past a man bleeding in the gutter, because of the 'on', and your saying he's wrong is of no interest to me – it's a value judgement, it's like a vote" – i.e. the old Halliday fallacy about culture-patterns; and "Social context governs everything – what do you do if a Jew comes to your door and you're a Pole? I'd turn him away and protect my family." I: "He's a human being before he's a Jew." T: "Nonsense" – i.e. the old essence before existence" fallacy. He called me a generalizer, an editorializer, and advised me to go and test my feelings of brotherhood in the Congo or not talk about them. I called him a potential mass-murderer, and said it was extremely dangerous to shrug other people's pain off or talk casually about "20 million people were killed in China so that their children could live without fear of mosquitoes". My point was: "It's not very nice for those who suffer the pain."

The entire conflict was about two different things of course. Tuohy was saying the writer should understand why things are, and I was saying that the man should act in the name of the way things should be, i.e. values. He put his point (with which I of course agree) too extremely, and did not mean what he said. When I left I said to C, "We'll cross over the road and if we see a man bleeding in the gutter we'll say it's of no interest to us and pass him by." Tuohy: "I never said that." I: "As it's in doubt I shan't quote you," and in spirit he is of course right.

14th November. Further points on Tuohy. His quotation of Dostoevsky's description of Siberia and his scorn for its lack of a sense of place. "Whether pain is justifiable or not is a non-question." I: "So Wittgenstein has explained away the suffering on the Burma railway?" Also: "Your disapproval is irrelevant. What good will it do Rhodesia?" Later: "There are two kinds of action. One is borrowing sugar from the neighbour in England, and the other is political – making more sewers." I: "There's a third kind, helping someone who's bleeding, mentally as well as physically." On ruling classes: "I could shoot Lady Rundall."

Tuohy's contradictions: (1) "You must respect people."... (2) "You must become more aware of human pain."... (3) "You must write in a tradition or else it's literature and Hagger" – and later saying I'm influenced by Eliot and should do all I can to find and preserve my own voice. (4) "You must look after your friends" (repeatedly in China).... Tuohy is a mess in some respects. To what extent, though, is he the consequence of his right-wing acceptance of pain? Is he not rather hard and pitiless as a man because he has accepted pain as being inevitable, and therefore says of the men on the Burma railway "Oh, they are unimportant – that sort of thing was bound to happen", or of p-o-ws who were vivisected, "They should have known about hara-kiri"? Can you care if you accept pain and are not "surprised" whenever it occurs, i.e. not appalled. I think caring depends on believing that pain should not happen, and futility too. Betterment comes out of that belief.

15th November. Thinking about Huxley's idea of "transhumanism", i.e. transcending humanity through the social environment rather than through the genes, which cannot transmit acquired characteristics, I thought about progress. My ideal is a world government by a group of elders formed into a council like the U.N. Each government should voluntarily hand over power and there will be no secessions. There would be a "religious" way of life for self-discovery, and all continents would be unified, there would be no hatred, man would devote all his negative emotion to loving his fellow man and discovering the silence.

A dream indeed! But think of the objections. (1) Isn't this the old 19th century idea of progress and doesn't the historical law of rises and falls of empires go against the eternal betterment of the social environment? Buildings and new towns decay, and there isn't the money to renew them and so squalor sets in; i.e. there are periods with healthy social environments and then periods with unhealthy social environments, and man somehow does not transcend himself. (2) Man will never progress to (e.g.) not being cruel: the 20th century A.D. is no less cruel than the 5th century B.C. Or rather, mankind will only transcend itself en masse in this respect if the genes can be controlled, and even if this happens what about (3) *Brave New World* and the joyless future that is promised in such a "bettered social environment"? There will always be rebels – man will always try to act against his own interests and destroy himself – and in such a new world I would become one of them, for I would be bored stiff and feel utterly futile.

These, then are the objections: history, human nature, and the joylessness of science. The first two are practical objections, and if they could be overcome so could no. 3. I must think about this new dream of the World-Lord for perhaps this is Britain's Shadow.

16th November. After writing *People like Masks* (Tuesday) and *Goatbeard in a Calm Sea* (Wednesday), talked about duck-netting with the Prince and reflected on the USE and the merits of a political rather than an economic union and whether Wilson is sincere.

Later I had a dream. Wilson had been killed in Parliament. I saw his body in a bag, I was present while the other conspirator opened the bag and identified it. He had been stabbed about half an hour after I last saw him. Then there was great joy, for the tyrant had been killed. I was appalled. The only other person to be appalled was Wilson's brother, a priest, who lay across the floor space of Wilson's grave and publicly wept. Later I was told a story by a Foreign Office man. His sister had been hanged with another man about six years before. He had died but she had miraculously survived and had been cut down and spirited out of the country by the executioners. I said: "You must be Harry Roberts then," and he said casually, "Yes." I was immensely interested. A murderer in the Foreign Office.

This is another image for the Reflection perhaps, an image I groped towards in *The Conductor*: the assassination of the ego. I kept thinking of

Cromwell, I remember. Does this mean that my revolutionary uncertainties are connected with the Reflection? Even if it doesn't, I think they still might be.

From Sunday November 20th. I have solved C's recurrent dream....*Fluid on the Knee* took me to this: I must be very blind if I can only see the answer to C's problems through art.

17th November. Wrote *Jewels of a Ruling Class* and then went to the Bank of Japan, where I put in five hours. Talked at great length with the Vice-Governor on trade with China, and got the lists for what Japan imports from China and copied them out. They include "oil from the paulownia tree". Worked on the Governor's speech to the Inaugural Meeting of the Asian Development Bank. It is being done in connection with the Gaimusho (Foreign Ministry) and the Ministry of Finance, and there is so much responsibility attached to it, because it expresses the Japanese attitude to Asia for the next 10 years, that I was offered sherry when I had finished.

Also, had my fortune told by Fukuchi. He held the 49 bamboo sticks over his head (one already being laid on the table to signify God) and divided them arbitrarily into 2 (heaven/earth). In my case the 2 processes (see 10th November) worked out at remainder 5 and 0 (=8) and formed hexagram no 46, "Shang". The variation worked out as no 32, "Hang". "Shang" means "earth-wind" (top-bottom) and "great progress and success", "advance to the south being fortunate". There is a strange insistence on ascent ("advancing upwards blindly") and on an empty city – two themes from *The Silence*. "This must be one of the best hexagrams in the *I Ching*." What a pity I do not believe in the Will of Heaven.

No. 23 is winter-spring and if this referred to England at war it would mean that at the end (in the last resort) there is always a Churchill. Line 5 is P.M. (Prime Minister), line 6 is one higher in rank but then not so powerful. No. 14, if applied to the Russio-Japanese war of 1904, would therefore be a signal to the P.M. to be passive and to concentrate the will of the whole nation. The similarity with Ikebana: heaven (left) – human being (the centre stick) – earth (right).

18th November. After three lectures at Tokyo University of Education and a lot of chores and letters, went to *Dr. Zhivago*, in spite of Tuohy's recommendation that we shouldn't, and found it very moving....His description of Bolt as a complete "phoney". He has certainly gone commercial, Bolt, but I don't think he is completely phoney.

What struck me was the way human beings were caught in the system and separated by soldiers. Perhaps no revolution can justify this; neither Strelnikov nor the beady-eyed People's Representative who took over the Zhivagos' home and who said, after some boys had been shot in the poppied corn, "It doesn't matter" – neither of these could justify the interference with the personal, and both had significantly left wives and children. Of course, the bourgeois case was put at its strongest. Lara and Zhivago did not want to separate, and autumn leaves and daffodils and Siberian frost, conventional enough images, also seem much fresher in technicolour, so that a poet's wonder does seem a more natural thing than trying to reorganise society.

Nonetheless, perhaps one is compelled to the conclusion that although a Revolution may be justifiable from the point of view of the efficiency of the whole, it is not justifiable if blood is shed and the quality of living is reduced, and the very fact that it never lasts more than twenty years makes its exponents save children. The best political position is in the Centre — I come back to this again and again.

From the Centre one can embrace both Right and Left, without favouring rule by the workers or the peers. As C said, however, the trouble is, no Centre has a dynamic policy.

21st November. At Tokyo University of Education. On what Huxley (J), Wells, Teilhard, Shaw, Bergson and Hulme have in common. Ideally, I believe in some notion of progress in consciousness/self in (i) myself and (ii) the human race, which will, I hope, be kinder and more civilised in future (="hominisation") and which will also affirm life more. Scientifically, I cannot accept the Life Force or Christogenesis, but this does not matter: they are good metaphors and to live/experience these ideas is the important thing.

I am, therefore, scientifically neither a mechanist nor a vitalist – I am in the centre, and whether or not there is an absolute difference between the animal and the human does not concern me. It is the living, vital consciousness I am interested in, the moments of saying Yes. As regards the application of this ideal to Western civilisation or the world, I am, reluctantly, not so optimistic (cf November 15th). History is against "transhumanism" or "hominisation" – civilisations rise and fall, and if man is to develop through the environment, there must be an environment that is constant and which preserves change. On the other hand, never before has man been in a position to control his own development (e.g. control the genes) and it may be that all history is not a precedent.

Have I then changed my attitude to progress since December 19th 1965? I wrote then: "I do not deny progress, but neither do I make a creed of it," and I was thinking of biological and material and humanitarian progress, rather than spiritual progress. Well perhaps I have inclined a little more towards progess in the last year, but I must not become positively optimistic – that would be absurd – I must only be negatively in favour of progress, i.e. see it in terms of progress away from despair. Yet even in negative terms, there must be something to progress towards.

23rd November. Since Saturday have written *A Crown of Thorns*, *Fluid on the Knee*, *A Light in the Canteen* and *A Knuckleduster Mind*, though I forget the exact order.

Accordingly, today I felt I could take a rest from the stories and return to poems. Prince Hitachi has invited me to his birthday party on Monday, and I thought I might write a poem *To His Imperial Highness on His Birthday*. However, I could not think of a suitable subject until in the end I hit on the idea of criticising the Prince, while seeming to praise him, by contrasting the unimportance of his birthday with the plight of less fortunate people in Asia. This is, after all, the reality, and what I feel. Out of this grew, in this one day (which was a national holiday) the very rough draft of a poem about Japan; the theme being that Japan has risen from the ashes of the war and is poised for economic empire through the Asian Development Bank, even though, to quote the Vice-Governor, "Japanese do not want to emigrate – perhaps we have lost our vitality to develop another country," and that Japan should work selflessly for a united Asia, leading ultimately to world government, and that the Prince should do all he can to help unite the opposites in Asia.

After I finished the draft I thought how little the Prince could do, and got discouraged. Would it not be better if I celebrated the Prince as a symbol of the new Asian spirit, e.g. by dwelling on his feeling for the Asians and so on? In any event, I shan't have the poem ready by Monday, as I had hoped, and if I do write it, I should present it to him later.

Otherwise it was a bad day, Aikosan breaking a lamp and N's mobile and the milk jug, and Ben (the dog) being sick, the cat getting a cut leg and so on.

24th November. Wrote *Blue Movies and Skim Milk* and then went to the Bank of Japan and had five hours of speeches for Sasaki's visit to Colombo for the SEANZA conference and for the Asian Development Bank.

I saw Sasaki for half an hour, to wish him a good flight before he went off to the Emperor's reception. He had been to the Asian Development Bank Inaugural Meeting and his opinion was that Japan had dominated too much. Fukuda, the Finance Minister, was originally elected Japanese Governor and when he was elected Chairman, Usami took over as Governor. Fukuda's English is not good, and he could not trust himself to make spontaneous arrangements at the Inaugural Meeting. Everything had, therefore, to be prepared in advance, in committee, and consequently proposals were rushed through at the ADB Inaugural Meeting, the other countries not getting a look-in. The U.S. delegate significantly had nothing to say and "did a Johnson", i.e. played himself down and sat on the edge as Johnson did at the Manila Conference.

Otherwise the Vice-Governor did feel the unity in the Conference Room. The President of the ADB is one of his best friends, Takashi Watanabe, and so I shall be able to "hear the low-down" on the ADB next year. When I told this to B, using those words and teasing him with a solemn face, his eyes shifted down and he looked over the rims of his glasses and said "Oh?"...His opinion on the ADB was that Japan will succeed economically where she failed militarily. Later did the 15 page economic report for SEANZA in one hour, after which I felt constipated with turgid language.

25th November. Saturday-Monday wrote *Dirt in a Bleeding Toe*, *Fils Under the Palms* and *Stool in a Bare Bar*. On Friday, Narita's "insensitivity" which is probably deliberate: showing me a photo of the party for Fukuhara to which I was not asked and which cost 2,000 yen. Strangely, B was very sensitive about it, and tried to hide it under some other photos of the baseball match, but Narita fished it out.

On Saturday afternoon I took C to Kitazawas and bought a historical atlas, and dreamt of the future of Europe, looking at the changes over the past few hundred years and trying to predict the next change.

I have meant to record a remark about A. When I showed Halliday my China articles, he pored over them and I couldn't get him out of them. When I showed A he barely looked at them.

26th November. On (Colin) Wilson. Whitehead offers three modes of experience: presentational immediacy, causal efficiency and conceptual analysis. This last is of little interest to me in so far as it is offered as a help to meaning. If a Rationalist comes to me and says "God exists, I have proved it mathematically, and the universe is a Unity," this is of little interest to me unless I can experience it. The moment when I feel and experience "Yes" as the result of perception is what I trust.

"Causal efficacy" is offered as a kind of meaning-centre in the consciousness of each of us: a centre which unconsciously selects meanings and which could one day perhaps, through evolution, become conscious, and through which we could perceive the essential Unity of the universe. Phenomenology uncovers this centre, or rather, its unconscious workings. The Unity of the universe is what it perceives, the moment of "Yes". This, experiencing through this meaning-centre and grasping the Unity of the universe – this is the solution to the Outsider's problem. He must stop being passive and locate his meaning-centre and say Yes to the Unity of the universe.

In so far as selection can become conscious and can be transmitted through society rather than the genes ("transhumanism"), meaning can evolve, and the Outsider is the man who evolves meaning, he is thus an evolutionary spearhead, and "the most powerful evidence of the reality of a new phase of evolution."

27th November. This is a remarkable thesis, and one that deserves much more attention than it has received. But to what extent, practically, does "evolutionary intentionality" solve the Outsider's problems? I am prepared to acknowledge that there is a grasping in my consciousness at times – I go along with the Maltese cross and the 4-petalled flower. But what evidence is there (1) that this grasping could one day become conscious, beyond a lot of talk about "drift becoming drive" and so on and (2) that this grasping is connected with the moments of illumination that I value highly – Roquentin listening to the negress, Meursault being happy, Krebs's moments feeling cool and clear inside, Lawrence's clear dawn, Nijinsky's "I am God", Nietzsche's "six thousand feet", etc.?

Furthermore, phenomenology uncovers the grasping – O.K., once I have uncovered it, what then? I have no further use for it, and here I sit in my window at Tokyo University of Education grasping the scene in front of me as a whole from trees to tiled houses. What do I feel? More aware, yes, and more observant, but the Unity of Everything? No, because unity (1) cannot be turned on by will, in spite of Wilson's constant reference to the "volume knob of consciousness" and (2) cannot be experienced through the conscious mind – as I wrote on October 25th, it has to come from underneath, through contemplation. I don't want to be dogmatic about this – I have often felt joy by looking nakedly and as sharply as my poor eyes will allow, but I have also felt joy by losing myself by the forest ponds or the Worcester lake, and it is certainly not true that blazing joy and unity come automatically from reaching out and grasping, though they do help.

28th November. After one class at Tokyo University of Education and work for tomorrow, went to the Hitachis to wish the Prince a very happy birthday. I had a few swigs of whisky in the taxi and was quite pleasantly drunk by the time my driver drove inside the palace walls, nearly peeing with fright.

The reception was in the room where C and I normally have dinner and a screen hid it from the hall. The Prince came to meet me, and we shook hands for the benefit of all those who looked. Then I walked right the way down to the birthday cake which said "Happy Birthday Prince Masahito" and took stock of some 50 Japanese who were drinking saké or beer. I spoke to Arai and then Narita, the ex-Ambassador, whom the Prince introduced, and then, being well plied with drink, to the Princess, who wasn't drinking. "You should drink" I said, and she blushed slightly and carried on talking. Later I said the same to the Prince and he obediently went off and got a glass. I spoke to the Princess's teacher and to the Prince's teacher when he was 9 and to Harada, the Grand Master of Ceremonies, and to Professor Arita of Todai Zoological Department and in the end wound up with a very drunk Kuroda hanging on my right arm, just after belting His Highness on the Imperial back.

Then another drunk began applauding, i.e. clapping for silence, and we all folded our hands in front of us and began singing the Japanese National Anthem, to his conducting, while the Prince stood in the centre of the room, with his hands by his side and his eyes shifting from left to right as I had always imagined Bonnie Prince Charlie during his exile. The anthem sounded very much like Zen or Gagaku, and when I told Harada so shortly after, he threw back his head and laughed from the belly, though he shut up later when I asked him about the Gagaku tadpoles and he didn't know. I left feeling elated. I was an utter fraud, and I had got away with it in the most respectable society imaginable.

29th November. Spent my first class at Keio on Dostoevsky's dialectic. Dostoevsky is on the side of the Underground Man's will (1864), against Chernyshevsky's reason, but later in *Crime and Punishment* (1864-6) Dostoevsky is neutral, between will and virtue and finally, perhaps, coming down on the side of virtue in the final dream of the disease of will and reason and Raskolnikov's conversion to Christianity; this only after the dialectic of Svidrigailov and Sonia has been fully worked out.

In a sense Dostoevsky created himself in *Crime and Punishment* – he found out which side he was really on. There is no doubt in *The Idiot* (1867-9), and in *The Devils* (1869-71) Dostoevsky is Shatov, believing in Christ but not God, and will in the composite personality of Stavrogin (spirit) and Verhovensky (act) is as doomed to destruction as is Kirilov, the image of the self-destructive nature of will.

In *The Brothers Karamazov* (1878-80) the dialectic is again between will and virtue, self-will and love, but both are within Ivan, just as both were within Raskolnikov: his essay on the Church and his "everything is permitted". It is these two parts of Ivan that form the subject of the novel: the crime and Ivan's guilt and responsibility – for his confession is in accordance with Zossima's "all are responsible for all". *The Grand Inquisitor* is about two kinds of virtue – socialist and Christian virtue – and the confession at the trial is, to Dostoevsky, the victory of Christ, the vindication of Zossima. Dostoevsky reached a conclusion, but to what extent is the triumph of virtue over will and reason relevant to us today, in an age when science has smashed religion? To a man concerned with suffering, it must be very relevant, and perhaps virtue in terms of Christ must be redefined as feelings, as in the case of Brady.

30th November. Yesterday, the terrible episode as regards Aikosan, which I wrote up as *A Nervous Breakdown*. It is an incredibly complex situation. The main point is that in May she agreed to stay another one and a half to two years, and she was paid three months' salary for doing nothing on that understanding. On November 9th we were informed that she was going back to Okinawa because she was physically ill. We knew this was a lie, and in exposing the truth, brought about a nervous breakdown. Had we been told, by Fumikosan or Fujikosan, that she had been having fantasies involving knives, we would of course have insisted on her going that very day, November 9th. If necessary, I would have paid her a month's salary to go. I had no idea we had a potential maniac in charge of Nan.

1st December. Finished *A Nervous Breakdown*, and then went to the Bank of Japan. Worried again about history and two views: history in terms of decades and history in terms of centuries. I incline, irrationally, to the second view, and my argument is: there have been past empires and when they decline there are certain "moral" symptoms which lead on to foreign conquest.

Of course there are objections in relation to Britain: (1) Britain did not depend on her empire as much as Rome, and the empire meant little to more than 10% of the population, in spite of the Boer war. (2) We should be glad we have managed to give our empire away, for it made us poor, not rich, and we are now better off than we were after the war (e.g. fuel crises). (3) A nation should think of its present generation and its children – who cares what happens even 100 or more years from now? (4) Britain will rise again, just as France has risen again, and look how much both won and lost from 1066 onwards through Henry I and II, Edward III and Henry V and VI, i.e. the Hundred Years' War. (5) The French had an Empire and they're up now – history goes in waves of up and down (cf China), not in Empire-organisms.

Of course, all these arguments are logical and certainly there will always be a territory "England" just as Rome re-emerged in 20th century Fascist Italy. But, thinking only of the next two generations, the traditional symptoms have begun to appear and it may be we are heading for foreign conquest like Israel under the Chaldeans. (Though the parallel is far from exact.) Who will the conqueror be? Hitler was a new Saxon, and was repelled. I wonder, will it not be the Danes, our traditional enemy, or the French? This is very fanciful, but: the symptoms have appeared.

2nd December. Taught *Epitaph for George Dillon* at Tokyo University of Education and in particular the long dialogue between George and Ruth. Osborne's use of words is clearly akin to that of Dylan Thomas: he breeds words out of other words, just as Thomas breeds images. So a second meaning will be enough to send Osborne off, and "bride and groom" will suggest "orgy" which will suggest "Druid" which will suggest "monument". That is one reason why I like Osborne so much. The other reason is his closeness to Eliot's vision. George's attack on the cocktail cabinet and on Josie's misapplication of mascara – both these are pure Eliot: the unreality of our modern commercial society, the way society makes us unreal unless we make an effort and strive to be alive. George's ideal is "having a mind and feelings that are all fingertips" and "the sound of the very wit of being alive". (Compare Jimmy's "burning virility of mind and body" and Archie's "dead behind the eyes".) George sees people spiritually, i.e. in terms of the quality of their life, whereas Ruth sees people economically i.e. in terms of their bodies. Which view is right? Clearly, both are right, and ideally one has both views. One wants to eliminate the human evils, and one wants people to live real lives.

Adrian on R. "He definitely has a chip on his shoulder." After the roulette party he said of the new language students, "A bit odd aren't they

– they've got accents," and A realised he had an accent for the first time. R's need to convert people into servants. "Adrian will now explain the rules" (to 50 people) and "Adrian will pay the money." The need to humiliate.

3rd December. Wrote *Yawns under a Sepulchral Sky* and then went to the Council to do the Scholarship interviews. Baker had said they would be from 2-5.30. In fact the time was 2.30 and they went on until 6. For the four hours I was paid (in advance) ¥3,000. A good afternoon's work by English standards, but, taking into account my taxi fares (¥400), only one quarter of what I earn for the equivalent time at MITI: ¥10,000 + ¥800 for taxis.

Bickley told us what to do in Tomlin's room after Suzukisan had buzzed around sexily and Taylor had said to me and Hill, "I shall be tempted to rape her this afternoon. Do you think the lavatory would be a good place?" The first two interviewees had to sit before Hill, Baker and Bickley, who conducted the interview, going redder and redder in the neck (for he is a red-brown man, like a squirrel, with a very ruddy complexion); while Taylor, Collcutt (surly as ever) and Guest (a barbarian in suede jacket and blue jeans and long hair) all sat along the back. After a while we repaired to our individual rooms and our candidates.

My most interesting candidate was a 35 year old judge, a sad-eyed man with the power to sentence to death. Do you feel for the man you sentence? I asked. Yes, he did. Usually he felt the criminal was not responsible: he was the victim of his background and upbringing. I also had a student of religion from Kyoto, and there was some doubt as to whether she is still a Christian. "I began John's Gospel because of my faith, but now I study and not because of my faith." There was also a budding secondary school teacher from Okayama who keeps a diary every day and who wants to write a book about England. Otherwise it was rather a case of *Yawns*.

4th December. Last night Adrian came and a lot of the conversation was on the way the British work together. Everything (at the British Embassy) is Christian names and no consciousness of age, and there is no overt demonstration of superiority, there is no equivalent of the bow. The assumption is that everyone is trying to do a job together, that outside the office everyone is equal and that certain limits have to be erected for the sake of the job. So it's "Adrian, would you mind doing such and such," and not "Do this." Reprimands are categorical, however: "That was careless, wasn't it," Dick Ellingworth says – the man who was miserable at his authority at the Emery's party – and A's reaction is to feel irritated that he should be so petty, though later, when reflecting on it coolly, he sees that the reprimand was justified.

Along with this hesitant conditional in requests goes the affability of a Baker or the unapproachable jokiness of a Hill, affability's more nervous brother. There must be no mention of the seriousness of the situation, there must be light-heartedness (Drake's bowls) and the chatter must not be directed personally, it must be rather detached; and addressed to the room in general, not any one in particular. So the barriers are underneath the situation and implied, and no one goes too far and oversteps them. One recognises them by "agreeing" to perform a request, and not refusing to comply with an order. There is a classless lack of jealousy in the Embassy, according to A, and the notion of a team, and the only drawback is doubt about the worth of many of the memoranda.

5th December. Did not go to Tokyo University of Education because of a sore throat. Stayed at home and wrote *Music in Running Water*, and was interrupted by a recommendation for Enozawa and a telephone call from Munekata who has, amazingly, got to the last 30 of the British Council Scholarships through G's inefficiency.

Went to the Prince in spite of my rough throat – it was pay day and I needed the money – and in the course of asking him what he had done, learnt "I went to the Korakuen Ice Rink. And Prince Mikasa did it." "Did it?" I echoed, wondering if I dared ask "in his pants?" "On the ice," Hitachi agreed, beaming proudly. "In the orchestra. To *The Sound of Music*." "I see," was all I could manage. I was bursting to laugh and did not dare trust myself to speak. What he evidently meant was that Mikasa conducted the orchestra.

I have not recorded a dream I had on Sunday morning, a dream possibly sparked off by my recounting the story of Angus Ward, which I wrote up today (Tuesday) as *A Crag and Bursting Stars*. I was high up in the mountains, and I can still remember their beauty in the night and their veined smoke. Adrian had visited C and me and I left the hut with him and we lay down in the cold to talk before he went down to the bottom and home. Suddenly he gripped me and watched over my shoulder. Someone was approaching. I could not see, but he could. I followed his eyes and could tell that it was coming nearer. Suddenly it was on top of us, and I turned as he flinched and yelled and ducked, and it was a black shadow of a person. I woke up instantly. I was wide awake and afraid. What was this shadow? Was it something I dread in connection with my fame – the rarefied air? Was it my past self I want to forget? And which Adrian has not forgotten?

7th December. I feel I am losing touch with my inner life. This feeling may be due to the minor bout of "flu" (rough throat, headache, aching limbs) which I have had since Monday and which kept me away from Keio yesterday; though it did not prevent me from writing *A Crag and Bursting Stars*. Nonetheless, I think I am right. Witness my preoccupation with "things in the world": revolutions, theories of history, Asia, world-unity, Britain and Mao, not to mention the extrovert nature of my stories, which are about other people.

Perhaps *The Silence* is a thing you can only write once – in creating yourself you become your progress to your Shadow and therefore emerge from the intense introspection and see the world as it is and live it. Perhaps, too, *The Silence* is among the best things I will ever write, just as (according to *The Observer* last Sunday) Auden's early poems are his best, and not his later ones. Because work written out of stress, tension and strain is better than work written out of "adjustment" and calm. (Alvarez's theory.)

Anyhow, I feel my personality is emerging from my withdrawn nature, and I am living more objectively, less subjectively. What should I do? Should I do anything? I think as long as I am writing stories about other people, this trend will continue: action at the expense of contemplation. I live more deeply in poetry than I do in prose. In prose I am perceptive, in poetry I am all-intuitive. Perhaps I shall finish my stories and then plunge back into meditation poetry and emerge again to write an essay on the need for spiritual reform and/or a novel.

On her way home from collecting Nan C saw a crowd on the bridge we always cross – the bridge before Edogawa bashi. She thought it was a suicide, so I went down to have a look and took Nan. A dredger had pushed up a huge mound of silt just below the bridge, and some half dozen dredgermen and a policeman stood on this mound, and they seemed to be pulling loose ropes from the water.

I did not notice the corpse at first. It was under a limp piece of bamboo and wattle matting, half in the water, half out. The current lifted the matting and revealed the ankles and I thought the corpse was bare-legged and white. Later they lifted the matting to photograph the face. I could not see the face, for it was back, but I saw the trousers, which had moved up to the knee, and the limp hands. After that there was quite a wait and I took Nan home (she had not of course seen the body) and returned.

Then the Inspector of Police arrived, with a lot of yellow braid round his blue cap. He stood alone on the bridge and shouted orders. The dredgermen then brought forward a plank-stretcher with handles, which they roped up. They then lifted the matting and lifted the raincoated corpse, which seemed rather stiff, on to the board. They put the matting over the corpse, and tied it up into a parcel so that it looked like a mummy. This with a red clothes line thrown irreverently by a man on the roadside wall and caught only a foot above the dead woman's face.

They then put the board on a small boat and two men pulled the boat across to the wall by holding the cross-wire. The stretcher was hoisted up the wall by men on top, and when the feet came level with my face (for I was by that wall now) I saw they were in worker's "tabe": dirty, white and canal-wet canvas socks with a divided toe. Was it a suicide or a murder, this death of a working man?

Later. It was in fact an old woman who jumped in on Tuesday night because her daughter-in-law had mistreated her and she was also out of work.

8th December. Finished *Dust and a Walled-In Queen* and looked back over the first 25 stories and realised that a pattern is emerging, a pattern that is both social and moral.

Went to the Bank of Japan and was confronted with five hours' speech-writing for the Governor's visit to Manila, which begins on December 17th. He is going to attend the opening ceremony of the Asian Development Bank on December 19th, and I had to write a punchy speech full of feeling: "...a concrete proof of the determination of the peoples of Asia to build a better future of themselves and for themselves. As such, the Bank is the first pan-Asian Parliament." The conception of the Bank as Parliament I decided on after making a list of all the images that could apply to the Bank, and perhaps I can use it in the poem *On His Imperial Highness's Birthday*.

I also had to correct a speech for the dinner Marcos is giving that evening. It was an atrocious speech, all about Japanese relationships with the Philippines, and nothing about Asia, and the impression could only be that Manila and Tokyo have cornered the ADB. So I told the Bank of Japan the speech was bad-mannered and diplomatically disastrous and as a result was given a completely free hand to rewrite the speech as I thought fit, cutting out various pleas for closer Philippine-Japanese trade ties and "I should like to thank you, Mr President, for the conveniences you have given the ADB". (When I asked "Has President Marcos coughed up any lavatories?" Ichiki looked shocked.) In the course of doing these speeches, and the statement at the airport (for Usami is representing the Japanese Government) I learnt that Japan intends to give the ADB more financial assistance.

9th December. Went to Tokyo University of Education and had to finish my 3rd lecture early because I ached and felt fluey. Was then bombarded by questions and people and ended up leaving later than usual. Had no lunch because of Bickley's telephone call to C. Haycraft and (Colonel) Hall intend to open a language centre in Tokyo and are looking for a Director. I have been short-listed. Would I be interested in staying in Tokyo after 1968? I said No, but telephoned Bickley and said I was better and that I could, after all, go to his buffet supper that evening. (C could not go because we have no maid.)

I went to Green Fantasia, Apt. 605 and met H and H outside 505. In the course of the evening talked first with Hall, about Japanese psychology, and then Haycraft about the same sort of thing and my desire to live in England for a bit. This was broken up by the dinner. Afterwards, talked to Bickley. Hannah on Baker's love of young women. Her production of *Everyman* with Tomlin as "confession messenger" and Tuohy as God. Left after arranging to see H and H in 5 months' time when they are here again.

10th December. Tuohy came with his first *Sunday Telegraph* article, a "rather general" affair, to quote his own words. Ironically enough, Tuohy's language tends to be more abstract than mine these days, (e.g. "thrumming") and he has changed his mind about Japanese war-crimes, which are now "unforgiveable" (see 12th-14th November). We talked about the future of

Japan and I said the economic vitality and strict manners will all break down, which will be a bad thing for the country and a good thing for individual Japanese. T: "But more people will jump in the Edogawa because there will be no manners to keep the daughter-in-laws in check." He: "I think the best thing that can happen to Japan is for Japanese to go abroad and to want to come back, because all the honorific stuff doesn't apply so much."

After he'd gone the post brought the Worcester College report 1964-6, and news that Jim Lowe and "Doughy" Rowe (the Worcester right-back) were both killed in separate car-crashes in 1964, along with white-haired Pickering who "died". Pickering I did not know very well – I can only just put a face to him – but I can remember one coffee session in Holdsworth's room when both Lowe and Rowe were present, and Collick (who came here in 1964), and could I have foreseen then that two out of the 7 would have met in Tokyo and another two would be dead by 1966?

The same feeling of progressing towards a horror has been with me since the *Iraklion* sank in the Aegean, after putting out from Channae, 230 being drowned. Could I have foreseen when I travelled to Crete on the *Iraklion* in 1958 that the rail I touched and the boards stained with vomit would be at the bottom of the sea in 1966?

11th December. On Saturday I wrote *Lumps under Snow*, on Sunday nothing as I tried to reduce the notes I have taken for *The Cynic* to some order. I spent the evening writing Christmas cards and thinking about the Husserl-Whitehead synthesis (see 27th November). Husserl advocates grasping, Whitehead unity through organism, and the synthesis definitely does suggest that it is possible "to grasp unity", a conclusion with which I emphatically disagree. The deeper self, the unconscious, annihilates all that's made to a screen image of unity; the process is not extrovert or aggressive.

I am not at all happy about (Colin) Wilson's idea of evolution, either: justifying effort in terms of the race. One must evolve towards one's Shadow in one's own life, and one may (by transhumanism) bring in the Superman in the course of it, but evolution itself is not a goal or an impetus if you don't believe in Christogenesis and as he says (p153): "The 'sense of oneness with the universe'... does not make for evolution." Who cares about evolution, and why should the outsider place greater emphasis on leading forward the human race than on feeling unity? If "the grasping" cannot apprehend unity, then the only evolutionary change will be greater observation, and who cares whether the Outsider leads the human race on to greater observation? In other words Wilson's solution "evolutionary intentionality" is no solution at all – it is all "ifs" and "possiblys" based on schematic logic – and in the course of arriving at it he has changed sides from Christ to the Grand Inquisitor, from religion to science, from pessimism to optimism.

12th December. After Tokyo University of Education went to the Prince and in the course of the history survey of England and France, raised the issue of insanity, he supposedly having inherited his grandfather's insanity. (His grandfather is supposed to have taken a speech from the chamberlains, rolled it up, and used it as a telescope.) Charles VI was insane, and Henry V was largely able to win at Agincourt (1425) on account of this, I said. The final wrong was that Henry V married Charles VI's daughter, and that his son, Henry VI was insane (i.e. the insanity moved from France to England) as a result of which Charles VII, Henry VI's uncle, was able to defeat Henry VI after they were both crowned King of France. When I had said this there was an embarrassed silence and I knew the Prince had taken the point. The Japanese are very sensitive towards themselves, but not towards others.

13th December. Spent a dismal morning trying to decide whether Hogan would make a play. The man obsesses me, I lose all sense of proportion when I contemplate him. I have already mentally written a novel about him and rejected it, and I was right to reject the play, I think. A play should be a slap across the face – a challenge to one's values. And the play I write should be a revolutionary play, an attack on the unreality of British society and a plea for the inner self which is stifled in the materialism of pop-music and machines. Perhaps it should be called *The Nightmare of*—, and perhaps the rise and fall of the British Empire should come into it, and there should be a "plot" which takes the hero throughout British society. Cf Langland. There must therefore be scenes from a church, and a cocktail party and so on. In fact, a dramatised, more modern version of *The Silence*; a journey through a decayed society, in quest of oneself, and the illusions which detain one.

The hero must be on a course of action; what course? Clearly a search for his own identity, a full-time search. It might be best, therefore, to make the quest ambivalent and suggest that X is adrift (cf Freeman), i.e. show him statically bound in situations until he pulls himself out and (e.g.) goes of his own choice into a monastery or sleeps in a doss-house. The beginning of the quest should be a glimpse of horror and freedom which results in his chucking a respectable career and coming to know humanity in parks, etc., until he wins his sense of progress and vision as an exile from society. The end of the quest should be the creation of a revolutionary or spiritual reformer, and after that a question mark. All this after singing "Happy Birthday" to Nan.

The point of the play must be the darkness and the loneliness and the "free choice" and the pursuit of the self, and perhaps I could show the inner being he projects? I think F should be of "the ruling class" and should end up as a revolutionary in the name of the real. So his "awakening" should take place in a ruling class situation and should be the notion of responsibility and suffering and death (=No). Having left "bourgeois" society he should emerge from his sense of suffering to a visionary's vision. In fact, the play should trace his progress from the vision of the rejector sleeping in the graveyard and meeting —, to the vision of the acceptor accepting life and revelling in modern society. The chorus of machines.

14th December. After a long morning on *The Monument*, went to the Prince and had a long battle with him. On greeting him I said, as usual, "Good afternoon, Your Highness." He said "Good evening, Mr Hagger." This was at 3.30. I had already had to stand around in the cold, waiting for a taxi that would stop, because he was sending "my" car to an Ambassador, and the palace stank of dinner from hallway to skylight, and I was in no mood to be messed around or pointedly contradicted like that. So when we had sat down I had a review of manners and told him that "afternoon" was from noon until teatime, and that evening was from knocking off time until bedtime. He: "What about 'Good night'?" I: "Literally it means 'I am going to sleep' or 'I am going to bed', although in its second meaning it is OK for Ambassadors."

After this we read some Betjeman and he was deliberately rather stupid about Dr. Ramsden's speciality, saying it was "The *Times* obituary" instead of "silk worms", and this rebelliousness became open defiance when, right at the end of the class, he refused to drink his tea and would not let me go, and just sat on with his poetry book open. So I said good-bye, in effect, and bolted for the door, and got away without putting in the usual unpaid 20 mins. About 9.30 though he rang up and, humming and hahing, asked me if I'd got the *Times* of December 13th, which contains Emery's attack on Japan: black mist, Sato unpopular, no democracy, complacency and future decline in shipping and so on. This was a most unusual interference in politics, and was probably prompted by Ambassador Narita. I rang Emery ("What a splendid response") and rang the Prince back after ten to tell him I'd bring the *Times* on Monday, and judging by the giggling I caught him in bed.

15th December. Spent the morning on *The Monument* and, while C typed Tuohy's second article on Japan (like Emery's an indictment), did some more speech-writing at the Bank of Japan and taped four speeches for Usami to rehearse. Two letters from mother: R has got his partnership in a firm called Hamlin, Grammar & Hamlin, and begins on February 1st; when he handed in his notice to Wilde, Sopte & Co., they offered him a partnership if he would stay. On Aikosan: did I remember "Marty the Swiss girl who threw herself in the Thames after she left us..., St. Thomas's hospital having to cope"? I take it she did not die?

16th December. Finished at the Tokyo University of Education. In the afternoon had Toyama. He stayed from 4 to 8.30 and first of all we discussed books for next year: Toynbee with the graduates; history from 1500; Stannard Allen; *Luther* or *Inadmissible Evidence*; and L. G.

Alexander's excellent book *Essay and Letter Writing*. He: "You are very popular with the students. Normally a foreign teacher is not respected – not today, when there are so many foreign teachers in Japan. You are an exception." No mention of the staff, I having refused to attend the staff party on December 26th (1) because it was Boxing Day, (2) because of the rudeness at the last Tokyo University of Education party (see 25th May). Later we got on to Hitachi and his telephone call on Wednesday.

As regards the *Times* article, Toyama thought Hitachi might have been put up to it by a right-wing group, or else the Household might be worried because if the JSP gets in their allowances will be cut.

17th December. Wrote on *Monument to a Phoney* and went out about 2 to collect my salary (and return Toyama's umbrella, Kimbara embarrassingly being in the staffroom), buy C's Christmas present from the American Pharmacy, and place an order for next year's books with Sanseido.

When I got back Tuohy came to collect C's typing, and he stayed for a drink. He was on pills and therefore aggressive, and I got off on the wrong foot by showing him Emery's article, which made him flush and which he debunked. ("There are too many figures"). This led to a conversation on Japan, in the course of which he said "Your standard here is lower middle class isn't it?" I: "In terms of space, Yes, but not in terms of food."

He then, somehow, got on to Tomlin (while I was getting a beer from the fridge), and told us how his manuscript has been stolen. It represents 10 years' work and the Ambassador has given him a month off to put down what he can remember. He: "I think it was probably the man who's been caught stealing books from the Council library and flogging them to China." I: "No, it's more probably a man with a grudge – a Council scholarship candidate – or a sexual rival or a case of blackmail."...

He was bleak. He envied our room, and so said it was middle class. He envied our Christmas tree and so said "Christmas is a depressing time – I don't want to be like Peter Warlock. He committed suicide on Christmas Day." He left, cold, with no warmth in him at all, and all Hyde, for a "party" (he was in a corduroy jacket) and his "payment" to C was passed-on Suntory.

18th December. Finished *Monument to a Phoney* and out of the left-over bits wrote *Love like Cenopods* which (predictably) C did not like. During the afternoon walked up to the church and was struck by images. First in the twilit tabernacle-tent there was a choir-rehearsal and the conductor's arms made great God-like shadows on the concrete drapes, while the choir's voices beneath the organ-pipes echoed. Then Mary, in blue and white, in the artificial grotto-Lourdes, near the crucifix pulpit. "Oh Mary, you are free from original sin."

19th December. An interrupted day. Nan woke up with earache and, having said she was OK and having gone to school, came home in tears and had to be taken to Morton as an emergency; I being afraid of mastoids, which are in the family. Of course it was only a spot, but the visit stopped her crying and it took up the morning. After that, went to Hitachi's and read the *Times*. His misgivings about Vietnam and democracy, his reluctance to give an opinion and his eventual admission: "This is fair but I feel a little unhappy" and "Some members of Sato's faction feel that this has been used as a weapon against them by Fujiyama's faction." Where does criticism end and insult begin? In the case of a decayed nation it doesn't, in the case of a dynamic nation this distinction is often childish.

"I hope Anglo-Japanese relations will not be affected," Hitachi said significantly and ominously, and, taking this as the burden of the afternoon, I rang Emery and distinguished the justice of what he had said from the impact and proposed a tongue-in-cheek statement disassociating the *Times* from the *Asahi Shimbun* (where the Sato faction had read a one-sided version of the black fog) and a declaration of independence in relation to the politics of foreign countries. Emery: "London couldn't possibly agree to such a proposal. Nonetheless this is very interesting and I'll get on to my friends in the Embassy."

Whereupon I rang P: "Oh how nice to hear from you. No, I'm not having dinner – the girls are here and we're leading a rather Bohemian existence. They arrived yesterday. As a matter of fact I was going to ring you. We're having an At home on December 26th, and if you can come...." After I'd told him about H he mentioned China. "London are very interested in you, you know...." And in the background the girls squealed.

20th December. Revised *Monument to a Phoney* and *A Nervous Breakdown*, and then wrote *A Sun Red and Orange and Neck out to Sea*. In the afternoon C went shopping and, after a walk in a high wind, (I) switched from stories (so far 38) to poems and the question of politics or spirit. The first problem is to show British society as it is, i.e. declining sea power and trade, loss of empire and loss of confidence of the ruling class, and its decadence and ineptness in terms of its determination to rule, the government's near-bankruptcy and the prosperous, materialistic society which forms its background.

The thing is, living is unreal – that is my criterion – and something must be done, either by reforming society politically (Pt 2) or by reforming the self spiritually (Pt 3). Political revolution is not the answer to the unreality – revolutions always revert to restorations and do not justify the suffering and death they cause; and physical energies for material ends do not last. Spiritual reform may be the answer, if "spiritual" means studying the self, finding one's centre, mastering the complexity which swamps one, i.e. all the confusions of our age. In other words, my two criteria must be (1) real being (2) preservation of life. And my method should be the visionary method, i.e. "seeing" solutions. Beginning with "Visions in Whitehall".

21st December. Tried to organise the poem and then went to the dentist and to Hitachi. The rather personal session rising from his poem, which was about a Princess in a German fairy-tale, standing by the river and dreaming of her student Prince who hadn't come back from the city. I advised him to try symbolizing, i.e. to abandon realism, and I asked him if he had any strong memories from his childhood. After a great deal of thought he came up with a black cat, which came in at night when he was small and which frightened him; a symbol for his inner fears, I suggested, if he were to write it up; and then, the recurrent nightmare of a revolution.

This took place when he was 10, i.e. in 1944, and was prompted by the French Revolution, he said, which he read about (when) young. In the nightmare the town was burning and he hid under the bed and was being searched for. Presumably this was fear of an American invasion, and not of a Japanese revolution? Anyhow, I probed him on revolutions to find out more and asked about the Ranas of Nepal, saying they were victims of a revolution, and wondered whether a revolution was likely in the future. In the end when I said goodbye he did not pay me the full amount for the month, this being my last time for December. There was no connection I believe.

I came back and, among other things, read Tuohy's *Special Relationship*. It starts off like a women's magazine story. What distinguishes it from women's magazines is the complexity of the feeling: first he's bored by her, then he unites with her against the play, then he is shocked by the fact she was married, then they separate finally, and there are offshoots in each scene; she saying he's detached ("blast you") and Sergeant Withers' wife and Roland's homosexuality and so on. "She" with shifted feelings – that's Tuohy, and his criterion is not "what happened" but "what did they feel"?

22nd December. A drab day. Went to see Nan as an angel. She was excited in the Bank of Japan car, but she cried in the stone "little theatre" of the Imperial Hotel. We went downstairs and drank beer and dry martini, C and I, and returned an hour later at 1 a.m., and sat in the 3rd row. The play was hilarious. Shepherds sat down, as did angels, when they felt like it; they forgot their lines, forgot to hold up their placards, cried out "Look there's Daddy" and trooped off stage when they should have gone to the crib. One shepherd swung his staff rather dangerously, and Ian led the angels off in the wrong direction. Nan followed Stephen and was a very good little girl: well deserved her Daddy's present of a bar of chocolate. She was, in addition, rather coy, and hid behind the others on the stage once or twice. She was clearly Sister's favourite.

23rd December. Spent the whole day indoors as C was ill. She lay on the futon by the gasfire, looking pale and getting up periodically to go and vomit, and I fetched and carried for her and cooked Nan's meals and answered the door and the telephone and also tried to draft out the new poem (which became *Old Man in a Circle*).

Perhaps I have not got used to the idea yet, or perhaps there was a certain amount of defiance in my determination – although I had planned to begin it now as far back as September. I could not get into it, I was cut off from my depths. Perhaps I have been off poetry too long – perhaps my stories come from upper me. In other words, for me, the writing of poetry is a spiritual act....The poetry itself is O.K. This feeling was reinforced by my contribution in the Eliot Memorial volume, three copies of which arrived. I am right. One's subject must be a quest through contemporary history, and the best form is "abbreviated narrative in a sequence of images". The problem as regards my new poem is how to get a narrative for a meditation on revolutions and reformations. Perhaps there should be a meditation in emotionally linked realistic images, but what about the structure?

24th December. Another day trying to concentrate on the new poem but still messing around on *The Death-Fires* as I now think of it. At 6.30 Tuohy came. He was rather subdued and he brought a lovely copper kettle with knobbles on the side, for us, and some beautifully polished sea-shells for Nan....Tuohy left at 10 to go on to a party in Roppongi and as we walked down the slope he asked me if I felt terror beneath the stars.

Earlier over dinner: "There are only two creative artists in Tokyo: you and me." The encouragement I needed.

25th December. Tuohy. On judgement: "Perhaps it's a Kafka thing and you're looking for a judge that doesn't exist." There is a story there. Also, his self-doubt: "Perhaps the *Sunday Telegraph* isn't taking my article – I should have heard by now, and I'm worried," and "My trouble is I can't think" – this being true, for I was always getting him back onto the subject in his China articles. The context: his reading philosophy at Cambridge. Also, his "cheating" over the *Observer*: "My copy hasn't arrived this week, who's recommended what for the year?" and then picking out Bayley's book on Tolstoy in a couple of seconds....He gave himself away by talking about Rothermere, Woolwich (I'm more Christian than most parsons it seems) and, especially, by saying of a report on Mao selling steel to the U.S., "I thought that was interesting, didn't you?" And it wouldn't have been carried anywhere else e.g. the AEN.

Buchanan came in the evening of the 25th. I was tired: I'd been awake all night – an effect Tuohy's alertness has on C as well as me – and Nan was awake at 2 whispering excitedly "He's been" and rustling her stocking. I was tired and we talked about his past, mainly: his Shiba dog, his American girl-friend, his gliding, the wolves in Trebizond and there should be some stories there.

26th December. Stayed at home and did not go to Miss Gegg's lunch, P's At home or the Tokyo University of Education dinner: having refused the first I could not go to either of the other two, and had no wish to go to the last. I worked on one of the nerve centres of the poem – the decline of the navy – and wondered if there were anything convincing in the anti-decline argument. (See 1st December.) Certainly we have never been better off but should the standard of living be the sole criterion? Perhaps it should.

27th December. Wrote rather unsuccessfully and then went to the Ward office to get my new Alien Registration Certificate and to report the visa extension. I was about a month late in reporting this, and as a result, I understand, a policeman will call at my house to decide what should be done. We also had our fingerprints taken, four of each with the index finger (forefinger) of the left hand. Owing to the clerks' inefficiency C's got put on two of my cards, and vice versa, for the girl could not admit her mistake.

We had to wait 15 mins after surrendering our passports/ ARCs/ 3 photos each/ 2 forms each, and sitting over the tiled floor in the drab government office I understood what aliens everywhere know: they have to wait in order to have the illusion of belonging, and the long counter which separates the clerks from them is a kind of barrier. I said to Nan, "If anyone asks what your father is, say 'He's an alien',," and I laughed when she did not understand ("What?") but my sentence confirmed my feeling of not belonging. I do not belong anywhere, and so I make visible my nature as an alien; I projected the Alien Registration Counter – it was to sit outside it, partly, that I left the U.K. The dismal pseudo-Dutch painting of industrial Tokyo with the fake, old gilt frame; the cubicles if you wanted to be private.

When I got back the Bank of Japan rang about two long letters to the Philippines, and later, looking at my desk, I knew I had lived this moment over before; perhaps in a dream three nights ago. For the poem I am working on my name was (= will be) grouped with another three as typifying the 20th century, and I believe one of the names is Paine; but I am not certain about that.

28th December. A lot of disturbances at front and back doors – a lot of cards and invitations from Milward and Tomlin in honor of the Eliot books.

29th December. Wrote home. From mother's letter: "Argie and I have been down to East Grinstead this morning. We left at 8.30 a.m., went to see Mrs. Coomber, put a wreath (holly) on Grannie's grave, visited Miss Walter in hospital, the Hoathers, and then home. Miss Walter fell a fortnight ago, and though she hasn't broken any bones, she has injured herself internally, which at 88 doesn't mend very quickly.... Do you remember the Clays have kept Chinese geese for the last ten years? They had got down to one goose, which slept on the backdoorstep every night, and a week before Roberts was captured, the bird vanished during the night. There was no noise, no feathers, not a trace was left. A goose previously got one of the others, and they heard the fight, and found the feathers, etc. They are sure that Harry Roberts (who was trained in the jungle) jumped on the bird and killed it before it had time to make a noise. They also think he gave himself up because a ten year old goose gave him such bad indigestion!"

30th December. I have not recorded a dream I had two nights ago. It was a long dream and I remember only one scene. I was with Tuohy in China and our guide introduced us to a man aged 210. He had a long beard. I asked him what he thought of Mao, and he began a terrific denunciation of Mao. I got Tuohy over to listen in. He spoke about the good old days, then he took us to the museum nearby. We were on a campus, and it was a university museum. He opened a book (he was the curator, I believe) and showed me some surrealistic pictures: men with bandaged faces and old hats and flowing cloaks. I was fascinated. "These," he said, "are foristic shadows." "Foristic shadows?" I echoed, and I realised he was referring to my own work, although I did not know the meaning of "foristic". "Look at these" I said to Tuohy, who was not very interested. Then I quoted Yeats' lines about Hades' bobbin and the winding-cloth, and I knew I was looking at a new image of the Self. When I woke up I looked up "foristic" in the OED, but could not find it. Perhaps my subconscious meant "forensic"? Anyhow, the dream had a great significance to me.

Last night I saw a World War I documentary, and I wrote 20 lines of poetry this morning on it: "Stuff Great Britain and consider the limbs of the people" – that was my theme. I am bored by Little England, and appalled by its decay, but it is a hundred times preferable to the hell of 1914, which was the price of Greatness: that should be my theme in the poems.

31st December. I have completed my rebuilding of myself, and I have deepened myself and escaped the tyranny of theories: see December 1st and 30th, where I have pulled out of Toynbee's view of things, although I still believe Britain is in a great crisis. I have also discovered myself as a short story writer and thereby extended my awareness of other people. I have also taken my theme from the individual to the nation (*Archangel*, *Blighty* and the present poem) and this is the fruit of my tour of China and my return to Britain.

In my assimiliation of 8th December, I said the main outstanding question was "Art or religion?" In so far as I have achieved any solution, it is in favour of art – I have not thought much about the Reformation lately – but the entry of November 2nd is significant: to unite all may be the solution. As regards revolution, I am definitely against from the international point of view, and, I think against from the domestic point of view (see November 18th). In my personal life I believe my main problem is to balance inner-outer, action-contemplation (see October 21st) and this is a problem for the future, for it is bound up with the role of the Artist in society. I cannot really think about this until I am an Artist, but possibly as Artist I could point towards bloodless domestic Revolution and Reformation, and thereby solve my self-division and unite myself. I am now more creative than ever before: witness the great burst of writing after China, and the freshness of the stories, and the compact entries in this *Diary*. I have rejected the old lumber.

What I must remember for 1967:

(1) In the poem I am doing now, I must see Freeman as a bloodless domestic Revolutionary of the Centre, who is between the "decline" theme of the Right and the anti-draft, pro-feelings theme of the Left. In short I must express the ambiguity and dialectic of our times in a lasting and eternal way.

(2) I must go into the history of Western civilisation since the Renaissance and finally decide about pattern.

10

BECOMING: CIVILISATIONS, DECLINE INTO
EUROPEAN UNION, ART
January – June 1967

1967

1st January. Yesterday we went down to Nobe. We had lunch at the house and spent the afternoon walking on the beach collecting firewood for the bath. In the evening we ate noodle soup and "crammed" Peking duck and lichis and drank saké, and I got stories. We had a final walk, and the moon was very bright, if a little oval, and just as there had been an orange causeway in the afternoon and red fire on the edge of the shot silk, smooth blue-brown-green water, so now there was white fire in the curl of the dark waves.

This morning the sky was snowy, and soon it began to rain and get cold, and all day we had the fall-out from Mao's fifth explosion, and we sat and huddled over the red oil stove and blew on our fingers and had "a Pope's nose" from time to time. And we discussed the mystery of life and Britain – Buchanan admitting that Little England might be nicer to live in than Great Britain – and world government, which, in his view, is the only way to end war, but which, he feels, can only be imposed by force. Then we came home to a dark, cold house, and Nan fell asleep straightaway.

2nd January. Wrote an awful lot. *Black Armband for a Teddy Bear* last night; and *Fire on the Water*, *Veins and a Resurrected Body*, *The Marquess and the Tram Standard* and *Tarts and Burnt Letters* today. Otherwise talked a lot about the future.

Late at night C asked "Could you say 'My life was happy,' as Buchanan could?" I: "No. An artist struggles too much. The burden of suffering and death gets heavier and heavier and after a time he cries out for rest and seeks to escape as a revolutionary or a spiritual reformer or as an overthrower of an empire. Into action. And at the end of it all he doesn't achieve all that much. As Wordsworth put it 'We poets in our youth begin in gladness/And thereof in the end comes despondency and madness.'" C: "You know about the escape, so you won't betray your art."

3rd January. Slept badly and was interrupted, before I'd begun on my poems, by the Jehovah's Witness, and straightaway wrote *A Kingdom and A Tear*. After that, fiddled around with the long poem, trying to think of a way of showing the decline of Britain since 1941. I failed to find a way because I tried to do it through an *Old Testament* denunciation, i.e. a spiritual perspective, whereas this spiritual perspective belongs to Part 3, Part 1 being about a purely national decay. Part 2 being from the point of view of material well-being (Galbraith) and the left wing attitude, which "I" oppose.

The poem is difficult because it is a survey of national decline and material prosperity from a spiritual point of view – "the vertical vision" – and Freeman should perhaps have an opponent to offer the antithesis of Revolution: the familiar "Reflection"-Devil, social man with material standards, who is in favour of Revolution, i.e. social action. In that case I would be detached, and there would be a dialectic. What I must do is establish the sickness of Britain – the spiritual sickness, not just the decadence, though the two are connected. For the Shadow, applied nationally, is an image of spiritual health, as opposed to national health or material prosperity. It is an alternative to the Church, an ideal of real being, whereas contemporary society makes for unreal living. This raises the law of unreality. The cause for our decline was partly economic, so to what extent does the other part, real living, solve the national and material problems? Also, to what extent are the masses capable of absorbing the cells of 10 idea; as opposed to the few who can absorb it?

4th January. After a morning on the decline of Britain and an afternoon buying a horse for Tuohy, to make up for the T'ang horse that broke and to repay the kettle, I went to Tomlin's party for the Eliot book. I went with Tuohy, after taking the horse round in a faroshki and having a second drink, and he said how awful Kenichi Yoshida's piece was. Very near Tomlin's house I said "That looks like Yoshida" and it was Prof. Iijima of Waseda, who is in with the Court. We picked him up and drove round and got thoroughly lost, whereupon the Professor got out to ask someone, and I nipped out for a pee. I had just finished when Iijima came back and asked, "Have you found it," and I pretended to examine the map. When I got into the car I realised my toecaps were splashed. When we got out of the car Tuohy said, "Mr Hagger teaches Prince Hitachi." "Ah so? Haw haw, Perince (sic) Hitachi? Do you teach Prince Hitachi too?" "No," said Tuohy. "I only teach at Waseda."

Tomlin was waiting by the door. Baker said, by the door, "Here come two distinguished authors." Tuohy puffed himself up and looked pleased, I grinned and said "Balls." I greeted Prof. Kuriyagawa and talked about Tuohy (not) having been killed in an air crash (Kuriyagawa's fear while we were in China), and Kenichi Yoshida and Prof. Narita, all of whom were slightly cold. They were embarrassed by my age, I think, and also by my attack on Winters which was not good etiquette; sensei are immune from criticism and I should know my place; also they hadn't understood what I had written. Narita once again asked Nadia's name, his usual insult, and this was coupled with the remark: "Prof. Nishiwaki did not know what this evening was in aid of."

At this point Tomlin made a speech, thanking the publishers and the contributers. He talked about the plaque (to Eliot) in Westminster Abbey (my poem sneers at this, "dying") and said he hoped the book would be well known "not only in Japan, but also in the – er – British – er, er – er, Commonwealth," while everyone waited tensely for "Empire". Miss Gegg wept – there was a large tear in her right eye and she was on my left. Did the plaque mean that much to her?

When Tomlin had finished we clapped and began talking again and I spoke to Kuroda and Bickley and then to Enozawa. I was intercepted by Takahashi on my way to Prof. Hijikata and met Emery, who is writing something for the *Times*. Later I was confronted by Prof. Nishiwaki who shook me by the hand, and I had a few words with Prof. Kuriyagawa and then went over to Tuohy and Kenichi Yoshida, who were talking about Pearl Harbour. Kenichi Yoshida: "Oh we bombed the U.S. because we had to make a clean sweep." I: "Why are you so perfectionist?" No answer. At this point Mrs. Bickley came over – "I've come over to see you" – and we talked about maids, sickness, and Japan, and the geisha parties Verner has to attend and which she doesn't like him to attend and so on. People are snobs: she didn't listen much in December (admittedly she was giving the party and was preoccupied) but she did now.

I went back to the hearth where Tuohy and Kenichi Yoshida were still talking, about China being France and Germany to Japan. This got us onto France and I said the French taught us about pavements but foolishly said Napoleon II instead of III. Tuohy: "Oh no, it was Napoleon III. Napoleon II was the Italian who died at 18."…He as the writer, had nothing to say on Eliot. Shortly after he excused himself and went off and I was left with Kenichi Yoshida.

In the end there was just Kenichi Yoshida and Tomlin and myself for a last drink, and Kenichi Yoshida called Tomlin "Freddie" and me "Mr Hagger" and asked Freddie to find me a maid so that Tomlin had to say "If ever you're stuck", etc. "How do you find such people?" Kenichi Yoshida asked "As Prof. Tuohy and Mr Hagger?" At long last I got him to leave and he suggested another drink. So I took him home to see "Alec Boyce's house", and we chattered all the way in the taxi, I forget what about. He tried to take his shoes off, and then he had to inspect the house (C had been warned by telephone) and he nearly fell down in the bathroom. "That's not an erotic bath" he said, and this got us arguing.

Later we talked about Pearl Harbour again, and I asked why. And he said "You're very young Mr Hagger, when were you born." And this led to the war: "You've never seen any blood perhaps." I corrected him and talked about V-bombs, and somehow he made the statement "You mustn't worry about blood – that doesn't matter" (Tuohy's attitude) and I said, "If you were in charge of a lot of POWs, you wouldn't shoot them, because you feel for them." Perhaps I said that first. Anyway his reply was "Damn, blood's nothing." I told him about the motor-cyclist's severed hand and he said

"Yes, such things do happen," and "I saw a lot of blood. I was in the army in the war." I suspect he was in Naval Intelligence, for shortly after C offered him some new potatoes (he is too alcholic to eat) and he said, "Did these come from England?" C said, "No, from Japan." He: "Oh, I thought perhaps you were a British spy, Mr Hagger," and his laugh was feigned, according to C who was watching his eyes. He: "I mean, I thought you got them from the Embassy." I: "Oh no, the Embassy potatoes are stale."

We quarrelled quite bitterly after this and I had to hold his elbow all the way down to the taxi. And I was drunk too. I was sick, and later I vomited in my sleep and nearly drowned in my own sick, like Lowry, and must not drink so heavily again. Now my hands are shaking and my eyes bloodshot (10.15 p.m. Thursday). I think we gave him whisky instead of gin, which is his usual drink.

5th January. At the Bank of Japan I asked Saito and Watarai what they had done over the New Year and the answer was the same: on January 1st they visited their wife's parents, and on January 2nd their go-betweens. Saito told me about his two refusals: he had first right of refusal and used it once, and the other time the girl refused him by letter. His veto was because the girl was "too intelligent"; and also because she was the eldest of three daughters, and as there were no sons in her family her parents wanted her husband to change his name and be adopted, to preserve the family name; as Saito is the only son, his mother vetoed the idea, and he obeyed.

Otherwise I showed the Eliot book to the Vice-Governor, and explaining the thesis to him filled me with confidence, and I felt there was nothing I couldn't do: "This is a revolution against the subject matter and technique of most poetry as it is written today. I don't want poems to be about modest trifles – I don't think poems should be about small-talk or flowers or animals or gardens, I think they should be about society or the meaning of life, about one's quest in life, one's search (and it is to emphasise this that I have included The *Riddle of the Great Pyramid*). I don't think technique should be so strict – metre, rhyme, mechanical form – a poem should grow like a plant through rhythm and image and cadence, and technique should be 'carrying on' – the servant not the master of the content or way of looking, just as in a Braque or a Picasso."

6th January. After writing *Blood and New Potatoes* and *A Thousand Feet and a Cage*, I went to Buchanan's party, with C and Nan. It was in a room at the Musashiya which had two tables, and everyone was Japanese save for us, the Emerys and the Giffards, who are going back in two months' time....I was sat between Mrs. Matsufuji and Mrs. Yamashita. We left rather early as Nan got tired, and next morning Tuohy rang and said nothing about the horse and suggested we get in touch with Miss Kobayashi of Waseda if we want to know about maids, whereupon he rang off in the middle of a sentence.

7th January. Reflections on the wave of terror in China. Red Guards have demanded that Chou En-lai be burnt alive, Tao Chu has been paraded through the streets, and clearly the Russians are right: "Sanity will return to China." Of course they are right, for they are further along the road, and China will reach their stage too, one day. Can it be that there is no such thing as lasting Communism, that "Communism" is just another name, like "Puritanism" or "Liberté, Fraternité, Egalité", for a process that happens when an old regime falls sick? Yes, it think it is possible, and I think it possible that there may be no such thing as Communism in the 21st century or 22nd century, although there will be something to replace it, for societies will always fall sick. Marx, then, merely varied an old formula that has always applied to decaying societies, and he was deluded in believing that it would be lasting: it is merely the transitional cure. And most of Eastern Europe must have been pretty sick in 1945 – there is no other explanation for the transitional cure which was Stalin's empire.

The process of revolution is, then, an indispensable part of the existence of societies. There will always be revolutions, and they will always be betrayed, i.e. effect a cure. And Orwell was right in showing us this progress, but wrong in understanding the total significance of revolutions. He should never have been in the position where he might be disillusioned. What I would like to know is, can a society go through a revolution twice? The French revolution was revived in 1830, 1848 and 1870, but it was not repeated; just as the English revolution's, perhaps, being revived today, though it will not be repeated. I would also like to know whether there is any connection between barbarianism and revolution, for there is a parallel between Genghis Khan and Mao, and possibly barbarian societies, in their expansive periods, are in the process of curing their innate sickness.

9th January. On Saturday and Sunday I worked on the beginning of the new poem, and on Monday morning I wrote *A Cuckoo at Casa Pupo's*.

I thought about my attitude to evolution again. There are two different things, the biological progress of man, and the subjective feeling of growth. I am interested in the second. Growth is the substitute for religion, embarking on a quest or search through self, society, history, civilisation, the universe and growing spiritually – deepening oneself and becoming less superficial. Growth towards a God-substitute, Growth without God – that is what I have to say, and although I am sure growth is reflected in society in forms, I do not look to any biological theory of progress for my energy. The important thing is not to be static, and (Colin) Wilson has recognised that. He has ceased to be the solitary interested in experience, though, and has become a spiritual "leader" of society who sees a solution through collective man and who is more objective than he used to be. This trend is typical of growth, but perhaps he should not have deserted subjective experience as he has.

Otherwise, I hailed the rebellion in China: Nanking, Shanghai, Canton

– there are some very brave people in China, if the reports are true, and what we are witnessing is not the beginning of a Civil War, but mostly a struggle which will repeat the fall of Robespierre. I told P that Mao could be out within one year from last October, and he said "You're crazy." Chiang Kai-shek is reported ready to return if "general chaos ensues", and perhaps P will come to understand that my judgement was not based on faith alone.

11th January. On Tuesday (10th January), the literary lunch for the Eliot Book, at Sophia House. Tuohy called for me, and in the taxi we talked about China. He: "I suppose the old Professors we saw have all committed suicide by now." We walked on the Sophia embankment, as we were early, and there was a military cheerleading session with a man holding a red flag in a great wind. The wind tugged my hair and as we walked into Jochidai and saw the Ambassador's Rolls arrive, I said, "If he's forgotten what Beatle hair is like he'll soon know."

Inside everyone was very hushed and embarrassed after the initial handshakes. We signed books, we talked in groups and Tomlin said he'd read my poems through and had got a bang out of them and had found them very exciting. Then we went to lunch. No one knew which fork to use for the crab, Milward made a very long speech, Kenichi Yoshida teased Father Rector's Deputy about heaven ("Please send me a cable so that I'll know what it's like"). Johnstone said "Poor Joyce", because he wasn't a Christian, Shinoda said Japan had ruined Blunden, Empson, Fraser and a number of other poets, and Milward knocked his glass over when I asked "But are you interested in Kipling?"

After six courses we adjourned for coffee in the adjoining lounge, and Hirai, Milward again and the Ambassador made speeches. The Ambassador spoke of originality and looked at me, and later he came by with a twinkle in his eye, and clearly wanted to talk.

On the way back with Tuohy I attacked the idea of judgement. People bring their biases and opinions and credos to a work and tell you about themselves, and there are no standards when you are trying to overthrow the standards of the literary establishment, I said, and Eliot and Osborne and all revolutionaries must have felt that. He agreed.

12th January. Tuohy's rejoinder before he agreed was: "Ideally there is a history of English poetry in the critic's mind, and you take your place in it in accordance with who you're similar to." Nonetheless, a critic who is purely interested in style, like Tuohy, will differ from a critic who is also interested in content, like Tomlin. And while I was at Hitachi's, Tomlin rang and told C that he had been very taken with my work and felt it ought to be published. I secretly felt elated, and grew accordingly. One can grow into a position, as I've discovered here, and I am sure that if I were published I would grow into the role of a major poet.

Before I went to Hitachi's I worked on the first long passage, the sun setting on the empire and the rise of the U.S., and I finished this on Thursday morning. At the Bank of Japan I had a long session with Ichiki, answering his uninformed questions about my contribution to the Eliot book, and getting him to agree that an image which tantalises and haunts for 20 years is better than a lucid line which lasts as long as a pop in the Top Twenty. His simple notion of poetry, "You see a bird, you feel an emotion," and his fear when I talked about death, or not belonging, or futility – feelings more or less unknown in healthy, united Japan perhaps.

13th January. A boring day at Tokyo University of Education and then the dentist, having my teeth cleaned instead of filled because there was a mistake and Besford was not there; also writing *A Scarlet-faced Ape, Minutes like a Mutter* and writing home.

14th January. On Thursday evening I listened to Radio Peking and heard the appeal to the Shanghai workers in English, and was particularly touched by the new terminology: "Respected Chairman Mao."

Today I got back to the poem and made a voyage through history, trying to get to the bottom of loss of empire and revolutions, and I saw the whole phenomenon in terms of unity and self-division. The rise of an empire, the energy which results in expansion, is connected with unification – separate provinces are united in a Union (cf USA, USSR). The fall of an empire, the self-satisfaction and decadence which results in contraction, is connected with the return of division, (as provinces throw off the yoke (cf Manchu, China, modern India.) After the loss of an empire, the society which founded the empire feels a sense of loss, and it is sick. Is it self-divided also? Is it true that a sick society which has just lost an empire can either concentrate and achieve unity and become domestically strong (Kamal, De Gaulle) *or* be self-divided and progress towards a revolution which makes it strong again? Is the second true of China? Of Russia? And is there any connection between the loss of the Spanish Empire and Franco?

Anyhow, what is certain is that there is always self-division before a Revolution – there has to be, so that there can be a rival government. What the Revolution does is to unite a self-divided nation. And there does not seem to be any great self-division in Britain, if you exclude the overtaxed Tories. On the other hand, whichever course Britain takes, she will become strong, and perhaps the key concept in societies is the drive for unity through a dictator or revolution. Compare the personal level.

15th January. On the drive for unity. The future of a sick society is either strength or death, i.e. unity or foreign conquest. The Shadow for Britain is, therefore, a strong, united Britain, and can it be that there is no law which foretells death? If not, then freewill is possible in history, and the Spenglers are wrong, and one cannot talk of "civilisations" dying; or even of "Western civilisation", although all countries in the Western world owe much to each other. I am still rather afraid there is such a law, and that one can talk in terms of growth and decay, and that unity and diversity are a feature of growth and disunity and uniformity a feature of decay.

In this case, my law of unreality was slightly wrong in its emphasis. Unreality is a symptom of disunity and uniformity and decay; reality is a symptom of unity and diversity and growth. Real living is not, therefore, an end in itself, but an indication of a healthy society, and unreal living is a symptom of an unhealthy, decaying, disunited society. One must be careful, here, to distinguish unity and diversity from unity and uniformity (Mao, Hitler), for the latter is barbarianism, and perhaps Eliot is right in saying that too much unity is a bad thing. (*Notes towards the Definition of Culture*.) Perhaps one always dreams of unity, but ideally permits diversity within a wider unity.

Anyhow, which theory is right – freedom or law? If only I knew. This would be the question I would ask my Mephistopheles: I would willingly agree to go to Hell in 24 years time if I knew the answer. Whichever is true, there are two views of sickness: either it is the effect of loss of empire, or it is (more generally) connected with materialism, i.e. it is a permanent disease of the soul, like flu, rather than an historical consequence.

16th January. At Tokyo University of Education. There are two criteria of sickness, the material-historical (as France's up/down) and the spiritual (i.e. any society is sick where the intensity of the individual's development is swamped by the material). There are two corresponding views of man, the humanist's – that man can be improved by social organisation and education and that material prosperity is a sign of progress – and the spiritual – that man is to be seen in terms of his possibilities and the growth of his mind and in terms of his own individual future rather than in terms of society or (e.g.) Mao. The first criterion of sickness believes that a civilisation falls sick when it ceases to be materially prosperous. The second criterion believes it falls sick when it ceases to be spiritually prosperous, even though it is materially prosperous.

What is the relation between the two criteria? I think no. 1 can involve no. 2, when it comes to health, but that it does not necessarily do so. Compare the Middle Ages with China, Japan, the U.S.A., where physical energy is different from spiritual intensity, i.e. where no. 2 is lacking. Thus, in the case of Britain, material historical ascendancy would only involve spiritual health if an independent spiritual effort were made. Trevor-Roper's attack on Toynbee is an example of no. 1 criterion berating no. 2.

Do civilisations decline for spiritual rather than material reasons? First can we talk of Western civilisation or only of generations which rise and fall? Taking account of the loss of the empires – France, Spain, Portugal, Austro-Hungary, Germany, Italy, Holland, Belgium, Britain, U.S. – I think we can talk of both, the civilisation being invisible behind the rise and fall. Perhaps the U.S. will be the last outpost of Western civilisation, representing a movement from East to West. Mesopotamia and Egypt, Hebrews, Crete and Greece, Rome, back to Byzantium and Islam, Holy Roman Empire, Britain, U.S. Perhaps on the other hand the broken and divided Europe which has lost all its empires is now heading for unity, for a "Universal State". If the first, what will destroy Western civilisation: Communism, which is surely not permanent, or Africanism, or even the Yellow Peril? If the second, what will save it? In any event, what will the spiritual interior be like? Will it (1) have decayed within so that it is ready to be conquered or (2) have recovered inner toughness so that it can survive? In any event, which will be responsible, spirit or matter? The answers appear to be different, depending on the fate. Destruction would appear to be due to the failure of Christianity, out of which the empires grew. Unity – a USA or USE or USW (= United States of the West, comprising both America and Europe) – would, on the basis of the Common Market, appear to be due to material things.

All I know at this stage is that, on Toynbee's analysis, which may be very wrong, past "civilisations" (if his distinctions are meaningful in any way) seem to break down for spiritual reasons and that we need a new religion to bind us together and give us sap. This new religion must be one involving the world and it must teach (1) wonder and (2) growth towards the Shadow of each individual. This is the national Shadow – a nation of individuals realising their Shadow. Revolutions and political solutions are not important – they belong to the first criterion and involve nations, not civilisations, and Britain must be seen within a USE or nothing. "The State should be within the Church" and the material does not matter so much as the spiritual: it passes away, whereas the spiritual survives, just as generations pass away and the tree outlives them.

18th January. On Monday (16th) I wrote *Like the Sea at Low Tide* and on Wednesday (18th) *A Monkey and a Peep-Seat*. On Tuesday 17th and Wednesday mornings I worked on the swinging London passage in the poem, and wondered if there is a parallel between the Regency and today. Then as now we had finished a European war and "Empire is no more". The point is of interest because of the background of the second generation of Romantics, a tradition I am probably carrying on in my neo-Modernist disguise. On Tuesday at Keio I did Blake, and I was struck by the fact that the centre of Blake's work after 1793 is the struggle between Los and Urizen-Spectre, which is of course an almost exact equivalent to my Shadow and Reflection.

Went to MITI for four hours.

19th January. I went to the Bank of Japan and had a long talk with the Vice-Governor about China. He claimed Russia is about to invade Manchuria and seize Dairen, which has an advantage over Vladivostok as a port in that the waters don't freeze in the winter. This would accord with Russian interests before 1905 (the railway the Japanese took) and it will be "a defence against Mao's aggression." I had read the report of troops being moved to the border and of Kosygin's visit to Vladivostok, but I was sceptical. Nonetheless if it comes to pass, the Vice-Governor's sources (he would not name this one) will prove extremely reliable.

We also read an article called *The Last Revolution*. This claimed that a revolutionary cycle that began in 1789 is now coming to an end with the Red Guards' Terror and Liu's revolt. I did not agree that there are such things as revolutionary cycles. What about the English and American revolutions, and what about the sickness society falls into from time to time? Are revolutions symptoms of sickness, or are they left-wing ideals which can go in cycles? I believe in the first. Yet what about the ideal of an all-out Communist offensive, e.g. the pincer plan of the early 1960s, the bridgehead from Saigon to Djakarta? Does this not suggest that Communism is an ideal that can be spread? Surely the evidence of Indonesia shows that Indonesia was not quite sick enough to need a revolution, and the general failure of the Communist offensives seem to underline the point. Communism is not a permanent thing – there can, anyway, be no such thing as a permanent revolution (see last summer) – and it can only "be spread" in sick societies.

Later I talked with Ichiki about the influence of the Tokugawa Japanese "house" on giri – hence the "loss of face", the reluctance to take responsibility, for these things could result in loss of surname. In the course of this I asked what would happen if he rebelled against giri, e.g. refused to make a contribution. He: "If often enough, I will be sent to Coventry." This got us onto rebellion, and I said that in the 20th century the West had not witnessed so much rebellion since the Renaissance. Future historians may well consider us as on the point of creating a new code of values, I said. There had not been so much destruction since the Renaissance, and the task was now to rebuild, and what is there to rebuild but a new European Union with its new values? Just as the Middle Ages feudalism passed into Renaissance ideals, so are Victorian Establishment ideals and values passing into new ideals and values, and Toynbee's Universal State is a possibility. All hail the European Renaissance in this age of overlap. We know our bugbears. What will our ideals be?

20th January. More thoughts on the European Renaissance. As regards Britain, there are three possible explanations from a long term point of view for Osborne. Either he has helped forward the breakdown and there will be decay; or he is the new Beaumarchais, signalling Revolution; or he is the destructive side of the overlapping, the breakdown occuring in 1910 and the rebuilding in store. There is an ambiguity in the mood of England today: there is both decadence and vitality, both old and new. The old Victorianism, Establishmentarianism and Christianity has been rejected and the new has not yet appeared.

BECOMING: CIVILISATIONS, DECLINE INTO EU, ART (1967)

Today at Tokyo University of Education Fubara said it was the new that pushes out the old, that you cannot destroy the old and then look round for the new, but if there is a renewal of an incomplete Renaissance in process, involving a more thorough rejection of Christianity, is the objective valid? What are the modern "barbarities" of medieval Latin and Gothic art – are they not Liverpool English and abstract art? (Compare T. E. Hulme on the medieval, the geometric.)

In 1964 I had trouble with T. E. Hulme, on 31st January 1966 I connected religion with striving. Clearly the old notions are out of date – "religion", "humanism" – but I am against Hulme and for the "many-sided man" in rejecting the subordination of man to God and in placing perfection on the human plane; and I am for growth, the Shadow, and against the "fixed and limited Reflection". Can it be, then, that a Renaissance vision can accommodate the Shadow and still be against other-worldliness? Is the Silence a Renaissance silence? Yes it is, for death is the end. But the key to the new Renaissance will not be scholarship, but a framework of livable ideas (cf the new Reformation) within the context of a political Union, and the place of origin of the new Renaissance will not be Italy but England, between the U.S. and the Soviet as Toynbee predicted.

21st January. For just as Christ appeared in a decaying community before a Union and preached at the beginning of the Union and later got accepted by that Union, so perhaps a modern teacher will do the same for the European Union. T. E. Hulme was wrong to make the Renaissance the enemy, just as Toynbee has been wrong to. The point is, the old distinction between humanism and religion no longer applies, for today death is the end, and religious growth and striving has to take place at a humanistic level, in terms of striving and secular-spiritual growth.

This point is of supreme importance for us in the 20th century who can now see the overlap, as Eliot and the other 1920s nihilists could not. For it means that T. E. Hulme was wrong about 1914, just as he was wrong in predicting a return to the religious attitude. Abstract art is not a sign of neo-materialism or of subordination to God, it is a symptom of the shattering of the old and the emergence of the new. We are now emerging from an age of transition, possibly the greatest age in all human history, and from now on religion must be seen in terms of "secular" growth, i.e. without any subordination to a God or reliance on a life after death.

And it is this redefinition of religion which will emphasise the European's moral superiority to the materialistic U.S. and the Communists. This renaissance is, then, a rebirth of the many-sided man, interiorised in the Shadow, and therefore of the idea of purpose and the meaning of life, and the new Puritans are the advocators of the anti-barbarous ideal, the rejectors of the new lightheartedness. They will possibly bear no relation to the political Puritans, the left-wing rebels against the Establishment who are now revelling like Cavaliers, and the Sabbath-observing middle class.

22nd January. Yesterday Tuohy came and was surprisingly respectful: called me "the poet" and agreed with me over pressure and over birds talking in Movement poems and, most surprisingly of all, over Winters. He was rather aphoristic: "discipline and Puritanism don't mix"; "wisdom is understanding, not knowing", and it is "not repeating one's mistakes". The main question is "How do you make people want to work?" and "How do you stop people envying and treating their children badly?" (i.e. re personal and social relationships).

Did some work on civilisations. Civilisations begin with religious thought and "progress" to abstract thought and materialism, yet religious thought is unacceptable and undesirable if it is medieval thought involving heaven and hell (or is this my abstract thought blinding me to medieval thought?) and so the ideal is the compromise of the Renaissance, the whole, many-sided man, not the divided man of 18th century rationalism. Certainly it is the striver who is the Los and the "fixed and limited" man of Hulme's medievalism who is the Urizen-Spectre.

What we need to do is to return to the Renaissance and have a revival of the Renaissance attitude, but believing that man must strive to become perfect, not that he's born perfect. As I said to Tuohy, "I am striving to get myself up to scratch, and up to scratch is an ideal I will never achieve. Many-sided man through awareness of one's imperfection – that is my ideal, and it is a Renaissance ideal, and so I am against anti-Renaissance ideas such as Hulme's and Toynbee's." They may be right about the decline of religion being a sign of decay, but who wants heaven and hell again?

23rd January. Yesterday thought hard on the poem, after writing the sickness passages; came up with the Great Year image after a feverish walk under a brilliant moon. I got into my futon and disregarded C's plea "Don't do any more, you won't sleep" – I found a diagram of the Great Year with the signs of the zodiac all round and was triumphant but paid the penalty with a night's throbbing waiting for dawn. And I wrote the passage before coming to Tokyo University of Education.

After that I pondered on the question "What is the role of the individual in the progress and decline of a civilisation?" Do civilisations decline when the individual loses his vitality or relaxes after responding to a great challenge? If they do, what of Europe? And of Britain? To what extent could I arrest the decline of Western civilisation, a question that is full of pride. Presumably, on Toynbee's view, by responding to the challenge of the collapse of Christianity and to the challenge of the loss of empire. (The theory of challenge and response is not discredited just because Toynbee was wrong about the Dutch lowlands.) One interesting point is that the Reformation came just after the Renaissance and affected the three countries connected with the Renaissance and beyond schismed Italy: the countries of Calvin, Luther and Henry VIII. So More had a foot in both, and the secular ideal of the Renaissance and the more secular ideals of the Reformation are connected.

25th January. After completing three days' toil on the opening lines – the failure of empire – I went to Hitachi and then on to P. M showed me in after a lot of swearing at the dog (the Burma figurine) and after a tense renewal of contact I reported the situation to date on China, and put forward my plan for relieving Liu Shao-chi. I had heard from the Bank of Japan that the Soviets would aggress to get Dairen. Let them aggress, and later withdraw – let them do anything to relieve Liu and give him a chance to make Lin Piao a Robespierre rather than a Stalin. Let there be a "blunder" from Brown at the Queen's dinner for Kosygin: "Now look here. What is going on around Khabarovsk, and why don't you go in and relieve Liu Shao-chi?" Nothing more – just enough to communicate the idea that we wouldn't take aggression in the name of defence to the U.N. Assuming that it is our policy to have a moderate government in Peking and not keep China and Russia divided.

P: "I doubt very much whether we've got a policy at all in that area." I: "We should have. Everyone complains we react rather than not – here's our chance to do something for once." P: "Yes but officialdom being as it is...." I: "Damn officialdom."

When I left M said "Nice seeing you" and I said "See was the operative word", an ambiguity to which she replied "One day we'll really get together," and P looked abashed.

26th January. Over breakfast I decided to leave Japan on October 17th. The situation is really very simple. If I stay until December or next April, Nan will be without school from June 1967. She is anyway insecure because of bullying and needs Sister Mary Batman to "look after" her, and she sees too little of others. She should therefore start as soon as possible after September 24th, the beginning of term at Oaklands. I can pay off the Bank of Japan at 9 months of ¥35,000, and there is a chance I can continue to work for the Bank of Japan in London.

27th January. At Tokyo University of Education I told Irie I would be leaving. His immediate reaction after I had told him about the closure of the school: "Ah, is there any other reason?" Possibly he was thinking of coldness from members of other factions than his, e.g. Saito, coldness possibly recently connected with my disrespectful treatment of Winters, who has a reputation beyond my position. (Yesterday I wrote *Is there a Rebel at the Lunch-Table?*) Later I wrote home, asking mother to persuade Miss Reid about Oaklands.

28th January. On drama. See 13th December 1966 for the "quest for identity" theme. Osborne and Albee convince me that the most electrifying drama is the product of a slanging match, so my hero must be an aggressive hero, and he must have a worthy opponent. Like Freeman, or George Dillon, he should be in rebellion against society, i.e. he should have rejected the things that (e.g.) Dillon rejects: the commercial theatre, the cliché and caricature behaviour of the Elliots, the cocktail cabinet and tasteless birds on the wall and the vile music that form their values. Of course there will be no sell-out from my "Outsider". He will not be the Outsider manqué who doubts himself into failure – he will carry on completely alone, blowing on his hands like Nietzsche or Spengler, having great thoughts. Perhaps he has to discover whether he is a revolutionary or a reformation leader: in either event opposition to society is his first move, and the problem becomes, how can it be improved. Perhaps I should write the history of the 2nd English Revolution. This should be a controversial enough theme.

Later I got the idea for a sequence of historical plays on such subjects as the Inquisition; Cromwell; the Reformation, etc. Of course, treating the subjects from my point of view and capitalising out of the violence the experience would provide. Why should I not do this? After all, Shakespeare didn't write about the Elizabethan Age.

30th January. At Tokyo University of Education (Monday) I discussed the problem of why there is growth and decay – "religious" élan and materialistic decline. I asked "Do civilisations flourish materially or spiritually?" i.e. because of economic pressures (Marxism) or because of the creative vitality of individuals like Eliot (Toynbee)? According to Tanaka, the economic state precedes the spiritual state – so a worker's consciousness will be less than a boss's, and material conditions determine spiritual levels. According to Fujihara the creative minority is the conspicuous part of the soul of the race and economic prosperity is a result of a growth process which is spiritual.

The implication in this is that spiritual movements produce economic prosperity. See my law of unreality. On Toynbee's argument, in the case of the Universal Church, this is clearly so, but is it so of the un-universal sects of the Reformation? Not necessarily, I think there is a red herring here. The creative individual does not create to advance material or economic prosperity – that is the Marxist fallacy. He creates spiritual energy to keep society and his civilisation alive, and he can affect his civilisation whether it is growing or decaying, i.e. he can give it a new lease of life. So if my "Shadow" could awaken people from their material sleep and help them master the complexity of their own living and respond to the challenges that face Britain (getting into Europe e.g.) then it will have affected Western civilisation. Anyhow, the main point is the relaxation, and the rottenness. Britain has relaxed and got out of condition and become decadent, it has relaxed in relation to the Shadow, and so is the most decayed part of Western civilisation.

So what is my message to Western civilisation? I think it is this. Stop considering the material criterion – the economic prosperity or otherwise of your society. Look for the deeper cause of our sickness – the spiritual relaxation, our low spiritual tension, our failure to strive. We have gone rotten and squashy inside: that is why our society is sick and we cannot solve our problems and we cannot respond to challenges with creativity. We no longer strive, so we react rather than act. First there is spiritual decay, then there is materialism. (Or does the materialism cause the decay?)

What we must do now is rise to the challenge of USE (United States of Europe), and, perhaps more important, recover our spiritual strength – get moving up towards the Shadow and be creative again. There must be a rebirth of the moving inner man, and existentialism will interiorise this new Renaissance. My law of unreality was right – real living is the thing, and if everyone lives authentically, then the West will be healthy and in control over its complexity, and for everyone to live authentically means a spiritual movement initiated by one or two creative men. The important thing is for people to be aware of who our leaders are, and to feel that rationalists like Russell and scientists are a poor substitute for "spiritual" leaders.

Whether a tightening up inside will lead to material health one cannot finally say with conviction, though it must be noted that there is a connection between the two. The spiritual leader cannot worry about that. His job is to replace Christianity by experiencing in his own life the substitute which Western civilisation needs for it to continue, by recording it and by creating a system (e.g. cells of 10) which people can follow.

31st January. A barren day, finishing at Keio and staring at my MS, the long poem, and achieving one idea, which is probably important: Revolution is the wish of the Reflection, whereas Freeman's task is to recreate the Shadow. Revolution is a cure for social sickness, but it is a transitory power, whereas the Shadow is a more permanent cure. So Freeman is waylaid by the Reflection, and the whole bit about Revolution is a kind of temptation which diverts him from the task he discovered in *The Silence*. Just as in man Urizen must be ruled by Los, Siva by Kali, Shopenhauer's idea by Will (he was wrong to think Will is enslaved by idea) – just as "Que meuro porque no meuro" ("And I die because I don't die", i.e. my Self dies because my ego doesn't die) – so in society Revolution must be ruled by Spiritual Reform. That is to say, Revolution is not wrong in itself – it must not enslave the Shadow and it must not violate the life of the Shadow with blood.

Later I got a telephone call from Sister St. John, saying that Sister Mary Batman will be there from 9.30. The care she poured on Nan went to my heart and I thanked her for her trouble. She: "We must, we are building the future." I was reminded of Mrs. Cheng in Shanghai District Palace: "Our children are our future." Sister St. John will not see any of the children after June, though, and so the love and devotion and personal attention and late telephone calls of now will be futile then, or will they? In her there is "the love of God", a force more powerful than my Shadow perhaps, and it fills me with tears of pity (for the futility) and admiration. Not movements: love, love, love is the most important thing.

I am tired, but I have felt love, pure love for the last two hours. I have

413

AWAKENING TO THE LIGHT

dipped into Underhill's *Mysticism* to explain my present mood, I have looked again at St. John of the Cross and I have reread Alyosha's love of the earth. Otherwise I have felt a great sorrow from the very bottom of my being – somewhere between my throat and my stomach, somewhere below my throat. Silence – that's common to Underhill, John and Alyosha. But this is love.

Even while I write this I feel I love everything so deeply that I want to cry. In fact my eyes have been watering on the verge of tears for the past hour. I cannot pin my love onto anything. I am existing in the depths of my being, I am pure feeling, and the feeling is love. There is a pop singer's life on TV. She has a miniskirt up round her waist and normally I would ogle her legs, but now, in this mood, I don't want to look. I just want to sit at this desk and feel this love. I have tried talking to my wife, and have even been slightly cynical. That was a meaningless pose. I am alive in my depths, somewhere at the top of my lungs, I think, and I feel as if I am going to burst into tears because everything is so good. My wife is clattering knives. That is good. Everything is good: the rattling window, the chord on the piano, the condensation on my window.

I have seen the very bottom of my being, and there is no abyss. Just a profound sadness and a great exaltation, at one and the same time. Man is nothing and all. Darkness and love, darkness and love of the earth and scaldingly hot, fresh tears I would be ashamed to confess to – tears of meaning and vision. Everything is good because my feeling is pure.

2nd February. On my view of art, and the old debate of the mirror and the resister. Clearly in a Stalinist regime (to quote an example from a letter by Philip Toynbee in this week's *Observer*) an artist cannot merely mirror: he must resist. Whereas in a healthy society, he does mirror, e.g. Elizabethan England. The appearance of the resisting Angries signified a breakdown in British society, for their resistance was more extreme than most artists'.

Are modern novelists resisting or mirroring, i.e. novelists since Wilson overthrew the Establishment? And this brings me to my career as a novelist. When I return to England, I want to write a novel about the new versus the traditional, the new technological versus the old amateurism and "general culture", and possibly the new revolutionary versus the old democratic. The framework should be my return to Britain last year, i.e. the ten weeks, and the Bazarov should be a scientist who has returned from abroad with new ideas (e.g. ideas picked up in Japan) and a left-winger who would like to see Britain reformed along Chinese lines perhaps. What values should I judge by? Values that are not mass values, values like freshness and real living and not being a cliché and finding yourself, values less decayed than the provincial values that Labour England has to offer. The decay of the old classical Renaissance ideal – seen at (Chigwell) school in Thompson.

BECOMING: CIVILISATIONS, DECLINE INTO EU, ART (1967)

3rd February. At Tokyo University of Education the politeness at lunchtime. "We shall be sorry to see you go." "We want your successor to be exactly the same as yourself. Some of us wanted a linguist, but they were defeated, and we want someone like yourself in every respect." Fubara's nasty question: "And will you go back to Cambridge?" requiring a monologue by me on my writing ambitions and on being "free" from all institutions. I: "Not one of you is free." Toyama: "I agree." (The others looking shocked.)

After that summarised the thesis – subjects, and treatments. In both novel and essay one can look for the attitude of the author; the extent to which his character is revealed (e.g. essay); the characterisation or portraiture, paying special attention to whether the character or portrait is idealised, i.e. whether both good and bad points are given; the dialogue, e.g. whether it carries the character forward, whether the character talks like that normally; the concreteness and freshness of the language; the emotional qualities of the situation, i.e. no striving after effect, no sentimentalism or tears (cf Richardson, Dickens), no falsification of a normal situation, e.g. a man talking too much in the presence of death; irony, i.e. saying the opposite of what you mean (Jane Austen and Thackeray e.g.); the pictorial accuracy or vividness and the details which may help us to believe what is being said; and (in the case of the essay mainly) whether style suits subject, e.g. De Quincey and Newman and Burke (law – legal imagery).

Later spoke to Hill to report my departure in October. His prefect's air, his bureaucratic jargon: "I'll notify London, and I'll let you know further on this one."

4th-5th February. On Saturday 4th Sizue came to look after Nan for two hours and get to know her, prior to baby-sitting. She is a shy girl with chubby cheeks, and she is patient and has a quiet voice. She looks the same as Nan's teacher.

On Sunday 5th Buchanan came, and he stayed until 11, and we drank well over a large bottle of saké, and talked at great length about Keikosan, who told him off for leaving his door open when she had a guest, causing a terrible loss of face. She is "the kettle without the lid", she boils over very quickly. "Don't argue with women, they're so illogical it's not worth it, and let them come round to commonsense on their own. In my experience it isn't the big things that annoy her – she won't say anything in a crisis, if I've been with another woman or when I went off with the geisha, or if there's a financial crisis. It's always the little things that she blows up at. Then she gets the paper and reads down for jobs."

6th February. At Tokyo University of Education. On the two themes in *Religion and the Rebel*. The historical theme is that civilisations grow through religion, their backbone, and decline because the creative minority loses its "religious" aim and purpose and falls into materialist, abstract, sceptical categories, i.e. ceases to be dynamic and regards man as static. The

415

civilisation then dies from the head down, in that the creative minority fails it, and the Outsider who reacts against the static materialism is therefore a symptom of a dying civilisation and culture.

The religious theme is that as a civilisation grows religion hardens into a "church for the weak" that is unacceptable to the Outsider. The Outsider therefore becomes a Rebel, and, later, the prophet of "religion for the strong", i.e. some notion of "existentialism" or growth, some view of man that is dynamic, not static, i.e. moving forward internally between the ages of 20 and 70, and not fixed in a social position or context.

Thus, the member of a creative minority at the end of the religious phase has a duty to react against the prevailing materialism and the established Church, and renew the early religious phase of the civilisation by holding up an ideal for "the strong" (to use the Grand Inquisitor's words), i.e. a dynamic ideal. This is what I have done, with the Shadow. The most crucial thing is that it is the "religion for the strong" that is the backbone of civilisation, not established Christianity, and it does not matter if Christianity collapses. So long as people are moving, so long as the creative minority (the head) is moving, the civilisation will remain in the vital "religious" stage.

So this is the answer to Revolution. It is not the environment that needs to be changed, but the self. A tyranny that changes only the environment and, into the bargain, enslaves its creative minority, can only collapse – there is no dynamic growth. Whereas the self that is moving will make discoveries (no discoveries, either geographical or technological, are made by static man) and the discoverer of "new things", the striver for the oldest things – he alone can provide the "soul-energy" that a broken-down civilisation needs.

Furthermore, this is the answer to the whole business of the Renaissance. The important thing is growth, being dynamic, i.e. moving, and if the Renaissance people included this in their ideal of the many-sided man, i.e. believed themselves imperfect until they had become many-sided, then they will be admired by the "Religion for the Strong." Other-worldliness is a bore: growth is the thing – "ripeness is all". (Shakespeare was a part of the Renaissance.)

And this brings us to the image. According to Kermode, the image is not just a joyous victory, it is also an expression of "Unity of Being", when soul-body were united and not dissociated (13th century, Pound and Hulme; 1450-1550, Yeats; 17th century, Eliot): hence the speaking body of the dancer and of Caroline ("her body thought") and the inward-looking "dead" Tutankhamun face and mask that expressed absence of thought, for the soul is in the body, a unity like the chestnut tree-work of art. Much of this may be a 1790s revolt against the 18th century mechanistic discourse (i.e. a revolt by Blake and Coleridge), but I am interested in Yeats's choice of 1450-1550, and Titian and Botticelli, whose faces are clearly as "visionary" and unified as the Byzantine faces Yeats admired. For it is the growth-principle that underlies this Unity of Being and unites "souls" and body, connects self and life, and this is Renaissance as well as Byzantine.

7th February. No, this is wrong. The inner life is found in Byzantine and Gothic art, and the image is first a yoke and then subservient to an idea, e.g. 13th century scholastic philosophy (p156, p185 of Bazin.) There is no inner life in Romanesque art, and there is much less inner life in Renaissance art than in Gothic: the eyes see, there is no religious symbolism (the world is now an image), there is no soul yearning or mystical intuition, man must know the world, man is the measure of all things (= humanism), rationalism is the main principle, along with lucidity, limitation, and the individual is supreme (p226). Although I admire this emphasis on the individual and on the many-sided man I do not admire the seeming abandonment of growth and the inner life (this may not be wholly true – scholars medievalize the Renaissance today and see it as being obsessed by Original Sin), and I affirm: there must be a kind of synthesis between Gothic and Renaissance, a left-wing Gothic as it were, affirming the need to grow in towering cathedrals (e.g. the choir of Cologne Cathedral) but at the same time growing into the many-sided man.

Perhaps it is terminology alone that divides me from T. E. Hulme. Perhaps what he calls Original Sin and limitation beneath God I call growth towards the Shadow on the human plane – the obverse side of the penny; just as what he calls classicism I call post-Renaissance balance between mind and nature through static forms. I don't know. Anyhow, whatever the historical truth about the Renaissance and Hulme may be, my ideal is the interiorised many-sided man and growth to him, and this ideal is not really in Renaissance art (Michelangelo?) for there can be no inner life in a body-culture. Hence Yeats's Unity of Being is an image of a body with the inner life implied, and it is implied more clearly in a Byzantine sage or Tutankhamun than it is in a flirting dancer.

8th February. And so in the period 1450-1550 it is so implied as to be often absent (Michelangelo). Hence the contradiction in Yeats between the sage and the speaking body, two aspects of one whole, two contradictions. Anyhow, to return to my argument, the image expresses Unity of Being, and my image expresses body-inner life-many-sidedness, and I find it difficult to make the mistake of identifying any one golden age in the past when this Unity was current, though I get hints from Byzantine and Gothic art and Michelangelo.

The essence of my Unity is the growth-principle, so growth is still behind my Unity of Being and the image. Is it too much to conclude that my growth-principle is behind all Unity of soul-body? I.e. the body is slack when there is no such growth, and taut when there is growth, i.e. the body is always a reflection of the striving of the man. Compare the idea that scientific and artistic creation are expressions of the same vital energy

417

(p471) – to what extent is creation connected with growth? If it is, how can static Tuohy create? (He can't incidentally – he has stuck.) And what of the fact that the 20th century has been very creative, yet seems to have lost touch with the growth-principle?

Anyhow, the point is, there is no complete Unity now, except in the case of an isolated individual here and there, and this seems to have little to do with creativity, which thrives through self-division. In fact, we experience "a schism in the soul" because our creative minority has failed us by abandoning growth and losing sense of the Unity of Being, and as a result we are creative in a baroque way, not a classical way. Classicism succeeds growth. After that everything splits up, e.g. the body (Puritanism) and the inner life (irreligion today). Cf the desymbolisation of the Renaissance, earlier, between growth and split.

9th February. Just as civilisation grows through a religion for the strong and declines into materialism, so it goes through Gothic – classical – and Baroque stages in art. Is this true? Anyhow, in terms of rise and fall alone, there is a progess from primitive/archaic (= Gothic?, soul and world muddled up); to classical (= Renaissance, when there is a balance between mind and nature in strict, static forms); to academic (too much respect for old forms); to mannerist (revolt against the conventional, creating an extreme world and feverish, caricatured expression, e.g. El Greco); to baroque (uneasiness and longing for freedom, fragments, organic not intellectual unity, pursuit of depth, rhythm, passion, grief and pain, e.g. Laocoon, love and death).

The main war is between classicism and baroque: classicism reduces nature to the human scale and records being and is interested only in mature, rational man; baroque is in a state of becoming, and is interested in all ages of man. This is a perfect definition of the difference between Tuohy and myself, and between discourse and image, and the whole Romantic tradition of Kermode, with its organicist view of the work of art, can be considered as periods of revived baroque.

The Modernists, then, are perhaps still in the "sickness of styles" (p527) and the experimentalism can be seen as the humanist prelude to a baroque proper. I quote: "The normal end of mannerism – its cure – lies in baroque. Once the spirit is again in contact with the world, the imagination drinks deeply... with an eagerness borne of long deprivation. The cosmos itself seems to be throbbing in the soul" (Bazin, p528). Perhaps Pound is a Mannerist, and I am one of the first of a new Baroque period that is Nordic rather than Southern (cf Tuohy). It is no accident that I wrote "this string of baroque pearls" (Spanish "barrueco") and that the baroque ideal is growth. It is clear who the academics are: the Edwardians and Georgians, and the Movement.

On sickness of styles: Greek, 4th century BC, French, 14th century AD and 1550-1600; Florentines, end of 15th century; Chinese sculpture under

Sung; 19th century French architecture. Mannerism: 18th Egyptian dynasty: Amenophis. Baroque: e.g. 50BC, 1534 and 15th century – eyeless head (p528). Byzantine art was "a new form of artistic expression and not merely a decay in technical processes" and "the creative value behind the artistic decline of ancient classical forms that resulted in the primitive forms of the Middle Ages".

10th February. While I was at the Bank of Japan yesterday C got me a book on the Renaissance and another on Michelangelo (1475-1564), and I looked for a connection between growth and the Renaissance. The nearest I came to it was in relation to Michelangelo's two visions "e son giganti" and "un gigante v'è ancor" (both 1534). Unfortunately there is a long poem, also 1534, which makes it clear that Michelangelo was against the giants: they are pride, and this is in keeping with his classicist limitation, which is opposed to growth – Baroque does not come until the artist approves of the giants, and Michelangelo is an early Mannerist. Possibly the giant is a criticism of the Pope or Christ, but I think the classicist explanation is sufficient.

How wrong Hulme was. The Renaissance was much more classical than the Gothic spires, much more limited in some ways. The Christian roots of Humanism, which Buchanan thought "balls". Hulme was nonetheless right. He saw that 400 years was coming to an end, though he failed to see abstract art as a Mannerist, pre- "baroque" retreat into another world – he confused Gothic and "baroque". And yet compare the Chicago Tribune Building to Rouen Cathedral's Tour de Beurre: 1928 and 1487 – he was not so wrong in predicting a return to medievalism.

What is the connection between Baroque and "Universal States"? Laocoon was 50BC – can one hypothesise about a United States of Europe from that? What about 4th century BC Greece? Anyhow, to turn to writing, I am sure that what Spender talks about, the Modernist turning away from reality, i.e. modern society, is a Mannerist withdrawal, whereas the Angry resistance to society is not Baroque – there is not enough throbbing celebration for it to be that. Baroque has to have a principle of dynamic movement and growth, and its advent in 20th century literature only really comes in my work. Sturm und Drang.

11th February. On Thursday 9th I wrote *Michelangelo and a Wheelchair Cross* – in fact most of it was written on Wednesday evening (8th). On Thursday (9th) and Saturday (11th) I tried, unsuccessfully for the most part, to write the defence of "religion for the strong" passage in the poems, and in the course of doing so discussed revolution very heatedly with C, trying to make a case for the "strophe". I: "The popular revolution will be the noblest revolution mankind has known, and there will be a referendum a year after seizure of power – a year to the very day. It will provide the only possible alternative to (Harold) Wilson (see Grimond's article on the absence of a practical opposition) and its aims are to raise the consciousness of the nation and effect a land revolution and redistribution of wealth that will get us out of our troubles." Why are people disaffected today? Think about that.

On Thursday night/Friday morning there was a fall of snow, and when I went in to my exam there was a patter on my umbrella like the rustle of polythene. By Saturday, there was a foot of snow and everything was quiet, save for the hissing gas fire and the occasional distant moaning of a plane. Nan built a snowman and was sad when I told her it would melt: "No, it will always be a snowman," she said, and I was aware of her innocence of time and death.

Mrs. Murata rang up on Saturday evening and asked me when I would visit her hotel to collect her present, the one she had brought up from the country this morning. (I did not know she was coming to Tokyo.) I said I could not visit her hotel. She: "When can I bring my present to your home this evening." I: "I will be out." We settled for leaving it at Tokyo University of Education. She is giving me an "on" so that I will correct her English or recommend her to the British Council. "Professor Seruizawa is the go-between."

12th February. After a morning in the local police station, after which I wrote *Paraffin Paper and Steam*, I groped towards a synthesis for the poems. The synthesis is in effect the growth principle of New Psychology (I had "forgotten" this until recently) and of Baroque and of Existentialism, and of the opposites of Reformation and Revolution, Saint and Leader, Church and State, head and body, Shadow and Reflection – an idea for which the *Archangel* Shadow on the Sky and Sir Thomas More are good images.

Particularly More, for like me he stands at the threshold of a new age – just as he is the first English rebuilder after the transition from the Middle Ages, so perhaps I am the first rebuilder (in art) after the transition from the "Modern Age" that More began. (Osborne being the last destroyer.) Moreover, the new "internationalist" period will probably last as long as the old nationalist period that began in More's time, and More is surely a good example of the interiorised many-sided man: lawyer, literateur (he knew Lyly), M.P., social theorist, master of requests at court and privy councillor, Lord Chancellor, art critic (he knew Holbein) and historian, he was in addition a scholar (a friend of Erasmus) who loathed the logic of the schoolmen ("milking a he-goat into a sieve") and who was sufficiently true to his identity of freedom and the spirit to choose his own death rather than compromise himself. A noble whole man and a "spiritual" man, perhaps he was the last (1478-1535) in whom the "Unity of Being" is to be found.

But just as diversity and self-division are the rule after 1550, so in the new era which confronts us there will be a new unity, and Unity of Being will be a practical and realisable existentialist principle for the Mores of the new Baroque "Renaissance".

13th February. And it is literally "Being". The Shadow is Being, and the Reflection is in Becoming, and one must grow into Being. That is why the new psychological principle is an existentialist one. Yet it is the oldest of principles – it is far older than the classics, the death of the ego and the birth of the self. The new Renaissance or "rebirth" will be of the growth principle and the many-sidedness it brings, and just as More and Colet and Erasmus thought of northern barbarism in terms of the classics, so will the new rebirth think of northern barbarism in terms of psychodynamic growth. And Unity – hence Libra in the poem.

Will there be a new "Elizabethan" Golden Age to rival Augustus's? It is possible. It is possible that it will occur within my lifetime – that the end of World War 2 was Actium and that I will take part in it. Anyhow, the new internationalist period will centre around a new conception of man, that I am sure of. In such periods there are generally Reformations and Revolutions, if the past nationalist era is anything to go by. It is doubtful whether there would be either of these, but it is worth noting that More was for the New Learning and against the rest.

What should my attitude be towards Revolution (a) as regards the U.K. before U.S.E., (b) as regards Europe – assuming that the "Revolutionary Era" has not come to an end, which it may well have done. In the case of (b) I would be against, bar the conclusion in *Archangel* (a People's Hall, benevolent, spiritual Leaders) but as regards (a) I am still in doubt, though I think in my centre I am against. Again like More after 1521.

14th February. Finished the defence of religion passage in the poem and then went to Keio for the exams. 200 papers to be corrected. A slow thaw continued. Snow impressions: chains on car tyres, snow hung on the fruit trees like blossom, and on the firs it was mountains. A lamp peeped over the crags like an afternoon moon.

On Monday evening I had a long talk with C, after she had complained she felt only "flashes of enthusiasm", and that people were not as nice as she had been brought up to believe. (Cf Tuohy's comment to the same effect three weeks ago, and my similar belief.) I told her that living wasn't easy, but that there was both good and bad, both beauty and horror, and that to see the beauty you had to wash your eyes clean and make an effort to overcome the enemy that lay somewhere between the forehead and the nape of the neck. I also said that for me the only way to keep fresh was through art, and that she should take her painting more seriously. I spoke for about 20 minutes, and what surprised me most of all was my authority and confidence, e.g. as regards growth.

The period of doubt and self-doubt seems over. When C said "Oh but everything seems so difficult – you are obstructed" I said quite genuinely and spontaneously that just as I had rejected bourgeois Loughton and so I could not depend on their help as regards living in Loughton, so I had rejected the poetic Establishment and therefore I could not depend on their co-operation. "I am twenty or thirty years before my time" I said. "It's like my hair. Everyone howled in 1957 when I grew it long and now it's much shorter than everyone else's. Not an exact parallel: there were plenty of long-hairs in 1957, though none in Loughton. Am I a Little Englander at heart for all my supranationalism?

15th February. A day correcting exam papers and going to MITI, where I learnt the Japanese intentions if Britain gets into the Common Market. The Japanese will form their own Market – surely this would be the basis for a new attempt at empire in the l970s?

Otherwise reread bits of Toynbee. Like Eliot, Yeats and Hulme, Toynbee has a theory that touches on the Unity of Being: the élan of growth (challenge and response) becomes schism in the soul ("a schism in the souls of human beings will be found to underlie any schism that reveals itself on the surface of the society which is the common ground"). In other words, there is self-division in "the disintegration phase of a civilisation" (Somervell, i 429). Toynbee tentatively dates the beginning of the phase to the Reformation, so there is a surprising similarity between his view and Yeats's, although Toynbee is against the Renaissance and is rather ambiguous as to whether it is the end of growth (cf 5th century BC Athens for art) or the beginning of breakdown.

What happens to this self-division in a Universal State, i.e. will there be a return to Unity of Being in a United States of Europe? The answer seems to be, from the point of society, "No". There are alternatives in a response to a challenge in this phase, and "as the process of disintegration works itself out, the alternative choices tend to become more rigid in their limitations, more extreme in their divergence.... That is to say, the spiritual experience of schism in the soul is a dynamic movement, not a static situation" (cf *The Silence*). After the dynamic process has been undergone, however, the individual can win for himself a measure of Unity.

The alternatives are in personal behaviour, as a substitute for creativity: abandon and self-control; in social behaviour, as a substitute for mimesis (passive) truancy (= desertion) and (active) martyrdom (= loyalty), rebellion and responsibility (truancy and promiscuity are "proletarianization" to Toynbee); in personal feeling, as a substitute for élan ("that movement of élan in which the nature of growth seems to reveal itself", Somervell, i 430): (passive) drift (= hostile universe of Camus and Hardy) and (active) sense of sin (= mastery of self); in social feeling, as a substitute for the sense of style (= subjective differentiation): (passive) promiscuity (eg lingua franca, syncretism) and (active) sense of unity (of mankind and cosmos and God); in life, as a substitute for a movement from Macrocosm to Microcosm (= self): on the one hand a violent pair, (passive) archaism and (active) futurism (i.e. Utopias, Revolutions) and on the other hand a gentle pair, (passive) detachment and (active) transfiguration (= Nirvana and the Kingdom of God which is "within you"). According to Toynbee, only transfiguration of these two pairs works – the others are cul-de-sacs.

Anyhow, the individual who chooses self-control and martyrdom (= responsibility) and a sense of sin (= mastery of self, cf Wilson) and sense of Unity (Alexander's Homonoia or Concord, a social thing) will be a unified man in a divided culture, and such a man will choose the gentle against the violent, the microcosm against the macrocosm, i.e. "transfiguration" against "futurism", and this choice is the subject of my poem: Reflection and Shadow, Revolution and "Reformation".

My sense of growth then is, to Toynbee, a way of life, which is how I've always thought of it – it is a substitute for the microcosmic way of life in a healthy phase of Western civilisation. Does Latin poetry of the Augustan age have the same preoccupations, e.g. the end of the first *Georgic*? And is it true that great art comes out of schism (dialectic) rather than growth, and that the abandonment of a traditional style is a sign of disintegration? What of my new Baroque? And Eliot?

17th February. A day of arrangements and touring Tokyo and letter-writing. Otherwise dipped into Toynbee again. The first interesting point is the relation between Universal States and spiritual vision. An external unity inspires such an inner unity (p 495). Then transfiguration and detachment are results of simplification in the macrocosm, = environment, and consequent gains in the microcosm, = self ("etherialisation"), and are therefore "symptoms of growth" (p 531): "every example of human growth will be found to have a social as well as an individual aspect".

Is this not a statement of my law of reality and of the idea that a few pour their being into the dead society of the bourgeois and keep it alive? Toynbee sees transfiguration-growth as having a Church-social aspect ("a society ... of some other kind", p531) and thus his law of reality does not assert that increased growth vitalises institutions. In fact he seems to be rather suspicious of movements back into the macrocosm: "geographical expansion coincides with deterioration in quality" (p 191), i.e. "geographical expansion, or 'painting the map red' is no criterion whatever of the real growth of a civilization" (p 189). "More often than not geographical expansion is a concomitant of real decline and coincides with a 'time of troubles' or a universal state – both of them stages of decline and disintegration. Times of trouble produce militarism..., the cause of breakdown" (p 190).

His criterion, then, is the microcosm, and expansion to him is a getting away from the self which leaves the nation enfeebled, as it has with Britain. I have always thought of geographical expansion as a sign of vitality. If I adopt the self as the criterion of growth, then I bypass the difficulty caused by the creation of the British Empire by materialists and I am really pleased that my principle of growth is the growth-principle of Gothic art and medieval civilisation.

19th February. On Saturday (18th) Tuohy came and was much more nice than usual; probably as a result of Tomlin's praise. More probably still because he agrees with my argument in the Eliot book. Certainly he is very much against Winters, and he bothered to quote a passage from *Encounter*: an article by G. S. Fraser saying that Empson had once said that rhythm was the one thing a clever non-poet could not fake. Rhythm and cadence being my strongest points.

Otherwise he made various points: the Renaissance was not invented until the 19th century – cf "I didn't know I was living in the Thirties"; Unity of Being as regards the past is a myth, and the thing to do is to detect it in a contemporary; is there a cosmic pessimism, to which I said "No", neither Hardy nor Camus ("benign indifference of the universe") is right, existence just is; on Buchenwald and the envy of Englishmen for the transforming experience (Krebs's, Conrad's Marlow's, the Ancient Mariner's) which is the justification for suffering – "I go into exile and suffer and deepen myself"; so Snow has no right to write about Paustovsky, for Snow has led a comfortable landlubber's life; also "there are no short cuts in writing, and those who seem to have taken a short cut are later disqualified"; and "*Notes from Underground* has no facts and is therefore unreadable" (disagree); and "According to Huxley, neither 'population' nor 'food' is mentioned in Toynbee's index – it's all élites"; and "since the French revolution, all revolutions are bound up with war, and there couldn't be a revolution in England because people have too much prosperity to lose."

We listened to Radio China, and Nan came through and we talked about childhood, and on the way down to the car we discussed the possibility of sharing a room in London after October, i.e. using it two days every three weeks or so.

20th February. Tried to write but I was worn out: the last two weeks have drained me – I have had several new leads and have, in addition, corrected some 350-400 exam papers. Also, the business of the Nixons interfered with my concentration. For although the affair makes me shake with fury – I am asked for £50 in the name of the family and am then spat at for sending it – I wonder if I do not create hostility in others, almost subconsciously, so as to keep myself and my family isolated. I am not certain about this, and certainly I do attract hostility (e.g. Ranger); I am provoked, that is the point. Certainly Adrian and Tony did the provoking, and they are primarily to blame for the mess-up in my relationship with them, but in general I find it extremely difficult to get on with people for a length of time, knowing them well, unless they think of me as a writer. So I never quarrelled with the Fitzsimmons, and I have never really quarrelled with Tuohy (except for reactions on my part to aggressions by him) and certainly not with Buchanan. It is the people who refuse to allow me to be who I am that I quarrel with. For I am fighting for my role. That is not strictly true, for it is also the people who impose on me (e.g. with money, for demands) and who challenge me or interfere with me (Adrian and Tony). On the other hand, perhaps they do not treat me as the genius I would like to be.

21st February. Yesterday I went to MITI and the Japanese in charge of all relations between OECD and EEC and Japan both confirmed what I learnt on February 15th. Accordingly today, after recording the English dictation for the entrance exam at Tokyo University of Education, I visited the Embassy, by appointment. The first man I bumped into was Adrian, who was sheepish. I said I was going to invite him anyway for Friday week, he said it was a pity I hadn't gone to the party because it "swung" and then he said, "Are you here on business?" and went. I read some of Ricks's reviews and then went for a brisk walk round the garden with P, who was in a white shirt. The walk took 5 mins, and I only had time to tell him about MITI. He: "I can't give our view of the EEC in relation to Japan; I will enquire what it is and let you know."

The recent secret Bonn-Paris deal has softened the impact of what I had to say. How can a wedge be driven between Bonn and Paris, using E. Germany and the French recognition of the Oder-Neisse line? Or German trade with E. Germany? Could we not form an alliance with Russia and E. Europe and so pave the way for East-West unity later by being a bridge between East and West? Raise this with P next time.

Otherwise I still felt uncreative, and not too optimistic about going home. I have sacrificed my career to my quest, and sometimes I wonder if I am not going to dry up, if my quest did not reach an end with *The Silence*. These are my moments of hell.

22nd February. "Not the height but the drop is terrible", says Zarathustra, and if the drop is self-doubt, how true. I wrote the passage that has held me up for a week – all 30 lines or so – and I was elated, and it did not matter that I was given a vile nerve cocaine injection at the dentist's, and that I fainted and had to sit with my head between my knees. The sensation: a sweat on a cold head, the dentist moving away, and myself powerless to shout out and warn, and a great ringing in the ears.

23rd February. I existed in my role as teacher, and not in my role as writer, and the agony. For it was the biannual British Council conference. I have always considered Cromwell an enemy for inventing the committee; who invented the conference? After Tomlin opened the session we moved into the Council-recruited teachers' three quarters of an hour. One is supposed to get grievances redressed. I have no grievances that can be solved (tax and transport for Nan are insoluble). So I said virtually nothing. Why should I say anything when I am leaving in October and have nothing to offer? Besides, the chairs were so arranged as to give a confrontation between speaker and the rest, and I had nothing to confront the Council with, and everything that was said was trivial and unreal and futile and a waste of time. "Conditions of service" was devoted to furniture and the need for the British Council to inspect lecturers' houses, and it was all hot air, and nothing was decided in the end.

After a break for coffee we heard out Bickley and Ann Gegg, and yawning with boredom I went off to see the book exhibition and then had lunch at the Swiss Chalet. On my table were Tomlin and Dr. Lloyd and Miss Woods and Peter Mann and someone else, and most of the time we talked about the rootlessness of the man who goes abroad, for Dr. Lloyd has been in Japan 15 years and he knows he will not be able to settle in England when he is compulsorily retired: a new generation has grown up, one he cannot understand. Tomlin was bored stiff, and he left early.

Afterwards I went to the Bank of Japan and proposed an Anglo-East European Common Market to Fukuchi and wrote out a Curriculum Vitae for Ichiki. I got home at 6.15 and Tuohy called and I went off with him and C to the Taylors' cocktail party near the Hotel Okura. The whiskies were large and after a couple I lit up and was full of confidence, talking with Alan Baker about Germany and the possibility of getting jobs there. Later I talked with Tomlin. I had just received a letter from him saying he had sent a copy of my letter to London "with the kind of recommendation for the future which, I trust, may bring about the results you desire".

After I had thanked him and told him I was quite moved, we got on to poetry. He said how good *The Death-Fires* was, and so far as I recall through my drunkenness, said I was a better poet than Auden because Auden has never written one poem he is remembered by, as Eliot did and I have. He was also very much in favour of Read's organic form – he agreed with Kermode about that – and he told me that Read is dying of cancer. He was quite cut up about it, as Read is a friend, "a good friend".

I left after admiring a Ross Thomas landscape, a gift for a wedding anniversary, and went back with Tuohy and ate spaghetti with Collcutt and the Guests, and again I caught fire. There was nothing I could not do or say, I was full of wit and made Guest giggle several times by being ironic about the British Council as regards its connection with the sons of Prime Ministers (Takahashi, Kenichi Yoshida). I got steadily more drunk and when I left at 10.30 I was reeling and I "rolled" down the slope, seeing Miss Hirose to a taxi, and was violently sick about four times before dropping off for a few hours.

24th February. I awoke at 4 or 5, and had a violent hangover, and attended the British Council Conference second day without being able to see or think, and with the memory of lurching, feeling a tingling in my nose and my inside topping over my throat. Peter Mann spent an hour on teaching with a monkey (he revealed he went to Australia after the war to work for immigrants from Europe, i.e. he is a Jew) and then Frank was called upon for his lecture, and for the first time he made me recognise his genius. His perceptions ("Japanese lack presentation and proportion", "they don't know that literature is not exemplary", i.e. that you can't call Macbeth wicked, and to a Japanese an emotion is produced by a work of art for sentimentality and "because it corresponds to their experience") had a weight that was almost Johnsonese. His aphorisms quite stunned me.

The evening before in the taxi he had said that "like all Englishmen married to a Japanese, Keene has a chip on his shoulder" and I had immediately objected, "Toff hasn't, and he came from the East End too," and Tuohy got very angry and lashed out, saying how sophisticated Keene's wife is, how she is a divorcée. (The British Council "call girl" was holding Keene by the arm, in between staring into Peter Mann's eyes.) He lashed out because I was right. There was no uncertainty like that in his performance today. He began in a panic – when Tuohy is flustered he hits out: aggression is his defence, as I know from bitter experience. And so he started badly, dismissing Peter Mann's lecture, saying he'd gone on too long (20 mins being the maximum he talks for) and then saying "When I went to the Shakespeare conference at Sendai Mr Tomlin gave a lecture and a Japanese said 'I know that already'. I said 'You shouldn't know it. It was all facts.'" Hardly a compliment to Tomlin. He also lashed out at the Eliot book: "You can see from it that the Japanese don't know how to present anything." It was all brilliant, but it was so near the bone, and clearly some people thought he'd gone too far.

"Blunt but true" was a comment last night when he said, "I thought Ann Gegg had tried to dress for her lecture, and I thought she looked awfully tired." "Blunt but true" – that is the nature of Tuohy's genius, or so I thought in my drunken hangover this morning. Honesty – that is his greatest gift. I have never met a man who is so dedicated to honesty. "Honesty – that's the basis of British culture," Baker said last night. If that is so, the British Council can have very little culture, for it is an extremely tactful organisation. But I can see what he meant.

What really subdued me was *Desirable English and Available English* a lecture that was handed round cyclostyled. Again, it was the authority and the weight that dominated me. And the imagery ("red wig" – does he wear that for God? – "toothbrush", etc.) is consistent. And the whole piece is a whole and is full of illuminations. I think it is his best non-fictional work. It has gained in maturity since China and the Japanese article and the Eliot book. It is also much more Angry, and perhaps this is my influence. He is now at his prime, having come through the difficult time of the last two years. Though he will always be a wasted genius. He shattered me, and I could not reform until after coffee, in Niblett's dry and patronising lecture, and then I had to go home and sit and brood for three hours. He had taken a pill, yes, but he had not slept. I had not taken a pill but I had slept, and I felt awful.

26th February. Possibly my exhaustion led to to overvalue Tuohy on Friday. Certainly I was so tired when I made that entry that I overlooked one thing. Tuohy has completely changed his mind about a writer having to say something, and that essay represents a conversion to my point of view, a conversion he had not undergone last summer when he attacked my poem because it was trying to say something. Perhaps all I have said about pressure – real experience pressing the words into meaning – has had an effect and I have influenced him. Perhaps too he is now through the arid spell and can become a major writer, like Yeats in 1916. I forgot to record some of Tomlin's words on Thursday: "If you can write three lines, as you can, you're one of the immortals"; "Eliot had exactly the same trouble as you"; "write to me from wherever you are in the future if ever you think I may be able to help you." Took C to see *Is Paris Burning*? which is the French *The East is Red*: lots of cheering liberator De Gaulle, lots of flag-waving.

Buchanan came. It was a dismal day, and he had "arhythmia", i.e. his heart has been beating irregularly, without rhythm. Consequently he cannot drink saké, and so we drank wine all evening, and discussed the old world and the prospect of an Eastern European Common Market including Britain, and Savonarola, and I awoke at 3 a.m. and was awake until 6, when I disastrously dropped off to sleep.

27th February. As a result I am utterly worn out today and cannot write a word. C has been sick and I have spent the morning taking Nan to school, and answering the door to tradesmen and feeling angry at the waste of time. October is closing up, and I am too worn out to write.

Went to Hitachi and did the Reformation, came back and thought about Savonarola (1452-1498). He was too asexual (a bit of the Rasputin itch would have done him good) and perhaps he was too puritanical a cleaner of cities, e.g. over carnivals, but the way he united the preacher and agitator should make him a hero, especially as Michelangelo was a disciple. (Hence Michelangelo's opposition to the Papacy in *The Last Judgement*, his first Baroque work.)

Savonarola was not ambitious; events brought him fame. He entered a convent in Bologna in 1475 and after failing as a Dominican preacher in Florence there were four years' withdrawal, 1485-9, in Lombardy. After his successful return he was made Prior of San Marco and came into conflict with Lorenzo and then his son Piero, and after Piero pledged Florence to Charles VIII in 1494 there had to be a revolution before Savonarola was thrown up to treat, and it was only after Charles VIII had gone back on his word after entering Florence that Savonarola was chosen first citizen (the parties being at war) and evidently felt embarrassed about going into politics: see his defence (Roeder p 57): "necessary for the health of your souls....Your reform must begin with the things of the spirit, which are above the material....If you desire a good government you must restore it to God."

In 1496/7 he went to extremes and rounded up prostitutes and enforced the moral law (p 78). This was a loss of grip, or else it must be seen as the normal consequences of a revolution, i.e. Savonarola (anticipates) the Cromwell tradition, and had to tighten his grip. It was his refusal to join the Pope's league that brought him down, along with the excommunication and the Arrabbiati. The Franciscan challenge to an Ordeal by Fire was immediately responsible for his arrest.

He caved in under torture and denied God, and his theoretical ideal ended in a dance under a gibbet until his slack corpse swung in the breeze and the flames leapt up and burnt it to ashes. Fra Silvestro had seen it all in 1489: "Three guardian angels linking these three hearts with a triple chain and dancing in the August sky" (p22). He had always been obsessed by death.

28th February. Went to MITI and was paid the equivalent of £13.10s for seeing five men in four hours, 40 minutes of which were breaks. As regards information, the most interesting was Kawasaki, who is in charge of the new plan to liberalise capital, and who spent 40 minutes telling me what he is going to do while I wrote it down. (Sorge's *Memoirs*: "A shrewd spy will not spend all his time on the collection of military and political secrets and classified documents. Also, I may add, reliable information cannot be procured by effort alone; espionage work entails the accumulation of information, often fragmentary, covering a broad field, and the drawing of conclusions based thereon" (Willoughby p64).

The most provoking was Maki, who is in charge of all Japan's dealings with the EEC, and who asked me what Europeans thought of Japanese industry, products and people. I pulled my punches and did not say: "The Japanese has replaced the Jew as money-grubber; he is a bore who is obsessed with exports and finding something new to imitate." I said there was genuine admiration, and envy, for such industries as shipbuilding, along with wonder as to how paternalism and efficiency could be combined so effectively (the answer being "on"); as regards products, I said that people no longer thought of "Made in Japan" as a sign of cheapness, as they did in the 1930s – it is now a sign of (albeit imitative) quality, and is often pushed at the expense of feelings and values e.g. in South Africa, Vietnam and Red Guard China (the Japanese wars in Canton); as regards people I said everyone knows they are the most polite of peoples, but after the initial politeness there is a question mark, possibly based on ignorance and distance. This was a polite way of trying to say that they are bores with their small-talk and faceless lack of individuality, after the initial charm of their Asian smile has worn off.

1st March. Finished the two Ages passage in the poem and went off to the Prince and spent the afternoon hearing him on Romanesque art. 1025-1190s odd – the period covered the Norman invasion but did not go up to Philip Augustus; not a distinguished period, I would have thought. Hitachi was most distressed at not having seen a Romanesque Cathedral (Ely, Peterborough, Durham, Pisa, Caen) and kept trying to convince me that Westminster Abbey, Notre Dame and the Rhenish castles were not Gothic. He also tried to convince me that the French châteaux were all post Francis I, which is not true.

On the way back from the palace my thoughts drifted back to the conference. The truth is, I am different from other people. I feel different from them, I sense their surprise when I said strange things (Alan Baker's surprise on Thursday evening when I talked about the Bonn-Paris Axis instead of the conference). I do not react as they do. Perhaps that is why I am a poet. My thoughts drifted on to my departure from Japan. What have I done here but tried to become "normal" – an insider? The leading private University, the leading public university (Todai), the Prince, the Central Bank, and the "most important Ministry" (Saito, last week on MITI) – is not all this an attempt to escape my difference and be a conventional Englishman and bourgeois? Perhaps what I secretly long to be in London?

Now I am turning my back on it all, and am choosing Nothing: the elusive pain of the familiarity of failure in the eyes of family. I can't rank the Establishment very highly, I can't lay very great stress on disguising my difference, can I? Yet I have vowed never to get a job where this difference will make itself known in all its nakedness – and teaching is not a bad disguise.

2nd March. To the Bank of Japan after drafting the bit about individual ideal. Had lunch with Ichiki, Saito and Watarai. The conversation began with universities and never got off it until I went to see their film on the Bank of England. On education in the modern age. Is more specialisation necessary, as the Japanese system has decided? I think the reverse; what is needed is a whole vision, i.e. there should be a basis which can be built on later. Such a vision is just as important for a politician as for a writer. The old Renaissance ideals of Latin and Greek are perhaps justly discredited, but the ideal of the many-sided all-rounder is not.

As a result of all this, in the evening made an important distinction. Savonarola, Cromwell, Mao and all the other Puritans impose moral rectitude, and this I am absolutely against. Women immodestly dressed, whores, pubs, racing, dancing, gambling, blasphemy, homosexuality, overeating, lovemaking on Sundays – all are quite all right by me, and their elimination should never be enforced by any government. To deny the body is to cut off all possibility of being a unity. On the other hand when pleasure becomes an end in itself people lose touch with themselves, and to live unreally is a bad thing in terms of one's existential criterion of living.

The modern prophet should not clean the cities morally – he should show people the way to themselves. Morality has nothing to do with prophecy or sainthood or being a visionary, an artist, a philosopher. It is an artificial code beside feeling and what is real, which are the criteria that matter. The senses should be fresh, and if you feel real and fresh by lovemaking in public, then that's all right. Only find the way to yourself.

3rd March. A crisis in my poetry. I am trying to write the individual ideal, which is to be followed by "the way of life" which can make it possible, the substitute for Christianity. This ideal must be expressed in an image. It must bear the relation to Freeman that perfection does to imperfection, so it should be imaged in a work of art, a sculpture of Michelangelo proportions. Freeman is the Existentialist Hero who grows towards the perfection, so this ideal Shadow must embody in its existence, just as Freeman does, the ideal qualities of the interiorised many-sided man, growth and "unity". From the thematic point of view, the sculpture should be in a Cathedral rather than a museum.

How do I do it? This has held me up all day. Perhaps I should do it by contrast, i.e. have Freeman looking at two figures, one a mechanical one, all bits of plate and screws and wires and cogs and pulleys and nuts and numbers (the Reflection), and the other a perfect giant, a creator united on organic lines, a unity of genius with a taut body. Do not look for a real equivalent, then; treat it as a vision and emphasise the strangeness, coming in a Cathedral; so it all passes away and the floor is bare? Perhaps the medieval man can be dying, and the towering giant can be seen against a tree on which appear saints' heads (the rose-wheel) like apples. His limbs can be associated with branches.

I am still not sure whether I shall use this idea – I have now got tied up with Archbishop Harsnett, the founder of Chigwell (School), and his bust in BS1 (Big School One) but I probably shall, even though it is not my original intention. Art is always different from one's original intention.

4th March. After a day of despair in my writing, not being able to write the individual ideal passage once again, Adrian came at 6.30 p.m. He is leaving the Embassy. Independence is his ideal now, I suspect because of me and because he is told off by Ellingworth, and also because there is no incentive for him to be real. "I drift through the day and keep up appearances." Most of the Embassy men lose their passion, but "Sydney Giffard is intensely real and he works hard". Adrian is going to Leukas this summer and he takes the bar exam in September. He will then go into Chambers and try to stay alive by fending for himself. A commendable decision from the existential point of view.

Otherwise he was a little apt to disagree for disagreement's sake: over the Japanese and over China, to give opinions which contradicted ones I have heard in the past simply to keep an end up or dominate. He asked me what I am trying to do in my writing and I told him I am aiming at a whole vision, and that my work must be seen as a whole, and there will be, perhaps, 10 long poems, all of which must be read in the light of each other. He asked what my quest was towards. I: "To myself at the age of 80, with certain ideal qualities vested in that Self." Which virtually echoed something he had said earlier: "You have chosen a career: at the age of 60 you will look back and remember the time you have written, not the time you have done other things."

Before he went I drank orange juice and that night the spring winds battered the bungalow like a typhoon and the heat went up and neither C nor I could sleep much.

5th March. On Sunday I sat around, worn out, and suddenly came to life and wrote the last block of the poem while the wind beat on outside. In the afternoon I went for a squally walk to the Cathedral, and got the idea for the ladder of perfection passage. We sat in one of the pews until a congregation began to drift in, and then we walked back, the wind tugging at the roofs and moaning in the telephone wires. It was a dusty, smoky wind, and it did not really make me feel fresh.

I went to Hitachi and learnt that Japan intends to press for peace talks later this year, about October he thought: "Our economy will be fine by then, whereas now it would be difficult." This was on Gaimusho authority, and I got the information because he volunteered a bit about disagreeing with the American Ambassador over Vietnam, in reply to which I drew his attention to Japan's £750,000,000 a year trade with America as a result of Vietnam.

In the evening I took C to see *The Quiller Memorandum*, the script being by Pinter. A realistic treatment of the spy's isolation, with the indifference of the controller exaggerated. A gripping comedy of menace, completely impossible but credible while it happened. The pain…was a bruise on the way home.

6th March. I don't consider my poems are aiming at targets: I don't see how an image-poem can aim at a target, and *Twilight* is not an "Angry" poem….I am determined my natural "genius" (i.e. poetic inspiration) should not be stifled by small groups of men in secure jobs who lay down the law about what is modest and what is overambitious. I will not write about pots or fauna or hedges. Why should I, when everyone else is, and it would be no more "me" than any hack article I have done is "me"?

7th March. Wrote the "spurting of iron" passage and decided to finish this poem as quickly as possible and then get on to the stories as soon as possible. Wrote other little bits later during the day, e.g. Churchill's funeral….Poetry is for me at present a very rewarding luxury that pays nothing. I want to return to poetry, but I know by experience how difficult it is. Poetry is, for me, agony, whereas I can write good, fresh prose in my sleep. Poetry is squeezed out of me. I shall move on to prose. So decisions are taken, as now: there is no conscious "I will", just a current that reveals itself, almost imperceptibly, and gains weight by accumulations.

8th March. After writing the individual ideal passage straight through, my emotion fresh, I went to Hitachi and taught him Gothic art. On Monday I learnt that the Japanese will sue for peace talks in October or later still, but learnt nothing comparable today. On Tuesday I went to MITI and learnt who the policy-makers are and, among other things, that MITI will impose a massive embargo on all EEC and UK goods if the Kennedy Round talks fail. On Thursday, after writing the passage about the rebel I went to the

Bank of Japan and learnt that Sasaki will in fact become President of the Japan Development Bank in April and will therefore control the shipbuilding industry finance and the Japanese plan to dominate the seven seas.

Otherwise I felt bruised. I was asked for £92 as second assessment of tax for 1966, and £109 Residence tax for 1966; by October I will have to pay 5/6 of the same amount or thereabouts for tax 1967; i.e. this year, I shall be giving about £400 in tax to the Japanese authorities, over and above the annual £200 which is deducted at source.

9th March. Tomlin's farewell for Baker. A packed room, a lot of shouting from menopausish women, claustrophobia; and I had "pinkeye" (conjunctivitis) which I caught from Nan. It was like a crimson sunset, and I wore glasses and M said almost straight away "You look studious." I confessed and she said "Get away" and then "Why don't you wear darks?" I said "I'd look like President Sukarno" and she said "Oh wonderful," and "I would like to see the daughter." Meanwhile I had spoken to P about China ("Do you think the Red Guard movement is being slowed down?" he asked) and one or two general things.

After talking to Kuriyagawa, Ann Gegg and Toff, I spoke to Baker-Bates. Stokes is learning Japanese in England, having gone home because Charlotte came up in rashes, i.e. had a psychological aversion to the Japanese. P invited me to lunch tomorrow. "Where in Tokyo would you like to eat?" I: "Somewhere where we can talk." Meanwhile M had come up to engage the boring Japanese women in talk, i.e. to liberate P. (P: "M will see to her" – before out talk.) When P told her I would be coming to lunch she said "Won't be in. I've got a hen party at the Okura." P said, "What a pity." I: "I'm sorry M won't be there." M: "Oh, you man you." Whereupon she hung on my arm until P patted her bottom. (Earlier she was kissed on the cheek by the Scientific Attaché, when P wasn't looking.)

On the way back I talked to Guest's wife and Kawawaki ("Let me babysit for you") and Ninomiya ("I enjoyed your article" – this in front of Tuohy). Later, after presenting a united back to Whitehead, we left with Tuohy. On the way out I realised I was going between two women and said "Oh dear, I'm going through the middle"; whereupon the left hand woman (who had red hair and was British) said, "There's nothing I like more than a nice handsome young man going through my middle." I was still protesting my amazement as Tomlin showed us out, and having felt C pick my pocket for the coat-tab, said to Tomlin "I could have sworn your maid picked my pocket." At which he laughed for a good ten seconds.

Tuohy did not say a great deal startling in Nicola's. The main thing was his Council report: Baker called him in and went red ("because he knew I wasn't on his side") and pleaded with him to change it for two hours. "London will be shattered if you send this." Tuohy: "He's gone down in my estimation; he's a timeserver." Yet Tuohy is probably wrong to put the truth before tact in a matter like this. He also set himself up against Pinter, having,

433

like us, seen *The Quiller Memorandum*. I had praised Pinter's one word dialogue, and Tuohy had to give us a set piece from himself to keep his head above water. I was very flattered that he should not have sent his address (Tumbler's Bottom, Kilmersdon, near Frome, Somerset) to anyone else in Japan except me. I got to bed late and did not sleep too well, and was rather dull on Friday morning.

11th March. After making the transition to Freeman as artist, I went and lunched with P. He was reading an airmail letter in crimson biro when his maid let me in, and he seemed preoccupied: "It was a nice party at Frederick's last night." He got me a Scotch with soda and ice and we sat and discussed China. We lunched on soup, steak and apple-pie – cheese (prepared by M and cooked by the maid). He drove me to the Embassy in his wide, long Zephyr and I left him going in to see Crowson.

12th March. On Saturday I wrote the bit on the pot and the need to build the spiritual "message" or value into it, and then thought about writing. Everything today has to be written through facts. The *Observer* was full of it. Bryden on Mortimer's sense of the 1930s (tennis, roadhouses, two seaters, ukeleles being the beginning of lack of seriousness, cf today's scampi, Majorcan holidays and Victorian chamberpots); and on *Howard's End* (what is missing from the stage play is "the sense of London, grey and rootless, rising and falling; the opposing life of grass and vine, green, rooted and timeless"); Gilliatt on Zeffirelli's film of *The Taming of the Shrew* (Shakespeare meant Padua so the cast behave literally like Italians); the new anthology of the Liverpool Poets, which is full of place names and so on; and the assumptions behind the new novels. Everything must be factual and realistic today, as Tuohy is always saying. So, Waley had to insert facts into impressionistic haiku he was translating.

Observation is important. One must be concrete and thingy, and not have too many ideas. (I approve of this.) One must not have "metaphysical come-uppance" or a point of view. The artist is a maker who is detached and who is trying to find out what a work of art is. He must not be "overambitious", he must "hit his target" in the sense that Osborne is aiming at a target. There has, in other words, been a fantastic movement from within to the external and outside.

On Sunday I wrote the passage on sick London, near the end, and talked Popes and subsidizing artists with Buchanan, who came in the evening. His long account of Penson.

13th March. Wrote the "self" part of the self in society summary – Freeman's rejection of action for vision, of movements for images – and then went to Hitachi. Read a passage from *The Wind in the Willows* and thought him Mole with his full stomach; was asked the meaning of "we will unit (sic)" – in a letter to Haneko from a NZ friend. Did Richelieu and Mazarin and the War of Spanish Succession.

Later went to Tomlin's to say farewell to Tuohy until tomorrow. The initial talk about the definite offer of a scholarship, mentioned by Baker and later Tomlin, which I have heard nothing about. Otherwise films and Harry Guest in *A Sleep of Prisoners*. The silences. Into dinner. Hannah and the IADC actor (Ken McDonald) did not turn up, so Ann Gegg was sat on Tuohy's right, C on Tomlin's right (as the only other Englishwoman), and Mrs. Guest on Tomlin's left. I had to switch with Guest and sit next to her and Ann Gegg, opposite Baker. The crippling dinner of five courses and two wines and champagne. Tuohy's attacks on Tomlin: "You are learning Japanese"; Waley; disagreeing over the family in China; "the Austro-Hungarian and Ottoman empires were not good empires." Tomlin's nostalgia for the 1920s. Noh, Tomlin not having read my report, and thus not knowing I did six translations.

I felt different. I felt as I did at the conference; what they were saying was a waste, a senseless, avoidable waste. Committees, conferences, dinner parties and amateur dramatics are the four most terrible of British institutions. After dinner we drank brandies without the ladies over a cigar. Tomlin reminisced about Leavis and Tuohy choked Guest off ("It's easy to sneer when you're young") and I said all the wrong things (how dilapidated the graveyard near the Brooke monument in Sciathos was). We adjourned to the main room and Tomlin sat by me and raised business, after which we were mercifully able to withdraw, having to relieve the babysitter.

14th March. Left the poems and went on to the stories and wrote *Antie Joone said Moosic* and *A Sun Setting in Blood*. In the evening Tuohy came, after seeing *Who's Afraid*, Elizabeth Taylor being Hannah. ("He's no good in bed.") I raised the offer of a scholarship, saying I had already made my decision, and was pleased Tuohy said "You'll never make much money if you turn it down, but I would turn it down." This got us on to "them", and the System. Tuohy: "Anyone who knows you're writing will try to get you in the System – they will want to destroy you because you've got something they haven't got." Of the dinner last night: "It was all unreal, and they are full of knowledge and opinions, not experience." I said I was different and raised the question "Am I different because I am a poet or am I a poet because I'm different?"

And after dinner we got on to my prose-poems. He read about 20 avidly, commenting on word-choice or focus or passages underwritten or overwritten, or overexplaining or shifts of sympathy or balance or garrulity, and said he liked several and that *A Gun-Runner in Danger* was "better than Hemingway – it is Hemingway without the self-consciousness". Earlier he challenged me over collecting them: "They are spasms and you can't have a hundred all together, or can you?" and "Is it 'things fall apart'?" To which I replied: "This is the evidence of pain and wonder, and it has to be presented in 100 separate items because they can't all be crammed into a novel." (He: "Quite right. You can't put anything into a novel – it's self-determining. Bits you get in because they're good generally have to be taken out later.") This he agreed to, though he wondered about art and the restriction of form, and he cited Francis Ponge and *In Our Time* as vaguely similar attempts to do what I am trying to do. And before he mentioned spasms, he asked if I was trying for "epiphanies", and after singling out what I am trying to do to the reader, said, illuminatingly, "I am not interested in how you came to write these – a reader can't be concerned with your problems of literary hygiene," which made me laugh.

He left finally well after 12, having advised me to get some of them published individually in *Cornhill* and the *London Magazine* before offering them as a book, i.e. talk to an agent, and as we walked down to the taxi we got back on to the British Council and their unreality and lack of experience and he said of the dinner on Monday: "You felt as I do when I talk to Japanese sensei and they end up thinking I'm a fool." I repeated "I may be a neurotic, but I am different from them", to which he said "No, they are the neurotics. They are all trying to belong to something, like Guest's acting or as you belong to a regiment, but what they are trying to belong to is all unreal." He left me an ally – he had consistently been on my side and encouraged me ("It's a sign of decay when a publisher can't recognise what is good") – and all through an exhausted Wednesday I turned over what he had said and went to Hitachi and taught him about Michelangelo's forerunners, Donatello and Masaccio (who died at 27), and I finally went to bed at 9.30 and (lay) for half an hour completely motionlessly until the body couldn't keep still any longer and the mind was brimming, until finally the mind spoke in the heartbeat of a swollen breast and the body in the gasp of arrested fulfilment, the gurgle of released death.

16th March. Just after 9 C and I went round to see Tuohy for the last time, and to collect two futons and a blanket he had said he would pass on. The bungalow was in chaos – bottles, presents and piles of left-behind books and pamphlets. Tuohy had a student with him to help. He was in suit and waistcoat and his hair was brushed very neatly and the atmosphere was very sad. He gave C a present wrapped up (a bowl) and he suggested I took the book on China education, which I did. The student went out to get a taxi and we picked up the futons and blanket and went out to meet it and got in. He spent a long time saying good-bye to C through the window while I went round to the front seat, and the taxi divided us and he said over the top of it, profoundly sadly, "Goodbye", in a kind of murmur, and I said "Until November" and got in and when I looked out of the back window he was standing limp, with his hands by his sides, and his eyes were slightly red. I have never seen him look so unhappy. As the taxi pulled away he stood on. Then he turned messily and walked back down his little path, and I felt tears coming and looked out of the front window.

And now (10.10) he is a dream and I have spoken of him as if he were dead: "He was always so real.... He was so much more advanced than anyone in Tokyo." Before I met him I was like Michelangelo's Adam, awaiting creation, and his touch was the touch of God that brought me into real being. I owe him so much, and I have never really been able to say so to him. Our relationship was very troubled last year, but it survived, that is the point, and now tears rise in my eyes, for I can't say with certainty that it will survive seven months' absence and a change to an English environment – though for my part I shall remember him until my white-haired November.

17th March. Thursday and Friday, two days of bits and pieces, during which I wrote *Skewered Pheasants under a Crimson Knife* very slowly. At the Bank of Japan I was brittle as a result of Tuohy's departure and rather unnecessarily compared rates and Residence Tax, as a result of which I discovered I do not have to pay Residence tax for 1967 as I shall not be in Japan on 1st January 1968. Otherwise no one said anything interesting, unless the shipbuilding industry's future can be regarded as interesting.

Went to BOAC to plan my trip home. I will have to pay only £12 odd extra for going via Hong Kong-Manila-Singapore-Saigon-Pnom Penh-Bangkok-Rangoon-Calcutta-Bombay-Karachi-Teheran-Cairo-Athens-Rome-Paris-London; this because there is a 1,000 mile free bonus for going via Singapore. The man sitting the other side of the slippery stone floor who spoke of "being drained in a bathhouse by a girl who wore forget-me-nots and used baby lotion". His lilting voice, his avid listener and her phrase: "You were oki, now you're a babysan," and there was something about the girl's having been married and saying "bye bye" to her husband.

Returned tired to unrecorded memories from the Prince. Two weeks ago there was a slow jazz number from the garage, and on Monday he started the class sucking a sweet and apologised: "Excuse me, I have had a drop." (Of Scotch?) Also the revolting frothy green tea served in the tea ceremony cup, without a picture. It pours down your throat in a viscous slime, like egg-white, and leaves a stain on your upper lip. You're supposed to swig it in three gulps and take about six to get it down. Then you look at the caves and the trees and try not to think of vomit.

18th-19th March. Went down to Nobe. It was a wet morning in Tokyo, and the rain stopped before Buchanan came, and the raindrops hung under the buds like white silk cocoons. The plum blossom on the way down, and the oleander buds, the camellia flowers; the freesia stalks and stock on the Drive-U-In tables. It was spitting slightly when we walked down to the sea. The black sea under a white sky, and the rollers in the wind: an oily rolling sea and spray like a mist of petrol fumes. The things on the beach: bladderwrack (cf English piers and barnacles and limpets and green weed) and seaweed like red and white flesh; a baby shark and squid-like sea-slugs and an occasional yellow thread of their eggs. A decayed crab shell, a shuttlecock like dead ribs and rotting bone (cf the intricate ivory on the Chinese junk in *Journey's End*).

437

Later we talked about this and that, I got three stories, but I was too relaxed and weary to give much in return. It is strange, but I was an overtalker, a monologist, when I came to Japan, and I couldn't really write; now I write a lot each day, and there is really nothing to say about anything, so I keep silence and listen.

We went to bed at 9.30 and were awoken by a rumbling earthquake at dawn (3 on a scale of 7 in Tokyo) and Sunday was brilliant. We had known it would be from our late night walk – the stars were very bright and the moon was on its back – and I went for a walk before breakfast and for another after breakfast, after which we went up into the valleys. The bees hummed in the camellias, the leaves shone after the rain, there were periwinkles in the hedges, and the voices of the peasants came from high up in the paddy fields, and we saw some belladonna (deadly nightshade), like green grapes; it's used as a heart stimulant and as an eye-lotion. On the way back we stopped at what Nan calls "the Coca Cola shop" and I heard the story about the hunting, shooting and fishing Englishman.

After lunch we slept and then I read *Playboy* and allowed myself the "holiday" indulgence…that hitherto I have not allowed myself in Tokyo, but which perhaps I should, and we left at 3.30 to get the village taxi at 3.45. Two other impressions: Japanese houses are like patched houses or quilt; and the naval hospital is a series of ramshackled wooden buildings with a decayed guardhouse with broken windows and a few tubercular patients wandering about. Buchanan got off at Kamakura to see Tabe and as the train sped into the grime of Tokyo I reflected on the intellectual thread of the week-end: which is better, the emotional depth of Doris Lessing's *Golden Notebook*, or the physical and sensuous immediacy of Hemingway's *Fiesta*? There is really no choice, as one appeals to the understanding and the other to the fresh, experiencing part of ourselves. Nonetheless Doris Lessing hit me hard enough to make me wonder, and one day I would like to write a comparable book. In the course of the discussion I asked Buchanan what novel he would write and he said: "It would be about the ridiculousness of life: it is futile and pointless, yet it is incredibly enjoyable." This sums up my feeling about life – death makes it pointless, but it is enjoyable. Once again went to bed before 10, and felt really well.

20th March. Dreams I have not recorded. (1) An earthquake swung me round and a child disappeared into the pavement. Then I was being burnt on a bed by Red Guards. I was strapped to the bed…and there was a fire underneath, and I was scorched and in agony. I cried out and was in hell. Then the fires went out and a tiger threatened to devour us. I lay still and it went away. I knew I was going to die. Later I heard I was going to be hanged. A man in Brisbane prison had been hanged twice because he had survived the first time, so this time there would be no appeal. (2) I went to visit P and was entertained by M who wore a mini. M made advances and actually got me into bed.

21st March. On Monday (20th) I wrote *Chickens like Judges, and Goats* and *Pipe-Clay Breeches and Geese* and then went to Hitachi and summarised Spain. His anxiety about the Indonesian Embassy, Mrs. Dewi being an embarrassment as she will be persuaded to stay in Japan by the Suharto-ites. Earlier rang Tomlin about my future and made three points on the postgraduate course: the money, the fact that I won't return to England until November, and my writing. In the evening I wrote this up in a letter which said: "I am all too well aware that I may have cause to regret this decision in the future...." I am choosing the individual against the System.

On Tuesday (21st) I wrote laboriously: *A Screw Manufacturer in Business* and *A Palace in Orange and Blue*. I then went to "Kiddyland" a child's department store, to buy Nan a "sewing book", and at the same time got a book on S.E. Asia. Read up on Thailand, which is perhaps the next place I should visit.

22nd March. Wrote *Like an Exorcised Witch* and *A Bathtub and a Falling Moon*, and then went to Hitachi, and in the course of teaching art, realised why I like Michelangelo so much: Christ is the Shadow, and man is strong yet powerless in relation to the Shadow (cf Rilke's Angel). The papal reading is ambiguous. The two traditions in the 16th century – Erasmus (Raphael and Titian) and Luther (Michelangelo and Tintoretto), with Bruegel, my favourite painter, uniting both in a picture like *The Triumph of Death* which has, for the last year, hung on my study wall; and alone resisting Mannerism. In the 15th century Gothic and Renaissance art got on all right, so this is the case for a Unity of Being broken in the 16th century.

A muggy day: too warm for a fire yet chilly without it – in between spring and winter. After returning from the Prince I reflected (over my evening drink) on what I discovered this morning, that I met M on Hallowe'en, 1965. I knew the face was familiar when I met her last year, and I'd forgotten I'd crossed swords with her at Emery's and asked her partner Mrs. Petrie-Hayes to dance.

23rd March. On Thursday I wrote *A Puppy like a Child*. It took more out of me than usual, and I went to the Bank of Japan tired and gave my views on Vietnam to Fukuchi: Ho is right if you don't recognise the Geneva Convention and see him as a pre-1954 Resistance Leader in all Indo-China, and Johnson is right if you do recognise the Geneva Convention. Talked to Saito about his child who is 18 months and who says "Bow" (= bowl) and "ji" (= "atsui", hot) and "shee" (= wee-wee) but nothing else. He is surely backward.

In the evening went to dine with Adrian and met Jean-Pierre Lehmann, whose father has been an importer in Japan for 18 years. He had had the (French) Ambassadress to lunch, a gorgeous blonde in her 30s, and she had played with her shoe and dropped it at the table and he had whipped it away

439

with his feet "to see what she'd do". She asked for it back. Otherwise the evening was all ideas and theories. He is in an economic publisher's here, and of course we talked a lot about de Gaulle and the Americans being too pushing over Germany and Kissinger's cuddling up to France and so on. On de Gaulle I said there are reactionaries today, and progressives, i.e. the nationalists and the internationalists, and de Gaulle is one of the first. He: "You can't rush these things." "It was right to make Britain wait to teach her the Common Market is a Club." He going to St. Antony's in October (via Spain 2 months and Italy 1 month, from June) and his proposed thesis is Japan's place in the Far East. Adrian seemed rather tired and said nothing after dinner.

24th March. Wrote *A Prodigal and a Sneer*, having learnt a bit more about its subject last night. Then just lay around and read in the afternoon, and in the evening got my official notice off to the Tokyo University of Education President (at Irie's request).

I really have very little to record while I am on stories. I do all my discovering in poetry and wrestle with great problems then. *Like a Boil* has thrown up an interesting idea. For without doubt, my poetry is the self-torturing ascent of the first paragraph, and my stories are the relaxed, pleasurable descent of the second paragraph. I am still divided – my poetry and my stories come from two opposite parts of myself. The Gigolo-Saint – that's me. Half thinking through the body and being sexy and longing for swinging London and beautiful women, and half ascetic, System-opposing self-surmounting. The Saint means more to me; perhaps the Gigolo will mean more to readers, judging by Tuohy's reaction to the stories at any rate. Ah well, perhaps no artist ever really knows what his "best" work is. I would put *The Silence* well beyond the stories. And perhaps my self-division is not so acute as it sometimes seems: perhaps unity is made up of opposites, i.e. perhaps it is living in opposite states alternately and not at the same time.

Something Tuohy once wondered. Have I any trace of acromegaly? Ezard has (his size 13 shoes) but what of my "enlargement" and "higher metabolic rate" (i.e. tension)? I think rather I have an overactive thyroid gland which gives me more nervous energy than most people and which helps me to burn myself up. "Some burn bright and fade."

25th March. Wrote *Like a Boil or a Mexican Vagina* and *A Bread Knife and a Lima Brothel* and in the evening took C to see an Uncle film…and relax. Otherwise thought about hyperthyroidism, or anyway, excess of thyroxin, and was reminded how much we depend on our glands. The chemical pattern is thyroid cells producing thyroxin (from tyrosine and iodine), which produce thyroglobulin (in combination with globulin). It is thyroxin that increases the metabolism of cells, and when there is too much thyroxin, the body weight decreases; there is excessive skeletal tissue, i.e. growth; oxygen is used more rapidly and therefore the blood flow is increased and also the cardiac output; it increases the heart rate; and the strength of the heart beat; and respiration; it increases the rapidity of thought i.e. nervousness and anxiety complexes, extreme worry, paranoias; it exhausts the muscles and causes muscle tremor (the paper nearly falls off when I try the finger test) because of increased activity in the hindbrain; it makes you feel tired "because of the exhausting effect of thyroxin on the musculature", but also it is difficult for you to go to sleep becuase of the excitable effects of thyroxin on the synapses; it also "increases the male sexual activities."

One of the dangers of thyroid surgery is that it can precipitate a "thyroid storm" i.e. your body temperature goes up and your pulse races and you "blow up". Is this it, then; have I located the reason for my nervousness? Is it glandular? I should check this with Morton, for interest's sake, not out of any hypochondriac desire to change my metabolism, on which my writing depends. If this is so, then no wonder I married C: with intuitive genius I understood that my life depends on reducing speed, i.e. on relaxing, and not on accelerating – if C is a hypothyroid, i.e.

26th-27th March. Wrote *A Clay Griffon and Whirring Storks* and then sat in the sun and got a headache. For the spring winds have increased the temperature. Then foolishly had a bath, which increased my metabolic rate, and was unable to sleep all night. I lay awake and listened to the battering wind and the rattling windows. C didn't sleep either, having very swollen glands under her jaw (is it glandular fever?)

On Monday I wrote fitfully *Flies and a Bed-ridden Wife* while C lay in exhausted pain on the settee, I answering the door and the telephone and generally coping with Nan's requests and so on.

After that went to get a haircut and to BOAC, and rerouted my trip home. Tokyo-Taipei (Oct 18) – Hong Kong (Oct 19) – Macao (Oct 20) – Hong Kong-Manila (Oct 21) – Singapore (Oct 23) – Kuala Lumpur (Oct 24) – Pnom Penh (Oct 29) – Bangkok (Oct 29) – Vientiane-Bangkok (Nov 1) – Rangoon (Nov 2) – Calcutta (Nov 3) – Katmandhu (Nov 4) – Delhi-Teheran (Nov 5) – Cairo (Nov 7) – Rome (Nov 9) – Paris (Nov 10) – London (Nov 11). There are various changes, but I have still not managed to fit in Seoul, which I would like to see before I go back. Perhaps I should go by boat from Nagasaki this summer, with C? Or perhaps I should pay the extra? (As this may be my last opportunity to visit Korea). Also, I have cut out the overland trip from Saigon – Pnom Penh. There are too many landmines. And the trip to Goya is out, too, and I have too long in Teheran. The next time I come East I must travel Cyprus-Israel-Karachi-Bombay-Ceylon-Indonesia.

Personal memories of the early post-war period: I carried a model of a battleship to Journey's End, our new house, on the last day of the war I think it was; I played army games in the air-raid shelter for old Polish and Japanese currency, and pre-Revolution Russian money (what has become of Robin Fowler?); Gwen Thomas took me to Barclays and I was allowed to go into the foreign currency room and take a handful of foreign coins – square Indian coins and Egyptian piastres with holes in them; I went for a walk in Brooklyn Avenue and the flash of falling bombs lit up the street as the siren wailed, and all was bright as day (am I reviving this by going to Saigon?); the sirens and the doodlebugs; mother pushing her bike on the first day at Chigwell in 1947, and my joke a couple of weeks later about basic fuel, for which we were all stood in the corner; and the time I played ships in Brooklyn Avenue, under the war map, and mother was a giantess at the kitchen sink, saying she'd seen my ship when she hadn't; and the blackout and the time the glass fell out of the windows and I sat on the stairs and laughed excitedly and told father when he came home "Daddy all the glass's fallen out"; and the time I lost Grandpa in a fog and he fell and cut his wrist and his cheek and I went out and looked for him and found him and felt guilty, because I had been scolded for causing his blood. These haunting moments, just some of my "Rechercher".

28th March. Wrote *A Virgin and Burning Etna*. And went to MITI. Had a long talk with Mr Endo about Japan's dispute with Britain and learnt that Japan does not consider her global restriction system unfair, and that she sees Britain's retaliatory 58 items as a discrimination. Also discussed the full background to the misunderstanding last October which led to the disastrous February 1967 conference in London, and which has hurt Japan's feelings so much. Also learnt from Mr Ogata that Japan has a new secret plan for the industrialisation of Asia, through regional co-operation. This is "top secret" (Mr Ogata) and I could not find out the details, only its general context and the fact that it exists.

29th-30th March. Wrote *The Museum of the Revolution*. On Thursday (30th) I wrote *A Gangway Boy in Love* and went to the Bank of Japan. The terribly embarrassing situation over the Vice-Governor. It was around 2-3 weeks ago that he would be Japan Development Bank President. This announcement was a leak, and he will now remain Vice Governor according to the *Japan Times*; and Fukuchi will become Vice-Governor of the Japan Development Bank. I feel sorry for the Vice-Governor. He is too honest, that is his trouble. Only corrupt people get on in Japan. When I said to Saito "He will become Governor of the Bank of Japan perhaps" Saito said: "But it is very difficult for him, to become Governor he must pay the Prime Minister money, and he has not much money and he does not like to bribe." The Governorship of the Bank of Japan and of the Japanese Development Bank – he has been deprived of both by his high principles, and he is an atheist.

Went to Ando's wedding. Arrived at the old Imperial (Hotel) in time for the toast, having nearly lost my way into the party next door: I saw Collcutt and thought they hadn't proceeded to dinner and had almost taken a drink when a waiter plucked my sleeve and led me down a brick and Angkor stone corridor to the wedding-room. The mess-ups: the music jarred during the cutting of the wedding-cake, and one of the speakers knocked the mike off, and the mike had earlier cut out from time to time.

I sat between Takahashi of Todai and Kawai of Tokyo University of Education (who shares a room with Minobe), and we discussed fascism and the fascist candidate who has threatened Minobe with Asanouma's fate (a knife in the stomach), and later the Principal of the Keio Primary School (who is 80) made a long speech, and he imitated Tojo. In Japan there are professional imitators. I: "Who did he imitate before Nishiwaki?" Takahashi: "What?" I repeated (my question). Takahashi: "Oh, er, Tojo." I: "I thought so. Is that usual – was he being critical?" "No, he was not being critical." I talked about *That was the Week* and English satire and said that in the West we imitated to ridicule, but he repeated that it was quite straight: "He was imitating his voice and tone and was passing on the message, and I cannot imagine how he can say such a thing without being arrested." Kawai told me that they all went into a pub in Monmothshire and that Ando had played naval marches on the piano (no one else being able to play)....After speeches by Kawai and Shumoto we sang the Keio song, like a bawdy song, and left; C having a headache and acute sinusitis.

1st-4th April. On Friday (31st) I wrote *Wet Rope on a Rubbish Dump* and *The Man who Liked Ugly Women* and rewrote *Tunnel*. On Saturday (1st) I wrote *A Liar in Paris* and *Barbiturate for a Bad Liver*. On Sunday (2nd) I wrote *Bleating Sheep* and *A Villa on Cap Ferrat*. On Monday (3rd) I wrote nothing.

I had drunk a lot on Sunday and as usual awoke before dawn and could not get back to sleep, and I was too tired to be fresh. So I made arrangements and rang people, got Irie and others moving about my departure, and went to Hitachi. On Tuesday (4th) I wrote *A Soul like a Blemished Nail* (number 87).

The episode of the light. As I was dictating *Tunnel* to C at 9.40 p.m. on Saturday, the light blew up and the heavy shade, supported by a chain on a hook, fell. It fell onto the end of the typewriter and scattered glass, but the radio took the full force and the bar across the top was completely snapped and the steel was crushed out into a bruise. I immediately protested to Irie, and on Monday there was a deputation, and they agreed to replace the radio. On Tuesday they came when I was busy and C was out and put up a hideous shade. It had bamboo leaves on the outside and the bottom was exposed, like a person's intestines, and it was rectangular, unlike the "spinning top" in my room. I created a fuss and said no, and that the spindle wasn't in the centre of the ceiling, and at lunch C and I talked about the hollowness of Japanese taste. They have imitated Western things without the long cultural history they need, so they just don't know what is nice and what isn't.

On Swinging England in terms of Shakespeare. What has happened is that Sir Toby Belch has kicked Malvolio down the stairs and Merrie

England has staked its claim against an intruding Puritanism. Malvolio must be one of the first Puritans in literature, and it would be interesting to trace the Puritan from 1600 to 1648. (Charles I thought *Twelfth Night* should be called *Malvolio*). Virtue is out and we are back to "cakes and ale" and seeing post-war Britain in those terms one is surely on the side of Belch; or rather somewhere in the middle but slightly inclining to his side. Yet he is a dull Insider in many respects, and has not felt the awful things that Malvolio has felt, for all his pride and silliness as "affection'd ass".

The modern Belch has seen deep and turned away from the horror, perhaps, and his sense of humour is outrageously angry and scores off Malvolio: "The English are pleasantly insane, which is not to say that the Japanese are unpleasantly insane"; "I felt a waiter pluck my sleeve and I felt virtue go out of me and said 'Who touched my garment?'" Or, "You can hardly have been out of bed at all," for the supreme Belch of modern times must be George Brown. Saying you did not know the Persian Ambassador was leaving at his farewell dinner is the same as raising Tojo at a staid party for Japanese, or even raising contraceptives. To be outrageous is a part of the new Merrier England: "my lady's a Cataian." And I must define this and contrast the two in my novel. The new misrule should be embodied in an "enfant terrible". Cf Bruegel's *The Fight Between Carnival and Lent*, and the old *Owl and the Nightingale*; Savonarola and Alexander VI.

Buchanan came and drank saké and told me about Emery's small party which turned into a quarrel on Vietnam. There were the Indian Ambassador and Ambassadress, who talked cricket; the Australian counsellor, who kept quiet; Stent, the Swiss journalist and his Chinese wife who has studied at Harvard, Cambridge and ICU – Stent having been a Swiss Corporal in the U.N. forces that signed the 1954 treaty in Korea and having met her while in Tokyo on R & R and having become a journalist to get out of going back to the Swiss Army; a left wing U.S. journalist who was pro-RFK; and Buchanan who was very right-wing. Emery is now living 25 kms outside Tokyo, near Stent.

One very interesting thing Buchanan said was: "Nine times out of ten, people judge you by the value you set on yourself. So if you depreciate yourself by bowing, people will have a low opinion of yourself. Whereas even if you're bogus, if you claim certain qualities, people will generally go along with you. One must be an imposter. It is like the test I did in the war, walking into the camp in Luftwaffe uniform. If you walk convincingly enough nine times out of ten people will accept you."

The magnolia tree, like a chandelier in the dark. The great eagle of the Cathedral stretching its neck and spreading its wings.

Miss Gegg's dinner. We went in and found four Japanese sitting in total silence: two Professors, a library man and a grim BBC researchman. After a bit of gush to fill the silence the Bickleys arrived, and Collcutt, and one or two other Japanese, including someone from the Ministry of Education. The terrible time until the end of dinner. The only interesting thing being

Bickley, who lived in Dulwich in 1962, in College Road, and who used to drink in the Crown. My plans to teach in England, which he said he would help me with.

Otherwise I smiled and started handing out bitter pills wrapped in glossy paper. I had a hit at Blunden ("the old boy") and Miss Gegg, through Mrs. Reuby's dog; and raised Tojo and said the Japanese were good imitators; and later I went through to the far room and took issue with someone over teachers' pay and demolished his argument by demonstrating liabilities which British teachers have to meet. Then I went on to the System and talked of the need to rationalise and exploded Professor Niblett's myth about the Japanese being hardworking, saying that callers and bowing made them inefficient. The little man in pinstripes who clasped both hands, sat back and said "Ah yes", then became a dummy again.

I also said that other countries were no less hardworking than the Japanese (e.g. the Italians were not "lazy" because a Japanese in Italy in April thought they didn't need a siesta). I told them about classes of ten in China and said it was a better system than the Japanese one of distance, and I also said that ceremony was a drag in the West (e.g. Princess Margaret sitting in the groundling section of the theatre and inviting students to use the royal box). Finally I had a hit at "erai" (important) phonies who return late from the bars, and had a hit at Collcutt's Christianity and Takahashi's rationalism and went. Miss Gegg sat alone in her chair and nursed her dog and did not talk to any Japanese.

4th April. Visited P via Sanseido and BOAC. He was late and I looked round his lounge: the pile of *Vogue* and *Life*; books on Kyoto; a dresser of cups and saucers; prints; dolls on a "tallboy" which turned out to be a desk; an invitation to the Hungarian Embassy. P: "Are you a soda, on the rocks or water man?" The book he is reading by Michael Foot, a book about spies he knows, so exciting that it's keeping him from the office. P: "One should use it on China – overthrowing Mao, ha ha ha," I having advocated this six months ago. P: "I saw Buchanan the other day. He didn't see me of course" (dusting his spectacles and looking at the ceiling). From this we got onto the local scene. On Tuohy he said "I've never shaken hands with him, I've often seen him but I've turned away." I: "Any special reason?" P: "No. He was in Poland wasn't he?" And the most farcical, "What nationality is Wittgenstein?" I: "Wittgenstein is the no. 1 British philosopher of the 20th century – what nationality is irrelevant."

5th April. More on P. His attitudes. It was "Have you got a slave yet?" (people have "slaves") and "Are you a soda, on the rocks or water man" (people drink whisky – "actually I'm a Kirin beer man"). Also, "R is not a particularly good friend of our organisation" (Embassy) and "M is a good friend" (people are enemies and friends), and "I feel sorry for R – he was disestablished and he didn't get a pension" (people are members of the

Establishment). Also "What nationality is Wittgenstein?" (people are only important in terms of their nationality). There is a very definite and rather nasty ruling class attitude behind all this, an attitude the System imposes on P, for he himself is very nice. Also "M comes back on the 23rd D.V." (perhaps she won't come back). His sceptical "In what way?" when I said Tuohy was brilliant because of his "weighty, aphoristic i.e. Johnsonese sentences which you remember for two years."

6th April. On Wednesday (5th) I wrote *A Camera against a Dream* and on Thursday (6th) *Rose-Leaves and a Madonna Lily*. On Wednesday I went to Hitachi and had a battle over Bruegel. I showed him my book and he took one look at the skeletons and the twisted faces of the blind and pushed it away, not wanting to be disturbed. I tried again with the *Carnival and Lent* and asked him the date. He read out the date, but same reaction. So I gabbled through the rest of what we were doing – the Italian influence on Europe (Durer, Holbein, El Greco) – snapped all my books together and sat for conversation for the last five minutes.

We talked about the Philippine Embassy he was going to. I raised the Easter week crucifixions and flagellations in Manila, and again he was disturbed (cf *Is Paris Burning* – too much action) and he asked "Nails between fingers?" and I said "Nails through the palms" and he winced. He has been sheltered from pain, and he must find pain disturbing; cf his dreams of revolution when he was ten. His reluctance to accept suffering – India, income tax – and his poem about suffering in Kyoto, generalised and Romantic.

After that we talked about the rare bird, the Tibetan hoopoe, which strayed into his father's palace gardens and which he had taken a bird expert to see. I asked "Did it escape from Ueno Zoo?" and he said it had flown from Manchuria. I: "Why should it stop in the Imperial Palace?" but he was not impressed. He showed me a picture of a brown-eared bulbul, which he recognised by my description of its long tail and loping flight, and I left without raising birds dying in an oil-slick and read Myshkin's account of the condemned.

7th April. Wrote *Dignity like Enamel* and *Bruegel and a Tibetan Hoopoe* and thought about Britain and noted a change in attitude during the last few weeks. I am on the side of the disestablished against the System and so I am in the Nonconformist tradition, an heir to the Whigs who were smashed by the Oates plot. I am anti-Tory, I am not royalist, or Anglican, and I do not stand for rule by a rich ruling class or for mannered smoothness, as Tomlin e.g. does. I am on the side of awkward Tuohy with his compassion against smooth Tomlin with his kind indifference. I am on the side of Labour where Labour is in opposition, but agree with Osborne's Maitland that Wilson is a votegrubbing little "catchf—" who wants to turn us into technological yes-men. Ditto: "Britain's position in the world.

Screw that. What about my position in Britain." People come before the nation, and the insulted and the injured on the highways and byways come before those who rule the System. R comes before P.

Then what of Cromwell and Charles? I am for the Merrie England of Sir Toby Belch and against Malvolio, but have a contempt for Sir Toby's "insiderishness" – he is as much a part of the System. I have always admired Cromwell's disestablishmentarianism, but I certainly despise his Puritanism, though I admire his seriousness. Oh dear, what an incredible tangle and how very difficult to sort out a positive attitude. Nonetheless I am an atheist, "Nonconformist" dissenter who is on the side of the disestablished against the System, of Merrieness against puritanism, of Freeman's values of wholeness and purpose against nihilism. And revolution?

8th April. Wrote *Far-Out Eyes in a Dream* and in the evening met Ruth Witt-Diamant, and after conversation about the photo unit with gaijin illustrations at Myogadani, and the coldness (we wearing coats, the Japanese going by the timetable), brought her back by taxi. Her presents: a Greek doll, a bottle of vodka; the San Francisco books. Over Scotches we talked about the McAlpines' desire to return to Japan to retire – he is 53 and retires at 60 and his pension is small and he can only be Representative of a 2nd (3rd?) class country, not Japan. I said I would intercede with Tomlin (which should provoke a reply to our unacknowledged Christmas card).

Her maid Haruko and her stay in the U.S. She made eyes at the husbands of Witt-Diamant's friends and said "Make same, make same" when Witt-Diamant ticked her off, and then she took up with cowboy Dave, whose wife is on the National Productivity Council and a friend of Witt-Diamant's. After turning a blind eye for a month she (Witt-Diamant) began to feel guilty at aiding and abetting – also she could never come home without finding them together – so she told Haruko to do it outside her house and she had a tantrum and screamed "My friend, my friend" and Witt-Diamant phoned Dave and he said "It's none of your business", and after that they carried on in his home when his wife was away on business, Haruko in "pants" and a paisley shirt. The mother found out because the 10 year old son began drinking the soup in Japanese fashion, and she said "Who taught you to do that?" and he said "Haruko", but she didn't do anything because there wasn't going to be a divorce, and after Haruko returned to Japan Witt-Diamant dropped her and she joined someone else and Dave still phones her twice a year trans-Pacific just to give her the hope that he will leave his wife for her, and she won't take anyone else as her "first sexual experience was with a Hindu" and no Japanese will do. (Witt-Diamant: "Why?" I: "It's in the *Kama Sutra*.")

Otherwise we talked about writing, she confessing she got no serious conversation because she's a woman (her stopping going to the poetry club after the second time because she increased their diffidence; her gift and the death mask of Dylan Thomas); and about the boy who asked her questions on the train, e.g. "Who's Mr Witt-Diamant?" She: "I said, 'He's a College Professor in Nevada.' And then I said 'This is my stop' and I got off." Her general insistence on sex. Her petticoat showed, she clutched at my hand, she told me about homosexual friends and novels, about geisha parties where they all lie down and do it afterwards, about her friend who wants to go to bed with a blonde and she said "You've only got to ask." (The Californian attitude). And about her friend in San Francisco who is carnivorous ("be eaten") and her lying awake all last night (1 a.m. – 4 a.m.) worrying for the name of a man I might write to, and who has...left the College.

10th April. On Sunday wrote *The Registrar and the Shrimp* and *Sour Ground and Ashes* and thought that Witt-Diamant is not a Peggy Guggenheim – she has little idea of others' poverty: e.g. "The Beats haven't got any money" (said cheerfully) and "Say you'll drop in for an interview next time you happen to be in California."

11th April. On Monday (10th) I wrote *An A-Bomb and A Knee*, and I went to Hitachi and asked him conditionals like "What would you do if there were an earthquake?" (Answer: "I would shelter under the table".) "What would you do if there were a big fire in Shibuya?" (Answer: "I would check that my house was all right.") On Tuesday (11th) I wrote *A Shrine under Sunset Point* and *Crocodiles and Armadillos*, and I reached number 97. I also tried to write a story on Gordon and discovered I have a play about British society – about the rich and the poor, the educated and the uneducated, the rebel and the established, etc. I shall write this when I have finished the stories and polished the one on Hogan. In the afternoon I went to MITI and learnt that K. Yamamoto is going to London to head the JETRO Centre in early 1968. I can look to him for a job in London.

12th April. Wrote *An Orphan in Prison* and *A Girl with a Twisted Hoop* and once again did battle with Hitachi, telling him that royalty have always been connected with painting and refusing to talk after 5.25. As a result he got awfully sulky and nearly went off to his room. I stood at the top of the stairs in an attitude of "Have you finished?" and he reluctantly came down.

On the history of painting 1050-17th century. France was an innovator until the 14th century (Romanesque, Gothic, Flamboyant), but after that did very little. From c1400 (after Giotto) until c1600 there was virtually no one to rival Italy: Donatello, Masaccio, Fra Angelico, Fra Filippo Lippi, Botticelli, Pasinello; Vignola, da Vinci, Raphael, Michelangelo, Giorgione, Titian, Coreggio, del Sarto, Veronese, Tintoretto, Caravaggio – what a feast. Spain and Germany did nothing until the 16th century: El Greco, Velazquez and Goya; Durer, Holbein, Rococo. Flanders was more creative: Sluter and van Eyck in the 15th century, Bosch and Bruegel (Pieter), and then, in the 17th century, Rubens, van Dyck and Bruegel (Jan). All England contributed during this period was the Decorated style c1280, the style which influenced Flamboyant in France. What lesson can one draw from all this? Especially from the artistic uncreativity of England before the 17th century?

Nan's shyness has been overcome. She restarted school on Monday and has not cried any morning. She's being studied by the sisters and they want C to supply material from the U.K. so they can complete their case history. Her problem is she is unwilling to try anything new; anything new that is not part of the routine worries her (e.g. the class photograph). Sister St. John said, "Don't mention your return to England." The effect of England and the maid, making her nervous of new experience. The responsibility of her lack of friends. Her demands at night: "get up tomorrow"; "put my potty out"; "hang mummy's coat up"; "put my clothes out"; and if we are going out "come back, come back – are you sure?" (though she's better over this). To get attention. Her sums; her "dice"-boxes. She has to link the 6 and the 6. Her fear of snakes and lions.

13th April. Rewrote *A Nervous Breakdown*, number 100, and then went to the Bank of Japan. The new carpets. The pile had footmarks all over it. It was a shiny mauvy-grey, and it looked like footsteps on slush. My last class with Fukuchi. He only told me today. He is going to become Vice-President of the Japan Development Bank, and he will be in charge of making loans for projects that are dangerous or non-profitmaking. His wet eyes, his urgent message in the middle of our class and his wet eyes again afterwards.

The Vice-Governor was restrained and asked for lectures on English culture, not on politics or economics....One can read a concealed intention into anything: Tuohy's choice of a Sphinx. Calpis is "fermented milk".

14th April. Rewrote parts of *Monument to a Phoney*, converting the prose-poem parts into situations, counted up and found I had 101, having miscounted somewhere, for I'd always included this in the 100. After that embarked on a terrific spring-cleaning, turning out exam papers and old newspapers and generally clearing out my head and making new piles of outstanding work: for my room is me, projected outwards.

After that took C down to the Ginza and walked through the lights and watched a man roll people's ¥100 notes in and a blank piece of paper out. ("I make your notes disappear for ¥300.") The pickpockets who worked nearby. From Kyobashi to Shimbashi: a few shops open, mainly men's "boutiques", a few brassy departos, one looking like ringmail, a few shop windows, but all said and done not much better than Bond Street. Not a patch on Oxford Street.

Went on to Nicola's. The difficulty in finding the place, near The Gaslight, just past the Russian Embassy. The Czech-looking man with the hunted look, and the three women he was with. His wife asserting herself by putting her arm round his neck, because she was the oldest. The other two spoke in American, but looked Iron Curtain. He looked hunted and kept looking over his shoulder for an escape. C as my mistress. We talked about the future and so on, while a Japanese couple next to us sat and read magazines over their pizzas, and then we went back....And I felt sad afterwards, so emptily sad, and I was in a coffin all the minutes before I fell asleep.

15th April. Reviewed the stories, made corrections, thought about the unifying device of Brewer, and the mood-link, which is progress towards death. A parcel came from Aunt Mary, a belated Christmas present, a navy sailcloth shirt for C and two books for Nan. No mention of me. Over lunch C and I talked about the problem. I don't mind, I am always rather glad when my Outsiderishness is confirmed. C said it was as if I were "from another race". "My family feels inadequate: you are the only one who's been to university, you're academic, so they feel you'll criticise them, and they always hesitate before inviting you, to take the dogs for a run in the park, for example. They always feel you'd rather sit in your room." I ironically cited Jimmy Porter and Bill Maitland, who have the same problem, and said Osborne's in-laws must have been crazy to treat him in the same way. C: "You and Tuohy are both Outsiders. Tuohy won't admit it because he's a bachelor and belonging is more important to him – he cares what Mrs. Barron will think and who he has to dinner. He's only an Outsider with us. But I would be the Outsider if you went to a literary lunch for people like Oxford. Those women are pretty intolerant, I should think."

16th April. Buchanan came and answered all my questions. He also told me that a beheaded head lives for one minute because it does not lose consciousness until the blood has dripped out. Hence Charlotte Corday, Marat's murderer, could manage a scornful smile when they held her up by her hair. Otherwise, arranged the stories in order.

17th April. The stories. The principles behind the arrangement are: (1) a movement from Russia to Japan, and a growing relationship with Brewer, who finally dies; (2) from summer to spring, Old Year to New, and the approach to death; (3) association of ideas. The whole is an image-poem, each image being one story, each one being linked by mood: exile, vividness, the cage of the System, love and sex, and mothers, and so on; my indictment and the reason why God can't exist. The Japanese stories are situations and the Western ones are memories. On Wednesday, I completed the arrangement, and when I try to sell them I must remember they will be useful for educational purposes and should make good bedtime reading, if the reader doesn't mind thinking about all the things I dread when it comes to bed. And there's always the odd train journey.

Senor Angel wouldn't talk to me at Keio. He has always said Hello, but now that Gibraltar's an issue between the British and the Spanish, and

Franco has threatened to declare war, he wouldn't look at me while I wrote out my names and he walked past me and out of the staffroom without a word. "Prof" Fujii wouldn't say Hello either, although he once gave me a lot of books. He talked to Angel in Spanish, and I suspect I came into their conversation. Later Angel read the *Japan Times*: was he looking for Gibraltar? Adrian's father is in charge of Gibraltar (for the Foreign Office).

18th April. On Sunday (16th) Buchanan tried to make himself out to be upper class: "demo-crazy" and "overthrowing the ruling class is a bad thing." I have come out left-wing, following Minobe's success in the gubernatorial elections. Tokyo belongs to the people, and not to any ruling class keeping power by using its connections.

On Monday (17th) Hitachi planted in my mind the thought that Minobe is "only 3% independent of the government." Minobe has power over Residence tax and demos and police, but Hitachi's police come partly from the Imperial Household and the other part could be drawn from the courts if Minobe turned nasty. I am against Hitachi's manoeuvrings to keep power and privilege, utterly against it, just as I was against the Sato faction's alliance with him. I am utterly against the Establishment, I will not take part in the System, and the same applies to England. I am against the Patterson, and the rich executive and the corrupt businessman; I am for the disestablished, the Buchanans and Pensons and Redmans, for all their personal faults – their desire to appear upper, their need to boast of things that they haven't done. Those likeable foibles so sadly missing in the arrogant and contemptuous men of power. And that applies to the Maoists and the Labour Party as well as the Tories.

The Tory is a nest-featherer, whether he is a Greater-Spotted Eden or a Lesser-Throated Heath. I am a progressive, rather a moderate one, but a progressive. Having been brought up Tory I do not trust the Tory. I reject my background. I shall vote Labour at the next election.

20th June 1970, after Heath's success. I am left-wing Tory now. Practicalities, realities. Not ideologies.

19th April. A day at home, because Hitachi went to Osaka. This was welcome after a strenuous Monday (17th) introducing history and an even more strenuous Tuesday (18th) at Keio. Ando's attitude towards the wedding. "Thank you for coming to my wedding – and you came earlier than you expected." I: "Yes, and did you get my present?" Ando: "Your what?" I: "My present." Ando: "Ah yes. A very nice present. Wooden bowls. They will be most useful and please give my best regards to Caroline." I: "Oh good, I wondered if it had arrived." Nothing about the second wedding to which we were initially invited. C: "I'd have said 'We kept the evening free and you didn't let us know.'" I: "It wasn't worth making trouble and he is a colleague, and Sanseido had just told me they'd only brought 30 copies of my book, when I'd ordered 90."

Otherwise on Wednesday I checked the papers and cut out four stories from the (West Essex) *Gazette*, including one pathetic one about a suicide to forestall a painful cancer death: the old boy was 73 and threw himself out of the lavatory window, having been in the lavatory during the night and said, "I've been looking at the lights of Essex." His wife: "He could only have seen a wall." Thought Osborne disturbs by giving us the opposite, I disturb by giving the facts of life: pain, suffering, death, not mistresses and men shouting at wives. Also in the *Gazette* was a story on a man whose mother, I believe, lives near me in Crescent View. He was killed when his Sea Vixen crashed during take-off and sank into the sea of Gibraltar. (Cf Senor Angel.)

On the 11 p.m. Wide show: "I think it should be the Wide-Awake Show."

20th April. A letter from home with a PS: "I have been meaning to ask you about Europe. Is it true that you need to take some sort of course before you could get a job there? If so, what sort of course is it and how long? Would you qualify for a grant, and suppose the British Council would know? Will it be worth doing it, if it is financially possible? Most courses have (very) short hours and very long holidays, so it might not interfere with your writing."

So far as I am concerned there are 5 points: (1) I will not write a thesis. (2) There are only two posts in Europe (Vienna and Berlin) and these are not often vacant. (3) Money-grants are inadequate. (4) I will not join the System. (5) I will not be told what to do.

While I was at the Bank of Japan Eloise Patterson came round with a record and complained because the Mumfords and Crichtons had not told Bruce about London's offer to post him to Istanbul, which he would have liked. I: "You should have told her that is one of the prices you have to pay if you go into the System." She didn't know Barron has become sole head of Shell.

21st April. Gave three lectures at the Tokyo University of Education, came home and slept while C went to Giselle's house. The Mongol boy was like a dog, coming up for affection. He sat on the floor and swung a basket all afternoon. Giselle's mother's Swiss friend who had been in Cuba. Her husband was Swiss and had a frozen-food store there. Their daughter was born in Cuba, and when the Revolution came and they wanted to get out, they were told they couldn't take the daughter as she was born in Cuba. The Swiss Consulate wouldn't issue a pass, because they didn't want any trouble with the new regime. Her husband was put in jail and she got the daughter out through the British Embassy, and the husband followed later. This was about one year after the Revolution, when it was clear things wouldn't settle down. They lost all their assets though. Their best friend, a Cuban, was shot against a wall, and there was shooting in the streets and anyone who broke curfew was shot. Her husband put his nose outside the door and was nearly finished off.

When I woke up there was a letter from Tuohy. There was a lot about the pairs on offer in Pnom Penh and Bangkok, the phalluses in Angkor, the sex-life of Nubians in Luxor.

Later we went to the Baker-Bates. They live in Kami-Meguro and we got there in 20 minutes with a "kamikaze" driver. We were the first to arrive and we talked about Kirkup and defending Britain, while Crystal flapped about drinks: a nice plain woman who has made up with intellect. Enter a New Zealand Embassy couple, the Atkins, then the Morrisons of Dodwells, a young boy in a shipping firm and Lindsay Fisher from up the road, the girl who was slashed by a burglar while her Chartered Bank parents were away: a stunning girl with killing eyes and a scar across her right arm who said "Pleased to meet you." We sat round the table in the Japanese house and I talked to Mrs. Morrison, who'd been born in Ceylon and had lived in China on and off until 1949 and who would always stay in the East. "It's in my blood." (She has also worked in the American Consulate in Hong Kong, in New York, and in Shell.)

Then I talked to Lindsay Fisher. I connected her experience in Japanese law with *Inadmissible Evidence* and Liz. She doesn't want to return to England: her friends are here and she wants to see the East. She has moved into a flat near Roppongi because her parents are going back on leave, and she is looking for a woman to share her flat with her; this flat was provided by the Wool Co. she began working with, the lawyers she worked with before not providing accommodation. According to Caroline, who talked with her after dinner, the President of the Wool Co. insists on everything being pale blue: he wears a blue-checked shirt and insists on his wife and children wearing pale blue; he has a pale blue Cadillac and calls the office building "Blue building"; his secretaries have to wear pale blue uniform, the men pale blue ties; he's got blue eyes and his wife and child have got blue eyes too. Why? What does blue symbolise – something like childhood happiness? Title: *The Man With a Thing About Blue*.

After that we had dinner. We got it in a room with Chinese prints and talked Nobe (for the New Zealand wife) and Japanese intransigence with Baker-Bates. Right at the end Crystal asked if I would like to see the baby. "Would you like to – no, I mustn't show off... but would you like to?" and I went through to a room with three futons and saw the boy's head (Jonathan – Jonachan). She: "It's super having a baby. There was all the unhappiness last year (the miscarriage i.e.) and now it's super, and my baby doesn't come up in nappy rashes and I feel guilty – I don't want to gloat." Earlier she described her homecoming with the boy. "Merrick had the shoji repapered and he put up those pictures and he had that tree put in the alcove and the garden floodlit and the table was stacked with presents for the baby, and I thought, 'Gosh, how wonderful to be back.'" Her talk in England for the Evergreen Society, with slides. Her mother being Treasurer. She and M are county people and do not know London.

23rd April. Miscellaneous. Once again Hitachi planted information. Last week it was about the 3% freedom Minobe has (see 18th April), i.e. the ballot is misleading, and this week it was the Tokyo University referendum on Okinawa. 47% of Okinawans want a gradual return to Japan, 41.7% an immediate return. Hitachi: "The 47% are from the younger generation and are right-wing (i.e. pro-American) whereas the 41.7% are from the older generation and are left wing (i.e. pro-Chinese, anti-U.S.) I thought, "You liar." For the 47% are left-wing and anti-Japanese and the 41.7% are right-wing and pro-nationalist, i.e. the Gaimusho (Foreign Office) is again saying "the ballot doesn't mean what it says" and is getting the ruling class in on it. Later Hitachi leant across the table to see Hanover on my atlas, and was caught by the lady-in-waiting.

Later still I saw the total eclipse of the moon (from left to right) and I remembered looking through smoked glass at the sun when I was a boy, and around this time cosmonaut Komarov was crashing to the earth with an unopened parachute on his spaceship.

Ena's story about the Indian. He was sent out as Representative of a Company which allotted funds from India. He spent it all on drink, so much so that one month he could not pay his only employee, his Japanese secretary, her full wages. He didn't turn up for three weeks and his secretary went to his home and found his wife and three children starving and cold (it was in the Japanese winter) and the wife had no coat, only a sari. The wife said she didn't want to go back to India as she would have to work for her husband's family.

24th April. A day on history. A survey of Toynbee's "civilisations", the criterion being that the history of England before 735 has to be explained in terms of Rome. Then a survey of the various empires from the Sumerians down to the Persians, showing how the Hebrew North Kingdom was smashed by the Assyrians, the South Kingdom by the Chaldeans. Then a history of the Hebrews: Abraham, Isaac, Jacob and Esau, Joseph, Moses (c1260BC), the war against the Philistines and Samson, the judges and Samuel, the choice of a king, Saul and David, Solomon's connection with Hiram of Tyre and Jereboam's revolt, the exile, the building of the temple (520-516), the Maccabees revolt 168BC, then the revolt against the Romans 68AD, the disaster (of Masada) 70AD, the hiatus until 1948.

Then on to the Prince and a lot on how Prussia took Silesia and England won Canada from France; and how Prussia, Russia and Austria split up Poland. Also a lot on Belgium, as he will be sitting next to the Belgian Ambassadress, a French woman, tomorrow: so, Leopold II won the Congo as a personal venture and left it to the Belgians when he died in 1908. Also a lot on Norway for the Norwegian Ambassadress, i.e. on Danish colonialism before 1815, and on Swedish colonialism until 1905. (What is there in Ibsen which suggests that Norway was a colony?) And when I got home, an interview in *Playboy* (which Caroline had bought because I like the busts) with Toynbee. Full circle.

As I left Hitachi I was presented with a bouquet of tulips. Higashizono: "These are from the Princess. She picked them in her garden." They were very phallic: the two red ones were forbidden penises, the two white ones virginal and the two mauve ones and the three yellow ones were experienced, one of the mauve penises being syphilitic with greenfly. *Greenfly in a Mauve Tulip*.

25th April. While I was at Keio Ena came to lunch with Caroline. Catherine's naughtiness. She drank her soup from the bowl, got straight down from the table, said "I want a sweet" and "Oh, I'll take one then" (Caroline: "I'm sure Nadia won't"), warred with the cat, and then ran off down the road, taking Nadi too. Ena puts her across the road when she teaches and lets her play alone in the playground, and Catherine calls when she wants to come back. Last week she was taken off to a Japanese woman's home and she wouldn't leave and was missing from 12 to 3.30, and Ena was in tears and got the man from downstairs to help her and they nearly rang the police. Ena: "Oh I couldn't be angry, I did that when I was a child." And she shrugged at ideas of kidnap and murder and talked about the £120 a month she earns teaching in her frightful accent (two doctors, two companies, and most sinful of all, a class of high school students at Hongo, all of whom will be corrupted). "I was brought up that way" – but because Ena had a slum upbringing, must Catherine?

G has run into difficulties over his 5th belt. He's got his 3rd "dan" (belt) and a competition is held every month for the 4th and he got his 10 points in two months, but he must reside in Japan for two years before he can try for his 5th. They don't want the "dans" to leave Japan: so he was 4th (belt) in England and was demoted to 3rd (belt) when he got here, and they made it difficult for him to get his 4th belt by putting him at the end of the line in competition, so he ran out of opponents and couldn't get the necessary number of points. They were taken out by Hanson-Lowe. He is the traditional right-winger, with his love of sport, patronisingly dining with his favourite jockey. (Ena: "He's rather well-spoken, isn't he.")

26th April. A letter out of the blue from the British Council (Mrs. Jackson), asking if I would be interested in being a candidate for Libya. The conditions are fantastic: £2,000 a year; tax 8%, furnished house 8%; 12 hours a week; gratuity of one month for each year completed, £230 for Nan; medical and dental expenses, no interview. On that I could travel back to Europe every summer and go by Algiers and Casablanca and Spain; or Malta, Sicily, Italy; or Crete and Greece; or Israel, Cyprus and Turkey; or Marseilles and the Riviera. There is a British Community School for Nan and riding facilities for Caroline. Local leave could be spent in Cairo. The only drawback is the time we should take up the post: officially this September, but probably not later than October/November.

I wrote back and said I'd applied for Libya in 1963 but got side-tracked to Japan but that I was still interested in Libya. I said I don't expect to get back to the U.K. until mid-November and that C and I would really like a little time to equip ourselves for any new post we may be offered. I asked if the University of Libya would be prepared to let me arrive in February if (for example) in return I guaranteed to stay until July 1970. When I told Buchanan he said "If I were you I'd snatch at that and go in October if necessary."

It is spring and the neighbourhood is screaming with tom-cats. Four of them sit on the garden wall and invade the Wretched: a black one, a black and white one, a tabby one and a "Persian" green and black. All have a short stubby tail. They fight and chase each other across neighbouring roofs. Ben (our guard-dog) is afraid of these, or perhaps he has a temperature from rabies still. He half-heartedly chases them off his territory, but barely did a thing when one tom put its nose in his hogswash and snaffled in front of his eyes.

27th April. Talked to the Vice-Governor about the mood in Britain and raised Figaro, Bazarov, Jimmy Porter as men who attack a sick, corrupt society and believe in rejecting certain aspects of its past. I said the new mood is to question everything and not to respect anything – to judge by intrinsic quality not by reputation or position. Is this true of the new generation? Certainly this is what my novel should be about. Just as the play is about the classes (loyalty and self-help) so the novel should be about a new generation of revolutionaries who powerlessly want to overthrow the whole structure of society, not in terms of self-interest and science (Bazarov) but in terms of justice. What is the basis of this creed? Is it nihilism or Russian anarchism (les justes)? Surely not – society has changed so much since then, and reform has removed most abuses. What is the basis of X's discontent with contemporary society – why does he want it changed and what is his dream? Is he just against?

Later. Either he is totally against a sick society and will become a revolutionary, or he is against its spiritual lethargy and will become a creator of the new European philosophy, existentialism, like Freeman. There is, then, a choice between matter and spirit, and the revolutionary is choosing matter (cf the Russian worship of the machine and Bazarov). So what is the new generation – one of more extreme destruction, or of creation? I think possibly the second.

28th April. Had an unexpected holiday at Tokyo University of Education for my second lecture: all students had to be convinced about the move of campus. Lunched with Buchanan, then wrote up Russia and Turkey. Buchanan on the younger generation: "What shocks me most is the lack of respect the new generation has, its bad manners and its brashness." Fine, this is so with every new generation. Bazarov shocked by asserting in a conventional environment that there are no principles or feelings, and that only science deserves study. This is the Bolshie attitude in its worst aspect:

lack of respect for anything not material. My Zabov was in the same tradition.

He is the soulless technological computer man (i.e. science destroying the old religious values) and he may also be the creator of a new way of life. I still have a novel on that. This novel is not the same one as the one on generations, however. Zabov has nothing to do with generations. Whether X in the generations novel is a revolutionary or a teacher, though, he is utterly against the indulgent luxury and ease of contemporary life – that is certain. He is against Merrie England and for Malvolio, whether he is a Jimmy Porter turned revolutionary or whether he's Freeman. Both share the same Puritanism, for all their promiscuity. He stands then for the new seriousness. The ease of contemporary society is a sign of sickness and he stands for something new, either materially and/or spiritually. Conventionality must therefore include that ease, or else there must be two conventionalities, one Puritan, one Merrie.

On Saturday night I dreamt I attended the wedding of Frederick the Great of Prussia. I knew this because he had an Alice in Wonderland pumpkin on his head. He told me he was going to "Spanish meadows" and I wrote it on my engraved chair dust.

29th April. Went to Nobe in pouring rain. Talked about the generations on the train down, and in the lunch-shop Buchanan mentioned *Fiore del Morte* = Death Flowers: chrysanthemums. No Italian will have chrysanthemums in the house – is this true of Libya? If so, perhaps I have the title for a sequel to the *The Death-Fires*. Things Buchanan remembered from his five hours in Benghazi, when he delivered a code from Tunis, a code for the 8th Army: on the walls, "Il Duce ha sempre ragione," and "credire, obedire, combattere" (= believe, obey, fight).

Later I went for a wet walk in the croaking paddies: they were under water and most of the frogs were bright green. Later the rain cleared up and we admired the green barley behind the house and walked by the sea. The mist slowly lifted. There was a very low tide – you could see all the rocks – and there was a lot of seaweed. There were blue cubs and girl guides with red scarves. We walked back via the village. The purple vetch, like sweet peas, and the frogs like castanets or clucking hens.

Back at the house we looked at Buchanan's dead pine. The pine-beetle burrows into the soil and eats the roots so that the tree dies. Blight is a bark-disease, from the outside. When we got back the first thing Buchanan did was to say "I think there's some music" and switch on the pops full blast, revealing his vulgar side. Cf on Tokyo Station: "We're right opposite a bar, so what about some beer?" which he drank from the can, having pressed the top.

Later the rain came on again and the mist descended and a ship tooted its foghorn several times around 9 p.m. Next morning we discovered that two ships (one 9,000 tons, one 18,000 tons, one being German) had collided

457

and knocked holes in each other, and the tooting was a distress signal. The shining leaves after the rain.

30th April. Awoke after a light sleep at 7, opened the window and lay on my futon and watched the birds flitting in a glorious morning, watched the hornets with trailing legs and the flies and the young daddy-long-legs. Breakfasted and read until 9.30, then went down to the beach and looked for the two boats. It was misty and the boats we identified turned out to be boats passing each other or coastal tankers of 2,000 tons on their way out from Yokohama. They had towed the crashed boats away.

After a long sit on the beach while Buchanan paddled with Nan we went to the local taxi shelter and went to Misaki on the tip of the promontory. The corrugated iron shacks on the way, the concrete, modern hotels and bars, the miniature Coney Island with its car-parks, lounging girls and litter. Misaki is a port and everything is a bustle. It is more like an Arab country than Japan. As we arrived a boat was leaving. The sailors were going tuna-fishing in the South Sea Islands and they would be away for six months. Wives and children held the coloured streamers. They didn't seem too perturbed, but one or two were sad, particularly one young girl with long shoulder-length hair in slacks who held on to her streamer until the very end. One woman looked like the local whore and she was pleased. The Blue Peter and the four signal flags; the national anthem as the anchor was pulled up.

Later we went to the fish-hangar and saw some 500 or more giant tuna in dry ice. They were all larger than Nan, they were as hard as white rock in the running water, and they looked like a hangar of bombs. The man with hooks, the blood and scraps and headless fish and perhaps the whore. After a sushi-lunch went back to Nobe and later came home. Buchanan: "Rosie Falkenstein lives in Masaki. She has a very elaborate place, we might go and cadge a drink." Dorothy Britton lives in Hayama, 10 miles away. Nobe-Misaki-Hayama. All along the coast.

1st May. At Tokyo University of Education. What is the major force, the individual, the masses or the rise and fall, spring and autumn rhythm of one's civilisation? If the individual, as with Existentialism, then there is no determining pattern, only a succession of waves, some weak, some strong, and all is Napoleon and Mao. If the masses, then the individual has no great significance as in *Darkness at Noon*. It is the denial of the individual that alienates me most of all from Communism, as it did Orwell in *1984*. If it is a relationship, then the pattern need not be completely determining. That is the best answer.

There are three forces, the individual, the masses and the pattern, and they all war, and ideally (from the Existentialist point of view) a responsible individual wins the consent of the masses and becomes a "creative minority" that resists the pattern, i.e. the pattern is subject to the freewill of the élite, in theory at any rate. There is no such thing as the "will of the masses" – the masses only possess will through the will of their "spokesman", an individual. That is one of the hardest truths of our time. Nonetheless the individual must carry the masses, so the masses are a force to be mastered rather than a force in their own right. This may seem cynical, but politics are cynical, and what is important is that politicians should be responsible men who understand the war between individual and pattern. The trouble is, all enlightened politicians choose the people against the pattern, and one would not want otherwise. So the more responsible the individual, the more he co-operates with the pattern and hastens on the decay. That is history: men becoming responsible and knocking nails in the general coffin. No wonder one is cynical and unhappy. One votes left and hastens what one dreads.

Later at Tokyo University of Education did the history of Britain up to 1066. The effect Denmark has had upon the English: the invasions of the Angles and Jutes, 5th century; the invasions of the 9th century – Danelaw – and the 11th century – Canute; and finally the Norman invasion, Wren's ancestor having been Rollo the Dane (= Robert). Harold's impossible task of defending his kingdom against the King of Norway and his brother (September) and William, Edward the Confessor's nephew and nominee (October). Well might he kneel at Waltham that autumn. Harold as a trapped man. How free was he, what about the masses, and what pattern determined him?

Later, did the history of Russia and Turkey with the Prince. The Mongol occupation of Russia (13th-16th century) and Iran's unification, cf Edgar and Danelaw. Is this a law, that unity is achieved after foreign occupation? Ivan IV's enslavement of the serfs, who were not emancipated until 1861. Is this too a law, that unity is accompanied by "irresponsible" tyranny (cf Mao)? The 18th century trouble with Sweden and Poland that got Livonia, Estonia, the Baltic Islands, Lithuania, the Ukraine. The Ottoman Turks were united in the early 14th century and the Turkish ruler of the Mongol Khans, Timur (=Tamburlaine), nearly put an end to them when he captured Bayazid. After the fall of Constantinople there were the 16th century wars with Venice and the 17th century "wars" with Hungary, which were not as successful as Russia's.

Looking at all this I despair and think, "These things happened, but they were not predictable." It is a necessary feeling – the feeling of freedom – and yet....

3rd May. Adrian came to dinner at 7. The car parked across our gate. His half bottle of Scotch. He immediately raised the theme of betrayal of trust and confidence...mainly in the context of Miss Ishibashi, the daughter of Rainer's landlady. When Adrian was in London he told Perry Anderson he didn't like Japan, etc, and P.A. repeated it all to Miss Ishibashi, who rang Adrian up when she came to Tokyo and who has told various people. It is sufficiently embarrassing for Adrian to want to take it up with Perry later.

We talked about the decline in moral values in the 60s, and I tried to explain it in terms of the new honesty. Tuohy is a man of the 60s because he will never tell a lie, not even on a government form. To Greene, honesty and innocence are vices which cause pain; to Tuohy and George Brown honesty is the cardinal virtue, and gentlemanly consideration for others' feelings is irrelevant. Cf Baker: "Honesty is what we've got to offer the world today." Perhaps, though, Tuohy was always like that, and I did not meet such people in the 50s because my friends were mild. Ranger is a man with a temperament, not a man of the 60s. Another feature of the 60s is the classlessness, and the way one is accepted as a member of the community in Britain, e.g. by the papershop and the bank.

4th May. (Adrian) thought Mrs. (B-B) doesn't like him. "I don't find her attractive and she senses this and is nasty and makes slighting remarks." I having said "Perhaps she's a little plain and has to compensate, and so she gives long monologues, and these can turn into stabs, e.g. her pointless remark to me that the British Council hasn't got a very good reputation." A: "All relationship is based on mutual attraction. We like people who like us." I.e. sex is at the root of everything. Later on B-B and Field, "they are the only people in the Embassy I really like." I: "They're the only two I do, and that's no accident."

The story about Whitehead....The normal severance bonus for a sensei is £700, and this one had taught for 30 years through the war and he wasn't in the System and Whitehead offered £20. Adrian, Field and B-B raised a further £50 with a subscription and challenged Whitehead over £200 from the winding-up of the commissariat (= buttery). As Chairman of the Committee, Whitehead wanted to give it to the Sacred Heart, and Adrian, Field and B-B stood up at the meeting of 70 and appealed to mass emotion and the Ambassador came in on their side, "bidding from £100", and the sensei got £200. Adrian: "A satisfying defeat of bureaucracy."

On his philosophy of life in relation to death. He is completely against the System and in favour of doing what one wants to do, e.g. write, go into the Foreign Office, the law or just sit on the beach in the sun. I, "Particularly that, because old men remember physical things, being largely cut off from them but surrounded by physical equivalents of the women and memories they loved."

5th May. At the Bank of Japan yesterday I was asked about Europe and the U.S.A., and I said the problem had to be seen in various terms. (1) Historical. On the pro-side was our common ancestry with the U.S. – the U.S. are former colonists – and on the con-side was their war-record, bankrupting us by selling arms for cash. Whereas with France, on the pro-side was our record of alliance in the 20th century, and on the con-side our long historical conflict. (2) Cultural. I said the U.S. made a greater cultural impact on Britain than France (did): washeteria are more common than

French wine, and this applies to books. On the other hand not all Britons like the supermarket image or the disc-in-slot feeling or the loud-mouthed, ignorant American grannie with her large camera. (3) Temperament. I said U.S. pragmatism was closer to our empiricism than was French theorising. In short the U.S. is closer to us than France, but there is a lot of anti-Americanism today. Our neutrality, our opposition to Vietnam.

6th May. Wrote the play (Noddies are against the Trustees) and then went to the doctor, about my conjunctivitis and hoarse throat, and the hairdresser.

7th May. A wet day. Worked on the play (*The Noddies* and the need to be "you") and then prepared Toynbee. Thought about "etherialization", the movement from macrocosm to microcosm in a growing civilisation, and the movement out into geographical expansion and industrial technique in a declining one; about the individual – do individuals originate growth; and about the challenge of the withdrawal. The basic message is inner vision – what I put into *The Silence* and what everyone rejects as being too ambitious for this age. I was right, I know it, but I live in the wrong time, and that is not an excuse, for I don't need excuses yet.

Later I felt the call from my future again, the terrible call to do something more than teach or write, the call to make a new version of the Church and society I have rejected, the confused stirring in the heart that pumps visions of new religions and revolutions into the mind. And oh, how carefully I listened, thinking of St. Benedict's three years in the wilderness when he should have been in university, and of Mohammed's 15 years as a caravan-driver today before the 7 years from the Hejira. As usual I said not "Lord here I am" but "Lord, not me". The mockery, the ridicule, my dread of microphones and TV cameras – I am not a revivalist or a changer of men or systems. I am just a quiet, retiring, average academic who wants to write, whose passion is writing.

It is a Hound of Heaven, this cursed call. Every two months it bays, and I listen and say No in spite of myself and it goes, and I go on living as before, against religion and for the tits in *Playboy*; against revolution and for an easy life for the people. Yet I know the life I try to defend is not a true life, and I feel sick, and I curse the fools who won't recognise the Silence, which defends the true life.

8th May. Mao, T. E. Lawrence – yes, it is the individuals who originate growth in a civilisation, by creatively responding to a challenge. Yet there is still something ambiguous about Toynbee's "creativity", which is a movement in the soul and not in the macrocosm, and which therefore has nothing to do with geographical expansion or machines that can reach the moon. For the poet and the scientist clearly create from the same source.

There is a secondary distinction to be made: the scientifically creative civilisation, like ours, can lose contact with itself and its soul because its

461

attention will be focused on the macrocosm, that is the point. So it is very difficult to say how creative we are today. In terms of science, we are very creative, but in terms of the soul and in our grasp over ourselves, we are barren. And is it the loss of such control (= "self-determination") that results in loss of growth, i.e. breakdown? Is a creative minority a self-controlled minority? I cannot say as yet, but this thesis must be connected with the ruling class's loss of confidence before revolutions.

One can see why Toynbee is so unpopular today – he is anti-Snow and the Scientific Revolution and the 19th century-type optimism, he is, like Leavis, pro-soul and the quality of life. The passage which could be on the Outsider: "If the creative genius fails to bring about in his milieu the mutation which he has achieved in himself, his creativeness will be fatal to him. In losing the power of action he will lose the will to live – even if his former fellows do not harry him to death, as abnormal members of the swarm or hive" (ed Somervell i p252). I.e. the Visionary/Prophet must return and make new the Church or Society he has rejected: it is a matter of life and death, as it was for the Outsiders who failed.

9th-10th May. On Wednesday 10th I got the idea, late at night, for 100 lyric poems of 12 lines each, or thereabouts, and I wrote the first one listening to the rain and suffering from pinkeye, and on Thursday I polished it, much to Caroline's annoyance. She wants me to get the play done, and she is right to drive me on that. For…I can only regard poetry as a luxury, even though it is more essentially me than stories or plays or novels. Nonetheless what I have planned is 100 poems on things seen and felt and experienced, on existence. This could be *Life Cycle*, or the group of existential poems I have long planned, the ones on death and pain and striving.

On Osborne and Shakespeare, or disorder and order in times of disintegration and growth. In Shakespeare, there is always a restoration of order, and even the dark period plays have a sense of justice. In Osborne there is only chaos, something is rotten in the State of Denmark and there is no cure, and the individuals are confused and turbulent and perhaps a little distorted with Mannerist suffering. They are not serene. The individual does not like the values of the society in which he lives, there is a sense (with which I sympathise) of the individual of responsibility being alienated from the society and this sense is not in Shakespeare.

In my play and other works, I stand for the self against society, and for the values of the image and self-knowledge and vitality and existential joy, but what do I think of the Beats, Ruth Witt-Diamant having invited C and me to meet Kenneth Rexroth on the 21st. I am in sympathy with their opposition to their society, but they are extremists and I am a moderate, that's the difference. They believe in total rejection, whereas I continue to live in society, albeit as a stranger, and I meet people and write about them from the point of view of my values.

462

BECOMING: CIVILISATIONS, DECLINE INTO EU, ART (1967)

Among other things I value what is real, and the Beats pose; I am against private jargon and for art, and therefore against the unsolid, spontaneous diarrhoea of much Beat poetry, I am for the Enterovioform of art. I'm against tired words, and though Freeman is perhaps pursuing the Beatific vision, I am against getting Beatitude with LSD or pot, because these drugs blind one to the pain and suffering of others, and these must be a part of one's world-vision. I am for the individual, but am against "cool" detachment, and I am against my society in a positive way, a reformist way based on certain un-nihilistic values.

11th May. At the Bank of Japan, lots of bookwork. Saito's silence when I raised Europe and his own question, "What is your attitude to it?" I: "I am in favour. Everyone is. Anything that will prevent a 3rd World War is a good idea." When I got home I read in the AEN that Japan has turned down the Kennedy Round U.S. plan whereby she would contribute $10 million a year to the world food aid program. "The Japanese feel the program should take account of their aid to hunger-stricken nations, notably India, in such forms as low-cost credits for items like farm-machinery and fertilisers. Japan spends about $6 million a year on such programs. It also pleads balance of payments problems generally in resisting the world plan."

In 1964, Britain gave around £300 million in aid, of which £154.1 million was to the Commonwealth, and £20.4 million to other countries (gifts were £9.1 million). Our balance of payments deficiency was £374 million. And we are going to contribute what Japan has refused to contribute. I shall raise this at MITI, as laughable evidence of the Japanese readiness to do business when they can get a profit, and of their basic lack of charity. I shall also raise it with the Prince.

The thing I will forget when I leave Tokyo. "Far East Network News on the hour".... (At the end:) "For further information read your *Pacific Stars and Stripes*."

12th May. At Tokyo University of Education, coldness from Narita, who didn't even acknowledge me when I entered the staff room, and who left without a word.

To Tokyo Medical and Surgical (Clinic) over my pinkeye. Saw Dr. S, as Morton is sick: a fuzzy-haired neurotic with rimless glasses and a moustache. He was against Morton's drops and recommended the Tsunematsu Clinic for a vision test.

13th May. Letter from mother. "Robert was elected for the (Loughton) North Ward yesterday (= 6th May) with a majority of about 400 over Archer, the chief Socialist opponent. It was quite an exciting day with a lot of coming and going and R doing tours of the polling-stations. Mr Biggs-Davison toured the committee-rooms. John Ezard was at the count, and

463

asked after your plans. I just said you were probably leaving Tokyo next winter."

15th May. Toynbee on growth. Growth takes place when individuals withdraw into solitude and discover things in themselves or about society or about their values, and return and pour their discoveries back into the society they have rejected, for the people to imitate through mimesis. Compare (Colin) Wilson. The Outsider is surely the Withdrawal and Return man who does not know himself, he is not a mere Romantic but the growth-factor in society (cf Hesse's Steppenwolf). Likewise breakdown (= termination of growth) does not take place because of declines in industrial techniques or foreign conquests – these are effects. It takes place because the leaders become infected by the mechanicalness of their followers, i.e. they become Reflection-ruled, static automatons with mass-tastes and they no longer reflect in solitude or strive for the Shadow or try to meet challenges with vital responses, and the people withdraw their support and create social disunity.

Clearly British society has broken down (cf Eliot on the loss of unity), though the challenge of Europe has restimulated us, and there is certainly very little class warfare at present, with the new classlessness.

What then is the position of the artist in such a background? It is, surely, to pour life into the mechanical society he has rejected. To what extent should he reject the past? We need the past to nourish our spiritual roots, so not extremely, but moderately. One should do an Osborne at the most, not a Bazarov or a Verhovensky or a Red Guard. And, within the context of USE (United States of Europe), a universal state, one should reject the breakdown as part of a "rally" or progress, but continue to draw spiritual nourishment from it.

Of course, Freeman and X in my play are both examples of Withdrawal and Return, though I have not written the Return. Perhaps I should – the 2nd poem and a 2nd play, The *Return of X*. This would have to be about a revolutionary or a religious reformer: perhaps instead I should write a series of history plays on the theme of Withdrawal and Return, using characters like St. Bernard and Savonarola to judge the present. The advantage would be that I'd get growth onto the stage. Also Lenin, Garibaldi, etc.

I have always been fascinated by the relation between self and society in Eisenstein's *Ivan the Terrible* (cf in *Hamlet*, and in Ionesco's *Exit the King*). I should like to write a play about a disordered King (self) and a disordered kingdom (society) and the effect of self-unification on that Kingdom. I suppose (King) Stephen would be inappropriate?

16th May. At Keio, a talk with Ando about Kirkup, who is delivering the opening lecture at the Japan Literary Society in Sendai on the weekend of May 29th. Ando: "I wonder what the British Council will feel, as Kirkup is giving the opening lecture – I wonder if they will feel anything." I: "Oh no, I shouldn't think they'd care at all. Attacking institutions is in the British tradition from way back in the 17th century and before, and more recently in the case of Osborne. The only feeling the British Council has is that Japan may not understand this – you don't attack your institutions, you're not informal towards your superiors. And clearly a lot of Japanese don't understand the first thing about British Literature or life."

17th May. Awoke at 6.50 a.m. to hear the FEN 7.00 news on de Gaulle's Press Conference. It was misreported, the announcer saying that de Gaulle had rejected Britain's application. I dozed off in a deep depression. Not since Suez have I felt so involved in a national issue; 1963 certainly did not arouse the expectations of this challenge.

Later the news adjusted itself. De Gaulle ruled out a veto and just stressed the practical difficulties. This can be seen as success for Wilson: for it is a sign of de Gaulle's weakness. (1) He could not apply the veto because his Parliament is unanimously in favour of Britain's entry, and the country is unanimously opposed to the emergency powers. (2) He had to adopt a hard posture at the beginning of the talks, whereas in 1963 he adopted a soft posture. (3) He has ruled out the veto, and unless he contradicts this statement he can only block Britain's entry by delaying the negotiations. Britain can force the negotiations through, or else withdraw the application and wait for the French people to topple de Gaulle, wait in a position of strength.

What we shall do I do not know, and I do not know if de Gaulle really thinks we want the Commonwealth in (the) EEC (*Yomiuri Shimbun*) or if he really lacks vision – his idea of the 21st century is closer to my idea of the 19th century than mine of the 20th century – but I have understood what sailors felt in fighting for Nelson, or Churchill, and I know that de Gaulle's not a great man, however great a national leader he might be. And it is the man that comes first.

18th May. On Wednesday evening I listened to tapes of Rexroth and Lowell's *Benito Careno*. Rexroth was all owls and water (cf Morton's pronunciation), and all the things he did in nature while he was young reminded me of *A Winter's Tale* (Thomas's). His rhythm is an *Old Testament* dying fall, and it is rather monotonous and can be rather pretentious, and although much of the diction is Saxon there are a lot of Latin words (uniformly, imperceptibly, interpenetration, poignant, vertiginous) and these make the poems unclean, as though someone has spilt oil over the page. The Saxon words aren't symbols and so his poems have no depth and can be understood the first time through, and some parts sound like poetaster Grisdale ("long decline of man").

How different from Lowell. The first half hour was full of words like "swab" and "puff" and the word "like" seems to occur in every other line ("sky like a grey wasp's nest", "like a Turkish bazaar"). The moaning of the slaves was fantastic, and even if the situation was drawn from *The Ancient Mariner* – the dead crew, the black tongues, the ghost ship – the rhythms haunted me all through the night, and I heard the U.S. captain's slow, ironic, subtle voice when I woke at dawn. This capacity to take possession of the subconscious is one of the unmistakable signs of genius, and I am not sure to what extent it was Lowell and to what extent it was the excellent actor who played the U.S. captain.

After the first three quarters of an hour it got a bit boring – the slave was a bore – and I had indigestion. You can only take so much of such compression, you need "like". Or perhaps he lulls you with his rhythms and subdues you like a woman, brings you up to orgasm, and the increase in the pace of his rhythm after that is merely fatiguing.

19th May. After my last lecture at Tokyo University of Education, a question. "Mr Hagger, I would like to ask you a question. May I? What is the boundary of language?" I: "Boundary, what's the meaning of boundary?" Later: "To communicate. Why, is this for your thesis?" Miss Narita: "Yes. That is the subject of my thesis." I: "Language is always bound by a situation. In Chekhov or Pinter a character says something ordinary but means something else. In *Camino Real*, the line 'Careful, I've got fragile mementoes' means 'My past is a sore point'. Dramatists and poets renew the language by renewing words in their situation." She: "I cannot agree." (Blushing.)

I went all out to smash. She: "'Being' and 'nothingness' are nonsense." I: "In terms of linguistic analysis or Wittgenstein they may be, but in terms of living and dying, this veined hand and my dead skull, Zossima's decaying body and Alyosha's kiss of the earth, they're not. Being (compare Heidegger's pure being) is defined in terms of consciousness." She: "But that is subjective." I: "This desk is not subjective. You know how Dr. Johnson refuted Berkeley. He kicked the stone and hurt his foot." She: "You trust experience?" I: "Yes, because there's no certainty in anything else. Meursault put a strand of a woman's hair before the casuistic certainties of the priest. What I am trying to say is, thought is a waste of time, for a good thinker. There is always pro and con, there are always two sides, and therefore there is no certainty, only sunsets and a woman's hair, and you can't think those. Empiricism, testing by observation – they are one's criteria. And getting back to language, everything depends on the situation."

I showed her a passage from Osborne about "technological nougat." "Nougat means architecture within this context," I said. "Your dictionary will tell you it means 'chocolate' ('sweetmeat'). The meaning here depends on the situation." She: "I will think about what you have said."

20th May. To Ruth Witt-Diamant's to meet (Kenneth) Rexroth. When we arrived two Japanese Beats were sitting in silence. They wore maroon shirts, one was bare-legged and had a moustache, the other a beard. They did not say a word all evening. The girl from Ochanomizu Women's University, a student of Shakespeare. The sculptress Aiko Miyawaki with her hair down to her breasts and her patterned stockings and her narrow lustful eyes. Her sculptress-composer friend from Okayama, who had come up for an exhibition at Matsuya 8th floor and who was a provincial (very proper and correct) trying to be avant-garde.

After Rexroth's arrival (see my story), the sculptress and the composer moved into the window, presumably to avoid the Beats to whom they had not previously said a word. In between talking to Rexroth I looked up and met the sculptress's eyes. Ruth: "She's been in New York and Paris – she's really a French girl now." In Japanese, "Nihon jin... don't like?" And she smiled. "Yes," Ruth said, "she's a real French girl now," and she took her hand. Later the sculptress said to me "I am interested in English sculptors. I find them very interesting." And: "I saw your bloodstone" (= stone spotted or streaked with red, as the one in my ring is).

During this time C heard about Sneider from Mary Rexroth. "He is a solitary Nature poet who is not interested in people and who just wants to walk in the woods and live cheaply on a Zen diet of whalemeat, but who always has seven or more people staying with him. He sent his sister some geisha combs and she keeps horses and thanked him for the lovely curry-combs."

Rexroth's two wives, his comparison of C to an Austrian tart he once knew. ("That's intended as a compliment – she was the most beautiful woman I've seen.") Something or other was "like custard."

21st May. Letter from mother of 1st May. On Libya. "If I were you, I would consider it was the way opening, and it would be very wrong not to take the opening."

Otherwise, wrote the story on Rexroth, *A World of Cops and Robbers* (or *A Mind like a Ribbon Tie*) and worked on Toynbee.

22nd May. Tokyo University of Education. Toynbee on breakdown and disintegration. Civilisations break down because the leaders lose their creativity i.e. they stop striving or growing, they lose Los and become infected with the dead, mechanical, habitual Spectre and the mechanicalness of the masses, they worship an ephemeral self (= the Spectre) and rest on their oars. Disintegration takes place when there is a split into 3: a dominant minority (civil servants and government officials); an internal proletariat (= anyone who feels he is "in" but not of his society, e.g. foreigners from the Commonwealth, members of the intelligentsia who feel uprooted from their homes and who have no place in society, cf Jimmy Porter, and ex-peasants who have gone to the cities and who are unemployed); and an external proletariat (= barbarians, e.g. Afghanistan, Saudi-Arabia, Nazis?) The Outsider and anyone who feels an exile are therefore members of this "disinherited" proletariat, and what they create is a Church, and as all religions come into being through alien inspiration; I, for example, should feel stimulated by my contact with, e.g., Japan.

Looking at myself in this light, as a Church-creating proletariat, I ask, "What should my attitude be about revolution?" The answer according to Toynbee would be to chuck the idea: "A revolution may be defined as a delayed and consequently explosive act of nemesis..., growth becomes hazardous." Revolutions happen when institutions refuse to adjust to new forces, i.e. the leaders' "great idea", and institutions being the province of the dominant minority and I not being a social leader, I should not meddle. Ditto United States of Europe. That is for others to build. I am a church-builder (hence *The Silence* and the Shadow) and as a poet I have glimpsed USE (United States of Europe), the universal state in which the Shadow will develop into an institution. I must not be infected with society's mechanicalness.

23rd May. Yesterday was my birthday. I am now 28, three years older than Keats or Owen. And what have I done? In so far as my poverty allows me to do anything perhaps I have done quite a lot, but I haven't done it well, that is the point. Still, Tuohy didn't finish anything until he was 27, so perhaps there is still hope. I am at least finishing things now.

Today I finished the first draft of *The Noddies*, having resolved to cut out the rewritten 2nd Act about X's conversation with Marshall, which rightly belongs to another play altogether. I must not clutter this play. In fact, so much am I emphasizing economy that I intend to eliminate Marshall as an appearing character, and, if I can, replace the boys' demand for Gordon's autograph by X. Thus there will only be two characters in the whole play, and everything will be concentrated on the relationship between X and Gordon, and on X's power of fantasy. X and Gordon are in a kind of limbo and they communicate through the Noddies, and Marshall's son and his suicide in Cambridge and his comprehensive-teacher daughter are quite extraneous to this play.

Closeness and apartness and the balance of sympathy and judgement – that is what I must concentrate on. The more characters, the more cluttered the play will be, and the less well we will know X and Gordon. The fact that a cast of two is harder work for the audience than a cast of six mustn't enter into it. How well we know the characters, and how realistically they are drawn – that is my criterion.

24th May. Wrote the story on Fujii and Senor Estévez, *Priests Like Veterans*, and prepared more stories for C to type. She got up to 78. Sunbathed for my spots on my back – I am slowly rotting away in this Eastern climate – and then went to Hitachi. Was told "I will miss you after you have gone."

It's no exaggeration: in the last year and a half he has more or less had a complete History of Western Civilisation, a History of Art, and (soon) a

History of Industrial Techniques and Communications (radio, TV, electronics, etc.). In addition I write out questions for him to ask foreign ambassadors. Last week I wrote out 50 questions for 10 ambassadors, and today the chief chamberlain came into the classroom to tell Hitachi that four ambassadors (including Rundall) would be dining with Hitachi on June 13th, i.e. I am now recognised by the Household as chief conversation-planner for Ambassadors. I shall think up some snorters for Rundall. (George) Brown is his boss, so I shall get Hitachi to ask about Brown's dealings with Princess Margaret, especially the hand round the waist. Lady Rundall strikes me as being ruling class, so I shall get Hitachi to ask if there was really a ruling class in 1956, "as Osborne says there was".

For all this work I get a paltry £4 per 2 hours, whereas for MITI I get £15 per 4 hours, three quarters of an hour being breaks between interviewees, when I stare out of the 9th floor window over Tokyo, or read.

25th May. A letter from Miss Meixner, as Mrs. Jackson is away: "We have been able to find sufficient suitable candidates to fill the posts in Libya from September, and we shall not after all be able to accept an application from you this year. Similar posts will almost certainly be available at the University from September 1968 and if you are interested we should be very glad to consider you."

I must confess, I am rather relieved. I was very eager last month – and it is certainly too good an offer to turn down – but recently (now that it has become hot) I have been thinking of the heat in Baghdad, and I have been waking up in the middle of the night and wondering whether it would be a good idea to sign myself away to heat for two and a quarter years (February 68-June 70) as opposed to one and three quarter years (September 68-June 70). Further more, Benghazi does sound a village, and I don't like the stifling effect of a small community with dozens of English people. In this respect I'd be better off in California – in N. California it would not be too hot, either – and certainly the standard would be better in California than in Libya.

Ideally I should in the meantime find some way of remaining in Britain on the conditions I want (i.e. 12 hours' work a week and no more). In other words, my withdrawal, to Tokyo, should be coming to an end, and my return will be final. This is only an idea.

26th May. At the Bank of Japan yesterday, talked with the Vice-Governor. He had read *Look Back in Anger*, and when I asked him, "Who's sick, society or Jimmy?" he replied without hesitation "Society", presumably thinking of Sato's corruption. Emboldened, I raised the System, and to my amazement he thoroughly agreed with me: "Yes, you must be independent of the System." His disillusion was in a matter-of-fact tone, there was no burning resentment, but he gave me a strange look that said: you're very young to know about the vanity of staking all on advancement. I think he will retire fairly soon and devote himself to history and culture and reflection.

An insight into Hitachi earlier this week. As I left, he going ahead down the stairs, he signalled to the Chief Chamberlain. His knuckles were by his trouser creases, and he beckoned with his left forefinger when he thought I wasn't looking, and the Chamberlain came scurrying.

On MITI. Met Mr Matsuda, a former student who is in the Coalmining Department. In the course of conversation Miyazawa, the Kennedy Round man, came up, and he defended MITI's protectionism, in refusing to take part in the U.S. wheat plan: "We must consider Japan first because our standard of living is behind yours in Britain." Then he added: "I think a lot of it is envy of Japan – all these requests I heard in London from your Board of Trade." Whereupon I tore in and demolished his argument, whipping out the figures from my bag, and a newspaper cutting from the wallet, and in the end he was speechless and could only say: "Yes, I think the Japanese have become selfish." (Earlier, Dolci and Friday lunches for Famine Relief.)

27th May. C on sexual feeling. "It is like a light bulb flashing on and off, like a lighthouse." I: "Or a heartbeat." She: "Yes."

A letter from mother of May 21st. "I had a letter from Mrs. Riley, who has been very poorly, to say she was going into a Convalescent Home on Thursday, so I set off to go up and see her. When I got to the top of the road I found it was closed for tarring, so I had to go all round by the Owl. When I got about a quarter of a mile from Mrs. Riley's I found that the road was also closed there, and I could only proceed on foot. I finally drove back past the Owl, moved the "road closed" sign, and drove so far, then walked.... Miss Moulton's sister spent 5 months in St. Margaret's Hospital, having her leg amputated. She came home about a month ago, and now Miss Moulton has fallen and broken her leg and is in Whipps Cross – isn't it unfortunate."

28th May. Friday 26th and Monday 29th are holidays from Tokyo University of Education, because of the festival, and it has got a bit cooler. I have taken advantage of this free time to finish the play and by Monday lunch I had got most of it through in final draft.

It is now in 2 Acts, not 3, and Marshall does not appear. I'm sure this is best; the imagination is much more powerful than reality. By dominating the boy, too, I now make the betrayal something entirely motivated by X. There is now no coincidence, or suspicion resulting from coincidence, and I throw everything onto the relationship. They are OK at the beginning, and they savage each other at the end, and no one else has come on the stage so something has happened between the beginning and the end.

The play is now fixed in the soul (I want to emphasise this by playing it in gloom, even though it is mid-summer). In spite of its interior nature, however, I abide by Realism and Concreteness, the two guiding principles of the stories. It was originally supposed to have been a story, so that is not surprising. X must remain X: he is unknown to Gordon, and he does not know himself. He is a new hero in so far as he recognises that the problem is in himself and not in society; for both Gordon and X have confused the self with society. (The Hagger theme.) Also X is an existential hero in terms of seeing, not acting. The quality of one's existence, i.e. one's seeing, is what is important; not acting.

29th May. After Keio, went to Aiko Miyawaki's flat (402, Nikkatsu Apartments, the first block). Aiko later said it was the first time she had entertained in her flat and she saw she'd had too many so quite clearly she was repaying her "on" to Ruth and she had to have a gaijin to keep her company and invited us. The blue cover over the doorway, the crammed apartment. Her "lights in brass reeds" or "elegant devices", looking like blocks of flats or telephone switchboards or even a stereo front.

The influence of technology, suggesting electronics and alloys and mass-production "wiping out all raw traces of work done by hand"; and computers; and mechanisms of square brass pillars and cylinders. Works of art that are at the same time means or devices, i.e. functional works of art, e.g. room-divider, fire-substitute. "The patterns have become 3-dimensional as well as mobile to the point where their irregularities can be rearranged or changed at will by the onlooker" (brochure). So technology and onlooker's participation are her main two features. She gets factories to cut the brass. The influence of repetition (and futility?) on her work. The flats or switchboard cells, compare "the similar repeated patterns seen in her paintings" (brochure). These she made with oil paint mixed with powdered stone or marble, a technique she discovered herself, she claims.

On her bookshelf were two pamphlets on Man Ray, the U.S. Dadaist, and inside one there was a note on a card "Aiko, I miss you very much, why don't you come back, love" and then an arrow pointing to a picture of Man Ray. She first met him in 1960, in Paris, and there was a photo, a lenseless Rayogram, of what looked like washers (Ruth: "those things you put on fawcets, washes that's right"; I: "washers"); or horseshoe beads. And I was sure she'd got the brass cylinder idea from Man Ray, just as Man Ray stole from Apollinaire (she: "Man Ray knew Apollinaire very well;" I: "Man Ray first went to Paris in 1921 and Apollinaire died in 1918 didn't he?" and he did); just as Max Ernst stole from Blake.

After admiring the various "works of art", including the pair of lips over the bed (red lips on a blue day) and the stockinged leg in the blue litter bin (lavatory?) by her desk we grouped ourselves round the join of the U: Yanagi, "a famous industrial designer" (Ruth), and later she asked Aiko for his name and line (he does milk jugs, and traffic-lights..., and he did all the new flyovers for the Olympics); an architect; C, me, Aiko, and Ruth. And we discussed art. Ruth said it was good that artists were creating out of the modern world because it was all around us, and there was no reason why art shouldn't be functional.

I said I was against art as mirror and for art as resister, and that the artist should condemn the modern world by putting eternal values in his art, and that such a work of art will be detached from the world, not functional. This clearly doesn't apply to architecture and Aiko is closer to architecture than art, and it might apply to Western civilisation or to societies in decline. Anyhow, I said in the West today we suffer moments of division and dialectic, and it is impossible to create peace and contemplation.

Ruth, on this relation between art and society: "You're making art sociology", and "Worthless societies have produced great art" and "Where is the art in *Guernica*?" I: "It's the complexity. Compare Beatles and a *Late Quartet* (of Beethoven's). Beauty and horror, the dialectic of the emotions." She: "But why is it beautiful?" I: "Our response can include several things: the shape of the pot/pipes/book; the picture it bears, the values it includes, etc. And the best work of art has all." She: "I don't think you can say it's the best." In the end I showed a picture of something Man Ray had done: a driving wheel and a broken gear, and I asked Yanagi: "Where does idiocy end and art begin?" He: "I don't care, I am only interested in the end result." He then said that Jackson Pollock wasn't art, "because a child can cheat". (Typical Japanese logic.)

Anyhow, throughout I was insisting that art is control and intention and shape, and is not something haphazard, like pulling out the brass stop, i.e. I was being well and truly pro-Joyce and anti-Dada. Aiko was clearing up the dinner and did not hear all. Ruth: "Mrs. Truitt hasn't spoken to me since I looked at her rod (= "presence") on the floor by the door and asked 'Why?'"

The dinner was, I think, vegetarian: pickled cucumber and coriander seeds (Greek style), tofu (= bean-curd); sushi (i.e. ebi – prawn) wrapped in bamboo leaves, Kyoto style, or in egg, Korean "flat peas"; asparagus and broccoli dipped in mayonnaise with ginger; saké, fruit salad (strawberries, Californian oranges); and coffee in a Yanagi cup. Ruth Witt-Diamant on Rexroth: he's uneducated and feels inferior and loathes academics, e.g. the time he walked out on Allen Tate; on herself. "My colleagues called me a casual rat. That's a tehnical term for the rat that gets the cheese by climbing over the gate and not getting hammered. I got my rank without submitting a thesis. I got bored, and I got out of it by having a baby. That took five years. I worked in the department and the law said 'PhD or equivalents are entitled to the rank of Professor', so I challenged the law and was rated grade 1 Professor, higher than some of my thesis (PhD) colleagues."

When I left Aiko insisted on giving me *Surrealism* (Thames and Hudson) to pay off the Liptons tea, and she would have given me *Dada* too. I feel she has talent but (as C put it) may have got stuck on brass pipes. Certainly pictures out of spaghetti in Milan are a complete waste of effort – consumable art. On the way there C had said that Aiko is the black-haired woman of her nightmares, the one who catches fire and may change into a bird. She didn't think so on the way back. I thought of her as a thinking body (she has an extremely alive body) and later read that she has been married and must be about 37, and I dreamt I was waylaid by her, that she was connected with Tomlin and rather cold, and that C cleared up the mess.

1st June. Wed. After Hitachi, and "Costa Rican coffee" (before he went to meet his brother from Brazil, Argentina and Peru), Ann Gegg's. Everything was in the garden and was quite pleasant until Lyn Guest. I talked to Taylor ("Are you thinking of going into the Council and being an English Language Officer? I wouldn't advise it, you get ropey posts, but you must think what you're going to do.")....Hill, who...said "I'd better move on, someone might be watching." I: "who?" He: "Oh, my conscience," but he meant Tomlin. Ignoring Whitehead I moved round to Mrs. Bickley, who is doing a recording at Keio. I: "Mita or Hiyoshi (campus)?" She: "I don't remember her name." Tomlin interrupted over some photos; he wanted to prove that a playreading had taken place to a British Council scholarship student.

After that I went over to Lyn Guest who was talking with Bickley. She said "You must be feeling rather at a loose end now that Frank Tuohy's gone." It was like a slap across the face and the meaning I took was that we had no other friends. "No," I said, "I went to China with Frank and I met him once a week to discuss writing..." and Bickley looked hunted under his squirrel eyebrows. She said: "He was a good cook, I will say that for him, but he was no good at places like this," and I should have said "Yes, he was the only one who talked to Japanese," but I didn't, I was still reeling, and we had passed on before I could challenge her. "Have you met Verner Bickley?" she asked, the implication being "We see so little of you, perhaps you haven't." "No, I don't think I have," I said. She: "Verner Bickley – Nicholas Hagger." I: "How do you do." He smiled and looked hunted, and her irony had backfired. After that I came back strongly and asked her if she knew about Rexroth. (C was talking to Guest and Guest had mentioned him first.) She: "No." I, to Bickley: "Kenneth Rexroth, the GOM of U.S. poetry." She: "Oh Rexroth, yeah." But I didn't stop or look at her, I spoke to Bickley, and I made him laugh by telling the story on the International House, and the CIA. (Guest had told C that he couldn't teach in the U.S. because he's leftist and the CIA would be after him.)

Later Bickley was taken away and I was left with her and I asked her what California would be like. She: "I wouldn't touch it with a bargepole, they elected Reagan. Go to New York." I: "I've got a friend in the U.N. and he loathes it." She: "Yeah, it's gone commercial. Don't go at all." I: "I think one should go and say No." She: "If you excuse me I'll go and ask Harry to take me some place to eat," and she went over and butted in on Guest and C, without saying a word to C, and Guest continued talking. (About how he was published in *Outposts*, by Dulwich Sergeant, and how he wanted to write and go to China but Lyn wouldn't let him, and how she would never sacrifice a week-end or do his typing.) Why did she behave like this?...Does she feel that we are "casual rats" – we got the cheese (e.g. the good jobs and Tomlin's recommendation) without the sweat (e.g. the summer school that G has been roped in for)? She doesn't like the way we keep ourselves to ourselves and just carry on – we disturb her in some way? C: "You must be on your guard. You must carry a tin of fly-spray."

Afterwards I went over to Tomlin and Toff said "Do you know this man didn't know the de la — Ensemble were here?" I: "I'd read about it." Toff: "And I suppose you don't know Max Adrian's coming." I: "I do indeed" (prepared for anything now), "we're going on the Wednesday. And," I said to Tomlin, "I'm very sorry we can't attend your party for Max Adrian but it clashes with Keio," and I could tell by Tomlin's eyes that Toff hadn't been invited. "Anyhow," I said, "I've advertised it to 200 students at Keio." "Oh good," he said, "come and meet McDermott and he'll give you particulars of another concert to advertise," and we left Toff standing. Ah well. I seem to be like some agent of truth who tramples on the tenderest spots of people's psyches, just by being me. To others I am an image, as Whitehead was to me.

At this point C came over and we went, via A. Gegg, who can't go back through Cairo because of the Middle East crisis and Nasser's aggression. Earlier, the Embassy secretary who'd been to Washington and Basra, who wanted to know what we were doing next....I: "Anything, if there's sufficient cash incentive."

Wednesday Oct. 11th, heard from Buchanan that Toff has been after my job and that he has been seen in the Tokyo University of Education corridors.

4th June. On Saturday C finished the stories, including the note to the reader, and now that it is all behind me I immediately felt that they didn't exist, and began preparing the play, *The Noddies*, for typing. So two months' effort just peters out. Like the effort that went into the poems. I live in a perpetual present. Though when Harry Guest telephoned with three addresses of small magazines I got a bit interested. And after L. G's rudeness, I was careful to put off the dinner invitation until some time next month.

At Tokyo University of Education (Monday) I discovered what might be the source for the name Brewer: copper-plated Indian-inked name on a "filing-cabinet" cupboard; I had "forgotten" there is a new teacher at Tokyo University of Education from Tsuda, one I've never met, an elderly US woman expert on Negro literature. Could I have "seen" that copper-plated name and connected it with Buchanan? Buchanan came on Sunday evening and talked about Israel, and my farewell party. Buchanan said Narita hoped I'd become "semi-permanent", like Buchanan.

5th June. At the Tokyo University of Education, on Toynbee and disintegration. What he is trying to do is to explain the soul in terms of the civilisation. So, in a growing civilisation, the creative people pass on and the masses imitate, there is élan and a style emerges (e.g. the civilisation is a mechanistic one), and there is a movement from the macrocosm to the microcosm, i.e. the soul. But when the civilisation disintegrates people don't worry so much about duty (= abandon) and they feel no causes are worth serving (= truancy), they lose direction (= drift) and there is a vulgar sameness in manners, art, language and religion (= promiscuity), and people dream of past and future Utopias.

This is the Age, and one must be against it, and the active man recognises the moral law through discipline (= self-control), he finds causes to serve to the death (= martyrdom), he feels he must control himself (= sin), he is aware of unity behind the pantheon (= sense of unity) and he withdraws (= detachment) but doesn't remain in his Nirvana, he is reborn (= transfiguration/ palingenesia), or twice-born, in William James's sense. Thus the states of mind in Camus and Hemingway connected with unreality/chaos/sickness/ waste are the passive attitudes of men (souls) living in a disintegrating civilisation, and the active reaction against the Age achieves what Toynbee calls the Kingdom of God: the second birth to real living/order/unity/the still point, the state of mind of the Superman and Rilke's Angels. For the Kingdom of God is within one's consciousness, it is a state of mind, an experience.

This pinpoints my long-standing attraction to, yet discontent with, people like Osborne, and Swinging London. They embody the passive, "helpless" attitudes of the age, even in their seemingly active rebellion. Their souls are passive, and mine is active and dynamic, not static. Which is why my soul, like the souls of all truly active men, is more independent of its civilisation than most.

6th-7th June. Wed. On Tuesday I took the day off from Keio, having been cheated, by fine weather, out of a holiday for the Keio-Waseda baseball, and I finished my polishing of *The Noddies*. With the exception of the climax, which is at present rather a jerk-off: too little delayed, warm, throbbing pain and pleasure that can't be held back any longer. X must ask G, "Will you betray me?" and not take it for granted that he won't.

Throughout the day listened to the Israelis' advance on Suez in hourly bulletins. I am a Dove, but every hour I was moved to sobs in the throat over the genius of Dayan, the one-eyed, black-patched Israeli general. He wiped out the air force of three states in one hour, overran the armies of five states (plus) in a terrific push forward, and when he broke into Jerusalem's Jordanian sector, the first thing he did was to pray at the Wailing Wall. His army behind him, and 2,000 years of hopes achieved.

How I would like to be Israeli. How secretly I hope my prominent nose is a sign of Jewish blood. It is the tradition of suffering I would like to inherit, the exterminations from Masada to Auschwitz, the rootlessness and the statelessness. Being a British subject, I have to be an exile to give outward form to the feeling, and what I inwardly know to be true. If I were wholly Jewish, I would be content. For my nose would be sufficient proof that I am an outsider and an internal proletariet, I would not need a language barrier. The Jew is my friend, the Jew everywhere, and I deeply regret not having met more Jews I can write enthusiastically about. Rose Falkenstein and Segal in the stories are the worst types of Jew, to be condemned like R or the worst types of the English, and I do not know any Jews I can praise: which is my fault, not the Jews'....

My father was always pro-Jew and used to refer to us (to my mother's disapproval) as part of the lost 10 tribes, and he used to joke about Haggai. My grandmother's grandmother was the daughter of a woman called Sarah (born 28th October 1776); her name was Hannah and her nieces and nephews were: Ebenezer, Robert, Jabez, Benjamin, (Hannah), James, Isaac. Did Messrs. Comfort, Burton and Harding neutralise Sarah's nose?...

To connect myself like this would be an identity, a link with the suffering of Dostoevsky. I would no longer be the isolated, cranky rebel; I would be a representative of all the suffering the world has known since Abraham left Ur 3,000 years B.C., I would go to Tel Aviv....When I raised it with Argie last summer she said "Oh no, Biblical names were common in the 18th century."...The deep, inexplicable, irrational emotion I felt during the Israeli Foreign Minister's speech to the U.N. And my unEnglishness, my metaphysical "seriousness."

8th June. On Wednesday I returned to *The Eternicide*. I rearranged papers I abandoned around 10th February 1965 (possibly later) and what defeated me from November 1963 till then suddenly fell into place, in one day. The reason was elementary – I kept back Z's MS till the end, after the destruction of BEATRICE (a brain machine), and posed the priest's doubts and desire for certainty as the main question.

Yet I could not have done this before February 1965, so much has my control increased since then, and so necessary was *The Silence* to my self-creation. I have moved back from my rationalism and have occupied myself. So in one day I did a Dayan and solved a problem that took two and a half years' struggle earlier, and the crucial point was my new technique of stating objective and disaster, character and opponent, and of numbering scenes backwards. I now feel that I can write anything and organise anything.

At the British Embassy, farewell to Rundall (the Ambassador) and the Queen's birthday. Adrian and Baker-Bates spoke to us on the way in (B-B on Plan B if it rained – "remove the pillars, they're only papier mâché") and, ironically enough we stood behind the Kiyookas, I having said we should beware of them, in the taxi, because I'd malingered on Tuesday. Mrs. Kiyooka, "I hear you're leaving" and all the polite things, and Kiyooka: "How many English are there in Tokyo?" I: "Around a thousand, if you include the environs." I later heard that 1,500 had attended the party, but that typical Japanese question was raised again with Taylor and Dupère, our first pair. Dupère: "I'd have said 1,232 – you should have given any number." (Later Kenichi Yoshida said: "The English are always quoting numbers at me," showing irony against the Japanese.)

We escaped and avoided Bickley and Toff....Then I saw Buchanan and we went up and got talking with Ozenberger. He fell silent when I came up and was puzzled when I said I knew him (I couldn't mention the Tokyo Medical and Surgical because Buchanan was there and he'd once gone to great trouble to take C to a Japanese hospital), and they resumed talking about Dayan. Ozenberger: "He's an archaeologist, you know. He is very interested in the ancient history." I: "He must be a genius. What's the latest? The last I heard was 70 miles from Suez." Buchanan: "Oh they've got Suez and they've broken the blockade at Sharm el Sheikh." Ozenberger asked me "How long have you been in Tokyo?" "I've been 16 years", he said, "and it's nearly time for my retirement, but I don't know what I shall do." I took a deep breath and asked "Why don't you go back?" It was an impertinent question, but Buchanan was there as a cushion, and he couldn't duck it. "Where to?" he said, and the whole tragedy of the Jews was in that reply. "Suez," I said, and I gabbled about how a new settlement would follow and how I'd be one of the settlers if I were in his position and then Kenichi Yoshida came up and I turned away from Ozenberger and began giggling with him and getting drunk while he discreetly tried to pump me on Israel in return for Fanny Hill.

I turned round to get another whisky and found myself face to face with M. She already had her hand out and she got in on our group. Kenichi Yoshida had said (presumably this was why he came over) that he was supposed to be going to England this year but that what he'd thought was "in the bag" had been cancelled because of the austerity measures. ("You give £100 million to lazy bums like me.") Consequently I asked M "What was London like?" "Terrible," she said, "foul, horrible," with long pauses between. "Why?" I asked. She: "There's no service and no politeness unless you've got money, unless you've got HH (= Hong Kong Hilton) on your bags." Kenichi Yoshida: "Oh, in the joints I know there's very good service." I: "You mean clip joints."

She broke off to ask him about his wife and (neurotic) daughter, which he didn't like: "She hasn't got out yet." M: "Come out." Kenichi Yoshida: "Yes, come out."

We went on about the new Britain and do it yourself and the new honesty. "It's Osborne, and George Brown who are the new men," I said. M: "Brown? You mean Brown?" Kenichi Yoshida: "Don't you like him, are you Conservative?" M: "Yes I am. He's foul. Horrible. Disgusting." All this time Tomlin was nodding and beaming over her shoulder and saying "Hello", and still the epithets piled up. I had just said, "In terms of the future Brown's refreshing, but in terms of Frederick Tomlin's standards he's a decline," and Kenichi Yoshida was saying "Speak of the Devil" and still M went on, "Disgusting. Gross. Ugly." "Ah, good evening," Tomlin said coming in. I said "We were just discussing the new honesty." M: "The new rudeness." Tomlin: "Very often it is, yes, yes."

Then Tomlin complained about his whisky, "This tastes like Suntory" and M took him aside to explain that it was Suntory, part of the economy measures. (I had earlier met Tomlin behind the red canvas "bar" and like him had been offered beer only.) Meanwhile Kenichi Yoshida was taking a whisky and a gin from the tray Tomlin had just taken his from, and at the moment the Queen struck up. C and I came to the shun, and M and Tomlin didn't realise. When Tomlin realised he looked up, bewildered, and came to the shun as if an RSM has called "Squad...," sticking his chin in and holding his head back, and I shook within, for he is the height of tradition, and he had been caught with his pants down. Meanwhile Kenichi Yoshida sloped back like a burglar and stood with his whisky and gin, and when Tomlin saw his frown grew and M started giggling all the way through the long Japanese anthem.

Later C and I were left with Kenichi Yoshida and an Indian squirt came up and took C over to talk to a small group of men and I had a word with Adrian, and then P came up and just as I was about to talk to him the Indian came back to apologise ("We were only joking, please to understand"). I chased P over to M, and P fled to C and took her away from the men (C: "I thought he was treating me as if I were a younger M") and I was left with M, and we went on about the new honesty. She: "I'm going to take my shoes off, do you mind?" I: "The new man would approve of that, taking your shoes off on the Ambassador's lawn." She: "Doesn't mean a thing." I: "Agreed." I finally got in a word about Kenichi Yoshida and mentioned his interest in Israel. She: "Oh yes, he is. Not connected with, he is." So my hunch was right.

12th June. On Thursday Ena rang and told C she's going into hospital for a week to have plastic surgery to her nose. "Ever since childhood I've felt inferior because of my lump on my nose. My family used to say 'Ena's the one with the lump'." She teaches a doctor who is a friend of this surgeon's. He arranged the meeting and the total cost of the operation will be £100, including £15 for the anaesthetic. She: "I couldn't say No after he'd worked it all out." Also: "I haven't told John yet." C: "Who's going to look after Catherine?" Ena: "Oh John will, John'll just have to." (Said irritably).

On the boat she was always on about "my husband." Now she is contemptuous. Her down on Catherine, and her fondness for Nadia. She is always holding Nan up as a model to Catherine....Her attempt to change herself now she knows another way of life. Her accent has become a mixture and she has friends who do this and that, and now her nose. It's a pity there is no plastic surgeon for accents. As Gordon would say, "She's gone up in the world."

BECOMING: CIVILISATIONS, DECLINE INTO EU, ART (1967)

13th June. At Tokyo University of Education, Monday on Toynbee and disintegration. The creative man is a conqueror in a time of growth – he conquers mimetic masses – but in a time of disintegration he is a saviour, and ideally a saviour from, not of. And when Toynbee invokes "the Saviour" he means the saviour-from as a type, the saviour who teaches a state of mind that can be experienced, and a real life. (If he means Jesus and not the typical, I am not interested.) This is just what Freeman will become, if he rejects the view of himself as an Artist that he reaches at the end of the 2nd long meditation; and if (as he does) he rejects the temptation to revolution, which is for the saviour-of (and the idealist always becomes a man of violence, cf Mao). He is not in any danger of succumbing to the other temptation, that of Russell and Sartre, of trying to make philosophers of Kings.

What the Saviour-from saves from is the negative view of life in a time of disintegration. It is interesting that Toynbee sees universal states as being founded for purely negative reasons, e.g. relief from war, and that he is very pessimistic about a USE, which is "out of the frying-pan of our time of troubles into the slow and steady fire of a universal state where we should in due course be reduced to dust and ashes" (ed Somervell i p629).

On Tuesday Toyama came to discuss education with Adrian, who wanted something different. Toyama on how cowardly the Japanese army was. "The Japanese army was very very coward and wash-brain." And his leftism. Adrian is gong to Geneva to study law and then he will go to Spain for a holiday. The well-educated Japanese bureaucracy, with its irritating insistence on regulations, as the source of "the Japanese miracle."

14th June. Went to the Max Adrian *Shaw* with Buchanan, who knew Shaw, his godmothers being Mrs. Patrick Campbell and Maud Gonne. Max Adrian was certainly not Shaw: Shaw's beard was redder, and his voice was more pipsqueak than Adrian's boom, and there was a lot of Shaw that was left out, e.g. the bits about the Life-Force and so on. Nonetheless, it is harder to do Shaw than Dickens; Dickens' observation and humour come across through different characters, whereas Shaw's abstract wit only comes across to a foreign audience if taken slowly. And Adrian raced, so that no Japanese understood.

In the interval even Toff complained he couldn't understand the connections the first time. ("Have you read any Shaw?" I: "Yes, all." T: "Cor, blimey.") Also spoke to Arai, who was as wooden and unreal as Watarai; his face lit up and went out, and he nodded before you'd said anything. From him I learnt that Wilkinson, HIH's former tutor, is back in Tokyo. He arrived this spring, having been out of Japan since he left five years ago. (Harker and me since.) He teaches at Aoyama Gakuin, and he...isn't on the British Council list. Arai was peeved at having been cut down to one class.

Lady Rundall belted over at the beginning, followed by Sir Francis and his handcrushing handshake, but she didn't change her expression throughout the entire evening. The drink upstairs with the Bickleys, Bickley buying them, and both looking harrassed, having been there the previous two evenings too, under Tomlin's thumb. And duty dinner with Buchanan after, at the sashimi shop. Ate jellyfish and a revoltingly sloppy oyster-like sea-urchin in seaweed. and the usual raw tuna. Buchanan didn't say much. We sat at the "counter", and we had to shout across C, so we drank and ate and talked as fitfully and tiredly as I feel now.

15th June. Yet another morning on the *Eternicide*; all my free time since 7th June has been spent on getting it straight. I am still only halfway through, and the heat has been awfully oppressive. The overall objections I have at present are (1) the fact that the characters are symbols rather than observed people, as per my stories, and hence their motivation may seem a little unreal (e.g. Conrad's *Heart of Darkness*); though these shouldn't be realistic every time, and the gains outweigh the lack of realism, and isn't it all realistic if Zabov is working a death-machine? and (2) the language; though the priest is stilted, and thus his language is in keeping with his character.

16th June. At the Tokyo University of Education. After my last class, the sadly headbowed Mr Ichimura, whose essay was wrong in every word. After going through it with him as kindly as possible I asked, "What are you going to write for your thesis next year? "Thesis?" he said and he wrote it out, "Thesis, next year." "What subject are you going to write on next year?" I persisted. "You want me to write this again?" he asked of his essay. "No," I said. "I'm talking about next year." "Next year?" he said. In the end I turned to one of the others and asked "What is thesis in Japanese?" "Thema," one said. "Ah thema," said Mr I. "My thema? Language. My thema will be on language." As though I should have known. "What aspect of language?" I asked. "English," he said, "Yes," I said, "but what aspect? Nouns? Verbs?" "Nouns, verbs?" he said, and he wrote them down. "Sah, I am sorry, my English is very poor, I do not understand." "Well," I said, only interested in getting away, "try and think about it," and he wrote it out in ink, on the bottom of his essay, "Try and think about it" until I fled in despair.

An image for a poet's mind: an orange tree, hung with sun-ripe oranges like lanterns, like the tree outside the window of our house at Nobe.

17th-18th June. Spent the morning and evening on *Eternicide*, Zabov's admission that he is self-divided. This is necessary for what happens after the conflict in the church, and at present I have decided that there is no sickness; Zabov eliminates the scientist in himself, which dies when he fails to kill the priest, and he is not up to the prophet in himself. He is caught between two stools....I used Z's mystical experience, which was first written in 1962/3, and the bit about the eyes like wells, which half-got used in the poems. The writer as editor. I am struck by the extent to which my themes are a repetition: in *The Silence*, *The Noddies*, most of the stories and now this novel, the theme is that we project our views of society and history, that all conflicts out there can be traced back to within here.

On Sunday I did the molesting of Te Deum and the priest's reaction. Afterwards I couldn't sleep....My first phase 1961-1963 (*The Molten Owl's Song*, *Tristy*, *Werig*, *Mandalas*, and *Juben* – which was never finished);...I went into exile and created my self in writing *The Silence*, and my second phase, 1965-1967 (*The Death-Fires*, *A Spade Fresh with Mud*, *The Noddies*, *The Eternicide*, plus)....I found my way back to my self and I inherited my past to become real. At least I am finishing things at present.

On work for Tokyo University of Education, how I wish I could visit the 1590s: Marlowe, Shakespeare, Jonson and Webster 1608/10 coming in the drama; Spenser, Shakespeare, and Donne in poetry; and Bacon in the essay (Sidney having been in c1581).

Waited for the hot rain to arrive (in fact none did) and, though worn out, spent the morning on the first part, and otherwise relaxed and read. Nonetheless did too much, especially on literature and as a result did not sleep a wink after dozing until 1 a.m.

19th June. At Tokyo University of Education, on Universal States and the pattern of the next 50 years if Toynbee is right. Universal States are built for negative reasons, although they inspire hope and the mirage of immortality. There is a great movement between classes and states, and there is a bloodless social revolution. There is standardization and uniformity through communications, provinces, the benefit of one citizenship with one law and language, one system of coinage and weights and measures. There is a strong civil service (composed of the former ruling class/aristocracy), and the process of weakening in the dominant minority is to be found in colonies and frontier-towns (e.g. Hong Kong) which help the barbarians to sweep in. Also the unmartial ideal of Concord and moral revolt.

Otherwise the main beneficiary is the internal proletariat, communications, the capital city, the language uniformity, etc. helping religious revivals. And one can see why religious revivals happen in such backgrounds. The more uniform and standardized everything is, the more negative it is. It exists to arrest the decay, it provides no drive, no purpose, no reason for striving. Also, the more uniform and world-wide the citizenship, the more rootless people are: local cultures get lost and all becomes cosmopolitan. In short, the more uniform everything becomes, the greater man's spiritual needs become, because the more negative and rootless he feels.

A spiritual crisis occurs, and man will listen to a gospel when he has the need. The need is arising now. Certainly the standardization is increasing, and it is not inconceivable that I shall live to be a citizen of a world-province that has replaced the parochial state of England. If there is going to be a new

481

religion, it will be a livable one, like Heideggerian Existentialism; not one that offers any metaphysical solution.

20th June 1970. This is what is happening in Tripoli now: The Arab War Council is the beginning of U.S. Arabia.

20th June. Worked on the first chapter of the novel, then went to Keio and lectured on the bankruptcy of will in Dostoevsky (the Underground Man, Svidrigailov, Stavrogin and Kirilov) and on the positive value of virtue/love (Sonia, Shatov, Zossima), i.e. social action is self-destructive, spiritual action regenerative.

Went to the Japan Travel Bureau and spent one a half hours changing my schedule with Koshi, cutting a day in Saigon for an extra bit in Angkor, and creating an alternative to Cairo via Istanbul (the Byzantine and Ottoman empires). Returned home and prepared for Hitachi's summary of the Holy Roman Empire 962-1806, including Italy, Austria/Habsburgs and Prussia/ Germany, Poland, the Low-Countries. The role of the Habsburgs: the first H was 1273, the most powerful Habsburg Emperor was Charles V 1516-56. The Habsburgs got Hungary 1699 (hereditary) and the S. Netherlands (1714-1797), but they lost Silesia to Prussia 1756-63. They finally challenged Napoleon and Francis II lost the title of Holy Roman Emperor in 1806, and became King of Austria-Hungary, his daughter marrying Napoleon 1807. Prussia became strong c1640-1815, and Poland-Lithuania became weak 1660-1795, the final partition between Prussia, Austria and Russia. Prussia thus won Silesia, Poland, and France. The N. Netherlands became independent of Spain 1587, the S. Netherlands going from Spain to Austria (1714) and thence to France (1747).

The Holy Roman Empire-Austria was quite separate, after 1866, from Prussia-Germany, so was Hitler trying to restore the H.R.E.?

21st June. After a sleepless night Nan started vomiting, a convulsive, involuntary, gulping throw-up of saliva. Her temperature was 38.5C (=101F) and she had a few coppery spots round the cheeks and complained of a sore throat....When I was out C took her to the doctor. Result, it is tonsillitis, which is akin to scarlet fever, and Nan will probably have to miss "Birdies can Fly" at the Hilton prize-giving on Saturday, the last day her school meets. And unless the sisters call here, she won't even see them again.

When I got back from Hitachi I offered treats without mentioning the disappointment: a firefly dinner at Chinzanso; Nobe; a ring or any other present she wants; TV in her bedroom tomorrow. "Pamper her without spoiling her," I told C. And when it was bedtime and she'd had her three medicines (brown for sickness, red for tonsils, white for sleeping) I held her hot hand while she snored herself to sleep, her breathing getting slower and slower. There are still no mushis (= cicadas that whirr) but it is hot and it is not a good time for fever: just under fan-temperature.

At Hitachi's learnt about the Romanian Embassy last night. Hitachi asked all my questions, e.g. "Do the Romanian people want to take Moldavia from the Soviet Union?" to which the Romanian Ambassador replied just "Thank you for asking," after a stunned silence. The chamberlains interpreted this as gratitude, not shock. Ditto the snap question to the Ambassadress: "What do you think of Carlot II?" She: "He was a good man," revealing her rightist tendencies. This morning he asked the Soviet Ambassador, "Is Eisenstein's *Ivan the Terrible* popular today?" and got the answer, "Yes," even though it's about Stalin. The Soviet Ambassador was made Assistant to the President by Krushchev, and has (I think) been exiled to Japan by Kosygin, so he is anti-Stalin.

11

LEAVING JAPAN: LOST INTENSITY OUTSIDE THE SYSTEM
June – October 1967

22nd June. A letter home on future plans. I shall arrive back about November 9th (possibly earlier). C will stay in Dulwich while I am travelling. As regards when Nan begins school; Miss Lord's plan I rejected in favour of Miss Reid's; as Nan takes a long time to adjust it is better for her to begin when she feels like it rather than in the last week in October, before I'm home. Though she should begin before Christmas, because of the festivities (carols,, etc.).

I have not recorded Kuramochi's letter of 30th May, about my scheduled departure from Japan "...The news struck me with a blow....We believe that leaving our country will be good for your future, while we feel a great loss at the same time. It is with a mixed feeling of joy and sorrow and the latter, I am afraid, is greater – that I am sending you congratulations on your more promising future. I wish you would lead days as happy as in Tokyo, or, rather, happier...."

Last night I lay awake, as I often do in this hot weather, and felt my "more promising future" close in: the NAB, and I seriously would not hesitate to apply for the dole if I thought it would be to my writing advantage. "Unemployed writer", battening off self-respecting citizens – yes, yes, yes. I am apprehensive about the future (10 months' nothing and then Leningrad, Paris or California, ideally) but it could be worse, it could be Auschwitz or Treblinka.

23rd June. A strike from Tokyo University of Education, but made little progress, being worn out from yesterday's exertions, a morning's writing; a speech and an article to correct, in addition to normal teaching at the Bank of Japan; and then the long letter home. Thought among other things about what, in my writing, is peculiar to me. (See 17 June.) For it occurs to me that I am reverting back to my style as it was in 1964, before the advent of Tuohy, i.e. that I am deliberately chucking the realistic style I have written in throughout my second phase; although I have learnt enough from it to deepen my earlier style and make it more realistic and convincing. I may be wrong – I am largely rewriting *The Eternicide* just to get a depressing accumulation of papers out of the way, and also because it riles me to think I might have wasted 1963/4 – but if this is so, then perhaps I have subconsciously, intuitively recognised all along that what I have to offer is an interior drama, i.e. that my characters (Zabov, Juben, etc.) were not completely real people "out there", and that this is my strength.

LEAVING JAPAN: LOST INTENSITY OUTSIDE SYSTEM (1967)

Last night I lay awake before dawn, turning my life over as usual and wondering if it is too early to start wondering where I've gone wrong, and I remembered Tuohy saying in China, "I've got enough impressions to dine out on for the rest of my life and I suppose you haven't noticed a thing," and I defended myself by saying (1) I don't like dining out and would refuse the invitations and (2) that my sensibility is an interiorised thing, that I get images from inside me and I write them, and don't depend on the external world as he does. That I said, was sophisticated journalism, we being in China as journalists. I am pleased with *A Spade* but perhaps what is me, as opposed to any other writer today, is the interiorised groping of a Freeman or a priest.

24th June. A visit to the Tokyo Medical and Surgical to see negro Dr. Johnson; the East has got into my body and I have begun to rot away on my back, a wasting...disease of a once ambitious spirit.

In the afternoon, to the Hilton Hotel, Akasaka, for Nan's "graduation ceremony." The plush room with a crown of thorns round the dome and coloured lights; the flowers and water in front of the stage, the modern armchairs. Nan's stage fright, shaking her head in row 3 for a quarter of an hour before the curtain went up. The seniors' performance, all about Sleeping Beauty and the redeeming prince.

Then Sister St. Mary whisked Nan away for the pre-kindergarten dance, and she did superbly – she was the first to take off and she whirled round the stage with great grace and unself-consciousness....Then came the prize-giving. She coyly received a prize for "dancing and conduct", glancing uncertainly down at C in the first three rows. The suppressed emotion and the man who thanked the sisters and teachers: calling this a "floor-show" and eulogising Sister St. John with adjectives before the presentation of the typewriter.

Sister St. John's reply. All mixed up, about the need to enjoy your children and leave the scolding to her, she does it for the best; and about the need to teach your children what is best, i.e. to scold them and not enjoy them, because you are teaching them to make choices, the right choices. Ending on enjoyment because generations change every 10 years today, and even the young ones may not understand their children and this is the age of liberty. Also on building the future, and we shan't be parted because we're all members of one family and we shall meet in heaven.

The farewells, my sadness with Sister St. Mary under a blinding, orange Hilton light. And the self-questionings in the taxi: how to cure Nan's traumas about going on stage; how to help her adjust to Oaklands.

25th June. Spent the morning on *The Eternicide*. Then thought about churches for the Tokyo University of Education. Toynbee is saying that churches are not only chrysalises between 2nd and 3rd generation civilisations; they are also the goals and justifications of the 2nd generation,

485

which are therefore to be seen as overtures which must die when the churches are born. The 3rd generation is therefore a regression, a decay, and the breakdown of the church is caused by the church itself. I do not agree.

There are three views of history: (1) that events happen, without pattern or meaning, (2) that there is pattern but no meaning (mine), (3) that there is a meaning or purpose in history (Toynbee's). I see churches as effects of universal states, but not as designed effects. Just as I see spiritual gains as benefiting the lives of men who belong to a species that came out of nothing and will return to nothing – and not as being the meaning of history. It is really a question of metaphysic and my metaphysic is, in the long run, nihilistic.

Furthermore, I do not agree that the Hellenic civilisation is justified by Christianity, whereas our civilisation since the Renaissance must be condemned as a regression. Similar conditions apply in both, and they must both go to hell together. I do believe that spiritually hard environments (= material prosperity, scepticism, reason, science) make for spiritual advances, i.e. that universal states produce churches. But I am anti-church and pro-experience, I am anti-institution and pro-spirit. Like Jung, and like Toynbee. I agree with Toynbee's view of communion with God (if God = Shadow), "The subconscious is the organ through which man lives his spiritual life... through which the Soul is in communion with God." The "One True God" is thus an experience of growth from the irrational depths, growth to the Shadow, but this, alas, does not justify history, which is meaningless.

26th June. The B-Bs' cocktail party. P came over. "And how are the distinguished Haggers?" My answer was "packing up to go," and we got onto more general subjects during his embarrassment, e.g. China. (He: "No one's allowed in by the Foreign Office at present – there'll be an incident and….") Hong Kong, the Summit meeting and Podgorny's visit to Egypt….After asking whether the new Soviet Ambassador was in fact sacked by the Kremlin (having been brought forward by Krushchev), I was interrupted by M. "You look as though you're plotting something," she said. I said, "Yes, the assassination of de Gaulle. I'm going to sit in the Champs Elysées with a machine-gun and (your husband's) going to be the stooge and we need you to go up and charm de Gaulle out." P gulped….

M said, "How's the Godhead?" (meaning the Muse) and "You're just the man I want to talk to – how do you get a defector through a tunnel when they are coming through from the other side?" She added "The book's called *Two Tunnels to Zushi*" and she hung on my arm and swung against my side while P looked even more embarrassed. After an indeterminate attempt to establish the time ("Four years back but there's no other way" – I: "Why not go to platform 12 on Tokyo station?") she said: "You're useless. (My husband) suggested a ventilator shaft. All tunnels have one, and the one I'm thinking of comes up in Mr Kobayashi's vegetable garden.

There isn't a pillbox on the hill, there's a garden." I asked if it was her first book. "I can't write it, because you see, there's got to be a lot of S-E-X," (hanging on my arm) "and my husband's going to ask 'when did this happen?' and the marriage breaks up. You see, it's not worth it." C had said not everyone'd read the novel...and that she should have a nom de plume ("Mildred —" said M) and I now said, "You can move scenes that have happened in Tokyo to London, and vice versa."

She was just going to reply when up came...Mrs. Mills, who said "Sorry to interrupt, but I've just had five dashound puppies." I wanted to say, 'Your womb must be rather tender, ma'am.' After a canine tipple, during which Mills vividly demonstrated how her fluffy dog had sunk its teeth into the upper part of her thigh (up went the skirt to add a bit of colour) Mrs. Mills, wife of a Hong Kong and Shanghai banker, asked "Are you a language student?" M winked. I said, "No, I'm a language teacher." "Oh, with the British Embassy?" I: "No, the British Council."...Short, cropped Mrs. M, who has nearly lost the glint in her eye, having been here 1954/6, first of all.

Then B-B took me aside to tell me that MITI have been difficult over the ban on exports from Rhodesia. Thence to...Kevin Garry and Nicholas B. Nicholas B fought Adrian H at prep school in the 2nd changing room. He taught Greek in Madrid before taking the European desk in Butterfield and Swire, and still dreams of Greek poetry. His wife was a nurse in the Chest X-ray dept. at the Radcliffe, Oxford. He was up 1959-63, and I remember seeing his photo in the AEN a week ago. He lives in the Imperial. (I: "Old or new?" He: "Old, of course.") He is tall and his wife is short and sensual.

Kevin Garry we came home with, after talking with two Australians. (The one who wants to get out of the Australian Embassy: "We'll help you Brits in Hong Kong," and "That's my wife in the pink dress, she's a pretty girl," and B-B stepped in and kissed her while he held the Moses basket, i.e. the baby). Kevin Garry was President of the Oxford Union 1959, but he wasn't a match for me last night: he was weak on China and Japan, and only had his stylish manner, e.g. not getting out of the taxi for 30 seconds, until he had finished what he was saying. Trattner...is now making steel in the U.S.

29th June. Prince Hitachi. On Monday I showed him *The Mistresses* on Alexander I and Fyodor Kuzmich, and after being fascinated he became aloof to put on the imperial dignity; which didn't work with a banging window (he making no attempt to put the hole on the spike). On Wednesday he wanted me to do the Franco-Prussian war and I had stopped on time, so after I stood up he remained seated in protest. The tantrum lasted 10-20 seconds. It was 10 minutes past my time and I don't get paid overtime, so I stood it out and admired the flowers and when he got up he was so rattled that he banged into the door with his walking shoes, and the crash echoed all round the palace. When I arrived I'd caught him in his slippers.

The smell of Mrs. Patterson's white gardenias.

30th June. Friday. Another holiday from Tokyo University of Education because of the strike (now 10 days old) which is over the move to "Tsukuba Academic City" in Ibaraki Prefecture, a move which will make Tokyo University of Education the number 1 university in Japan..., and then went out to buy two world travel books and got a haircut.

It occurred to me as regards my phases (see June 17th) that in most of the works of my first phase the development is geographical, not spiritual. This was M's error of last Monday, and is surely a sign of our decline – that geographical, macrocosmic progression comes more naturally than internal development. Note James Bond, e.g. *You Only Live Twice*, which C and I saw on Saturday. The story very strongly suggests neuroses escaping the subconscious (= crater) and returning and the descent into the self and the fight with the "world"-dominating ego, who is nearly one-eyed, but the fact that it is done geographically rather than more symbolically is a sign of decadence, assuming it could have been done non-geographically. So in my work, Caban goes East, Tristy dreams of Djakarta, etc., Werig goes up on the moors, Zabov goes to Russia and his successor in *The Lost Englishman* goes to Ghadames in the Libyan desert, and Juben goes to Paris via the Middle East.

In my second phase however the characters (Freeman, X, Zabov) develop within, and the geographical move is subordinated to that development. This is a gain, it means I have found my way back to the soul. Compare also my harmony with C. The last real row I had with her was on 4th December 1965, my insight then having led to one and a half peaceful, tranquil years. Possibly there was a development on her side about the same time, but I attribute the development to *The Silence*.

1st July. Worked and then B came, uninvited, and drank beer. His tiredness: "I feel like a swimmer approaching the shore" (= vacation), in spite of the strike. His readiness to die, he is like a ripe apple ready to drop, and even the thought of going down to Nobe is too tiring for him. Though he did say at the end, "If you can't go down midweek, I'll go down with Arai – she said she wanted to." (The strange omission of the "Miss".) He told us about the Japan-British farewell to the Rundalls.

His grandfatherly assumed interest in Nan's prize ("I see you've disobeyed the colours on the opposite page – that's a sign of independence") and her granddaughterish pride in showing it off. Her numbers and small letters in C's book, for which she gets a star a day if she gets them right (4 stars = 1 sweet). Her request that when I come back from "China" (= my trip home) I bring her "a thin little bangle to go round my wrist". Today she astounded me commenting on a Fiji military parade on TV, "They're Red Guards."

2nd July. For Tokyo University of Education. On Spengler. He certainly argues from a metaphor to a law as Toynbee said; so "cultures are organisms" instead of "cultures are like organisms."

The essence of his theory is that cultures harden into civilisations, and the soul-power of cultures hardens into the intellectual (i.e. rational) power of civilisations. So a civilisation is the destiny of a culture, and if we have the misfortune to be born into a civilisation we should become engineers instead of poets or saints, i.e. we should be for our time (amor fati) and not against it through the active Toynbeean response ("a transfer of power from Economics to Religion").

It is all terribly inevitable, just as old age is inevitable, and one is more on Toynbee's side, in spite of his absurd singling out of the interregnum at the end of the second generation as the high point in history, one that the first and third generation interregna are equally distant from – the absurd deification of the Incarnation. On Heroic Ages Toynbee is saying that barbarians inevitably spill over the dam, but that they are only good at destroying and cannot create (cf China's destruction of the family and traditional values) and that they collapse suddenly to be followed by a "dark age", as did the regimes that surrounded Beowulf and Agamemnon, and that the judgement on their ages can only be severe.

After this Toynbee is saying that the civilisation ceases to be a unit in history during the disintegration phase: there is a lot of intermingling in the uniformity of a universal state and there are contacts between civilisations. Certain places act as "roundabouts" for civilisations (e.g. Syria, Oxus-Juxartes) and in these places higher religions grow; the response of transfiguration being one of the responses of a conquered people, the other responses being anti-West, Slavophile "Zealotism" (archaism) and pro-West Westerniser "Herodianism" (futurism). A St. Paul of cosmopolitan origins (Greek education, Roman citizen, Gentile Tarsus Pharisee) chooses transfiguration.

3rd July. Further thoughts from Toynbee; on Russia. Is Russia a Western country or a barbarian country, the universal state of the Tsars having ended?* This is the crucial question in understanding the modern world, for the Soviet Union is the first power, since the Ottoman attack on Vienna of 1683, to threaten the West; 1683-1945 and then Stalin. Moreover, anyone in England would have agreed during the 1950s that if there were a frontier against the West it was down Europe; i.e. the frontier against the barbarians (which are closing in) is now Eastern Europe and the Mediterranean nations. In this case Russia has always basically been Slavophile, and the Westernising of Peter-Lenin is a superficial thing, connected with the way a growing society charms a barbarian power; until it ceases to work. In which case also the view of Europe I presented in *Archangel* is wrong – a European universal state will never include Russia – and de Gaulle is wrong too (in foreseeing a Europe stretching from the Atlantic to the Urals).

Again I ask, is Russia a Dacia (i.e. a province in a new universal state), or is it a Parthia, to be fought with the desperation of the 1st century Romans after Carrhae, and finally to be coexisted with until it no longer matters? If

Russian Orthodox is anything to go by, and Dostoevsky and the Western context, Russia is a member of the West, and I have always been right about it.

Would that I could read the future. Last night I lay awake from 2 to 6, during a storm, and as in 1965, images began to rise, at first patterns, but later visions of Chinese cities and fortresses and even a dateholder saying "July 1". At one stage I attempted to get control, and I asked to see the world 700 years from now, and all I got was a honeycomb city in a hill like a cross between Libyan hovels and Petra. Possibly the H-bomb will bring that about; anyhow, there was nothing on the future of Russia – only China. Though I have understood some of Nostradamus's power.

(*One of my areas of disagreement with Toynbee.)

4th July. Thoughts, again, on Wilson's *Outsider*, one of the worst (thought-out and written) books since the war, yet the one I can never escape because it's so much a comment on my life. The theme of the book is an anti-rationalist one, that the reason is a Blakean Spectre that holds one's drive to the Shadow in its power, i.e. prevents the miserable "Outsider" from realising his destiny as a prophet. The Spectre is the internal enemy that lies across the path to Los/Superman/Angel, and this makes one's inner life seem unreal. Hence the world seems unreal, in accordance with the theory I have developed, the theory that all problems are in one's inner life and that these are projected out into history and politics and ideas (cf Eisenstein's *Ivan the Terrible*, whose unification of his kingdom is an expression of a drive to inner unity). So a Ricky complaining that life is futile is static within, and can't develop to the Shadow and the visionary.

It is Romantic, this view of the Reason-Spectre (since Goethe and the 1770s reason had been overthrown in favour of energy and spontaneity and spiritual drive), but the man in the grip of his Spectre, the Oblomov, is even more of a Romantic than Blake. And this brings me to Tuohy, who wrote me a warm letter last week. Tuohy is a brilliant observer, and he makes you think all the next day after you've been with him, but…the surface glitter conceals a deep emptiness that he himself has admitted. ("Perhaps I haven't the courage to descend into myself.") Tuohy is in the Spectre's power: hence his block and his hatred of the anti-rationalist tradition (e.g. Jung). I have known both Wilson and Tuohy, and both are geniuses in their own way; with Tuohy I have always said "True", with Wilson "Exciting." Tuohy affects my attitudes, Wilson my way of life, and I belong to the post-Blakean Romantics of whom Wilson is one.

5th July. A day when it got hot and the first cicada started running, like a water-cistern in a lavatory. I was worn out from Keio yesterday and I went off to Isetan (not having Hitachi) and got a flash for my camera and got my watch repaired and bought an alarm clock and then went to Maruzen and bought two files. Meanwhile C had Ena over.

6th July. A cooler day. I have not recorded the letter from Reggie. "The events of the last few weeks, culminating in the sudden death of your Auntie Ruth, are still hardly believable to me, and as the days go by I begin to feel the loss of her Dear Person more than ever. I realise that I will have to come to terms with myself in this matter, and this I fully intend to try to do, but it will not be easy. 30 years of happy married life are not so easily forgotten...."

7th July. Another holiday from Tokyo University of Education, which is still on strike. Worked. In the evening took C out to eat. Went to the Imperial Garden Bar and watched the rain in the puddles under the lanterns. After that went on and ate in Nicola's. Arrived at a busy time and sat in the bar. C: "There's a black-eyed beauty." (A heavily made up girl)....

The transitory air in both places. The Vietnam wife and friend in Nicola's, the girl with the parted hair who looked up at me as she went under my arm in the Garden Bar door. And what I diagnosed later in the gents mirror as an autumnal beauty. I suppose it had flowered by 1960, yet how different my life might have been if it had seen an early summer and flowered in 1956. Five years before Pat M described me as the most beautiful man she had ever seen. I would, undoubtedly, have become a businessman.

Cain and Abel on the radio, recalling me to *The Molten Owl's Song*. How odd that Cain's land of Nod, in my play, should have been Japan, and how could I understand what I was getting at – ...Cain being a fugitive and a vagabond.

8th July. A letter from mother. "Argie has had some infection in her fruit trees, she has had to have three down today, which is sad and expensive too. A fourth tree is being treated...."

9th July. A wet day, got overtired. Otherwise reflected on my nervousness.

Undoubtedly, if I have a wound to compensate ordinary mortals for my immortal bow, then it is in my nervousness. Yet can I really be anti-Freud and say that the bow came first – is it not something I've striven for to ease the awful torture of the wound? I suspect it is. My attitude towards it, though, is ambivalent. I want to discover the cause, find out the source of the anxiety neurosis, if it is that; whether it's an early trauma or just a "lack of practice" (for it has got worse since I came to Japan). Yet I want to preserve my creative powers, and I know the two are in some way related. My paralytic terror at Tomlin's, at the conference – if I lost these I would lose the power to write, I am sure of it. And so I do not try to lose it (i.e. the wound).

But having it, what should my attitude be? Should I make a show of resisting it, or should I accept it? In my Existentialist (Activist) Oxford days, I denied it and fought it, and became a teacher to conquer it and

491

perhaps I succeeded temporarily, to a certain extent. Should I do that now, or should I parade it without shame, like a scar? There are few who will parade their scar. Sometimes I start shivering, I go completely paralytic and want to withdraw; other times I bubble over with assurance and conviction and genius. I cannot say which is the true "I". I am divided. I can say, though, that the self I experience most often, outside my house, except with a chosen few people, is the former.

10th July. A stormy night, typhoon Billy having hit Kyushu and killed 250 odd (+150 odd missing). Although it was downgraded to a tropical storm before it struck, it pushed an enormous rainbelt in front of it, and I could not sleep, and at dawn watched the whirling russet clouds reveal a deep blue sky, and in the morning wrote *And after that came the storm.*

Later went to Hitachi and did the First World War with him – the carving up of Austria-Hungary among 7 nations, and, strangely, the pinching of 5 nations (including Poland) from Russia. After that did the U.S. – in addition to the slavery issue 1861-5, the creation of the U.S. from Louisiana 1803 to the Treaty of Oregon 1846. After that did Latin America, which threw off Spanish rule 1808-1830 in the order Colombia and Venezuela, Argentina, Chile and Peru, Mexico; Brazil being a Portuguese empire 1825-1889. After Brazil tried to annex Uruguay and her, Paraguay engaged in a 3-sided war (Brazil, Argentine, Uruguay) and lost her entire male population and half her female population, 1865-70. All this was while Shizukosan came to play with Nadia. (Nan: "If you go out on Wednesday, I'll cry.")

In the evening I was too tired to do more than ring Narita. Who has at last recognised his "on" (regarding his visit to Britain). "It is almost entirely thanks to you," said three times. He is going to meet Ruth and the McAlpines in Highgate, and is going to seek out Baker at the (British) Council. "Where is Professor Tuohy now? Has he settled down finally?" Our giggling over the telephone, I trying to avoid offering him my family to visit. His mention of eels his wife is sending. "With my card."

11th-12th July. A day of little progress, and working for Hitachi. On Wednesday, a day of fantastic effort, prompted by a letter from Komano giving us an estimate for packing....Rang various other people before going to the dentist, a large filling having fallen out when I bit my toast in the morning, at breakfast. Had a temporary filling and then went to Koshi to get him to send a packing "certificate of reservation on JAL" to Komano. This will mean our luggage can leave on August 26th instead of the day after our departure (October 19th), the Japanese law.

Thence, to Hitachi, where we revised Prussia 1640-1871, Austria 1806-1866, Austro-Hungarian empire 1866-1918, and the unification of Italy 1848-1870. (Piedmont's rebellion in favour of Lombardy and Venetia 1848, Milan 1859, duchies, Naples and Sicily 1861, papal states 1861; 1st unification except for Venice 1866 and Rome 1870, in 1861.) Also did

Africa and colonisation and especially the French empire (Algeria 1830, Tunisia 1881, Morocco 1912.)

At the end of the class Hitachi asked me for an English teacher and on Thursday a.m. I spent a long time telephoning Bickley; Tomlin and Buchanan. My first candidate was Bickley – who would be good at all three subjects, language, culture and questions – but after he expressed interest Tomlin said no, as he is on the diplomatic lists and is too busy. The cultural department of the Embassy had its drawbacks shown up – "he's on the diplomatic lists". I vetoed Tomlin's suggestions...and plumped for Buchanan. Tomlin "We'll back him if we're asked." B: "Oh, I thought my name was mud with the Council." B may not be strong on language, but he would be strong on cultural affairs, which are most important.

On Tuesday night I did not sleep because of the heat and overwork and while I lay awake I thought. After the day's exertions I was worn out before B-B's party for Adrian had even started. Shy Shizukosan, Sizue's deputy while she is on holiday. When we arrived Adrian and Rosemary Woods were present. Soon after the B's (of the Australian Embassy) arrival, and Figgess.

I talked to Adrian and B-B early on, and then sat with Mrs. B and Figgess, who said "You've been here three years?" in a tone that was a more perfect replica of Tomlin's. Could Tomlin have modelled himself on Figgess, i.e. be Figgess with hesitations? He has the same domed head and hooked nose, and the same lack of aggression and confidence. I said "Four", and asked "How long have you been here?" He: "Oh, twenty, thirty, I don't like to count exactly," and I suddenly knew.....(When introduced he said "We have met once" and "Good evening Mrs. Hagger.") I said I could understand how people stay a long time, e.g. Buchanan, and he countered, "Oh, but he's not involved in Japan, he's just here because he couldn't do anything better in England isn't he?" I: "Oh no, he has a lot to do with Japan. He teaches a lot of interesting Japanese, and he's treated like a daimyo in Nobe, and, most important of all, he reads voraciously. He must have some 2,000 books, and there comes a time when you just can't move. He: "Oh, I'd be happy to give away my books." I: "No, it's a psychological thing. Some people shed themselves and their books, and others hoard themselves and their books, and he's a hoarder." Everyone agreed and he was isolated, but not unpleasantly.

Later, during dinner (soup, paté in jelly, beef and stuffing, meringue and water melon, the whole prepared by the Ambassador's cooks and washed down with an inadequate supply of red wine) he had a go at mini-skirts and said how dreadful they looked on some people "even a certain person here who shall remain nameless." Crystal pulled down hers, but he meant Rosemary Woods.

Later still I asked Adrian what he thought about France's withdrawal from AFVG, and said de Gaulle seems to have been outflanked by the WEU's receiving the application to enter the EEC. During the forthcoming

493

argument (Adrian: "But it could have been handed over in a pub."; "But what difference will it make – de Gaulle's not going to jeopardise the six") Figgess took my side: "I'm most disappointed – you talk so rousingly, and yet you say there's only a 50-50 chance of our getting in."

Later we got onto films and Figgess liked *A Man for all Seasons*. I: "But isn't it too rational? People don't talk like that, in complete sentences, and they don't say what they mean." Silence, F: "Yes, you could say that, but I'm not an expert, like you..." Said genuinely. I took it as my due. Later B-B got going on A. J. P. Taylor, for the second time getting out the books and persuading me to read them. I: "Amis, George Brown and Taylor make a corner." F: "I quite agree." (Also the bit about Catholics and Protestants in Europe, and the Common Market as a Catholic plot. Catholics as a social group.)

14th July. Arrived at Nobe at 8.15. The absence of taxis at the station (after having to belt down Zushi platform because half the train was taken off); I thought it was because of the beginning of Bon, but Buchanan thought it was the anniversary of Commodore Perry's landing in Kurihama, and this was evidently right as we learned later that Nobe follows the old calendar, i.e. that Bon falls on August 13th-16th.

With Buchanan we had saké, and sashimi (raw fish, "yellowtail" – "inaba") and the sandwiches and biscuits we took, and after that I went for a walk to look for Bon lanterns. We had seen some from the taxi in Tokyo: red, yellow, blue-green. After that we went to bed, at 9.30, and I awoke at 2 to look on a hot fog from the sea, and, sweating, went to the fridge and drank the only bottle of beer inside.

15th-16th July. After a semi-sleepless night, and a lot of time spent watching for the dawn over the thatched roof nearby, staggered up and ate and went down to the beach. Roasted myself purple in between a couple of swims, and sat around in a temperature of over 90F. One and a half hours' shopping and drinking and waiting for chopped sashimi, then ate and slept and woke for a further trip to the beach. I was weary, and could hardly walk* past the stilted stage near the fishing-ramp. Sat, and then returned to the house and shopped for black tye and sashimi, and then ate and drank saké and talked about being against your time. Got thoroughly drunk and after a lone walk among the dark hedges and the dimlit houses, went to bed and vomited three times* outside the sliding window, on the slope down to the thatch, and finally dropped off, feeling empty, and slept till 7.

Woke with a clanking head to shrieks of "Yuriko" from the thatched house, got up gingerly, and then, as yesterday, read Fitzgibbons' biography of (Dylan) Thomas until beachtime. It was by this time 33C (92F) and I felt drained. I sat and roasted, dressed, on the beach – the dead turtle – then went back and changed for a swim. After that felt weak. Shopped for beer, and drank, and then ate crab (tinned) and slept until 3 and sat around.

LEAVING JAPAN: LOST INTENSITY OUTSIDE SYSTEM (1967)

Yesterday Nan had some sparkler fireworks – she was frightened by the bangers on Friday – and today we bought a thunderflash. Buchanan set it off. It wouldn't ignite at the top, so at C's suggestion he lit the fusewire, bending down, and the thing blew up in his face. He was covered with sand and ash, and so were his glasses, and the foot long carton disintegrated like a grenade. I: "That's what it feels like to be blown up." He: "That's the nearest I've come to it."

On the way back, the wait at the "coca-cola shop" for the taxi. The first class carriage on the train. Later, the sushi shop in Jimbocho, and the hermit crab.

Earlier B's story about Istanbul. He was in a café, drinking raki (i.e. ouzo, cf arak – it turns milky when you add water), a boy of 16 asked him to move to another table and then shot one of four nearby sideways on from about 20 yards. "He just fell forward onto the table – he didn't know." The others started screaming, the boy just sat and waited for the police. It was a vendetta thing, and the police winked at that. He was under age, so they told him to go away and not be a naughty boy again."

The way Nan picked jellyfish out of the sea, imitating Uncle Brian (Buchanan); while I watched (as when the fireworks were ignited) terrified of getting hurt.

*Were these symptoms of heat exhaustion? I think so.

17th July. An active day, broken by collecting salary. Otherwise thought about a poem whose theme I unwittingly stated suddenly yesterday at breakfast, after gazing at the hill over Nobe: "Nature, like history, has pattern but not meaning. Agree or disagree?"

After Buchanan agreed I thought out the poem. It is first of all about the mess in Nature and history, symbolised by the Nobe rubbish dump. (Boxes, petrol cans, firesticks, paper, and an ant with a shadow, a mallow, cannae and the purple flower, pine bristles and wires like bars; and cicadas like a sawmill.) This mess is given a pattern by the hill, which dominates it and unites it, making everything relate (meaning is why, pattern is relation); like a mandala, all round the centre. So Nature is given a pattern by evolution, and history by Empires.* In other words, the hill stands for the principle of striving which runs through Nature and history; and the self. For ultimately the mess is given meaning by striving in the self. This hill is, then, the Shadow.

Finally there is a statement of subjectivity, that "isness" only has a meaning in my brain, in that without the observer it is merely pattern, and not meaning. Nature and history seen within the context of the self ("my sliding doors") are transformed into something new, they are not futile but the highest quality of life, i.e. striving ("climbing" to the Shadow). And man, so far from being futile or meaninglessness – each man is the meaning in the universe, for him; because the mess of the rubbish heap can become an image, a pattern seen in relation to climbing, i.e. the hill, the highest existential fulfilment and "meaning" (i.e. realisation). And so the chaos of stanza 1 is to be transformed into the rich order and purpose of stanza 3, and the rubbish dump becomes the hill.

* No, by civilisations.

18th July. Worked but not very successfully, and then went to MITI. The man who learnt Chinese and admitted "MITI believes that within 5 years China will be our number one market, and so I had to learn Chinese full time for six months"; the chief who coughed disparagingly and fluttered his eyelids and who didn't know one of his staff when I mentioned him – I marked him down for bad relations with his staff; the man who had been in France and who thought Brown's method of applying to the Common Market childish. I: "After the French pulling out of AFVG, there was no other way." He, later: "We Japanese sympathise with the underdog, i.e. the weaker, and so we sympathise with Britain."

The same day came Britain's announcement that she will pull out of Singapore and Malaysia 1973/7, and that Antigua is now independent. This latter item of news is just a bore, but what about East of Suez? I am a little divided. On the one hand, I am not interested, personally, in serving in those countries, nor do I think funds spent in them are spent profitably. On the other hand, our withdrawal is a diminution on our status, as the U.S., Australia and New Zealand have recognised, and that is a pity. For as our status goes down, so does our position with the U.S.

We are undoubtedly living in a time of fantastic decline – none of the local Embassy lies about progress can prevent me from seeing that. Yet it is with a great deal of sadness that I record that, as a writer, I have so far been right. Even now, I would give anything for us to get into Europe and prove the mood of *Blighty* wrong.

19th July. Worked, but experienced the same symptoms of heat exhaustion as I did on Saturday, and did not write much. In the end lay and read the *Observer* (our diminishing status with Washington, and the need to devalue), then went to Jimbocho, where I bought three books relevant to *Mandalas*: Sierksma's *Tibet's Terrifying Deities*; Fouchet's *The Erotic Sculpture of India*; and Coedès's *Angkor*.

These books should, between them, contain the thesis of X, the man who replaces Zabov in the new version of *Mandalas*. The point is that Truffer puts forward the religious interpretation of Eastern religion (OM/mandalas = meditation and self-perfection); whereas X puts forward the erotological interpretation (OM = satisfaction of desire, Siva = lingam not ego, Kali = yoni?) This interpretation is an interpretation of the modern generation, for ours is The Sexual Age, and Truffer is out of date; though half right, for the mystical and sensual are one – see Rica, the Kali. So, academic attitudes reflect their personal ways of life, in relation to Rica she is still, they move. X sleeps with her, Truffer contemplates her. Is there any text which treats a mandala as a sexual orgasm? The woman and bull symbolism in some of the mandalas Sierksma offers, which suggests that even mandalas are about sexual neuroses. What about Nepal? Which fuses Hindu and Tantric Buddhist beliefs? Mandalas are Buddhist so what relation is there between erotological Hinduism and woman-bull?

20th-21st July. Worked without getting anywhere, went to the Bank and then, alone (because of C's leg and boil), went straight on to Ellingworth's party for Adrian in No. 5 House. No one over 2nd Secretary, other than Ellingworth: no Figgess or Tomlin. The Georgian interior, wooden boards. Decayed E whose eyes took in my nervousness. "I'm wifeless too, my wife's gone to Chuzenji for the summer." I: "There's a colony there." Nothing else to say, so I said "I'll go through." Then my wound opened and bled, and I had the shivers, I wanted to turn and run away.

I stood in the doorway to the stone veranda and was introduced, by an aggressive Gaimusho man, to Adrian Thorpe, a beefy man who looks like (Harold) Wilson and has a lisp. The Gaimusho man, "Mr H is teaching, or studying English at the Tokyo University." I: "Of Education, I've left Todai." He spoke in such an affected accent that I misunderstood something he said, i.e. misheard a word. I: "How long have you been here?" He: "Twenty months." I: "It's strange I haven't run into you before." The Japanese: "But you have. Mr Hagger was at B-B's, and Mr Thorpe...." I: "Wasn't there."

The Japanese retired two paces. I: "Are you in Information?" He: "I succeed John Field in a week's time." I: "Ah, I've been asked to find out who got the Suez Canal dues before 1956." He "What?" I repeated. He: "Jews?" I heard "Dues" and repeated. He: "Oh, dues. I thought you said Jews. The Suez Canal was owned by the Anglo-French Board and so the money went to them." "But did any of it remain in Egypt? The point is, did Nasser seize the £2 million a week from us, or was the money invested in Egypt in some way?" He: "Oh, I see what you mean. I don't know." A lot of wind and arrogance and confidence and moreover, no knowledge.

I went through and talked to Mrs. B-B about some Canadian method of taking exercise. I was so bored, and constricted, that when the Barbers arrived ("How's the Prince?") I muttered an excuse and beat it over to A.... Was introduced around, and was left with...Claire McIntyre of the Australian Embassy. Talked about language; then the plight of the English teacher now that we are pulling out; then about the Malaysian base, and the British decline; China and Prince Hitachi. C.M. had handed in her resignation that day; she can stay on three months to get half fare (only being here one year, she has broken her two year contract), i.e. until mid-November, and wants to go outside Tokyo and do pottery. I: "Why did you resign." She: "Boredom." She reads *Time* and just sits around until 5.21, and has no travelling because she lives in the compound. She doesn't regret coming to Japan. Australia is so suburban and deadly. She is independent and lives 50 miles south of Melbourne.

Got back thoroughly drunk and ate C's sashimi and admired the erotic pictures in the books on India and Tibet, which she'd been reading, and went to bed.

On Friday finished the bit about the strong and the weak, and the old lady. Then rang B-B about the Dodwells couple, see April 21st. The power of the institution. When I read about the death of Jock Morrison in a *Japan Times* advert on June 8, I was sure it was the one we met....I was right – Jock Morrison it was we met on April 21st, a rather randy man with a moustache and glasses who said "I don't care what anyone says, Wilson's done his best." He went swimming in Hong Kong, had a heart attack. They got him to the shore, and he died before the ambulance arrived. They were going on leave, so Betty was there. She was an Embassy typist, and she married in her late 30s, i.e. 1964, so she is a widow after three years; and her mother died just before. She has not returned to Japan, and "has the East in her blood," so possibly will.

I have not recorded Fitzgibbons' book on Dylan Thomas, which I read last week-end. This is full of the Ms, and some of the telling juxtapositions make it clear that Helen M slept with Dylan Thomas. Cf April 8th, what Ruth Witt-Diamant said....Ruth Witt-Diamant is also mentioned in the book as being Dylan Thomas's hostess in January/February 1951. I suppose she couldn't have been "Sarah"? Like Sarah, Ruth Witt-Diamant went to London in October 51, and went on to Swansea. "Sarah" is supposed to have been a publisher's employee.

21st-23rd July. On Friday evening (21st) I took C to Nicola's (restaurant) while shy Shizukosan tried to cope with Nan. C's Pallas Athene helmet hair; the small tenor (alto) saxophone, like an opium pipe, and me defending my trip and thinking of Michael Caine ("I watch until they think they've got me, then I end it"). Later, the smell of red incense – lotus blossom – and their similarity with "halma men".

On Saturday (22nd) and Sunday (23rd) two days of tremendous energy. I have a strength that no one can break, I have an inner core and conviction that carries on whatever happens. In bed later C said, "The moon's caught in the branches of that tree." Earlier, "I've been watching it for the last three days, and it's moved round to there, on the opposite side of the house", i.e. over the Hatamuras, and she was suddenly depressed; by the "cruelty of the world", though, as a result of a programme she had watched on TV, by emotions like anger and hatred.

I said "One must keep a sense of proportion, they are of little importance to the universe," and suddenly I was talking as Krishna did to Arjuna. People got angry and had negative emotions, I said, and in London someone wrote a letter saying "No", but ultimately, it was of little importance to the universe. She: "Yes, but then you become hard." I: "No, you live between Yes and No." She: "And cruelty can't be ignored because it's of no importance to the universe." I: "Agreed." We both agreed that as we were alive, we should fight cruelty, but, I said, it was worth remembering that dozens of generations of agonies were dead, for there was comfort in the thought, and one could derive strength from the thought.

"My strength depends on the indifference of the universe," I said. She: "Well you needn't make love now, because the universe is indifferent." I: "I'm going to die and you're going to die, so to us now it's important, though in a few hundred years from now it will admittedly be a matter of indifference to the universe as to whether we did or not," and...I quoted "The grave's a fine and private place/But none I think do there embrace." And as I lay over her and affirmed her the moon got free from the branches of the tree, and it sailed up like a balloon, and it shone down with a supporting, universal joy.

24th July. Novel. Zabov is looking at the skull-handle in the antique-shop; and the reproduction of the *Last Judgement*.

After C came back from Kinokuniya with ice-cream packed in dry ice, I watched the dry ice dissolve in water (0_2 + H_20?). It bubbled and poured out unreal, white smoke. The bubbles swelled into fried eggs and popped into smoke, and evaporated, and with a universal vision I watched a generation's conversation and emotion.

Sounds. The squeak of a cicada, like a cork being pulled from a wine-bottle; without the pop.

26th July. A hot day. I felt tired, too tired to do much work. C went to Dr Morton about a red bump on her face. I minded Nan and corrected Kawai's bibliography pieces....C came back and said it was an abscess, i.e. a cyst, that Morton had tried to lance it, but without success; and that if it had not gone down by Friday, it might need surgery. Also, that Nan's white cell count taken from her ear was "not right" and that though it might be because of her tonsillitis, she should have it done again. My heart sank. And I read the book later, while Nan (who doesn't miss a thing e.g. "Mummy's orange pills – are they nice?" and "What's this towel for?") protested "I don't want to see the doctor." It said that white cells are up when the tonsils are infected (and get white spots on them?), but these are the symptoms of leukaemia. M said, "I should take Nadia to a blood specialist when you go back to England." Does this mean that he suspects leukaemia? Sick with fear I gave into every request she made, and when I got back from the travel agents (rerouting via Istanbul-Budapest and planning hotels) I sympathised with her splinter ("I think I'll pick it") and she was more loving than usual, and hugged my neck and wouldn't let me leave her room. Later dipped into *Astrology* by Mac Neice for my third poem, and I felt afraid from a distance; having suspended emotion until after Friday and the results of the test.

27th July. Slept badly in the heat and then tried to write, and thought. Then went to the Bank of Japan and heard about Oshima's wife. Two years ago she had a child at the K—Hospital. Saito, "She had been to an American college" (she was a student of Todai) "and she was a modern woman, she did not like pain, and so she had an injection to kill the labour pains." It never unfroze. Watarai: "Last week it was worse, then it was better, then it was worse and she died." Last Saturday. The negligence theory about the injection is only a conjecture, for Oshima has not said anything. "He is cheerful, he does not mention his troubles, I admire him." The other theory is that the doctor made her stand up too quickly after childbirth, and that this produced complications, but this is untenable. Short of an unknown disease there can be no other explanation. I: "It's awful."

Saito, "Yes, and my best friend was killed two weeks ago. He was unmarried and he had been on a date. He had seen his girl-friend off at Shinjuku station. It was raining. He crossed the road – not at a pedestrian crossing – and a car hit him and threw him and two other cars coming the other way hit him and rolled him over. It was in the paper. Three cars is very rare." I, later, "It makes me feel old. Ten years ago I would have been shocked, and I would have been surprised, but now nothing surprises me. I feel anger and sorrow, but not surprise, for the human condition is evil, cruel, and that sort of thing must be expected to happen. As in the case of Morrison...." He: "Yes, I agree. It is terrible that I sit next to a man and then he is dead." Finally, "Today has been somewhat gloomy, but it is the truth." I: "Yes, and it is better than pretending." He: "Yes."

28th July. Took C and Nan to Kabuki. We arrived in time to see a woman throw herself off the cliff, after a man, and to be redeemed by an "angel"; the man losing his blindness. After a long interval *Kangincho* (= "scroll for temple funds") began. The 20 square-shouldered men sitting on a bright red "platform" at the back. Six musicians in front, five barrier guards in front of them, including Togashi in a Christmas party hat. Bamboo left and right, a pine like three clusters of cloud at the back, and a striped cloth over the door like a bathing-hut front or a shower curtain, and striped downwards like a Franco-Belgium flag. The music was saucepans and kettles, with occasional suspenders and garters and a few rubber bands.

Benkei, the servant in a master's role, looked like a bumble-bee – he was all black and yellow and buff and when he got angry, which was frequently, he buzzed and looked like Mr Efficiency himself, the bungling Nakagawa. He got drunk out of two gourds which looked like monstrous peanuts. Yoshitune, the master dressed as a porter, had a lampshade on his head and he wore the yamabushi's (= mountain priest's) bulging trousers; he looked like a round doll, centre of gravity in the middle, and when he beat it at the end, he looked like a pregnant washerwoman. Bits of gripping intensity and stretches of boredom when they stood and talked; these being nothing like the Kyogen that followed, where there was no attempt at voice-projection.

Left and went to the doctor where Nan had a prick in her ear and C's abscess was pronounced improved but still hard and in need of surgery.

Nan's yells while they took a test-tube of blood and several smears. "I want to see" and "Is it a light?" The blood looked so scarlet it was incredible it could be so white.

29th July. At the doctor's on Friday; Nan's fear of going in. C took her to the ladies to tell her to get a grip on herself, I stood outside the Medical and Surgical Clinic door, and two Greyfriar (?) nuns came out, with squat, square crosses high up, and babbled away in Italian. Eventually one asked, in English, "Aren't you the doctor they sent us to?" I: "No, I'm afraid I'm not." More babbling in Italian, whereupon I asked (having half-recognised one in milky glasses), "Are you from the Cours Saint Louis?" (My daughter's school). She: "You go in and write out your name and address." I, having done this a hundred times since 1963, smiled and bowed and said "Thank you," and they smiled and they bowed and they were happy, and they went off smiling benevolently, having done their good turn for the day, while I was left shaking my head.

In the doctor's waiting-room, the fat American with crew-cut, silver hair. There was groaning from behind the consultation room, the groaning of a dying man, and he turned to me and said "Better him than us ay?" and I giggled at his cynicism. Later he announced to the waiting-room in general, "First day in my life I've been sick, I've never been to a doctor before." (He must have been over 60.) No one responded and he was called through, grumbling about how awful it was going to the doctor, and during his absence a woman came in. When he returned they greeted each other as Americans do when they've met each other socially. "I've got a gall bladder," he said. "Got a pain down here." "Oh yes?" gasped the woman, not feeling his crotch. "Took me at 11.30 yesterday," the American said. "Came up in a cold sweat and I couldn't breathe, and was here 12 to 1 and 4 to 7 yesterday, and 11 to 12 today, and now." "Making tests are they?" she asked as he was called through again and she whispered to her daughter, who was mini-ed, "He is the manager of the Bank."

Saturday. Wrote until all grew dark and a storm approached.

It was the most vicious storm I have ever experienced; the only three that rival it are the one before I took "A" level; the one in Greece when I nearly got drowned between Rhodes and Turkey; and the blue storm here two years ago. The rain lashed down, the trees bent, and the lightning, at first like lights being turned on and off almost continuously, suddenly turned to bolts. They echoed down after brilliant "phuts" in our very room, and some six bolts fell all round the house.

The most vicious I flinched from before it began, and from the French windows I followed its track from high up all the way down over my shoulder, clutching Nan; a jagged fork aiming at me. It struck a scaffolding just beyond our garden wall, some ten yards from me, and everything seemed to blow up in a ghostly white glow. With my stomach sinking and my knees knocking I went on telling Nan a story about Nobe as my father used to tell me a story about Peter and his dog during the V-bombs and, earlier, the doodlebugs. Another bolt fell ten yards behind us, and knocked a concrete clothes line down in the Hatamuras', and burnt all the washing. Not a peep out of them – they put up the shutters and hid in their futons, and the washing was still strewn on the ground when blue sky returned.

Then the cicadas started up again, and all was cool, and the cat crept out from under the settee, thoroughly cowed by the big explosion, and the dog plucked up the courage to go outside, and, looking at the trees for a blasted bole, I realised they were all black under the lashing rain. Everything was a fresh, melanistic black, and I was drained, emotionally exhausted by contact with primeval fear.

30th July. Sunday. Wrote and prepared *The Noddies* for typing, then went for a walk to the Cathedral and went down the stone steps to the dark corridors of the catacombs, and finally (via a Virgin pointing forward) to the moist floor of the crypt. The glass door marked "Exit", the dark in the centre, i.e. not near the doors or the altar. The pews in storage, the thick candles like night lights in glassholders on the altar. The recesses at the side, like the slabs higher up. The catafalques, small, medium, large; I: "For children, Japanese and gaijin (foreigners)."

Outside the wedding arrival, and the guest who lost her glove and said "Thank you." Later Chinzanso and the crowds in the swimming-pool and the café, under umbrellas; like Margate beach, or Bognor. In the evening I tore up 80% of my newspaper cuttings – four years' worth – and filed the remainder. On Monday: I wrote a bit more but mainly concentrated on the play. Was interrupted by Tokyo University of Education, who came to renew the washer in the "fawcet", and at the same time refused to buy our second-hand china. In Japan everything has to be new. C flogged it to Ena (as from October 16th) while I was at MITI.

1st August. C and Nan played hospitals, plasters on the nose (and tears). Meanwhile at MITI I had a man who goes home (like all of them) at 11 p.m., and who hadn't had dinner with his wife more than five times in the first six months of their marriage; the typical marital situation. I: "You should leave MITI or go abroad." On Japanese work, in relation to the Trade Policy Sections. The Chief sits in the middle of the room, with his back to the window, and the Deputy Chief beside him.

2nd August. On Tuesday I went to the dentist and was told I would have to have a wisdom tooth pulled. Went on to Bank, hairdresser, copier, pharmacy, then came home and worked. On Wednesday I spent a weary day sweating fitfully…and doing *The Noddies*.

3rd August. After discussing my successor with Ichiki returned to B. He had just come up from Nobe, having gone back specially yesterday because his Tokyo neighbours got the date wrong; he was supposed to be welcoming them this morning, and he could not ask them to wait until next week. Also he left the fridge on 7, and Keikosan said it would blow up if left a week. He was full of Rumichan, who had been to stay, and poor Nan stood by with her rubber ring and her memory of swimming with her Uncle while he sat, cut off, and sang Rumichan's praises. I nursed Nan and made a fuss of her, and in the end B paid her the attention she'd looked forward to all day.

After that she went to bed and we discussed British reserves (£997 million) and overseas assets (£8,000 million). Buchanan: the overseas ones can't be sold without great difficulty. Also devaluation, and the rebellion of the Isle of Man.

Otherwise we discussed travel. This took him on to his experiences about 1935 with Edward Luns and, later, with his own car-hire business, C. H. Challis of Bond Street (now). He had to take a party of Maynooth priests and Jays (dress shop) girls to Bruges, after which he handed them over, and "there was so much fornication on the train that night that one of the priests came and said he was worried at what I'd do." B: "What happened? I saw nothing".

He took a party of Vassar girls round Europe for six months. They went Denmark-Greece, Poland-Spain, and had two weeks in Paris, during which they slept with the liftboys, and a long time in Naples. The two dates, Guiseppe the Vesuvius guide, and his pal. They drove the girls into the hills and they petted. Then the girls said No, so the men left them to walk ten miles back through the dust. Buchanan: "They were sitting in the lobby with the tears rolling down cheeks that were white with dust" – the dust that covers everything in the summer in Naples. In Scotland they all bought Glencarny bonnets (with strings) in Princes Street and wired or "sent a cablegram" to Pop when money ran out. They bought Buchanan a $1,000 silver dish at the end, for turning a blind eye, and presented it coyly. (The leader of the group and B's mistress is now President of that Women's University.)

He had to take a party from Lugano to St. Moritz. You have to go via Italy, and he went via the Maloja pass. After they were through a thunderstorm washed it away, and there was a choice between staying in St. Moritz or risking the hairpin bends of the Bernina pass. It was night and wet, and the driver wouldn't go – it was a 40 seat bus. Of the party of 30, only two wanted to stay. Buchanan said he would drive. The driver protested to the police. The police advised against it but said, "If you write out a note saying we're not responsible, we won't stop you." Buchanan did it, backing up to precipices at each bend, then going forward; this with the aid of a girl. They all took photos and got in at 3 a.m. to find the bus-owner pacing up and down, having received a call from the driver saying: "The guide's stolen the bus." Buchanan: "What are you worrying about – your bus is here." He took (Sir Stafford) Cripps to Oberammergau, and the Duke (and Duchess) of Norfolk to Italy. Buchanan: "He was a bit drippy. We'd be in Italy and he'd

503

look out of the window and say 'Isn't France lovely', and things like that. And she said things like, 'Oh, where are my lorgnettes', and she'd be sitting on them."

This got us onto Hercy Belville and Georgina Tennant (an Asquith), and Charlotte Bingham. Buchanan: "The Binghams come from an Irish peerage, Lord Lucan. He quarrelled with Brudenell over the Charge of the Light Brigade in the Crimean war. Lucan was in command of the cavalry in Crimea, Brudenell was a divisional commander under Lucan, and he deliberately misunderstood Lucan's vague orders. Brudenell belongs to an English peerage, Lord Cardigan, the inventor of the cardigan. His family now does Bronco toilet paper."

On the future. If we go to Milan we should live near Como and commute; we shouldn't live in Venice because the canals are malarial. Would it be worth becoming citizens of Liechtenstein, to avoid tax? (Cf Graves). Are there any openings there, for teachers of English? What are the tax laws there?

4th-5th August. On Friday, I spent the day (4th) trying to finish *The Eternicide* and correcting bits of *The Noddies*. On Saturday (5th) I did the same, in a gruelling heat of about 100°F, and wrote to Tuohy, and in the evening Sizue came and Nan didn't cry (as yesterday, when C went to see Morton about her abscess); and C and I went to see *A Man for all Seasons*. More's nobility seemed too perfect – I'm sure he saw that Wolsey failed to move the Pope and that he himself could not succeed. Henry VIII was a cross between Dick and the Kohinata ginger Tom. I did not know he died of syphilis; this would account for Catherine of Aragon's five miscarriages. Otherwise my feeling was that it was all far too rational and considered. I would have stuttered or hesitated once in a while.

7th August. Images. Sunburn, gone into holes; the tree stump, like an eagle, spreading its wings; "lichis" – white fruit after the skin (red) is off. Nan: "Put a ladder up to the sun and swing on the sky and then put a floor over it so it won't be hot."

8th August. At MITI, encouraged my five conversationees to leave MITI and put leisure/individual before nation. They all said they would like to, but that it would be improper and wrong. Mr Kuroda who began by saying that British institutions were old, and who got sat on. I: "Which is better – to have leisure or to have a sound balance of payments?" Mr Yokoyama whose time is largely wasted by callers and unnecessary meetings, and who has to do his work after 5, i.e. until 9. Six days a week he only sees his boy's head; his hours in the house are 8.30 a.m. (when the boy is asleep) and 9.45 p.m. (when the boy is asleep)....

Meanwhile C took Nan to the doctor to see if her blood-infection has anything to do with her tonsillitis. It clearly has, i.e. it is not leukaemia, which is a relief. My propaganda before, teaching Nan about the body – the blood and the bones and the meat – from *Duden* and other medical books. Her fascination, looking for things connected with the groin, the tummies, and bottoms. Nonetheless it worked. She was about to cry when Morton said "Hello", but then she said "That's a stethoscope" (thinking of a picture in *Duden*) and everything was all right.

9th August. After a deep sleep I had a hilarious dream. Most of it I've forgotten, but I remember sitting down in the road, near a station, and meeting the Randolph set, e.g. Graham Wallis, who said, "We can go to Stratford and walk down to see Leyton Orient play soccer." I was in a Japanese yukata, over Western dress, and I led the way and sang Gregorian chants (?) like an Orthodox Patriarch with a beard; I was carrying a cross, and everyone in the streets bowed down, and I was in fits that they should take me so seriously. I was still laughing when, on the train, Shillito asked me about Miss Arai. Then there is a hiatus. Later I went to see Rob's houseboat. I was expecting a house and began wading in knee-deep water before I realised it was a boat in dry dock. Inside it was an office, and two rooms were connected by a coal-shoot with an iron flap.... Later I woke and lay awake, then dozed.

When I got up I couldn't shower – I'd run out of razor-blades. I had the most brilliant day I have ever had. Is this proof of the theory that we need REM's more than hours of sleep; i.e. a full quota of REM's and you're at your best? First I changed the "eyes" image in the play from frogspawn to crabapples, which is just right. (It also gives the passage a double meaning – balls, cf "penal".) Then I finished the novel by writing *The Paschal Lamb* – Christ for the Many and for the Few; then by revising *The Truthful Era* and building it in;...and finally by getting the idea for the Prologue....In the course of all this Komano rang to say I have to have a ticket before my luggage can go off, and I thought up the brilliant ruse of buying a ticket to Taipei, and of the getting the JTB to deduct the money I pay from the final ticket if JTB agree. Oh, if only I were like this every day. Even so, I have finished the novel once through in two months (Wednesday 8th June-Wednesday 9th August), which is not bad going.

10th-11th August. Nobe, the wind and the cool on Thursday (10th). Last thing Buchanan and I went out to the Kennedy's "night-club" and ate long hot-dogs and drank beer. The décor: Jacobean chairs and a juke-box, antlers and ship's lanterns, a tapestry Dutch painting, a large salad spoon and fork, hanging "strings" with beads you see over Chinese entrances, strangely by the inner wall, a rubber plant, and a large, high bottle of Chianti. Buchanan: "I think it's petting at the back and more upstairs." The boy at the bar confirmed it is open till 6 a.m. throughout the winter. Buchanan: "It's a brothel upstairs." The exorbitant lunch. I: "Do you find coming difficult? I understand it gets harder at 40." He: "Oh no, that's psychological. You can go on till your 80s."

Next day (Friday 11th) it was the hottest for four years: 99.1F in Tokyo. At 8.10 a.m. the tide turned and it clouded over at the exact moment: lunar attraction? So there were clouds over the surf as plus became minus. Nan asked, "Has the sun gone to the coca cola shop to have a drink?" Out at sea is a rock by which you measure the tide. A south-westerly wind whipped across the beach blowing beach umbrellas and rubber rings and balls and clothes, and the waves came in in great rollers, and all was clean. The pine trees die from the top.

12th August. Searched for an image for God as a limb in Lacroix's *Science and Literature in the Middle Ages and Renaissance* and did not find it. I wanted the idea of growing something because we needed it, it now being useless and dangerous, but only got: the appendix; a wisdom tooth; cancer in the stomach (the seat of happiness along with the liver) and in the brain, i.e. a tumour; a racial image (cf father and mother), a memory like an accretion of brain cells/tumour, perhaps that is the best.

Also read a fascinating book, Kemble's *Idols and Invalids*. It is about the medical history of various figures. So Columbus's crew brought syphilis to Europe in 1473 (Columbus dying of it in 1506). Cesare Borgia got it 1500/3 but was killed in 1507 before it had any effect (and Alexander VI was not poisoned but died of malaria). Henry VIII got it in his youth, hence Catherine of Aragon's miscarriages. He died of a syphilitic ulcer and a ravaged heart; Edward VI and Bloody Mary both had it, and Elizabeth was probably barren from it, i.e. one night wiped out the glorious Tudors. (N.B. the spirochaete responsible was not discovered until 1905, by Schaudinn and Hoffmann.)

Also, Mary Queen of Scots was four months pregnant before she eloped with Bothwell – the miscarriage was not conceived one week after the wedding as is officially believed. Queen Anne married Prince George of Denmark in 1683, when she was 19, and had 17 children in the 25 years before her menopause. What she had was a varicose ulcer; hence, no heirs. Milton had glaucoma, and wrote his poems in two short periods early/late; Byron died of uraemia. Catherine the Great had one husband, who was impotent, 12 lovers (including Rimsky-Korsakov) and five children, between the ages of 23 and 67. Louis XVI was impotent until he was circumcised for plimosis in 1777. And America was misnamed after Amerigo Vespucci, a beef and biscuit merchant; Walter Walseemüller mistook him for Columbus in 1507 ("Americus Vesputius").

13th August. The account of the wandering Jew: Joseph Cartaphilus, who struck Christ. This was when Cartaphilus was 30, and a doorkeeper at Pilate's praetorium. Ever since he has wandered the earth, and when he reaches (the age of) 100 he returns to 30. The story was first told at St. Albans in 1228 by an Armenian archbishop. The Wandering Jew is a rejector of Christianity, like myself.

LEAVING JAPAN: LOST INTENSITY OUTSIDE SYSTEM (1967)

Otherwise, Buchanan on Compton Packenham ("Pack"). It began with thatching. He built a thatched house in Tokyo, and no one knew how to do it, so he had to get an expert from Kyushu. He was *Newsweek* correspondent during the Occupation, and a descendent of General Packenham, Wellington's general at Waterloo. He was critical of the Occupation, and MacArthur chucked him out. Truman got him back, and MacArthur wouldn't speak to him and a year later MacArthur went. It was at his house that Buchanan met Dulles. He was invited with Alison, the U.S. Ambassador, and "the King of the Kanto", a Major-General, gatecrashed half way through the evening and held out his glass. Asked, "Say who are you?" Dulles: "I'm vaguely connected with the State Department." He died of a stroke.

Also Sid Brooks, Reuters until Garry. He was hauled out of his car by a cop and given the bag test. He blew so hard he burst the bag, and the cop laughed so much he let him go. Mrs. Aoki, Buchanan's neighbour, is the daughter of Admiral Yamamoto, who was shot down while reviewing his fleet in an aircraft during the war.

14th August. Spent Sunday and Monday on the "society is sick" passage in the play, polishing the imagery. e.g. crypts – steeples. Also polished the bit about the "groovy generation", which was not good in the first version. Otherwise felt well and worked aggressively, as I always feel and do after Nobe.

15th August. Wrote and then dictated the note to the reader. Then went to "get the chop." Nan asked "What's the chop?" and she was appalled at the idea I'd have a wisdom tooth pulled from the lower left jaw.

The worst part of the job was the anaesthetising: two into the tooth and jaw requiring six jabs, and later one on the inside gum. After that Besford stood over me, holding a "screw-driver" like a spanner, and with a mechanic's arm, began levering. When the resistance came he took over the "pliers" extractors and pulled. The X-ray had shown only one root, but there were in fact three, and one snapped. He then had to fish around in the socket with his "tweezers". He tried about five different sizes. ("Slightly larger. No, slightly smaller.") At length he came up with the last fragment, a chip of a root that would have infected the gum. Then he blew away the blood ("Spit but don't rinse") and swabbed and thrust packets containing the tooth and cotton clamp (if the socket bled) into my hands and out I staggered.

In the taxi I was stung by a bee; I sat back, and it stung me in the back of my left arm, and when I got home I was more worried about that than my tooth. Having had only one wisdom tooth pulled and one bee sting in my life before, I had both within an hour today. By the time the bicarbonate of soda had worked, however, my jaw unfroze, and I had to dose myself hourly with three aspirins plus one bufferin, the best combination.

On the wisdom tooth as a symbol: the tooth-buds of these, the last molars, come through between the ages of 21 and 25, and sometimes do not come through and remain "uncorrupted". Cf God?

16th August. A dopey day, overdrugged with a total of some 12 aspirin and 4 buffarin; which, after a letter home in the afternoon, almost seemed an overdose. Otherwise prepared for the packer, i.e. stuck photographs in, went through old manuscripts and vowed to rewrite *Tristy* as a novel, making Louise a girl-friend and having the relationship begin with mother's funeral. He can't suffer for his mother, but he comes to suffer over her. Bring him up to date, make him a man of the 60s, scornful of the System, resisting the pressure everyone (e.g. Barnard) brings to bear on him to get a job. A Jack of all trades and master of none. Make him a Wandering Jew, using the Cartaphilus theme of August 13th? Explain his rejection and scorn, i.e. why he is a rebel, why he protests, why he looks down on "the ease and luxury of contemporary society" (my "note to the reader" of *The Noddies*). A new Puritan. Make him a Little Englander.

Some figures from *Britain 1967*, which I am going to send off. Overseas aid 1965, £195.7m. (£55.9 in gifts). Effect of Second World War: British domestic capital – £3,000m; overseas investments – £1,000m; external debts + £3,000m; exports in 1944 – one third of 1938. National debt, 1914 £651m; 1918, £7,435m; 1939, £7,131m; 1946, £23,637m; 1966, £31,327m (£1,795m repayable in currencies other than sterling). Defence 1966-7, £2,280m = 29.5% of the budget (=£7,728m). Balance of payments 1964, £406m (£314m in 1966 *Handbook*); 1965, £136m. Reserves constant around £1,000m since 1950s (1964 fell by £122m). External liabilities (p410) paid to governments, £1,334m. External assets, gross £10,000m. External liabilities, because of Second World War, £2,500m (£1,849m to other governments).

17th August 1967. Finished typing the play, then went and collected my salary from Tokyo University of Education, ran into a sensei and then Kuroda and stood in a near 100° temperature and gave an account of myself for 20 minutes and sweated so much that in the end it was running out of my cuffs. Paid another £30 residence tax (every month now I have to pay about £30 in tax, along with £35 to the Bank of Japan) and then went to the Bank of Japan....The technique of not announcing until the last moment is a typically Japanese one, and I must be prepared for the Mombusho to refuse me first class fares just before I am about to leave. I can outmanoeuvre this by asking Irie to confirm that Koshi's estimates will be met. My excuse for asking can be that the packers will want to be assured that the temporary ticket will be covered in accordance with the estimates. I know the Japanese well enough to know the few seconds per months when they are being genuine; and the stretches of days when they are not.

LEAVING JAPAN: LOST INTENSITY OUTSIDE SYSTEM (1967)

18th August. A very busy day. Did some packing, then went to the dentist. Was held up by a demonstration. Besford met me in the waiting-room 10 minutes late, "We're waiting." Two fillings without cocaine; I thought he was giving me an injection, and it was the drill.

Afterwards on wisdom teeth, as an image for God. They have always been there and they were once bone-crunchers and grinders as opposed to flesh-tearers (carniverous fangs) – the molars more up and down and round. One day they will be gone. Always there, connected with primitive cannibalism, one day gone – that's God. But what of Christ? What limb have we acquired? Tonsils, appendix?

I could not get round to this; the four girls were waiting at the door and phoney B had finished his lecture. Phoney because he didn't answer my questions and talked self-importantly. After that to the Post Office. Then to Koshi of the Japan Travel Bureau to change C's flight to the 16th so that she can go over the Pole and cut 12 hours off the flight and so that Nan can avoid cholera jabs. Thence via Ginza 4-chome and Arabian phalluses of lanterns, Chinese tables and Lesbians, to MITI. Mr Matsuda on the way the public servant served the Emperor in the 1930s, not the public. Mr S. Yamomoto on his disillusionment because Britain and the U.S. talk of free trade theoretically but do not permit free competition from Japan. I drew his attention to the human factor, and said that if cotton dumping at x-y yen puts 4,000 people out of work when 600,000 are unemployed, it is a bad thing, just as Scotch would be if it put 4,000 Japanese out of work. I said, "The human factor always comes before a theory about free trade that you learnt at university."

19th August. The packers came, 9.30-2.30. They packed everything up in cardboard boxes, and wasted as much space as possible by stuffing in bits of newspaper. The more space they wasted, the more cubic footage they got paid for. They put books in ridiculously small boxes so that there was 6 inches spare at the end, and said they couldn't use larger boxes as they would be too heavy to carry. They tried to put two lampshades in one box, with nothing else, and I made them open another box and stuff some clothes in the lampshades. They were then for sealing the other box, without inserting anything where the clothes had been. In the end they got it up to (or I kept it down to) 29 boxes; yet even so the cubic footage was only 80-90, much less than the 154 of the estimate.

Meanwhile C went to see Dr. Langstone and learnt that Nan's tonsils will have to come out very soon, to get her blood right.

After all this I was exhausted and I lay in a stupor and dozed and all Sunday I was half asleep from the strenuous preparations of last week....I have learnt about myself and I have defined the differences between me and (my family), between cosmopolitanism and provincialism, between the theoretical and the practical, between the moral and the cynically indifferent, between my world and their other world. Rejectors and acceptors.

509

20th August. A dark cloud came up on a sultry evening and as the raindrops fell and the cicadas fluttered indignantly through the dancing gnats C asked "Is this the end of the summer?" And as I inhaled the fresh smell of the earth I was aware that I was living through an image. Rain, and the early end to a hot summer.

Another image I remember. Two weeks ago I went and peed, and the water in the white basin frothed up and I thought I was peeing acid; it was in fact bleach that had not been flushed. Acid in the body.

21st August. Spent the morning on the telephone over the Mombusho money. Irie came back on August 16th; the title of his address in Concord, U.S. was *The Role of Emerson and Thoreau in International Goodwill*. It was in fact on Emerson and Quakerism.

22nd August. On Monday evening I took C out to Nicola's and we sat in the cage and amused ourselves at the vagaries of Tommy Palmer, who yawned and looked at his watch and stared at the ceiling and was bored stiff. He looks like a doctor or a solicitor, not a jazz musician with a sax like an opium pipe. At drinks time he and the pianist talked in one group, and the harmonium player (a thin Dickensian caricature of a Japanese) and the Japanese drummer talked in another group. Things don't change much.

That night I had an REM just before I woke up. Tuohy and I were in Peking (?)* and he invited me to see the antiquities museum; it was mainly Aztec, etc. with some Chinese pavilions. There were two open exits in each wall on the ground floor, and into one of these charged the Beast, a cross between a hog and a unicorn, in so far as it was upright, on two legs, and had a pig's head. It was grey, for the dream was in colour. This Beast chased all the people out into the corridors and it chased C, who was there, and finally it turned on me. I ran out into a courtyard and met a knight, who gave me a lance-cum-spear. Just as I was turning to face it and fight it, like St. George and the Dragon, Nadi came and woke me up.

Did it symbolise my own desires, the "id"? The pursuit of C, and the aggression towards everybody, suggest that it did. In that case the knight is the "Superego" and censor, and the lance is what I must resist my lower self with. In other words, I have too little "ego" (which judging by my shyness, is true enough); I am all superego and id.

When I awoke I felt energetic. Worked on *Tristy*. I reduced it some sort of a shape, even though it seems a little thin. Now, it is about the relationship between Tristy and Louise, and it is about the break-up of their marriage, if they are married. The question is, "Will Tristy suffer?" and it is answered by his inner weakness: Louise wants affection and she can't get it from Tristy or her family, so she goes back to her former lover. He loves Louise, and destroys himself – out of pride? because he can't share her pain, can't "stoop" to that?

He is now a kind of eternal student, like Trofimov. He lives off National

510

Assistance and dreams of being a kind of Wandering Monk, against ease and luxury. This becomes a reality? The point is, he has utterly rejected the System without even trying it, and he is too concerned with living to worry about a job. Barnard as Merrie England; Peverett as Great Britain. I think it should be written in the first person. Should begin with mother's death or with meeting Louise? I think the first: then it can be an explanation for the break-up. Thus, first emotional closeness, then emotional distance…, then irritation, anger and detachment….

After that took C and Nan to the doctor, and had cholera and typhus jabs. Agreed with Morton that Nan should have her tonsils and adenoids out, as they are infecting her blood. Morton's watchful look, as though I were the father of a doomed girl, and his grey face, like Besford's or Taylor's. He will die soon.

*This must have been dreamt around the (time of the) attack on the British Embassy, Peking.

22nd-25th August. Tuesday evening (22nd), from the doctor's to Nobe, C having been psychic and "known" that Rumichan was going to have a cold and couldn't go as planned. When we arrived there were bugs everywhere, as usual.

That evening we spent waiting for typhoon Louise. It never came. The talk ranged from dulce and carageen seaweeds, which are to be found in Ireland (Carageen in Galway); Sikorski and D. W. Brogan, who are mentioned in an exceptionally good *Encounter*, both of whom Buchanan knew. Also Kessler, Sartre putting Revolution before Peace and being too extreme for the PCF, and Stoppard's crummy, excessively literary idea for his play on Hamlet; and *At Swim Two Birds* by Flann O'Brien.

Later we talked about being independent, how the one may be right and the 99 out of step, and we got on to information, and Buchanan said how useless the Embassy was….He: "I don't waste my time; if you tell them something they feel inadequate – they should have known it, they might get into trouble; it goes straight in the wastepaper basket. I don't waste my time, I'm shiranai otoke (i.e. wise and know nothing like a Buddha) whenever I pick up valuable bits of information. My first loyalty is to my friends."

Later he said the most extreme suffering is loneliness, especially a widow's, and "All unhappiness is connected with our relationships with other people – in ourselves we're happy"; but that life is mainly happiness. And when we went out to drink at the Kennedy's he raised Arai (his girl-friend) and said Keikosan (his housekeeper-mistress) had said "Enjoy the change", and that when he goes off to a hot spring she says "Don't pay more than 3,000 yen." "And the tarts are nicer than in England. I remember Boyce saying to me his pick said to him, 'Any more familiarity and the f—'s off.'" She has no jealousy as regards the act, but would create hell if she thought Buchanan were going to leave her for Arai, e.g. "Oh, you get on well with Arai because she speaks English and I can't."

When we returned, via the sea, he fell over by the thatched barn; in his jinbe and with his legs in the air he looked like an insect. "No harm done," he said as I helped him up, and we rolled back together, he more drunk than I, he being able to take less than me.

I slept heavily, and the next day, Wednesday (23rd), was overcast. We shopped at 12 for the typhoon, but, despite some rain in the afternoon it didn't come as expected. ("The typhoon's slowed down and increased, like a woman," Buchanan had said.) C and Nan and I went for a walk to the graveyard, that's all, and the next day Nan asked "May I go for a walk? I'll just have a word with those Buddhas, about those dead men that got die." She knew, possibly because I was moved by the non-hero's grave: sand, a bamboo, knee-high fence; two vases with everlasting on either side of a half-buried pebble. No upturned rice-bowls, no expensive saké pots or incense "fireworks" for him. Buchanan on her regular verbs: "'Cutted' – yes, very sensible."

Otherwise, we were plagued by his wretched dog, Komorichan ("bat"). It sat by the ankle-high table and yapped like a bully for food; it wolfed Nan's cheese and trod over my bare feet and then snapped at them and sniffed me when I lay down after the meal. Buchanan fawned over it and talked to "him" and in the evening I lost patience and told the thing to shut up.

On Thursday (24th), there was a brilliant dawn, and drops of rain on the pine-brushes shone out, and everything was fresh; a spider's thread ten yards away was slightly pink in the middle. The sea, however, was in an aggressive mood, and later, on the beach, we watched great rollers crash down and spread the foam yards in. I composed a poem in my head, "The sea is like an eiderdown"; I did this watching from behind darks under a beach umbrella.

Then I swam with C and Nan. I suppose it was silly: the red flag would certainly have been up in England. The first time was O.K., but the second time we all got caught in a great roller, just out of our depth, and as I grabbed at Nan in her rubber ring and she clutched my left little finger, my bloodstone ring came off and sank. Immediately after we were crashed under, with such a force that C's top-knot piece of false hair was torn from her head and lost. One wave and two losses.

Later Buchanan took Nan in again, and I went in to protect in case he had a stroke. Nan got cold. I waited until the 15th and 16th (large) waves had gone, and then swam hard for the shore. I couldn't make it – I was pushing her with one hand – and a great roller came up at least four foot above the sea. In desperation I turned into it, holding Nan by the arm. It crashed down on us. We both went down and came reeling up in boiling foam, and I surfaced and saw another of equal height bearing down. I held Nan high above my head and took a deep breath, and the full force hit me on my back and knocked me onto my side. But still I held her up and she just got a mouthful, that was all. After that I came out.

LEAVING JAPAN: LOST INTENSITY OUTSIDE SYSTEM (1967)

Those two waves were by far the largest of the morning, and Buchanan thought it lucky we weren't drowned. "You can tell your friends you were nearly drownded (sic) in the sea." After that we ate and dozed and returned at 4.30, via the Kadola sushi shop. Buchanan went on.

28th August. On the way back I thought up a possible source for new material. O'Brien's novel had earlier made me wonder if I haven't got a rich, tapestry novel about, for example, Oxford; on inner life and mythological background, in accordance with a myth for the 1960s more positive that the old, "sick" themes of Oxford....I am inclined to feel that this is a novel about Ricky and our two respective attitudes to life; about a latter-day Oblomov and Stolz, about drifting and choice....The question is, "Will R be persuaded by the Stolz to do X?" and the answer depends on R's resistance and his anti-heroic lament. The anti-hero and the hero. Later it occurred to me, just as Shakespeare took plots like *Hamlet* and *Lear* from history or legend, could not I do the same? If so, I would not use the Arthur legend – people have to be real today, and what the Gawain poet did is no longer possible; nor is what Tennyson did. No, I would take my plots from 19th century history. So Alexander I could be treated as a kind of Lear; the youthful whoring becomes a spiritual movement that ends in renunciation. I could de-Christianise Julie de Kordener and concentrate on the renunciation of Fyodor Kuzmich. Also, Louis Napoleon could be a chooser, a kind of Existentialist hero who dreams and brings into action. The objections are, how tied should I be to a sense of history, and how much should I stick to historical fact. I don't want to be tied to either, I want to create a renouncer, a chooser, and draw on Alexander and Louis Napoleon purely as convenient material for a plot. What I make them will not be what they were. Should I change their names? Should I get rid of particular time and place, i.e. period, or should I have them behave in modern ways with ancient customs? I must make history into legend, and make past societies relevant to our own.

29th August. On Friday (August 25th) I fixed up Nan's tonsillectomy for September 8th and went to MITI and battled for 5 hours with anti-British, anti-Hong Kong officials, and on Saturday I couldn't sleep properly for overwork. After an afternoon spent crouching like a cur through another violent storm (the "firework" explosion a few houses up the road, a vicious bang before the flash; and the vacuum I spoke to Nan in during the 20 flashes a minute period of the storm) I reviewed the poems.

It seems to me that *The Silence* lacks uniformity. Perhaps this is what Tuohy meant when he said it doesn't come up at you as a whole. One way to solve this problem would be to have a narrator connecting, and linking, all the different moods. There are two possibilities. Either I have "the author" sitting with his beads, thinking of each bead as a picture, and imagining an exhibition within his mind. (Or the author sitting alone with

513

his beads, imagining an inner guide escorting him through the gallery of his soul?) Or else, I have another man, an ironical commentator, talking in prose, attracting the reader's attention and escorting him round the exhibition; in which case, what of the beads? Or has he numbered the beads to refer to the pictures he painted?

The disadvantage of the first is that I really need the ironical detachment, to distance Freeman. The disadvantage of the second is that it's a meditation, and should take place within the author's mind. I could take the first if I treat Freeman as an artist, who has left a record of his work, as opposed the treating him as a meditator. In any event, perhaps I should scrap the numbers for italicised narrative, indenting 20, and perhaps I should also scrap the glosses. I want a unifier, but how expressionist is the Magic Theatre of the soul?

30th August. On Sunday (August 27th) worked on the author's commentary. I decided that I must keep *The Silence* solemn and that the "I" must be the private Freeman, "Freeman" being the public one. Thus I should provide what I previously "phased out". Freeman's mind meditating on and narrating in images, his quest and self-realisation. As this is later in time, he is detached from his earlier, old self, and can comment on the lack of feeling, moral blindness, narcissism, pretentiousness, earnestness, seriousness, etc. He is now human, but believes you must go through this sort of quest if you're born into a sick society. He ends with the question "Am I an artist or, as this meditation has suggested, a saviour?" (Answer, in the next meditation, the first.) At present the meditation has been withheld; only the raw material of the memories has been provided. I need the meditating mind to unify the experiences and hold them at a distance.

This raises form, and I was struggling with form this afternoon, when I walked up to the Cathedral. There I saw a rosary in a glass case, and having left, I went back and looked for it, and began counting the beads (59). Two Japanese girls went off, leaving a young nun, and after a massive does of arithmetic I said "Sumimasen, I have no money, next week." She: "You pay next week." And she handed me the rosary (cost, ¥500 – 10/-). I took it, moved.

I came straight back and, abolishing the numbers, "redrafted" the poem into 5 out, 10 decades and 4 paternosters, and 5 back; a form that's more satisfactory than my present one. I have still to write in the meditating mind, but if the poem is now published and becomes a part of the English heritage (as it should), then I shall have owed much to a nameless Japanese nun. For without her kindness, everything would have been different. I must remember to pay her the ¥500 next week.

31st August. On Monday (August 28th) I worked on the narration; I decided to have mood passages based on the glosses for the 8 paternosters; the 2 junctions (out and back) and the 2 crucifixes. The beginning, then, is the end, and in between the initial futility has been transcended and justified in a triangle. My one doubt at present is whether I can blend the poetry and the prose.

Later went to the Tokyo Medical and Surgical and got cholera 2, TAB and Tetanus. While I waited, the full room, the Californian man and his Malayan secretary with a mini round her hips. She put her hand on his knee; then a fat woman with dyed hair shuffled out. She had cuts and scratches all down her left arm, and she said "I can't fly for two weeks – I've got to stay here for two weeks." It was her right leg. She sat next to me, and the man (her husband?) wrote out a cable. I read it over his shoulder. "Helen Tenant grounded. Will not be able to walk two days...." The secretary talked loudly and aggressively, said "I don't want to stay in Tokyo another two days – the food's too good here." She and the man exchanged glances when the wife said she'd be able to fly back and join them.

Later the wife and the secretary went out to the X-ray, and when they came back there were only two seats; one next to the man, one three down. The secretary sat next to the man, and the wife had to sit apart. Earlier she had buzzed around, asking questions that the wife (and the man) ignored. The man and the wife conversed. He: "How many X-rays have you had?" She: "Seven." He: "You might be radioactive" (i.e. I can't come near you, only my secretary). The secretary carried on writing her letter. She finished it and sealed the envelope. It was to a Mr Martin someone in California, and she was obviously delighted to be the cosmopolitan Californian in unsophisticated Asia. Later Morton snapped at the girl, who interrupted to ask if the man could see his X-rays at 1.45 p.m.: "O.K., but I won't have seen them, or if I have they'll be wet." She: "Better tomorrow?" He: "No let him come in if he wants to, I'll imagine what his X-rays are like." Later still, when I was paying a bill, he emerged with the same girl and pretended to clunk her on the head.

When I got back C told me that Eloise had brought a yellow strip that contains Vapona insecticide; a Jim Ranger invention for Shell that has yet to be marketed, and which kills all mosquitoes for three months.

Later, I went to Kiddyland with Nan. The child's world. Yesterday (Sunday) she saw the balloons go up from the Universiade opening ceremony and wondered if one'd come down here: "Will it go to Kinokuniya and get some meat and then get in a taxi and come here?" Now she operated monsters that roared and remote-controlled cars and wanted to see new things. The child's world is completely self-centred (everything is there for it), and it is full of immense curiosity, e.g. "I want to see a hospital, I want to go to hospital. Will there be one in this book?" The athletes in minis; their wedding rings. They walked through the children's departments and stared at all the men. Nan's "froggie puppies"; which are lifted from *The Wind in the Willows*. "Moguchan" = mole.

2nd September. Tuesday (August 29th). Waking in the night, my left arm red and swollen on the inside from TAB, and sore if I didn't keep it bent,

515

I was utterly alone....Then everything was rather pointless, and the sweat of my endeavour seemed rather ridiculous or absurd in comparison to the vice and pleasure I might have given myself to. On Wednesday morning, however, the sun and Nan and C swept all that away, and I resumed a blinkered, illusory existence cut off from the truth, and in the afternoon met Irie at Tokyo University of Education to sign some papers authorising my gratuity. Irie: "I have had a letter from a graduate student saying 'Mr Hagger is very severe, but every lecture is of the highest quality, and I do not know what I shall do after he has gone.'"

3rd September. Back to the *Eternicide*. I have decided to call Zabov Faraday, which is a good name for a futurist-scientist and expresses his lean intensity. The main problem, however, is what to do with Marty.

4th September. On Friday evening I took C to Nicola's and we ate to Tommy Palmer. I still had a swollen arm from the TAB. On Sunday we went up to the Cathedral to pay off the nun. She wasn't there, and I had to buy some postcards and write a note in borrowed pencil on the envelope and drop the ¥500 in the porch-box. Afterwards, staring at the postcards, I began to write a poem, and an hour later I had finished the first draft of *Night: Cathedral and Tower*. Otherwise I have spent since Wednesday typing the beginning of *The Eternicide*. I have decided to eliminate Marty, and I have preserved the oranges image.

5th September. Went for an afternoon walk while a purple cloud loomed. And passed. When I got back found Eloise sitting, talking to C. She looked very brown and had her hair in a pony tail, and her dress was a bit mini. John was playing with a new kind of balloon; you blow it up, release it and it makes a loud noise like a mouth organ chord. Conversation was on the children first....I: "Has C been telling you about our packing?" She: "No about Henry VIII and neurosyphilis. And Sir Thomas More." I: "There's something missing from Bolt." She: "Yes, when we did the play it seemed so deep at first and later Ken McDonald said 'I don't like this man'...." After that she demonstrated John's reading ability and I defended the imagination and said the child is father of the man and was against the chains of reason, and she agreed. "I've only met Cortazzi four times, and we've talked about nothing, but he thinks of the Japanese as the Enemy too, like Bruce."

6th September. On Tuesday evening Buchanan came and described how he had a testicle removed. Mother Mary, "You'll be able to go at it better than ever before." The injection into his spine, the nurse who held his hand while they cut it out. Keikosan's two boys (his two boys?) had their tonsils out for ¥250 (= 5/-) each, and came away one hour later.

On Wednesday I went to the Prince and set him 6 summaries out of 7 classes. We did Italy and Germany 1921-39, and to my amazement he knew nothing about Mussolini or Hitler; didn't know when they came to power, didn't know what countries Hitler finally invaded (Rheinland, Austria, Sudetenland, Czechoslovakia and finally Poland). He told me in detail where he'd been this summer, but wasn't interested in where I'd been. Royal egotism.

8th September. Got up early and took Nan to hospital to have her tonsils out. The Seibo Byoin (International Catholic Hospital), "staffed and operated by the Franciscan Missionaries of Mary" said the brochure. We arrived at 8.30, queued at the Reception Desk for 10 minutes and were then taken to the office, and thence, via the old lift with a floor like a jig-saw puzzle, and by a Japanese nun, to the 2nd floor and room 231.

It was bare, save for a crucifix. There was a high bed surrounded by two curved rails, and a yellow cot. Cupboards lined the wall behind which stood the bathroom. The door that wouldn't close, the view over the tin roofs of the chapel cross, a line of elms. In such a room Buchanan must have sat when N.G. was dying. Nan got into the cot happily enough, and drew. When I left a Japanese nurse came in with a bowl full of implements. At the pool sat Mother Mary, a gaunt and erect octogenarian. She was talking with Ozenberger, the "connoisseur on spiders" (*Entre Nous*). I met C at 12.

The operation went off at 11 as planned (tonsils and adenoids), Nan was in the room when C returned from her beer with me. In the afternoon, the emptiness, the silence, while I tried to write and waited for news. My relief that all was all right. Wrote home, and received a child's doctor's set from Giselle's mother (her smile and alive eyes). Nan was miserable and sleepy, so I did not visit until 7. Nan: "Daddy I had a prick (= injection) in my bottom." Otherwise she was pale and limp, and slept. No interest in presents, and just an occasional nod.

I whispered with C and left some books and went out and ate. The businessman who made calls from the corridor. The comings and goings in the hospital corridor, the crash of a tray around tea, like a broken relationship, and the sweepings of dust-pan and brush: use this as an image.

Next morning C was woken at 6 by chapel bells, and more giggling and talking at the nurses' pool. Dr. Langstone visited Nan around 10.30, and, wanting to return to Hayama (having spent the night in Tokyo on me), booked her out. I went to collect them, said "Thank you" to a nun like the one in Okayama, and paid the bill: ¥23,870 (Dr. Langstone excluded).

9th September. Could it have been the nun who made such an impression on me in 1964? Sister Frances of Okayama? She would have had to change from teaching to nursing, and from the blue robes of Notre Dame Seishin to the "dirty" white robes of the Franciscan Missionaries of Mary, but it's essentially Mary she's serving if it is, and she told me in 1964 that she would be moving to Tokyo. Certainly, to me this morning, the face under the wimple was immediately familiar, and mine to her, as I asked "Is there anything else? I mean do I pay the bill now or will it be sent on to me later?" and, the Japanese nun not understanding, she replied, "You can get the office to send it on to your home if you want." (In fact I paid.) She had the same lilt as the nun who said in Okayama, "Let's face it, these students aren't geniuses, and they want background: they got it."

A face under a wimple – it haunts me. I wrote her into *The Silence*, I made her the centre of my whole "Live by Metaphor" doctrine. Why? Because she is an image that corresponds to a part of me, some need in me. Ironically enough, if it was Sister Frances I saw there is a parallel in Ako of Manos, the one I met with first Fitzsimmons and then Tuohy: she corresponds to a part of me, the other part of me, the gigolo aware of his Shadow, not the saint. I am all screwed up. My tight trousers on my slim hips get all the looks, and yet I am in love with their blackness, like Masha in *The Seagull*. "Why are you wearing black?" "I'm in mourning for my life."

Early waking, reluctance to work manually, a withdrawal (like mine of 1961), a feeling that I am a writer rather than a teacher – all these are schizo-symptoms on the Reflection's view....Gigolo v saint.

10th September. Yesterday I spent the afternoon sitting on my futon beside Nan, who was on the settee-divan-bed. Earlier she had had a temperature, and it was like sitting in front of a fire. Later she bucked up and played with her presents ("hospital is like a holiday"), but she still smelt of stale blood.

I read the *Gazettes*, and a picture of Britain began to emerge, a picture of British provincial life. How much more squalid it is than Chekhov's or Dostoevsky's. It's all chairs that are piled on top of one another, chairs with canvas backs in empty, brightly lit rooms, and smiling, public matrons in coats and hats. Everything has to be done for the community, and so it's all chairmen and awards of merit, dancing displays and community association club dances. This is an environment that traps: its squalor is an emotional one, not a physical one. Frightful old ladies and nauseatingly well-fed bourgeois in sheepskin coats. England is now a rabble of official positions, of committees and councils, of conferences and dinners and amateur dramatics.

In the upper strata, intelligence has to be shown through the trivial, as in the case of a report of a party in the *Japan Times*: Figgess and the Danish Ambassador graduated the others in useless knowledge, then give them little caps with ribbons and badges. You prove the height of your IQ by exchanging unnecessary facts, it's all I.Q. and triviality, with nothing serious allowed, it's all carefully studied light-heartedness. And it's deathly.

From bottom to top, then, from Community Association through magistrate Bob Foster to Figgess and Co., English society is debilitating in its "quality of life", and the background is congratulations on retirement from work colleagues, work in a System which you neither control nor own, and an economic Battle of Britain II. All else is voluntary service of the community (Church, councillor, etc.). What else can one do except withdraw and be an individual? And reject?

11th September. More on Britain. I have overlooked the part played by societies and their annual dinner-dances. So, the Angling Society, the Church Women's Guild, the Horticultural Society all have "spring" functions, and the British Legion women have a Branch birthday supper, and the (Debden) Community Association have a cheese and wine party, everyone holding drinks with unaccustomed self-consciousness. The (Loughton and Buckhurst Hill) Caged Bird Society had its 5th annual dinner, and there's always the Mission Fair jumble sale that raised £45.

So we live for the "occasion", life leaves the routine and takes on significance when there's an "occasion", and there's "death-watch beetle and woodworm at St. Michael's church", and the kinetic values are placed in the individual.

And what does the individual think? Anti-Maoists are being executed round Canton, 150 U.S. soldiers are dying each week in Vietnam, and there's F in a camel-hair jacket standing under a tree. He hasn't suffered, he doesn't know about the suffering in the human condition, he's closed his eyes to it, and my God won't he criticise people who haven't, won't he criticise people who don't laugh along with Barbara Kelly at the local "What's my Line?" Japanese man thinks he can be Western by owning a pipe, a car and a set of golf-clubs, but all he really needs to do is to shut his eyes to suffering, and then he's there, in a big way.

Recognition of suffering requires a world-vision, and modern Britain is utterly provincial at heart. Yes, I seriously intend to go on National Assistance when I return to England. Not because I've done a lot to help Anglo-Japanese relations and Britain hasn't done anything for me except take my tax; rather because the Gordons are nicer that the Fs and the Ps. Oh how well I understand T. E. Lawrence. Of course he turned down the Governorship of Egypt and elected to be T. E. Shaw. The ordinary man is so much nicer than the bourgeois.

12th September. Went to Keio during typhoon Opal's advance downpour, and gave two lectures. Then went to the Rantei, 6 4-chome, for Inoue's on-discharging dinner. The four Bank of Japan men were in the private room when I arrived. I make my first blunder within 10 seconds. After shaking Inoue's hand, I shook Watarai's (no. 3) instead of Ichiki's (no. 2). Then I sat down at a rough oak-table like an unedged, knotted garden seat and facing a giant kettle suspended over a sunken centre-hearth by bamboo. Inoue: "What would you like to drink." I: "Beer and saké." He: "Not Black and White?" (Disappointed.) I: "It doesn't go with Japanese food." (He had it later.) Then, "This is the menu, what would you like." He offered me a choice, so I chose, and it was all compulsory. I redeemed the situation by saying "So much the better, I would find it very difficult to choose," and we fell to discussing the 10-course meal.

The first course was "Debira" sole and chestnuts, "Kuwai Sembei", pine vermicelli, gingko leaves, maple fu. Mainly bits of trees, in short. When it arrived I picked at the gingko, which was green within a shell, and said, "It's a nut isn't it." Ichiki "Yes," and he then pointed out the mistake to the manageress. To change the subject I said, "Fu – isn't that Chinese?" Stony silence. Inoue. "No, it is Japanese." I: "I'm thinking of egg foo yang. "Haw haw." I was right, maple fu is maple and egg.

Having eaten a pine "wish-bone" I got through to course 6, and then I was dying to pee. So I asked if I could go to the lavatory and no one understood. In the end, busting, I said "toy-ray", and immediately I was rushed out to the toilet. Later I had to give my main impression of Japan. I had to say something, so after joking about the Bank of Japan I said it was my first impression of the way Japanese live in the back room and come out to entertain. When I left I shook hands with Inoue and turned to Ichiki. Inoue: "No, he's coming with you." I turned to Watarai. "No, he's coming with you too." So when I turned to Saito I asked, "Are you coming too?" S: "No, I am going with Mr Inoue," so I shook his hand.

13th September. Spent the morning correcting Bank of Japan material for the Rio IMF meetings, then went to Hitachi and took him through Britain/France/U.S. between the wars. He was in his shirt-sleeves, all podgy-armed and brown, and when I left I explained I was meeting C at Kaigado, and he spent about 5 minutes talking with the chauffeur trying to decide the way.

While I waited for C outside Kaigado (which had closed at 6) I wanted to pee, and I went round the corner and peed, just out of view of the chauffeur. Who, when C arrived, drove us to the Broinowskis. There were about 10 present when we went in. Alison was in a long red, orange and brown chintzy hostess-gown, and she took my case and put it on the stairs and said "Will it be all right – I mean it hasn't got any State secrets in it?"

I went through and spoke to her and then to him. About Adrian and law and independence. He: "I'm a qualified lawyer and there isn't much independence in it, but I'm content here, I've got a good boss. The Australian Chargé d'Affairs." I progressed on to a German solicitor. Then B-B came up (Crystal, "Where's your better half?" which could have been ironical), then we went over to the corner to eat, and we began talking future plans.

Then F came up, and we got to the future of English teaching – places like Singapore. F: "I think Asians will prefer English to American long after 2000AD," and I realised he was defending what he believed in, as ex-Information no. 2. By saying we'd become Little England, I'd trodden on his values. B-B walked off then, and F and I began a discussion on Britain, e.g. Aden and Hong Kong, and foreign wars. F: "Europe's our future".

I raised the empires and the new Renaissance, and at this point Ranger came over, hoping to score off me. "Ten empires in Europe?" he said "What do you mean by that?" "European empires" I went on, and I raised the German empire. "German empire? What German empire." I: "In Africa," and I went on about the Italian one in Tripolitania and the Belgian one in the Congo and so on and we got onto Portugal. I said that ironically the Portuguese Empire was the first to crumble and the last to yield. Ranger "Portuguese empire? – Where?" I: "Macao, Angola, Mozambique, Timor, various enclaves in India" and he was utterly crushed. "They're good psychologists (though bad humanitarians) the Portuguese," I said. "They know that a survivor has to be inconspicuous." Ranger: "Good cocktail party fodder, but I wonder."

Then we got onto China, I believe via Macao, no. Che Guevara. Ranger: "Why should Che Guevara choose Bolivia?" (scornfully). I: "Because it's the next place to go." R: "But there's nothing there for anyone, there are no spoils." I: " Guevera's a T. E. Lawrence who loves fighting." I said Guevara is a new T. E. Lawrence, and Field asked me what country I would overthrow if I were Guevara and I said "Mao because the job's half-done." R: "Oh, I disagree there. This State could go on for another 60 years." I: "Then in 70 years from now there must be a revolution." R: "But if you have a sense of history -" I: "You compare with Cromwell and Stalin and Robespierre." Having compared the puritanism in China with the 17th century I ended that Mao is either a Stalin or a Robespierre. Ranger: "But in Canton now, this Trade Fair's coming up and my Japanese contact said the Maoists and anti-Maoists would declare a truce." F and I: "Rubbish, they're executing people in the streets. The Army may ring the city, but there won't be a truce. Brigands will continue to roam the countryside."

Then an Australian China expert came up, a balding blond called Gill. He promptly went off, and we continued on China, I saying I was the first to get wind of the Cultural Revolution, but that I hadn't made any money out of it. Ranger: "You should've tried the CIA." I: "I'm sure *N—* is CIA. I don't want to impute anything but I'm sure someone sees all the stuff. On the other hand you can carry this to extremes," and I raised Rexroth and his departure. I: "He's wrong of course, but you can tell a CIA man by the size of his car. That's what the *New York Times* articles said." At that moment an American came up, Bob Reu—, who, I later found out, was Personal Assistant to (Ambassador) Reishauer. After the introductions there was a silence and I said "We were talking about the CIA." Field gasped. R blushed and said, "Oh, that's strange. I was at a party the other night and a G.I. said he thought I'm a CIA agent." I: "Are you?" He: "I'm afraid I can't boast that," a double entendre. I: "The *New York Times* says you can tell a CIA man by the size of his car. Is that true?" F: "All Americans have large cars." Reu—: "I cut those articles out but I didn't read them. I'm in the clear in that case, I haven't got a car." And at that very moment an American came in and said to Reu—, "I'll have to park the car round the corner, the police say

I'm obstructing the road." I: "He hasn't got a car, he's got a chauffeur – he must be a Superintendent in the CIA." Whereupon F and Ranger collapsed and I was spluttering helplessly and Reu— blushed scarlet and left – he shook hands all round.

I went over to proclaim my total victory to C and was interrupted by Dearlove, a young language student who was a cross between Stokes and Richard. His diffidence and respect for my age, his wife with sexy eye-shadow, who had earlier hung on Ranger's arm. A budding M. After talking to C I went and stood by her and found out she'd been in Hong Kong from 2 to 20, and that it was a small place and people wanted to get away, e.g. to Japan. But she went back for Christmas. Told her about China and the Prince. (She, "You are mean" with a nervous little laugh.)

Then Alison came in with a large marmalade cat up to her breasts, and without a word she put it up on my shoulders, in an unmistakeable symbol of the way she felt, and while she looked with a deep, deep mirth I stood and felt like a pirate with a parakeet on my shoulder. Then a small white-haired blonde – her hair was like a bird's nest hat – came over and fondled the cat, and I asked her if she wanted the wretched, and so I met the Baxters; she all frizzy red-haired and orange and Welsh (Celtic like Ena?), like a nurse, and he small and squirrelly, with timid nut-brown eyes. She wanted the cat, he didn't. Then it emerged that he used to go to the Forest School (in Essex), and often swam against Chigwell, especially against a blond "b—" called Beverley Clark, and I told him about the *Gazettes* (after the *Observer* and Guevara) and Princess Margaret's visit, and he, being Aussie, felt a little homesick. I: "They call it the old school tie."

After that I saw F coming over, and I broke off to check Reu—'s name, and F said "He's over there, he's come back." I went over with C and at the first opportunity went over the previous situation: "It was strange the way you came up, because we were talking about the CIA in connection with my visit to China...." He rose to the bait and stepped aside. I told him about the information I'd had, and how no one'd buy it for £2,000. He: "You should've asked ten, and you should've kept it hidden." I : "I'll do that, if I go again." Then, to change the subject, he said of the record on the gramophone, "That's her," and he turned and cuddled a blonde, and then left again, and she said she was on a tour of U.S. camps, and that she'd just been in Vietnam, and that she's going to London this December, and that she's here for a week and only sings British folk-songs, and I raised Tomlin.

Then a Japanese came up, a singer too. With him was an oriental (Japanese?) in a Chinese shamsung (slit dress). Then everyone stood and sang "Once a Jolly Swagman" to the Japanese's guitar, while I knocked back my 8th (?) whisky, which I had filched from the kitchen, and I noticed that the Aussie singer lacked "presence". She sang "All together now", etc, but no one really looked at her. Then everyone drifted through the door and up the stairs, and I went into the upstairs "toy ray" to have a pee, and when I came out I found everyone sitting in a circle in the bedroom, staring at the wall. Broinowski said lights, so I turned off the light and sat down next to C with the noisy oriental woman breathing down my neck and putting her hand across to a chair. Then the projector whirred.

The film was about Broinowski in the Embassy, and may have been shown straight. Certainly several people found it humorous and ridiculous, while one or two of the Embassy girls tried to be nice and enthusiastic. My ironic digs at C, Broinowski's conscious glances to see how I was reacting. When it was over the lights came on and B wound the reel in his hand and Alison sat on the bed. B: "There wasn't any sex in it – just a secretary's legs," and everyone thought about Alison sitting on the double bed. Also the farewell kisses on the film, when B left Tokyo. I believe that was the end of his first term, and he married while on leave.

After that we came down, and Alison looked through me and said "I'm sorry you're leaving, but I'm glad we caught you before you went." C: "It was a good party because they aren't the usual people and they were all young." And how much nicer the Aussies were than the English. Dearlove and F have gone quiet and hollow, like Adrian and Tomlin; they don't think with passion, as Tuohy does, putting his being into his thought. They go through the motions, they are detached, and wary so then they have to move on. Adrian is not taking his law exam because he hasn't done enough background reading; Emery is now Manager of the Singapore office, which is promotion.

After Ranger went F asked, "Will you write a novel about Japan?" I: "No, there are no relationships in Japan. Though I suppose you could write a novel about an absence of relationships." On a man married to a Japanese wife?

14th-18th September. The typhoon did not come. Earlier I'd asked Ichiki "What happens if it comes when I set off?" He: "The Bank of Japan is safe," i.e. Jack's all right.

On Monday. Hitachi's beaming when I asked if the Imperial family would be shocked if he said, under the nose of the Emperor at lunch, to the Soviet Ambassadress, "What do the Soviet people think of Stalin today?" He may ask it.

On Tuesday I went and gave my last lecture at Keio; had classes of 74 and 146, and when it came to giving advice I told both of them that I felt unqualified to give them any advice, but that if I wanted them to remember me by anything, it should be by a spirit of independence. I told them that I have taught at MITI and the Bank of Japan, and that I've seen how the System can absorb an individual, so that he has no leisure and does not get home until after 10 p.m. If I have any hope for you, I said, it is that you should trust in your individual judgement, that you should not be afraid to regard yourself as right and the System wrong, and that you should value leisure and the virtues of an independent life. And if I have any hope for the women, it is that you should marry men who will appreciate you as human beings, and who will be prepared to sacrifice the System for you, and make you happy.

There was a spontaneous outburst of applause when I had finished: I had clearly touched a nerve that was sympathetic rather than painful.

18th September. A novel on Japan should be the one Tuohy should be writing, on the gaijin community divided between the System and someone like me; or a "solitary's" confessional novel, like *The Lost Englishman*, in which there is an absence of relationships, or possibly just a relationship between the man and the girl; or a spy novel, the central action taking place in China (a discovery of the Cultural Revolution). In short, a Durrell; a Rilke; or a Greene in type. Given the time I would like to do all three. Meanwhile, Thursday-Sunday, faced problems in Pt. 1 of *The Eternicide*.

19th September. On Sunday, on Toynbee's Law of Nature or Law of God. The point is that objectively, the world just is, it is meaningless, it is ruled by certain laws of nature like growth and decay, the seasons' wheel. Subjectively, however, I am free, I can image meaning, I can see the universe as a whole.

This, then, is my philosophy, law and meaninglessness and isness out there, like the "fee-fee-fee-fee-feeee" of a cicada that will die; and vision and unity and love and freedom inside my senseless being. This glimpse came to me as I went out for a walk, and saw the local people in workers' bags milling around and shouting under a golden holy of holies near the sacred cockerel's drum, and I will get no nearer to the meaning of life than this, the stance of Freeman....I am a creator of meaning in a brutally meaningless world. Not a desiring mind in a world that disappoints (Camus), and not an insecure mind in a contingent, lawless world (Sartre). My quest, then, is for what I see, and what I am free to see depends on the way I look; on myself.

What of social laws and the individual? Are broken down civilisations doomed, or is there an escape through an individual, a de Gaulle, a Stalin, a Mao? History suggests there is no escape, and I have a sneaking sympathy for the "all our yesterdays" view of Macbeth: that people strut around and puff their chests out and act big, and it's all nothing – that if it were anything one would try and get in on it. Yet, as an Existentialist, I am forced to believe in such an escape, in for example, a Napoleon; although my sympathies lie with the people, against the System. Perhaps my brand of Existentialism requires me to believe that history is a farce anyway, that the historical out there is a "law of decay and meaninglessness and isness", and that the individual embodies meaning by resisting the decay. It may be a creed of decay, but I am a historical determinist against my time, I believe in historical determinism in spite of phoney, tinpot optimists like (Harold) Wilson.

On Tuesday morning I had a long dream. I think it began in a (Japanese) bar. C was there, and girls kept sitting against me. The boiler was going to blow up and everyone was evacuated onto the street. Mrs. Nixon was trying to turn it down and was turning it up. I turned it down and saved the day. Then I was in the Pattersons' house. They lived in a kind of windmill, and (Mr) P went down the winding stair (= subconscious) and brought up John from a floor below. He held something which he dropped. They gave me a gallon of beer which I nearly dropped.

The room was full of women – it was a kind of orgy – and I remember M lying on the bed, hair all round her, and a wig over her loins. Then I saw a photo in a newspaper I'd been carrying with me. (In the bar?). A famous pop singer was the centre of a giant military ceremony in a vast hall. I went through the photo into the ceremony, and later I was with C and her in my bedroom in Journeys End, Loughton. C was asleep in the cupboard bed, I was on the window bed. The singer hadn't got into her sleeping-bag. She was clumsy – she burnt the lampshade and dug something in the curtains. Then she stood up in bursting bra and panties and rehearsed a speech about how "what's done to me here and here is what I like, and people are prudes". C slept on, though she stirred a little.

Then the singer came and sat on my bed in her sleeping-bag and presented her breasts and, looking at C, I got out of bed, and with the singer's aid began to clean my teeth at the basin. The toothglass was full of soapy water. I put the toothbrush back in it and turned, and saw C's head on the floor. There was no body and it was grimacing. No blood. Then I realised: it was severed. I didn't see her body on the bed, but the singer was crouching behind the head of her bed, and there was a large ham on a plate, with the family carving knife and fork in it. The singer stood up for love – the severing was a casual thing to her. I shrieked "No, no," and rushed for the door, which was locked. The singer closed up behind me with the knife.

The dream was clearly about the suffering I would cause C if I acknowledged my subconscious or about a death-wish. (I had not slept for three nights, not properly.) The dream was probably inspired by Dusty Springfield (who is on TV) and a picture of the guillotine in Larousse. Also a memory of Sonia of Loughton?

Later I rang P and M answered and said "I think I recognise that voice." I: "Who is it?" She: "Nicholas," and I was reminded of the bed and the hair.

20th-21st September. At Tokyo University of Education (on 19th), on Toynbee. He is saying that renaissances summon up the ghost of a dead civilisation (cf archaism, the ghost of the present civilisation), and that they have a sterilizing effect on artistic genius. Is this true – can the Gothic revival during the Industrial Revolution be blamed on the Renaissance? And if it is true, isn't the Revolution justified by Michelangelo?

On "Law or Freedom in History", Toynbee is saying there are two ways of regarding the law. As a cause when it is a law of God as it is in a time of growth; and as an effect, when it is a law of Nature (wheel, Greek gods), as it is in time of disintegration. What he means by law I mean by pattern in the triad: (1) waves/chaos, (2) pattern, (3) meaning as applied to history. Toynbee explains the pattern or regularity in terms of the soul or psyche, i.e. though believing that 18th/20th century metaphysical attitudes are determined by their political systems, cf the Universal State; and Homonoia (p293 of volume 2 of Somervell's abridged *A Study of History*), he believes "the social laws...are reflections of psychological laws governing some infra-personal layer of the subconscious psyche" (p317). This is my projection theme, that society is a reflection of the self as regards our way of looking.

Toynbee is wrong however in his application of the theme. He explains the variety of the growth phase by the fact that will and reason are making free choices during this time; and the uniformity of the disintegration phase by the fact that the subconscious has taken over in the disintegration phase (hence Freud, Adler, etc.) and there are fewer choices. So Freedom (i.e. choice) is in the growth phase. Generalisations aside, I think Toynbee is wrong from the personal viewpoint. Rational control of the Will (i.e. Self) is not necessarily a good thing, and isn't growth a deeper thing, proceeding from the depths of the psyche? This view of growth as a series of choices responding to challenges is attractively Sartrean, however, and Toynbee is right to root all growth of society within the self of a chooser. Toynbee the Existentialist (p318).

So once again, what about the determinism out there, and the freedom of the individual within it? Living in a time of disintegration, I do not believe that the individual can affect the laws he is victim of, not if he is living in a disintegrating society at any rate – this law may not apply to a growing society like Israel.

This was the idea in *The Conductor*. Presidents and Prime Ministers go "fee-fee-fee-fee-feeee", like a cicada, but they are subject to the law of growth and decay, and they can do nothing really to prevent the decay. Could Churchill? Thus the "freedom" of line 1 of the previous paragraph is not a freedom of action (that only applies in the growth phase, and Toynbee may be right in what he writes about Freedom – from the point of view only of the growth-phase). No, it is an internal freedom, a freedom of vision, and therefore of a spiritual way of life.

The individual is the repository of all meaning. It is the individual who creates meaning in a meaningless world. Meaning is an image, a spasm, a sudden throb of joy, a sudden glimpse of unity. Out there is meaningless isness and pattern, but in here is a glimpse of meaning. Yet this does not mean I am distorting things or deceiving myself through this irrational sense of unity which is not out there. Vision and the thrill of meaning are always superior to boring, unreal pattern. The way I see is controlled by the way I look, and if I am unreal, in a meaningless world I despair; whereas if I look for meaning and glimpse it, I have penetrated through to something in myself. I am a man seeking unity and meaning in a world I know to be meaningless. What I see is the truth. Not what science shows me, but what I see. An Existentialism of the eyes. Of the image.

Wednesday. I can't keep up with what is happening; perhaps I should abandon the outside world and return to my "dream" novels – the world is too exhausting and demanding. After Hitachi, went to Kawawaki's and Tomlin's party at Hongo for Bickley's new magazine, the *Journal of English Teaching*. Free copies inside the door, which we clutched like little red books. Tomlin on tonsils: "how sensible of you to get it done here." On to Guest, who will leave next year or March 1969. His question and answer technique and lack of statement....Thence Taylor on Angkor "Vat". Then on to Buchanan and a decayed, beaten-up, freckled, rather donnishly-looking man. He: "Oh yes, I've heard of you – aren't you leaving?" Then: "Hardwicke." I: "Where are you?" He: "British Council, I'm Alan Baker's successor." I: "When did you arrive?" He: "Three months ago." (In fact one month.) Later Shimaoka, Bickley, Field, Mrs. Bickley, who kept coming up and introducing people with a flamboyant "Darling, may I introduce Mrs. ...," while Bickley looked sullen....

I went over to Tomlin, and we got talking about how everything is governed by Movement and realistic attitudes, a symbolist like Golding being an oddity. Buchanan joined in, and we got on to the decay of Britain. Tomlin: "It all began with Wain and Amis, and now the Angries are there in the centre, they *are* the Establishment. Yeats defined decadence as 'passionate intensity', and that sums up the Angries. Now they've lost their passion. Tynan earns £50,000 a year." On C. Osborne, number 2 in the Arts Council, and the 51st book we could do without. "Levin's right, he's a twit." "The trouble is everyone's so conventional," he said, meaning conventionally Angry? And everything he said defended his outlook, of passionless ceremony and detachment.

We got on to the future of Britain. "We won't end up as an Austria, I think we'll end up as a Spain, with a cultural empire." He repeated his remark at Tuohy's farewell dinner, "I think the Ottoman and the Austro-Hungarian empires were jolly good ones: they were liberal to the extreme. Like Spanish Morocco." I asked, could there be a revolution, with over 60,000 paid-off soldiers queuing discontentedly at Labour Exchanges? He: "By Jove, that's an idea, I hadn't thought of that. Yes, by Jove, I must think about that." But he doubted it. "It couldn't be a left-wing one, and no one would tolerate a right-wing one – Mosley was unpopular in the 30s." I: "Couldn't we do a Greece? Greece was the birthplace of democracy." He: "But they put Socrates to death", etc. I: "But that grew out of the end of the Peloponnesian war." He: "Yes, you're right there, yes there is a similar mood. What concerns me is the general moral collapse," and I felt as if I were with my Superego. Liberalism and tradition.

After that he got round to Turkey with Buchanan, and the consulate in Trebizond that was a "listening-post to Russia" (Buchanan), and I left them for Bickley and Brammah. Later Brammah: "I'm in sole charge in Malaysia. I can publish what I like. But it's a responsibility. If the sales go down by only 0.5 per cent, I feel personally responsible, and guilty." He's been there 10 years.

Eventually Buchanan and I left. It was raining, and we hadn't umbrellas, so we went back upstairs to order a taxi and Tomlin offered us a lift. After a pee between Bickley and Tomlin, and a discussion of earthquakes (Bickley: "A big earthquake today"; Tomlin: "Yes, an horizontal one"; I: "I thought it was vertical"; Bickley: "The biggest I've experienced"; Tomlin: "Not as big as Niigata") we went down to T's car and Mrs. Bickley sat in the back in the middle. I said to Bickley "You get in with your wife and I'll go in the front." He: "No I'll sit in the front," as she craned like a flamingo. Tomlin and Buchanan sat on either side of her, and I spoke to Bickley and he didn't say a word to his wife. He talked about making out in England and how he'd had to tear himself away, and the chauffeur, who had boils over his face, got us thoroughly lost, and it took us about half an hour to get back to my place, after we'd passed Buchanan's front door. I: "We're continuing the party; it's a pity there isn't a drink's cabinet by the gears."

After we'd got back Buchanan came in for Wienerschnitzel and salad and martini, and he remarked, "I saw Mrs. Bickley on Nobe beach the other day. I was with Arai, and she was with Rogers or Rogerson of the Embassy (= P, I discovered September 26th). He came over and told me about her – she was in the water. He said they'd been further down the coast but it was too oily to swim, so they'd driven along. (In fact jellyfish like white-blue bellies with trailers; M was stung five times; Portuguese men o'war?) They were in a party."...C: "He's away and she doesn't like being in that flat alone." I think half the trouble is the absence of the children. She doesn't like Japan (she told Buchanan) and she's only here for her husband's sake, and there are no children to stabilise the marriage, which is therefore a floating thing. That is why Patty is not as "clutchy" as M or Mrs. B. John is an anchor.

At least that was what I was saying at breakfast on Thursday, when the dustcart bell went. I dashed out with the large dustbin, and though it was raining, returned to take the two smaller ones. I was wearing my black shirt and patched bomb-disposal sand trousers. Beyond the dustcart was a black car with someone like Bruce inside. The other side of the dustcart was an orange taxi. Patty was getting out and paying it off. She wore a green raincoat and carried a small umbrella and seemed to wear goloshes. She slunk along the far wall, all pony tail, and I called, in cheery English and style, holding a dustbin, "Coming back from a night out on the town?" She chuckled, all the way into her front door, saying nothing, and then I realised: she couldn't have taken John to school – that road is one-way.

24th September. Sunday. On Thursday I was briefed over tax by Saito, on Friday (after my last lectures), I tried to get Nakagawa to prepare this tax slip for October. It came out, through his technique of writing things down in Japanese and modifying what was on the paper, "Mr H does not want any salary for October" and later, instead of "I will collect my salary on October 17th", "All must be finished by October 17th."

Saturday and Sunday to Nobe, two idyllic days. A clean beach after the typhoon rollers, gold light on the wet sand, and I a shadow against it; spiders green and yellow and red, on enormous threads, and peasants threshing and winnowing among poles of drying rice; true blue periwinkles and vetch, and hosts of autumn lilies. (= cluster of amaryllis) red and flamboyant with curly, orchidaceous tongues like opened fingers, a kind of snapdragon? (Like fiore del morte, you can't bring them into the house. They were like splashes of blood round the imperial moat.) They were everywhere in the valleys, on Sunday morning, along with the London pride and the tree-buds, under the kites and the soaring kestrels, on the silence and the precarious sound of the brown cricket.

On Saturday, the sea was like a distempered wall, and huge anvil clouds came up, and later Buchanan's bath smoked, being bunged up with soot. The early night (at 8), and I tossed and turned, feeling failure and forcing myself with my will to believe that I'm free, and in the end I got up and went down to the Kennedy night club at 9.20, and was taken out of my despair by a sentimental song on the juke-box ("You don't have to tell me that you love me"). The girl's sadness I felt, the deserted bar, sand and insects throughout the night.

Buchanan's sadness the next day, because we're leaving. His story on Wednesday I forgot to recall. He'd been given a free ticket for a concert to St. Mary's Cathedral (cf the huge praying mantis he said was like it) and he'd been in Chinzanso at a party and had a lot to drink, and he went in with a cigarette and thought he saw the ash-tray; he realised he shouldn't smoke in a church and dropped his cigarette and it was the holy water.

On the way back, the two men I thought had come from Vietnam, whom Buchanan thought sailors. One, a tough guy who read *An Easy Way to Die*, was a pilot, and the other was a soldier near the DM Zee. It was bloody, but he was more interested in getting to Australia by signing on for another six months and getting the 40 days R-R in any city, and in Los Angeles, where he's going back to in three weeks from now, after doing another two and a half weeks in Vietnam.

Later, the meal in the sushi shop: salmon roe (orange) and sea-urchin, like small yellow tongues, and tuna and prawn and seaweed in green-veined slabs, washed down with saké and beer.

Toynbee on the middle class. Before the Industrial Revolution there was private enterprise everywhere. After, the industrial workers were regimented, and after 1914 the middle-class lost their profit motive through taxation, inflation, etc., and as a result lost their ethos of zest for work and thrifty saving. The rising cost of living reduced families, and so the middle-class mother lost importance. There has been an exodus into public service and the corporations, and as a result capitalism has lost its drive, and this may mean the doom of the capitalist system. "The atmosphere of progress is the only one in which capitalism can survive." The same trend has removed leisure, i.e. the creativity of minorities and the middle-class culture, and the result has been (along with the result of a raising of the working class to the material standard of the middle-class) "a proletarianization of the life of a large portion of the middle class on the spiritual plane" (Somervell ii p382).

Certainly the old bourgeois life has gone: large houses with walls and maids and gardeners, imitations of higher estates; numerous children, formal meals with gongs; Sunday morning walks to church; great security, business and respectability to those outside one's walls (an ideal impossible in a "petit bourgeois" world of terraces and semi-detacheds); and going to the right parties, a part of this. It has gone, and Buchanan laments it, but do I? Certainly what has replaced it is neither Communism nor capitalism, a static, profitless capitalism that is tedious, but I am utterly anti-bourgeois. True survivors: Uncle George and the business, the Fs, and their cardboard Galsworthy values.

25th September. More at Tokyo University of Education on Toynbee. On the prospects of Western civilisation. He says one must not be optimistic or pessimistic. Past experience suggests we have broken down through war, and begun to disintegrate (schism into 3), but there are good signs, e.g. democracy and social justice, and there is the unprecedented mastery of Nature and social change, and perhaps a World Order is possible, perhaps the disintegrating class-conflicts will be solved by socialization, which is already replacing private enterprise.

If there is going to be a salvation, if we are not going the way of the previous 20 (civilisations), the salvation will be through a creative minority making use of leisure, and transferring power from Economics to Religion, winning freedom from law. This view of freedom is really Vitalist. The determining law of Nature is the passive approach to disintegration, the drift of the subconscious, perhaps the automatism of T. E. Hulme and Gurdjieff (cf the "mechanicalness of mimesis"), and the creative few must win their freedom from this mechanicalness, must become conscious as opposed to automatic, must resist their time and not go along with their time, like Spengler. I think Toynbee is too generous in his suspension of judgement. He was anyway writing in 1950, when Western civilisation was still in Africa; though perhaps the "contraction" since 1957 is not a contraction in clothes and techniques, and is to be seen, as he sees it, as the split between anti-colonial internal proletariat and ruling class imperialists (like the Communist movement). Possibly things are weighted against us a little now.

What one takes away from Toynbee, however, is his sense of the free few who create for the automatic, determined masses, and a sense of pattern – and clearly one rejects the 2nd generation high point nonsense – but as regards today, his pattern of decline and his vision of behaviour within it corresponds to my pattern and vision.

Met C at Kinokuniya....On to P's for a drink which turned out to be a dinner. M in a braless short dress, so when she bent you could see her nipples. The underdrift was on sex. It began when M was doing the drinks. She said, "I can do martinis, I'm a double 07 girl." I: "Oh yes, I read in Wynne's memoirs that Penkovsky kept the secret service girls busy. Does that go on?" M: "That's what I do all the time." P: "So that's what you do in London." M: "But I'm discreet, I keep it quiet." P: "Oh that's all right, so long as you keep it quiet." This was a new, independent, complaisant P: "As a matter of fact I do know a bit about this....It would have been arranged."...

We then went through and dined off Japanese plates: shrimp cocktail, duck, pie and red wine out of one of M's lop-sided, but nice pots. And (via art and Anne Truitt) we got onto Callaghan, Brown and M asked "What do you want to be, Foreign Secretary?" and "I've seen so many men who've been hurt by having dreams and ideals, and they've never happened. Like your dreams of revolutions and nervous energy and so on. I: "I just want to write, etc." She: "That's reasonable." I: "Who are these men?" P: "Yes, who are they?" M: "You don't know half the men I've known." I: "I'm sure I haven't." P: "I'm sure you have." M: "Not half." Then she went on about her father, who had dreams that never happened. Later she told C she always wanted to be a teacher and have her own school. P: "I'd like to have been a military man." (M's father's dreams and ambitions were military?)

I said I just wanted to live outside the System on a £15 per week job. M: "You can get more than that." C: "But what's he got to sacrifice for it?" M: "You can get more than that just by talking, as an ideas man." Then, "I've believed in the System 20 years, and I'm disillusioned with it. Don't go into it." (Earlier, P: "The System? There are several." I: "*The* System is a type, like *the* priest.") I: "Muggeridge is right, you have to screw money out of the System."

Later, over coffee, P said he couldn't sleep, and I said "You need to take a walk, and then you need...." P: "Yes, but when you get to my age it gets a bit difficult, and when you've got someone like M....Nicholas, may I get you another drink?" We got back onto Penkovsky. I: "What do the 007 girls do, persuade or just oblige?" and "I shouldn't have thought Penkovsky would've fallen for it." M: "They do, every time." I to P: "What would you do?" M: "He'd help himself and take it like a meal and enjoy every minute of it." P: "If it were in the interests of my country, I would."

Then we talked individually, and M told C she had an ulcer operation when she was 26, and she would rather die than have another, and that P only had £250 (£50?) when they married and she still isn't used to drinking, but her doctor says it's good for the juices, and that after she's rowed with P, she ignores him. And I told P about Grivas, Callas and Niarchos. P: "Monica had a Greek boy-friend who was a shipowner. He was called Odysseus. That was in 1965, on leave. M: "No, Ulysses." P: "Odysseus." M: "I'll get the card." And she fished out of the desk and showed me: "Ulysses A Papandreos", and Ulysses was crossed out and Odysseus written above (in Greek). M to P: "Yes, you're right."

531

After that P came up with some retsina and M imitated Kenichi Yoshida and P looked on in disapproval, saw C looking at him, and turned on a smile, made it into a joke. Like Ricky's, his suffering was only tolerable if he disguised it as a joke. Later M clutched my fingers and said "I'm uncontrollable" and I said "One must screw money out of the System, screw is the word, will you arrange it?" and P said "Your new boy-friend while I'm away" (October 6-18) and hailed a taxi, chuckling, and I wondered if they were seriously divided, or whether they were playing a game for our benefit, because they were old (he's 46) and we're still young enough to do such things.

26th September. One thing I said at P's: I come from a complex generation, I am torn between Great Britain and Little England; I envy someone like Tomlin who became mature during our period of greatness, I envy him and resign myself to be the last of a turbulent generation. And so I looked on a TV showing of the Welfare State, all arrows on the roads for traffic, all traffic-lights and no thought outside one's place or time, and not in it either, and I loathed it; and, regarding Japan, the U.S., Russia, I felt that all no. 1 countries have placed the individual beneath society, and I was full of loathing for them, and part of this loathing of Japan was connected with an absence of welfare, a sacrifice of arrows. Pro and con beat through my veins.

Perhaps it's also because I live in a divided time caused by the vacuum that took the place of the Austro-Hungarian and Ottoman empires; a vacuum that first Hitler and then Stalin filled, finally splitting the world in two. Anyhow, I feel pulled apart, that's certain, and I don't belong. I don't belong to Great Britain or Little England, any more than I belong to Capitalism or Communism. Hating the System, loathing the alternative pettiness and materialism, I am in between. And perhaps the key to myself is in my not belonging.

If I were a Jew I could understand why I do not belong, why I am different from the British, why I am bursting with energy and lack cynicism and decadence and manner. If so, I have discovered who I am, and have found that suffering tradition for which I crave. If so, I know why I am psychologically stateless and rootless, and my historical salvation would be not to lead a revolution in Britain, but to go and build in a growing civilisation, in Israel. On 7th June I wrote, "Perhaps the stigma is ancestral, not moral." However, perhaps one's self-discovery is never purely historical or racial, and perhaps this wish of mine is a form of self-deception.

26th September (Tuesday)-3rd October (Tuesday). A week of chores. Exams at Keio and Kyoikudai, an invitation to a Keio party from Ando, whose wife can't come as she has left him. "She is expecting a baby in February or March." (She is a R.C.) He asked me to sumo, and I couldn't go; and then he asked me to his house, his new house, and he can't fulfil his on. His forgetfulness, his loss of confidence. Then Kuriyagawa asked me to resign as of 30th September and I asked Ando to act as go-between and said I would stop correcting exam papers on 30th September unless I were paid for all October. Again his fumbling.

Buchanan has been turned down by Hitachi and the Bank of Japan. It was C's birthday on Thursday, and I went to Kinokuniya on Wednesday and got her a cake, a book on costume, a ukiyoe. Nan's excitement. "Can we sing happy birthday?"

On Thursday, I was briefed at the Bank of Japan for tax, on Friday I spent four hours in the tax office, arguing with four men. My attitude: I could have left Japan in March 1966, I chose to stay because the Bank of Japan wanted new information, I visited England for this reason and as a result Sasaki was able to talk to Callaghan in London. I forfeited ¥400,000, which had to be paid back, and now I am being taxed on it – is that fair? In the end, after I'd refused to take No as an answer, the chief told me to get "compensation for information for MSS" written on the slip, in place of "compensation for lesson fees." Saito did this on Saturday but phoned when I was at the tax office getting £24 cut off, asking me to wait until Ichiki had given his approval. On Monday, of course, Ichiki didn't; proposed a combined "withholding receipt" with both entries, as if it mattered. This the tax office looked like accepting. On Monday I got the Keio papers off, and a letter of thanks for Kuriyagawa's on-discharging silk cloth; had an exam at Tokyo University of Education and went to Prince Hitachi.

Then on to Gengo and Fukuchi. The cheap sushi bar: Gengo: "It's like an English fish and chip shop." Thinking this a crack (he'd earlier said Fukuchi arrived in Hamburg to the finest weather of the century, and it was then pouring) I retorted "Fish and chip shops have been put out of business by instant steak houses. English people prefer steak." Which shut him up. On the future, F: "Perhaps Gengo will want me to retire, he is a very bad friend of mine." G: "My ears are temporarily blocked." The falseness of Gengo's earlier praise, about how the rain stopped for F? (The more extravagant the praise of a Japanese is, the more critical it is.) All this grew out of a conversation in the Palace hotel bar ("Have you read 'The Sun Risen' in the *Economist*?"), looking out of red and yellow lights in the rain. "Ah Vienna", etc. and G said later in the car, "Mr F and I met in Vienna."

In the sushi bar, the wriggling prawns, the garlic, the prawn-heads you crunched, trying not to vomit, the slipping sea-urchin, the tea-cups of saké. It was called "Edinburgh", and Figgess (of the British Embassy) often goes there, so the white-hatted chef said. (Ex-Prime Minister) Ikeda used to visit the place. "Don't put your horse-radish in your soyu."

On Saturday afternoon (30th) took C and Nan to the Matsuzakawa Departo, Ueno, to see the Dalai Lama's exhibition. The first seven 17th century (Tibetan) mandalas (out of about 100). The moth-eaten silk covers, the bands (or strips) down. The 7 stages of satori, with the central meditator (blue hair and orange skin) sitting holding a blue egg with a white spot, like a bowl. Feet up, right hand down, a red and gold cloak. Number 1 begins in the world; with blue gods, i.e. desires; number 7 ends in vision, the clouds having withdrawn, flames (yin-yang) consuming everything, flames and death (represented by skeletons) together.

The lantern with sun-wheel, white elephants, birds with tusks. Red god above, blue god below (later, positions reversed), and later (after the 7) the blue god has a red mistress, and he has receded into the distance (signifying detachment) and there is no centre, all is scattered. A sage, spinning tops, peonies (pink flowers), snakes growing out a woman's back. A rosary. Deer, peacocks, bluebirds, cranes and swastikas on the silk border. The world seen in a mirror (representing unreality). A girl warding off the blue god in fire, tigers under the seat. A pot-bellied god like Benten with flames and a thunderbolt in his hand, snakes round his shoulders. Skull-drums, Turkish teapots, Hindu-Persian writing. Buddhist hierarchy in a tree, with "a shadow" on top. One large centre in red and gold (= Shadow) with lots of small repetitions on the silk. Baghdadi turquoise (blue stone); tomato stones (jade? amber?). A lot of sex under the blue god.

3rd October. Went to the tax office to settle the final return; at 3 music clanked up and all the clerks stood up and did arms raise knees bend, while I sniggered.

Later went to the Hitachis for dinner. Nan fell and cut her eyelid before we left, and we kept their Highnesses waiting. We went upstairs and shook hands with them. The sitting-room with the Takashimya dolls (advertisements) and old Masters. The Household women who pestered you with nuts and cakes, over a compulsory sherry. Talk on England and future plans. Then downstairs to dinner, Haneko walking carefully in her kimono. The bright room with the ladies-in-waiting peering round the door. Hors d'oeuvre, fish, soup, roast beef, salad, cake-pudding, fruit (melon). Both C and I dropped gravy on the cloth, Hitachi sent his knife and fork flying with his sleeve, a maid dropped the salad bowl upside down on the floor.

Talk on flowers, dragonflies ("ako tombo"), peonies and pottery, opera and horse's eye plates, black butterflies and Portuguese men o'war. Anything more intellectual (China, modern Britain) soon collapsed under Haneko's disapproving flutter of her lids. Haneko agreed that "ako tombo" are red, not "green and blue" (Bush) but said the *Japan Times* had made "a misprint, not a mistake". (Compare in the tax office; I: "Last year I made a mistake." They: "No, you did not make a mistake." I: "Then you must admit my argument." The Japanese refusal to believe in mistakes.)

Hitachi and Haneko nearly fell out over sweet potatoes, but she was respectful, more so than a year ago, and they seemed happy. They talked about children quite freely, without embarrassment, which is strange (bearing in mind that they do not have any). After dinner they came up with a borrowed "shitimus" (?) (i.e. coronation token) and ear-rings for C and a vase with his "signature", an "ogatama" (a kind of magnolia from Kyushu).

The Emperor sat in a temple where Hitachi was born, and the magnolia was in front of him. Came home. Sizue, "Haneko is very beautiful."

The next day, to Hitachi after correcting exam papers. His sadness (at our last meeting), his present of the Gagaku record. His description of his Household (12 staff, 6 at night), which seems like Olivia's in *Twelfth Night*. Higashizono the Belch, the mentor being Malvolio. He does not feel watched. The girl who brought in the final tea ceremony; Hitachi flirted with her and told me she's resident and not married. His sadness at the end. "I shall remember you until I die."

6th October. And later on Wednesday, the trouble over a successor. Wednesday-Friday. Matthews, who had been approached by Kuroda's son, an ICU student, was arrogant and high-handed to me over the phone, so I decided to force B through, "if Mr M is too busy" (ironic Kuroda). On Thursday (5th) M telephoned to decline, and later Kuroda accepted B. At the Bank of Japan, my kindness to Ichiki, and no mention of the episode of the withholding receipt. Ichiki's attention to the letter of the law being the most maddening thing about the Japanese bureaucracy.

Later at Keio's party: the Kyobashi restaurant, Kyobashi. Aquaria downstairs, sawdust and a light brown wood "bar"; silence when I entered the room upstairs, Kuriyagawa and Ando and Yamada and the two Iwasakis all looking down and fluttering as K mentioned my salary. They had a saké vat, and you could taste the wood in the saké, but I got stuck on beer, and no one had any. The wait while I, as guest, awaited a signal from the host, English style; and they did vice versa, Japanese style.

Small fish, a knobbly shell in flaming salt, upside down ("like a knuckle"); the sole on the ship-plate. It was so fresh that it was still alive (like Fukuchi's prawns), and it looked at me rather dolefully through two Picasso eyes, took a couple of breaths and wriggled its bare spine and the fins at the edge and slightly flipped its tail. Its body was on our plates and I felt disgusted and I looked at its eyes and I wanted to say "I am sorry." Then it watched me eat its body, looking slightly hurt, and when I'd chewed through the last piece, it gave a reproachful squint and died.

Ando got drunk and referred to the hostess as his mother-sister and made no bones about the fact that his wife has left him; covering up as a womaniser. He and K and I talked modern Britain and syphilis and history, while the others sat in total silence, one I couldn't bring them out of; it was because their superior was present. K wrote down Progoff's book because his father introduced Jung to Japan in a porn-book, and he and I took a taxi back to Iidabashi, and Friday's visit to a sad Morton, danger at the Tibetan exhibition from indignant leftists and cold-blooded corruption from a desire to degrade.

7th October. On Thursday at the Bank of Japan (and at the Keio party) I was asked for my impression of Japan. What are they? I think, what I said.

First, there is an overwhelming sense of growth. This is an educated society and everyone is striving beyond himself, unlike Britain, which is static. The reason (education) is debatable, but if it is so, one of the strongest factors is the educated bureaucracy, with every clerk fulfilling everything to the uttermost. This thoroughness is explained by "on" and "giri", and also by losing face and fear of "mistaking." (The reason why departo girls giggle when they are embarrassed).

Perhaps the key to Japan is its Victorianism. From Hitachi's household, through Prince Hiro's sailor uniform and butterfly collars and the 8-course meals, to the love of work and the walling round and the hierarchy, Japan is thoroughly pre-1914. That is why the Tomlins and the Buchanans will never really leave. Yet it is a strange Victorianism, an Americanised, permissive Victorianism. Perhaps it goes back to feudalism, but there is a definite centre to Japanese society, as there isn't in England, and this is connected with the subordination of the individual to society, e.g. in work, England preferring leisure. There is a pro and con to all these, just as there is in England.

On the worst type of the English. Understandably it's the R, the man who loudly questions others, but not his own ignorance. There was a letter in the *Japan Times* by an English woman who wants to know why Japanese girls giggle, i.e. why aren't they English? The answer is in Ruth Benedict: they must fulfil a customer's request to the utmost, they might not understand what he asks, then they lose face in front of client and chief, so they smile to sooth the client's feelings and hide their embarrassment. But she made no attempt to discover the meaning.

Compare the new determinism, the men like George Brown and Bill Maitland who thrash around without control (e.g. Brown's dance-hall row) and have excuses made for them (e.g. "he's under pressure"). C: "They're all vulgar basically." Katherine Whitehorn: "I don't want to hear excuses, I want to hear a deserting husband told 'You louse.'" One sympathises yes, but they are really awfully ignorant and spineless.

7th-8th October. Saturday (7th) to Nobe. A wet, misty day with all the tints a darker green; a little red. Ate a large lunch of inaba (yellowtail sashimi), raw ham, lichis, Cheddar and fruit, and slept until 5. Then discussed Hitachi with Buchanan, my successor. (He: "I don't want to be an éminence grise and advise a coup d'état, I'm not a Rasputin, like you.")

On Sunday (8th) it was brilliant and we sat on the beach and Buchanan recalled his mother bathing from a cage pulled by a donkey, and wearing bloomers and puffed sleeves tied at the ankles and wrists, and frills over the breasts. Also cycling bloomers. Later we went into the valleys. The amaryllis were dead, but there were blue water orchids in the paddies, and periwinkles and "safety matches" and harebells, and one water snake and lots of frogs.

Later we ate near threshing, and I stared at the tubs of grain and the pile of chaff while a woman picked chaff from purple beans, and I felt sad, I felt I was leaving the closeness to the earth.

In the evening we went to the Jimbocho sushi shop, Nan singing "favourite Uncle Brian", and Buchanan was depressed. ("This is a cheerful place" and "I'll send Nan some 'nori'" – seaweed.) But all day, and in the coca cola shop especially, I'd been psychic, and I knew we would return to Tokyo.

9th October. A morning on the telephone, the afternoon with the Bank, visiting for tax clearance certificate, and buying Christmas cards. From Friday and Dr Morton; my nipple (right). I have mastitis, i.e. inflammation of the breast tissue which occurs rarely in the male. It is really an activation of normal breast (mammary) tissue, i.e. rudimentary ducts which secrete occasionally have become congested and swollen as a result of injury. In one in 1,000 cases there is malignancy (cancer) and it has to be cut out. Pulling the shirt over one's head, or a woman's excitement generally cause it (in my case both); but it can also be regarded as a feminine characteristic. I said, "Am I turning into a woman?" and Morton laughed. Increasingly swollen.

From my correction of Kawamura s essay on Toynbee. I wrote: "I think you are right in treating Toynbee as a subjective imaginer, as a man with a vision; like Blake. As a questing soul rather than as a man who has set down what happened objectively. *A Study of History* is really on a level with *The Brothers Karamazov*; it is an attempt to create meaning out of history (compare "The Grand Inquisitor"), and it therefore tells us more about Toynbee than history; which is meaningless. All the greatest souls have refused to accept the meaninglessness of history. On the other hand, those like Dostoevsky have always had an awareness that history is, after all, meaningless, and it may be a criticism of Toynbee (or of his medium) that in refusing to accept the meaninglessness of history, he has actually denied the meaninglessness of history."

This, unconsciously, reflects my view of the soul in history. Faced with meaninglessness, he defies it and tries to transcend it (e.g. in the form of the Shadow), but he never allows himself to forget it. This is the twentieth century hero.

10th October. I did not record the Baxters' visit last Friday. They came to take away the cat. Gaybe was Welsh and looked like Lady Hamilton with her hair all over the place. Keith was squirrelly and English until (with a degree in Japanese) he was recruited by the Australian Embassy two years ago. G's parents had already left to emigrate to Australia by sea. On Wednesday 11th October, the cat got off the lead on the football pitch.

On Tuesday we went to the Nelson exhibition at Mitsukoshi. To get to it we had to go through the British sale and found our way to a corner crowded with Japanese who were staring nervously with solemn eyes. On display were an old boiler, like the one that burst in Journey's End, £25; a couple of old family fire-buckets, £9 each; a Watney's sign, £5; a couple of garden saws, £5 each; a pair of pincers and a carpenter's rule; and various other odds and ends.

Odds and ends I have not recorded....Why did the Ambassador Rundall return? Clickerty click printing machines near Edogawa Bridge. Water-ripples from the canal, like yellow streamers. Image, peeling/gone into holes. The place of the spirit in history.

11th October. To the Bank of Japan for licence to transfer money – I having been refused permission to keep my deposit account open and thereby escape losing in the likely event of an EEC devaluation. Mr Torii's assistance, the walk in Mitsukoshi again and the monkeys and parrots; while we waited.

In the afternoon took B to meet Hitachi. His nervousness in my sitting-room. The show of books, B cringing a little and calling H "Sir", as he must have buttered up his superiors in the Army. B said, "I was in this room eight years ago, teaching the chamberlains for the Crown Prince's tour to the West." H: "That was for the coronation, fourteen years ago I think." B put his head in his hands and said "God, fourteen years," and I thought back to when I was 14 and in the under 15 at school, being caned by Venn; on that very day, perhaps. B was in the room where we drank brandy on Tuesday 3rd. Bridges. Later (after Greeks and Bulgars) I said, "Teaching someone like H is like snakes and ladders. We got up to 90 and went back to 10."

Later the Tokyo University of Education party in the Mikasa Khaikhan. The foyer, Nakagawa in the pay desk. The square of unmovable settees, no spaces for the legs. My TV smile, my self screaming "phoney". Later, the room with chairs round the walls and a food-laden buffet table in the centre. Caroline and I stood as if awaiting execution before 20 people in our one solitary corner while Sakuraba, Irie and Fujii eulogised....S: "I must apologise because (Prof. Irie) arrived late." Irie: "I think Mr S has said all I want to say." In short, the three visitors. Buchanan's eulogy, how I was the best teacher Japan has ever had, and the finest and most charming colleague he has ever had in his life and so on.

My speech after the toast ("Please make your reply now" after I'd said "I hope to reply later"). I spoke about arrangements and the future, my reasons for leaving and my trip; and then about my impressions of Japan. The meaty bit was about my unorthodox vision of education, a joint search for true values, a true "leading out", not the teacher passing on dead knowledge to a student. Also about my values possibly being unJapanese, in which case (assuming the students rejected them) I hope I've made them more aware of their own values. Lively discussion (e.g. Tanaka's book on the Mediocre) and a departure to banzais after the presentation of a doll and a tour round the 20.

12th October. From yesterday, I forgot to record B dropping his chopsticks on the floor, and the nightmare episode of the lift. While I went round the 20, Buchanan stood impatiently by the 5th floor lift saying "Come on Shelley", and when eventually I got in the door closed and Buchanan nearly got left behind; then when we arrived on the ground floor, there, standing to greet us was the man who bid us farewell on the 5th, Sakuraba, the chairman of the party. He had come down in the adjoining lift. C: "It was Ionesco, a pantomime. All the Japanese are unreal somehow."

On Thursday to Koshi. Tokyo University of Education has asked for a receipt for my million yen/ticket....

Last weekend I read at one sitting Muller's *After all, this is England*, a very human account of how "it" could happen in England, and a very interesting attempt to explain a concentration camp commander in terms of the collapse of his personal life and in terms of his impotence and latent homosexuality. Ronnie makes it clear that Smith is projecting in a background of decline and decadence, that what is wrong is Smith's soul, not England. Perhaps this is the corresponding English vice, a reluctance to be thought abnormal (cf Osborne's "Thank God I'm normal"). The hostility to the Outsider and the Rebel. The refusal to be who one is.

13th October. Took Ben to the JSPCA. He was excited because he thought he was going for a walk – he carried his lead in his mouth – and he followed us trustingly into the execution shed, like the Polish children who followed that Polish martyr. He will clearly be put to sleep. As Maekawa said, he is too old for anyone to want him....

Later, to the Sanbancho Hotel to meet Tomlin for a brief drink, 5.00-5.35. The new Ambassador, Pilcher, was holding his first meeting, and protocol had to be observed. The talk was on Taiwan, trips, writing, and then Kirkup. Kirkup has written a book called *England, that Sick Country* and he attacks the British Council staff by name (Alan Baker is without manners for inviting K to a party without having been introduced) and tells a lot of "untruths" about Britain. Tomlin: "I'm having it translated, and I may consult my solicitor." His idea was that we should all club together. I was not keen on this, but I said I would put my name on a letter disagreeing with K's view of things, and I suggested a new book *New Britain* to correct K.

Later, over a meal at Nicola's next to two Russians, I told C there are three things: anti-Britishness, lies, and defamation. My attitude to K is complex, because I agree with his overall view of Britain, though not with his illustrations, and I would defend his right to say that in Britain. On the other hand, I don't think anyone should drag Britain in the dirt before foreign students who take it as gospel, without giving them the other side (which is what I do), and I don't go along with defaming people out of spite, though I must admit to having a sneaking sympathy with Kirkup here. Once again I am torn, once again I am in the middle. K is too extreme, but I am, at heart, a moderate Kirkup – less one-sided, but on the same side in relation to the System.

14th October. The Tokyo University of Education factionalism becomes clear in the light of yesterday. Fukuda wrote to Kirkup when he was in Kuala Lumpur and invited him to the Tokyo University of Education. Narita (prompted by Buchanan) said no, and went to the British Council, and as a result I appeared. So there was, from the outset a pro-Kirkup faction, and a pro-Hagger faction. Sakuraba was in the first, and edited Kirkup's second book; I silenced him by sending him to Britain through the Council. Now Kirkup's anti-Council activities are really directed at me. I am amused, and rather sad for him. If the only way he can find an outlet for his creative energies is the lampoon and a minor poet's tinpot Osborne rhetoric, then he belongs with the Gay brigade and the Dadas, not the Toynbees and Joyces.

Anyhow, all this makes last Wednesday's party clear. I prefer a stand-up to a sit down party, with few speakers, but by Japanese etiquette this form (and the lack of a present) is a poor effort. Strong, Fitzsimmons and Mayer all had sit-down parties and presents. Narita telephoned this morning, having arrived last night, and he said among other things, "I hear they treated you disgustingly, they didn't give you a present." and quite clearly in Narita's absence the pro-Kirkup faction took over, and with Japanese "subtlety", i.e. with the manners of Kyoikudai breeding, had a hit by making the speakers the visitors (only those with "ons" will speak) and by making the present for my daughter (we appreciate her more than you).

Buchanan came at lunch to bring a book on Angkor, and he came again in the evening, and he agreed. This explains why Sakuraba was distressed, why he bought the cuff-links and came down in the lift. Like Toyama, he is torn. When he is alone with me, he is nice; when his faction is around, he must be a little detached. If all this is true, Wednesday was a big triumph for me. They were rude, and I defeated them with kindness and scornfully ate nothing but sandwiches. No wonder they were uncomfortable when I went round and shook each one by the hand; and talked to the ex-graduates rather than the sensei.

15th-16th October. Packed all morning and got off to the International House, where we arrived at 3.30. Nan's excitement, exploring the corridors and bouncing on the beds in this, room 208. A walk in the garden, where I conceived *The Expatriate*; four years were under my feet, and I felt different from the youth I was then, and I was not sure I'd lost vigour and energy. Later the silence over tea in the puritanical lobby, and the Quakerish atmosphere in the "study-bedrooms".

An early night, which I got up from, insomniac, at 10. I went down to the bar and stood behind the bishop from Albany, and the barman served a Japanese first. It was a brandy cocktail. With great panache the barman poured in the milk, etc. and began to shake. His hands moved in opposite directions, the end of the shaker flew off, and the brandy-milk splashed on the bar and dripped by the bishop's shoulder. I stared with a serve-you-right look while the wretched man cleared it all up and went out to buy (?) some more milk and did it all again. The bishop was ruffled. He asked for the "check" three times, each time a little more impatiently.

On Monday (16th) I rushed around. First to the Hong Kong and Shanghai bank to collect the licence and Torii. We were going to persuade the Bank of Japan to let me open a dollar account in New York, on which I could draw in London; this as a precaution against devaluation. (In fact it had to be sterling travellers cheques, marked for use in any country in the world, i.e. convertible sterling.) On the way Torii said "A new Bluebird – a new model." I asked him if he drove a car. He said later that at weekends he flew, and that he was a flying instructor. In the war he was a pilot. Over Borneo, Samoa.

"In fact," he said, as we walked up the Bank of Japan steps, "I was a kamikaze." ("Kamikaze" originally meant favouring wind, like the one that destroyed the Koreans and Mongols in the 12th century, and the Spanish Armada.) And he told me about the March 31st raid on Okinawa. (The first and most famous?) 378 went and only three returned alive, of which he was one. They had to fly low over the U.S. ships three times. It was squally, and a low cloud saved him the third time. His reaction was shame. He had lost face by not dying, and didn't want to go back. So he flew around until he saw another plane. Then he plucked up the courage, and they both returned, and the three were declared heroes. They built a monument in Kamakura, costing 2,100 million yen (air force money), and visit it every March 31st. How they were chosen. They were all lined up. "Eldest sons out; those with dependent mothers or children out. Right, the rest of you will go." For ages I've wanted to meet a kamikaze, and, ironically, he was there all the time, just the other side of the bank counter.

Met C, who signed the travellers cheques while Nan changed all the figures on the stock exchange board. On to the Imperial to buy some pearl ear-rings and have a last drink there. Later, a meal and a brandy and a drive to the airport.

C was all right during the weighing in (under 40 kg) and the unaccompanied baggage and the quarantine, but after that she was a bit subdued. We had seen both Buchanan and Irie. The problem was to find Buchanan while avoiding Irie. I found Buchanan in the bar, but Irie found us, so we sat and had a deadly drink, Irie gushing and preventing either Buchanan or me from saying what we thought or felt. On the red carpet I kissed C good-bye and Buchanan said "Bless you" and I knew C was moved.

We went into the spectators' enclosure, and looked through the glass. A Japanese sat down on his bottom and everyone laughed. C and I talked through the grill as through the mesh of an electronic confessional until she was called. She was the last on the plane and she sat just behind the left wing. On the roof Irie said, "I think she is under the "S" of "Japan Airlines"," but, because she was supposed to be 1st class and up front, I said, "No, I think she's in the third window from the left."

Then the plane taxied off, red light blinking like an ambulance, and turned, and the hot gasoline fumes from the deafening jet-exhaust tousled my hair and later it was a red spot in the sky and I felt depressed and alone and had to put up with Irie chipping in in the car with "Would you like the window up?"

17th October. My last day in Japan. What do I feel? I wish I knew. For my strongest feeling during the last month has undoubtedly been one of dissatisfaction with my way of life. I have lost myself. I have been fallow, and all the parties and meetings have merely taken me further away from myself. The person I have been recently is not the person who wrote *The Silence*.

I must withdraw from society once again, and get myself back into last summer's frame of mind. For this social life is unreal, it is a pantomime. And the only glimpse of the true life I have had recently is in the nights. Waking at 3 a.m. I have known my death, with a sinking, undermining in my stomach I have confronted my death. During the last month I have become a teacher. I AM A WRITER who wants nothing but to be left alone to write. I AM NOT A TEACHER. Sometimes I feel I am losing all my intensity. Once the depth of a Dostoevsky was ahead of me, and now I am growing old or filling out in the flesh, and the hoped-for results are harder to credit.

These doubts have occurred during the last few unreal weeks. But tonight I feel they have been caused by my overworked, social life. If I can sleep well and have time to myself and get untired, then I will produce work of quality. My change is in my favour, not against me. That is what matters, not what I (as a teacher) feel about leaving Japan. Forward to the airport; people appearing for unreal reasons, people making outward gestures: "Oh, did he show his respect by appearing at the airport?"

12

AN ARTIST-THINKER: TRUTH AND VISION, GOD AS
THE GOAL OF THE QUEST
October – December 1967

18th October. Tokyo-Manila. The departure was a farce. Saito and
Enozawa got me to the airport by 10.30. At 11.10 Irie and Narita rolled up
and said SAS 984 departure time had been changed from 12.10 to 11.40 and
I would have to board. So I left before anyone really turned up.

On the plane I felt creative again and wrote 11 lines of a poem. I arrived
among all the preparations for Sato (the Japanese Prime Minister): red,
white and blue bunting, Japanese and Philippine flags still being knocked
up on the telegraph poles. I left before Sato's arrival and drove in my
"limousine", i.e. battered minibus, to the beginning of a chaotic (traffic)
queue.

Manila at first sight is Baghdadi. It is sprawling and flat, all shirt sleeves
and flies and army. The next impression is of Californian Victorianism.
From the "glarney" yellow and green "bazes" with streamers to the Wild
West 1890ish stores, the Californian buses and the voting adverts on the
telegraph poles, this place has Irish roots. After that you are aware of the
decay. You crawl among peeling buses past palms and mud tracks and
corrugated iron hangars that have gone rusty. You pass a decayed helicopter
and rusty oil drums and the earth is scarred and tracked. Later it's long grass,
and one man standing hopelessly with a scythe. Then it's corrugated houses
on stilts on a brown river, two fighting pyes in the mud; a market with
canvas roofs and standing crowds; an avenue of large white, stone "European"
type residences under palms, and long grey walls. Finally Manila Bay and
the long sprawling Roxas (Boulevard) that finally comes out at the National
Park. All very Baghdadi: from suke to open space.

Yet, wandering in the Park later, having tried to see Intramuros, I saw
Manila as a kind of China. Dozens of men were sweeping autumn leaves
off the beautifully kept grass, notices said "Keep OUR park clean," and the
effect of the short-sleeved strollers, no one hurrying, was like Canton; and
in the centre, "no loitering," was Rizal's monument. This place has energy
in a way. Yet the only traffic light (a noisy one too) is here, and the rest is
children in the fig-trees and touts; group-taxis (converted U.S. jeeps with
Polynesian designs) like small cattle-trucks and taxis with long, bendy,
decadent aerials; and pillboxes and children being chased away from army
lorries. Manila, in short, is backward, quaint and decayed and yet some
attempt is being made to cohere the people's energies.

19th October. Manila. A day on suffering. Took a private car round Manila in the morning; San Augustin church (1599-1606) which was desecrated by the British (1763). "JHS", Jesus Has Suffered, flame-trees or fire-trees and a picture of St. Augustine riddled with bullets from the war. Then on to Fort Santiago (built 1590-1739, i.e. over 149 years). The Japanese underground dungeons for torture (fingernail-pulling and hose in stomach); the cave flooded by the sea. The dungeon where 600 corpses were found in 1945, the Japanese commander fulfilling his "on", preventing the prisoners from escaping. The execution wall nearby. Prof. Oben's brother must have been shot there; "on 23rd December 1944, with six others." The concentration camp of 10,000 Americans outside the University of Santo Tomas. (1,000 died.) The guide escaped the Death March from Bataan to Capas, Tarlac, was shot through the cheek, left for dead ("it felt hot") and rejoined the guerillas, liberated Intramuros and the camp. The Rizal prison; the patriotism and talk of national heroes is all very Irish. Were the cars and stores Irish-Californian, or pure Spanish?

After lunch, and a short siesta, Prof. Oben rang and took me to Fort Bonifacio to see the thousands of graves of the U.S. war dead. "The solemnity of the place," and my question, "What is the justification for suffering?" On to Paco cemetery (once Rizal's). The bones are disinterred after five years and placed in "alcoves" as in the San Augustin crypt, and Oben's father after five years had hair and leather on him, but was otherwise "just a handful of bones." Oben obsessed with the war, having dressed as a woman to escape being thrown into a burning apartment with roped up Filipinos. He saw children bayonetted for pleasure by Japanese ("How low human nature can sink") and his father's first class apartment (his life savings) was burnt. His obsession also with his family and Catholicism, like the sincere student. ("My father was a Catholic, I am a Catholic too" – very Italian.)

Later he took me to Quiapo. The bus broke down (like the car this morning), and the comments of the passengers were wonderfully unJapanese. "Shall we push or pray to heaven?" "I'm not pushing, I'll get appendicitis." "We want our money back." The bus girl was in fits, as was the driver, and the bus was abandoned.

Quiapo square: beggars, candles, hawkers, and arum lilies like rosaries. There was a service on, and the faithful were standing any old how a hundred rows deep, fanning themselves, chattering and praying to icons, and the women had black or white veils on their heads, for "they must cover their heads". In the porch, a queue wiped black feet (of a statue) and kissed them; inside another queue swooned over a broken (Spanish) Christ on his back, and people knelt under all the icons. We went down to the altar. There, right knee down, cross over right shoulder, was the Christ who appeared, black, to an 18th century Spanish parish priest. Underneath NPJN (Nuostro Padre Jesus Nazareno, i.e. Our Father Jesus Nazarenus), and the singing was united and full of emotion. The decay, the Irish/Californian/Spanishness, the social consciences, the patriotism and the Catholicism, and the family – these factors, along with the money-grubbing, make up the Republic of the Philippines. And suffering is very much among them. The black Christ would have been in Fort Santiago, and he is clearly Filipino. But, and I repeat, what is the point of the suffering? "Cui bono?" ("To whose advantage is it?")

20th October. Friday. Manila-Hong Kong. And in Hong Kong, more suffering. At Manila I was told Cathay Pacific was full and my name was not on the list. I managed to transfer to P.A.L. and in fact arrived sooner, as it was delayed. I spent the afternoon getting into Room 822 of the Grand and visiting black marketeers, i.e. "money exchangers". I bought a lot of S. Vietnamese and Indian money. No one had any Cambodian or Nepalese. After that I went across the water to Lane Crawford's and Caroline's perfume (which cost $62HK).

Had a drink at the Mandarin, then took the ferry back and encountered a crowd near the Peninsular. We had to wait about an hour for the bomb-disposal squad to arrive. We stood 50 yards away from the "danger" sign and the red can, at either end of the street. They packed sandbags round it, announced that it was gelignite, and then (I think), shot it up with a pistol. The sound was like a thunderflash. There were two more round the corner. The blast of the second one was bright yellow; I was 50 yards away when they blew it up. The Chinese laughed, the English either looked excited or disapproving in a suburban sort of way. My impressions of Hong Kong are much less vivid than my impressions of Manila, probably because I've been here before.

21st October. Hong Kong-Macao-Hong Kong. Got up early after lying awake, brooding on love and bones, and caught the 9 a.m. hydrofoil to Macao, which I immediately liked.

It is surrounded by the sea on three sides and linked to China by a widish isthmus, and, unlike skyscraperish Hong Kong, the front is quaintly Portuguese. I found a taxi-driver who'd take me for $25 HK, and we went to the border, which is open, letting the Chinese enter quite freely. The significance grew as we went up to the fort, which was deserted and used as a radio station, the Portuguese having moved out last December; down to the East India Company Building and the statue defaced "Long Live Chairman Mao", and on to the church on Penha Hill via the former British consulate, which is covered in slogans and deserted, and an armless first discoverer.

For all the Governor's house and office in pale pink, and the Leal Senado (Loyal Senate), for all the red flowers and purple bells and Portuguese slat shutters and banyan trunks in Ching Buddhist temples, this place is run by the Chinese. Mao's music blares out of Communist offices and propaganda shops, his portrait and poems are on every wall, there are notices denouncing

British imperialism all down the main ("Rashid") street, everyone is taking to Maoist dress, the children are following suite, and the police can do nothing. Even the guide seemed brainwashed. He fled China in 1947, but even he maintained that it is the British police that have caused the trouble in Hong Kong – thus gullibly swallowing "the people dogma" – and he refused to speculate as to whether Mao had died. "Oh no, he's still alive." He was also rather anti-Portuguese. E.g. he told me that four years ago the Portuguese took the beggars before a public holiday and put them in prison for 2-3 days, and then released them. And so the beggars always disappeared when there was a holiday – they had no home to find. That ended two years ago.

After lunch I walked among the Communists and asked one propaganda shop if they had Mao's thoughts 1966-67, and left when I'd made my point that Mao folded up in 1965. Then I went to the floating Casino and watched some games of Big and Small, and I could imagine it ending up like the Empress Dowager's stone boat in Peking.

I took a pedicab to the ferry, and was alone on deck. We sped off among Greek hills. There was a blue sky with tank tracks across it, and the long wake expanded to right and left and became a causeway of setting sunlight, beckoning to the misty black of the distant Chinese mountains. I stood for over an hour, my hair tousled, and as Hong Kong came up ahead I felt as I did in the Gulf of Corinth, I was happy, blissfully, ecstatically happy.

22nd October. Hong Kong-Singapore. In the morning I went on a tour of Hong Kong. We went up to Victoria Park, overlooked the Wanchai district and Happy Valley, and via the hideous Tiger Balm Garden, went to Repulse Bay (named after the wooden British destroyer which drove back the Chinese ships in 1840/1), Deep Water Bay and Aberdeen, with its junks and sampans strangely like Canton. What impressed me was that Hong Kong is a stratified society (it is all millionaires' houses and trees and slums), and that the trouble will continue until independence. And, I almost believe, rightly so: the Europeans are only 1% to 99% Chinese (90% being Buddhist), and there are too many ragged children and beggars for things to continue in the present way.

From a terrorist's point of view, there can be very few districts where he can plant a bomb that will get the message across to Europeans. Jardines where I saw the three exploded, is in one. Only the country club and the Repulse Bay Hotel are reasonable targets on the largely wooded south side. If I were a terrorist I would keep the bombs in Chinese villages on the south side, and take them into the European-areas (including Victoria Peak); but I would not plant them to kill, I would plant them to make a bang and frighten, no more. And that is where I part company with the terrorists. I acknowledge their right to protest, but I do not acknowledge their right to kill.

The hideous all-cure Balm Garden built by two millionaire brothers to repay the public. The gaudy yellow and green dragons and peacocks, the monkeys, and all on painted rock. The red columns and green Chinese-style tiles, the suburban British red brick in the middle; about as Ching as the Moscow-like moon-lamps like heaped up cannon balls. There was only one thing to do and that was to drink beer, which I did with a New Zealander businessman.

I got to the airport at 2.15 for my 3.35 flight to Singapore, and discovered it had been cancelled. Tried to get on to the 2.35 which had been delayed, but missed it by one seat. Protested to Malaysia Airlines, and was taken (with a Swede and a Dane) to the Hotel Miramar, where I consumed a large Skoll watching colour TV, and in whose luxury room I now sit, waiting for the 8.00 Cathay Pacific.

23rd October. Singapore. I arrived at midnight, having seen a guerilla sitting in the road with a gun in his back as I left Hong Kong. He wore a vest. We passed over Vietnam. Phan Rang was like a snow-white battlefield in the moon, and there were great bare tracts. The temperature in Singapore must have been well over 90, and humid, and it has stayed like that all day.

I do not like Singapore. It is flat and most of it looks like the outskirts of London; the British military base "new town" seems to be everywhere. The city is a cross between old colonial red and icing-sugar Raffles, and the arcades along Rashid Street. There is little of interest. City Hall, where the Japanese surrendered, that is all. Otherwise it is all Tiger Balm Garden and Jade House, the two hideous monuments to Mr Aw Boon Haw the tiger and his brother Mr Aw Boon Par the leopard. Jade, transluscent alabaster, crystal, black jasper, quartz, fake marble – these are what these two vulgarians crammed their ugly house with, and how beautiful some of the pieces are.

In the afternoon I went to Johore. The causeway that General Yamashita crossed, the house over the trunk road where Singapore surrendered to him, Kranji cemetery, like that Fort in Manila. Otherwise it was the Sultan's palace, and the young boy who liked the Sultan, and the Moslem graveyard of round tombstones for men and flat for women. Johore has 37% Chinese to Singapore's 75% (and 14% Malayans, 8% Indians, 2% Europeans). The swarthier skin and Moslem mosques were the only outstanding differences between the two sides of the water.

The rubber plantation. The trees are planted in rows, over 200 acres. A tree must grow five years before it produces, and it is only good for firewood after 40 years. Women do the tapping and the men work in the processing factories. The women tap 6.30-11.00 a.m. in the cool, and they get half a cup per tree and do 60 trees a morning, each. You start 6 feet up and work downwards, and you cut one tenth of an inch off the bark for the early morning flow.

Later, the end of the fire-walking. A temple like an Elizabethan theatre, with galleries, crowds of 400 milling Indians, the yogis in yellow with ashen feet, a pool on the ashes of the fire. The small bananas on a leaf, with ashes on them. The yogis barefooted with their admiring friends.

24th October. Singapore-Saigon. I left Singapore at 10.45 and arrived at Saigon through shelling I didn't see at 12.55. Had to wait an hour before I was allowed through. I couldn't get into (i.e. have a feel for) Singapore, as I told the Chinese Wong at the airport. (He, "I've always been an outsider" – hence his noisy explanations of cameras, watches, how to get promotion to buddy Anderson.) But I like Saigon, although it's even more of a con-town than Manila. I know, I have just been fiddled on a black market deal – 2000P for $10, he offered me, and when I opened the wad I found 400P. Elementary and I was taken in, being, as usual alas, too trusting; not thinking he'd whip most of the notes away after he'd counted them all out.

Saigon, as I told C, is a city ready for war, but the war doesn't seem to be happening. So there's barbed wire everywhere, the pill-boxes are manned, everything is under an army guard, there are jeeps and lorries, but there are no bangs, and it is all like a Field Day at Chigwell (School). After booking in at the des Nations, I went for a drink at the Continental. This took me along Tu Do. After that – after the bamboo chairs on the terrace and tables five rows deep and the man who tried to flog me dirty pix inside an art book – walked down to the Central Market and waited for terrorists, but none came. So I went up to Independence Palace and then along to the Basilica, where sisters and local beauties knelt and mourned a man inside a coffin up front. After that I walked back to the Continental, and it was on the way back to the "Nations" that I encountered the robber. If I'd been able to get a taxi, it wouldn't have happened, and the annoying thing is that I had a large dinner afterwards, in the belief that I'd actually profited out of it. The jargon in Vietnam. They say two "hun" (hundred) and two "thou" (thousand), and everything is contrasts, e.g. "Mamma money changer number one, he number ten, no good." In this they are like the Singaporis, and they are also as repetitive. Also "same-same".

Later the CIA agent by the Oscar lift, the roof and the kitten, the flares and the thump of guns and the big flash of a bomb across the river, near Bien Hoa. And later I was awoken by the thump of guns, which was nearly drowned by the air-cooler's chug, like a ship's engine.

25th October. Saigon. Spent the morning getting to the Passport office at 335-337 Vo Tanh, persuading them (in the light of information gleaned last night at the Hotels Caravelle and Brinks) that they should grant me the exit visa immediately as I was going to Bien Hoa. ("Ben Whaa") at 1.30 on the U.S. military bus. This worked. "An exit visa is only necessary for Cambodia, but if you are going to Bien Hoa, that is all right." I had to wait an hour, though, to get my confiscated passport returned. Stood next to Mark Frankland of the *Observer*.

After that visited the river and the bombed-up Floating Restaurant, and then went to Bien Hoa in an American army bus with anti-grenade mesh over the windows. Travelled with several American GIs in uniform. I was in civilian clothes, but no one asked if I should be with the military. Over the river, with its slums on stilts, then over flat ground with dump trucks and jeeps and dust like a mist and stretches of water and low, lush palm fronds. Feather duster palms behind. A well paved road, a lot of traffic: loaded vans and civilian lorries and U.S. everything. Then there are hovels on the swampy left, and over the sandbagged bridge; past a few villages with melon stalls, you come, on the right, to several bases enclosed in barbed wire. Transport planes. The further you go, the more pill-boxes there are, the higher the sandbags, the browner and dustier the earth. The effect is a defence of the right against the left.

Inside the barbed wire the bus put off the GIs, more got in, I sat tight and we returned.

No stopping in the villages after the turning off before Phan Thiet. I would like to have stopped; there were about seven Roman Catholic churches, with old facades like the one in Manila. Otherwise corrugated iron hovels, wooden shops in the centre of the road, very low and dirty. The VC prisoner of war camp, skull and cross bones at the corners, and, strangely, a lone Drumcliff type cross almost buried in rank weeds. The question I have asked myself all day. Why did I go to Bien Hoa – why do I have this self-destructive mania to risk myself? What is its origin? Why should I get involved with the VC – why why why?

The bus put me off in Cholon. The unfriendly streets and the storm. I took refuge in the Colisseum. An American GI waved me in without checking my security and I sheltered from the rain and read all the security notices and notices on VC grenades. A GI called "Help yourself to a beer from the fridge", so I had a beer though I hadn't a coupon. The phone rang. "Answer it," a GI called. It was an American General who asked: "Have you got the address of the Annapolis Trenching Billet? It's on the board in front of you." I looked at the board and gave him the address. Then a GI called "Your bus is here." I got on another military bus and returned to Saigon.

Over dinner, the man who was divorcing his wife, and who thought "Oh s—" about anything she did; her financial demands. Later, the Hanoi bartender saying you trusted no one in Saigon as anyone could be VC, and saying first (loudly and indignantly) "You are not our friend if you want to meet a VC" and later, "You'll get your throat cut if you try." Outside the white-haired currency dealer agreed to take me to a VC for 100P. I had to return to the des Nations to get it, and in the intervening four minutes he changed his mind: "How should I know" (shrugging). Later, the talk with the Oscar CIA agent about not being content with one's job. To bed late.

26th October. Saigon-Siem Reap-Angkor. A walk next morning, a stroll past a guarded exhibition hall, breakfast at the Le Royal. Then off to the airport in a military bus ("a TSN"). It took me to the military personnel shed, and I had to cross the runway to get to the civilian entrance. Then there was one and a half hours delay until we left at 1.45 on a Caravelle. The CIA agent who met me.

Arrived at Pnom Penh 20 mins later in time to get the 1.00 plane, which had been delayed, to Siem Reap. It had lots of ribbons and wires, and inside you went up hill. Sat next to Dr Tinker, who has finished two months' voluntary work at Chou Doc, and who is against the U.S. effort. His theory of aggression and competition, his concern with U.S. aggression. When Chou Doc was "hit" he was "in the latrine with his pants down". He cowered on the floor.

At Siem Reap, after agreeing to share a room with him, drove to the Grand through a lush countryside of flooded paddies like ponds, and gum trees, and palms. Immediately went out to Bakong in a motorcab, a box hooked on to a motorbike. Buffaloes, hens, herons or storks. Siva prepuces, old stones and silence under the hiss of cicadas, the whoop of parakeets, cow bells. The sutras of orange-clad Theravada monks, the repetitive note of the godless usurpers. The headless figurines of the earlier Buddhists; the heads were cut off and replaced with linga after Jayavarman VII. These were guarded by long broken limbs under a pyramid form. Old stones and a new, bare people, the new Khmers of "the good" dictator Sihanouk, who permits no opposition and who shoots all critic exiles if they return.

27th October. Angkor. To stay in Cambodia is to think about dictators. After the spiky helmeted apsaras' rather tedious dancing at Angkor last night, I got talking to a man who claimed to be related to the Khmers, and who agreed that Sihanouk is a new Jayavarman VII who will make the Khmers powerful again. All this in French. Later I got a hotel boy to eulogise Sihanouk in the bar. His brother is Prime Minister, he magnanimously makes gifts out of the taxes, and his enemies are those who refuse to agree that Phanom Dong Rak is a part of Cambodia. (It is on the Cambodian map I picked up here, "Dangrek".) China is one of them, though the Chinese built Siem Reap airport and inspired the militia that looks for (anti-Sihanouk) bandits in the jungle. I think Sihanouk may be doing a Sato, and challenging a divided China for (in his case) influence in Indo-China – hence his separate support for the VC. Anyhow, the Thais and the Vietnamese Chams still threaten the Khmers, and the leader is thought good because "there is no fighting" and he gives people money. (This and the Eastern respect for the family keep him in power.) Nothing much has changed since Jayavarman VII (c1181-c1218).

Angkor Thom visited after 8 a.m. this morning. The giants' causeway, slit-eyed gods and round-eyed "Tibetan" demons holding 7-headed cobras. The Bayon, a temple-tomb and image of society. There are 52 "chapels", the one at the top being for the god-king, the ones at the bottom being for the cowboys. To each his place. Each of the 52 has four faces in the likeness of Jayavarman as Buddha, and the 208 faces took 26 years to build. And when this megalomaniac died the people refused him a funeral and threw off Buddhism, thereby revealing him as the dictator he undoubtedly was.

Later, drove round three more of his temples, Preah Khan, Neak Pean and Ta Som, all of which were overgrown, and then three Siva temples: Mébon Ord, Pré Rup and Prasat Kravan. The lingam symbolism, Siva as destroyer on his bull; Visnu as protector, 8-armed, on his garuda, which eats naga (cobra); and Brahma the creator on his sacred goose. The holy water of the lingam cures the sick, just as the leper king became sick by killing the cobra (cf the albatross), but in Angkor Wat the lingam is a symbol of life and death. For Suryavarman II (1113-c1150) was cremated and his ashes were put under the topmost lingam, which is thus the creator of life and the monument to death and a symbol of the unity of life and death like the Michelangelesque frieze of heaven and hell, the figures in action and everyday under 18-armed Yama of the Dead; and of Visnu making the ambrosia of immortality – it is a wonderful transcendence of death at the behest of a tyrant. For Angkor Wat took 50,000 workers 50 years.

28th-29th October. Angkor-Pnom Penh. Spent yesterday evening talking with Tinker, and got up at 6.30 this morning. Was at the airport by 7.15 but the plane did not leave until 9 because the troops had to get things ready for Sihanouk. When I left they were standing in the hot sun, and when I arrived in Pnom Penh, other troops were waiting for Sihanouk in the hot sun. We had to wait over half an hour (all roads were closed). Then his convoy approached, like (the Iraqi) Kaseem's: all sirens and motorcyclists and headlights blazing in the bright morning, and applause. All I got was a glimpse past the President of Mauritania. There sat the tyrant, the man who is supposed to be so good but who needs his army to keep in power, and when he got down among his generals I was reminded of the Angkor Wat frieze of the procession to the new capital.

Drove in to Pnom Penh, and to Le Royal, with a fat Englishman, had a drink and lunch, and then took a trishaw round Pnom Penh. It seems that all the pagodas house members of Sihanouk's family or the army; the posh flats down to his palace belong to the army. Otherwise I was most interested in the wreckage of a U.S. plane that had intruded (cribbed, like the railway station, from China); and in the VC Embassy. This was closed today, but I shall go and find out Ho's peace terms tomorrow. The rest was a leisurely wheel through a French village cum town on the (rivers) Sap and Mekong, the only remarkable buildings being the Central Market (cf Saigon) and the rather dull museum. Except for a couple of lingams with figures inscribed on the heads, the statues were rather drab, perhaps because they need their context in Angkor Wat. After Saigon the people, too, are drab; they are much more drably and poorly dressed, and there are a lot of bare feet. The primitive Chinese "cupping" has given a lot of them the bruised appearance of autumn apples, and I have not heard any really warm things said about the dictator in Pnom Penh.

Later I drove past the sarong and sampot weavers to the only opium den in town. Opium is "inderdit" so the trishaw driver backed off out of sight.

It was a private house, mostly dark. I went up the path and knocked on the door. No answer. I opened it. A light showed through a grille on the far wall. I went back down the path and up some stone steps, did not turn left but went down into a yard. On the right was a corrugated iron shed with a raised platform. A hammock had been swung in front of it, and in it, by a charcoal fire, sprawled an old woman, dead to the world. A sheet hung on a line formed a cubicle on the stage out of which came clouds of smoke.

The houseboy agreed (in French) that opium was being smoked. Then came the old lady, and all the children went and sat on the platform, along with the houseboy, and I was on my own. In French she said there wasn't any opium around ("Pas ici"), after asking if I knew how to smoke it. That was really as far as I got for she withdrew into the house and left me with the houseboy. "Elle a peur," I said, and the boy agreed.

I went out and found the trishaw driver. On the way back he told me he'd been to Saigon and the U.S. with an American: "Jack Halliday was my patron." But that now there was no U.S. Embassy. I: "Do you like the U.S. better than the Viet Cong?" He: "I no say, I too small. If I say policeman handcuff me and take me to prison."

On Sunday (29th October) I saw how such a (small) person acts. After a morning spent arguing with the doorman and official of the VC Embassy – it was closed until 8 a.m. Monday and they would not permit me to meet the English-speaking Mr Van before; and trying to enter the royal palace, in vain because the President of Mauritania was having a look; I went out at 4 to try and buy a small silver gift.

I took my "cyclo-pousse" boy, number 1947, and we encountered the procession for the President's departure. The bend of the road was lined on both sides with schoolchildren, soldiers and people. The children wore white shirts and yellow scarves (the Yellow Guards); they also wore soldiers' pointed hats, "le militaire d'enfants". The army did not carry guns – that was left to the guards at all the corners. My boy parked his trishaw, and we ran and joined in.

Then they came, first a car, then another, then motorcyclists, and then standing in the back of an open car, the President, and Sihanouk, smart and unsmiling in a white coat. There was terrific cheering and clapping, and my boy leapt up beside me, clapping his hands over his head. Immediately the procession had gone (i.e. after the next 30 cars and jeeps) he was quiet again. What did it matter to him that Cambodia and Mauritania are getting together, when he is so small?

This country is ruled by fear, fear of the police in the Ministry of Interior, fear of the army, fear of "the policemen" (my boy) in this hotel. Everyone says Sihanouk is good because they are afraid; which was my first impression, spoken to the fat Englishman.

30th October. Pnom Penh-Bangkok. First thing this morning I got off to the VC (Viet Cong) Embassy, and rang the bell as directed and went into the garden. An old woman told me to get out ("partis"), and she was later supported by an old man and a fearsome young tough who bundled me out of the gate. The bell was on the outside, so I rang again, and threatened to go on doing so until I saw Mr Van, all the while jabbering in French about U.S. atrocities. In the end the old woman went in and came out with a form, "Fiche", which I filled in outside the gate. "Motif": "To obtain a visa for NFL territory so that I can tell the British people the truth about American atrocities in Vietnam." Five minutes later she returned, smiling, with a dog, and I was admitted to a room with a glass case. There was a replica of Tran at the stake, a picture of Ho and various books, but nothing about Mao.

Then in came Mr Van, a monkish, smiling man with a parting down the middle, and very mild. He wore a dark blue shirt, and his hands had a terrorist's clumsiness. I explained, he wrote details about me: my profession and jobs, when I went to China (revealing the VC connection with China), my address in England. Of course it would be difficult to get me into NFL territory, but he would refer it to H.Q. and write to me. He was rather optimistic though. I asked if I'd get to "du sud ou du nord" and he interpreted "nord" as North Vietnam, indicating that he regards Vietnam as one country, the north of which is presently under Ho. In the end, still smiling that Chinese informal smile, a people's smile, he shook hands and outside the three chuckers-out smiled and saluted, and now, to them, I was a friend, I had used the jargon: "atrocities".

I took a cyclo-pousse to the market and wandered among people dear to Van: squatters near baskets of vegetables, a woman weighing fish and knocking them on the head to kill them as they were sold, live fowls, a woman having lice picked out of her hair by her children. They were dear to me, too, these victims of Sihanouk the good, and after getting the 1.00 plane and arriving in Bangkok soon after 3.30, and seeing a city like Tokyo – all taxis and concrete buildings and no cyclo-pousses – I understood what the Vietnamese war was about. Mr Van's agricultural world is one of squatters and gardens and boulevards and relics of old colonial rule, the Indo-Chinese world, and that has nothing to do with the industrial Americanised West that Mr Van is fighting against and (ultimately, in the sense of industrialisation) wants to become.

31st October. Bangkok-Calcutta. Last night, I got round Bangkok between 6.30 and 8.30, and got an idea of the structure of the city; from Asdacy Road to the end of Rajdamnoen Road seems to be the centre of the city. I thought I would like to teach there, although it lacks the charm of Indo-China.

This morning I got up at 6 and visited the Floating Market. The brown-green water of the tributary ("canal"), palms and wooden hovels on stilts, sampans laden with bananas and melons and vegetables, and débris: bamboo, fruit, one dead pye on its side with its legs in the air like a money box. Chinese and Thai temples. Later went to the Temple of Dawn, a

Buddhist temple in Hindu style. The bulging eyes of the demons which came from China 1180/90: in Angkor through Jaya, and here because the Thais were pushed out by Kubla Khan in 1190. So the Chams-Chinese are the demons, who are simply the enemy; Kubla having bulging eyes.

Went on to the royal palace. Lots of red and gold, and roofs of snakes like antlers. Emerald (in fact Jasper) Buddha; the Michelangelesque wall of Mother Earth, under Buddha, repelling the demons "from the Ramayana"; they couldn't be the enemy too could they? A bit late for Khmers, but they could be the Burmese, who were the threat then. No photos allowed, just as you had to wear jacket and tie, "out of respect", even though no one lives there.

Got the 2.00 plane to Calcutta. It was Thai Airlines' last flight on that route, and I lunched well and drank wine in sympathy. From the airport Calcutta is like outer Saigon: green paddies and palms. The people don't seem poor. There aren't many. Then you notice the absence of traffic, the bare-footed stragglers and squatters. the cow in the road. Then the city begins. You see bare-footed rickshaw drivers and carters, an imploring crowd outside a "Ration Shop", slumped and despairing tousle-haired bodies under a wall-sign "CPI" (Communist Party of India) and a hammer and sickle, and red and white paper for a Hindu festival. No wonder they're going Commie or world-renouncer. You go on through a hell of smoke and dust and look at the hopeless, limply propped against trees or, penises showing, lying around on steps, and you feel you are at a zoo, and you feel brotherhood.

Later Mr Ray, the (Aryan) Brahmin and ex-law officer, showed me the O.K. things: Dalhousie Square, the Hooghly (Ganges), the Victorian monument, Chowringhee Road, but even so we stumbled on to a dark dockers' meeting (candles and incense and squatters on the grass) and on chaotic bus queues, and nothing could erase the impression of pink and dirty stucco and balconies, shorts and bare feet and honking horns, and the prison waggons. And I had to admit that the labour unrest is leading to Communism and Mr Van.

1st-2nd November. Calcutta-Katmandhu-Delhi. Later, the Brahmin said the caste system would be gone in 100 years, but that predestination wouldn't, and later still I went out with an old hand called Baxter, who I met over dinner. We went through streets exploding with firecrackers for the birth of the goddess (Dussehra) as a sacred cow, past slumped sleepers, to Job Charnock's tomb. The slither of a cobra beyond the beam from the gateman's torch. No one slept in the graveyard.

Next morning I got up at 4.45 and drove through quiet streets and dawn sleepers. Some did not even sleep on rags, some had not even bothered to look for cover, but slept in the open, near a protuding porch or arcade, as if the instinct for self-preservation no longer mattered. It was to this cesspit of humanity that the goddess came. And yet, suddenly we came out to a long stretch of rice under a low mist, and a crane stretched its neck, and my disgust and horror vanished and I knew that basically life was good, and I was glad the goddess came.

The flight to Katmandhu was a vivid one, and I wrote a poem with Everest bright white on blue in the distance, the top of a range like snow cleared off the road onto the kerb. Katmandhu was medieval. A fresh air life among the hens and sheep of Durbar Square, the barn-like houses near it, the agricultural life of a Cambodia that I yearn for and yet am unhappy in when I begin to settle there. They too were waiting for the goddess, being a day behind Calcutta, and all the temples were closed. So I wandered among mild, butting cows in Hanuman Doka, looked at the red monkey and the erotic phalluses, and saw Taleju (temple) from a distance.

Here I was accosted by a Tibetan refugee. I had been looking at a thanka, and he had a guerilla friend who had another. I asked for a mandala, and we trooped off to his hen-coop of a first floor, and sat on sacks of oats and looked at mandalas on the straw. The guerilla was beginning 15 days' walking into China, over Everest, in an hour's time, and he wanted money for food, so he let me have the one I wanted for just $8. The oath that it was 100 years old – the importance of the Tibetan promise.

Later, after visiting the "Romeo and Juliet" Machendra Nath, after seeing the goddess (a child of 8, well made up, and no relation to the cow) in the window of the House of the Living Goddess; and having stared at the curly-eyed Buddha "clock" (square tower) at Swayambhunath; I took a discontented ex-British Army (Gurkha?) private, a Nepalese, and bought a thanka of Berbheirau for $30 (much reduced) from a Mr Cama, with whom I may go into business. And when I got back the small poxy men from the curly-eyed Buddha square were at my hotel, and after extensive negotiations on the 1st floor of another barn, I bought a 400 year old cosmic clock mandala for $21. There are hundreds around Katmandhu – would it be possible to act as an agent for antique shops, i.e. be a middleman and supplier?

All this took place in streets exploding with squibs and lined with candles. My guide: "The fireworks are to wake people up to the cow." In Calcutta, the festival made me angry – sacred cows among the starving beggars and lepers – but here I felt at peace: the girls of 8 were all excited, trying on their special bangles, and I have one image of a boy walking beside his peasant father, dressed in the same Mr Pastry R.A.F. hat and drainpipes and boots, and holding his hand and looking up and smiling with joy; and the father looked down and smiled back. Here was happiness, and the cow was good, the hats hanging like butchers' joints, they too were good. And all was pure in this fresh mountain air.

This morning (2nd November) I was up at 6.30, and, having successfully resisted the scrounging of my guide, left for Delhi and the Imperial Hotel, which turned out to be on Pan Am, I having grumbled about leaving in the middle of this coming night. After lunch I got out and visited old Delhi: the

Asoka Pillar, the Jama Masjid, and, most interesting, the Red Fort (from 1638), the old Moghul palace with the obsessive Persian couplet on the marble Private Audience room: "If there is a Paradise on earth, it is this, it is this, it is this."

What ecstasy can have led to these words? Wandering in the garden, between the baths and the judgement throne, near the cobra-charmers and under the vultures in the elms, I thought I knew, and I did not believe the guide's cynical explanation that the Moghul Moslems wanted their paradise in this life. To me, it was the height of Moghul civilisation, the creator of that couplet and the man who sculpted it among the marble flowers. The self-confidence and self-belief.

Delhi is an attractive city, full of gardens and boulevards and old colonial buildings, and I could be happy working here for a while. I want to get to know India, just as I want to get to know hell. Hell is a very warm place, in the emotional sense, that is. India has the excitement of the 6-line ruby I nearly bought in one of the Moghul palace shops.

3rd November. Delhi-Istanbul. After a lone dinner and the man in the bar who made a point of not seeing anything of India to spite the sauce company in Switzerland that had sent him out, went to shop and got up at 3 for the 5.15 Pan Am. Travelled via Teheran and Beirut. The Malaysian physiotherapist going to the U.S., the bearded French engineer, the timid Tibetan going to study for five years in the U.S., never having flown before, or even seen a plane. Will his religion and subject of study (Tibetan religion) survive the U.S. life? If he is in a community as he was in Delhi, with the Dalai Lama, perhaps it will.

At Istanbul got straight into a taxi and went, via the Andrianople Gate of 1453 and the Aqueduct of Valens, across the Golden Horn to the Park Hotel. Got straight out and saw the Sultan's Palace and Hareem (Abdul Hamid, the murderer of the Armenians, lived in the Vildiz Palace); the Blue Mosque, which has an English grandfather clock; and Aya (Hagia) Sofia (= Holy Wisdom), the church that Justinian built, and where he and Theodora were crowned, Theodora upstairs in the gallery. The 6th century mosaics and ceilings have been done up in the 8th, 10th and 12th centuries, and the Moslems sacked the place in 1453 and put up quotation from the *Koran*. Finally the Topkapi Palace, begun by Mehmet the Conqueror. The main inpression I had was of loathing the Ottoman Empire for makings its vassals curry favour with vast and (I assume) often unappreciated gifts, e.g. from Egypt and Damascus. The gifts from Russia being different.

After that visited the suke. The leg-puller of a currency man who offered 2,000 liras for 1,000 yen, and who had Eisenhower's autograph. The other fiddler who sends dollars to his machine-tool company in Germany. After that all is a tired dream. The long visit to the U.S. consul, which ended in the car getting stuck by the water, and a total stranger casually getting in to add to the weight, so we could go up the ramp; then getting out. A long argument in the hotel over the fare, the driver wanting 100 lira, I saying it should be less because we agreed 50 for the sightseeing and he didn't know the way. In the end I said, "Here's 90 for the sightseeing and 10 tip for being so helpful," which mystified everyone.

Then a drink. When I paid the waiter brought me change, thinking I had signed a chit, and then accused me of trying to welsh. Then a dinner during which the lights went out twice and a creepy and pretentious string-orchestra carried on playing classical-pop; and during which a waiter polished a glass so hard that it broke in two. Finally an argument in the lobby because they insisted I paid my bill at 5 a.m., an argument that ended in the man giving me 11 lira a dollar on the black market. Such things only happen when you are drunk or tired from 23 hours without sleeping.

4th November. Istanbul-Budapest-Vienna. The Turkish inefficiency. I had to wait from 5-5.15 a.m. for my bill, then there were no bridges (they disappear from 1 a.m. to 6 a.m. but no one told me); and finally I was given a boarding-pass I didn't need to show. The Turks gesture a lot with their hands, but the impression of vitality they give is misleading. Is it the same with all decaying countries – Britain, Hungary? This combination of inefficiency and superficial vitality?

Arrived in Budapest with a U.S. travel agent who talked about his conference; got a lift into the centre with the Publicity Director of Malamud's film *The Fixer*. Set off in rain from the Royal hotel by taxi and visited November 7th Square; the Heroes (of 1896) Square; the Pest castle; the opera; the Basilika. It was then that the guide stopped, and on entering she dipped her hand in the font. Later she admitted she was a Catholic and "not Communist"; that the people are not Communist in their hearts. She did not fight in 1956 because she had a baby. On to a Soviet monument and the Parliament building, then across to Margaret Island and Buda Hill: St. Matthew's and the castle, the 1849 citadel and Russian flags. Home via Vaci Utca, the street with the profit motive, the unclassless street.

The people seem well off, but the streets are grey and draped with red flags, and there are all too few Baroque buildings to relieve the chipped fronts caused by "Hitler" (my guide) and often Stalin. Left with an Australian pharmaceutical company worker who said the trouble with Britain in his experience is complacency and lack of initiative. So his three room-mates sat around moaning and didn't get an extra job to cover their ski-ing holidays as he did (answering the phone for a doctors' tax free).

When I arrived at Budapest airport I was told that, in spite of what they had said when I checked in at 9, the plane had left at 11.30. Rerouted to Vienna via Belgrade and tried to squeeze a taxi fare out of Hungarian airlines. Did not get it – "Eastern Europe is different". Got into the Bristol hotel at 6 to find letters from C and mother (Argie's appendicitis). Had a bath, then went down to the bar and to the dreamlike unreality of yesterday evening: a large dining-room, napkins starched on the tables, a pianist, and no one there. Sat by the piano; the pianist, "I don't like playing here, I am a composer not a pianist." Michelangelo Sculptor.

5th November. Vienna-Paris. Got up early, had an unreasonably expensive breakfast, then sought out the Habsburgs. The Kapuziner church with its monk attendant. The stillness in the vaults as you walk from the 17th century past Marie-Thérèse and "Franciscus Imperator", the last Holy Roman Emperor, to whom Hitler paid homage; to the three coffins on their own. Elizabeth's and Rudolf's are the same and have marble crucifixes and wreaths on them. Francis Joseph the First's stands on high, on a marble pedestal. The skull and crossbones on the coffins of the earlier Habsburgs, as if the coffin-maker were mocking the solemnity and regal splendour of the vault.

After that, went out to the Schönbrunn (Summer Palace) and walked in the Baroque, white and gilt rooms, and then went to the Hofburg rooms at Michaeler Place (Platz), with their more drab, more Flemish tapestried rooms. The main impression I had concerned the beds. In the Summer Palace, where Kathy Schratt had the first 4 rooms, Francis Joseph had a large double bed; in the "Winter Palace" he had a miserable bedroom with an Oxford jug and bowl for a basin and a very narrow single bed; as did Elizabeth, who also had a shrine and a rosary.

The rooms were not warm and cosy; with their parquet floors and Hampton Court-like doors at each end of the room, their large baroque stoves, they somehow suit the bleak, forbidding coldness of Francis Joseph's eyes. Rudolf's rooms were unfortunately closed. Later I went over to Ballhaus and looked in on where the Congress of Vienna took place. It was closed. (The Congress also took place at the Schönbrunn.)

As I left, Vienna was faded green cupolas on baroque walls, above hundreds of strewn yellow-green autumn leaves, and modern Europe was out of reach, difficult to grasp from the past, unlike everywhere east of Istanbul. And so modern Europeans live at one remove, alienated in their superiority, making less contact with each other than the Indians or Turks.

In Paris I stayed at the Madison, in St. Germain des Prés. I had a couple of beers in the Bonaparte, and another next door, and I was struck by the phoniness of the dandy show. A "Maoist" uniform, a woman with long blonde hair and a wasp mink coat, they were out to impress because they had nothing else to belong to. Alienated, they belonged to their rebel group and strutted with Bohemian girls as if they were Regency lords, and they strutted past enormous chalked letters outside the church, on the kerb: "On est en le Bonaparte, nous."

6th November. Paris-London. Got up early, rang London, then went for a walk down the Rue de Seine to Pont Neuf and the Square du Vert Galant, where I spent so many lonely mornings and afternoons in March 1959. On through the Louvre and the Tuileries to Concorde and the Elysées palace.

Then up to the Seine. Longed to live in Paris, for I could be free here on the waterfront. Went to the Rue des Ecoles and the crummy, glass room which is the British Council, Paris, and got particulars about the British Institute from Mrs. Cooper. She thought I'd find work if I just turned up in Paris. The Parisiennes like to complicate things: you have to push a button instead of simply opening the door, and the airport bus departs a whole paper-chase away from where it arrives, and there is no one to ask.

Arrived at Heathrow at 1.30, and was met by C and Nan, both of whom looked different. Mother drove us back while I recounted what I had seen on this swing through guerillas and palaces. The rush of emotion I felt when I saw C and Nan, and earlier when I landed, gave way to a willing acceptance of what I saw, and there was none of the hatred for England that I felt last time, on June 11th 1966.

The afternoon was spent in unpacking, tearing up, and distributing presents, and after dinner I went round to Journey's End with Rob and Frances who came for me. Rob asked me questions about my trip while mother listened in silence, and we ended up by discussing Tibetan mandalas and their markets in London.

Rob drove me home, and we went into the Standard for a couple of beers which he paid for, and got onto the changes in Britain: the sameness and lack of initiative-reward. I said it was a sign of decay that people like myself were not a part of the ruling system, and Rob agreed and agreed too that I was right to be a part of the brain drain. I said one should try to know everything and act as if one were one's own ambassador, turning one's back on the System that has already turned its back on one, and, to my surprise, again Rob agreed.

7th November. Spent the morning trying to cope with my mail, while C shopped. When mother brought her back she asked if she could have a word with me over J: "I feel you could diagnose what's wrong." After going to Chiswell's and buying a desk and a chest, because there's nowhere to put anything in this tiny place, I went round to mother's and heard the story. Thompson felt J was not doing enough last Christmas, i.e. J was having a good time at school and not reading much. After France last August he said "Thank goodness I'm not going to university" but he has since changed his mind. The three week course at West Kensington was tough and J was very depressed after three days; he later found out there were only three school-leavers on the course and he got the tutor to explain things and passed with flying colours. Edward Moore: "We've never had a beginner who knew so much." Then he was sent on credit to Victoria Station (1 week), Basingstoke (2), Holborn (2) and Wolverton (3) and he has been very depressed: "I've just ticked all day." (One calls, the other ticks.)

Nan went to school; cried briefly on this her first day at Oaklands, but stayed late dancing at the end.

8th November. Went up to London with C to try and change convertible sterling travellers cheques to the value of £560 into dollars. Completely failed at the Hong Kong and Shanghai, Chase Manhattan and the Bank of America because I cannot prove that I am a non-resident; I have no emigration visa on my passport. One can be non-resident for tax purposes, but resident for exchange control.

Went on to the Bank of Japan. Fujimoto, like Kiyooka; Shimamoto, the squirty Japanese who insists on what is convenient for him, and blushes. There I got fixed up for 2/3 classes on a Thursday afternoon, £2 a class. Classes to be on Modern Britain and Europe.

Then I went to Sotheby's, and saw a tall Oxfordy man like Andrew Baring, called Thompson, and a smaller man, called Lawson. My thanka and mandalas are worth £30/£100 if the condition is good and the outside cloth is old. I might make £10 profit on each one, and I should write to my contacts in Nepal to try four.

Observations on London. No one really knows anything (e.g. the bankers). The faces reveal a strange kind of emptiness. As in the case of the pop-singers, their eyes almost have the emptiness of a dreamy love. It's all hippie of course, utterly different from the sharp-eyed penetration you had to have when I was young. Otherwise, the people look so frightful. It is as though there has been a massive degeneration in the national physiognomy. And there are more accents than not.

9th November. Got back to *The Eternicide* (having been off it since September 18th), and found it difficult to concentrate because I am still tired and because there is no room. The electrician came and stood on a chair to read the meters, and did his sums kneeling on the floor, 4 months' standing charge; 4 guineas back on £7.10s – over half. "Yeah, the calibration is too high, but let's leave it till January because electricity's going up this month."

10th November. I have not recorded my meeting with Ezard on Wednesday. We met in the Standard (Loughton); he wore a black corduroy jacket and a blue sweater and had long curly hair. Almost immediately he asked how my writing was going, and said I'd be among the top seven novelists today if I wrote a novel. I told him about my thinking, he told me about being between jobs; he starts on the *Guardian* on Monday. "I've got to the top of a profession I entered by accident" – he went to the *Gazette* office to apply for a post as library assistant. "The library girl you once met found you the most attractive man she'd ever met." I: "Not attractive but different."

Otherwise we talked about saying, etc. He: "You've got something to say – you can count the people who have on one hand. It's a very rare quality." I, in conversation, "All my heroes are Outsiders." One of those flashes of intuitive knowledge that constitute self-knowledge, i.e. surprise at the obvious.

On Saturday I met him again, in the company of Pamela Brett, ex of the *Gazette*. The talk began on *The Quiet American* which was "boring" and later got on to what the younger generation is like. I stuck my chin out and said that in the 1950s everyone's eyes were penetrating into the social surroundings, whereas today they seem rather empty, and that it's Hippie love that's behind it. "Something's snapped in here." They disagreed in a mild sort of way, saying that everything has to be about people and what makes them tick today; and pro-love and anti-war and anti-unemployment. The Love Generation, as I said.

But can you love people in the abstract, or only in particular? (The Greene theme.) Anyhow, the new alertness and tolerance. The rest of the time we talked about religion, beginning with the new romantic interest in Yoga as something mysterious; going through Nothing and the after-life. Ezard's Wittgensteinian attitude towards "the meaning of life"; which comes from Cambridge. Kingsley, and the 1960s world which Ezard and I helped (in 1958) to bring in.

Ezard's friend Leslie is now a surgeon and is still writing.

12th November. On Saturday evening (before Ezard) I went to Oaklands for the fireworks. Nan stood on the iron fence. The sparklers, the rocket that dived over the far hedge and hit a cyclist. Rob Edwards joking about Japan ("The Rising Sun"). The peacock tails and scarecrows in the wind, while I watched through a hawthorn bush.

Afterwards, coffee and juice and bangers in the tennis courts, and Miss Lord dragging a box of crisps across the hardcourt ground. Afterwards, to the school, and upstairs to a room I have not been in for 20 years. I felt old.

13th November. I drove C over to Dulwich. Went out to the Crown and Greyhound with C.

14th November. Spent the morning working on the novel and the evening typing it and writing letters to the U.S. In the afternoon visited Argie. She was in bed in her back room, and she told us she wants to have the windows replaced by modern ones.

On Lucy. Her visit to Ireland with Argie. "Of course I don't have the view." Her visit to Scarborough. She (Lucy) took her mink stoll and her emerald dressing table set because she was afraid she'd be burgled in her absence, and the lot was taken when her suitcase was whipped from the boot. Argie to the police, "This is not serious, I haven't broken any limbs and material possessions are unimportant." On Lucy "They're her god." "She paid lip-service to my idea, but did not agree with it deep down." Her (Lucy's) psychiatrist. Why can't she sleep in the dark – is it a childhood neurosis, or is it self-loathing and guilt, i.e. inability to be by herself? Just as self-loathing people have accidents, so self-hating people imagine burglars or fear the silence and have to put the radio on during the day, as Lucy does.

Three walks in the forest among falling leaves. The copper beech leaves underfoot, and the sun through the trees, and later the moon, like a yellow balloon. Those obsessive falling leaves, a generation dying one after another.

15th November. From yesterday, a programme on dying. "In dying you can become a person," said the matron of one hospital for the dying. The challenge of death, finding a way of accepting it and transcending it, becoming a person through it, living at a more intense level. I think the actual moment of death must be a painless, even pleasant thing. Like going to sleep when you're very very tired. So many have died, and the last breath does not seem to be painful in natural death: witness dying in your sleep.

Mother's story on Mrs. Lee. She visited her on her 94th birthday, because Argie couldn't go. She said "I'm sorry, I don't know you dear." And kept repeating it. So mother reminisced and said she lived next to Dr Mautner, etc. In the end, "Oh you're not Mrs. Broadley's sister are you?" Mother thought, "Near enough." Then Mrs. L asked after Rob and Nadi.

This is very revealing of the nature of the memory: one idea opens the way to everything else, because the memory is stored in clusters, and as soon as one cell lights up, the others do too. So, in writing this *Diary*, I could not remember what happened on Monday until I remembered "Dulwich". Labels....When the memory fails like this, as in the case of Mrs. Lee – is dying the bringing to birth of a person then? The answer is No. One must die at the right time, that is the point. Death the bringer-to-birth.

I am reminded of Nan. The night I returned from my travels she asked, "Will you grow old and will you die?" I could not answer. "Will I die?" I: "Not for a long time, and then you'll go to heaven." She, sceptically "Where's heaven, I don't know about heaven. You get dead and go under the earth." A child's vision is very true. The curse of deception is a thing one learns, and I could only deceive her, I could not allow her to live in the melancholy way I do, not in the years of innocence. For me, death is an undoer-of-birth. Hence my despair.

16th November. Wednesday. The conflict between a homosexual old priest and a young scientist. They are kept respectful by the age barrier, and neither is nervous with the other. The priest is exhausted, F is energetic....The man behind the ideas then, is an egoist, and he will be polite to the priest, his elder. The priest pursues F partly because he wants to kill the old doubt in himself, and partly because he sees F as a new generation that he must come to terms with. Mainly, I think, because he wants to prove F mistaken. An old man trying to prove that a young man is mistaken, and wrongly being aware of the indignity of the situation – that is the basis of the relationship between the priest and F.

18th November. On Friday afternoon, visited Miss Reid. Her near blindness (cataracts). She chattered and played with Nan, embarrassed by me; asked a lot of questions and complained about the deep ray treatment she has five days a week and which is very painful. "I have Saturday and Sunday off. It's irritating being stuck here, I'm very energetic normally." She is going to Gloucester for Christmas and then she will be O.K....When we got back, C discovered that two pairs of her bloomers and one pair of Nan's frilly "duckers" ("knickers") had been taken from the line, clothes pegs and all: and yet my mauve "with-it" shirt (4 guineas) had not been touched. To the police, over the phone, I said "It's clearly a fetishist." He: "Yeah, a fascist."

On Saturday. Took C to the Washeteria and had tea at Journey's End afterwards and asked after Miss Moulton. Mother: "She's dead." She broke her leg twice and her sister had her toes cut off, then the foot, then the leg amputated, last November. Miss Moulton had never had any responsibility, and this June she began wandering in the street and getting up in the middle of the night, thinking it was day. She was put in Whipps Cross hospital, and, because she was taking up a good bed and was only there because of (Mr) Oatley, she was transferred to Claybury. She was remote and answered questions politely, "Yes, quite all right thank you," and spent all day counting, but she never got beyond 1300, and went downhill and died the day before C got home. She was cremated and then had a memorial service. She was a school friend of Mrs. Rhodes's.

Mr Llewellyn is also dead. Mrs. L nearly died in Argie's car. She'd been up for treatment at the London and Argie got her back to the house and she died that night. Then Mr L "hung up his hat to Argie," but Argie felt she couldn't have Grannie and Mr L. He then married a merry widow called Peter Pan and lived in Clacton. It was a question of whether he or his brother would die first, and he did; his brother died six weeks later.

Also Herbie Burrows. He had the decorators in and he said to his wife "I'll be back to help you clear up" and he was found slumped over his office desk in his coat and hat. He'd just sat down on getting in. Perry is a chartered accountant, Bedwell has had a stroke.

In the evening mother came and baby-sat and we went and watched *Wuthering Heights*, the last instalment. It was not good. TV is a realistic thing, and the atmosphere of the novel is in the prose style, and the borderline between life and death seemed stagey and unconvincing. I prefer radio to TV when it comes to doing novels. There is so much more room for imagination: "No Bill, not the club Bill," is one of the most evocative memories of both my childhood and Rob's. Later went and drank in the Standard with C....

Quoted a judgement on the radio, that writers in advance of their time are always hated; also the old idea that prophets find no honour in their own land. I may be going schizophrenic, but I believe this now, and I believe that I must just carry on and complete what I have to complete. When my time catches up with me, I will win recognition, and recognition is not important to me now; and if it is important, it is important for all the wrong reasons.

"Young man everywhere," as Rilke put it. ("Profit from the fact that nobody knows you.")

19th November. Went to lunch at Journey's End, and spent lunch discussing yesterday's 14.3% devaluation. Rob had no sense of attitude. When I said, "There's a short-term view that devaluation reduces the number who will have to be unemployed," Rob cut in very angrily and noisily, "But Nick, that's rubbish," and so on. (F: "Keep your voice down.") I: "I did not say I agree with this view, I did not express my attitude to it, I merely said there was this short-term view. In fact I take the long-term view, that it's part of our decline."

20th November. I wrote and in the afternoon a man from the NMLAS (National Mutual Life Assurance Society) called Buckingham came. He had a red Shavian beard and announced at the beginning that he'd had too much beer for lunch. He was supposed to be telling me how I could get a pension at 65, and in the end we did agree that I'd have to assure £2,000 now (annual payment £63) and another £2,000 in 10 years time (additional annual payment £81) and that together these policies would bring in just under £10,000, i.e. £10 a week for 20 years after 65.

Otherwise he told me about his time with the air force, fighting the Communists in Malaysia and blowing up bombs. Also about his wife. They have lost a child and she works. Their rent and rates come to £41 a month in Hampstead. He was a broker before he went into insurance. He was earning £2,000-3,000 a year but was working 105 hours a week. He now earns £1,300 but has a car. "I don't want to live in this country, I pay one third of my salary in tax. I want to go to Geneva."

22nd November. Spent Tuesday in London. Mr Nakata and Mr Sato, four hours between the two. Shabby white curtains stretched between top and bottom of the windows, and underneath, Speaker's Corner and Hyde Park and Marble Arch and the Cumberland.

On to the British Council. Arrived early and saw Miss Davidson, all rosy-cheeked and embarrassed, and the dreaded Meixner, a tall rather aggressive girl with shoulder-length hair parted down the middle, a mini-skirt and boots.

After that, went into Prescott in room 117B. Prescott, a meek Collcutt, began by explaining the Council system. I said I'd been to Iraq and Japan. "Oh, so you'd know." He then explained that it was impossible to say what posts were coming up where as not all candidates let the Council know before March. I: "I regret to say I'm one of them." After that I told him about China and the U.S. and Japanese tax. He: "In a way you needn't have come today, and I'm afraid you won't have learnt anything."

Spent Wednesday on my novel.

23rd November. Went to MITI and the Bank of Japan. In between walked near the Salisbury and went in and had shepherds pie and beer....The antique dealer, the girl with her arm in a sling. In the evening, when I was exhausted, Frank phoned. Will meet him on Monday or Tuesday. Watched a rather nervous Wilson on TV, then slept.

24th November. Wrote. In the afternoon Flo came. Mother: "Nick still hasn't got any clothes because of the dock strike." Flo: "Oh, I expect he'd look gorgeous, you know, with his fig-leaf." She had blue hair and as we went out to the car, C telling her about the theft from the washing-line, Flo said "How infuriating, I expect they're like these aren't they?" and pulled up her skirt to reveal her bloomers. This was for my benefit. C: "It's to shock."...We do the opposite of what we are. Life is a perpetual tension between being and doing, between who we are and how we try to deny it.

25th November. After a wearying morning on the novel, went for a drive in the afternoon and pinched firewood from the forest: whole armfuls of logs and bushwood. Had tea at Journey's End, in the course of which I was asked if I would speak to (a) Parents Association on China. I: "No." Reasons: no one is interested in things outside England, not in the provinces, and it would be pointless....Mother: "Oh no, that's a generalisation." Whereupon J let loose ("I went once and it was a waste of an evening, I was bored to death, no one was interested in the speaker") and I let loose on a certain expression on the English face, the stand-offish look down the nose of bourgeois....To my surprise mother agreed, and even said it was coming to a revolution: the Welsh liberation army; the fact that no one can have a party without a gang of 100 gatecrashing and smashing all the windows and coshing heads if they aren't let in; the wrecked telephone kiosks; the decay in education, accent no longer mattering and everyone being dragged down.

Later still J drove me home and said, "I must inscribe on my wall 'I will not go into the System'," showing that he is a convert of mine. Later still C and I sat and discussed Tom and John – John being a JP now. C: "All these provincials are eager to serve on committees because they're outside London, they haven't quite made it. Being a JP or being on a committee is a status symbol – it's class in the end. The middle class suffer from it most, because they are a class who have never made it. We used to live next to a working class family that was rich and owned a chain of stores, and they never tried to pretend they were 'better' than they were, and nor does the upper class – they don't serve on committees."

An image for the artist I forgot to record: an oyster. For a grain of dirt enters its shell and irritates it, and self-protectively it converts it into a pearl. Creation out of pain.

27th November. On Sunday evening, with J, after the Nixons' visit to put up prison bars in the windows. Made notes on the Revolution....It will be a central revolution, neither leftist nor rightist; one aiming at changing the whole structure of British society, which has failed; one also designed to solve the leisure problem in an automated age, basing all values on the individual. The following must be changed.

1. Money and capitalism; into a units system, whereby you get houses and cars for units earned and accumulated, i.e. profit, but whereby incentive units help you get these things quickly.
2. There must be a land revolution with a maximum of 10 acres per private dwelling.
3. The State and bureaucracy; these will be replaced by 12 provinces (districts) that will only be under Whitehall control as regards financial aid and foreign policy. Tax will be related to units and amount, i.e. the more you put in, the less tax you pay.
4. The power complex. No post in the 12 or the centre can be held for more than one year, to give all citizens a chance. Ostracism is to be revived.
5. Education; every adult must put in the equivalent of 3 years' evening university in 5 subjects before 65; units being the incentive.
6. Christianity; to be replaced by my cells of 10, for knowledge of self and society.
7. Bourgeoisism; everyone must earn 5 contribution coupons a month (meals on wheels, committees) and these earn units.
8. Law; a new code, and punishments geared to loss of units/working for society.
9. The Welfare State; this is to be run on a district basis with an annual competition that earns units for every member of the winning district. Patients pay 1-3 units per month, doctors get units per consultation.
10. The people; each district will have a central forum with statues and the library/leisure services will be there, and earn units.
11. Work; units are given for the amount not time, and a skilled manual worker does a maximum of 4 hours a day and earns units for leisure activities; all mental workers must do 1 hour unskilled work a day. Bonuses?
12. Monarchy; abolished for a republic.

The aim of this 12-point plan is to create an entirely new System, non-capitalist, non-Communist, tying profits to work. Otherwise, within the system everyone is free not to accumulate units, and democracy is increased if anything, because more people have a say in the running of the country's affairs. All this to be pushed through by Parliamentary means.

28th November. And on Monday came de Gaulle's second veto, making this system more of a possibility by making the Common Market more remote; and this sort of platform would only be accepted if we declined in solitude, aiming at a technological future: nuclear power, neo-plastics, automation and fast transport, and no influence at all.

I learnt of the veto on the tube as I was going to meet Tuohy at the Salisbury. He'd been to a Bunuel, "The girl's just like Caroline." We sat in the backroom of the Salisbury and talked, he about driving and his village and about the death of the Council scholar who stayed with him, from nephritis; Baker's daughter is marrying an "undertaker" (Tuohy), i.e. underwriter at Lloyds; "Tomlin's manuscript, he told a London mistress, was pinched from his hotel in Kyoto, this being a lie to cover up the fact that the theft from his house was by a mistress, i.e. Tomlin keeping the mistresses apart." He has been working on a novel (?) he began before he left Japan, does not seem to have written one on Japan: "I toyed with the idea of doing one on Tomlin getting Kirkup killed." The conversation was inevitably bitty, and he has not changed: waistcoaty and glasses subsiding to the gentle.

We went on to the Yorkminster, which has a tactless notice by de Gaulle on the wall, and then round the corner to an Italian restaurant, the Capannina where we had duck/pigeon/chicken and wine. He told me about his meeting with Hartley, about his snobbishness and how the late Lord Hilton had got better since the war and about Portugal and so on, but we never really got to grips on England. He paid for the meal and we then walked to the Wheatsheaf, Maclaren Ross's old haunt, and thence to Tottenham Court Road station.

I called in at Journey's End and had a long argument with Rob over revolutions, he saying it's a good idea and requesting further details. As a result I couldn't sleep. Tuohy has that effect on you – he heightens your awareness and makes sleep impossible – and I went to work this morning literally not having shut my eyes, and somehow got through four hours of classes.

1st December. On myself, after a long time off it. There are at least two people in me: a reactionary and a revolutionary. The reactionary's vision prevailed in *The Death-Fires* and the revolutionary's vision prevailed in *The Noddies*....Which is me, God only knows; that was the struggle in the poem that is the sequel to *The Silence*. The reactionary is religious, the revolutionary is iconoclastic and long-haired and scornful of all established ways of thought, including Christianity. It is something of a romantic; it goes to China and Saigon, and wants to get into VC territory in Vietnam, whereas the reactionary merely wants to write. And I must rein in on the revolutionary, without denying it full expression I must rein in on it; for the reactionary is the artist in me, and the artist and the revolutionary are as distinct as the poet and the dreamer.

What matters to a part of me now is form and structure, and the other part that deals in the structure of society is an extroverted projection from the basically artistic concern. Politics are a projection, for me, I must never forget that; I am fundamentally an artist, as I am fundamentally married. This self-division connects with my view of the novel, my theory of fiction. For all my characters are divided characters, and there is a perpetual dialectic in their souls as struggle leads to choice. Perhaps it is here that my voice is to be found; and perhaps I should concentrate on this.

Odds and ends: "Tynan's two opposites, the dandy and the leftist. I wouldn't want the two reconciled because that's Tynan – would anyone else?" Answer: Yeats. Cf C. Day Lewis: "Some things are unwritable about, because they're removed from feelings; like Government cuts or the Common Market."

2nd December. In the afternoon went to the forest and walked near the winding stream. Came home, Nan grizzling and feverish, and had tea. Later went to the Owl, and heard from the publican that Mrs. Darby of Fairmead died four months ago. Mother thought cancer. The house was built specially for her by her builder husband, so that she could go in and out easily. Is she buried in the forest church, where she was on the flower roster?

Mother was at school with Zelda McAlpine, Bill's sister? She was bottom of the class, like the Blackwall Tunnel twins: a "third generation clerk" (Mrs. Barron quoting Sir John Sims).

3rd December. To lunch at Journey's End, I deaf in my left ear, which is swollen inside. Over lunch R mentioned Susan Hampshire's word-blindness, mother mentioned Galsworthy (she having starred in that) and I got onto Galsworthy's values and how he ended up being on the side of the bourgeois and liking an order that had already passed away.

4th December. Went to the Great Peter Street Salvation Army doss-house. It looks like a barracks in three storeys, and there is a modern building opposite with two cranes on top. You go in by St. Ann's Street, a redbrick affair that has a church. There's a "stable" and you turn right in a kind of portico and, while men sit desolately or drink tea in the yard, you inquire of the receptionist behind glass. His order book, the notice at the back, in yellow on red: "Bed Book Office". Then "An official form of identity MUST be shown by all booking in. Please state surnames and Christian names. Date of birth. Dormitory Bed Prices 6/- a day, 37/6d a week." A Scotsman answers you behind glass, and you can't hear properly. 6/- includes bed and breakfast.

There is a notice inside the stable door, "Sorry – Hostel full", and if all the Hostels are full you go to the Reception Centre, Gordon Road, Peckham. They stay permanently or a week or so, and no one cares if they don't turn up, though if they've booked their bed for a week, it's kept for them. The meals are cheap: 2/- for peas, potatoes and meat; 6d for rhubarb and custard; 4d for tea. The upstairs is open after 6, and the man in charge is called "Manager". His name is Brigadier Moore. "Jus' the Brigadier."

AN ARTIST-THINKER: TRUTH AND VISION, GOD (1967)

On the way out I thought I'd get a reaction from one of the inmates, and I followed an old man in a tatty overcoat and beret after he'd turned right down St. Ann's Street. "Excuse me," I said, and he shouted at me, in Italian I think it was, something about "Non parlare" the English. It was his tone and manner that made me sad: I was an enemy to him, because of my overcoat and my lavender shirt and my black bag and my shiny shoes, I could not fraternise with him. I came away with a determination to put on old clothes and have lunch in that canteen with its tables and despair; also to spend a night in the Peckham doss-house. I must also find out what official form of identity has to be shown. (Insurance card?)

6th December. On the family. John (b1867, April 16) and George (b 1870, Mar 11) started the tailoring business. Their father was Benjamin, and he must have been born about 1840. Benjamin was a Methodist minister. His wife was a Nettleton (Charlotte?) and they were a family of farmers. In 1910, or around then, he travelled down from Macclesfield to baptise, or christen, Flo – Argie can remember that.

I am not sure whether I have recorded it, but on Monday mother brought a drawer of photos round, and there was one of mother's father and George sitting on the beach, and George looked just like J. I wonder if that was when Lucy sat on the railings, at Eastbourne, and Harold picked her up. There was also a photo of Tom, the RFC volunteer who died like Robert Gregory, and to my horror, he looked just like JP John. I...understood why J is divided between art (me) and business (George).

The next day, Thursday, mother took C shopping and C asked her what sized stockings she took. In the course of her reply mother said "Dad" (her word) "used to buy me the most expensive kind – 25/- with embroidered tops. I used to go back and change them without his knowing, change them for 5 pairs." C: "I thought how like your mother – very practical; but how nice of your father to want to buy her the best." She also said it was a pity he has no grave. "He just disappeared – I'd always bury your ashes somewhere."

7th December. At the Bank of Japan, discussed the new values, following a letter in *The Times* from Jacquetta Hawkes. It said in effect that Lord Reith is of the old generation in finding war fun – he stands for a "personal and national competitiveness and success" and "belligerent national self-interest" whose disastrous results have alienated the young. The young, supposed to be suffering from "moral decay", find the war memoirs of the old "morally offensive", the Hippy love-ideal and voluntary surrender of the Empire constituting for us, a real change of values. So we should make this "deliberate choice of a new direction" known to the world, i.e. presumably cut down on defence and imperialism and retire from the world ("renunciation"). Otherwise, their values balked in an old-value world of pragmatism and consensus, the young will continue to dream of emigration.

I feel there is a lot of truth in this. Our older generation have failed us: they've produced war and economic crisis and wrong attitudes to other human beings, and no matter how bad the new values are, we can only try them, for we must have an alternative.

8th December. Snow. It fell first on Wednesday, but more heavily on Thursday evening, and in the afternoon I went for a long walk in Epping Forest. It was on all the trunks, and the horse-prints were frozen, and the leaves all crunchy, and there was a hot golden sun in my head. The ponds were half ice, half snow on ice, and I drank the cold air as if it were beer. I had ruddy cheeks, I felt bursting with energy, I took great strides in my calf-length mosquito boots. Smack, crunch, crack – on through the forest, a glory, until at last the frosty tiles of the cottages showed through the trees. Nan's imagination. "The snow is saying 'Help help help me fall down'" – that's what she said to me when I asked her what it was doing, and my God, she is right, that is exactly what it is saying.

Later, after typing…, J came, and together we attacked bourgeois life: the fussing, the rushing; the earning money and not being able to spend it (Reg: "people are more interested in making money than in spending it"); the false values if you live their way; the senseless caring about what others think. Argie and mother forgot to put a wreath on Grannie's grave on her birthday this year, and because it is a custom and Miss Walter and Mrs. Hoather would have gone and laid flowers and been shocked, they had to write a letter to each saying that with Argie ill they had been too busy, but would be going. A dying bourgeois custom.

9th December. More snow. Drove over to Dulwich and almost immediately went over to Peckham to search of the Camberwell Reception Centre. I found Gordon Road and first of all went to the Salvation Army. Went back past the railway bridge and there on the left it was: an outhouse looking like a tower guardhouse, and lights on behind pink curtains in Georgian rooms, and spear-railings over the basement. A man asked "What number you looking for" and I went in with him and a family, and found myself lined up to play billiards; in another room there was a children's party. I went outside and looked again at the notice; it said, "Enquiries in Consort Road entrance: first left and first left again." I walked under another bridge and turned left and left and under another bridge – I missed it. I was directed back. It was by the bridge, there was a new brick wall and it was set back.

It looked like a prison under snow. I went to the Enquiries and got shown in to some official who tried to contact the Deputy Warden. Both he and the Warden were at the party. While everyone dithered I pumped them. There are 300+ here, and a number are more or less permanent. When they come in they are asked if they have any money, and if they say they haven't they are marked "destitute". There was no "smell". They sleep in a long dormitory. I could not establish what they have for beds, or what food they are given. (I must ask the Ministry of Social Security.) They have to work until noon. When I came away the snow was falling, and I passed an old tramp shuffling along under the bridge and I looked for my car. The hopelessness.

Later, dinner. M's silence, trying to get you to talk so she can knock you down. My silence. Her techniques: oh but; and if you've been somewhere or are interested in something, "I've got a friend who...." If I had to choose between that tramp under that bridge, and M— if I were God, I know who I would choose.

10th December. A visit to church. I didn't know which book was hymn and which was prayer, and had to stand through the presentation of flags and sing a verse of the national anthem. The hymns and service I found utterly formal and routine and stale; full of words like "dreadful". The only relief was Nan getting a book for her birthday; a small girl who ran riot and offered people books ("Book?") and called "Cuckoo" throughout the prayers. (Vine's child once crawled under the altar.) I came out feeling spiritually deadened, following a patronising direct method talk on Communication and the Indians.

There I was introduced to Mrs. Taylor, who, as DB (Domestic Bursar), apparently took me home after my finger got crushed in the BSI door. (A. O. Dean was sitting in front of me – he must have been head boy then? Bridges – he having acquired a...son, she a husband, I a wife.)

Went to lunch at Journey's End and did not bait Rob. Except over the failure of the older generation and the farce of the war. He: "We didn't go to war over Czechoslovakia or Poland." I: "Ro-ob" Earlier, he: "Frances, what do you make of this?" In the slow, taken-for-granted solicitor's manner.

12th December. A profitable day in London. Went to St. Giles-in-the-Fields and spoke to the deputy verger for half an hour. Got him yarning. After that went to the Lost Property Office (Sales) in the Haymarket and had a long talk with the sandwich man, a talk all about his working conditions and daily routine and past memories. In the end I tipped him half a crown for a drink, and he said "You don't have to do this you know." He was eating out of dustbins and sleeping out and I had an overcoat and a bag, but he still said that.

Later I went to St. Martin-in-the-Fields and had a look in the crypt. Came home footsore and exhausted, my head packed with images and new impressions. Lay on the sofa all evening. I kept willing myself to come through and sit down and write, but my body would not respond.

C on the English. She took some paraffin on a bus and was told to get off, so she went and got on the next bus. "It's a proper little police state." Rob disagreed and said it was very reasonable. C: "He wants to go abroad, he hasn't had enough experience. He doesn't realise how petty everything here is." Which is true. All the running around and urgent talk is, in terms of foreign systems, petty and unimportant. Also on the awfulness of the English. Everyone is complaining, no one enjoys living here, the whole place is so depressing somehow. And there are just too many regulations.

13th December. Things learnt from TV plays. Characters must be strong, i.e. a moaner and a nagger; they must talk in their own distinctive way. Though my "complexity of character" approach does not lend itself easily to such superficial "types". Again, there must be cause and effect. So, a secret is told over champagne, and as a result someone eavesdrops and learns it, and as a result there is a row and a cripple is accused of being mean, and as a result the cripple attempts to escape the house. Again, everything must be action, as in the Muller play, *Death of a Private*. The hero's mistress must *kiss* the pop-singer, he must *knife* her, a soldier must *strike* him, he must be caught *giving* money to his son, he must *jump* off a roof. Action, action, action – something happening, that is the secret of drama.

Mrs. Gray and Mrs. Smith are both 88, but neither will speak to the other because Mrs. Gray is old Indian imperialist, and is a cut above Mrs. Smith; who nearly died this week. She came over, believing Mrs. Foley still lives here, and complained of not feeling well. Mrs. F gave her some brandy. She still thinks she owes C some rent. Mrs. Gray goes out to Hubbards for lunch and then denies she's been out, and sometimes she does not answer the health visitor. Mrs. Curry, the cockney foster mother of two West Indian children, had the key to the commercial storehouse; where we stored the double bed.

14th December. A look back over the year, assimilative. The themes that recur are, the ideal of the unified man (16th February); the growth ideal (5th February); the anti-puritanism (2nd March); the tension between reactionary and revolutionary (1st December); the need to be against the System, which is both decayed and needs progress; opposition to the zeitgeist; the historical themes often inspired by Toynbee; "refuse to accept but never deny the meaninglessness of history" (9th October) and the individual creates a meaning of vision within a meaningless, determined history (19th-21st September); the few being anti-automatism; and certain ideas about England e.g. new values, the decline of the bourgeois, the new honesty, etc.

Last year (8th September and 31st December 1966) I thought my main problem was "Art or Religion or Revolution" and I solved this in the idea of a unity between all three, the centre being the artist. (see November 1966). I think I have become an artist in this last year – witness all the entries on art and my preoccupation with structure and my present ability to finish things. I have not, however, really solved, in my living, the relationship between Religion and Revolution. The growth ideal for the strong has rather been neglected, for "Religion" I express in my poetry, and I have not written much this year. I have moved out of the growth of self into the environment, with my 12-point plan for social revolution (see 27th November) and I express this in my novels. I have solved both problems of Religion and Revolution as ideas – there must be two new movements. I have not solved the balance between them in my living; I act for neither, and I have become more extroverted in the last year, witness the entries on historical and social themes.

I think I was right not to act – I am an artist not an actor; but I have neglected my spiritual side (= the Shadow) because I have neglected poetry. And my art has still not brought me any success. What am I to do about this self-unity – how can I unite myself? Only in an image in a moment of time?

16th December. From 14th December. No, not in an image. In my life and all that I write. For man has religious needs and social needs, needs relating to the self and to the environment, and my unification must be experienced in my heart, behind my temples, not in any artificial image that is "superior" to life. Experienced, but done, achieved? Acted out? On 14th December I wrote "I think I am right not to act" – was I right? For the need is there.

What holds me back? Shyness, my wound – nervousness – and perhaps fear of being thought ridiculous. For the man who sets himself up is ridiculous. Also, character deficiencies. I am not a tub-thumper – I could doubtless make myself into one, but at present I am not. And yet action would be so easy. As regards Revolution it's as easy as posting a letter. As regards Religion, I don't know how I'd launch the movement I suggested to Ricky last summer, a movement possibly to be connected with a school for self-knowledge and self-discovery. But my reflections in August-September 1966 are a pointer for action there. And I felt strongly enough about it then to write to my mother in early September proposing I should do something about it.

For the truth I have to teach is so simple: it is that God is what you search for and never find, God is the unknown, the image that acts as the goal of your quest, which you never achieve; what I have called the Shadow, but also the ultimate mystery of things, the quality which the Shadow possesses: vision in one moment of time of the whole mystery of life and the universe. In short God is an experience of vision that is denied me. Is action a temptation or a call away from art and the self?

19th December. A day in London. The "find the King" episode and "do you want a knife in your throat?"

20th December. The day when the luggage arrived, a day spent unpacking and sorting through papers and throwing away. Books and treasures and papers, and china and toys – these were the main things. Mother came round and was rather bothered by impressions and did not comment.

22nd December. I have not recorded that I wrote a poem, *A Poet Reads the Fire*, on Tuesday evening. This will go in 50 lyrics I plan to do; to be called *Fiore del Morte*, the death-flowers. These poems must accentuate vividness and death and artistic logic and form. They must gleam with a brilliant freshness, and stick to the homely and the everyday. They must raise the deep questions of human existence and the human condition in everyday terms. They must wrest truths out of the sockets of a skull.

Images to become poems: a body rejecting an organ it doesn't recognise as being its own, even though the organ will save the body (i.e. immunology); the wind blew the water across the pond, my heart was a frost-trodden; the wind sent the water flickering, my heart was frost-trodden snow (i.e. about the reflection, and my mind). Repetition, the power of repetition. Compare the formula for all plays: meeting (= introduction) – development (= change from the seeds in the beginning) – conclusion (= goodbye). An image: Fair Isle three tone knitted pattern.

Otherwise David Frost and the triviality of an English Christmas party: paper hats and crackers and riddles and lots of comments about dressed up geese – "Oh, they're very fine geese"; how I hate it all. Just as I deliberately wrecked M's whispering game here at Dulwich, by talking across it.

24th December. A visit to Dulwich, after Nan had been to church with Grannie and I had returned her to Journey's End.

25th December. Slept until 8.15 and consequently could not go to the carol service Grannie had tried to persuade me to go to. Opened presents. Nan's scooter, cot, hobby-horse, etc. from dozens of people.

To lunch at Journey's End. A giant turkey, things like bread sauce and cranberry sauce; and champagne. Plum pudding with sixpences in it. Afterwards, presents in the lounge. Then Nan's cries, while I gave F a class. How to work backwards when writing an essay; get the development of the central idea first, then mention this in the introduction. Afterwards tea. Cake and chocolate biscuits, without the little red men, the trumpeter-cake decorations. Discussion of the Queen's speech. Her listlessness, the lack of form of the speech.

26th December. Went round to Journey's End for a Boxing Day lunch: cold turkey….Later, at tea, Rob said: "Vine must get fed up with communion over Christmas, for 61 at 7, for 80 at 8." I: "Remember Bickford," and priests are as dependent on "meaning" ("feeling") as poets….R said: "Vine is a very interesting speaker. If you hear him." I: "I heard him last summer, he denounced the congregation and told them their reading of the *Bible* was perfunctory and shallow. I agree. I know the *Bible* better than most regular church-goers. I've been doing a lot of work on Penguin scholarship. You know, every verse in the *Bible* has been dated, and all the references to the resurrection are 250AD whereas a lot of the rest is 100-150AD. Rob nodded. And there's the bit in the *Sunday Times* supplement about "virgin" being "young woman." A mistranslation. Later I said, "And Jesus had brothers and sisters according to the *Bible*," so that's anti-Catholic....I: "Anyway, Christianity needs to be de-mythologised. That includes the ceremony."

29th December. A programme on robots that shows what Faraday is trying to do. At present a mechanical engineer can make a mould of a person in plastic and metal (the "Sin 1" of the Stanford Research Institute, California). This is to train student anaesthetists, and the level is of a person on the operating table about to go to sleep; it moves its eyeballs and has reflexes, but nothing else. Its actions are picked up by electronic sensors and a computer analyses them, and the operator can ask for a print-out of every action that's been taken since the beginning of the operation. It is fully programmed – you don't need to press a button.

31st December. Taking stock. It has been a disappointing year in many ways, but I am more confident than ever before that I am destined for greatness; though it may take me at least another 12 years before I even begin to get across. Last year I rebuilt myself and deepened myself, this year I have fulfilled pledge two of last year – I have gone into the history of Western civilisation and I have decided finally about pattern, and Toynbee. Otherwise I have developed myself as an artist. I have moved from the unshapen poems and stories to the shape of *The Noddies* and now of *The Eternicide*; a shape in which ideas are a part of the pattern, and not ends in themselves.

This year, the artist and thinker in me have come together, and that is a thing of enormous importance. It is the answer to the question of last 31st December, "Art or Religion?" but I still feel I could act more on religion and revolution (see December 14th and 16th). (This is an escape, 2nd January 1967). The Artist ideal of uniting these (see last December 31st) is no nearer, but I no longer write, "I cannot really think about this until I am an Artist."

What I must do now is go all out for my own voice, my own slime. I must look at what is me as opposed to anyone else, and that means writing in the way I have already written and paying attention to the stock Hagger themes: perfection, striving, meaning, love and death. I must also concentrate on conflict and self-division.

What I must remember for 1968: find my own voice.

BIBLIOGRAPHY

(Books referred to in *Awakening to the Light*)

BAZIN, Germain, *A Concise History of Art*, Thames and Hudson, UK, 1961

DOSTOEVSKY, *Notes from Underground* or *Letters from the Underworld*, translated by David Magarshack, Everyman, J. M. Dent, UK, 1957

JAMES, William, *The Varieties of Religious Experience*, Fontana, Collins, UK, 1960

JUNG, *Modern Man in Search of a Soul*, Routledge and Kegan Paul, UK, 1962

NIETZSCHE, *Thus Spake Zarathustra*, Everyman, J. M. Dent, UK, 1946

OUSPENSKY, P. D., *In Search of the Miraculous*, Routledge and Kegan Paul, UK, 1964

TOYNBEE, Arnold, *A Study of History*, vols 1-12, OUP, UK, 1962

TOYNBEE, Arnold, *A Study of History*, 2 vols, abridged by D. C. Somervell, Dell, New York, 1965

WILSON, Colin, *Beyond the Outsider*, Arthur Barker, UK, 1965

INDEX

INDEX

Belgian Ambassadress 454
Belgium 230, 302, 303, 354, 406, 454, 521
Belgrade 557
Belinsky 220
Bellow 141, 237
Belsen 144
Belville, Lord Hercy 504
Ben (dog) 380, 539
Ben (cousin) 49
Ben Bulben 325
Benedict, Ruth 536
Benedicte 305
Benedictine 40
Benedictus 327
Benelux 30
Benghazi 457, 469
Benito Careno (Lowell) 465
Benjamin 476, 569
Benkei 500
Benten 336
Beowulf 489
Berbheirau 555
Berdyayev 110
Bergman 80, 171, 281
Bergson 91, 93, 233, 242, 379
Berkeley 60, 466
Berlin 302, 303, 331, 336, 452
Bernina 503
Besford 405, 507, 509, 511
Betjeman 127, 391
Betty 498
Between Ormuzd and Ahriman 31
Beyond Good and Evil (Nietzsche) 214
Beyond the Fringe 375
Beyond the Outsider (Wilson) 173
Bible 301, 319, 476, 574, 575
Bickford 143, 574
Bickley, Verner 353, 373, 385, 388, 401, 426,
    444, 445, 473, 477, 480, 493, 527, 528
Bickley, Mrs. 401, 444, 473, 480, 527, 528
Bien Hoa 548, 549
Big Ben 306, 311
Big Brother 258
Big Buddha 73, 80, 169
Biggs-Davison, Sir John MP 40, 463
Bingham, Charlotte 504
Black Armband for a Teddy Bear (Hagger) 399
Black Magic 85
Blackwall Tunnel 568
Blake 37, 62, 63, 76, 207, 208, 231, 233, 234,
    235, 238, 291, 312, 320, 349, 370, 407,
    416, 471, 490, 537
Blakean Romantics 490
Blakean Spectre 490
Bleating Sheep (Hagger) 443
Blighty (Hagger) 116, 303, 309, 313, 314, 354,
    358, 359, 397, 496
Bliss, Sir Arthur 100
Blood and New Potatoes (Hagger) 402
Bloody Mary 506
Bloody Tower 318
Blue Mosque 556
Blue Movies and Skim Milk (Hagger) 380
Blue Peter 458
Blunden, Edmund 70, 90, 95, 230, 298, 306, 312,
    313, 328, 361, 404, 445
Blyth, R. H. 96, 98, 101, 129, 177
BOAC 727 254, 437, 441, 445
Board of Trade 470

Bodländer 132
Body of the Idea 22
Boer 384
Bognor 102, 318, 319, 322, 502
Bohemian 393, 558
Bolivia 71, 521
Bologna 428
Bolt 378, 516
Bombay 437, 441
Bon 494
Bonaparte 558
Bonas 297
Bond, James 359, 488
Bond Street 449
Bonn 425
Bonn-Paris Axis 430
Book of Urizen (Blake) 233
Borgia, Cesare 506
Borneo 541
Bosch 448
Bosnia 230
Botah 77
Bothwell 506
Botticelli 416, 448
Bottrall 95
Boulevard 543
Boyce, Alec (Tokyo University of Education) 59,
    401, 511
Boys' Brigade 99
BP 6
Bradbury, Jill 22, 23, 36, 43, 312, 327, 328, 331,
    351, 362
Brady 278, 282, 283, 296, 322, 383
Brahma 551
Brahman 33
Brahmin 554
Brammah 354, 527
Braque 402
Brave New World 377
Brazil 473, 492
Brearley, Mr 96
Breath Smelling of Violets (Hagger) 374
Brecht 41, 277
Breen, Michael 325
Brentano 349, 365
Brest 302, 331, 332
Bretall 83
Brewer 450, 474
Brickdale, Francis 107
Bridges 132, 140, 538, 571
Brink, David 307
Brinton 373
Brisbane 438
Bristol 557
Britain 131, 144-45, 148, 167, 180, 191, 204,
    217, 220, 235-36, 238, 243, 255, 258-59,
    263-64, 267-70, 274, 278-79, 292, 298-
    300, 303, 305-307, 309, 316, 318-19, 332,
    341, 343, 347-49, 365-67, 369-70, 384,
    386, 397, 399, 400, 405-408, 410, 412, 414,
    422-23, 428, 440, 442, 444, 446-47, 453,
    456, 459-60, 463, 465, 469-70, 477, 492,
    496, 508-509, 518-20, 527, 532, 534-36,
    539-40, 557, 559
Britain, Modern 144, 146
Britain, New 150
Britain Today 348
Britain's Shadow 377
Britannia 138, 222, 229, 251, 312

580

INDEX

581

INDEX

Chowringhee Road 554
Christ 8, 26, 27, 31, 39, 46, 90, 103, 111, 112,
    116, 120, 121, 141, 168, 184, 195, 217,
    218, 221, 228, 231, 258, 262, 263, 267,
    271, 328, 333, 334, 354, 383, 389, 409,
    419, 439, 505, 506, 509, 544, 545
Christ, (Spanish) 544
Christ Recrucified (Kazantzakis) 84
Christian Society 293
Christian West 20
Christianity 5, 8, 20, 35, 38, 39, 43, 45, 48, 57,
    59, 64, 79, 86, 93, 99, 108, 114, 116, 117,
    119, 120, 141, 142, 143, 149, 155, 169,
    179, 181, 201, 203, 208, 213, 216, 221,
    228, 229, 231, 233, 241, 254, 263, 264,
    269, 271, 279, 288, 291, 327, 345, 349,
    364, 370, 383, 385, 395, 404, 407, 408,
    409, 410, 413, 416, 419, 430, 445, 486,
    506, 513, 566, 567, 575
Christmas 311
Christmas Carol (Dickens) 103
Christogenesis 379, 389
Christologist 54
Christopher 321
Chung, Mr and Mrs 255, 257
Chunnel 299
Church 103, 111, 168, 169, 229, 264, 293, 318,
    322, 327, 383, 400, 407, 416, 420, 423,
    461, 462, 467, 468, 519
Church Hill 306
Church Women's Guild 519
Churchill, Sir Winston 30, 141 226, 230, 341,
    368, 378, 432, 465, 526
Chuzenji 497
CIA 252, 473, 521, 522, 548, 550
Cinderella 8
City 99
City Hall 547
City-life 99
Civil War 311, 326, 404
civilisation 107, 110, 114, 119, 123
Civitas Dei (or *City of God*; St. Augustine) 119
Clacton 563
Claire 35
Clare 68, 70, 306, 313
Claremorris 325
Clarence, 48
Clark, Beverley 522
Classicism 109, 113, 242
Claybury 563
Clays 314, 396
Clayton 251
Clough 68
Clov 208
Club 440
Clutterbuck 318
Clyde 304
Coal Hill 260, 261
Coalmining Department 470
Coates, Mrs. 38
Cobham 319
Cocteau 8, 167
Coedès 496
Cognac 224
COI 154, 158
Colchester 351
Cold War 301
Coleridge, Samuel Taylor 14, 25, 54, 136, 296,
    416

Colet 421
Coline 80
Colisseum 549
Collcutt 109, 295, 385, 426, 442, 444, 445, 564
College 9, 448
Collick, Martin 113, 389
Collooney Bridge 325
Cologne Cathedral 417
Colombia 492
Colombo 380
Columbus 506
Comfort 220
Commodus 326
Common Market 407, 422, 440, 494, 496, 566,
    568
Commonwealth 141, 236, 309, 401, 463, 465,
    467
Commune 262
Communication 571
Communism 32, 65, 148, 216, 218, 236, 250,
    256, 257, 258, 270, 272, 303, 305, 313,
    314, 347, 403, 407, 408, 409, 458, 530,
    532, 545, 546, 554, 557, 564
Communist Party of India 554
Community Association 518
Community Centre 48
Como 504
Concluding Unscientific Postscript (Kierkegaard)
    211, 212
Concord 423, 481, 510
Concorde 558
Concreteness 470
Coney 458
Coney Hatch 70
Confessions of a Rationalist (Hagger) 44
Confucius 263
Congo 106, 110, 376, 454, 521
Congress of Vienna 558
Connecticut University 245
Connolly, James 65
Connolly, John 324
Conquest 184, 275
Conrad, Josef 110 172, 174, 219, 233, 277, 338,
    424, 480
Conservative 305, 477
Conservative Public Opinion Poll 36
Constantinople 459
Contemplator 363
Continent 43, 147, 152
Continental 147, 548
Coole House 325
Coole Park 324
Coomber, Mrs. 396
Cooper, Mrs. 559
Copenhagen 270
Corbett 297
Corbett, Harry H. 135, 142
Corday, Charlotte 450
Coreggio 448
Corinthian 315, 333
Coriolanus (Shakespeare) 63
Cornhill 436
Coronation Street 246
Corpus Christi 305
Cortazzi 68, 516
Corvo 40, 41, 254
Council of Europe 30
Counter-Renaissance 93
Cours Saint Louis 214, 501

583

INDEX

INDEX

INDEX

INDEX

Milward (see Father Milward)
Mimesis (Auerbach) 102, 107, 108
Mina 11
mind 121, 122, 129
Ming 257, 259, 260, 261
Minister (Methodist) 5
Ministry of Education 107, 148, 260, 444
Ministry of Finance 378
Ministry of Health 310
Ministry of Interior 552
Ministry of International Trade and Industry (see also MITI) 273, 360
Ministry of Social Security 571
Minobe 443, 451, 454
Minsk 301, 302
Minutes like a Mutter (Hagger) 405
Misaki 458
Mishima 274
Mission Fair 519
Mississipi 358
Mita 473
MITI 272, 273, 296, 360, 365, 385, 407, 422, 425, 429, 430, 432, 442, 448, 463, 469, 470, 487, 496, 502, 504, 509, 513, 523, 565
Mitsubishi 156, 264
Mitsui Club 347
Mitsukoshi 537, 538
Mitya 218
Miyajima 76, 101
Miyamoto 340
Miyawaki, Aiko 467, 471, 472
Miyazawa 470
Modern Age 420
Modern Britain 227, 362
Modern Britain and Europe 560
Modern Man in Search of a Soul (Jung) 107, 147
Modernisation 127
Modernism 106, 109, 124, 125, 162
Modernist 124, 126, 136, 162, 184, 187, 192, 407, 418, 419
Moderns 184
Mods 6
Moghul 556
Mohammed 112, 267, 274, 461
Moldavia 483
Mole 434
Moll Flanders (Defoe) 217
Mombusho 139, 508, 510
Mongol Khans 459
Mongols 452, 459, 541
Monist 71
Monmothshire 443
Mont Orgeuil 31
Montaigne 35, 93
Montgomery 47
Monument to a Phoney (Hagger) 392, 393, 449
Moore, Brian 338
Moore, Brigadier 568
Moore, Edward 559
More, Sir Thomas 410, 420, 421, 504, 516
Morita, Miss 77
Moritani 125
Morocco 493
Morrison, Jock 453, 498, 500
Morrison, Mrs. 453
Mortimer 434
Morton, Dr. 94, 151, 152, 154, 169, 170, 207, 208, 236, 393, 441, 463, 465, 499, 504, 505, 511, 515, 535, 537

Moscow 225, 270, 301, 302, 303, 332, 333, 343, 547
Moses 454, 487
Moslems 547, 556
Mosley 316, 527
Mother Earth 554
Mott Street 306
Mottram, V.H. 61
Moulton, Miss 470, 563
Mount Bandai 71
Mount Fuji (see also Fuji) 95, 139
Moussorgsky 3
Movement 97, 124, 218, 282, 286, 311, 357, 358, 410, 418, 527
Mozambique 521
Mozart 60, 241
Mr Bleaney (Larkin) 212
Muggeridge 531
Muir 163
Muller 539, 572
Mulligans 324
Multiple Personality 137
Mumfords 452
Munekata 57, 78, 79, 101, 103, 173, 178, 386
Munich University 92
Murata, Mrs. 420
Murder in the Cathedral (Eliot) 65
Murdoch, Iris 83, 121, 167
Murphy 145
Musashiya 402
Muse 486
Music in Running Water (Hagger) 386
Muslim 274
Mussolini 517
Muto 82, 97, 106
Myamoto 360
Myogadani 57, 447
Myshkin 446
Mysticism 364, 414
Myth of Sisyphus (Camus) 165
N. Africa 362
N. California 469
N. Netherlands 482
N. Vietnam 352, 367
NAB 484
Nagano Prefecture 85
Nagasaki 129, 190, 441
Naito, Mr 243
Nakagawa 500, 528, 538
Nakajima 69
Nakata, Mr 564
Nakhodka 270, 299, 300, 301, 333, 334, 335
Nanking 257, 258, 259, 403
Nanking University 257
Naples 492, 503
Napoleon I 156, 230, 237, 458, 482, 524
Napoleon II 401
Napoleon III 401
Napoleon, Louis 513
Napoleonic Wars 237
Nara 120, 121, 128, 133, 183, 359
Narziss und Goldmund (Hesse) 148
Narita, Professor 53, 54, 56, 59, 60, 75, 76, 85, 90, 94, 96, 98, 134, 148, 154, 157, 169, 190, 193, 203, 275, 294, 297, 353, 381, 382, 400, 463, 474, 492, 540, 543
Narita, Ambassador 391
Narita, Miss 466

INDEX

Ochanomizu Women's University 67, 90, 467
October Street (No 25) 302
Odawara 81
Ode on a Grecian Urn (Keats) 245
Ode to a Nightingale (Keats) 60
Oder 425
Odi et Amo (Hagger) 107
Odysseus 531
OECD 425
OED 337, 397
Ogata, Mr 442
Ogilvy 195, 200
O'Hanlan 325
O'Hanlan's Dream (Hagger) 372
Ohashi 140
Ohta 294
Okayama 73, 96, 100, 385, 467, 517, 518
Okinawa 374, 383, 454, 541
Okura 433
Old Man in a Circle (Hagger) 144, 255, 394
Old Testament 117, 141, 171, 214, 222, 268, 399, 465
Old Vic 89
Olivia 535
Oloroso 305
Olympic 78, 254
Olympic Film 147
Olympics 471
Ommayed Sunnites 274
On 365
One 61, 186, 201, 234, 291, 337, 340, 345
One of our Spies is Missing 360
One Self 345
One True God 486
One World 60
One-force 61
O'Neill 18, 244, 245
Oneness 60
oneness 18, 389
Opal 519
Opportunity H 31
Orc/Oothoon 233
Ordeal by Fire 429
organism 122
Orientals 251, 352
Original Sin 105, 106, 241, 332, 417
Orsett Hospital 351
Orthodox Patriarch 505
Orwell 175, 254, 286, 403, 458
Osaka 101, 156, 296, 451
Osborne, John 21, 118, 175, 223, 277, 278, 288, 289, 329, 384, 404, 408, 411, 420, 434, 446, 450, 452, 462, 464, 465, 466, 469, 475, 477, 539, 540
Osborne, C. 527
Oscar 548, 549
Oshima 125, 167, 190, 205, 499, 500
Ostend 303, 310
Oswald 91
Othello 213
Ottoman Empire 556
Ottoman Turks 435, 459, 482, 489, 527, 532
Our Lady 305
Ouspensky 238
Outposts 44, 473
Outsiders 450, 462, 560
Ovid 35
Owen, Wilfred 24, 70, 124, 134, 136, 340, 468
Owen, Alun 24

Owl 70, 306, 313, 328, 330, 470, 568
Oxford 1, 6, 16, 17, 45, 53, 65, 69, 75, 77, 95, 96, 100, 131, 132, 161, 169, 170, 173, 174, 247, 253, 297, 303, 308, 327, 328, 329, 331, 351, 356, 365, 450, 491, 513, 558, 560
Oxford Book of Rhyme 39
Oxford Mail 308, 310
Oxford Radcliffe Camera 35
Oxford Street 449
Oxford Union 487
Oxus-Juxartes 489
Ozenberger, Dr. 70, 235, 239, 245, 477, 517
Ozymandias (Shelley) 106, 247
P 343, 346, 347, 354, 368, 369, 393, 395, 404, 411, 433, 434, 438, 445, 446, 447, 478, 486, 519, 525, 528, 530, 531, 532
P—, Marsha 150
P.A.L. 545
P.E.N., Keio 190
Pacific 59, 447
Pacific Stars and Stripes 463
Packenham, Compton 507
Packenham, General 507
Paco 544
Padua 434
Pagan 43
Paine 396
Pakistan 232, 354, 362
Palace 149, 168, 170, 180, 533
Palace Hotel Crown Lounge 250
Palestine 141, 171
Palinurus 233
Pallas Athene 498
Palmer 44
Palmer, Samuel 311
Palmer, Tommy 510, 516
Pan American 265, 555, 556
Pan, Mr 254
Pantheism 87
Pao-hsi 366
Papacy 349, 428
Papandreos, Ulysses A 531
Par, Mr Aw Boon 547
Paradise 161, 325, 556
Paraffin Paper and Steam (Hagger) 420
Paraguay 492
Parents Association 565
Paris 4, 6, 160, 230, 332, 358, 425, 437, 441, 467, 471, 484, 488, 503, 558, 559
Park Hotel 556
Parliament 146, 223, 264, 315, 316, 368, 377, 465, 557, 566
Parliamentarian 220, 223
Parthia 107, 489
Partisan 5
Party 15, 256, 258, 262, 270, 315
Pascal 88
Pasinello 448
Pasolini 353
Pasternak 299
Pater 287
Patterson 139, 375, 451, 525
Patterson, Eloise 131, 452, 487, 515, 516
Paustovsky 424
Pax Americana 107, 150
PCF 511
Peace 511
Peace Museum 101
Pearl Harbour 401

600

INDEX

409, 410, 412, 420, 422, 423, 428
Reformations 421
Reg 570
Regency 315, 407, 558
Reggie 491
Regicides 311
Reid, Miss 311, 317, 411, 484, 562
Reishauer 521
Reith, Lord 569
Religion 61, 214, 316, 370, 489, 530, 572, 573, 575
religion 113, 122
Religion and the Rebel (Wilson) 415
Religion for the Strong 416
religious 116, 120, 123, 125, 129
Religious Attitude 241
REM 505, 510
Renaissance 88, 93, 106, 170, 215, 228, 237, 241, 263, 271, 363, 398, 408, 409, 410, 413, 414, 416, 417, 418, 419, 420, 421, 422, 424, 430, 486, 521, 525
Renaissance, German 141
Representative 203, 447, 454
Reprieve (Sartre) 38
Republic of the Philippines 545
Repulse Bay 546
Repulsion 187
Rescuing Woman 290
Residence tax 433, 437, 451
Resistance Leader 439
Resnais 145
Responsions 77
Restoration 141
Resurrection 87, 319
Return 464
Reubens 311
Reuby 29
Reuby, Mrs. 445
Reu–, Bob 521, 522
Reuters 507
Revolution 263, 264, 270, 274, 315, 316, 359, 370, 379, 397, 400, 405, 408, 413, 416, 420, 421, 423, 452, 511, 525, 565, 572, 573
Revolution Museum 333
Revolution, Russian 441
Revolution Square 302
Revolutionary 398
Revolutionary Era 421
Revolutions 270, 315, 421, 422
Rex 97, 142
Rexroth, Kenneth 462, 465, 466, 467, 472, 473, 521
Rexroth, Mary 467
RFC 310, 569
RFK 444
Rheinland 517
Rhenish 429
Rhodes 501
Rhodes, B.D. 24
Rhodes, Mrs. 563
Rhodesia 224, 242, 376, 487
Rhymers' Club 315
Rica 496
Richardson 415
Richelieu 434
Richie, Donald 247
Ricks, Christopher 45, 187, 307, 425
Riddle of the Great Pyramid (Hagger) 402
Riggio 92

Right 314, 316, 373, 379, 398
Right of Centre 314, 315
Riley, Mrs. 306, 470
Rilke 43, 55, 88, 108, 113, 127, 129, 132, 207, 208, 209, 211, 212, 217, 234, 241, 283, 296, 439, 475, 524, 564
Rimbaud 288, 290
Rimsky-Korsakov 506
Rinne 235
River Map 366
Riviera 455
Rizal 543, 544
Rizzio 322, 353
Robartes, Michael 21
Robbe-Grillet 114, 357
Roberts, Harry 327, 328, 329, 330, 377, 396
Roberts, Mr 301
Robertson, Bill 96
Robespierre 404, 411, 521
Robin Hood Lane 197
Robinson 168, 169
Rococo 448
Roderick 270
Rodin 83, 209
Roeder 428
Rogers 528
Roghudi 92
Rohlfs, Professor Gerhard 92
Rollo 459
Roman 92, 145, 246, 250, 273, 364, 489
Roman Catholic 549
Roman Empire 106, 224, 285
Romanesque 448
Romanesque Cathedral 429
Romania 483
Romans 107, 156, 454, 489
Romantic 48, 106, 140, 143, 167, 184, 187, 203, 226, 233, 244, 288, 418, 446, 464, 490
romantic 167
Romanticism 109, 113, 135, 167, 212, 241, 242
Romantics 184, 357, 407
Rome 104, 105, 237, 268, 324, 384, 407, 437, 441, 454, 492
Rome Treaty 30
Romeo and Juliet (Shakespeare) 555
Room at the Top (Braine) 11
Roosevelt 368
Root, Miss 317
Roots (Wesker) 147
Roppongi 395, 453
Roquentin 347, 382
Rose 146
Rose-Leaves and a Madonna Lily (Hagger) 446
Rosedale 37
Rosier 167
Ross, Maclaren 567
Rosse's Point 325
Rotation Method 86
Rothermere 395
Rouen Cathedral 419
Roundheads 223
Rousseau 241
Rover 2000 321
Rowe, "Doughy" 389
Roxas 543
Royal 557
Royal Albert Hall 325
Royal Mile 323
Royal Standard 307

INDEX

605

INDEX

Venezuela 492
Venice 237, 285, 459, 492, 504
Venn 269, 538
Verhovensky 214, 215, 383, 464
Verner 401
Veronese 448
Verrio 322
Versailles 239
Vespucci, Amerigo 506
Vesputius, Americus 506
Vesuvius 503
Victoria 303, 331
Victoria Park 546
Victoria Peak 546
Victoria Station 29, 559
Victorian 226, 300, 332, 333, 408, 434, 536, 554
Victorian Establishment 408
Vienna 452, 489, 533, 557, 558
Vientiane 441
Viet Cong 208, 252, 261, 552
Vietnam 148, 163, 230, 252, 259, 347, 353, 393,
   429, 432, 439, 444, 461, 491, 519, 522,
   529, 547-48, 553, 567
Vietnamese 250, 365, 553
Vietnamese Chams 550
Vignola 448
Vildiz Palace 556
Vine 327, 571, 574
Virgil 36
Virgin 502
Viscount 73
Visionary 462
Visions 393
Visnu 551
Vitalism 64, 66
Vitalist 530
Vivien 326
Vladimir 220
Vladivostok 299,407, 408
Vogue 445
Volga 264
W. Berlin 303
Wailing Wall 475
Wain 218, 281, 298, 527
Waiting for Godot 2
Waldo, Ralph Trine 181
Waley 434, 435
Walker, Dr. 31
Walker, John 132, 135, 150, 355
Walley 35
Wallis, Graham 35, 505
Walseemüller, Walter 506
Walston, Lady 146
Walston, Lord 146, 200
Walter, Grey 122
Walter, Miss 396, 570
Waltham 359, 459
Waltham Abbey 307
Walthamstow Avenue 371
Wan-li 259
Wanchai 546
Wanderer 170
Wandering Monk 511
War 98
War of Spanish Succession 434
Ward, Angus 386
Ward, Stephen 43
Warden 570
Warlock, Peter 392

Warrington Gardens 34
Warsaw 197, 302, 322, 332
Waseda 281, 286, 374, 375, 400, 402, 475
Washington 474, 496
Waste Land (Eliot) 43, 58, 64, 133, 155, 158,
   203, 275
Wastelanders 65
Watanabe, Takashi 380
Watarai 402, 430, 479, 500, 519, 520
Waterloo 42, 507
Waterstone 77, 78, 84
Watkins, Vernon 207, 234, 235
Waugh 133, 278, 283, 297
Way of Contemplation 364
Weber 235
Webster 481
Welfare State 220, 223, 277, 307, 532, 566
Wellesley, Lady 188
Wellington 368, 507
Wells 279, 287, 290, 379
Welsh 522, 537, 565
Weltanshauung 218
Weltschmerz 72
Wendy 7
Werig 481, 488
Wesker 27, 146, 147, 150
Wesley 223, 349
West 50, 57, 74, 80, 86-87, 105, 110, 112, 119,
   141, 144, 177, 180, 197, 199, 214, 216-
   17, 221, 228-29, 232, 237, 239, 244, 249-
   51, 256, 262, 264, 267-68, 270-73, 278,
   280, 289-90, 303, 311-12, 333, 365, 379,
   398, 405-408, 410, 412-13, 423, 425, 443,
   445, 450, 472, 489-90, 505, 519, 530, 538,
   575
West, Christian 168
West Indies 43, 240, 572
West Kensington 559
Western civilisation 105, 110, 119
Westerniser "Herodianism" 489
Westland Row 323
Westminster Abbey 312, 401, 429
Westminster Hall 311, 312
Wet Rope on a Rubbish Dump (Hagger) 443
WEU 493
WG (Warrington Gardens) 322
WG Association of Tenants 34
Whales 189
What is to be Done 212
Wheatsheaf 567
Where Angels Fear to Tread 146
Whigs 446
Whippies, the 28
Whipps Cross Hospital 31, 41, 42, 470, 563
white light 162, 165, 201, 203, 228, 234, 239
White Tower 318, 350
Whitechapel 275
Whitehall 310, 311, 393, 566
Whitehall Palace 311
Whitehead, Alfred North 61-62, 65-66, 93, 107,
   122, 150, 228, 349, 365, 381, 389
Whitehead, Mr 352, 460, 473, 474
Whitehorn, Katherine 536
Whitworth, Miss 96
Whole 209
Whole Man 119
wholeness 1, 17, 126, 188, 205, 216, 244, 280,
   447
Who's Afraid of Virginia Woolf 312, 435

INDEX

NICHOLAS HAGGER
WORKS REFERRED TO IN THE *DIARIES*

INDEX